SO-AIN-521

COMPANION TO RUSSIAN STUDIES

1. Introduction to Russian History
2. Introduction to Russian Language and Literature
3. Introduction to Russian Art and Architecture

AN INTRODUCTION TO
RUSSIAN HISTORY

EDITED BY

ROBERT AUTY
FORMERLY PROFESSOR OF COMPARATIVE SLAVONIC PHILOLOGY
UNIVERSITY OF OXFORD

AND

DIMITRI OBOLENSKY
PROFESSOR OF RUSSIAN AND BALKAN HISTORY
UNIVERSITY OF OXFORD

WITH THE EDITORIAL ASSISTANCE OF
ANTHONY KINGSFORD

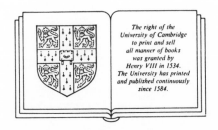

*The right of the
University of Cambridge
to print and sell
all manner of books
was granted by
Henry VIII in 1534.
The University has printed
and published continuously
since 1584.*

CAMBRIDGE UNIVERSITY PRESS

CAMBRIDGE

NEW YORK   NEW ROCHELLE   MELBOURNE   SYDNEY

Published by the Press Syndicate of the University of Cambridge
The Pitt Building, Trumpington Street, Cambridge CB2 1RP
32 East 57th Street, New York, NY 10022, USA
10 Stamford Road, Oakleigh, Melbourne 3166, Australia

First published 1976
First paperback edition 1980
Reprinted 1987, 1989

Printed in Great Britain by the
Athenaeum Press Ltd, Newcastle upon Tyne

British Library Cataloguing in Publication Data

Companion to Russian studies.
1: An introduction to Russian history
1. Russia — Civilization
I. Auty, Robert   II. Obolensky, Dimitri
III. Kingsford, Anthony   IV. Introduction to Russian history
947   DK32   75-10688

ISBN 0 521 20893 9 hard covers
ISBN 0 521 28038 9   paperback

CONTENTS

List of maps ix   *Preface* xi   *Transliteration table* xii

1
The Geographical Setting
D. J. M. HOOSON
Professor of Geography,
University of California, Berkeley

Introduction 1 The natural habitat 2
Growth and peopling of the Russian state 14 The location of
economic activities 20 Distribution of population 31
Regions 40 Guide to further reading 46

2
Kievan Russia
A. D. STOKES
Lecturer in Russian,
University of Oxford

Early history 49 The Normanist controversy 52
The origins of the Kievan state 54 The beginnings of
Russian Christianity 58 Svyatoslav 59 Yaropolk 61
Vladimir I and the conversion of Russia 62 Yaroslav 65
Yaroslav's successors 67 Vladimir Monomakh 70 The decline of Kiev 71
Guide to further reading 75

3
Appanage and Muscovite Russia
NIKOLAY ANDREYEV
Emeritus Reader in Slavonic Studies,
University of Cambridge

The Mongol invasion 78 Alexander Nevsky 79 The 'appanage system' 81
The rise of Muscovy 82 Moscow, Lithuania, and Tver' 86 Vasily II 89
Ivan III and the hegemony of Moscow 90 The church 94
Vasily III 96 Russian society 97 Ivan IV: the Muscovite tsardom 98
The 'Time of Troubles' 105 The Romanov dynasty 109 Tsar Alexis 111
Guide to further reading 116

CONTENTS

4

Imperial Russia: Peter I to Nicholas I

MARC RAEFF
Bakhmetoff Professor of Russian Studies,
Columbia University

Introduction 121 The empire 130 The government 141 The economy 153
The social classes 158 Westernization 170 Tensions 173
Guide to further reading 183

5

Imperial Russia: Alexander II to the Revolution

JOHN KEEP
Professor of Russian History,
University of Toronto

The burdens of empire 197 The efflorescence of secular culture 209
Economic and social change 215 Government and opposition 233
Guide to further reading 248

6

Soviet Russia

H. T. WILLETTS
Lecturer in Russian History,
University of Oxford

The February Revolution 272 The October Revolution 275
Civil war and foreign intervention 278 The NEP 282
Stalin's rise to power 286 Collectivization 287 The Purges 290
Soviet foreign policy between the wars 292 The Soviet Union in the
Second World War 295 Stalin's last years 296
The ascendancy of Khrushchev 298 The fall of Khrushchev 305
Guide to further reading 308

7

The Church

JOHN MEYENDORFF
Professor of Byzantine and East European History,
Fordham University;
Professor of Church History,
St Vladimir's Seminary, New York

Doctrine, liturgy, spirituality, and missions 315
Intellectual trends 318 Schisms and sects 320
The Russian Church and the Soviet state 323
Guide to further reading 328

8

The Structure of the Soviet State:
Government and Politics

L. B. SCHAPIRO
Professor of Government,
London School of Economics and Political Science

Historical factors 331 The Communist Party of the Soviet Union 333
The Constitution of 1936 338 Organs of control 344
Conclusion and prospects 345 Guide to further reading 347

CONTENTS

9

The Structure of the Soviet State:
The Economy
ALEC NOVE
Bonar Professor of International Economic Studies,
University of Glasgow

The system before 1928 350 The Stalin system 351
A centralized, command economy 358 The Khrushchev period 359
The economy under Brezhnev and Kosygin 361
Guide to further reading 363

10

The Soviet Union and its Neighbours
HUGH SETON-WATSON
Professor of Russian History,
School of Slavonic and East European Studies,
University of London

The Russians and neighbour nations 366 Periods of Soviet
foreign policy 370 Germany and eastern Europe 372
The Middle East 377 China and the Far East 380
Guide to further reading 386

Appendix 389 Index 393

MAPS

1 The USSR today   xiv
2 The northerliness of the Soviet Union   xvi
3 The Soviet Union and its hemisphere   3
4 The frame of land and water, and the impact of
   freezing conditions   4
5 Distribution of accumulated temperatures   8
6 Distribution of effective moisture   10
7 Natural regions   12
8 Territorial expansion from Moscow, 1260–1904   16
9 Ebb and flow of the western frontier since 1914   19
10 Farming regions   22
11 Industrial regions   27
12 General pattern of transport freight flows   32
13 City growth by regions, 1939–61   36
14 Distribution of population, and regional units   38
15 Kievan Russia in the eleventh century   50
16 Russia about 1396, and the rise of Moscow, 1300–1584   80
17 The expansion of Russia, 17th–19th centuries   122

PREFACE

The *Companion to Russian Studies* aims at providing a first orientation for those embarking on the study of Russian civilization, past or present, in its most important aspects. It lays no claim to cover them all. While we hope that it will be of use to university students of Russian language and literature, Russian history, or Soviet affairs, it is equally directed to the general reader interested in these subjects. Each chapter seeks to offer a self-contained introduction to a particular topic; but the editors have not wished to impose a uniform pattern, and each author has been free to approach and present his subject in his own way. Particular care has been taken to provide up-to-date bibliographies, which are intended as a guide to further study.

As is the way with collective works of this kind, the *Companion* has been some years in the making. We should like to express our gratitude to the contributors for their forbearance – sometimes sorely tried – in the face of difficulties and delays which have held up the completion of the enterprise. Economic considerations beyond our control have made it necessary to divide the contents of what had originally been planned as a single book into three volumes. The first is mainly concerned with the history of Russia and the Soviet Union; the second with Russian language and literature; the third with art and architecture. However, the three volumes, for which we share the editorial responsibility, should be regarded as complementary parts of a single whole.

We are grateful to all those at the Cambridge University Press who, over the years, have been involved in this project. Above all we wish to record our debt to Mr Anthony Kingsford, whose great experience in book production, unflagging energy, and expert knowledge of many aspects of Russian studies have been of the greatest value at every stage.

R.A.
D.O.

Oxford
1975

TRANSLITERATION TABLE

	1	2
А а	a	a
Б б	b	b
В в	v	v
Г г	g	g
Д д	d	d
Е е	ye/e	je/e
Ё ё	yo/o	jo/o
Ж ж	zh	ž
З з	z	z
И и	i	i
Й й	y	j
К к	k	k
Л л	l	l
М м	m	m
Н н	n	n
О о	o	o
П п	p	p
Р р	r	r
С с	s	s
Т т	t	t
У у	u	u
Ф ф	f	f
Х х	kh	ch
Ц ц	ts	c
Ч ч	ch	č
Ш ш	sh	š
Щ щ	shch	šč
ъ	–	–
ы	y	y
ь	'	'

TRANSLITERATION TABLE

Э э	e	e
Ю ю	yu	ju
Я я	ya	ja
(I i)	i	i
(Ѣ ѣ)	ě	ě
(Ѳ ѳ)	f	f
(V v)	i	i

The transliteration system given in column 1 is used in all sections of the *Companion* except Volume 2, chapter 1, *The Russian Language*, where the 'philological' system given in column 2 is employed. The bracketed letters at the end of the alphabet were discontinued by the spelling reform of 1917–18.

ye (*je*) is written for Cyrillic e initially, after vowels, and after ъ and ь. *o* appears for ё after ж, ч, ш, щ. In proper names final -ый, -ий is simplified to -*y*.

Proper names which have a generally accepted anglicized form are usually given in that form, e.g. Alexander, Archangel, Beria, Dimitri, Khrushchev, Likhachev, Moscow, Nicholas, Potemkin, Pugachev.

Map 1: The USSR today

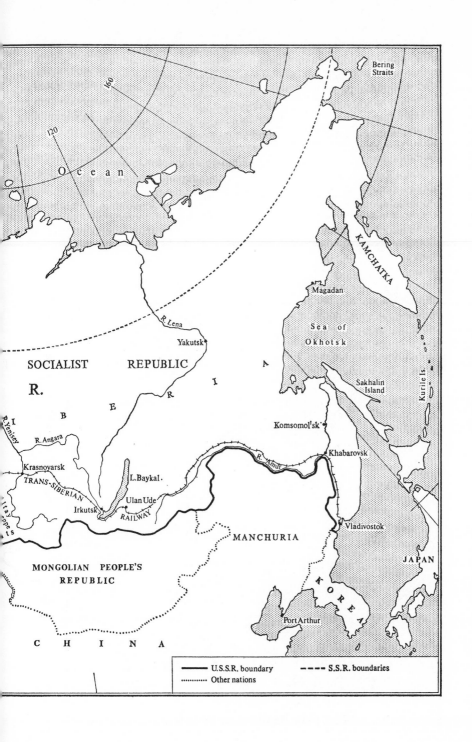

Bering
Straits

160

120

O c e a n

KAMCHATKA

Magadan

R.Lena

Sea of
Okhotsk

Yakutsk

SOCIALIST   REPUBLIC

R.

Sakhalin
Island

Kurile Is.

I
B   E   R   I   A

R.Yenisey

R.Angara

Komsomol'sk

Krasnoyarsk

L.Baykal

R. Amur

Khabarovsk

TRANS-SIBERIAN

Ulan Ude

Irkutsk

RAILWAY

Vladivostok

MANCHURIA

JAPAN

MONGOLIAN PEOPLE'S
REPUBLIC

K
O
R
E
A

C   H   I   N   A

Port Arthur

———— U.S.S.R. boundary   – – – – S.S.R. boundaries
··········· Other nations

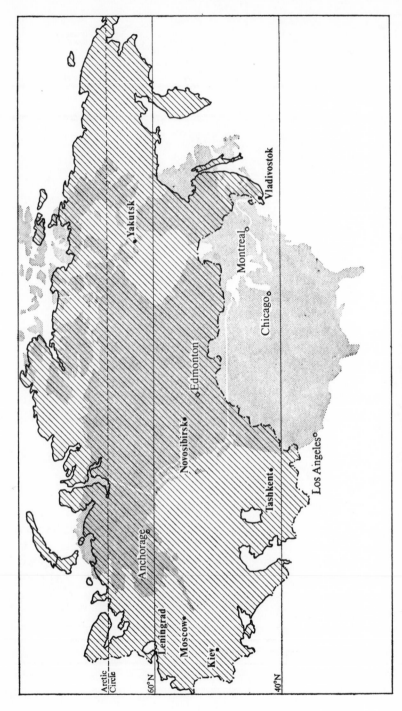

Map 2: The northerliness of the Soviet Union

The USSR compared with North America

1

THE GEOGRAPHICAL SETTING*

D. J. M. HOOSON

INTRODUCTION

The Soviet Union – powerful heir to the old Russian Empire – is a geographical phenomenon of paramount significance in the contemporary world. It covers more than twice as much land as any other country; less recognized but more significant, however, is the fact that it contains a greater range of the world's major landscape and cultural zones than any other country. The greater part of its territory is more similar to North America than to any other part of the world, both from the point of view of its natural conditions and in terms of the youth of its settlement, its pervasive 'frontier' spirit, and the country's underpopulation in relation to resources and potential. All these qualities, apart from the European origin of the inhabitants of this 'American' part of the Soviet Union (largely Siberia), sharply mark it off from Asia, of which it technically forms a part. Soviet Middle Asia (Turkestan) and Caucasia, on the other hand, brought under Russian colonial rule in the nineteenth century, do qualify as parts of Asia in any meaningful sense of that word. If one looks at the world as a whole, Russia is above all a European nation, like the United States, in its dominant influences, origins, and ways of using the land.

THE GEOGRAPHICAL APPROACH

Since geography concerns itself with a mass of heterogeneous phenomena in the worlds of both man and nature, its proper organization and understanding require the recognition of a meaningful focus for it. Some historians (and others) have considered geography as consisting merely of the physical environment and have talked about 'geographical' factors as if they were synonymous with physical factors, and some historians of

---

* Some sections of the text of this chapter and most of the maps have appeared in similar form in the author's book *The Soviet Union – a systematic regional geography*, published by the University of London Press, 1968. Map 10 appeared in the author's article 'Industrial Growth – where next?' in *Survey*, no. 57 (October 1965), pp. 111–24. The publisher and author are grateful for permission to reproduce maps based on the original copyright material.

1

Russia have long shown a propensity to overstress and oversimplify the role of the physical environment.

Far from concentrating on the study of the natural landscape *per se*, or promoting environmental determinism, the main geographical questions today are concerned with patterns of human activity. In the long-term interaction of people and land, economic factors are of immediately over-riding significance. Therefore, consideration of the various branches of the economy figures prominently among the separate topics discussed here on a national scale, and the growth of cities and industries, which expresses what is most dynamic and internationally significant about the USSR today, needs to be dwelt upon.

Geographical interpretation does not fully come into its own until all the various strands – natural, historical, economic, political, etc. – are integrated in a particular, manageable, regional unit. Thus the following thumbnail sketches of particular regions of the country consider the distribution of population, the culmination of the long struggle of people to find themselves in relation to a particular piece of land with a specific location – a general theme that has lain at the heart of the story of Russia.

POSITION IN THE WORLD

At first glance sheer size strikes one as being the most fundamental geographical characteristic of the Soviet Union. Indeed, the fact that both in area and population it is larger than the United States and Canada combined is worth keeping in mind in current world comparisons. The USSR is most comparable to Canada in terms of latitude (Map 2). Moscow itself, with 7 million inhabitants, is only just south of Edinburgh and further north than Edmonton, Alberta – the most northerly city of any real importance in Canada – while Leningrad is on the same latitude as the Shetlands and southern Alaska. In winter almost the whole Soviet coast-line is frozen, and most of the country's land is quite unfit for farming.

The country's location can be understood fully only on a globe and in the context of the significant concentrations of world population (Map 3). Although it appears to be squarely astride the land hemisphere, with three-quarters of its area in Asia and bordering most of the other Asian countries, the bulk of the Soviet population still live in Europe (west of the Urals).

THE NATURAL HABITAT

The Russian landscape – more than that of most countries – is stamped in the image of its climate. The natural units that meant most to man as

2

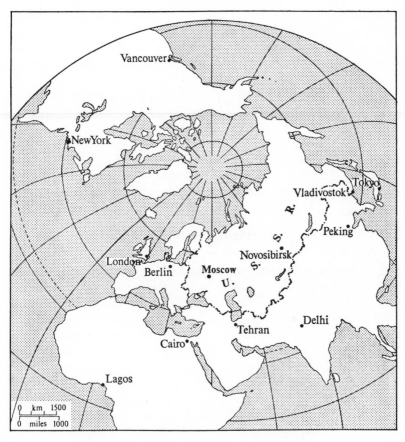

Map 3: The Soviet Union and its hemisphere
An equidistant projection, centred on Moscow

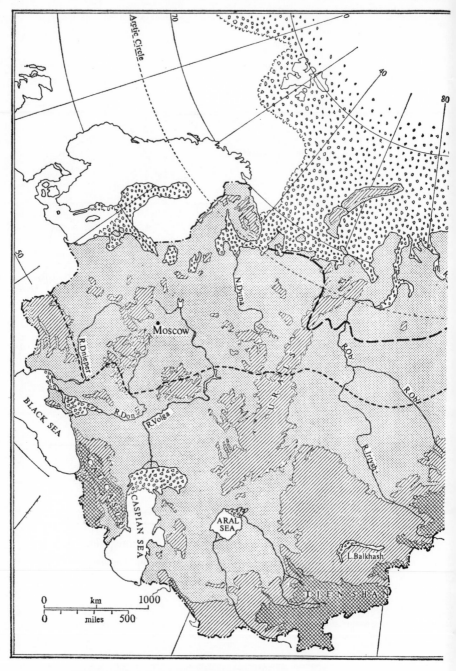

Map 4: The frame of land and water, and the
impact of freezing conditions

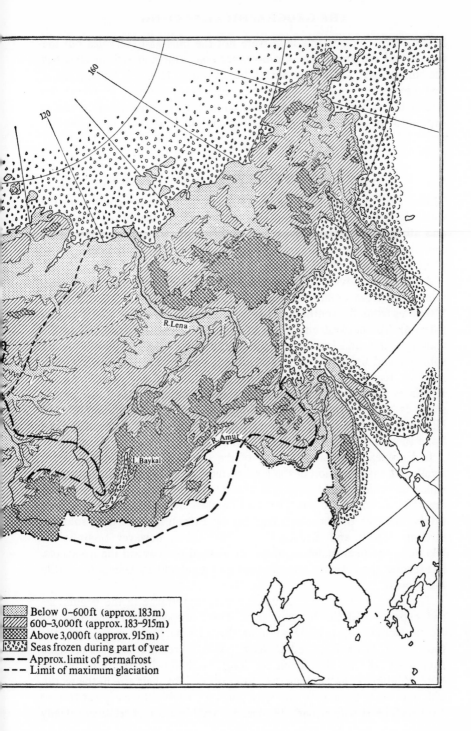

160

120

R.Lena

R.Amur

L.Baykal

Below 0–600ft (approx.183m)
600–3,000ft (approx. 183–915m)
Above 3,000ft (approx. 915m)
Seas frozen during part of year
Approx. limit of permafrost
Limit of maximum glaciation

he strove to colonize this land were not the hills and the vales but the forests and the grasslands. On no other comparable stretch of land has the climate been able to use such a broad brush. Thus it is not surprising that nineteenth-century Russian scientists were the first to reveal the interacting system that encompasses climate, soil, and vegetation and is expressed in the familiar 'natural regions' such as the steppe, tundra, etc.

THE FRAME OF LAND AND WATER

While it follows that climate exerts the most pervasive control on the total significant natural conditions of a country, the broad alignment and altitude of the landforms in turn exert a considerable influence on the climate, as well as acting as the skeleton upon which the flesh – soil, plant, and animal life – has formed.

A line in the Soviet Union dividing high land from low land follows the river Lena from mouth to source and then runs parallel to, and about 300 miles from, the southern border of the country as far as the Black Sea (Map 4). To the west and north of this line, covering two-thirds of the country's area and housing nine-tenths of its people, the landforms are subdued and unspectacular. Most of this area lies below 600 feet (and nowhere reaches 6,000), giving some credence to the popular image of Russia as a land of vast plains. To the south and east, however, the landscape is quite different. Jagged Alpine ranges – with some peaks of Himalayan stature – glaciers, volcanoes, earthquakes, and the mile-deep Lake Baykal create a landscape of 'un-Russian' variety and grandeur.

In European Russia the legacy of the Ice Age accounts for the most significant basic division of the land surface. The glaciated northern part, which coincides roughly with the present forested area, has an unkempt drainage system, with marshes and shallow lakes and great morainic ridges, such as the one well trodden by French and German soldiers, through Minsk and Smolensk. To the south, however (mainly the Ukraine), the finer material, blown or washed out beyond the ice-sheets, has formed the basis for a thick mantle of good soil, especially the fertile löss (loess).

The river systems were of fundamental importance in the beginnings and expansion of the Russian state. The European rivers (notably the Volga, Don, Dnieper, western and northern Dvina, Neva), radiating to the four seas from a hub around Moscow, played a crucial role in the ultimate supremacy of that city. Even the long Arctic-flowing rivers of Siberia (Ob', Yenisey, Lena), among the most crippled for their size in the world, did, with their tributaries and easy portages, enable the early fur-traders to cross Siberia with remarkable speed. Partly because of relatively steady flow and good gradients, the Yenisey is the most useful of the Siberian river systems, as the Volga is in European Russia.

In the south of the country there is a natural inland drainage area, almost as large as the USA, from which no water reaches the oceans. The major rivers in this region flow into two large, slightly saline bodies of water – the Caspian and Aral seas. The level of the Caspian in particular has been falling in recent decades, largely owing to a reduction in the volume of its main intake river, the Volga. This has had far-reaching economic results, and many ambitious engineering remedies have been proposed, though none has yet materialized.

No country on earth is as crippled by its coastline or shut in by its own seas as is the Soviet Union. Either because of winter ice, lack of good harbours, imprisonment in land-locked seas, or distance from economically responsive territory, no point of the very long coastline has the same value as does New York, London, or San Francisco. The only direct year-round access from the Soviet mainland to the high seas is obtained through Murmansk, near the Norwegian border, kept ice-free by the moderating airs and currents of the North Atlantic, among them the Gulf Stream.

CLIMATE

The mountain rim along the southern border of the Soviet Union effectively shuts out the tropical air from the Indian Ocean, while to the north the country is wide open to the Arctic. Three of the principal general characteristics of the Soviet climate are its continentality, uniformity, and dryness.

The continental nature of the climate (as measured by range of temperature between summer and winter) results from the sheer mass of land involved and its position in the northern hemisphere. The general westerly airstream makes the Atlantic, not the Pacific, the tempering influence, and continentality is intensified across the country from southwest to north-east. The difference is due mainly to the steep drop in the winter temperatures, reaching a 'cold pole' January average of – 60°F only 300 miles from the Pacific at Oymyakon. In fact, winter is the dominant season in the USSR – a heavy cross that the Russians have long learned to bear. Over half the Soviet area experiences continuous freezing temperatures and snow-cover for over half the year. This huge area, mainly in eastern Siberia, has *merzlota* (permanently frozen ground), sometimes to a depth of hundreds of feet – a considerable obstacle to all forms of construction, as well as agriculture (see Map 4).

The 'uniformity' of the Soviet climate is illustrated by the fact that while in midsummer almost all Russians can be happy in shirtsleeves, in

7

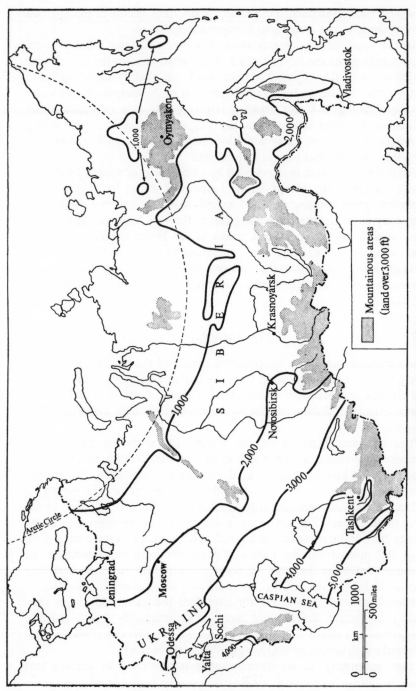

Map 5: Distribution of accumulated temperatures
Day-degrees, centigrade, above 10°C (50°F)

Mountainous areas
(land over 3,000 ft)

Oymyakon

Vladivostok

Krasnoyarsk

S I B E R I A

Novosibirsk

Tashkent

Arctic Circle

Leningrad

Moscow

U K R A I N E

Odessa

Yalta Sochi

CASPIAN SEA

1,000

2,000

1,000

2,000

3,000

4,000

5,000

4,000

1000

500 miles

km

0
0

midwinter it would be perfectly feasible to skate on the rivers from the Arctic to the Caspian, or sledge from Leningrad to Vladivostok, although there are one or two sheltered havens along the Black Sea coast (Yalta, Sochi, etc.) with a type of Mediterranean or reasonably subtropical winter.

A facet of the climate often overlooked but no less significant is the dryness. Whereas the whole of the British Isles and well over half the United States have a rainfall of at least twenty inches each year, less than a quarter of the Soviet Union reaches this level. Add to this the variability from year to year of the rainfall, especially in the marginal areas, and the fact that the wet areas for the most part are in thermally crippled zones, and one sees that drought is a more pervasive problem in the USSR than it is in any other large country except Australia.

In a country most of which is short of either heat or moisture, or both, the climate can be summarized from a human (very largely agricultural) point of view by considering (a) the accumulated temperatures during the growing season and (b) the effective moisture, i.e. precipitation minus evaporation. The most meaningful comparisons are with North America.

The outstanding reservoir of heat (Map 5) is the desert of Middle Asia (Turkestan), which is comparable in this respect, as in its dryness, to Arizona. However, the most productive farmlands of the country, in the greater Ukraine, have heat budgets rather similar to those of the US 'winter wheat belt' and fringes of the 'corn belt' in Nebraska and Minnesota, while the 'virgin lands' of western Siberia are more comparable to the Canadian prairies in this respect, as are the old farmlands of the Moscow region. Over half the country, to the north of these regions, does not have enough heat or an adequate growing season for normal agriculture.

The tragedy is that the greatest surplus of moisture occurs in these northern heat-deficient regions (Map 6). Conversely, south of a line from Odessa to Krasnoyarsk, where there are good soils, shortage of moisture is a limiting, if not a prohibitive, factor for farming. Thus the zone of overlap between adequate and reliable provision of both heat and moisture is a narrow one, following the natural zone of the 'wooded steppe'.

NATURAL REGIONS

Moisture and heat are the elements that create a particular soil, first by breaking up the parent rock and then by providing suitable conditions for the growth of a particular type of vegetation, which in turn helps to build up and modify the character of the soil. Thus, given time and fairly stable climatic conditions, natural regions emerge with a distinctive combination

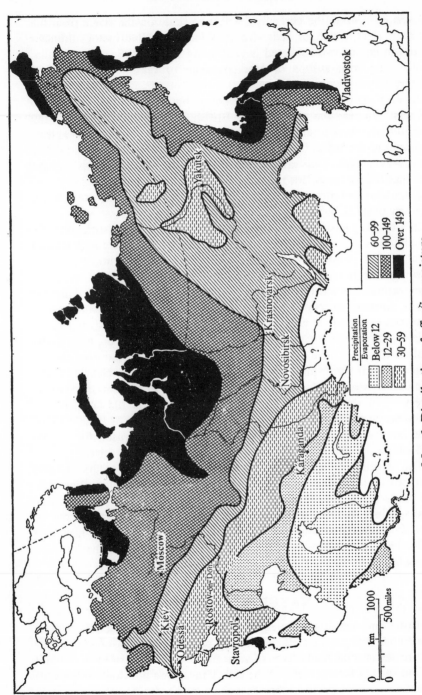

Map 6: Distribution of effective moisture

$$\frac{\text{Precipitation}}{\text{Evaporation}} = \text{Equilibrium (after Ivanov)}$$

Precipitation
──────────
Evaporation

Below 12
12–29
30–59
60–99
100–149
Over 149

Vladivostok

Yakutsk

Krasnoyarsk

Novosibirsk

Karaganda

Moscow

Kiev

Odessa

Rostov-on-Don

Stavropol

km   1000
500miles

0

of soil and vegetation characteristics, reflecting in each case a particular balance of heat and moisture, and generally ironing out, on a continental scale, variations in the bedrock.

Dividing the country once again by a line from the western Ukraine to the neighbourhood of Krasnoyarsk on the Yenisey, to the north there is adequate moisture but inadequate heat, the soils are acidic and leached of their soluble salts, and trees are ubiquitous. To the south, except for the small Kolkhida basin on the Black Sea, there is enough heat but not enough moisture and the soils are well supplied (sometimes too much so) with soluble salts, while grasses and drought-resisting shrubs characterize the generally treeless landscapes.

There are seven major natural regions in the Soviet Union (Map 7). Firstly, there is the 'wooded steppe' – the most densely populated and agriculturally productive of the natural regions, in the zone of maximum overlap of heat and moisture and of grass and trees. To the north of it stretch three regions, each progressively colder and damper than the other, and to the south three regions, each hotter and drier.

The tundra forms a continuous strip along the entire Arctic coast of the USSR. Its southern edge is the tree-line, since beyond it the summers are too cool (less than 50°F) to allow the growth of trees. With the very long winter, permafrozen soil, and low evaporation, the soil is waterlogged, unformed, and acidic, supporting only mosses, lichens, and dwarf shrubs. There is a dense insect and bird population in summer, as well as many fur-bearing animals, but the principal animal of the tundra is the reindeer.

By far the largest of the natural regions, covering nearly half the country, is the *tayga* or coniferous forest. It has a long and harsh winter, but relatively high summer temperatures allow for the growth of trees. However, excessive moisture from the winter's snow, often prevented from percolating away by the permafrozen or 'hardpan' layers, coupled with the poor humus content of the pine needles and cones, produces a heavily leached and acid *podzol* soil, which is only cultivated where there are special incentives or subsidies. It was the small fur-bearing animals that first lured man into the *tayga*, but the more valuable of these have retreated further and further eastward.

In European Russia the milder winters have allowed the penetration of a wedge of deciduous trees from Europe proper, around Moscow and near the Baltic coast, where they are mixed with the northern conifers. The presence of these leafy trees, together with the longer summers, has allowed the formation of a brown-earth in this region. It is still relatively poor and acidic but, unlike the soils of the *tayga*, it has been considered worth cultivating from the early days of the Slav settlement. This so-called 'mixed forest' region is typically transitional, with deciduous trees increasing in dominance from north to south. So is the all-important

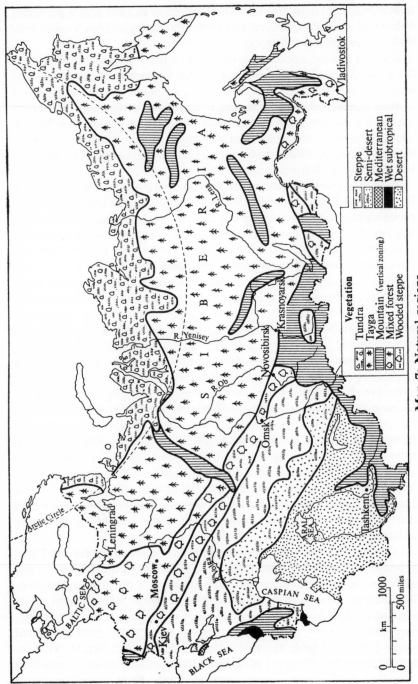

Map 7: Natural regions

Regional divisions reflecting vegetation

Vegetation

Tundra
Tayga
Mountain (vertical zoning)
Mixed forest
Wooded steppe

Steppe
Semi-desert
Mediterranean
Wet subtropical
Desert

Vladivostok

S I B E R I A

R. Lena

Krasnoyarsk

R. Yenisey

R. Ob

Novosibirsk

Omsk

Tashkent

ARAL SEA

CASPIAN SEA

Arctic Circle

Leningrad

Moscow

R. Volga

Kiev

BLACK SEA

BALTIC SEA

km   1000

0   500 miles

'wooded steppe' already mentioned, which is composed of tree clumps, mainly of oaks, interspersed with patches of grassland or steppe. The soil is mostly *chernozyom* (black-earth) as in the steppe proper, but the region receives a greater amount of effective moisture than the latter, which accounts for the existence of trees and the generally reliable crop-ripening conditions.

The steppe itself is one of the really fundamental and distinctive of the country's natural regions. Since little of the original vegetation remains, it is the black-earth that expresses the region's character. This is one of the most productive soils in the world, the Soviet Union has more of it than any other country, and it carries well over half of the present Soviet arable acreage. The blackness of the soil is an indication of its rich store of humus, built up over centuries of annual decay of tall grasses and further preserved and enriched by the acquisition of lime and other constituents of the parent rocks. The critical factor is that evaporation exceeds precipitation, so that there is a gradual net accumulation of plant foods in the topsoil. But the climate that has created such a good soil often fails to provide enough moisture to ripen its crops.

The southern parts of the steppe, notably the 'virgin lands' region between the Volga and central Siberia, experience high variability in moisture conditions, which nevertheless are sufficient to encourage a farming gamble. As the climate becomes drier toward the Caspian–Aral depressions, however, and the black-earth and grasses change to the less fertile 'chestnut' soils and sparse bushes of the semi-desert, this ceases to be a temptation. In the Middle Asian desert proper, the surface material varies a great deal, from the fertile *löss* of the piedmont area to *solonchaki* (salt crusts), clay basins, slabs of limestone rock, or sand-dunes. Vegetation varies accordingly but few areas are entirely bare of drought-resisting bushes, which have some value as forage.

The natural regions of the USSR have their counterparts in North America, but it is useful to note how large each type looms in each continental unit. In proportion to size, the Soviet Union has much more tundra and coniferous forest, and slightly more black-earth grassland and arid lands, than North America. The mixed forests of the Moscow–Baltic region balance those of north-east America, while there are even miniature analogues of Florida and California along the Black Sea coast. But there is no equivalent in the Soviet Union to the extensive, well-watered, and at the same time well-heated forest land of the south-east quadrant of the United States.

GROWTH AND PEOPLING OF THE RUSSIAN STATE

The character, extent, and position of the natural regions, summing up as they do the more significant features of the natural environments, have had a profound effect on the history of colonization in Russia. However, in the process they have themselves been significantly modified and have presented to each succeeding generation a face that is fresh and yet enduring. Thus in any survey of the geographical saga of the human occupation of particular places, the natural conditions must always be kept in mind, although their influence must not be exaggerated or personified, since the impact of nature must always be viewed through the prism of the cultural appraisals, techniques, and stages of development of the people concerned.

The Soviet state is both old and new – a Europe and a North America rolled into one. Russian national consciousness emerged from a melting-pot of immigrant peoples and took geographical root at about the same time as this was happening in England. On the other hand the 'frontier', in the social rather than the strictly political sense, has been as pervading and continuous a feature of national development as it has been in North America.

BEGINNINGS

The pre-Russian occupation, such as it was, is to be seen in relation to the later stages of the Ice Age, with which it overlapped, and the gradual establishment in the post-glacial period of relatively settled climatic regimes and resultant natural regions. On the southern fringes of what is now the Soviet Union there had arisen some well-organized settlements, in the two or three millennia B.C., such as Samarkand and Khiva in Middle Asia and the Greek trading settlements on the Black Sea coast. These were climatically favoured but, more important, were on the beaten track of the ancient world. They also proved very vulnerable to the various 'hordes' of livestock-rearing nomadic peoples who moved out from Mongolia and neighbouring areas along the steppeland route toward Europe. The inhabitants of the forested lands north of the steppe were few and scattered and engaged in hunting and collecting.

Slavonic-speaking peoples were moving eastward from east-central Europe into the Russian mixed forest region by at least the seventh century A.D. They followed rivers like the Dnieper and upper Volga and their tributaries, hunting, especially for furs, and practising 'shifting cultivation' on burnt-over patches of better-drained forest land. As

14

population, organization, and opportunity for trading increased, towns grew up at well-defended sites, well located in terms of routes.

Kiev was the earliest and most successful of these and became an effective centre of Russian nationality. It was located in the fertile wooded steppe, just below the confluence of several tributaries with the Dnieper. However, agricultural and trading facilities were not enough – defence was a vital factor, and Kiev's location on a high bluff overlooking the river, coupled with the comparative cover of the wooded steppe as against the steppe proper, seemed good. But the pressure from the nomads eventually grew so intense that this attractive but rather exposed position became untenable, and the city was sacked by the Mongols in 1240.

Novgorod, which had grown up in a much less attractive site on the edge of the northern coniferous forest, but near the start of the all-important water-road 'from the Varangians to the Greeks', managed to survive as an important political and economic centre for over two centuries after the eclipse of Kiev. There was an inevitable shift of the centre of gravity of the Slavonic people well to the north, and in particular to the heart of the mixed forests between the upper reaches of the Volga and its tributary, the Oka. To the refugees from the Kiev region this must have seemed an unsmiling land, with its marshes and chaotic streams, heavier, stonier soil, and denser forests. But by that stage the people were more concerned with finding a sheltered haven for gaining subsistence than in trading, and this land, though poor by Kiev standards, was not beyond the pale, as was the great forest to the north. Gradually this region, placed at the hub of great rivers radiating in all directions, became the nucleus of the modern Russian state and Moscow established its hegemony over other focal points within it.

In the thirteenth and fourteenth centuries Moscow was very centrally situated in relation to the total Russian world and the communications of the time. Its princes certainly made the most of the possibilities of their location, which was unusually advantageous. By the end of the fifteenth century the Muscovites had solidified their position and established their external independence as well as their internal supremacy. From this base they began to build a vast continental empire just as several of the maritime states of western Europe were also finding their feet and preparing to set out across the oceans.

THE DIRECTIONS OF IMPERIAL EXPANSION

It remains to outline the main phases and directions of the Russian imperial expansion (Map 8). By the latter part of the fifteenth century the Muscovites had become strong enough both to conquer Novgorod and inherit its northern forest realm and also to refuse tribute to the Tatars.

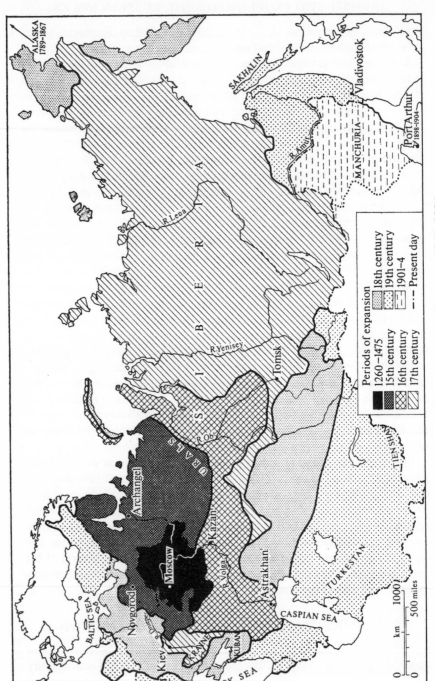

Map 8: Territorial expansion from Moscow, 1260–1904

Periods of expansion

▓ 1260–1475	▒ 18th century
░ 15th century	░ 19th century
▨ 16th century	▦ 1901–4
▨ 17th century	- - - Present day

ALASKA 1789–1867

SIBERIA

R. Lena

R. Yenisey

Tomsk

R. Ob

URALS

Archangel

Kazan

Moscow

R. Volga

Novgorod

Kiev

Astrakhan

UKRAINE

R. Dnieper

R. Don

R. Kuban

BALTIC SEA

BLACK SEA

CASPIAN SEA

TURKESTAN

TIEN SHAN

R. Amur

SAKHALIN

MANCHURIA

Vladivostok

Port Arthur 1898–1904

km   1000

0   500 miles
0

This led to the two most significant advances of the sixteenth century – the foundation of Archangel as Russia's first seaport and the arrival of Chancellor's trading ships from England, and the capture of Kazan', the stronghold of the Volga Tatars, which opened the way for the rapid Russian advance down the river to Astrakhan' and also to the low passes across the Urals to Siberia. However, although Russia had gained access to the Arctic and the land-locked Caspian, it was still effectively denied access to the Baltic by Sweden, to the Dnieper river by Lithuania, and to the Black Sea by the Crimean Tatars backed by the Ottoman Turks.

THE DASH ACROSS SIBERIA

By the mid seventeenth century a few Russians, mainly concerned with making their fortunes in fur, had penetrated to the Pacific, using the conveniently aligned river systems and portages, and encountering little opposition from the few natives *en route*. This feat made the Muscovite Empire by far the largest in the world, but entailed very little in the way of permanent colonization, since the penetration was confined entirely to the *tayga*. The Manchu Empire barred the way to the Amur valley and the Tatars still held sway in the Siberian steppes, but in any case the Russians in Siberia were not yet interested in agricultural settlement.

By the accession of Peter the Great in the late seventeenth century, Russia had undergone a displacement into Asia, was still confined almost exclusively to the forests, and had little contact with Europe. Peter inaugurated a radical shift in orientation toward the West with his conquests on the Baltic, the brand-new capital of St Petersburg that he planted there, and the modernization that he set in train. This westward momentum was intensified during the eighteenth century and by the end of the Napoleonic wars the empire extended deeper into Europe than the Soviet Union does today.

The most significant and insistent direction taken by Russian territorial expansion in the nineteenth century was to the south, as that of the previous century had been to the west and the one before that to the east (see Map 8). This southerly extension involved two relatively new concomitants: permanent migration and colonization by Russians outside the forests, and the incorporation of long-settled communities of non-Slavonic peoples into the empire.

The first and most valuable of these acquisitions, following the establishment of control of the northern coastlands of the Black Sea in the second half of the eighteenth century, was the black-earth steppe of the Ukraine ('New Russia'), which supplied most of the massive wheat exports of the nineteenth century, and became the site of Russia's first modern development of heavy industry. The final defeat of the Crimean

Tatars, supported by the Turks, ended, in European Russia at least, the struggle between the farmer and the nomad which for centuries had lain at the heart of its history.

From this Black Sea vantage-point Russia moved to conquer the Caucasus region already long settled by Georgians, Armenians, and many other national groups. This was a colonial, rather than a settlement operation, and in mountainous and subtropical environments quite foreign to the Russians. In the classic colonial manner they attempted to Russify the people and to set up tea and other plantations; they also had to subdue dogged mountain tribesmen in much the same way in which the North West Frontiersmen of India were conquered.

A similar juxtaposition of colonization and colonialism about half a century later took place beyond the Urals and the Caspian. A few tentative settlers entered the better black-earth, wooded steppe region of western Siberia in the eighteenth century, and the trickle turned into a steady stream following the end of serfdom in 1861. However, the flood did not come until the 1890s, when exceptional famines in European Russia and the saturation of peasant migration to the Ukraine and Kuban' coincided with the construction of the Trans-Siberian railway and the beginnings of governmental encouragement of free settlement in Siberia.

The conquest of Middle Asia (Turkestan) was facilitated by the establishment of vantage-points in the Siberian steppe to the north and in the Transcaucasus to the west. The irrigated *löss*-lands had been occupied for centuries, but some Russian Cossacks were settled in the Semirech'ye region north of the Tien Shan mountains. 'Indirect rule' through local emirs and khans, and the promotion of cotton specialization, were the familiar hallmarks of the Russian occupation of this region.

The last arena of Russian nineteenth-century expansion was the Far East – the Amur region and neighbouring Manchuria. The Russians had been barred from this region by the Chinese for two centuries, but about 1860 the time for a reassertion of Russian influence seemed propitious: Chinese power was crumbling, the Japanese had not yet asserted themselves, and the Russians were about to surrender their North American holdings. Although not much settlement was effected, and despite the fact that the land was second rate agriculturally, the acquisition of Vladivostok, Sakhalin Island, and other strategic points significantly strengthened Russia's position as a Pacific power. This strength seemed to be growing very fast when the Trans-Siberian railway reached the Amur at the turn of the century and the Russians obtained concessions for it to take a shortcut across Manchuria and also for an extension to ice-free water at Port Arthur. By this time Mongolia and other parts of north-west China effectively had come under Russian influence as well.

The year 1904 saw the high-water mark of the Russian Empire, when its

Map 9: Ebb and flow of the western frontier since 1914

area was larger than that of today's Soviet Union. The Russian expansion over the previous four centuries, viewed in such a context and in that particular year, must have seemed ominous. However, in the following year the clay feet of the colossus were rudely exposed by Japan, which forced Russia to retire from Manchuria behind the Amur river, and laboriously to begin to build another railway to Vladivostok, a project that took another ten years to complete.

19

EBB AND FLOW IN THE TWENTIETH CENTURY

The unprecedented setback to Russian expansion caused by the war with Japan in 1905 led to a series of revolutionary outbreaks, which widened the cracks in the foundations of tsarism. By 1921, after seven further bitter years of external and civil war, the young Soviet Union, while still just surviving, was severely truncated geographically, having been forced to relinquish stretches of former imperial territory in eastern Europe from Finland to Bessarabia, amounting in all to twice the size of Britain. The Russian frontier on the west had reverted roughly to what it had been in the eighteenth century (Map 9).

However, during the 1930s the Soviet Union built up new strength as a world power and during the period 1939–45 it regained most, though not all, of the territory of the old Russian Empire, besides two small areas, Transcarpathia and the Königsberg district, which had never been Russian before. In addition, the years immediately following the Second World War saw the Soviet Union extend an effective control further into central Europe than the Russian Empire ever did. In the long contact zone with China, Mongolia is still within the Soviet sphere, while Manchuria and Sinkiang, where Russian influence has at times been strong, are firmly within the Chinese orbit. The Chinese are now reasserting their former claims to sovereignty over the Amur region, and encouraging the Japanese to press for the return of the southern Kurile Islands. Thus while the European frontier of the Soviet Union traditionally has been the most unstable, it now appears possible that the long Soviet border with China, although superficially more 'natural' than the European one, may stand the test of time less well.

THE LOCATION OF ECONOMIC ACTIVITIES

The most immediate and powerful link between the distribution of people and the fundamental character of the land (in terms of natural resources as well as climate and relief) is the pattern of economic activities. It is a rapidly changing pattern, but one that is heavily influenced by the inertia of former patterns of population and cultural traditions, as well as one responsive to technical and resource discoveries and, particularly in the Soviet Union, governmental policies. All that can be attempted here is an outline of some of the more significant gross patterns of farming and industry, and of the all-important transport network on which regional specialization depends.

FARMING

Little more than one-tenth of the Soviet Union's national acreage is cultivated, in spite of the massive plough-up of the 'virgin lands' in recent years. A further one-fifth is classified as pasture or hay-meadow, leaving at least two-thirds unusable for farming. Although the area sown is still larger than that cultivated in the USA and Canada combined, the average quality of the land as well as its productivity (per acre or per man-hour) is considerably lower. Nevertheless there is little doubt that, given a high level of organization and investment (a proviso hitherto notably lacking), the Soviet Union ought to be able to feed its population adequately from its own land for the foreseeable future.

More than two-thirds of the arable land in the USSR is in black-earth country. The axis of the chief agricultural belt follows the wooded steppe from the western Ukraine to the foothills of the Altay mountains, extending southward into those parts of the steppe proper that receive adequate moisture and northward into the warmer and less leached parts of the mixed forests. This black-earth country, now so dominant in the Soviet agricultural scheme, remained dormant for many centuries while the early Russian farmers struggled to make a living in the much poorer forest clearings to the north of it. This was because the steppe and the relatively open wooded steppe were the domain of the livestock-herding nomads and, so long as their power persisted, farming settlement in their territory was clearly out of the question.

By the early eighteenth century two-thirds of the Russian population (almost all rural) was still to be found in the *podzol* forests around Moscow and in the north-west. This proportion, however, had been reduced to one-third by the mid nineteenth century. The intervening period, therefore, saw the great southerly shift of the Russian peasants into the black-earth zone of European Russia, down to the Black Sea and the north Caucasus. Finally, since the late nineteenth century the movement has been eastward along the narrowing part of the black-earth wedge toward central Siberia. The last chapter of this long drawn-out story seems to have been written with the over-ambitious 'virgin lands' extension of the mid twentieth century. Henceforth it is probable that further investments in agriculture will be more wisely put into improvements in land already proven reliable and productive, rather than into further attempts to cultivate virgin land. In fact, it would be realistic to envisage in the Soviet Union in the future a retreat from some currently over-extended pioneer fringes, as has happened in similar areas of North America.

Russian agriculture has always been heavily biased toward grain,

21

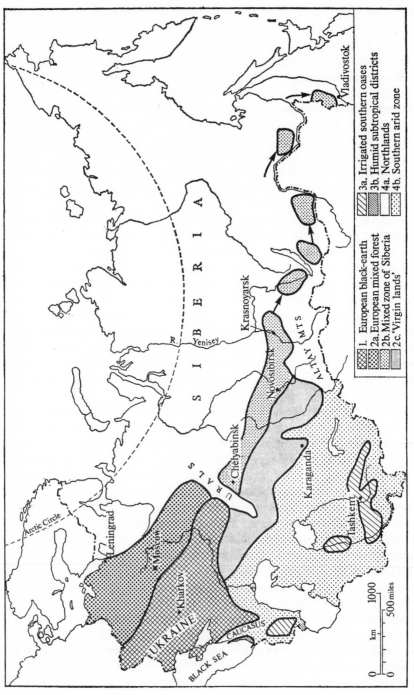

Map 10: Farming regions

1. European black-earth
2a. European mixed forest
2b. Mixed zone of Siberia
2c. 'Virgin lands'
3a. Irrigated southern oases
3b. Humid subtropical districts
4a. Northlands
4b. Southern arid zone

Vladivostok

S I B E R I A

Krasnoyarsk

R. Yenisey

Novosibirsk

ALTAY MTS

Chelyabinsk

U R A L S

Karaganda

Tashkent

Leningrad

Moscow

Kharkov

UKRAINE

CAUCASUS

BLACK SEA

Arctic Circle

km   1000

500 miles

0

which even now accounts for two-thirds of the sown area. However, the proportion was nine-tenths in 1913, and there is a continuing trend toward more emphasis on fodder crops together with (in the grain category) a shift from the traditional wheat and rye to maize (corn) – all this being directed toward increasing the size of the livestock component in agriculture. However, because of the relative scarcity of climatically well-endowed land for these crops, the potentials are limited.

FARMING REGIONS

The following is an attempt to summarize Soviet agriculture geographically, by distinguishing regions that stand out for their relative productivity and importance to the whole economy, as well as for their specialization (Map 10). Regions 1, 2a, 2b, and 2c, wedged between the northern forests and the southern deserts, are in the main agricultural triangle, which produces the overwhelming proportion of the nation's food.

1. *The European black-earth region*

This is the agricultural heart of the country, accounting for about half its output by value. Although heat and moisture vary significantly, the whole region has fertile soil and a relatively intensive mixed-farming economy. It produces the great bulk of the country's winter wheat, barley, maize for grain, sugar-beet, sunflowers, fruit and wine, pigs and poultry, and probably a majority of the cattle, potatoes and rye as well. It is the nearest Soviet counterpart to the US Middle West (though appreciably poorer in natural endowments) and probably represents the soundest potentiality for increasing the national food output.

2a. *The European mixed forests*

Although this was the only area the Russian peasant knew until the seventeenth century, it is now recognized as being very second rate, although not beyond the limits of economic farming. The traditional emphasis on rye, oats, potatoes, and flax is giving way to dairying and intensive market-gardening around Moscow and the other growing urban markets.

2b. *The mixed-farming zone of Siberia*

Although largely black-earth, this strip along the Trans-Siberian railway is more comparable in over-all productivity to region 2a than 1, owing to the long severe winters and the cool summers. Dairying and spring wheat are the dominant branches of farming. East of the Yenisey there are just a few patches of poor farmland, often on permafrost.

2c. *The 'virgin lands'*

This new region has been laid out largely as a monocultural spring wheat producer, but the short growing season coupled with persistent drought and 'dust-bowl' propensities have meant that productivity is low and very variable. Nevertheless, the cultivation of this region has facilitated the intensification of agriculture in region 1.

3a. *The irrigated southern oases*

These are limited areas of first-class land with a good heat budget, but dependent largely on the availability of irrigation water. Cotton is the dominant crop in most of the oases, with fruit and alfalfa also becoming prominent.

3b. *The humid subtropical districts*

These tiny enclaves are the only parts of the country that escape regular frost and also have heavy rainfall. They produce tea and citrus fruits, but extension of the latter is discouraged by quite frequent killing frosts.

4a. *The northlands*

This vast area, covering nearly two-thirds of the country, is an agricultural wilderness, making a negligible contribution to food production. Reindeer-herding, hunting, fishing, and forestry may be said to be the only commercially viable activities (apart from mining) that the environment permits. There are, of course, highly subsidized 'farms' near mining camps, etc., which are there to produce fresh food at any price, but the incentive to farm in this difficult area has to be strong.

4b. *The southern arid zone*

Outside the irrigated oases, and south of the 'virgin lands', this area supports only very sparse grazing for sheep and camels, herding of which is traditionally based on nomadism.

The roughly triangular Soviet farm base (Leningrad–Yenisey–Black Sea), in which most of the output is achieved and where most of the new investment no doubt will be placed, is really the 'effective national territory' from all points of view, industry included – which underlines the continuing fundamental importance of agriculture to the location of economies and population. The Soviet Union could be virtually self-sufficient in food, but whether it will, or should, continue to strive for this – with its growing industrial exports – rather than import those foods that are appreciably cheaper on the world market, is at least arguable.

INDUSTRY

Industrialization has been the ultimate end, in a sense almost equated by Lenin with communism itself, of most of the frenzied efforts and sacrifices made in the Soviet era. Farm collectivization has been seen not only as a means of ensuring the urban food supply but also the initial capital accumulation for the industrial plans. The scientific-educational drive, the magic of 'electrification', railway construction, imports of foreign personnel, capital equipment, and raw materials – all these and more were primarily bent toward the industrial goal. Moreover, whatever the human cost, the cumulative fruits of this single-mindedness in terms of national power and the transformation of the Soviet Union in world status in the last three or four decades have been impressive. The rate of industrial growth has inevitably slackened recently but the 'plateau' of superpower status has been reached, and this level must bear a close relation to the degree of success that has attended the country's efforts at industrialization.

The chief geographical issue about Russian industry is its changing locational patterns; a major trend in the last century, and particularly in the Soviet era, has been, as with farming, a gradual dispersal within at least the triangle of tolerable farmland. One can say that the first significant dispersals of industrial activity beyond the confines of the Moscow region, to the metal-bearing Urals and to his own innovating capital on the Baltic, were set in train by Peter the Great. But more far-reaching was the late nineteenth-century shift of fuel and modern industrial production to the 'new south', notably to the coal and iron fields of the eastern Ukraine and the oilfields of Baku.

The scale of industrial dispersal has been greatly extended since 1930. At that date, as in 1913, there was very little industry of national significance east of the Urals, or even east of the Volga. Stalin's 1930 decision to institute the so-called 'Urals–Kuzbas Combine', involving a resuscitation of the Urals iron industry through the exchange of iron ore and coking coal with the Kuznetsk basin (1,500 miles away, in central Siberia), set in train the modern phase of industrial dispersal. The full impact of this easterly displacement, however, came only after 1939 with the approach of war, and clearly has been slowing down within the last decade or two. Its scale has been greater than that of anything comparable in Russian history and, although its force may now largely be spent, a new type of zone, authentically Soviet in character and stage of development, has been created between the Volga and Lake Baykal – the chief industrial reception area of the last three decades. However, it should be

25

noted that even now about two-thirds of all Soviet industry is located in European Russia (if one includes the Urals), in spite of the fact that the easterly dispersal probably has been the dominant force in this century.

ENERGY AND RAW MATERIALS

With this framework in mind it is necessary to look at some of the physical patterns affecting industrial location. The most basic of these is energy, which lies at the heart of the current 'east–west' controversy over the government's regional policies. About four-fifths of the estimated energy reserves are in Siberia while, as has been noted, the bulk of the market for it in terms of population and industry is in European Russia. However, one can easily exaggerate the significance of this lack of geographical coincidence: for one thing, a large proportion of these reserves, notably of coal and water-power, though technically available, are really inaccessible from an economic viewpoint, because of such impediments as distance, climate, or rugged, permafrozen terrain. But just as important is the fact that oil and gas have recently become the most favoured types of energy, and the present easily accessible reserves of those are mainly in the European area, in spite of notable recent developments in western Siberia.

The change in the energy balance is worth noting here, since it has been so fundamental, rapid, and overdue. Although Russia was the world's chief oil producer at the beginning of the century, the Soviet Union under Stalin became exceptionally, and by then quite archaically, dependent on coal – and this cost the hard-pressed Russians dear. In the mid 1950s oil and gas accounted for only about one-quarter of the energy generated in the USSR, compared with two-thirds in the United States. In the post-Stalin period a concerted plan has been followed to approximate the US energy balance by the mid 1970s, and already oil and gas account for well over one-half of a vastly increased Soviet energy output.

All this has been reflected on the map in a spreading out of energy production in the last decade or so (Map 11). The geographical shift has been most dramatic for oil. In 1941, when the Germans invaded, over four-fifths of Soviet oil came from the vulnerable Caucasus region, especially Baku. Now at least two-thirds of the much larger output comes from the extensive new Volga–Ural fields.

Natural gas production has expanded even more rapidly, most of the output coming again from southern European Russia – much of it being absorbed by the Moscow region. Even larger amounts from sources in Middle Asia are piped to blast-furnaces in the Urals, while extensive reserves have recently been exploited in western Siberia. If the European

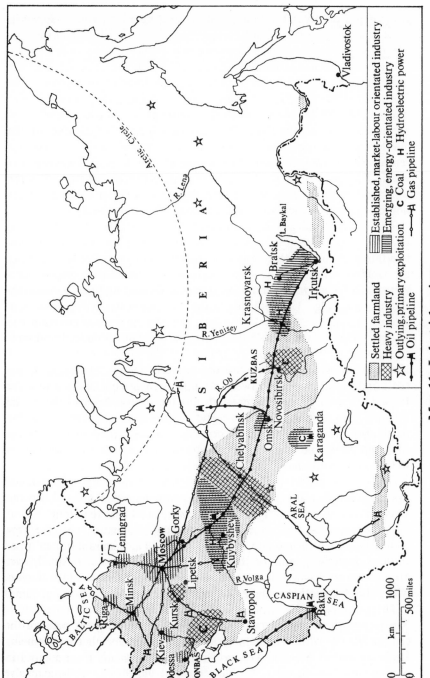

Map 11: Industrial regions

Established, market-labour orientated industry

Emerging, energy-orientated industry

Settled farmland

Heavy industry

Outlying, primary exploitation ☆ Hydroelectric power H
C Coal

Oil pipeline ⊶⊶

Gas pipeline ⊶⊶

Vladivostok

S I B E R I A

R. Lena

L. Baykal

Bratsk

Irkutsk

Krasnoyarsk

R. Yenisey

KUZBAS

R. Ob'

Novosibirsk

Omsk

Chelyabinsk

Karaganda

ARAL SEA

Leningrad

Gorky

Moscow

Kuybyshev

Minsk

Lipetsk

R. Volga

Riga

BALTIC SEA

Kiev

Kursk

Odessa

DONBAS

Stavropol'

CASPIAN SEA

Baku

BLACK SEA

Arctic Circle

1000

500 miles

km

0

gas supplies do become exhausted in the next decade or two, as forecast, these Siberian reserves should become the chief national suppliers of this cheap energy source, which is booming all over the world.

Dispersal also has taken place in coal and hydroelectric power since the war, and now accords more closely with the location of reserves. The Donets coal basin (Donbas) in the Ukraine, which was providing two-thirds of the Soviet output when the Germans overran it in 1941, now accounts for only one-third, the difference being largely due to the development of other fields such as the Kuznetsk basin (Kuzbas) in central Siberia. When Stalin died almost all the developed hydropower was in European Russia, whereas now some of the largest stations in the world are operating (e.g. at Bratsk and Krasnoyarsk) or under construction on the rocky reaches of the Angara and Yenisey rivers.

The accumulated geographical result of this dispersal has been what might be called a new 'energy axis'. At the time of the German invasion two-thirds of Soviet energy was generated within a belt of country joining the Donbas with Baku. Now three-quarters of the output comes from a very much longer zone, stretching from the Donbas and nearby gasfields through the Volga–Ural oilfields to the coal and water-power sources in central Siberia, west of Lake Baykal. But although the orientation has changed, the greater part of the energy is still both produced and consumed west of the Urals and integrated into the European electrical grid. However, the greatest storehouse of long-term energy (black and brown coals and water) remains between the upper reaches of the Ob' and Lake Baykal, an area recently integrated into the central Siberian grid. The eventual plan is to join these two grids, in order to make full use of the much cheaper Siberian energy. When this is done, some four-fifths of the country's accessible energy and over three-quarters of its people will be welded into a formidably effective national territory.

As for raw materials, only a few points can be made in the space available. Firstly, although there were acute shortages not only in the 1930s but even in the early 1950s, it now appears that the Soviet Union has adequate reserves on its own doorstep of virtually all the raw materials needed for modern industry, which cannot be said of any other country. However, some of them are of less than first-class quality, or are awkwardly located in relation to one or another of the factors with which they have to be combined.

The chief centres of iron ore mining are in south-central European Russia and the eastern Urals, with a minor region of great potential in central Siberia, while the main area of non-ferrous metals runs from the Urals to central Siberia. The growing significance of oil and gas by-products as raw materials for the chemical industries (petrochemicals) has led to their rapid localization in places like the middle Volga or the northern Caucasus, or in the Moscow region at the hub of the pipeline network.

Obviously, physical resource factors are not the only ones in industrial location. Population, both of labour and consumers, is of great importance, as are transport facilities; both of these phenomena will be considered later on. It is clear, however, that the axes of accessible energy and most raw materials do coincide roughly with the axes of population and reasonably good agricultural land in the USSR. Industrial specialization is quite marked within this effective zone, of course, and an attempt to distinguish the main categories of industrial regions will now be made, disregarding ubiquitous industries of purely local importance (see Map 11).

The first category is also the oldest, being made up of well-established centres of market-oriented, labour-intensive industries. Moscow and Leningrad are obviously the most important of these, depending heavily on political patronage, invested capital, and a reserve – particularly precious in the early Soviet period – of skill and literacy. In the case of Moscow the city's central position in earlier times at the hub of the river system has been succeeded by a similar position with regard to the railways and now to the pipelines, so that high-value manufacturing, depending on skill and assembly of varied raw materials, can thrive. On a smaller scale Riga, Kiev, and Odessa have similar advantages, including the security of a well-populated regional hinterland, whereas Leningrad, without the latter, must depend more exclusively on the momentum of a privileged past.

Those regions in the second category – the centres of heavy industry – are obviously very different from the first in their youth, historical development, and present industrial capacity, but together they may be said to be about as important. They have been fundamental to the rapid advances of the industrial revolution from the late nineteenth century onward. Pride of place goes to the eastern Ukraine (Donbas–Dnieper), both chronologically in terms of modern steel development and, though only just, in terms of current output. Its dominance in the early Soviet era has been greatly reduced since 1930 by the resuscitation of the Urals as a steel region – and incidentally of the Kuzbas, mainly as a concomitant of the need of the Urals for coking coal. Recently a steel complex has been established in central European Russia, using the almost inexhaustible ore of the 'Kursk magnetic anomaly', which had been known about but technologically out of reach for a century. This has obviously great market advantages over central Siberia, but coking coal is more expensive.

Except for this Kursk area, all the industrial regions so far mentioned were founded before the war, and by any yardstick they still account for the bulk of the country's manufacturing. But there are several others whose industrial significance was slight before the war, but which have begun to emerge since as industrial regions of national stature. In this third general category, related primarily to affluent energy resources, the most important region is the great oil-bearing one of the Volga–Urals, which before the war had a fuel deficit and only locally significant industries. With oil, gas, and the new Volga hydro-dams, it is now the largest energy provider of any Soviet region. It has become a major centre for the petrochemical industries, and its position near the centre of gravity of the Soviet population gives it a crucial advantage in consumer industries over the energy-rich regions further east. The most important of the latter is the mountainous region of central Siberia between the Yenisey river and Lake Baykal, where the giant dams are situated, as well as the country's largest and cheapest brown coal deposits. In spite of these great assets its future is not assured, because of handicaps of distance, severe climate (effectively, just beyond the broadly settled farming belt), and labour shortages. Nevertheless, the whole region is integrated in a grid and has attracted some energy-intensive, labour-saving industries. In the last category can be lumped together the few, widely scattered industrial settlements outside the effective national 'triangle'. They are mainly concerned with mineral exploitation in the north, processing of agricultural products in Middle Asia, or fish processing in the Far East. Many of the mineral workings were started with forced labour and at a time of acute scarcity; now the future of some of them is in doubt: labour has to be bribed to work there, minerals have been found more frequently in the broadly settled belt, and the government is becoming more hard-headed in the matter of costs.

In conclusion one may repeat that about half Soviet industry remains west of the Volga in European Russia, and about three-quarters if the whole Urals and Caucasus regions are included. Equally outstanding, however, in the industrial dispersal of the Soviet planned era since 1930, has been its extension into the funnel of farmland east of the Volga and as far as Lake Baykal. Even if, as seems likely, this easterly movement has by now run its course, it has already led to a permanent extension of the country's industrial base, compared with the pre-1930 period.

THE TRANSPORT NETWORK

The Soviet Union may well have the most overloaded transport system of any major nation, and its inadequacy has often proved a critical factor in limiting the scale and specialization of economic activities. The ton-mileage of freight has increased more than fifteen-fold since the Revolution, while the mileage of railway (which still carries over two-thirds of the total national freight) has scarcely doubled. However, the coming of the pipeline for oil and gas and the high-voltage electrical transmission line have taken the pressure off many of the bulkier hauls, particularly of coal. But there is still a considerable need for improvement, by western standards, notably in the development of a good road transport network, which is still in a quite rudimentary state.

Until about a century ago, the great bulk of Russian traffic, other than local everyday hauls, went on the rivers. The Volga has been pre-eminent ever since the early days of Muscovy, opening up the riches of the Near East and China as well as the iron ore of the Urals and the furs of Siberia. It is still by far the most important of the Soviet waterways, accounting for about half the ton-mileage of their total freight, even though the latter amounts to barely one-tenth of the railway freight.

The railway network, on which the Soviet economy is still so dependent (even though less so than a decade ago) is most adequate to the demands placed on it in European Russia and least in the newly developed Volga–Baykal zone. Consequently almost all of the railway building done since the Second World War (the Soviet Union is one of the very few advanced countries still actively extending its railways) has been in this eastern zone.

Generally speaking, the greatest density of freight – largely on the railways, but generally paralleled by the pipelines and transmission lines – follows what may be called the 'economic spine' of the country from the eastern Ukraine to Moscow and thence eastward, through the middle Volga and the Urals to central Siberia (Map 12). Dominant directions of movement are northward from the Ukraine and westward from Siberia and the Urals, which reveals the Moscow region in its historical role, at the receiving hub of a radiating system of rail, river, road, and pipe. Thus its central position is constantly being bolstered in the same way as is that of Paris or London.

The very character of such outlying regions as Middle Asia or the Far East is bound up with the adequacy and distance of their transport links with the 'effective national territory' and with the conflicting claims of specialization and self-sufficiency. It may well be that the arguments for concentrating on the perfection of a closely integrated network within the boundaries of the proposed National Electricity Grid, from the European border to Lake Baykal, will prove, as in the case of economic activities generally, more and more persuasive.

DISTRIBUTION OF POPULATION

The population on the land now comprising the Soviet Union (over 240 million) has more than doubled during the present century. The

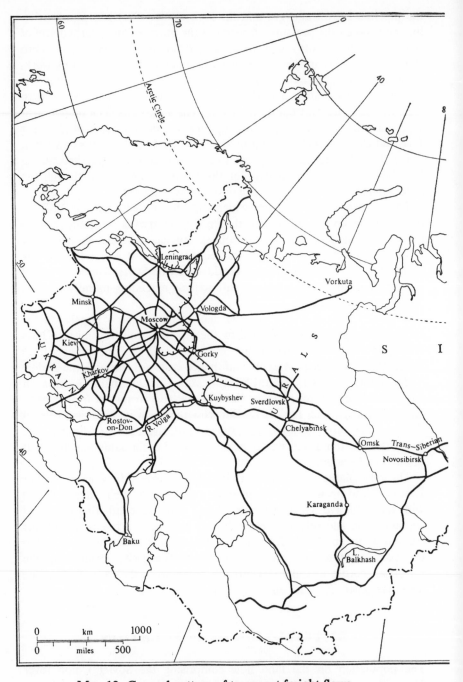

Map 12: General pattern of transport freight flows

Based on recent estimates, ignoring lines of communication where annual freight
seems to be less than 5 million tons

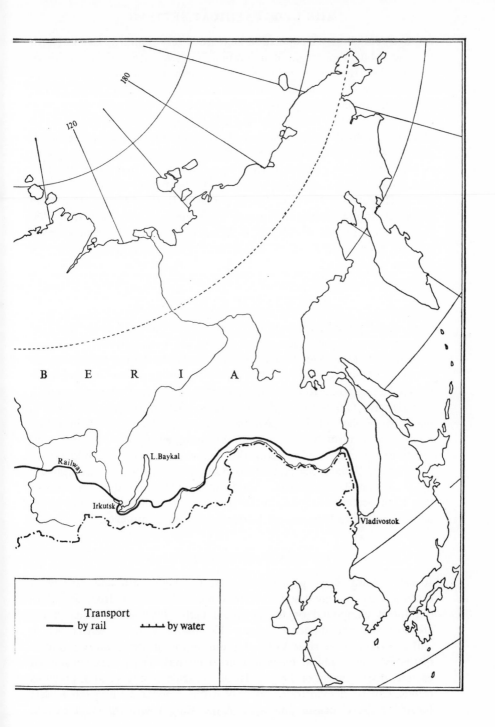

180

120

B E R I A

L.Baykal

Railway

Irkutsk

Vladivostok

Transport
by rail ┅┅by water

average annual rate of population increase is very similar to that in North America, but the tragic demographic consequences of the military catastrophes that have befallen the Russian people in the twentieth century show up in the fact that there are nearly 20 million more females than males among the over-forty age group.

It is also vital to realize that the Soviet Union is still in the throes of carrying through the fundamental changeover from a rural to an urban society, which has virtually been completed in North America and most of western Europe. Before 1928 at least four out of every five Russians had always been tied to the soil, as most people of southern Asia are today. However in 1962, for the first time in Russian history, the urban population outnumbered the rural, a stage which Britain reached in 1860 and North America around 1920. Since the rural segment now has a notably older population, its decline will probably be rapid in the next decade.

THE ETHNIC STRUCTURE

The official federal structure of the USSR draws attention to the fact that the population is composed of many cultural groups. However, although it is true that one can find people in the Soviet Union related to the Persians, Mongols, Finns, and even the North American Indians, their national as opposed to their local significance can easily be exaggerated. The decisive fact is that more than three-quarters of the population is made up of that Slavonic-speaking amalgam that has spread into, and established control over, the main Eurasian triangle of valuable land mentioned earlier. Undoubtedly the regional character of Middle Asia (Turkestan), Transcaucasia, and the Baltic republics is influenced greatly by their non-Slav majorities, but it so happens that they are regions that have become marginal in the economic as well as locational sense, and the minority Russians wield disproportionate influence.

MIGRATORY DIRECTIONS

It has already been pointed out that the eighteenth and nineteenth centuries saw the great southerly movement of Russians from their age-old forest compound on to the much better black-earth lands of the Ukraine and neighbouring regions. The majority of the Soviet people still live west of the river Volga, but during the present century the most distinctive geographical phenomenon so far has been a very substantial easterly displacement of the population. Its scale, and reversal of previous trends, can be demonstrated roughly if one compares European Russia (north of the Caucasus and west of the Volga) with the chief eastern 'reception area' between the Volga and Lake Baykal. During the half century before 1911 the population of the European zone increased by about 40 million, compared with 10 million (about half of them after 1897) in the Volga–Baykal zone. However, during the half century 1911–61 the Volga–Baykal zone increased by 25 million, i.e. more than double the contemporaneous gains in the European area. Of course, the wars, which affected much of the European zone, and the consequent easterly evacuation of part of the population, were mainly responsible for the hectic speed of this change, but the scale of the net redistribution is still remarkable, considering that the European zone had about four times the population of Volga–Baykal in 1911. Therefore even if, as seems likely, this displacement is now coming to an end, it has effected a fundamental change in the population map, and has virtually completed the story of the occupation by the Russians of the permanently habitable triangle of their huge domain.

THE GROWTH OF CITIES

The combination of speed and volume of city growth in this century, and particularly the last four decades, is probably unparalleled in the history of urbanization. There are now more than three hundred cities of over 50,000, housing one-third of the Soviet population, compared with about fifty such cities (containing one-twentieth of the Russian population) in 1900. Whereas the rural population has declined absolutely since 1926, the city population, so defined, has increased over five times in the same period, involving a net addition of 55 million people (the total population of Britain today) to the cities of the Soviet Union.

During the interwar years, when the Soviet Union was basically building on foundations bequeathed by tsarism, the booming cities (i.e. those with populations over 50,000 that doubled) were mainly in the Moscow region and the greater Ukraine. However, in the two decades after 1939 two-thirds of such boom cities were situated east of the Volga – over half of them, and the larger ones, being in the Volga–Baykal zone. The map of regional rates of city growth (Map 13) shows that all the groups of cities within the Volga–Baykal zone, but none outside it, doubled their collective populations, a phenomenon comparable to what happened in many California cities at that time.

As elsewhere in the industrializing world, the presence of the really large city has become a dominant feature of the Soviet scene. There were over thirty-five cities in 1972 of more than 500,000 people, compared with three in 1926, and a dozen with over a million – which is about as many as North America had during the Second World War. Moscow and Leningrad were roughly the same size in 1913, but Moscow, since it

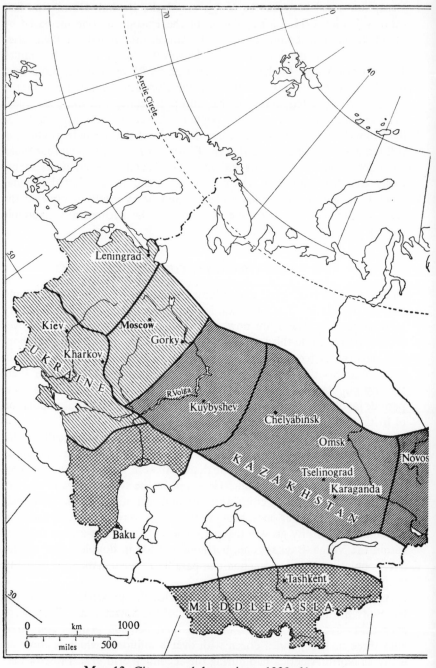

Map 13: City growth by regions, 1939–61

In the 1960s growth was more evenly distributed, but with Kazakhstan
and Middle Asia showing the most rapid increase

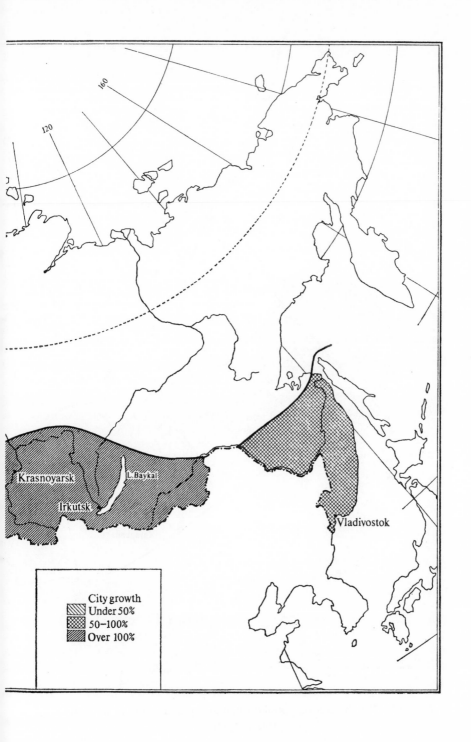

City growth
Under 50%
50–100%
Over 100%

Krasnoyarsk
L. Baykal
Irkutsk
Vladivostok

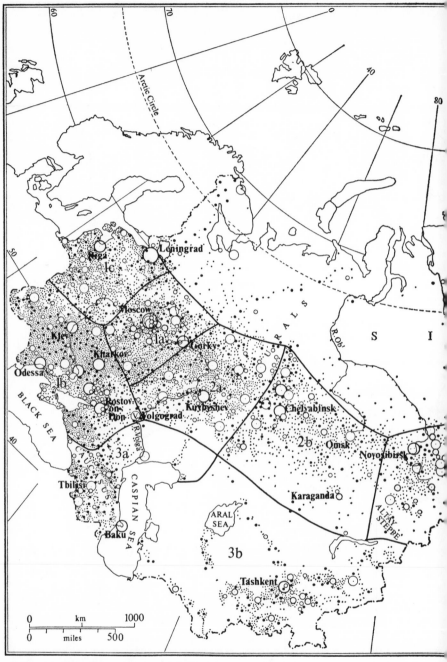

Map 14: Distribution of population, and regional units as defined in
this chapter

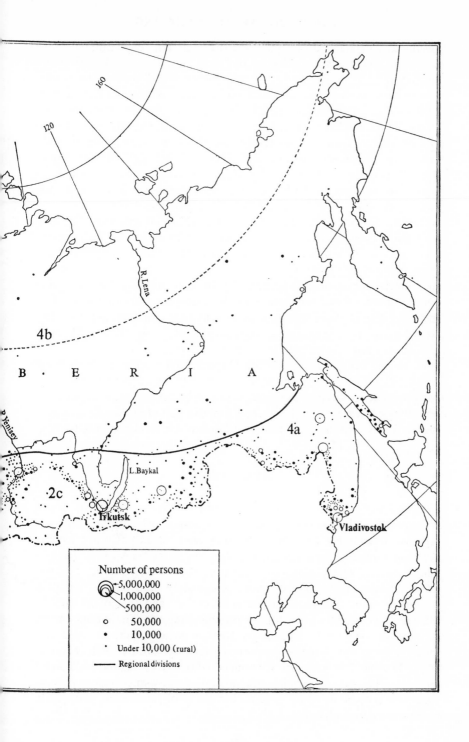

160

120

4b

R.Lena

B · E · R · I · A

R.Yenisey

4a

L.Baykal

2c

Irkutsk

Vladivostok

Number of persons

○ 5,000,000
○ 1,000,000
500,000
○ 50,000
• 10,000
· Under 10,000 (rural)

──── Regional divisions

resumed its capital status, is now twice as large. With eight million people or so, it now takes its place as the most northerly of the half-dozen mammoth cities of the world. Of cities in the Soviet Union with at least one million persons, five are in the older parts of European Russia, west of the Volga (Moscow, Leningrad, Kiev, Gor'ky, and Khar'kov), three are in the Volga–Baykal zone (Kuybyshev, Sverdlovsk, and Novosibirsk) and two on the southern margins (Baku and Tashkent). This dispersal of the large city – Tashkent was the only city east of the Volga with as many as 100,000 persons at the beginning of this century – is one of the most significant features of the Soviet era, and urbanization is still at a relatively early stage by American or west European standards.

The distribution of population as a whole (Map 14) reflects in a striking way the continuing influence of climatic deterrents – cold in the north and east and, to a lesser extent, drought in the south – in confining the great majority of people within the long triangle from the western border that tapers out in central Siberia. It also demonstrates the continuing concentration of the population in the European part of the country including the Urals, although comparison with a similar map for 1890 would show an impressive easterly drift within the funnel. The city clusters are now the critical locations to observe, and the Volga–Baykal zone stands out from most of the long-settled European zone in being much less rural in structure. A certain equilibrium in terms of the east–west population see-saw, however, seems to be the present situation, and one cannot foresee a time when the European part of the country, including the Urals, will have less than two-thirds of the total population.

REGIONS

No particular scheme of regional divisions within the Soviet Union can be expected to be the correct one for everyone's taste; furthermore, the regional boundaries can rarely be thin ones. Boundaries are usually zones of transition, and attention should always be focused on the core and essence of each region rather than on its edges. Two rather cut-and-dried schemes of regional division have mainly been used – that of a country's 'natural regions' (as outlined earlier) and that of its current officially recognized administrative–economic regions. The former can be justified in view of its impact on Russian history, but, as cities and industry loom ever larger in importance than agriculture, such 'natural' zones become less and less coincident with today's significant human regions. The use of official administrative–economic regions makes statistical accounting more precise, but many of these areas make little or no sense geographically.

Thus another scheme is outlined below – essentially one of dividing the Soviet Union into human regions, though of course reflecting natural conditions. Some of the criteria for this delimitation are (a) rate of population (especially city) growth; (b) scale of contribution to the national economy and of proven *accessible* resources; (c) dominant economic specialization; and (d) common bonds of historical or ethnic associations. Obviously a good deal of compromise and subjectivity is involved in accommodating such varied phenomena in one coherent scheme, but the resulting regional divisions are no less real or vital.

THE SCHEME

The following ten regional divisions are set in the framework of the generalized culture worlds – European, Asian, 'American', and northern – that were hinted at at the outset of this chapter (see Map 14). Space allows for only the briefest characterization of each region here.

1. *The established European base*

The well-populated area of European Russia, west of the middle Volga and north of the Caucasus, its present character established in pre-Soviet times, accounts for about half the country's population as well as its agricultural and industrial output. Though growing more slowly in recent decades, and much less dominant nationally now than it was, it is still comparable in national significance to the important north-east quadrant of the United States.

(a) *The Moscow region.* Unlike most Soviet regions, this one owes its importance and form to legacies of the distant past. Poor in resources and transitional in nature, it derives whatever coherence it possesses from the dominating presence in its midst of the 'heart of empire' – originally, the hub of the river system, and later of the rail and pipeline networks. Within the region, the Oka river marks off two distinct landscapes: to the north, high-value, skilled industrial cities, pine forests, and niggardly, city-subsidized agriculture; to the south, better soils and climate, a dense rural population and, until recently, very little non-agricultural industry. The metropolis binds these two even more closely into a functional unity.

(b) *The greater Ukraine.* Taken as a whole this is the best-endowed, most productive, and most populous of the Soviet regions. With well over 50 million people, it has the numbers and industrial power of West Germany and the farmland and population density of France, while it is well located in regard to climate and by comparison with other significant European regions. It was the main target of the Germans in 1941, being the country's chief agricultural and industrial base, and was entirely

41

overrun for a time. However, its proportion of the national population and production has steadily declined throughout the Soviet period.

It is, in a sense, homogeneous naturally and culturally, since it is almost all good black-earth country and most of the people classify themselves as Ukrainians. However, a significant division stands out, roughly along a line from Odessa to Khar'kov. To the north is the relatively well-watered wooded steppe, a crowded peasant land, still largely non-industrial with some ancient settlements, notably Kiev. To the south and east is the steppe, developed only in the nineteenth century, heavily industrialized (notably in the Donbas–Dnieper belt), with a drought problem and much lighter density of rural population. The recent intensification of agriculture through the maize–livestock drive and the large reserves of natural gas indicate that the Ukraine is well equipped to adapt itself to the new economic priorities.

(c) *The Baltic region*. Compared with the other two regions, this one is small and marginal in its contribution to the national economy, as well as in its location in relation to the mainstreams of Soviet economic development. Most of it comprises Estonia, Latvia, Lithuania, and White Russia. It has been traditionally part of the east European shatter-belt, caught between a number of expansionist empires, and has a very complicated ethnic structure today. The inherited skills and capital of Leningrad and of one or two Baltic towns have kept them important manufacturers of precision machinery; though on a much smaller scale than the Moscow region. It is a watery world, laced with rivers (not now as important as in the days of Novgorod and St Petersburg) and marshes, and cool summers restrict the scale and range of agriculture. Its future prospects may depend considerably on the extent to which Soviet overseas trade develops.

2. *The Volga–Baykal zone*

This is the effective, viable part of the vast 'eastern regions' and is, in contrast to the European area, to a large extent a creation of the Soviet period. Although mainly in Asia, it bears more resemblance to the newer parts of North America. It is distinguished by ample resources of energy and industrial raw materials and by unusually high rates of city growth in the last few decades. However, it still possesses less than one-third of the Soviet population and industry, and it is doubtful whether this will increase in the foreseeable future.

(a) *Volga–Ural*. This roughly covers the oil- and gas-bearing region which, together with the large hydroelectric stations, has converted it since the war from an energy-deficient region to the most affluent in the country in this respect. It had been transformed since the late nineteenth century from its traditional role as a 'frontier' between Asia and Europe, the desert and the cultivated land, to a position near the centre of gravity of the Soviet population and well connected by communications with the important regions of the country. Its present petrochemical and energy-oriented industries thus have a good market as well as resource base, and the region is very well situated for further growth. Kuybyshev has become much the most important city in this recent expansionist phase.

(b) *Ural–Ob'*. This includes the metallurgical eastern flank of the Urals as well as the climatically habitable part of the west Siberian plains up to the Ob' river. It is essentially a new region, having been settled agriculturally under conditions and during periods of time very similar to those of the Canadian and American prairies, maintained up to the present in the 'virgin lands' project. Its industrial component is based largely on steel and non-ferrous metals, and its modern development dates from 1930, with the rejuvenation of the once very prominent Urals iron industry that had been eclipsed by the Ukraine in the late nineteenth century. Its cities and industries grew at an unprecedented rate during the last war, when the Urals acted as the main reception area and arsenal, and afterwards, with the continuing policy of encouraging disproportionate investment in the 'eastern regions'. In the production of steel and wheat – the twin staples and traditional indicators of the Soviet economy – it closely compares with the Ukraine, which was unchallenged in this respect before the war. Nevertheless, the Ural–Ob' region is finding it increasingly difficult to retain skilled labour in a rather unattractive environment, and its rate of growth has inevitably been slowing down.

(c) *Central Siberia*. Within this region of mountains and foothills, where all the great rivers of Siberia have their source, is to be found the Soviet Union's greatest reserve of accessible energy. This alone sets it apart from its neighbours, notably from the Far East area, in spite of their many historical, climatic, and ethnic continuities. The twin cores of the region are the Kuznetsk coal basin and the Yenisey–Angara–Baykal water-power zone, and they seem to be growing together and becoming more interdependent. The Altay Steppe, on the western edge of the region, is the tail end of the continuous Russian agricultural triangle. Most of the region is therefore chronically in a difficult marginal state as far as agriculture is concerned, and it is certainly the most fluid of the Soviet Union's great frontiers. Development of energy, and the railways and grids to facilitate this, continues to be rapid, but problems of labour and of distance from the markets are likely to set clear limits on its future growth.

3. *The southern borderlands*

The Caucasus–Caspian and Middle Asian regions, while different in many ways, have much in common. They are both areas of ancient settlement, whose population has been in contact with the civilized world for much longer than have the Russians, and they were both conquered by the latter in the nineteenth century. Non-Slavonic peoples are heavily in the majority, and national and religious feeling is still evident. Physically, too, these regions are quite different from the Russo-Siberian lands, with great contrasts between Alpine ranges, subtropical forests, and sandy deserts, and an absence of severe winters, which are such a basic characteristic of the Russian land. Also they are both still basically agricultural and more rural in structure than the rest of the USSR, and their main function now, apart from tourism, is to grow crops such as cotton and tea for the Russian market. Both are essentially marginal within the Soviet scheme.

(a) *Caucasus–Caspia.* Before or during the Second World War this area could hardly have been considered marginal economically, since the whole Soviet economy depended critically on the oil from Baku. But now oil is even imported into the region. The Caspian Sea, which used to meet most of the Russian fish requirements, is now relatively unimportant, and the level of the lake itself is falling. Even exotic crops like citrus fruits and tea are less well based and extensive than they might appear, and tourism (a growing Soviet industry), because of the mountains, Riviera-type seascapes, warm sunny winters, and ethno-historical colour, will probably turn out to be the most profitable specialization for this region in the long run.

(b) *Middle Asia.* This human group, as large as that of Canada, is the most isolated one of any size in the Soviet Union, separated as it is from the others by a broad desert. Drought is its chief problem, and the bulk of the population is concentrated at the junction of the two major landscapes – mountain and desert – on the irrigated *löss*-lands, where cotton is the major crop. Natural gas has been found recently in large quantities, but it is being piped largely to the Urals blast-furnaces. There is very little industry in the region itself, other than the processing of agricultural products. It will remain agricultural, though the conflicting claims of specialization and self-sufficiency, and of cotton and fruit and vegetables for the national market, have still to be resolved.

4. *The northern marginal lands*

These areas are liabilities in the general agricultural and industrial sense, but contribute primary products – fish, timber, and especially minerals – to the national economy, and possess considerable strategic importance.

(a) *The Far East.* The four million inhabitants of this region live next door to one-quarter of the world's population in China and Japan, while they are four or five thousand miles away from their own centre of government and most of their kinsmen. The attitude of China is crucial to the development of the natural resources and trade of the Soviet Far East, and the present hostility of the Chinese, coupled with their territorial claim to the whole area, has stultified development in recent years. Although agriculture is possible in some places, the region is chronically dependent on grain imports (now mainly from Canada). The only major economic contribution made by the area is fish – and operations recently have extended all over the North Pacific. But as a Russian window on the Pacific it has obvious strategic significance.

(b) *The north.* This region, beyond the effectively settled belt, occupies nearly half the country's area, but contains only 2 per cent of its population. Since it lies entirely in the *tayga* or *tundra*, and since most of its ground is permanently frozen, agriculture can hardly exist without a subsidy. Distance, transport hazards, and shortage of skilled labour (with the reduction of forced labour) compound the difficulties and expense of any operations. In the long run, only scarce or particularly valuable minerals – the north is now the chief source of gold and diamonds – can pay their way, apart from the fishing bases and forest operations on the accessible edges of the region. In these operations, the European north has a distinct advantage over the Siberian north, apart from its rather milder climate. But the north should by no means be written off entirely. In the early days of Muscovy it mainly filled the national coffers, and it remains a considerable asset to the Soviet Union as a reserve bank (especially for minerals), a strategic insulator, and also an integral part of the national image, symbolizing enterprise, virility, and expansive opportunity.

SOME CONCLUSIONS

In summary, then, it is possible to recognize an 'economic spine' or an 'effective national territory' for the USSR. These terms denote essentially the major area of the country which consistently produces a surplus in relation to its population and which, by implication, seems at least partially to be supporting the rest of the country. In terms of output of food, energy, and industrial raw materials, this spine runs from the Ukraine directly to the middle Volga and on to the Urals and central Siberia, following the black-earth area most of the way. However, a glance at Map 12 (pp. 32–3) makes it clear that any such spine is deflected *en route* toward the Moscow region, which in any realistic reckoning must be included in it. Thus the Ukraine–Moscow–Baykal zone, including five of the ten regions described above, accounts for some three-quarters of the country's urban population (almost all Slavs), as well as of its agricultural and industrial output, and an even greater share of the accessible industrial resources.

Beyond this spine, the other regions comprise 70 per cent of the country's area, but their contribution to the national economy is secondary and relatively dispensable. They are either heavily rural and largely non-Slavonic in composition, with a decidedly colonial character, or pioneer mining communities, often operating in difficult conditions and therefore apt to be temporary.

Within the economic spine, a basic distinction has been drawn between the old-established European core and its recent funnel of expansion between the Volga and Lake Baykal. The question of where the future emphasis in terms of population and economic development will lie between these two segments is still in doubt, since policies concerning energy, market, skilled labour, raw materials, transport, etc., are in a state of flux. Probably there will be a period of comparative equilibrium, on a greatly broadened base, a situation that would particularly favour the Volga–Ural region, which combines some of the character and advantages of both east and west.

Obviously the effectiveness with which the Soviet Union exploits its really usable land (which approaches the total area of the United States) and deploys its resources and manpower will be one vital factor in the country's continuing 'competition' with the United States. Like the United States, but quite unlike China or India, the Soviet Union is not an overpopulated land in relation to the means of livelihood. The United States has a markedly better agricultural base, but the Soviet Union has potentially a greater range of industrial resources, and while it remains well behind in overall productivity and standard of living, it does possess the necessary endowments – human, natural, and locational – for long-term 'Great Power' status. There is no compelling reason why the present gap between the USA and the USSR – partly a matter of historico-economic lag (the Soviet growth since 1930 has been compared to the American from 1880 to 1914) – could not gradually 'wither away' as the present century advances. That this has not actually been happening in the post-Khrushchev years – the gap may even be widening – underlines the crucial importance of institutional reform to the full realization of the country's rich physical and human resources.

GUIDE TO FURTHER READING

There is, of course, an extensive literature on this subject in Russian, becoming ever more voluminous. Apart from books and atlases, there are four national geographical periodicals that appear six times a year, as well as regional and semi-regular ones. Since 1960 a selection from the periodical literature has been translated in the monthly journal *Soviet Geography: Review and Translation*, published by the American Geographical Society and edited by Theodore Shabad.

The editor also compiles 'News Notes' of geographical developments and, all in all, this journal provides the most effective means of gaining insight into the character of Russian geographical writing and keeping the factual material discussed in this chapter up to date.

Atlases

R. C. Kingsbury and R. N. Taaffe, *An Atlas of Soviet Affairs* (New York, 1965) is an imaginative and concise paperback atlas covering most aspects of the geography of the country, in words as well as maps. G. Kish, *An Economic Atlas of the Soviet Union* (Chicago, 1960) is organized on a regional basis, and there are concise verbal summaries opposite the regional maps; the maps have a great deal of symbolic information but are rather insufficiently quantitative. The *Oxford Regional Economic Atlas of the USSR and Eastern Europe* (Oxford, 1960) is organized by topics and is attractively presented, with useful textual accompaniment, though it is somewhat out of date now. Of the many excellent atlases in Russian, the best, most up-to-date, and most easily manageable on the general and regional geography of the USSR are: A. N. Baranov *et al.*, *Atlas SSSR*, 2nd edn (Moscow, 1969), which has the full spectrum of physical, economic, and regional maps; A. N. Voznesensky *et al.*, *Atlas razvitiya khozyaystva i kul'tury SSSR* (Moscow, 1967), with a very wide range of maps – topical and regional – on economic and social themes; *Atlas sel'skogo khozyaystva SSSR* (Moscow, 1960), a very comprehensive atlas of Soviet agriculture; and *Fizikogeograficheskiy atlas mira* (Moscow, 1964), the most comprehensive atlas of physical geography in existence.

General Surveys

C. A. D'Almeida, *États de la Baltique, Russie*, vol. 5 of *Géographie Universelle*, P. Vidal de la Blache and L. Gallois, eds. (Paris, 1932) is a comprehensive, readable, and beautifully illustrated description of the Soviet Union at the outset of the first Five-Year Plan. D. J. M. Hooson, *The Soviet Union: A Systematic Regional Geography* (London, 1968) consists mainly of the detailed regional analysis of ten regions, as delimited in the latter part of this chapter, preceded by a topical introduction. P. E. Lydolph, *Geography of the USSR*, 2nd edn (New York, 1970) is a lavishly illustrated and up-to-date textbook, starting with the official regions; there are some good maps, including many from the magnificent *Soviet Atlas of Agriculture*. R. E. H. Mellor, *Geography of the USSR* (London, 1965) is a comprehensive, factual survey, organized by topics rather than regions.

The Natural Habitat

A thorough survey of the interrelated phenomena in each 'natural region', by a scholar who was prominent in both tsarist and Soviet geography, is L. S. Berg, *Natural Regions of the USSR*, English language edn, J. A. Morrison and C. C. Nikiforoff, eds. (New York, 1950). The most authoritative detailed reference work on climate is A. A. Borisov, *Climates of the USSR*, English language edn, C. A. Halstead, ed. (Chicago, 1965). A mine of information on a timely and little-understood topic is P. R. Pryde, *Conservation in the Soviet Union* (Cambridge, 1972). S. P. Suslov, *Physical Geography of Asiatic Russia*, English language edn, J. E. Williams, ed. (London, 1961) is a detailed and well-integrated description of the natural conditions of this region, and a good example of the way in which Russians traditionally have approached this subject.

Growth and Peopling of the state

J. R. Gibson, *Feeding the Russian Fur Trade* (Madison, 1969) is a detailed and interesting examination of a specific phase of Far Eastern settlement. C. D. Harris, *Cities of the Soviet Union. Studies in Their Function, Size, Density and Growth* (Chicago, 1970) is the most comprehensive analysis of Soviet urbanization processes. W. H. Parker, *An Historical Geography of Russia* (London, 1968) is a readable and well-illustrated survey, containing a large number of excerpts from contemporary observers, domestic and foreign, at various periods.

Location of Economic Activities

S. S. Balzak, V. F. Vasyutin, and Ya. G. Feigin, *Economic Geography of the USSR*, English language edn, C. D. Harris, ed. (New York, 1949), although doctrinaire in many ways and now obviously out of date, is still a very thorough survey of the location of economic activities on the eve of the Second World War. N. N. Baransky, *Economic Geography of the USSR* (Moscow, 1956) is a translation of a carefully done, in general objective, and primarily regionally organized survey; the last edition of the most widely used secondary-school textbook for several decades. A stimulating and accurate survey, with emphasis on the economic aspects and with up-to-date statistical analysis, is J. P. Cole and F. C. German, *A Geography of the USSR: The Background to a Planned Economy*, 2nd edn (London, 1970). A. Lavrishchev, *Economic Geography of USSR* (Moscow, 1969) is a translation of a recent Soviet standard text. T. Shabad, *Basic Industrial Resources of the USSR* (London, 1969) is a thoroughly detailed and up-to-date survey, mostly by regional divisions, of developments in this crucial sector. L. Symons, *Russian Agriculture. A Geographic Survey* (London, 1972) is the most authoritative and up-to-date survey of this subject.

Specific Regions

T. E. Armstrong, *Russian Settlement in the North* (Cambridge, 1965) brings together a mass of material, historical and ethnographic as well as geographical, in a readable way. V. Connolly, *Beyond the Urals. Economic Development in Soviet Asia* (London, 1967) is a comprehensive, well-written account, mainly of Siberian development. W. A. D. Jackson, *The Russo-Chinese Borderlands* (Princeton, 1962) is a good survey of the background to this potential area of friction. D. J. M. Hooson, *A New Soviet Heartland?* (Princeton, 1964) is a detailed consideration of the significance of the Volga–Baykal zone as defined in this chapter. A. Nove and J. A. Newth, *The Soviet Middle East* (London, 1966) is a perceptive study of distinctive non-Russian southern republics of the USSR including comparisons with neighbouring non-Soviet lands.

2

KIEVAN RUSSIA

A. D. STOKES

Four distinct stages of development can be seen in the earliest period of Russian history. The first, prehistoric stage is concerned strictly with the Eastern Slavs rather than with the Russians, for it is only at its close, in the ninth century A.D., that the Rus', who were to give a collective name to the Eastern Slavs, their territory, and their political community, make their first appearance in historical sources. Russian history proper begins with the second stage, extending from the middle of the ninth century to the seizure of the Kievan throne by Vladimir I in 978, and marked by the birth and formation of Kievan Russia. The latter achieves its maximum power and development in the third stage (Map 15), the reigns of Vladimir I (*c.* 980–1015) and Yaroslav the Wise (1019–54); while the fourth witnesses its decline, interrupted only in the reigns of Vladimir Monomakh (1113–25) and his immediate successors, and is brought to an end by the Mongol invasion in 1237.

EARLY HISTORY

Our knowledge of the early history of the Eastern Slavs in particular, and of the Slavs in general, is fragmentary and imprecise. The exact location of the original Slav homeland is disputed. It certainly covered an area of eastern Europe to the north of the Carpathians, and may indeed have extended from the Elbe to the Dnieper, but conclusive archaeological and philological evidence is lacking, and the early Slavs did little to attract the attention of contemporary writers. In the period of the great migrations their role appears to have been largely passive. While successive waves of invaders from the east and north – Cimmerians, Scythians, Sarmatians, Goths, Huns, and Avars – occupied or swept through the southern Russian steppes, the Slavs who fell under their dominion were more often than not known to the outside world only by the names of their conquerors. But although positive identification is difficult, archaeological

Trade route "from the Varangians to the Greeks".

L.Ladoga

R.Volga

N.Dvina

URALS

R.Kama

Novgorod

L.Il'men

Pskov

R.Volkhov

[Suzdal']

[Vladimir]

W.Dvina

Gt.Bulgar

BULGARS

Polotsk

Smolensk

R.Desna

Vladimir-in-Volhynia

Lyubech

Chernigov

K H A Z A R S

Kiev

Pereyaslavl'

POLOVTSIANS

R.Don

R.Danube

CARPATHIANS

R.Dniester

P E C H E N E G S

R.Donets

R.Volga

R.Dnieper

SEA of AZOV

Pereyaslavets

Cherson

Kerch Straits

Tmutarakan'

BULGARIA

BLACK SEA

CASPIAN SEA

CAUCASUS

Byzantium

| 0 | km | 800 |
| 0 | miles | 500 |

◫ Kievan Russia

▨ Mountains

[ ] Principalities important in the 12th century

Map 15: Kievan Russia in the eleventh century

and other indirect evidence suggests that Slavs may already have constituted a large proportion of the population of western Russia before the Christian era. By the first century A.D. they are known to the sources as Venedi, but they emerge fully from their anonymity only in the fifth century, when, having moved southward toward the Black Sea into the vacuum left by the passage westward of the Huns, they came into direct contact with the East Roman Empire. Sixth-century writers distinguish three main groups of Slavs, adding two new names – Antae and Sclaveni – to that of Venedi. The latter appears to have been the common name given to the Slavs by their neighbours, probably the Celts, and used by the Goths and Greeks to designate the Slavonic tribes beyond the Antae and Sclaveni of which they had no direct knowledge.

Historians of Russia have paid particular attention to the Antic federation of tribes. Though their name is not Slavonic, and has been taken to indicate that they were first united as a result of their subjugation by the Alanic As, they were certainly Slavs. The area they inhabited in the sixth century, bounded roughly by the Black Sea and the Danube in the south, the Dniester in the west, and the Dnieper or possibly the Don in the east, suggests that they were Eastern Slavs; attempts have therefore been made to discover a connection between Antic and Kievan Russian history, to identify the Antic federation, a 'military democracy', as the initial stage in the development of the Kievan Russian state. But the Antae disappear from historical sources after the destruction of their federation by the Altaic Avars in 602 and, since the archaeological evidence is both meagre and ambiguous, this hypothesis, which has a particular attraction for those who favour a Marxist interpretation of Russian history, must for the present remain a hypothesis. Indeed, any reconstruction of the history of the Eastern Slavs between the seventh and ninth centuries can be only conjectural.

Increased pressure from the east combined with the revolts of subject peoples to weaken the Avar hold on southern Russia; but even the destruction of Avar power by Charlemagne in 796, a momentous event in the history of other Slavonic peoples, appears to have led merely to a change of masters for the Eastern Slavs. Bulgaria exercised control over the tribes of the south-west, while those between the middle Dnieper and the Don soon became the tributaries of the Turkic Khazars, whose expansion westward had contributed to the downfall of the Avars. The Khazars, however, proved capable of establishing a more permanent and economically viable state than had their predecessors and their rule was relatively mild, leaving no bitter legends, such as those by which the Avars were to be remembered, to be recorded by later Russian chroniclers. Their empire was founded upon trade rather than upon the exploitation of subject peoples. With its political centre on the Volga delta from early in the eighth century, it was able to take advantage of changes in the pattern of trade between east and west, enforced by Arab domination of the Mediterranean, which made the great waterways of Russia – in particular the Volga and the Don – important links in an alternative route to Asia. Thus Khazar dominion, which may have been exercised over the Slavs by Magyar tributaries of the Khazars, brought a relative stability to southern Russia, imposing upon the subject East Slavonic tribes a unity that was later to distinguish both them and their territory from the rest of Kievan Russia.

It was probably also in the eighth century that the Swedish Vikings or Varangians discovered the opportunities for trade with the Orient offered by the rivers of Russia. When they first began to probe eastward along the western Dvina and the Volga, they made little impact on the Eastern Slavs; but in the ninth century Byzantium became the goal, and the Dnieper route that they followed took them through the East Slavonic heartland. The change in the direction of the Varangian thrust coincided with the emergence of the Kievan state and inevitably poses the question of the relation of the two phenomena, the subject of the age-old 'Normanist–anti-Normanist' controversy.

THE NORMANIST CONTROVERSY

What appeared to be a clear-cut 'Normanist' answer to the question was given by the *Povest' vremennykh let* (*The Primary Chronicle*), the twelfth-century Russian chronicle, which is the single most important historical source for the period. It places at the beginning of Russian history the summoning by the Novgorod Slavs of three Varangian brothers – Ryurik, Sineus, and Truvor. They and their men, according to the chronicle, were the original Rus' from whom the Russians took their name, the first Russian princes, who brought to the Eastern Slavs the order and stability that they had been unable to achieve on their own. The narrative that follows seems designed to demonstrate that Kievan Russia was the creation of Ryurik's descendants (Sineus and Truvor having died soon after their arrival in Russia, leaving no heirs), and that the Ryurikide princes alone were the legitimate rulers of Russia. With the authority of the chronicle to support them, some eighteenth-century historians portrayed the Eastern Slavs as barbarians to whom the Varangians had brought culture, civilization, and political organization; others, reacting sharply to what they considered a slur on their country, argued that the culturally inferior and numerically insignificant Varangians had nothing to offer the Eastern Slavs except their services as mercenaries.

Increased knowledge of the period has led to the abandonment of the more extreme positions. It is now clear that the Varangians did not leave the indelible imprint on Russian culture that the claims of the early Normanists would lead us to expect; that few significant traces of Varangian influence can be discovered in Russian law, political institutions, social organization, religious beliefs, language, or literature; and that therefore their cultural role in the development of the Kievan state must be minimized. Neither can it now be maintained that the *Povest'* itself lends unqualified support to the Normanist thesis. It was precisely the contradictory nature of its evidence that prompted A. A. Shakhmatov to embark on the close study of the chronicle that established that it had in fact been written by a number of hands over a period of about a hundred years. Since each individual contributor had had his own point of view (and some were annalists rather than historians, not concerned with the larger issues of origins and causal connections), the reasons for its inconsistencies and contradictions are apparent; but they remain to supply arguments both for and against the Normanist view.

In recent times the discussion has focused particularly on the identity of the Rus' and the origin of their name. Here the evidence of Constantine Porphyrogenitus's *De Administrando Imperio*, which gives the 'Russian' and Slavonic names of the Dnieper rapids, would appear to be decisive. The 'Russian' names prove to be unmistakably Scandinavian; it is therefore difficult to escape the conclusion that the earliest Rus' were Varangians. The origin of their name is less easy to explain, as all efforts to trace it back to Scandinavia have been inconclusive. It must, therefore, have been adopted by the Varangians after their arrival in Russia; the most widely held view is that it derives from the first element of *Róps-menn*, a local term still found in the name of the Swedish region Roslagen, and in *ruotsi*, the Finnish name for the Swedes. This is a philologically sound solution, but it has some questionable historical implications. The fact that the term became associated with an area of southern Russia, when it had been in the north that the Varangians first established themselves, has led some scholars to cast doubt on this theory, but a more convincing alternative to it has yet to be found. G. V. Vernadsky's attempt to reconcile the Normanist and anti-Normanist positions by postulating an Alano-Slavonic Rus' and a common Alanic–Tokharian background for the Rus' and the Norsemen long before the Viking era is too hypothetical to be acceptable. Soviet historians, on the other hand, who are generally anti-Normanist and who have therefore looked for the Rus' among the Eastern Slavs, have only been able to produce cognate river names in support of their thesis. These could indicate that an East Slavonic Rus' had inhabited the areas in question before the coming of the Varangians, but they are no substitute for the positive identification of the tribe itself. Other evidence that they adduce can be disputed, depending for its interpretation upon an initial Normanist or anti-Normanist premiss.

THE ORIGINS OF THE KIEVAN STATE

Behind the Normanist controversy lies the larger issue of the origins of the Kievan state. The original Normanist thesis held that the activities of a comparatively small number of Varangian merchant-adventurers had created a state in a short space of time out of a primitive society; it thus denied the primacy of socio-economic factors in such a process. It can easily be understood that the essentially anti-Marxist nature of this model invites the criticism of Soviet historians; but it is also true that much effort is still being expended in demolishing positions that have long since been abandoned. Belief in the Scandinavian origin of the Rus' is not nowadays part and parcel of the naïve understanding of historical processes characteristic of the early Normanists. In this sense the terms 'Normanist' and 'anti-Normanist' are obsolete, and the Soviet historian B. D. Grekov is expressing a common view when he asserts that 'the prerequisites for the formation of a state had matured and yielded positive results in Russia long before the ninth century'.[1] These prerequisites were the erosion of the tribal form of organization, a resultant differentiation of society, and the accumulation of wealth and power in the hands of a native aristocracy. Thus it could be generally agreed that social and economic developments among the Eastern Slavs had made the emergence of new forms of political organization a question of time; nevertheless, it is clear that in the event it was the Varangians who acted as the catalyst.

Yet the story of the coming of the Varangians, as told in the *Povest' vremennykh let*, must be treated with some caution. Ryurik, Sineus, and Truvor may be no more than mythical figures, the stylized symbols of the unrecorded events that by the middle of the ninth century had established Varangian rulers in Novgorod and Kiev, the two most important cities on the great waterway 'from the Varangians to the Greeks'. Recorded Russian history begins rather with Askold and Dir, whose seizure of Kiev was a prelude to their attack on Constantinople in 860; and the political foundations of the Kievan state were laid in 882, when Oleg, the rival Varangian prince of Novgorod, united the north and the south by defeating Askold and Dir and proclaiming Kiev his capital.

Foreign trade, which had first drawn the Varangians to Russia, is the

---

[1] B. D. Grekov, *Kievskaya Rus'*, vol. II of *Izbrannyye trudy* (Moscow, 1959), p. 359.

underlying theme of the accounts in Russian and non-Russian sources of the activities of the early grand princes of Kiev – Oleg (*c.* 882–913), Igor (913–45), and Svyatoslav (964–72). Constantine Porphyrogenitus describes the annual winter expeditions that yielded the goods for their commerce – furs, wax, and honey, in the form of tribute from the subjugated population, and also slaves; the assembling and equipping of the large fleets of *monoxyla* (dug-out canoes) at Kiev in April and May; and the hazardous journey down the Dnieper and along the coast of Bulgaria to the markets of Constantinople. The *Povest'* records the campaigns against Byzantium of 907, 941, and 944, which secured for the Russians the right to sell their goods in the city and to buy in exchange luxury items, such as silks and wine, and includes the texts of the Russo-Byzantine treaties of 911 and 944, which confirmed and defined these rights and regulated the relations between the two countries. That trade was the primary concern of these Russian princes is also amply demonstrated by the events of 944, when the offer of a commercial treaty was sufficient to halt Igor's army on its way to Constantinople, even though the terms were less favourable to the Russians than were those of the earlier treaty of 911. And in 969 it was the commercial potential of Pereyaslavets-on-the-Danube that inspired Svyatoslav's abortive plan to make it the new Russian capital.

Neither was the eastern trade route forgotten. But with Byzantium and the south absorbing the major part of their energies, Khazar control of the lower Volga presented too formidable an obstacle to Russian expansion to be tackled by Oleg and Igor. They did, however, try to circumvent the Khazars and gain footholds beyond them in three campaigns to the Sea of Azov and the Caspian, all of which are mentioned in oriental sources. The first, in 909–10, was an exploratory raid that produced no tangible results; the second, in 913, was more ambitious and, though the returning Russians were treacherously attacked and routed by the Khazars, they had succeeded on the outward journey in establishing a base at Tmutarakan', on the eastern side of the Kerch straits, which was to become the centre of an important Russian principality. It was from here that a third, overland expedition was despatched in 943 to create another stepping-stone to the east at Bardaa in Azerbaijan. The venture ended in failure and Tmutarakan' remained the furthermost Russian outpost in this direction. Even the opportunities offered by Svyatoslav's destruction of the Khazar Empire in 965–6 were not exploited.

The emphasis on foreign trade in the written sources has been held by many historians, and foremost among them V. O. Klyuchevsky, to indicate accurately enough the economic foundations of the Kievan state. In their opinion the majority of the population were not tillers of the soil but found their livelihood in the forests as hunters, fishermen, and beekeepers; it was the development of trade in the non-agricultural products of the forests that led to the growth of markets and towns. In time the more important centres of international commerce on the major waterways were fortified to protect their increasing wealth, a native aristocracy of merchant–soldiers emerged, and the cities then became the masters of the surrounding areas that had created them. The process had been largely completed by the time the Varangians appeared on the scene in the ninth century. They found a Russia already composed of fortified towns and satellite areas and introduced no change in the pattern of economic life, eventually merging with the native aristocracy, whose interests and activities coincided with their own.

The opposing view is best represented in the work of B. D. Grekov and other Soviet historians, whose concept of Kievan Russia as a feudal society subsumes a closed economy with a predominantly agricultural base. They argue that agriculture, practised by the Eastern Slavs for centuries, was the main occupation of the population in the Kievan period. Towns sprang up with the emergence of classes as a result of improvements in agricultural techniques. Originating as tribal centres, they became the citadels of local chieftains, and only later developed into towns in the proper sense – permanent settlements with commercial suburbs created by merchants and craftsmen – when progress in agriculture had produced the surpluses to stimulate both internal trade and the demand for specialized occupations. This stage was reached in Kiev, the most advanced city, no earlier than the ninth–tenth centuries. Foreign trade was an additional factor, which explains the particular prosperity of a limited number of towns in favourable geographical positions, while the average Kievan town functioned in a natural economy, its artisans and merchants serving the needs of the surrounding agricultural area in which there was little demand for imported goods. In such conditions land was the main source of wealth, and therefore the wealth and power of the native aristocracy must have been based on the ownership of land and the exploitation of those who cultivated it.

For the most part Grekov's theories have the support of the more recent archaeological and other research, and undoubtedly present a truer picture of Kievan Russia's economic life. Agriculture was its mainstay; trade with other countries was primarily the province of the princes and their retinues; and non-agricultural products constituted the bulk of the exports for the good and sufficient reason that they found a readier sale in foreign markets. The interest of foreign sources in the commerce that brought their countries into contact with the Russians needs little comment, while its prominence in Russian chronicles is explained by the concentration of the latter on the activities of the princes.

Less convincing is Grekov's conclusion that the ruling class had derived its economic strength from the land since pre-Kievan times. Of this there is no direct and undisputed evidence for the period before the eleventh century. In the tenth century tribute, booty, and trade were still the principal sources of income for the princes and their retinues, but it is possible to see the germ of land-ownership in the allocation of rights in particular areas to particular individuals. Sveneld, a *voyevoda* or general under Igor and Svyatoslav, was granted the tribute from the tribes of the Drevlians and the Ulichi on two separate occasions. Olga, Igor's widow, who occupied the Kievan throne during the minority of her son Svyatoslav (945–64), set aside for herself hunting and fowling preserves and, in organizing a more systematic collection of tribute, established local centres of administration. These presumably had permanent agents who maintained themselves at the expense of the local population.

Large-scale land-ownership by the ruling class implies at least a more organized control of the rural areas than was achieved in the tenth century. It developed with the putting down of roots, with the evolution of permanent institutions of government and administration, as the *druzhinniki* (members of the prince's *druzhina* or retinue) were given civil responsibilities that drew them out of the towns and into the countryside. But in this second period of Russian history there was no stable state territory, and the very term 'state' can be applied only in the loosest way. In the reigns of Oleg and Igor a firm hold was kept on Rus' proper – Kiev, Chernigov, and Pereyaslavl', with their satellite areas – on Novgorod, and on the main towns of the waterway between them. Yet for Svyatoslav, Rus' was still a base for further expansion rather than the permanent centre of his realm, as his readiness to abandon Kiev for a new capital on the Danube demonstrates. During his absence in Bulgaria, Kiev could not call upon forces sufficient to raise the siege of the city by the nomadic Pechenegs, for outside the garrisoned towns Russia was ruled by rebellious chieftains and princes who were held in obedience only by periodic military expeditions. The country was united by brute force, and united only in the sense that its people were all tributaries of the Varangian conquerors and supplied troops for their more distant campaigns.

In these conditions it would be idle to look for any more than rudimentary government. The grand prince, as his title implies, was the senior of a number of princes who combined forces for foreign campaigns and reached joint decisions in matters of common interest, such as the negotiation of the treaties with Byzantium. Another influential element in the grand prince's counsels was his *druzhina*, the sole source of his personal power. It was on its advice that Igor abandoned his march on Constantinople in 944 and accepted Byzantine terms for peace; it was in trying to satisfy their demands for better clothing and equipment that he met his death in 945; and his son Svyatoslav refused to accept Christianity for fear of his *druzhina*'s mockery. Such examples of the *druzhina*'s influence over the grand prince indicate that the bond between them could easily be broken at the will of the individual *druzhinnik* and typify the loose structure of early Kievan institutions. The business of government was confined almost exclusively to the organization of the annual trade caravans to Byzantium and the gathering of tribute; but even this was conducted in a purely arbitrary way until the extortionate demands of Igor provoked the Drevlians into killing him. It was the lesson of his death that prompted his widow Olga, the most far-sighted of the early Kievan rulers, to lay down a fixed scale of tribute and create local outposts of Kievan authority in the Drevlian land and the Novgorod principality.

THE BEGINNINGS OF RUSSIAN CHRISTIANITY

Of no less importance for a future genuine unification of the country was Olga's encouragement of Christianity. There had probably been individual Christians among the Eastern Slavs from the time of their earliest contacts with the East Roman Empire, but the first large-scale conversion of Russians to Christianity occurred in the ninth century, a period of phenomenally successful Byzantine missionary activity among the Slavs in general. The new victory for the Byzantine Church was announced by Patriarch Photius of Constantinople in 867, seven years after Askold and Dir's first Russian attack on the imperial city. It is generally assumed that there is a direct connection between these two events; that Askold and Dir were the first Russian princes to accept baptism; and that it was Kiev that received first a bishop and later an archbishop from Constantinople. These promising beginnings were largely nullified when the pagan Oleg captured Kiev in 882. The church hierarchy disappeared without trace, but individual Christians survived to form the nucleus of a Christian community that gathered strength throughout the tenth century. Renewed contacts with Byzantium and Bulgaria, converted in 864, swelled their numbers, and the pagan state discovered the value of literate Christians in its dealings with other countries. By 944 they were able to worship in their own church of St Elias in Kiev and they played a prominent part in the negotiations for the treaty with Byzantium concluded in the same year.

When Olga became regent on Igor's death, the position of the Kievan Christians was further improved, as she herself accepted Christianity in Constantinople in 957. Russian and Byzantine sources do not agree on the date of her baptism, but preference must be given to the evidence of Constantine Porphyrogenitus, the reigning emperor at the time of Olga's visit, from whose description of her reception in *De cerimoniis aulae byzantinae* the date 957 may be deduced. Since there was already a church and priests in Kiev – the priest Gregory is mentioned by Constantine as a member of Olga's suite – the reason for her long and dangerous journey to Constantinople at the age of over sixty is not immediately apparent. The most likely explanation is that she wanted her personal baptism to be followed by the conversion of her country. To achieve this aim she had to convince the pagans in Kiev, who were still in the majority, that the introduction of Christianity would not entail a meek surrender to Byzantine influence. No doubt the example of Bulgaria, a Slavonic country with its own national church and a Slavonic liturgy, suggested a solution; for the Kievan priests were almost certainly Bulgarians. In this case Olga would have travelled to Constantinople in the hope of obtaining from Byzantium a similar independence for a Russian national church; and perhaps she calculated that a solemn profession of faith before the emperor would aid the success of her mission. Although it is clear that the aim was not achieved on this occasion, the hypothesis is supported by the events that followed. In 959 a Russian embassy to Otto I asked for a bishop and priests to be sent to Kiev, and the inference must be that Olga was again following the example of Bulgaria in seeking from the Western Church what had been refused in Constantinople. Since Byzantium would have had no reason to reject a request for an ordinary bishop, it can be assumed that Olga was asking Otto I for a bishop or archbishop with the authority to organize the Russian Church as an autonomous diocese. Otto, perhaps deliberately, misunderstood the proposal, and it was a bishop with only limited authority who set out for Kiev two years later. At all events he met a hostile reception in the Russian capital and left as quickly as possible. The emperors of both East and West had failed to realize that the political implications of an overtly Byzantine or Latin Christianity made the religion unacceptable to the Russian pagans. Olga, her influence declining as Svyatoslav approached the age when he could assume the throne, abandoned her efforts to build a Russian national church and baptize her people; and Russia had to wait another quarter of a century for conversion.

SVYATOSLAV

Svyatoslav's reign made no recorded contribution to the internal development of Russia. More interested in making war than in governing, he spent little time in the country and after Olga's death (969) delegated authority to his sons. By this first division of Russia among the ruling family, Yaropolk was to rule in Kiev and Oleg in the land of the Drevlians. Curiously, according to the *Povest' vremennykh let*, no provision was made for Novgorod, in spite of its distance from the capital and its vital importance for the Dnieper trade route. The Novgorodians themselves had to ask Svyatoslav for a prince and were sent Vladimir, the youngest son. This story may be no more than a legend, but it seems typical of Svyatoslav's lack of foresight and concern for his own country, a failing for which he was bitterly reproached by the people of Kiev. In retrospect each of his two wars can be seen to have had an inner logic, but they were impulsive and opportunist in conception, the strategy and aims developing as they progressed; and they brought few calculated benefits to Russia. The destruction of the Khazar Empire (965–6) sprang from the discovery that the East Slavonic Vyatichi were still its tributaries, but the conquered territory was then left unoccupied, to be seized in the eleventh century by the Polovtsians, a new and more formidable enemy. The initiative in the trans-Danubian campaign (967–71) came from the Emperor Nicephorus Phocas of Byzantium, who evidently felt that the defeat of the Khazars had brought the Russians dangerously close to Byzantine possessions on the Black Sea and therefore diverted their attention from this vulnerable area by hiring them to attack Bulgaria. The plan was ill-judged, for Svyatoslav immediately saw in it the opportunity for more permanent Russian gains in the Balkan peninsula than the emperor had intended. But only later did the war become an over-ambitious attempt to create a huge empire of Southern and Eastern Slavs, with Pereyaslavets-on-the-Danube as its capital. An easy victory over a weak and divided Bulgaria was followed by a challenge to Byzantium itself and ultimate failure. Outwitted and defeated by the Emperor John Tzimisces in 971, Svyatoslav was forced to accept Byzantine terms for peace and to relinquish all that he had won. He withdrew from Bulgaria with insufficient troops to repel the Pechenegs lying in wait for him at the Dnieper rapids, and met his death at their hand in the spring of the following year when he tried to break through to Kiev.

Nevertheless, the wars had some positive, if unintended, results. Firstly, they undoubtedly helped to spread Christianity in Russia, in spite of Svyatoslav's own refusal to accept his mother's religion. His men, who were mainly Slavs, had spent four years in Bulgaria, a Christian country whose people spoke a language very similar to their own, but one with a higher standard of culture and civilization to give concrete proof of the material benefits of conversion. Moreover, Christian Bulgarians and Greeks had been brought back to Russia as prisoners, or came voluntarily as refugees to escape punishment for their support of the Russians in the war with Byzantium. One such prisoner, a former Greek nun, became the wife of Svyatoslav's son and successor Yaropolk; others were probably taken for their skill as craftsmen, since new handicraft techniques, such as glass-making, enamelling, and the production of glazed ceramics began to be practised in Kiev from about the time of the Balkan campaigns. All these were skills that had flourished in Preslav, the Bulgarian capital. Secondly, Svyatoslav's probing expeditions had at least established the natural frontiers of Russia. From now on the Russian princes were to settle down within the territory inhabited by the Eastern Slavs, their energies more and more absorbed by internal problems of government, the perennial struggle for power among themselves, and the constant threat of the nomads from Asia – first the Pechenegs, later the Polovtsians, finally the Mongols.

YAROPOLK

At Svyatoslav's death, his son Yaropolk was already ruler of Kiev, appointed by his father in the expectation that he himself would remain on the Danube; Yaropolk therefore assumed his father's title. There is, however, nothing to suggest that his younger brothers recognized or accepted the right of primogeniture. It was to be a frequently recurring situation in Kievan history, one to be resolved by conflict and the elimination of rivals, rather than by law or by family unity and loyalty. On this occasion it was Yaropolk himself who brought about the death of his brother Oleg in the belief that he was forestalling the latter's plans to overthrow him. When news of Oleg's fate reached Vladimir in Novgorod, he fled to Scandinavia to gather an army for the continuation of the struggle, leaving Yaropolk as the sole ruler of Russia.

Yaropolk's reign should perhaps be placed more properly at the beginning of the next period of Russian history, since the little that is known about his policies and activities suggests that he showed a concern for the welfare and security of his country more characteristic of his successors than of his predecessors. He carried the war to the Pechenegs, instead of waiting for their attacks on Kiev and the trade caravans along the Dnieper; and he was the first to apply the later much practised and successful policy of taking the nomads into his service, settling them in frontier regions as a first line of defence against their own people. Amicable relations with Byzantium and Rome, sustained by embassies to and from the Russian capital, may be evidence of a willingness on Yaropolk's part to consider the conversion of Russia, but any such plans were not allowed to mature. His reign was brought to a violent end in 978 (980 according to the *Povest' vremennykh let*, but there is reason to prefer the earlier date) by the return from Scandinavia of Vladimir, whose achievements as Grand Prince of Kiev were to make the Russian chroniclers forget or ignore the possible merits of the brother whom he deposed and killed.

VLADIMIR I AND THE CONVERSION OF RUSSIA

From the outset Vladimir's actions were those of a ruler with a stake in his country's future. His attitude to Kiev differed significantly from that of his Varangian mercenaries. Having taken the city, they considered that it was theirs to plunder and demanded a ransom from the population. But to Vladimir it was his capital, and he felt sufficiently secure in it to reject the Varangians' demands and to send the majority of them away to find service in Byzantium. The few whom he retained were encouraged to settle by grants of land. Kiev was further protected by the building of a ring of new towns, strongholds against the Pechenegs, which were settled with Eastern Slavs from the north.

The apparatus of government created by Vladimir was rudimentary, consisting of a network of provincial centres in which he placed his sons. Their main duty was to collect the tribute from the local population, keeping a third for themselves and their retinues, and delivering the remaining two-thirds to Kiev. It was a system that was sufficiently effective – thanks to the size of Vladimir's family – to make the political unity of Russia a reality throughout most of Vladimir's reign, but later the absence of any centralizing institutions of government was to be a continual source of weakness. It allowed the growth of separate and increasingly independent principalities that were only loosely connected with the Kievan centre. Russian unity was dependent on family loyalty, common economic interests, and the personality and military strength of the Grand Prince of Kiev. Even Vladimir's authority was challenged in the last year of his life by his son Yaroslav, prince of Novgorod, and war between them was averted only by Vladimir's death. As the ruling house multiplied and proliferated, family loyalty was superseded by family feuds and family jealousies. As less and less trade flowed along the Dnieper waterway, owing to the attacks of the Polovtsians and changes in world trade, common interests became harder to find. The principalities evolved their own individual patterns of economic life, and the princes and their boyars discovered a new source of income closer to home in land-ownership. Ultimately only the personal power of the grand prince was left, and in the years that followed there were to be few grand princes who could summon up the resources and the strength of personality needed to hold Russia together.

Of far greater consequence than the impermanent political structure completed by Vladimir was his conversion of Russia to Christianity. His reign began with a pagan revival in Kiev and the building of a pantheon to the East Slavonic gods. Though in itself this was a step backward for Russia, it clearly reflected Vladimir's understanding of the value of religion as a cohesive force that could bind together the Eastern Slavs. Soon he turned his attention to the religions of the civilized world around him – eastern and western Christianity, Judaism, and Islam. Each was examined and discussed by the grand prince and his *druzhina*, although the previous long history of Eastern Orthodox Christianity in Russia made the final choice almost inevitable. The story of the conversion in the Russian chronicle has many legendary elements and gaps, but from non-Russian sources it is evident that a request for military aid from Emperor Basil II of Byzantium brought matters to a head. The emperor's need was urgent, and Vladimir was therefore able to set a high price on his assistance – the hand of Basil's sister Anna – but he also had to agree to accept Christianity for himself and his people. On these terms a Varangian corps was dispatched to Constantinople, where it arrived in the spring of 988, in time to enable the emperor to crush the rebellion that had threatened his throne. The *Povest' vremennykh let* has it that Vladimir was baptized in the Byzantine city of Cherson in the Crimea in 989, but other evidence suggesting an earlier date carries more conviction. Vladimir would surely have been left in no doubt that a Byzantine emperor would in no circumstances send his sister to marry a pagan and that the mere promise of a pagan to accept Christianity after the arrival of the bride-to-be was insufficient guarantee in a matter of this delicacy. It therefore seems more likely that Vladimir first gave proof of his good faith by being baptized in the presence of the Byzantine envoys at the time that the agreement was concluded – i.e. in the winter of 987. In all probability this took place near Kiev in Vladimir's own village of Vasiliev ('Basil's'), since Basil was the Christian name that he adopted at his baptism in honour of his future brother-in-law. But the conversion of Russia was delayed by Basil II's unwillingness to fulfil his part of the bargain. The following year Vladimir waited in vain for his bride at the Dnieper rapids, the point at which a Pecheneg ambush might be expected; it was not until he had captured Cherson in the summer of 989, and threatened Constantinople with a similar fate, that the reluctant and weeping Anna crossed the Black Sea. After the marriage ceremony Cherson was restored to Byzantium, and priests from the city accompanied Vladimir and the new Grand Princess Anna back to Kiev, where the pantheon was destroyed and the mass conversion of the Russian people began.

The early history of the Russian Church is almost completely ignored in the Russian chronicles. In an entry *s.a.* 1039 the *Povest' vremennykh let* makes its first reference to a Russian metropolitan, the Greek

Theopemptus, which is proof that by this date the Russian Church was under the jurisdiction of the Patriarchate of Constantinople; but there is no information about its status during the first fifty years of its existence. Many theories have been advanced to explain this puzzling silence, most of them based on the assumption that the chronicler–monks were concealing facts about the position of the church that they considered derogatory. Thus, it has been suggested that it was subordinated in the early days to one of a number of neighbouring archbishoprics – Ohrid in Bulgaria, Tmutarakan', or Cherson; that Vladimir had appointed his own primate, without reference to Constantinople; that Rome was responsible for the initial organization of the church. In recent years, however, it has been conclusively established that a Russian metropolis was erected by the Patriarch of Constantinople soon after Vladimir's conversion; and that the first metropolitan arrived in Russia from Byzantium at some time between 989 and 992. Consequently, there are no circumstances connected with the early status of the church that could explain why the Russian chroniclers avoided a topic of considerable interest to them. Possibly the solution lies rather in the struggle for power that developed after Vladimir's death. There are grounds for believing that he had made Pereyaslavl', not Kiev, the first Russian metropolis, but that the seat of the metropolitan was transferred to Kiev in 1036, when, after a long period of strife between Vladimir's heirs, his son Yaroslav finally emerged as the sole ruler of Russia. If Yaroslav's role in this turbulent period was less creditable than the chronicler would have us believe, if he was in fact the aggressor rather than the avenger, the gaps in the chronicle's history of the church could be seen as the by-product of a concealment of evidence that would have cast a slur on the progenitor of all the later grand princes of Kiev and Moscow. This remains a hypothesis, but a wholly satisfactory solution to the problem has yet to be found.

Eastern Orthodox Christianity brought to Russia the rich Byzantine heritage that has left its imprint on every aspect of Kievan civilization. It also distinguished the Russians from their neighbours – Jews, Muslims, and pagans to the east, Roman Catholics to the west – so that the name Rus' came to mean the country, its people, and its religion. The coincidence of ethnic, political, and religious boundaries fostered in the minds of individual Russians a consciousness of belonging to a wider community that could be destroyed neither by the divisive feuds and wars of the Russian princes nor by two centuries of Mongol domination. Moreover, from its foundation the Russian Church upheld and justified the authority of the grand prince, adding new substance to Kiev's claims to supremacy among the Russian principalities. As the seat of the metropolitan, the capital was not only the heart of a huge centralized institution that covered the whole country and vitally affected the lives of all its inhabitants, but also, through such centres of learning and literature as the Kievan Monastery of the Caves, the inspiration of Russia's vigorous cultural life. Indeed, Kiev's ecclesiastical and cultural significance survived the decline of its political power. This fact reflects the relative durability of Vladimir's achievements as, on the one hand, the baptizer of Russia and, on the other, the creator of a political system.

YAROSLAV

After Vladimir's death in 1015, twenty-one years were to elapse before the whole of Russia was again controlled by a Kievan grand prince. For the first four years the throne was occupied by Vladimir's eldest surviving son Svyatopolk (1015–19), but apparently he felt so insecure that he had three of his brothers assassinated. Two of them, Boris and Gleb, became Russia's first saints, because of their Christian humility in offering no resistance to the murderous brother whom they freely acknowledged to be their father's rightful heir – which makes it difficult to understand why Svyatopolk as Grand Prince of Kiev in 1019. In his turn Yaroslav was were avenged by Yaroslav of Novgorod, who defeated and succeeded Svyatopolk as Grand Prince of Kiev in 1019. In his turn Yaroslav was challenged, unsuccessfully, by his nephew the Prince of Polotsk, a principality that was to remain outside the Kievan federation, and in 1024 by his brother Mstislav of Tmutarakan'. In this struggle Mstislav was the victor, but the refusal of the Kievans to accept him as their prince made him come to an agreement with Yaroslav in 1026. Russia was divided between them along the line of the Dnieper: Mstislav held the left bank with the important cities of Chernigov and Pereyaslavl', Yaroslav the right bank and Kiev. The division lasted until 1036, when Mstislav's death restored a reunited Russia to Yaroslav.

If the single episode of Boris and Gleb's assassination is excluded, the Russian chronicles provide only the barest outline of this internecine war, leaving the motives of the main participants far from clear. Svyatopolk is cast as the villain of the period, Yaroslav as the avenging hero, driven to seize the Kievan throne only by righteous indignation. But it has to be remembered that this part of the chronicle was almost certainly written in Yaroslav's reign; that only a civil war could have cleared his path to power; and that in 1036, when he finally became the undisputed ruler of Russia, ten of his eleven brothers were dead. Sudislav, the only surviving brother, was imprisoned by Yaroslav in the same year and remained a prisoner throughout the rest of his reign. When one also remembers other examples of Yaroslav's ambitiousness and ruthlessness, such as his rebellion against his father in 1014, scepticism about the accuracy of the chronicle's strangely uninformative record of these years seems justified.

Nevertheless, Yaroslav was a worthy successor to Vladimir. While not in any sense an innovator, he built with energy and purpose upon the foundations laid by his father and brought Russia to a position of equality in the European family of states. Contemporary European rulers acknowledged her power and influence in the marriage alliances that made Russian princesses queens of Poland, Hungary, Norway, and France, and foreign princesses the brides of three of Yaroslav's sons. Russia was kept united and free from invasion throughout his reign. In the south the Pechenegs suffered a crushing defeat that put an end to their raids on Kiev and secured safe passage for Russian merchants on the Dnieper. In the north and west Yaroslav took the offensive against the Finns, Lithuanians, and Poles, but the latter became his allies after the marriage of his sister to Prince Casimir of Poland in 1043.

With Byzantium relations were close and culturally fertile, though the subordinate position of the Russian Church was not allowed to restrict the country's freedom of action *vis-à-vis* the empire. Indeed, after the death of Metropolitan Theopemptus, Yaroslav attempted to assert Russia's independence in ecclesiastical affairs.[2] In 1051, Hilarion, a native Russian priest and one of the most erudite and talented writers of the whole Kievan period, was elected metropolitan in succession to Theopemptus by a council of Russian bishops. He was the first Russian to achieve this distinction, but it had been done without the authority of the Patriarch of Constantinople. Shortly afterwards Yaroslav evidently agreed to depose him in favour of the Greek Ephraim, who is referred to as the metropolitan in the *Povest' vremennykh let s.a.* 1055. The marriage of Yaroslav's son Vsevolod to a Byzantine princess of the royal family in 1052 or 1053 is certainly a sign that by this date the Russian Church had returned to the fold; it was probably the price that Emperor Constantine IX paid for its submission. More violent was the dispute that occasioned the fourth and last Russian attack on Constantinople in 1043. The details have not been conclusively established, but it seems that it must have been linked with the death in Constantinople the year before of a number of Russians in a brawl between Greek and Russian merchants. No doubt the original friction had been caused by some change for the worse in the conditions of trade enjoyed by the Russians; Yaroslav had hoped that a military expedition would lead to a treaty that would restore the privileges that had been lost. The attack was a complete failure, but it underlines the continuing importance to Russia in this period of her commerce with the empire.

[2] The view that Yaroslav tried to make his church independent of Byzantium is not accepted by all historians. For a different view, see vol. 2 of this work, ch. 3.

But Yaroslav earned his title 'the wise' in other fields. His is the credit for the compilation of the first Russian legal codex, *Pravda russkaya* ('The Russian Law'). It probably originated with the charter granted to the people of Novgorod in 1016 for their support of Yaroslav's cause in the war with Svyatopolk. The charter offered them redress in the event of the sort of persecution that they had already suffered the year before at the hands of Yaroslav's Varangian troops. On that occasion their only remedy had been an uprising, for which they were savagely punished by their prince. Now there were to be payments of compensation, as an alternative to blood vengeance, for the murder of free men of various categories, and also for assault and affronts to honour. Further clauses may have been added in 1036, when Yaroslav installed his son Vladimir as prince of Novgorod, and later the whole charter was applied to Kiev and the rest of Russia. By this time the original payments of compensation were developing into fines to be paid to the prince, carrying with them the notion of penalties for a breach of the sovereign's peace and leading to the creation of a judiciary and the appointment of law officers. Since *Pravda russkaya* is a collection of laws promulgated over a period of time and in response to particular events and circumstances rather than a general codex, it is a valuable but somewhat erratic and haphazard source of information on Kievan society; the added difficulty of its language and terminology raises problems of interpretation that make it possible to cite the codex in support of widely differing conceptions of Kievan history.

The lasting monuments of Yaroslav's reign are the products of his patronage of the arts and learning, of the many cultural activities that had been brought to life or stimulated by the adoption of Christianity. Kiev was the main beneficiary. After Yaroslav's accession to full power in 1036 it became once more the undisputed capital of Russia and, in all probability, for the first time the seat of the metropolitan. With the aid of Byzantine skill Yaroslav set about making it equal to its new status, a second Constantinople. It expanded rapidly: new walls and a new citadel, the famous Golden Gate, were built, and among the many new churches the magnificent St Sophia cathedral. Here Yaroslav, himself a bibliophile, assembled scribes and translators to create a library and a centre of learning that made possible the rapid flowering of a native Russian literature.

YAROSLAV'S SUCCESSORS

The Kievan state had reached its highest point of development in Yaroslav's reign, and its decline began with his death in 1054. Klyuchevsky and other more recent historians have claimed that Yaroslav tried to make some provision for the continued unity of Russia by instituting the so-called 'ladder' or 'rota' system of succession. In their opinion Yaroslav's sons were meant to rule Russia as a family: Izyaslav, Svyatoslav, and Vsevolod, the three eldest, constituting the first generation with authority over the rest, the younger sons to be regarded as the second generation and on a par with nephews. As individuals the members of the family, according to this system, would own no particular area that they could bequeath to their heirs, but in their lifetime they would have the right to hold a portion of the country, determined by their relative seniority in the family. When the death of a prince left a throne vacant, it would be occupied not by his eldest son but by the next most senior member of the family. The system envisages constant movement from principality to principality and, in theory, continued unity for the country as a whole: for each prince would recognize that it was in his own interests to preserve a unity from which he too might expect to benefit when the passage of time had brought him to the senior throne of Kiev. In practice the system could have worked only with a family of limited size, and one whose members died in strict order of seniority. But in fact neither Yaroslav's so-called 'testament' nor any other source substantiates the view that such a system of succession was conceived by Yaroslav for his descendants. It is true that a list of the occupants of the Kievan throne between 1054 and 1113, the period in question, suggests an underlying principle of succession by rota: Izyaslav (1054–68, 1069–73, 1077–8), Svyatoslav (1073–6), and Vsevolod (1078–93) followed each other as Grand Princes of Kiev in order of seniority; when Vsevolod died it was Izyaslav's eldest son Svyatopolk II (1093–1113), the senior prince of the second generation, who came to power. But when we consider in more detail how and why these changes on the Kievan throne took place, it becomes apparent that the 'rota' system is a myth. It is a *post factum* theory to explain an apparent pattern, not a principle devised by Yaroslav and accepted by his sons to guard against the disintegration of Rus'. Usual family law determined the fate of Russia in 1054: undivided ownership was required only in the case of an undivided family consisting of a father and a number of sons; the death of the father was followed by division among his heirs and complete separation. And this is what occurred after Yaroslav's death. His eldest son Izyaslav had been named as his heir in Kiev, but Russia as a whole was divided into a number of patrimonies among all his sons. In his 'testament' Yaroslav simply urged them to accept Izyaslav in his place and to support each other.

Such a division of Russia made it impossible for a prince of Izyaslav's calibre to wield the same power and authority as his father had done. Nevertheless, for nearly twenty years he and his brothers Svyatoslav and

Vsevolod, who had received the principalities of Chernigov and Pereya-slavl', acted in concert by voluntary agreement. Between them they held the original Rus', Novgorod, and other important territories, and their collective strength enabled them to impose most of their decisions upon the junior princes. But the voluntary nature of the bond between them made it too fragile to be enduring. With Vsevolod's aid Svyatoslav deposed Izyaslav in 1073 and installed his own sons in all the major principalities except Chernigov, which went to his accomplice Vsevolod. Once more it seemed that the political unity of Russia might be reforged by force, but Svyatoslav died three years later and, in spite of the strong support given to Vsevolod by his son Vladimir Monomakh, the country experienced a period of bitter internecine strife that ended only when Vladimir himself acceded to the Kievan throne in 1113.

The absence in these years of any single source of authority is empha-sized by the attempts of the princes to reach agreement among themselves. The urgent need for an end to conflict was all too plain, for not only were the princes themselves ravaging their own country, but they were also leaving her open to the attacks of the Polovtsians, the new nomadic scourge, which had made its first appearance on her south-eastern borders in 1061. Indeed, there were those princes who were so indifferent to the interests of Russia that they used the Polovtsians to augment their armies in their family feuds. The first congress of princes was held in Lyubech in 1097, when it was agreed that they would care for the Russian land 'as one heart' and abide by Yaroslav's original division of the country; i.e. they confirmed that the territories inherited by Yaroslav's sons were the patrimonies of their descendants. But the peace that had been established did not last out the year. The Grand Prince Svyatopolk II, incited by David of Vladimir-in-Volhynia, seized and blinded Prince Vasil'ko of Terebovl'. The sequel to this episode illustrates the changed status of the grand prince. Svyatopolk II was summoned by his peers to answer for his crime and forced to punish his accomplice. He tried vainly to justify his action on the grounds that he had believed that Vasil'ko was plotting against him; but he was sternly told that it was not for him to act on his own initiative and on mere suspicion: Vasil'ko's guilt should first have been proved to the satisfaction of his assembled brother princes.

The collective and individual weakness of the Russian princes was paralleled by the growing strength of the internal forces in the princi-palities and, in particular, of the towns. In the provincial capitals the focal point for the expression of the will of the population was the *veche* (the town assembly), an institution that had its roots in the pre-Kievan period but that had had little chance of exerting any influence on affairs in the days of the more powerful Kievan rulers. All heads of families had the right to participate and they were summoned by the *veche* bell to hammer out unanimous decisions on important issues of common interest. In 1068 the Kievan *veche* rose in rebellion when the Grand Prince Izyaslav, defeated together with his brothers by the Polovtsians, refused to give the Kievan militia fresh arms to continue the battle. Izyaslav was deposed and replaced by his prisoner Prince Vseslav of Polotsk, whom the mob had freed. At the same time they besieged the house of Izyaslav's *voyevoda*, who was probably the head of the town administration, and released the fellow citizens whom the grand prince had previously imprisoned. This seems to indicate that there had been an earlier history of conflict and opposition to the grand prince's rule, and that the Polovtsian victory had brought matters to a head. That part of the *Pravda russkaya* that is known as the *Pravda Yaroslavichey* ('The Law of Yaroslav's Sons'), and which doubles the fine for the murder of the prince's retainers and officers, is considered to be a direct response to this social unrest.

VLADIMIR MONOMAKH

The activities of the Kievan *veche* also decided the question of the succession in 1113, when the death of the unpopular Svyatopolk II was followed by rioting in the city. Once again it was the prince's officials – the head of the town administration (now with the title *tysyatsky* or chiliarch) and his subordinates (*sotskiye* or centurions) – who, together with the rich Jewish merchants and moneylenders, were the targets of the *veche*'s anger. An urgent message was sent from the *veche* to Vladimir Monomakh, inviting him to assume the throne. He refused – probably because Kiev was the patrimony of his uncle Izyaslav's descendants, but a second invitation made him change his mind. It carried with it the warning that the next victims of the mob's violence were likely to be Svyatopolk's widow, the boyars, and the monasteries, and laid the responsibility for their safety on Monomakh's shoulders. The *Povest' vremennykh let* has it that the rioting broke out after, and as a result of, Monomakh's rejection of the throne, but since it was the agents of the prince's administration and the moneylenders who were attacked, it is clear that social grievances were the primary cause of the riots. Monomakh was summoned after they had begun as the one man whose popularity and firmness could deal with them. This hypothesis is confirmed by the legislation enacted by Vladimir immediately after his accession at a meeting with his *druzhina* and the chiliarchs of Kiev, Pereyaslavl', and Belgorod. His additions to the *Pravda russkaya*, known as the *Ustav* or Statute of Vladimir Monomakh, are concerned with such

matters as extortionate rates of interest and the enslavement and in-
denturing of debtors, the grievances that had lain behind the riots.

When the gathering strength of the centrifugal forces at work within
Kievan Russia is taken into account, Vladimir Monomakh's achievement
in restoring a temporary unity to the country must be judged to have
been far greater than that of either his grandfather Yaroslav the Wise or
of his great-grandfather Vladimir I. It is true that he began his reign with
the advantage of the reputation he had established in the days of his
father Vsevolod and his cousin Svyatopolk II and which had led the
Kievans freely to choose him as their prince, also that he was able to
control a number of the major principalities directly through his sons;
but once more the country was to be held together largely by the personality and energy of an individual. Significantly, there was no need to hold
congresses of princes to reach agreement on common policies in
Monomakh's reign. This is not to say that his authority alone was sufficient to preserve order and unity. His whole life both before and after his
accession was spent in a long series of wars that crushed the offensive
spirit of the Polovtsians and left feuding princes in no doubt that breaches
of the peace would bring upon them swift retribution. It was as a result
of his readiness to respond to every challenge that the principle of the
grand prince's seniority acquired a new vitality and meaning. The Russian
princes were forced to accept the idea that their right to a share of
Russian land carried with it the obligation to support the grand prince
whenever he might call upon them to do so; and that they would be
punished and deprived of their territories if they failed to obey his orders.
To Monomakh's skill in war and his ability to lead men must be added
the breadth of vision that enabled him to think of Russia as a whole, to
show concern, for example, for her reputation abroad, and the grasp of
political realities that made him realize the need for popular support.
These qualities are evident in his *Poucheniye* (testament), written for the
guidance of his sons and successors and preserved in the *Povest'
vremennykh let s.a.* 1096.

THE DECLINE OF KIEV

Monomakh's name continued to be respected and to exert an influence
long after his death. His son Mstislav was able to succeed him as Grand
Prince of Kiev in 1125 without any opposition and at the latter's death
in 1132 the throne passed with equal ease to Mstislav's younger brother
Yaropolk II (1132–9). But Monomakh and his sons had merely delayed
the disintegration of Kievan Russia, and after 1139 the process continued
with renewed vigour. The struggle for the Kievan throne over the next

71

thirty years was at least proof that it was still considered the supreme prize; but the bewildering speed with which Kievan princes came and went demonstrated unambiguously that the prestige conferred by possession of Kiev was a memory of past glory rather than a measure of contemporary military and economic strength. In the two-and-a-half centuries of Kievan Russia's existence before 1139 there had been only fourteen grand princes of Kiev: between 1139 and 1169 the title changed hands seventeen times.

These rapid changes were also, of course, a sign of the individual weakness of the contestants. As the ruling family of princes proliferated, it broke up into a number of branches and sub-branches, fragmenting and localizing political power. At Monomakh's death there had been two main groups, the Monomashichi, the descendants of Monomakh himself, and the Ol'govichi, the descendants of Oleg Svyatoslavich of Chernigov. Soon there were Volhynian, Smolensk, and Suzdalian Monomashichi, while the Ol'govichi subdivided into Chernigov and Novgorod–Seversk branches. The branches grew further apart and became increasingly dependent on local strength, on the forces that could be put into the field by the major town in the principality, and that were loyal to the town rather than to the prince. When Prince Svyatoslav Vsevolodovich was forced to flee from Novgorod–Seversk, part of his *druzhina* – presumably his personal retinue – went with him, but the rest of his men, who were local troops, left his service. The princes found that they could no longer simply command the obedience of their armies. In 1185 Prince David of Smolensk wanted to lead his men from Trepol', near Kiev, to the relief of Pereyaslavl', besieged by the Polovtsians. The troops called a meeting of the *veche* and rejected the proposal, saying that they would have been ready to help in the defence of Kiev, but that they were tired after their journey south and would go no further. Obviously the towns now had more to bargain with in their dealings with princes, and it became common practice for their relations to be formally established by treaties guaranteeing the rights of the citizens and thus limiting the powers of the prince. As Klyuchevsky has pointed out, the chronicler who describes the system of government in the principalities in the middle of the twelfth century does not find it necessary even to mention the role of the prince. He records that decisions are taken by the citizens of the major towns, gathered together at the *veche*, and are accepted as binding by the minor towns in the principality.

Novgorod is an extreme but striking example of the independence of these city states. Its geographical position gave it many natural advantages, which its energetic citizens exploited to the full. In the early days its easy access to the waterways of Russia, coupled with its proximity to the Varangian homeland, had made it the natural base for the conquest of the rest of the country. From here Oleg had launched his successful campaign in 882; Vladimir I and Yaroslav the Wise had each in their turn been able to gather in safety the armies with which to depose their brothers. And for their support of Yaroslav the citizens of Novgorod had been granted a charter – the nucleus of the *Pravda russkaya* – which was a first step toward their independence. Thus, both for political and economic reasons, it was necessary for the grand prince to control Novgorod. The latter, however, since it was not economically dependent on the Dnieper trade route, did not feel the same need for close links with Kiev. When the incursions of the Polovtsians, the increased use of the Mediterranean for commerce between East and West and, finally, the capture of Constantinople by the Crusaders in 1204, had robbed the Dnieper of its international trade, Novgorod continued to flourish as a commercial centre. Indeed, it is precisely in the twelfth century that her merchants become particularly active. The powerful St John's guild of merchants was formed soon after 1130 and quickly secured for itself a monopoly in the weighing, measuring, and taxing of the goods bought and sold in the city. Through the enterprise of these merchants Novgorod became the main centre for Russian exports to western Europe, and Novgorod charters of the early twelfth century make it plain that goods from Kiev and the south were not a significant element in this trade. It was the wealth of Polotsk, Smolensk, Suzdal', and of its own vast territories, the harvest of the northern forests, that Novgorod merchants carried to the island of Gotland and the Baltic ports with which reciprocal trading agreements were concluded. The principality's need to import grain was certainly a potential weakness, but it could be exploited only if supplies were cut off both by Kiev and Suzdal', the main grain-exporting areas. When Kiev could no longer dictate the policies of Suzdal', the possibility of exerting such economic pressure on Novgorod became more remote. Novgorod thus had no interest in delaying the disintegration of Kievan Russia. She herself suffered little from the internecine strife in the distant southern principalities and, in absorbing the energies of the more powerful princes, lessened the likelihood of outside interference in her affairs. A strong Kievan state, on the other hand, would have offered her continued political subservience with no economic benefits.

Already in the reign of Svyatopolk II (1093–1113) the principality had twice demonstrated its readiness to take advantage of weakness at the Kievan centre by refusing to accept the prince appointed to rule over it; after the death of Vladimir Monomakh power began to pass rapidly from the prince to the *veche* and its representatives. The most important administrative posts, those of *posadnik* (mayor) and *tysyatsky* (chiliarch), ceased to be appointments made by the prince and became elective offices. From 1156 it was also the *veche* that chose the three candidates from whom would be elected the bishop (later archbishop) of Novgorod, a figure of considerable influence in the life of the principality. A prince was still needed as a military leader, and also as an outsider who might be expected to administer justice with greater impartiality than a local judge; but gradually he was reduced to the status of a paid official.

The year 1136, in which the Novgorodians deposed and imprisoned Prince Vsevolod Mstislavich, was the turning point. Over the next six years there were eight changes on the Novgorod throne, enforced by the citizens themselves, not resulting from the usual movement of princes from principality to principality. Princes of Novgorod now assumed the throne at the invitation of the *veche*, which could also dismiss them. In doing so, they were obliged to sign treaties with the principality that restricted their authority, guaranteed the rights of the citizens, ensured that the administration of the city and principality remained firmly in the hands of Novgorodians, and sought to prevent the prince from gaining any sort of foothold in the territory over which he nominally ruled. The earliest extant treaty of this type dates to 1264, but there can be no doubt that the custom sprang from the first real exercise of power by the Novgorod *veche* in 1136.

Elsewhere in Russia the *veche* did not achieve a similar dominance, and Novgorod remained the only 'republican principality' until the fourteenth century; but everywhere the principalities were developing in ways that made the old ties with the Kievan centre an anachronism. No longer was there even a common enemy. Galicia and Volhynia were concerned with the Hungarians and Poles; Polotsk with the Lithuanians; Novgorod with the Finns and later the Teutonic Knights; Suzdal' with the Bulgars; the original Rus' – Kiev, Chernigov, and Pereyaslavl' – with the Polovtsians. The Grand Prince of Kiev summoned the Hungarians to his aid in his war with Suzdal' and Chernigov; his enemies called upon the Polovtsians. Rus' was the constant battleground, but it had less and less of real value to offer to its conquerors. In 1159 Prince Svyatoslav Ol'govich described his possessions as 'Chernigov and seven empty towns inhabited by kennelmen and Polovtsians'.

The myth of Kievan supremacy was finally destroyed by Vladimir Monomakh's grandson, Prince Andrey Bogolyubsky of Suzdal'. For his father, Yury Dolgoruky, the old, original Rus' had still been the prize; and in 1139 he had been prepared to exchange Rostov and Suzdal' for Pereyaslavl'. His son Andrey was more of a realist, and recognized the greater potential of Suzdal'. In 1151, after Yury had suffered a defeat in Rus', Andrey had urged him to quit the middle Dnieper, where they had 'neither war nor any other business'. Succeeding his father in 1157, he chose as his seat neither Rostov nor Suzdal', the two most powerful and ancient cities in his principality, but the relatively junior Vladimir, where there was no vigorous and unbiddable boyar aristocracy to demand a voice in the conduct of affairs. It was in Vladimir that he planned to build a magnificent new capital to supersede Kiev. Consequently, when the latter was captured by Andrey's army in 1169, Andrey himself did not move south, but gave the city to his younger brother Gleb, after it had been sacked and plundered for two days.

Kiev never recovered from this blow. Nominally its princes were to remain 'grand princes', but the title was now also assumed by the rulers of Vladimir–Suzdal'. Under Andrey's successors, particularly Vsevolod III (1176–1212), the latter retained and strengthened its position as the most powerful principality in Russia. Indeed, if it had a rival in the years before the Mongol invasion, it was not Kiev, but the principalities of the south and west, Galicia and Volhynia, united by Prince Roman in 1199. Vladimir–Suzdal' is the link between the earlier Kiev and the later Moscow; but, like Galicia–Volhynia, it was essentially a regional principality, pursuing its own regional interests, not the focal point of a movement to reunify Russia or to marshal her resources against her many external enemies. A fragmented Russia could still meet with varying success the individual challenges of Polovtsians, Hungarians, Poles, Lithuanians, and Teutonic Knights; but she had no chance of resisting the Mongol onslaught of 1237.

GUIDE TO FURTHER READING

Bibliographies

P. A. Crowther, *A Bibliography of Works in English on Early Russian History to 1800* (Oxford, 1969) is a valuable, up-to-date, comprehensive, and well-arranged bibliography of English-language works on the period.

Original sources

V. P. Adrianova-Peretts, ed., *Povest' vremennykh let* (2 vols., Moscow–Leningrad, 1950) is the most important single source; this edition has the original text, a modern Russian translation, detailed commentaries, and a study of the *Povest'* by D. S. Likhachev. The English translation by S. H. Cross and O. P. Sherbowitz-Wetzor, *The Russian Primary Chronicle: Laurentian Text* (Cambridge, Mass., 1953) has its inaccuracies. For the period after 1117, see the continuation of the *Povest'* in the Laurentian and Hypatian Chronicles: *Polnoye sobraniye russkikh letopisey*, vol. I, pt. 2, 2nd edn (Leningrad, 1927, repr. Moscow, 1962), and vol. II (St Petersburg, 1908, repr. Moscow, 1962). Constantine Porphyrogenitus, *De Administrando Imperio*, ed. and with English trans. by Gy. Moravcsik and R. J. H. Jenkins (2 vols., Washington, 1966, and London, 1962). Of particular interest is ch. 9, with its contemporary account of the trade route from Kiev to Constantinople, which raises many controversial issues – e.g. the identity of the

Rus'. These are very fully discussed in the excellent commentaries by D. Obolensky in vol. II, and preceded by a comprehensive bibliography.

General works

G. Vernadsky, *Ancient Russia* (New Haven, 1943), and his *Kievan Russia* (New Haven, 1948) together represent the fullest treatment of the period in English. They are valuable for the presentation of evidence from sources in many languages, for the detailed discussion of numerous controversial topics, and for the emphasis laid on the importance of Russia's links with Asia; but the author has a tendency to overlook the distinction between hypothesis and fact. B. D. Grekov, *Kievskaya Rus'*, vol. II of *Izbrannyye trudy* (Moscow, 1959), the standard Soviet history, has a socio-economic approach, and readers unfamiliar with the period would be advised to turn first to the outline of political history in the book's last chapter. The English translation, *Kiev Rus*, cannot be recommended. For a Marxist study of the earliest period, see P. N. Tret'yakov, *Vostochnoslavyanskiye plemena*, 2nd edn (Moscow, 1953). V. O. Klyuchevsky, *Kurs russkoy istorii, Sochineniya*, I (Moscow, 1956), the work of the great nineteenth-century historian, is out of date in many respects, but is still well worth reading. The English translation, *A History of Russia*, trans. by C. J. Hogarth (New York, 1960) is full of mistakes.

The origins of Kievan Russia

A. Vucinich, 'The First Russian State: an Appraisal of Soviet Theory', *Speculum*, 28 (1953) discusses the hypotheses of leading Soviet scholars, and the premises on which they are based, with the essential bibliography in the footnotes. V. P. Shusharin, *Sovremennaya burzhuaznaya istoriografiya Drevney Rusi* (Moscow, 1964) gives the opposite point of view, but covers a much wider range of topics. For a balanced, but anti-Normanist interpretation, see D. M. Odinets, *Vozniknoveniye gosudarstvennogo stroya u vostochnykh slavyan* (Paris, 1935). No serious work on the period can avoid discussing the role of the Varangians, but see in particular, for the anti-Normanist case, V. A. Ryazanovsky, *Obzor russkoy kul'tury* (New York, 1947); and, for the Normanist view, V. Moshin, 'Nachalo Rusi. Normany v vostochnoy yevrope', *Byzantinoslavica*, III (1931); the same author's 'Varyago-russkiy vopros', *Slavia*, x (1931); Ad. Stender-Petersen, *Varangica* (Aarhus, 1953); and 'Varangian Problems', *Scando–Slavica*, Supplementum 1 (Copenhagen, 1970).

Russia's relations with the outside world

For a very good summary of Russo-Byzantine relations in the period to 1018, see D. Obolensky, 'The Empire and Its Northern Neighbours', *The Cambridge Medieval History*, vol. IV, pt. 1, 2nd edn (Cambridge, 1966), ch. xi. See also, by the same author, *The Byzantine Commonwealth: Eastern Europe, 500–1453* (London, 1971). A fuller treatment of the whole period is M. V. Levchenko, *Ocherki po istorii russko-vizantiyskikh otnosheniy* (Moscow, 1956). Kievan Russia's links with all other countries are dealt with by V. T Pashuto, *Vneshnyaya politika Drevney Rusi* (Moscow, 1968).

Christianity in Kievan Russia

A. P. Vlasto, *The Entry of the Slavs into Christendom* (Cambridge, 1970), ch. 5, covers in outline the whole subject and summarizes the conflicting views on the many controversial issues. A more detailed exposition of the author's own views on the early status of the Russian Church can be found in A. D. Stokes, 'The Status of the Russian Church, 988–1037', *Slavonic and East European Review*, XXXVII (1958–9).

Social and economic history

These topics command the particular attention of Soviet historians: see A. Vucinich, 'The Soviet Theory of Social Development in the Early Middle Ages', *Speculum*, 26 (1951). The standard Soviet works are Grekov's *Kievskaya Rus'*, and the same writer's *Krest'yane na Rusi s drevneyshikh vremyon do 17 veka* (Moscow, 1952). For other views, see G. Vernadsky, 'On Feudalism in Kievan Russia', *American Slavic and East European Review*, VII (1948); and J. Blum, *Lord and Peasant in Russia from the Ninth to the Nineteenth Century* (Princeton, 1961). A very important monograph on Kievan agriculture, which reveals the weaknesses of the more schematic Marxist approach, is R. E. F. Smith, *The Origins of Farming in Russia* (Paris and The Hague, 1959).

Kievan culture and civilization

See B. D. Grekov and M. I. Artamonov, eds., *Istoriya kul'tury Drevney Rusi* (2 vols., Moscow–Leningrad, 1951); B. A. Rybakov, *Remeslo Drevney Rusi* (Moscow, 1948); N. Andreyev, 'Pagan and Christian Elements in Old Russia', *Slavic Review*, XXI (1962); G. Florovsky, 'The Problem of Old Russian Culture', *Slavic Review*, XXI (1962); D. S. Likhachev, 'Further Remarks on the Problem of Old Russian Culture', *Slavic Review*, XXII (1963); and B. D. Grekov, *The Culture of Kiev Rūs* (Moscow, 1947).

The system of succession, 1054–1113

An exposition of the generally accepted view can be found in Klyuchevsky, *Kurs russkoy istorii*, vol. I, 169–89. For objections to it, see A. D. Stokes, 'The System of Succession to the Thrones of Russia, 1054–1113', in R. Auty, L. R. Lewitter, and A. P. Vlasto, eds., *Gorski Vijenac: A Garland of Essays Offered to Professor E. M. Hill* (Cambridge, 1970).

3

APPANAGE AND MUSCOVITE RUSSIA

NIKOLAY ANDREYEV

THE MONGOL INVASION

The Mongol (or Tatar)[1] invasion – whose main events were the first encounter between the Russians and Tatars on the river Kalka near the Sea of Azov in 1222 or 1223, the invasion of north-eastern Russia in 1237, and the sack of Kiev in 1240 – created a new political situation in eastern Europe: Russia fell under the rule of the successors of Genghis Khan's (c. 1155–1227) immense empire, becoming in fact its north-western province. It was governed by the 'Golden Horde' from its capital Saray on the lower Volga, which later became an independent state. This situation created a number of problems in Russian politics, as the country's interests had necessarily to be combined with the aspirations of the Mongol conquerors; Russia began to develop into a European state oriented toward Asia (a fact that was to determine her future for a long time to come), and suffered the first onslaughts from the west, which also influenced the course of her history.

The Russian administrative system was not altered by the conquerors, but the grand princes now had to obtain a *yarlyk* (charter) from the 'Great Khan' confirming them in office, obtainable by obligatory travel to Saray and Mongolia to pay humble obeisance and offer rich presents. The Mongol authorities took a census of Russia's population and imposed on all except the clergy a tribute to be collected by Tatar officials under the supervision of Mongol *baskaks* (agents). Sometimes, as in 1257–9, the local khans demanded Russian military detachments to reinforce their army. All this was resented by the Russians and seen as humiliation; in a number of towns there were protests and revolts, which were cruelly punished. Some relief did come later, however, when certain Russian princes were allowed to act as collectors of the tribute.

---

[1] The armies of the Mongol conquerors consisted very largely of members of the Turkic nomad peoples whom they had subjected. In the territories of the Golden Horde the Mongols became largely assimilated to their Turkic subjects, and the official language was a form of Turkish (Chagatay). The term 'Tatar' has been used for different Turkic peoples; and there is consequently some confusion in the use of the terms 'Mongol' and 'Tatar' in Russian historiography.

After the fall of Grand Prince Yury (son of Vsevolod III) in 1238 in the battle on the river Sit', his brother Yaroslav came over from Kiev to rule in Vladimir, and was finally confirmed in 1243 by Khan Batu. He died in Mongolia three years later. For a short time he was succeeded as grand prince by his brother Svyatoslav (1247–8) and then by his son Andrey (1249–52).

Prince Andrey, who in 1250 had married a daughter of Prince Daniil of Galicia, shared his father-in-law's dream of a union of north and south Russia with a view to overthrowing the Mongol yoke. After years of tenacious struggle with his aristocracy, Daniil became supreme ruler of Volhynia and Galicia and hoped to conclude an anti-Mongol alliance with the neighbouring western states, but negotiations with Poland and Hungary proved unsuccessful. In 1245 he had to submit to Khan Batu. Through the intermediary of Plano Carpini, papal envoy to Mongolia, he established relations with Pope Innocent IV, promising him to bring about a reunion with the Roman Catholic Church. The Pope sent him a royal crown and Daniil was crowned in 1255 at Dorogichin. However, he obtained no practical help from the West, though he had himself taken an active part in the affairs of central European countries. Some encouragement for his anti-Mongol plans was received by Daniil from the Lithuanian Prince Mindovg (d. 1264), the first prince to unite the Lithuanian territories in one state. Nevertheless, under the threat of armed reprisals from the Mongols, Daniil was forced in 1260 to dismantle his fortresses and to abandon his anti-Mongol projects. In spite of this, Galicia prospered under his rule and his reputation stood very high. His successors were unable to keep, still less to increase, their inheritance, however, and by the middle of the fourteenth century the principality of Galicia was absorbed by Lithuania and Poland.

ALEXANDER NEVSKY

Alexander (1219–63), another son of Yaroslav, is known as Alexander Nevsky in commemoration of his victory on the banks of the river Neva on St Vladimir's Day, 15 July 1240: at the head of the Novgorodians, he defeated the Swedish army commanded by Birger, who was threatening the Novgorodian territories. Contemporaries considered this event to be a victory of Orthodoxy over Catholicism; the 'free city' of Novgorod, however, fearing an increase of the victorious prince's power, let him go back to his own principality of Pereyaslavl'. A further threat to Novgorod, coming this time from the Teutonic Knights, rulers of the Baltic provinces (who, after capturing Izborsk and Pskov, had been plundering merchants under Novgorod's very walls), impelled the Novgorodians to

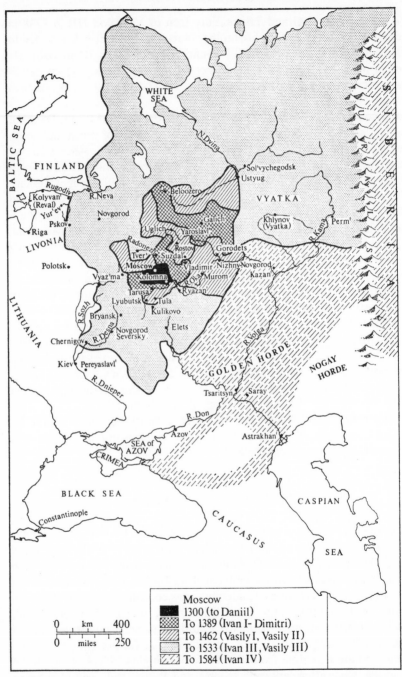

BALTIC SEA

WHITE
SEA

FINLAND

SIBERIA

URAL

Rugodiv
Kolyvan'
(Reval)
Yur'ev
Pskov
Riga

R.Neva

Novgorod

N.Dvina

Sol'vychegodsk
Ustyug

VYATKA

LIVONIA

Beloozero

Uglich   Yaroslavl'
Galich

Khlynov
(Vyatka)

R.Kama

Perm'

LITHUANIA

Polotsk

Radonezh
Tver'   Rostov
Moscow   Suzdal'
Kolomna Vladimir
Vyaz'ma   Murom
Tarusa   R.Oka
Lyubutsk   Tula
R.Sozh   Kulikovo
Bryansk

Gorodets

Nizhny Novgorod

Kazan'

Novgorod
Seversky

R.Desna

Elets

Chernigov

Kiev   Pereyaslavl'

R.Dnieper

GOLDEN HORDE

R.Volga

NOGAY
HORDE

Tsaritsyn   Saray

R.Don

Azov

Astrakhan'

SEA of
AZOV

CRIMEA

BLACK SEA

CASPIAN

Constantinople

CAUCASUS

SEA

Moscow

1300 (to Daniil)
To 1389 (Ivan I- Dimitri)
To 1462 (Vasily I, Vasily II)
To 1533 (Ivan III, Vasily III)
To 1584 (Ivan IV)

0   km   400
0   miles   250

Map 16: Russia about 1396, and the rise of Moscow, 1300–1584

beg Alexander to return. He came back a year later, freed the Russian towns, and in April 1242 routed the bulk of the Knights' army on the frozen Lake Pskov. Between 1242 and 1245 he also secured the safety of the territory of Novgorod and Pskov from raids by the Lithuanians, inflicting on them several defeats on Russian as well as Lithuanian soil.

All these armed encounters with Russia's western neighbours impressed on Alexander Nevsky the absolute necessity of a very cautious and realistic policy toward the Mongols: Russia could not afford to fight on two fronts. Therefore, in 1252, when the Tatars forcibly replaced Andrey as Grand Prince of Vladimir with Alexander Nevsky, he made complete submission to the Khan, who then stopped a punitive expedition the Mongols were preparing to launch against Russia, and thereafter remained strictly loyal. In 1261, as if in recognition of this conduct, the Khan consented to the creation of the Orthodox diocese of Saray, and gave its bishop the right to make converts. In 1262–3 Alexander succeeded in persuading the Khan to cancel another punitive expedition against Russia, where a strong spontaneous movement had been starting against the Mongol 'infidels' and their Russian supporters. Alexander died, on his way home from visiting the Horde, on 17 November 1263, taking monastic vows on his deathbed. He was canonized by the church 117 years later, and history has perpetuated his name as that of an outstanding military leader, a far-seeing statesman, and a passionate defender of the Orthodox faith.

THE 'APPANAGE SYSTEM'

Internally, life in Russia at this time was dominated by the strengthening of the appanage system. Under this system, during the thirteenth, fourteenth, and part of the fifteenth centuries, the right of succession to the principality of Vladimir remained with the members of the ruling dynasty, according to established tradition. The other principalities belonged to the individual princes, to do with as they pleased. Each principality was frequently divided among the heirs and each had its own dynasty, which habitually fought the numerous other princes for the title of grand prince. This appanage system led to endless internecine struggle. It was in these circumstances that the Russian Orthodox Church, which was not involved in this struggle, acquired its particular importance as a national institution untainted by politics. It was at this point that it became entirely the church of the people, of the masses, losing its previous, chiefly urban character.

In 1299 the metropolitan's see was transferred to Vladimir from Kiev, now utterly ruined, thus emphasizing the fact of the migration of Russia's spiritual centre toward the north-east. Vladimir, however, was only nominally the official administrative centre of the grand prince. From 1263 to 1375, when it became clear that the centre of the nation had moved to Moscow, the struggle for political power in north-eastern Russia was constant.

THE RISE OF MUSCOVY

In the 1280s and 1290s a struggle broke out between the two eldest sons of Alexander Nevsky – Dimitri of Pereyaslavl' and Andrey of Gorodets. Both applied for support to the Mongols, who seized this opportunity to ravage Russian territories mercilessly. In the circumstances the importance of Tver' was greatly enhanced. Tver' had developed rapidly in the thirteenth century and had attracted a large number of people fleeing from the lands laid waste by the Mongols, and at this point it seemed that the future belonged to her; but ninety years later the leadership had passed to Moscow.

Many explanations have been offered for this shift (Map 16). N. M. Karamzin attributed the success of Moscow to 'the help given by the Khans'; Moscow 'owed her greatness to the Khans'. M. P. Pogodin considered that the geographical factor was decisive. S. M. Solov'yov elaborated on 'Moscow's felicitous key position' as 'the meeting place of important ways of communication'. Fully aware of the importance of the geographical argument, V. O. Klyuchevsky emphasized the commercial advantages enjoyed by Moscow and the expansion observed in the economic exploitation of the princes' patrimonial lands, which in turn gave birth to the idea of the autocrat, fostered by Byzantine politico-ecclesiastical literature. The same line was followed by P. N. Milyukov, A. A. Kizevetter, and S. F. Platonov. I. Vishnyakov suggested that the personality of the Moscow princes was also important. A. E. Presnyakov added the important concept of the 'centralization of power' in the formative process undergone by the Russian state. M. K. Lyubavsky thought Moscow's chief strength was its population: every kind of encouragement was given to the influx of immigrants from other Russian territories, these measures contributing to the formation of the Great-Russian people. N. A. Rozhkov believed that the rise of Moscow was due to the disruption of natural husbandry and to the transition to monetary transactions. M. N. Pokrovsky placed as paramount the part played by 'trade capital', which, concentrated in the hands of the Grand Prince of Moscow, financially exploited the other Russian territories, creating 'trade privileges' for Moscow. A number of Soviet scholars, refuting fully or in part their predecessors' theories, explain the rise of Moscow in terms of the 'beginning of the liquidation of feudal fragmentation'.

It would seem that Moscow's rise is best explained by the combined effect of a series of factors – geography, internal policies, external politics, economy, as well as the personalities of the gifted Danilovich princes, who succeeded in combining firmness with flexibility and were endowed with correctness of intuition about immigration policies and a judicious attitude to the church, an institution of outstanding importance in the Middle Ages.

The first mention of Moscow occurs in the Chronicles under the year 1147. At that time it was merely a fortress on the southern limit of the Suzdal′ territory; it could in no way be compared in importance to such Russian urban centres as Vladimir on the Klyaz′ma, Novgorod, Rostov-the-Great, Suzdal′, Ryazan′, Chernigov, Nizhny-Novgorod, or the principality of Galicia–Volhynia. The then insignificant principality of Moscow was situated on the middle course of the river Moskva and included neither its source nor its mouth. Besides its Finnish name, Moscow was also known as Kuchkovo (from the name of the boyar Kuchka, who owned an estate on what became the future site of the city). This name survived in the area known as 'Kuchkovo Fields', later Lubyanka. The location of the little township was hardly geographically felicitous and can scarcely be considered to have been the chief reason for Moscow's rise. In 1263, when Alexander Nevsky died, he bequeathed the town to his youngest son, Daniil (1261–1303), who did not share this low estimate of Moscow's potential. In 1300 he seized Kolomna, the property of the Prince of Ryazan′, where the Moskva joins the Oka. In 1302 the childless Prince of Pereyaslavl′ bequeathed to Daniil his principality, which was rich in fisheries, timber and – above all – salt pans (salt being a very important article of trade at the time); Daniil's brother was unable – though he tried – to wrest it back. Daniil's son Yury (1303–1325) took the Prince of Mozhaysk prisoner, and thus became possessor of the whole course of the river Moskva. After the death of his uncle, Andrey, Yury tried, in spite of the advice of Metropolitan Maxim (d. 1305), to become Grand Prince of Vladimir, but the Khan bestowed his charter on Andrey's cousin, Mikhail Yaroslavich, Prince of Tver′ (1304–17), because Mikhail had promised the Khan a larger 'present'. The measures Mikhail took in order to increase the tribute paid to the Horde by Russia made him highly unpopular. He realized the importance of the metropolitan see and tried to have his own candidate appointed to the see of Vladimir. This provoked the enmity of Metropolitan Peter, who had been appointed by the Patriarch of Constantinople. Peter, a native of the principality of Galicia, became a supporter of Moscow, where he made long stays; he foretold that Moscow would unite all the Russian territories and declared his wish to be buried there. His successor Feognost (Theognostos) officially transferred the see to Moscow, a measure of exceptional importance, since for the Russian people Moscow thus became the centre of church administration and something like the spiritual capital of 'All Russia'.

Both these metropolitans won approval from the khans, who exempted from tribute the regular and secular clergy and their families, as well as all those connected in any way with the monasteries and convents. The ecclesiastical courts presided over by the metropolitan had sole jurisdiction over the clergy and all their dependants, and the metropolitan was empowered to admit to the religious enclaves anyone 'wishing to lead a life of prayer'. This privileged position of the church naturally greatly enhanced its authority. History does not record a single conflict between the church and the Mongols, even after Islam was adopted as the official religion of the Golden Horde in the reign of Uzbeg (1313–41). Whenever the church's rights were violated, the culprits were always the princes, the boyars, or the *veche* (citizens' assembly) of the republics of Novgorod and Pskov.

In Moscow Yury continued his father's energetic, dynamic, and not excessively squeamish policies. Taking advantage of a change of khans in the Golden Horde, he became Prince of Novgorod, one of the richest centres in Russia, which extended him financial support. This immediately caused a conflict between Yury and Mikhail, and the former was required to go to the Horde, where he spent two years, returning with the charter of a grand prince, granted by Khan Uzbeg. He also became the Khan's kinsman by marrying his sister Konchaka, who was baptized Agatha. At the end of 1317 there was an armed encounter between the two grand princes, and in spite of the military assistance given to Yury by the Mongols, Mikhail was victorious and took Yury's wife as a prisoner to Tver′ where she died. Both princes were called to the Horde, where Mikhail was accused of having acted against the Horde, and was therefore executed in 1319. Yury remained grand prince until 1322, when Mikhail's son Dimitri accused him of having concealed part of the tribute owed to the Great Khan; Dimitri was rewarded for this accusation by being given the charter of a grand prince himself. In 1327 the two princes met at the Horde, where Dimitri killed Yury to avenge his father's death. Uzbeg then had Dimitri executed for having taken the law into his own hands, and the principality was given to his younger brother Alexander. In 1327 an uprising took place in Tver′ against the Mongol tax-collectors; Uzbeg then ordered Yury's brother Ivan Kalita to 'punish' the inhabitants and gave him a strong Mongol army. Alexander fled to Pskov and from there to Lithuania, his brother Constantine becoming Prince of Tver′. In 1328 Ivan Kalita received the charter of grand prince. The nickname Kalita, or 'moneybag', was given to him because he was generous to the poor, to whom he used to distribute copper coins from a bag. To the family traits common to the Danilovich princes he added remarkable financial and administrative acumen, which formed the basis of his political power. He sought the support of the Mongols, diligently collected the Khan's tribute, and very ably managed his own finances. He acquired three towns (Uglich, Beloozero and Galich), and the principality of Rostov was in a great measure dependent on him; indeed all the territories, including Great Novgorod, had to reckon with the will of the grand prince, who tended to limit or suppress the independence of the individual principalities and whose actions were frequently coercive. At the same time he contributed to the improvement of the administrative system in the country and the eradication of brigandage, and – above all – he averted the disastrous punitive expeditions of the Tatars.

Like Mikhail of Tver', Ivan Kalita styled himself Grand Prince of Vladimir and of 'All Russia'; henceforth, with only a few exceptions, the grand principality remained in the hands of the Danilovich princes. Their power was not only formal but had real significance under the Tatar yoke: the Grand Prince of Vladimir was the only one to 'know the Horde' – to have the right to maintain direct relations with the Khan, and to 'intercede for the Russian land'. The princes had to pay a tribute for their principalities and also a special tax for the grand-princely charter. The practice of this 'appointment of the princes' diminished the role of the veche, the citizens' assemblies in the towns. Sometimes an appanage charter would be bought from the beneficiary by a wealthier prince. On the death of Ivan Kalita in 1340, his son Simeon the Proud (1340–53) was only sixteen years old, 'but all the Russian princes were subject to him and he was enthroned at Vladimir'. He visited the Horde five times and usually obtained what he wanted. He also made several territorial acquisitions: in a letter addressed to the Novgorodians he calls himself 'Grand Prince of All Russia'. But the Suzdal'–Nizhny-Novgorod principality arose as a new rival and serious danger also began to threaten Moscow from Lithuania, whose Grand Prince Olgerd (1345–77) tried to persuade the Khan to join him in an attack on Moscow in pursuit of his energetic efforts at expansion toward the east. Meanwhile, Simeon and Metropolitan Feognost succumbed to an epidemic of the plague. Simeon was succeeded by his brother Ivan Krasny (1353–9), and the metropolitan by Aleksey (of the boyar family of Pleshcheyev), one of the outstanding politicians of the time. Olgerd wanted to create in western Russia (which was almost entirely under his control) a metropolitan see independent of Moscow, and in 1358 Aleksey went to Lithuania to defend his rights and was kept there by Olgerd for two years. Aleksey was appointed, under the terms of Ivan Krasny's will, de facto regent during the minority of the nine-year-old Grand Prince Dimitri (the future Donskoy, 1359–89). The succession to the grand principality was first decided by the Horde in favour of Dimitri Konstantinovich, Prince of Suzdal' and Nizhny-Novgorod, but thanks to the efforts of Metropolitan Aleksey and to the great political confusion of the Horde, the grand prince's charter was in 1362 transferred to Dimitri Donskoy. Dimitri Konstantinovich twice attempted armed rebellion but his intrigues at the Horde were unsuccessful and in 1365 he formally renounced all claims to the grand principality. In 1371 Moscow defeated Prince Oleg of Ryazan'.

MOSCOW, LITHUANIA, AND TVER'

The struggle with Lithuania and Tver' proved much more strenuous. In 1361 Olgerd seized Kiev, making his son prince, and subsequently seized other territories of the former Kievan state, thus becoming the immediate neighbour of Moscow. In 1368 his troops appeared at the walls of Moscow, but were unable to fight their way through the stone fortifications built during the preceding year. Another expedition in 1370 also proved unsuccessful, and in 1372 when he again marched on Moscow he was defeated at Lyubutsk, was forced to ask for an armistice, and abandoned his plans of overrunning north-eastern Russia.

In 1368 the Prince of Tver', Mikhail Aleksandrovich, concluded an alliance with Olgerd and in 1370 obtained from the Mongol ruler Mamay at the Horde a charter as grand prince, but Prince Dimitri did not let him enter Vladimir. Mikhail sought Olgerd's help in vain. In 1375 Mikhail again obtained from the Khan the charter for the grand princedom, but Dimitri sent a strong army against Tver', consisting of troops drawn from nearly all the north-eastern principalities, including even several small appanage holders in the principality of Tver'. Realizing that the whole Russian land was up in arms against him, Mikhail hastened to conclude peace and recognized Dimitri as his 'eldest brother'. This campaign, remarkable for the loyalty shown to Dimitri by the majority of the princes, clearly showed the significance of Moscow. Reliance on the orientation of Tver' toward Lithuania had proved a miscalculation. Olgerd died in 1377 and his son Yagaylo (Jagiełło) was refused recognition by his elder half-brothers, Andrey of Polotsk and Dimitri of Bryansk, who went over to Moscow where an open break with the Horde was maturing. For some years there had been armed frontier collisions between the Russian and Mongol troops – with varying success. In 1378 the Tatars burned down Nizhny-Novgorod, but one of the Tatar armies sent by the Khan was defeated on the river Vozha. Mamay, who was governing in the name of the puppet-khan Muhammed Bulak, decided to subdue Moscow and bring Russia to heel. He concluded a military alliance with Yagaylo and the Ryazan' Prince Oleg and in 1380 mustered an army of some 200,000 men, which included mercenaries from the northern Caucasus and the Crimea (there were even some Italian colonists from there). Dimitri had about 150,000 men, but neither the princes of Tver' and Suzdal'–Nizhny-Novgorod, nor the people of the republic of Novgorod took part in the campaign, though Andrey of Polotsk and Dimitri of Bryansk brought their troops. The grand prince took the initiative and met the Mongol army beyond the Don before it could join up with the Lithuanians, and on 18 September 1380 on the field of Kulikovo inflicted a crushing defeat on Mamay. Yagaylo retreated; Oleg of Ryazan' failed to arrive.

The moral significance of the battle of Kulikovo was immense: the Horde lost its reputation for invincibility. According to Klyuchevsky's famous formula, 'the unity of Russia was born on the field of Kulikovo'. Mamay was killed soon after in his struggle with Tokhtamysh, the khan of the 'White Horde' (whose territories lay beyond the Volga and included part of western Siberia), who had seized supreme power at Saray. Tokhtamysh informed the Russian princes that he had 'vanquished Mamay, his rival and their foe'. Grand Prince Dimitri and the other princes sent him valuable gifts but did not go themselves to Saray, thus showing that they no longer recognized their subjection to the Horde. In complete secrecy Tokhtamysh prepared an attack on Moscow. In 1382 he burnt the city and cruelly ravaged the Russian territories, which had not had time to recover from Kulikovo. Dimitri, who had gone to the northern provinces to assemble an army, did not meet Tokhtamysh in the field, but had again to recognize the supremacy of the Horde. All he was able to do was to keep the charter of grand prince in his own hands. Tver' and Ryazan' became active again and Dimitri and his advisers remained loyal to the Horde, playing a waiting game in preference to rebellion and further military encounters. Until his death Dimitri directed his government's efforts toward the economic recovery of the ground lost in 1380 and 1382.

The Moscow territories were enlarged by the addition of Vladimir and its lands, Galich (north of Kostroma) and Tula, which was at that time Russia's southern boundary, and these policies continued under Vasily I (1389–1425), Dimitri's eldest son. For the first time since the Mongol invasion, a grand prince had nominated his successor, the Khan giving his approval. A year later, Vasily visited the Horde and there bought a charter for the Suzdal'–Nizhny-Novgorod principality, an area finally incorporated at the end of his reign, and to these territories he added Murom, Meshchera, and Tarusa. He also tried without success to incorporate the Novgorod lands on the northern Dvina.

Relations with the Horde and with Lithuania were complex. Tokhtamysh, with whom Vasily – like his father – was on good terms, was turned out of the Golden Horde in 1395 by the new Mongol conqueror Timur or Tamerlane (1336–1405), whose armies penetrated into Russia and ravaged Elets. Vasily was waiting for the Mongols with a large army on the shore of the Oka, but Timur unexpectedly turned south to Azov and the northern Caucasus. This was attributed by the Russians to a miracle – the intercession of the Virgin, whose ancient icon, Our Lady of Vladimir, had on that very day been brought to Moscow, where it has remained ever since. Nevertheless the Persian historian Sharif-ad-Din described Timur's fictitious victory over Vasily, thus leading several western historians astray.

The Golden Horde was now ruled by Edigey in the name of Timur-Kutlugh. He exacted heavy tribute from the Russians, but between 1395 and 1405 Moscow completely severed her ties with the Horde, though she still had recourse to the latter's help in her struggle with Lithuania. In 1408 Edigey and his troops unexpectedly appeared at the walls of Moscow, but could not take the city. He limited himself to exacting a 'ransom' and sacking the neighbouring districts and several other towns. On Nizhny-Novgorod he 'bestowed' independence under a prince appointed by him. When in 1411 Edigey lost his command over the Golden Horde, he had not succeeded in breaking the power of Moscow.

Under Gedimin (1316–41) and Olgerd (1345–77) the principality of Lithuania had grown more and more Russian: some 90 per cent of the population were Orthodox Christians, and the official language was Russian (and remained so until the end of the sixteenth century), but the ruling class was Lithuanian and was opposed to complete Russification. The crux of the matter lay in the form of Christianity that the still pagan Lithuanian élite would adopt. Louis of Anjou, King of Poland, died in 1382, leaving a small daughter, Jadwiga. A marriage was arranged between her and the Lithuanian Grand Prince Yagaylo, who was baptized into the Catholic Church (most of the pagan Lithuanian nobility following suit), and he became King of Poland. In Lithuania, after a struggle, Witowt (1392–1430) became grand prince. He unified all the territories from the Baltic to the Black Sea under Lithuanian rule and aimed at the unification of all Russia under his rule. In 1395 he seized the principality of Smolensk and the town of Lyubutsk on the Oka. After Tokhtamysh's fall he had sheltered him in Lithuania and now began to fight the Horde with a view to reinstating him, but in 1399 his army was defeated by the Mongols on the river Vorskla, and in 1401 the Russians retook Smolensk. Fortunately for Moscow, however, Witowt's attention was diverted to the west by the German *Drang nach Osten*, which ended in an overwhelming defeat of the Teutonic Knights at Tannenberg in 1410, and after that the question of the unification of Poland and Lithuania forced Witowt to keep his eastern plans in abeyance.

VASILY II

On Edigey's fall in 1411, Vasily renewed relations with the Golden Horde under Jalal-ad-Din, a son of Tokhtamysh. Vasily himself was succeeded by his son, the ten-year-old Vasily II (1425–62). His right to the throne was immediately contested by his uncle Yury of Galich, who considered that under the terms of Dimitri Donskoy's will he was entitled to the grand principality, Dimitri having decreed that in the case of his son Vasily's death the Moscow appanage should pass to his next eldest brother. But this will had been made by Dimitri Donskoy when Vasily I had as yet no direct heir. On the side of Vasily II were Metropolitan Foty (Photios), four of his uncles – among them Andrew of Mozhaysk and Peter of Dimitrov – the entire population of Moscow and, above all, his guardian, Grand Prince Witowt of Lithuania, to whom his daughter Sofia, Vasily II's mother, had appealed for help. Fear of Witowt temporarily stopped Yury, and Witowt welcomed this opportunity of intervening in Russian affairs, although taking little account of Moscow's real interests. In 1427 he concluded an alliance with the Prince of Tver', and in 1429 the Ryazan' Prince Ivan Fyodorovich took service under him, thus becoming a vassal of Lithuania. Witowt again encircled Moscow from north and south. He wanted to break with Poland and took steps to be recognized as King of Lithuania by the Holy Roman Emperor.

Immediately upon Witowt's death in 1430, Yury again raised his claim to the title of grand prince. In 1432 the charter had been given to Vasily II, but Yury, with his sons Vasily the Cross-Eyed, Dimitri Shemyaka, and Dimitri the Handsome, now began a fight for the grand principality, which lasted for two decades and was marked by acts of the utmost cruelty. Vasily II blinded Vasily the Cross-Eyed in 1436, and was in turn blinded by Dimitri Shemyaka in 1446. During this time Moscow changed hands several times, but the final victory went to Vasily, supported by the majority of the people. This was a definitive victory for the principle of succession from father to son as against the former practice of succession (where priority was given to uncles over nephews), and it paved the way for political centralization of power, which was evidently popular in the country at that time.

During these upheavals, the Russian territories continued to be overrun by the Mongols. The Golden Horde, however, had begun to disintegrate, and the first half of the fifteenth century is marked by the emergence of the Kingdom of Kazan', which very soon became a constant menace to north-eastern Russia. Fighting back one of their inroads, Vasily II was himself taken prisoner (7 July 1445), but on 1 October he was set free after consenting to pay a considerable ransom. To collect it a number of

Mongol princes and their armed retinues accompanied Vasily back to Moscow, and some later remained and took service there – the first time that Mongols had sworn allegiance to a Russian prince. In 1452 Vasily gave Kasim, the Kazan' khan's brother, the townlet of Meshchersk on the Oka, which became known in Russian history as Kasimov, the Mongols in Russian service being dubbed 'Kasimovites'. Kasim led a bitter fight against Kazan'. At the same time, the separate khanate of the Crimea was formed, independent of the Golden Horde, but in the third quarter of the fifteenth century it became a vassal of Turkey. Between 1450 and 1461 another khanate was formed at Astrakhan' on the Volga estuary. The territories east of the Volga and up to the river Irtysh in Siberia formed yet another Mongol state – the Nogay Horde. The Golden Horde was still based on Saray for several decades, but though Khan Ahmad directed campaigns against Moscow in 1451, 1455, and 1456, it already showed definite signs of weakness.

IVAN III AND THE HEGEMONY OF MOSCOW

Vasily II was succeeded by Ivan III (1462–1505), sometimes called 'the Great' by later historians, though his own contemporaries' opinion of him was divided. Even as a child he was a pawn in his father's political game, the seven-year-old boy becoming betrothed to Maria, the five-year-old daughter of Prince Boris Aleksandrovich of Tver', to whom he was married five years later. Vasily's blindness made him appoint his son co-ruler with the title of grand prince. On Ivan III's accession, his lands were surrounded by a number of independent Russian territories, such as the republic of Novgorod and the principalities of Tver', Rostov, Yaroslavl', and others. At the end of his reign, Pskov and Ryazan' alone still maintained a semblance of autonomy: Moscow had assumed the leadership of all the other Great-Russian territories. The political picture had completely changed: Ivan III had in effect become the sovereign of northeast Russia. The process begun under Dimitri Donskoy – the crystallization of a national Russian state – was now complete.

The policies of Moscow now underwent a number of alterations. Ivan III's aim was to abolish the old appanages, even those belonging to his own kinsmen. From his brothers he demanded unconditional obedience, and in his testament he submitted his younger children to his eldest son as mere officials. He enlarged the central administrative machine; court life was radically reformed and etiquette introduced to enhance the grandeur and dignity of the grand prince's power. It was indeed under Ivan III that the Grand Prince of Moscow was transformed into an 'autocrat'. The desire to achieve a harmonious relationship with the boyars, which had characterized the majority of previous rulers, was now replaced by the concept of absolute authority. The fall of Byzantium in 1453 left Moscow in a certain sense the bulwark of Orthodoxy. This idea can be fleetingly glimpsed in a letter addressed by Ivan III to the Novgorodians in the 1450s and was taken up and fully developed in the 1490s by Metropolitan Zosima, who compared Ivan to the Byzantine Emperor Constantine the Great and referred to Moscow as the new Constantinople. In the special circumstances of the end of the century it was given a still more ample justification in the writings of the Pskovian monk Filofey. It may well be that this idea played its part in the modifications introduced by Ivan III in his later policies.

Ivan III had to face several important problems of fundamental significance to Russia. The first was Novgorod: all the Moscow princes had tried to take the area 'under their hand', nominating subservient princes as Moscow's viceregents. On a number of occasions the Moscow army had moved against Novgorod in reprisal for disobedience to their grand prince and usually imposed a levy, thus re-establishing Moscow's authority. Vasily II had forced the Novgorodians to conclude a peace treaty in 1456 at Yazhelbitsy that limited the city's autonomy. Novgorod continued to pay tribute to Moscow 'as in olden times' but lost the right to proclaim the legislative resolutions of her *veche*; the city's seal was replaced by that of Moscow's grand prince; and the towns of Vologda, Volokolamsk, and Bezhetsky Verkh came under Moscow's control. Novgorod's leaders contemplated reaching an understanding with Lithuania and Poland and sought the support of King Casimir of Poland; the masses, however, sided with the Muscovites. Ivan III decided to lead a kind of crusade against Novgorod and attack it immediately: the Novgorodian army was defeated on 14 June 1471 on the river Shelon'. Novgorod was left a semblance of independence, but in the treaty it signed it was for the first time called a patrimony of the Grand Prince of Moscow, forbidden to deal directly with Lithuania, and forced to pay an enormous tribute and to cede to Moscow certain of its territories. Discontented or affronted Novgorodians began to appeal to Ivan, asking him to come to Novgorod to try their causes, sometimes going to Moscow themselves to seek redress. On one occasion in 1477 two Novgorodian officials addressed Ivan III as *Gosudar'* ('sovereign') instead of the usual *Gospodin* ('lord'). Ivan seized the opportunity to subject Novgorod to a blockade, in which he was aided and abetted by the Pskovians, demanding to be recognized as sovereign master of all Novgorodian territories. In January 1478 Novgorod agreed to his demands that there should no longer be either a *posadnik* (elected head of the free city) or a *veche*, that the city should be ruled by a Muscovite governor, and that the special

Novgorodian privileges should be abolished. Also ten Novgorodian districts, half of the lands owned by the six richest religious houses, and the town of Torzhok with its land became the personal property of the grand prince. A large number of boyars' and merchants' families, among them the Boretskys, headed by Martha, widow of the last *posadnik*, who had become the symbol of the fight for Novgorod's freedom, were deported to various towns in the Moscow principality and their places taken by Muscovites. The bell of the *veche* was removed to Moscow and all the territories owned by Novgorod became subject to the grand prince. The town of Vyatka resisted but was subdued in 1489. In 1498–9 Ivan III confiscated for his own benefit immense tracts of monastic lands in the Novgorod territory, this act spurring Elder Filofey to evolve his theory of 'Moscow, the Third Rome'. Ivan also dealt a severe blow to the chief source of Novgorod's riches – trade – and suppressed the Hanseatic offices in the city.

Tver', for long Moscow's rival, lost its independence in 1485. Her prince, Mikhail Borisovich, took part in Moscow's conquest of Novgorod, but in 1483 he concluded a treaty of mutual assistance with Casimir IV, King of Poland, and Ivan III sent an army to ravage his lands. Mikhail then recognized Ivan to be 'his eldest brother' and promised to sever his ties with Poland and Lithuania. In 1485, however, he again started secret negotiations with Lithuania, after which Ivan III laid siege to Tver' and, when the Tver' boyars began to defect, Mikhail fled to Lithuania. The principality of Ryazan', at that time virtually ruled by the Grand Prince of Moscow through his nephews Ivan and Fyodor, was annexed to Moscow. The Yaroslavl' and Rostov princes 'bent the knee' to Ivan, transferring the ownership of their lands to him but remaining on their estates. Ivan III had achieved the abolition of the appanage system.

During the reign of Ivan III, Moscow's political attitude toward the Mongol states underwent a radical change: from defensive it became offensive, remaining flexible at the same time. Toward Kazan' Moscow employed both persuasion and coercion, on occasion marching against the city, but at other times seeking to have Moscow sympathizers appointed as rulers and encouraging the pro-Russian elements in the khanate. With the Crimea, under the Girey dynasty, Ivan had concluded an alliance; he ably directed the Crimeans' military fanaticism against the Golden Horde, Poland, and Lithuania. The Golden Horde, in the person of Ahmad Khan (who had formed an alliance with Casimir IV of Poland), made a last attempt to change the course of history by military action: in 1472 and 1480 the Mongols' efforts ended ingloriously. In 1480 the Russian and Mongol armies faced each other across the river Ugra. This so-called 'stand on the Ugra' caused much anxiety in Moscow, brought forth sharp criticism of Ivan III, who was accused of cowardice, and ended in the retreat of both armies. Negotiations in progress with Ahmad were broken off and Ahmad himself was killed by the Nogay Mongols. In 1502 the Khan of the Crimea, Mengli-Girey, completely destroyed the Golden Horde. The majority of Russian historians consider 1480 to be the date of the final liberation of Russia from the Mongol yoke.

The growth of Moscow's power, and discontent with the pro-Catholic policies in Lithuania, caused members of the Lithuanian ruling house and the Chernigov–Seversky princes to side with Moscow. In a peace treaty of 1494 Grand Prince Alexander of Lithuania acknowledged the new *status quo* and agreed to the inclusion of Vyaz'ma and part of the Smolensk region in the territories of Moscow. Peace was reinforced by the marriage of Alexander to Ivan III's daughter Yelena. In spite of this, the strengthening of Catholic activities in Lithuania caused further migration to Moscow. A new war started with Lithuania in 1500 and ended in 1503 with an agreement to refrain from hostilities for six years. Moscow received the entire basin of the upper Oka, the whole course of the Desna with its tributaries, part of the lower Sozh, and the upper Dnieper.

In the same year, Ivan III made peace with the Livonian Order, which under its Grand Master Plettenberg had unsuccessfully attempted to seize Pskov. By the terms of the peace treaty the Order undertook to pay an annual tribute to Moscow for the Yur'yev (Tartu) region, which in the past had belonged to the Russians. In order to ensure the safety of the Novgorodian territories, Ivan III built a strong fortress named Ivangorod on the deep-running river Narova, opposite the Livonian town of Narva. This was the beginning of the stubborn Russian struggle for an outlet to the Baltic sea, a fight which was to last right through the sixteenth and seventeenth centuries and to succeed finally only during the reign of Peter the Great. In the last quarter of the fifteenth century Ivan III added to his title of Grand Prince of Moscow just three words – 'and All Russia' – and thus laid claim to all those Russian territories that in the past had formed part of the Kievan state ruled by the descendants of Ryurik.

The growth of Moscow had been duly observed by the Holy Roman Empire which, through its envoy Nicholas von Poppel, offered Ivan the title of king, in the hope of using his armies in its fight against Poland, which was attempting to wrest Bohemia and Hungary from the Empire. Ivan III refused: 'We, by the grace of God, have been sovereigns of our land from the very beginning, in direct descent from our forbears and, as our fathers held their investiture from the Lord, so do we hold it. . .and in the same way as we have wished for no subsequent investiture from anyone, so do we now continue not to wish it.' Instead, he offered to conclude an alliance. During his reign political and trade contacts were established with the Venetian Republic, with Denmark, at that time engaged in fighting the Swedes, and with the towns of the Hanseatic League. Diplomatic relations were entered into with Georgia, Turkey, and Persia.

In comparison with Ivan III's constant preoccupation with the 'gathering of Russian territories' and questions of foreign policy, problems of internal reorganization received less attention. He did, however, reform the *duma* (council) of the boyars: it now comprised representatives of the titled aristocracy on whom the grand prince bestowed the highest rank, that of boyar. Second in rank to them were the *okolnichiye*; in the sixteenth century other ranks were created. The duma set up *prikazy* (departments) to administer the country. Under Ivan III, the system of communications, already efficient, was further improved. In keeping with the growth of the state, the grand prince increased the number of civil servants (*d'yak*, *pod'yachiy*, and *pisets*). Towns and districts continued to be ruled by appointed administrators, but Ivan took pains to determine the limits of their power and to control their activities. A judicial code was compiled in 1497 (probably by B. Gusev, a *d'yak* of noble descent), which introduced a uniform system of legal procedure and administration for the country as a whole.

Internal trade flourished during this period, since most of the territorial frontiers between principalities had been eliminated. Foreign trade, on the other hand, was hampered by the refusal of Russia's neighbours to let Russian merchants cross their frontiers and gain access to the sea. However, a small but important amount of foreign trading did exist and was carried on through the intermediary of Italian settlers in the Crimea. Ivan III started building activities in Moscow on an ambitious scale and involved many architects, master masons, and artisans from western Europe.

THE CHURCH

From the start of the Mongol occupation the Russian Church had become the focus of a striving for a national identity. The church, which in the pre-Mongol period had been decidedly urban and oriented toward the educated classes, was now felt to be the church of the people and the expression of their aspirations; there was a new spiritual awakening in Russia. Monasteries began to be built in forests; a need was felt for silent, contemplative prayer and for a fuller renunciation of the world than had been practised in the Kievan period. These new tendencies can best be personified by Blessed Sergius of Radonezh and his disciples (of whom at least eleven are known), who played a leading role in the development of Russian monastic life. St Sergius played an active part in the formation of the Russian state, and the close collaboration of high-ranking Russian churchmen with the sovereign was a constant feature of the period.

In 1448 the Russian Church became autocephalous. Metropolitan Foty, primate of Russia, had died in Moscow in 1431, and was replaced by the Greek Isidor, a nominee of Byzantium, who took part in the Council of Florence (1439), at which a union was concluded between the Greek and the Roman Churches. On Isidor's return to Moscow, Vasily II dismissed and imprisoned him: Moscow was fiercely antagonistic to an agreement with western Catholicism. Isidor was, however, allowed to escape to the West. In 1448 a council of Russian bishops, neglecting for the first time to seek the prior sanction of the Patriarch of Constantinople, elected Iona, Bishop of Ryazan', to be metropolitan.

The Mongols' tolerant attitude toward the Orthodox Church had contributed to the rapid increase in ecclesiastical land tenure. In the second half of the fifteenth century two contradictory points of view arose in ecclesiastical and secular circles on the future of the church and its relationship with secular power. The 'Non-Possessors', also known as the 'Trans-Volga Elders', were led by a monk of the Kirillo-Belozersky monastery, Nil Sorsky (of the Maykov boyar family). They opposed ecclesiastical ownership of land, and preferred to live a simple life, as hermits or ascetics. The adherents of the opposite trend, the 'Possessors', also called *Iosiflyane* after their leader, Iosif Volotsky, stood for extensive ecclesiastical landownership and for disciplined, organized monasteries ruled by their abbots. The decisive collision between the two movements took place at the ecclesiastical council held in 1503, victory going to the Possessors. This decision was, in fact, a reaffirmation of the close partnership between the official church and the grand prince. Ivan III, who prior to the council had felt in sympathy with the Non-Possessors, now realized the advantages of being provided with a basis for his sovereign rights by Iosif Volotsky's theories of theocratic absolutism and of the divine origin of power.

Echoes of the pre-Reformation in the West had reached Russia and, as was to be expected, their first repercussions were heard in Novgorod which, more than any other part of Russia, had always been open to the West. In the fourteenth century the rationalistic heresy of the *Strigol'niki* – the shearers – had sprung up there, and the 1470s saw the appearance of the heresy of the Judaizers. It seems that the latter was a movement analogous to Protestantism in western Europe; its adherents rejected a number of rites, monasticism, and the veneration of images and relics. In 1490 they were anathematized by an ecclesiastical council and in 1504 the heresy was condemned a second time.

VASILY III

Ivan III was succeeded by his eldest son by his marriage with Sophia Palaeologina, Vasily III (1505–33), but the accession was preceded by the 'dynastic crisis' of 1497–9. By his first wife, Maria of Tver' (d. 1467), Ivan III had had a son, Ivan the Young (1458–90), whose name appeared in all the documents on a par with his father's, thus emphasizing the hereditary nature of the grand prince's power. By his second marriage, with Sophia Palaeologina in 1472, Ivan III had six sons and five daughters, but in 1497 he suddenly dismissed Sophia from his presence and in 1498, apparently suspecting some kind of plot, he solemnly crowned his grandson by his first marriage, Dimitri, as grand prince. Six people were executed, and Vasily, his eldest son, fell into disgrace. After some time, however, Ivan III altered his attitude to Sophia and in 1503 she was reinstated, and Vasily was again given the title of sovereign and grand prince. Dimitri and his mother, on the other hand, died in prison. Historians have advanced several hypotheses to explain these sudden changes; Ivan III gave his own explanation. When asked by the Pskovian envoy what had caused his grandson's disgrace, he replied: 'Am I then, the Grand Prince, not free to dispose of my sons and my throne? I shall give it to whom I please.' According to the terms of Ivan's will, Vasily III was proclaimed grand prince with precedence over his brothers. The principle of *yedinoderzhets* (sole ruler) was henceforth no longer in question.

Vasily III continued his father's policies. In 1510 he forced Pskov to give up her *veche*, government being henceforth vested in a *namestnik* (governor); three hundred of the city's foremost families were resettled elsewhere and their places taken by Muscovites. In 1517, what remained of the principality of Ryazan' submitted to Moscow. A struggle had been going on for many years with Lithuania and Poland for Smolensk and several other principalities, including Starodub and Chernigov–Seversk. Smolensk was annexed by Moscow in 1514, though an armistice was concluded only in 1522, pending a peace treaty 'for ever and ever', which actually was signed a century later. Friendship with the Crimean khan had become a thing of the past: troops had to be sent every year to the southern border, to guard against sudden attacks by the Crimean Tatars, and several stone fortresses (Kaluga, Tula, Zaraysk) were built at the same time. Relations with Kazan' underwent frequent changes and as a rule the Russian border regions were in constant danger. Moscow continued to develop her diplomatic relations with foreign countries – with the Pope, the Sultan of Turkey Suleiman I the Magnificent, and even with Babur, founder of the Mogul empire of India.

Though Vasily III dealt despotically with the descendants of the independent Russian princes and the nobility, high-ranking Russian families continued to emigrate to Moscow from Lithuania, among them the Princes Glinsky. Departure from Moscow, however, was considered to be treason, punishable by death. Under Vasily III the German free settlement in the suburbs of Moscow, first established under Ivan III, showed considerable growth. There, foreigners (mostly artisans) could live in accordance with their own customs.

RUSSIAN SOCIETY

The social structure of the Moscow state has been compared by some historians to a pyramid. The apex is represented by the grand prince or, as he was now more and more frequently called, the tsar (a term derived from the Latin Caesar). Under him were the descendants of the former appanage princes, sometimes called 'princelings'. They considered themselves superior to even the highest-ranking boyars and there arose constant disputes and quarrels between them and even among the 'princelings' themselves, since it was not clear whether the offspring of Ryurik, the supposed founder of the Russian dynasty, or those of Gedimin, the Grand Prince of Lithuania, took precedence, or what was the exact rank of the descendants of Lithuanian and Russian princes and of Tatar khans. To complicate matters, rank was also based on services rendered in the past by members of the princely or boyar families. This *mestnichestvo* ('place order') often hindered state administration. In wartime the grand prince often gave the order 'to be without place', i.e. to serve without regard to rank or descent. However, on the whole disputes arising from this system served the grand prince's interests, impeding the formation of an organized aristocratic opposition to his authority. Though the 'princelings' no longer enjoyed political independence, they owned large family estates, which in some cases comprised the entire territory of their former appanage. They had numerous 'servants' (dependants or vassals), who were either free, under agreement, or who were villeins – slaves in fact. The number of these was decreasing, but on the other hand a new kind of slave arose in the persons of *kabal'nyye lyudi* (bondsmen), who for a determined period sold their freedom for money. Analogous, though without social pretensions, were the constantly growing monastic lands with their peasants.

The population was divided into two categories: *sluzhilyye lyudi* (servicemen) and *tyaglo* (men of burden). To the first, besides the princelings and boyars, belonged the *dvoryane* (gentry) bound to life-long military service, for which they received lands to hold during the period

97

of their service. They were required to enter their sovereign's service armed and mounted and with an armed retinue. The obligation of military service also extended to the hereditary landowners – the princelings and the boyars. The gentry were interested in receiving agricultural lands, of which in consequence less and less remained available. But land was useless without agricultural workers, hence the constant aspiration and necessity to bind the peasants to the land. But the peasants were free to move as they pleased. The 1497 *Codex* (§57) had fixed a certain period of the year for their migration from the estates, determined by St George's Day, 26 November. A peasant was free to leave the estate on which he was working during the week preceding and the one following that date. Before 1497 these migrations could take place at any time, which often paralysed work on the farms. The second category – *tyaglo* – consisted chiefly of these rural peasants and of the merchants and artisans in the urban population.

Because Vasily's marriage to Solomoniya Suburov was childless, and because he was unwilling to leave his throne to his brothers Yury and Andrey, Vasily took the decision, with the consent of Metropolitan Daniil, to repudiate his wife and send her to a convent. He then took a second wife, Yelena Vasil'evna Glinsky. In December 1533 he died. His three-year-old son Ivan IV (1533–84), later to be known as 'Grozny' (commonly, though somewhat incorrectly, translated as 'the Terrible'), was proclaimed grand prince. Yelena Glinsky, who on her mother's side was descended from an illustrious Serbian family, became regent. The regency council was constituted by her uncle, Prince M. N. Glinsky, and representatives of the higher-ranking boyars. Vasily III's brother, Yury of Dmitrov, who was considered a dangerous pretender to the throne, was arrested, and died in prison. Very soon Yelena acquired a favourite in the person of Prince Ivan Ovchina-Telepnev-Obolensky. He dismissed Prince Glinsky (who later died in prison), and was given the highest rank in the land, all power being centralized in his hands. In 1537 an attempt at armed rebellion was quelled; it was led by Vasily III's other brother, Andrey of Staritsa, who hoped to incite the Novgorodians to rise in revolt. He was imprisoned and thirty of his partisans were hanged on the Novgorod roadside. In 1538 Yelena died, apparently of poisoning.

IVAN IV: THE MUSCOVITE TSARDOM

A fierce fight for actual power began to rage around the seven-year-old Grand Prince Ivan and his sickly brother Yury. From 1538 to 1546 the country was ruled in the name of Ivan IV by a number of princes and boyars, each trying to set aside the influence of his rivals or to eliminate them. Chief among the contestants were the Shuysky princes (foremost among the Muscovite aristocracy, descended from the princely house of Suzdal') and Vasily III's cousin Prince Ivan Bel'sky with his kinsmen; a little later on the Glinsky princes, uncles of the young sovereign, also entered the fray. They all sought the help of the metropolitans, whose support varied: Daniil and Ioasaf were for the Bel'skys, while Makary, though appointed by the Shuyskys, would not be drawn directly into the struggle.

At the end of 1546 the young Ivan showed his mettle. Influenced by Metropolitan Makary, an enlightened and firm supporter of autocratic rule, he decided to adopt the style and title of tsar and on 16 January 1547 was crowned with great solemnity, thus stressing both the dignity of his power and the importance of the Russian state. He married Anastasia Zakhar'ina-Koshkina, daughter of a boyar family that had come to the forefront under Dimitri Donskoy, and an ancestor of the Romanov dynasty. The marriage was a happy one, though Ivan was criticized by members of the older aristocracy for having married an 'upstart'.

The reign of Ivan IV has been given many interpretations by historians, not all of them convincing. This is due not so much to the complexity of available data as to the destruction of a great quantity of documents belonging to this period in the great fire of Moscow in 1626. The young tsar's first measures were directly influenced by Metropolitan Makary's views on the necessity of autocracy and were coloured by a desire to bring justice to the country in accordance with the idea of a Christian state current in Byzantine ecclesiastical circles. Makary began by calling two church councils (1547 and 1549), which produced a church calendar of Russian saints ('all the Saints who had shone in the Russian land') and regulated worship at local shrines. The so-called *Stoglav* (a statute book of one hundred chapters) was adopted in 1551; it aimed at the unification of all aspects of church life and it finally – after much discussion by the council – brought some order into the question of ecclesiastical land-ownership.

In June 1550 a new *sudebnik* (code) was issued which, instead of the sixty-eight articles of the 1497 statutes, contained one hundred. It was carefully edited and its chief aim was to limit arbitrary methods practised by the *namestniki* and their assistants. Under its rules, representatives of the local population were to be present at court proceedings; a procedure was established for complaints against governors; acts of brigandage were to be investigated by special magistrates elected from the gentry; bribery was to be severely penalized; capital punishment was to be restricted to certain grave crimes, although on the other hand torture was permitted in cases of murder and theft; landowners were to be subjected to the jurisdiction of central courts, but could themselves judge and pass sentence on their peasants, except for the gravest crimes; and the peasants' right to migrate on St George's Day was confirmed. The 1550 code was approved in 1551 by the *Stoglav* council, which was attended by both the clergy and laymen.

According to the majority of historians, the so-called *Izbrannaya Rada* (elected council) played a part in these reforms of the 1550s. This council was apparently an unofficial group of statesmen headed by the tsar's closest friends, Aleksey Adashev and the priest Sylvester, who were inspired by the idea of creating a truly Christian state. They were joined by Metropolitan Makary and a number of others, though the precise composition of the council is not known, and in any case official authority was vested in the *Blizhnyaya Duma* (privy council) working with the tsar.

In 1550 important agrarian reforms were effected and laid down in a charter, enumerating the duties of the population and fixing legal fees and costs. Most historians believe that this charter was intended to benefit the independent peasants and the urban population. In 1555 the custom of paying dues to the governors and their assistants was abolished. Justice and the collection of taxes passed into the hands of local representatives, elected by the *tyaglo*. The offices of judge and court secretaries were likewise made elective. These measures ensured ample self-government for the *zemstva* (elected organs of rural self-government). The only representatives of the government in the provinces were the *voyevody* (military commanders) in charge of the garrisons and the 'city agents' who administered state property in the towns. Local government and the judiciary were in the hands of elected officers except for affairs of extreme gravity, which were reported directly to Moscow. The entire rural population now paid into the state treasury fixed taxes or dues, out of which the sovereign paid his civil servants' salaries.

Ivan IV gave particular attention to the military servicemen. In 1550 he ordered the election of 1,071 'best servants' from the gentry and boyars' families, listed in a special book (*Tysyachnaya Kniga*). These 'best servants' were formed into a special regiment of 'Moscow nobles' and were expected to be ready for service at any time. In 1555 (or 1556) a 'service statute' fixed with great precision the duties to be borne by the servicemen in accordance with their land allotments. On the death of the holder, his *pomestiye* (benefice) passed to his eldest son, who entered service at the age of fifteen. For every hundred *desyatiny* (*desyatina*=2.7 acres) of arable land a mounted and armed man was to be supplied, in default of which the *pomestiye* was taken back and the owner punished. Besides land allotments, the servicemen were paid a salary (fluctuating from 4 to 1,200 roubles a year), which was not paid annually, but given to the servicemen before starting on a particular campaign. In order to keep a record of the armed forces, the gentry was mustered annually in the districts under the control of Moscow. The armed forces were reorganized and were now divided into hundreds, commanded by 'heads'. In 1550 a corps of musketeers 3,000 strong was formed from 'selected marksmen', and were paid 4 roubles a year. Military technique was developed and a remarkable artillery park created.

The number of administrative departments was increased under Tsar Ivan IV. In 1549 a *posol'skiy prikaz* (office for foreign affairs) was created, but it was in the 1550s that Ivan took the first steps toward transforming the Moscow body politic into an empire by including foreign states within its framework. Kazan', which had for so long been a thorn in Russia's side, was conquered in 1552 and its considerable dependent territories were gradually absorbed. In 1556 Astrakhan' surrendered without a fight to the tsar's armies. The Volga now ran all its course through Russian territory; the country's eastern regions at last knew peace; a direct road to the Urals was opened; and rich new lands were made available for agriculture. Contemporaries took these victories as a first manifestation of the triumph of Christianity over Islam. Russian folk-songs made Ivan IV their epic hero; even icon painting reflected these achievements, as for instance the famous icon of the 'Church Militant'.

The tsar's advisers were bent on starting a war against the Crimea, and were supported by the church. But Ivan chose rather to engage all the country's forces and resources in a fight for an access to the Baltic Sea to which Moscow had tenaciously aspired since the times of Ivan III, as Russia's vast hinterland had as yet no ports. War over Livonia started in 1558 and was to last, with varying success, for twenty-four years. By 1561, under the blows of the combined Russo-Tatar forces, Livonia itself had disintegrated: Estonia had submitted to Sweden, Latvia to Lithuania. In 1566 Lithuania made offers of peace to Ivan, ceding Polotsk, but the *Zemskiy Sobor* (national assembly) decided to continue the war in pursuance of its aim. The campaigns of 1572–3 and 1577, personally conducted by Ivan, were particularly successful. But the war had lasted too long; Russian military reserves were depleted and the country was exhausted. Ivan's rival, Stefan Batory, King of Poland since 1576, invaded Russian territory, but failed in his attempt to take Pskov or the Pskov–Petseri monastery, and did not succeed in routing the Russian army. Nevertheless the tsar's armies could not overcome the united forces of the coalition, and the courage and enormous sacrifices of the people proved to have been in vain. In 1582, through the intermediary of the papal legate, Antonio Possevino, a ten-year armistice was signed at Zapol'sky Yam by which Ivan IV lost all the fruits of his earlier victories. In 1583 an armistice was signed for three years with Sweden at the price of ceding the Russian towns of Kopor'ye. Yama, Ivan-gorod, and Korela (Keksholm). Russia's failure to attain either her military or her political goals has been attributed by many historians to a lack of internal stability due to the activities of the *oprichnina*. Ivan himself in his *Sinodik* (*c.* 1583) listed 3,300 innocent victims whom he had had put to death.

At the end of 1564 Ivan divided the Russian state into the traditional *zemshchina* (state territory) and the new *oprichnina* (lands belonging to the tsar himself, referred to ironically as 'dower lands'), which could be used to defend the tsar's person and interests. The *oprichniki* (the servants of the dower lands) constituted a special police corps and wielded extraordinary powers, which they frequently abused. The tsar's ill-will and cruelty are considered by many to have been the reason for this division, but others have thought that such policies were a step in the process toward absolute monarchy. In many countries at that time a fierce struggle was going on between the sovereign and the nobility; in Russia, Ivan IV's ideal was the Byzantine conception of divine right.

Before the beginning of the Livonian war no dissensions are known to have existed between the tsar and his counsellors. During the tsar's grave illness in 1553 it was made clear that some members of the Council of Boyars feared a new regency and would have preferred to have as his successor his cousin Prince Vladimir of Staritsa, the last appanage prince in Russia, rather than Ivan's infant son Dimitri. The tsar went so far as to accept the compromise of creating for such an eventuality a regency council that included Prince Vladimir. The serious error committed by Aleksey Adashev in advising an armistice with the Livonian Order in 1559–60, the death of the Tsaritsa Anastasia in 1561, the replacement of Sylvester and Adashev by other councillors, the death of Metropolitan Makary in 1563, Ivan's politically motivated marriage to the Caucasian Princess Maria Temryukovna of Kabarda, all contributed to the tsar's new policies. The flight to Lithuania of Prince Kurbsky, formerly the tsar's closest friend, in April 1564 and his taking the field against Moscow in the following September awakened the tsar's mistrust in the loyalty of the nobility as a whole both toward himself and in connection with the Livonian war. In December 1564 Ivan left Moscow for the Aleksandrovsky suburb, accusing the princelings and boyars of disloyalty and even threatening to abdicate. The crisis was mitigated thanks to the intervention of the church and the Moscow citizens, but the tsar's decision to divide the realm into two parts was carried into effect. The *oprichniki* (numbering less than 6,000 men) became in Ivan's hands a formidable weapon against those who were in favour of placing Prince Vladimir on the throne. In 1567 Vladimir himself and Prince Ivan Miloslavsky voluntarily confessed to the tsar that a plot to do just that had indeed existed. At this point Ivan even considered emigrating to England and started negotiations to this effect with Queen Elizabeth I, but her answer was non-committal. A wave of executions ended in the poisoning of Prince Vladimir in 1569, and the following year the tsar devastated Novgorod, where he had sensed pro-Lithuanian sympathies. However, in 1571 by an oversight the *oprichniki* let the Crimean Tatars slip through almost to the walls of Moscow, and a year later the *oprichnina* was officially abolished.

A revision of the landowning rights of the bishoprics and monasteries was carried into effect in the 1570s. In 1575 Ivan had appointed Prince Simeon Bekbulatovich of Kasimov to be Grand Prince of Russia, but revoked this measure a year later. It is possible that this was done in order to allow for the reallocation of church property: many estates were surrendered by the church and became crown lands. Ivan may have thought it unwise to order this himself as a crowned Orthodox monarch, but his appointee was a recent convert and looked on by his subjects as little better than a heathen (although the prince later became a monk).

The economic upheavals caused by all the changes introduced by Ivan were quite severe. To this must be added the catastrophic devastation of the villages and farms from which manpower had been drained by the recurring annual exigencies of war. In the second half of the 1570s Muscovy suffered a severe economic crisis; a large number of discontented Russians fled to the Cossack settlements on the Don and in the Ukraine, and Ivan found himself facing the utter failure of his own policies. This explains his readiness to consent to the demanding peace terms with Poland and Sweden.

With a view to overcoming the crisis, the church council held in 1580 transferred to the tsar large tracts of monastic lands and the control of such lands was generally tightened up. In the same year 'interdicted years' were introduced, during which 'Saint George's Day' was temporarily cancelled, to stop the migration of rural workers.

The favourable aspects of the beginning of Ivan IV's reign were blotted out by subsequent failure. Friendly relations with England, where Muscovy was 'discovered' in 1553, led to the granting by Ivan of numerous trade privileges to English merchants, these measures being politically highly unpopular in Russia. 'Your English Tsar is dead', exclaimed Shchelkalov, one of the heads of the Foreign Department, to the English envoy when Ivan died. The only consolation was the defeat inflicted on the Siberian khanate by Yermak's Cossacks, though the struggle for this territory continued until the end of the sixteenth century. (Yermak had been called in in 1581 by the Stroganovs, a powerful Russian merchant family, to defend and enlarge their vast territorial and mercantile acquisitions beyond Urals.)

Ivan IV died on 18 March 1584, a man 'of marvellous great understanding', outstanding talents, and unbridled passions. His favourite son, Ivan, had died in 1582, having been fatally wounded by his father in the heat of a discussion concerning the prospects of the Livonian war. Ivan was succeeded by his son Fyodor (1584–98), a man of mild temper, indifferent health, great devotion to the church and, like his father, a composer of church music. During his reign a semblance of a regency council was formed which consisted of his uncle N. R. Zakhar'in-Yur'yev, Prince I. F. Miloslavsky, Prince I. P. Shuysky, Prince V. Yu. Bel'sky, and the new tsar's brother-in-law, Boris Godunov. One of the first acts of the council was to exile Ivan IV's youngest son Dimitri, his mother Maria Nagoy (Ivan's seventh wife), and their relations, to Uglich. Dimitri had no right to the succession but the Nagoy family were known as intriguers and possible complications had to be foreseen.

Very soon Boris Godunov became the tsar's sole counsellor. In 1588–9 the boyar duma empowered him to conduct negotiations with foreign countries, and he became the highest-ranking dignitary in the land; the English rightly called him the 'lord protector'. After the death of Stefan Batory (1587) the Lithuanian magnates upheld Fyodor's candidature to the Polish throne, but the crown was won by the Swede, Sigismund Vasa. The armistice with Poland was extended by a further fifteen years, and after a short and successful war with Sweden the towns lost by Ivan IV were in 1595 returned to Moscow. The southern border of Russia continued to be defended throughout this period. The Crimeans made their last aggressive appearance at Moscow's walls, but were met by the army headed by Godunov and retreated.

In 1589 Godunov realized the long-cherished dream of the Russian Church by setting up its own patriarchate. Although after the fall of Constantinople the Greek Church stood in need of moral and financial assistance from Moscow, it had not been inclined to establish a fifth patriarchal see in addition to the four existing ones at Jerusalem, Antioch, Alexandria, and Constantinople. Godunov succeeded in obtaining the agreement of Jeremiah, Patriarch of Constantinople, to a 'Patriarchate of All Russia'. The Russian churchmen elected Iov (Job), the then Metropolitan of Moscow, to be the first patriarch, and he was confirmed in this dignity by the Council of Patriarchs, assembled in Constantinople in 1590.

The government tried to limit the peasants' 'migration' from their place of work and their tendency to bind themselves to richer landowners. The 'interdicted years' were continued and in 1597 a law authorized landowners to recall for a period of five years those peasants who had left them after 1592.

With the death of Tsar Fyodor in January 1598 the Danilovich line of the Ryurik dynasty came to an end. The throne was offered to his widow Irina, but she took the veil. Patriarch Iov and the government over which he presided then offered the crown to Boris Godunov, who refused it. A national assembly was then convened which, in February 1598, elected him anyway; he was popular with the servicemen, who formed the majority in the assembly. However, Boris delayed his coronation until September, seeking assurance that his election was indeed acceptable to the people. Godunov's ultimate accession was a severe blow to the nobility, the majority of whom were in opposition to the new tsar. Their leader was Fyodor's cousin, Fyodor Romanov, nephew of Ivan IV's first wife. In 1601 Boris committed all five Romanov brothers to trial; they were all exiled and Fyodor and his wife forced to take monastic vows. Boris did not trust the nobility, and the system of denunciations, especially by servants, flourished during his reign. He clearly wished to be a popular sovereign, but famine and plague in 1601–3 sharply aggravated the country's social problems. Boris distributed food to the hungry and began large-scale building in Moscow in order to provide employment, but the flight of peasants to the Ukraine increased and brigandage was rampant. In 1603 a number of malcontents, commanded by the Cossack Ataman, Khlopko, attempted a march on Moscow.

Boris was an admirer of western educational methods. He invited foreigners – technicians and doctors – to Russia, and his son Fyodor received an exceptionally sound education. He sent a number of young men to the West to be systematically trained there, hoping later with their assistance to open in Moscow schools run on European lines. He introduced into the regular army regiments recruited among foreigners and encouraged trade with the West.

THE 'TIME OF TROUBLES'

In 1603 there arose a new danger – the appearance in Poland of a pretender to the Russian throne. In 1591 Prince Dimitri, the youngest son of Ivan IV, had died in Uglich. A court of inquiry, presided over by Prince Vasily Shuysky, had established that Dimitri, who was subject to epileptic fits, had mortally wounded himself while playing with a knife. Among the people, however, it was rumoured that he had been killed by Godunov's agents. The Pretender affirmed that he had miraculously escaped the murderers' knives. He found ready support among the Polish nobility, King Sigismund III, and the papal nuncio Rangoni. In October 1604 he started a military campaign against 'the usurper Godunov'. In Moscow it was declared that the Pretender was a certain Grigory Otrep'yev, a runaway monk, son of a serviceman. Historians differ in their opinions, but it is clear that the Pretender was a native of Moscow and sincerely believed in his royal descent.

Boris Godunov died unexpectedly on 13 April 1605. The sixteen-year-old Tsar Fyodor (Godunov) II and his mother were forsaken by nearly all their subjects and killed. On 20 June 1605 the Pretender, at the head of his troops, solemnly entered Moscow. The patriarch was deposed and replaced by another; in July the Pretender was crowned tsar. In the words of a contemporary writer, Prince Katyrev-Rostovsky, 'he was a man of keen intelligence, educated in bookish learning, eloquent and daring'. In Poland and to the Jesuits he had made lavish promises, but now delayed fulfilling them. He recalled from exile all those deported by Godunov. Prince Dimitri's mother, the nun Martha, formerly Maria Nagoy, acknowledged the Pretender as her son. The 'Pseudo-Dimitri' clearly sought popularity, chiefly among the servicemen, but he was surrounded by too many Poles and Lithuanians to be successful in this. His marriage to Marina Mniszek, a Pole who refused to be converted to Orthodoxy, celebrated – contrary to the Orthodox canon – on the eve of St Nicholas' Day, aroused great irritation. The church was apprehensive of Jesuit influence in the Muscovite state. In these circumstances, Prince Vasily Shuysky, who had several times altered his statements on Prince Dimitri's death at Uglich, and had been sentenced to death and reprieved, now headed a rebellion against the tsar. The Pretender was killed on 17 May 1606, his body burned and the ashes fired from a cannon pointing in a westerly direction, whence he had come.

On 19 May the boyars and people of Moscow, assembled in the Red Square, proclaimed Prince Vasily Shuysky to be the new tsar. For the first time in Russian history the ruler swore an oath to render justice jointly with his boyars, not to confiscate estates or property belonging to the heirs of men condemned to death, and not to listen to false testimony. The Metropolitan of Kazan', Germogen, was appointed patriarch; Shuysky was hastily crowned on 1 June. On 3 June the real Prince Dimitri's body – now declared a holy relic – was brought from Uglich and Dimitri himself was canonized. In the name of the tsar and the nun Martha, proclamations were sent throughout the country, explaining the late Pretender's usurpation and heresy, stressing Shuysky's dynastic precedence, and announcing the canonization of the holy relics of St Dimitri of Uglich, 'Godunov's innocent victim'. Tsar Vasily Shuysky hoped that these measures would put a stop to unrest in the country, but civil war started in the autumn and nearly half the population rebelled against him.

The period from 1606 to 1612 was somewhat complex. A powerful peasant movement arose, led by the energetic and courageous Ivan Bolotnikov, who fought not only against Shuysky and the landowners but also against the whole system limiting the peasants' freedom. For a time he was joined by the gentry; Shuysky's armies were hard put to defeat him and even after his death the peasantry remained rebellious. In June

1607 a further rebel movement arose, headed this time by a second Pretender, 'Pseudo-Dimitri II', who allegedly had escaped from Moscow. He based his operations on the village of Tushino, twelve miles from Moscow, where he was joined by his 'wife' Marina Mniszek, by the opponents of the tsar, and by a large number of Cossack detachments from the Ukraine and the Don. The Metropolitan of Rostov, Filaret (born the boyar Fyodor Romanov), became patriarch at Tushino, where the Pretender held 'court' and formed his own boyar duma. Supported by the Lithuanians and Poles, the Tushino forces tried to blockade Moscow and took several towns. Anarchy reigned in several regions of the country – in the north, the Volga, and western Siberia.

Shuysky's government was saved by the Swedes, who came to his help in return for a number of towns previously ceded to them in 1583 by Ivan IV. They provided Shuysky's nephew, Prince Mikhail Skopin-Shuysky, with auxiliary regiments which, together with Russian troops from Novgorod, liberated the north from the Tushino armies and forced the second Pseudo-Dimitri to escape to Kaluga. On 12 March 1610 Prince Skopin-Shuysky and the Swedish General de la Gardie solemnly entered Moscow.

In September 1609 Poland had openly entered the fray. Sigismund III had laid siege to Smolensk and a delegation from Tushino, led by Saltykov, arrived at Smolensk to beg Sigismund to let his son Vladislav ascend the Moscow throne. On 14 February 1610 a treaty was signed by which Vladislav was to rule together with the boyars and the whole land, i.e. with the help of the *Zemskiy Sobor*. Provision was made for safeguarding the servicemen's interests, but not those of the nobility. Orthodoxy was to be protected from Roman Catholic encroachment, but permission was given to build a Catholic church in Moscow. On 24 July 1610 an army commanded by Dimitri Shuysky, the tsar's brother, was defeated by the Polish troops at Klushino. The Polish hetman, Żółkiewski, marched on Moscow, which was simultaneously being attacked by the second Pseudo-Dimitri. De la Gardie retreated to Novgorod (Skopin-Shuysky had died a month after the liberation of Moscow). On 17 July 1610 the Muscovites rebelled against Tsar Shuysky; he was forced to become a monk and was later sent to Poland with his brothers, all of whom died in captivity.

Disputes now began in Moscow over the crown. In August a new treaty was signed with Żółkiewski, and the people of Moscow took the oath of allegiance to the Polish king's son Vladislav. A 'Great Embassy' of 1,200 was sent to Sigismund, among them several high-ranking boyars, including Prince V. V. Golitsyn and Metropolitan Filaret, whose presence in Russia might have been dangerous to Vladislav. In Smolensk the members of the embassy learned that Sigismund himself wanted to ascend the throne of Russia. Żółkiewski could not make him see reason and resigned. In the Kremlin seven boyars ruled in Vladislav's name, but in fact they took their orders from Gonsevsky, the man who had replaced Żółkiewski and whose behaviour greatly irritated the Russians. On 11 December 1610 'Pseudo-Dimitri II' was killed by one of his men. This gave full scope to those who, fearing the spread of anarchy, had hesitated to start an open fight against Sigismund. The new move was headed by Patriarch Germogen, who in his Christmas message overtly called on the Russian people to oppose Sigismund. Gonsevsky arrested the patriarch, but the latter's aim had been achieved: one after another the Russian towns were rising in revolt. The first enrolled army of *opolcheniye* (volunteers), under P. S. Lyapunov, Prince D. Trubetskoy, and the Cossack Ataman Zarutsky, moved toward Moscow, where on 19 March 1611 an anti-Polish rising had broken out. Gonsevsky with his Polish troops had barricaded themselves in the Kremlin and Kitay-Gorod, which were besieged.

The country during this civil war was ruled by the leaders of the volunteer army, but sharp dissensions arose among them; Lyapunov was killed and in the following autumn the corps disintegrated. Of the 100,000 men, some 10,000 Cossacks still remained who continued to besiege the Poles. Political anarchy was at its height. Prince Miloslavsky with some of the boyars called on the people to submit to Vladislav. The Poles were still entrenched in Moscow after a two-year siege; they had also taken Smolensk and were preparing to continue the war. The Swedes, after the appearance on the scene of Vladislav, became openly hostile and occupied Novgorod. Trubetskoy and Zarutsky swore allegiance to 'Marina Yur'yevna' (Marina Mniszek), 'Tsaritsa of All Russia', and her little son Ivan by the second Pretender.

At this moment of utter confusion, the voice of the church proved to be decisive, urging the people to stand up for their faith and country. Proclamations to this effect were sent out by the Abbot Dionisy, and Avraamy Palitsyn, the Cellarer of Holy Trinity Monastery, as well as by Germogen from prison. A movement inspired by patriotism started in September 1611, when the Nizhny-Novgorod merchant Kuz'ma Minin, a remarkable organizer and gifted politician, incited the citizens of the north and Volga regions to form a new army of volunteers, and succeeded in collecting the necessary funds; the citizens of Nizhny-Novgorod, for instance, donated one-third of their property. Prince D. Pozharsky, who had already distinguished himself in the field and had been wounded in Moscow in the fighting with the Poles, was nominated to conduct the army. The corps of volunteers included men from many regions and even Tatars and Volga Finnish tribesmen. In a proclamation, the army repudiated the second Pretender's son and the 'Lithuanian King' (Sigismund), and proposed, after 'marching together against the Poles and Lithuanians', to elect, assembled in a body, 'the tsar that the Lord would indicate to us'. In September 1612 this second army of volunteers approached Moscow and on 22 October took Kitay-Gorod by storm. An attempt by the Polish army to save their garrison was unsuccessful. The Poles in the Kremlin capitulated.

THE ROMANOV DYNASTY

Preparations were immediately set in motion for a national assembly, which was opened in June 1613 and was fully representative, with delegates from every class of people, including peasants. Foreign candidates to the throne were rejected, and discussions among the members of the assembly on the eligibility of the Russian candidates ended in the election of sixteen-year-old Mikhail Romanov (1613–45), son of Fyodor Romanov (Metropolitan Filaret), still a prisoner in Poland with other members of the 'Great Embassy'. For a considerable time Mikhail's mother withheld her consent to her son's accession, but yielded on condition that 'the whole land would help him'. One of the reasons for his election was the kinship of the Romanovs with Ivan IV's first wife, Anastasia. The Cossacks, among whom the Romanovs were popular, also supported him.

Paradoxically the first Romanov tsar, by tacit agreement though without any written document, derived his right to reign from popular election by the people as a whole. Indeed, the national assembly continued to sit uninterruptedly during the first ten years of Mikhail's reign. The difficulties facing the new tsar's government were many and arduous. Relentless war had to be waged against bands of adventurers who continued to plunder the population, and the Swedes were still at war with Russia. Here England offered to mediate, and in 1617 peace was signed at Stolbovo: Novgorod and its territories were returned to Russia, but the entire coast of the Gulf of Finland remained in Swedish hands.

Sigismund III and his son refused to acknowledge Mikhail as Tsar of Russia. In 1618 Vladislav invaded and reached Moscow but failed to achieve his aims. An armistice for a period of fourteen and one-half years was concluded at Deulino; Smolensk and the Novgorod–Seversky territories were ceded to Poland. The Poles did not renounce their pretensions to the Russian throne, but consented to exchange prisoners. Metropolitan Filaret returned to Moscow in 1619 and became Patriarch of All Russia, with the same title as that of the tsar: *Velikiy Gosudar'* ('great sovereign'). Until his death in 1633 the metropolitan controlled the country's affairs, including his son Tsar Mikhail himself.

In 1632 war with the Poles was resumed and ended in the capitulation of the Russians under the walls of Smolensk, which they had been besieging. This defeat paralysed Russian foreign politics for twenty years. In 1634 'eternal peace' was signed at Polyanovka: Vladislav gave up all claims to the Russian throne, but all the Russian territories occupied by the Polish army passed to Poland.

In 1637 the Cossacks of the Don and the Dnieper (Zaporozh'e), who were constantly raiding the Crimea, seized the Turkish fortress of Azov on the Don estuary, because the Turks prevented the Cossack boats from reaching the sea. The Turkish army laid siege to Azov in 1641, but could not drive out the Cossacks, who begged the tsar to take the town under his protection – which would have provided Russia with an outlet to the Black Sea. However, the national assembly considered that the country's economic situation was too unfavourable to allow such expansionist policies.

Relations with the West were developing satisfactorily: James I of England granted a loan of 20,000 roubles to the Russian government; the Holy Roman Empire mediated in the peace negotiations with Poland; and the Danish Crown Prince Waldemar wished to marry Irina, eldest daughter of the tsar (although the marriage did not take place because of religious differences).

Mikhail's internal policies were primarily determined by the country's disastrous financial and economic situation. External and internal loans helped the government to start restoring solvency. The agricultural system – the basis of Russia's economy – had to be reconstructed. According to contemporary registers in the 1620s, seventy per cent of the farmsteads were derelict. A series of measures were taken by the government to remedy this: extra taxes were introduced; by 1627 hundreds of thousands of acres of crown lands had been distributed to servicemen; the time during which peasants who had left the estate on which they had worked could be forced to return was extended from five to ten years and then to fifteen; taxes, instead of being calculated on the area of arable land, were now levied on the individual farmsteads, regardless of the area under cultivation. But it was only in the middle 1630s that work on the land returned to normal. Trade was given every encouragement. In 1614 Mikhail exempted English merchants from taxes throughout the country and reduced to a minimum those paid by Dutch traders. A large number of western technicians were hired and foreign doctors attended the tsar's family and the boyars. Administrative reforms tended to intensify centralization and bureaucracy. In the provinces the governor's authority was again strengthened and local self-government was gradually limited to tax collecting.

The strong personality of Patriarch Filaret, who intentionally diminished the national assembly's importance, contributed to the emergence of authoritarian government. During Mikhail's reign and that of his successor, the power of the tsar was limited by the decisions of the assembly, but as its power had withered away, the semi-constitutional rule of the first Romanovs was gradually replaced by an absolute monarchy, which as in the past sought its guiding principles in the Byzantine tradition of the 'great Basileus' and which, in its Russian seventeenth-century aspect, leant on the servicemen and the urban population.

TSAR ALEXIS

Tsar Alexis (1645–76) was sixteen years old when he succeeded to the throne. He was called *tishayshiy* ('the most gentle'); though he was quick-tempered, kindness and intelligence were – according to contemporaries – his predominant traits. He married Maria Miloslavsky. His tutor and mentor, the boyar Morozov, promptly married another daughter of this patrician house, thus increasing his influence at court and making himself virtually the ruler of the country.

A census was taken in 1646 to determine the economic situation of the population as a whole, and, answering the repeated requests of the landowners, it was intended to put a stop to peasants leaving their employ. An attempt was made in 1640 to raise the salt tax, but seven years later this measure had to be cancelled as its only result was increased smuggling. The government also tried to lower the salaries of servicemen, which gave rise to much discontent. The increase of bribery in the administration was an open scandal. In June 1648 there was intense unrest in Moscow, as well as in many other towns, directed chiefly against Morozov and his assistants. Several members of the ruling clique were summarily dealt with. The tsar saved Morozov's life but removed him from office. Authority now passed to Prince Nikita Odoyevsky, a man of exceptional intelligence and statesmanship. He was entrusted with the task of drawing up a new *ulozheniye* (legal code). A national assembly, composed chiefly of representatives of the provincial gentry and the urban population, was called to discuss this.

This new body of laws was finally adopted in 1649 and 2,000 copies were printed – an exceptionally large number for the time. The code represented a victory for the middle classes: by its terms, the clergy was precluded from acquiring further lands and lost some legal privileges; the boyars and clergy were no longer allowed to admit bondsmen (see p. 97) to their service and no time limit was set for recalling peasants escaping from estates; foreign trade was to be concentrated exclusively in Archangel, to the satisfaction of Russian merchants; and the peasants were tied to the land on which they worked and their right to change their place of employment on St George's Day was cancelled. The code contained new articles on state crimes, including crimes against the Orthodox Church, for which the death penalty was introduced. Both the upper and the lower classes were extremely displeased with the new code and peasants fled from their employment in unprecedented numbers.

In 1650 violent revolts broke out in Pskov and Novgorod as protests against the export of grain and money to Sweden in compliance with the provisions of the 1617 peace treaty. Pskov was surrounded with troops and a national assembly had to be called as the tsar wanted to avoid bloodshed. A special delegation of the assembly was sent to persuade the Pskovians to submit, explaining that these exports were not treasonable but the implementation of state treaties. In 1654–5 plague ravaged the country, temporarily paralysing everything, and shortly after there was an acute financial crisis because of the decrease in the influx of foreign silver as a consequence of the protective trade measures. Instead of the silver *kopeyka* and *den'ga*, the government began to issue, from 1656 onward, copper coins valued officially at the same rate as the silver. The value of these copper coins almost immediately began to fall, and severe inflation drove the population in 1662 to take part in the so-called 'copper' revolt, forcing the government in 1663 to call in the copper coin issues and to use its silver reserves.

As a consequence of the measures binding the peasants to the land, the Cossack territories, especially on the Don, were overflowing with refugees, who were no longer admitted as fully-fledged members of this military Cossack republic. Azov barred the way out of the Don estuary. Therefore all these hapless would-be Cossacks moved further on to the Volga region and thence to the Caspian Sea, plundering Persian territories. They found a talented leader in Stepan Razin. In 1668–9, fighting the Persians, he gained a widespread reputation and was able to create a Cossack army. In 1670 he led a revolt on the Volga against the Muscovite administration and the landowners. The movement expanded swiftly, gaining the peasants' sympathy as well as that of the poorer servicemen and townsfolk. Simultaneously an anti-Russian movement started among the Finnish tribes of the Volga region. Razin declared that he was not against the tsar, only against the gentry, and that this was the peasants' reaction to their enserfment. The rebellion was broken by regiments of foreign mercenaries, and in 1671 Razin was executed, but the social problem that had created the revolt remained unsolved.

During the reign of Tsar Alexis a crisis arose in the Russian Church (see pp. 320–1), sparked off by the question of formal errors or inaccuracies in the Orthodox rites and the liturgical books. The upholders of 'ancient piety' categorically rejected any alterations or corrections as heresy. The Russian Ecclesiastical Council of 1654, on the other hand, approved the proposed amendments. The Greek patriarchs likewise confirmed them first in 1655 and later in 1666–7 at a 'Great Council' held in Moscow. The dissidents, however, would not retreat from their categorical rejection of any deviation from tradition or ritual ceremony. They preferred to face suffering, undergo the fiercest reprisals, and even immolate themselves on burning pyres rather than 'lose their souls' by accepting reform. In 1668–1676 the rich and populous Monastery of Solovki on the islands of the White Sea went so far as to offer armed resistance to the tsar's troops. This schism weakened the Russian Church and divided Russian society: the dissidents or 'Old Believers', in the absence of bishops, finally split into numerous sects, some of these without clergy, and were considered by the government, to a certain extent, to be second-class citizens.

This ecclesiastical schism coincided with a crisis in the patriarchate. In 1652 Metropolitan Nikon of Novgorod was elected patriarch. He enjoyed the tsar's special confidence and friendship. Nikon wanted to make the office of patriarch as influential and strong as it had been in the time of Filaret. He was granted the title of 'Great Sovereign' and virtually became Alexis' co-ruler, and he considered himself the tsar's equal. At the same time he attempted to establish the priority of the spiritual principle over the secular. However, he overreached himself, forgetting that Filaret had been the then tsar's father, whereas he was no more than a gifted peasant from the Nizhny-Novgorod region. The tsar began to feel the weight of his strong personality, and in 1658 Nikon, infuriated by the taunts of the tsar's courtiers, departed from Moscow without having first sought permission to do so, but he did not resign his see. An extremely complicated canonical situation was thus created. In 1660 a council of the Russian clergy resolved by a majority of votes to deprive him of his patriarchal rank, the minority considering, however, that a local council was not competent to take such a decision. The tsar agreed with the minority. Finally, the Great Council that assembled in Moscow in 1666–7 was attended by the patriarchs of Alexandria and Antioch and by representatives of the two other sees of Constantinople and Jerusalem, as well as by the Russian hierarchy. The council deprived Nikon of patriarchal and sacerdotal rank and sent him into retirement to the Ferapontov Monastery. In 1681 he was released and died on a boat on the Volga on his way to the Voskresensky Monastery, which he had founded.

Foreign affairs under Alexis were dominated by the inclusion in the Russian state of 'Little Russia' – the Ukraine, which had belonged to Poland. Its inhabitants were irked by the Polish way of life and irritated by the conclusion in 1596 of a union between the Roman Catholic and the Orthodox churches (in accordance with the Brest agreement), by which the latter kept its liturgy and rituals but recognized the authority of the

Pope. The Cossacks played a leading part in rebel activities and acquired much popular support. They had created on the Dnieper islands beyond the rapids a military community of their own, the Sich. There was also the quasi-military organization of the 'Registered Cossacks', who lived as free peasants in the Ukraine and were administratively controlled by the Polish authorities. By the end of the sixteenth century the Cossacks had repeatedly revolted, and when Sigismund III had become involved in Russian affairs, they succeeded in wresting certain rights from the Poles; an Orthodox metropolitan see was even restored in Kiev. The systematic introduction of Polish influence in the Ukraine was countered from 1630 onward by further Cossack risings, all of them, as in the past, cruelly crushed. Many Cossacks and other Orthodox Ukrainians escaped to Russia. In 1638 King Vladislav abolished self-government for the 'Registered Cossacks', limiting their number to a bare 6,000 men and appointing Polish commanders to the Cossack formations. Polish garrisons were sent to various towns and the spread of Polish culture was further intensified. In 1648 a rebellion was started by the Cossacks on an unprecedented scale, in which the whole population of the Ukraine joined. It was headed by an outstandingly gifted leader, Bohdan Khmel'nitsky (d. 1657), who after many vicissitudes sought support in 1648 from Moscow. In 1654 the Cossacks achieved their ends. Tsar Alexis and the national assembly agreed to incorporate 'Little Russia' in the Muscovite state, although this meant the end of peaceful relations with Poland and heralded a difficult war. Fighting lasted until 1667 when, by the treaty of Andrusovo, the lands on the eastern bank of the Dnieper were ceded to Russia, although the western-bank territories, excluding Kiev, remained in Polish hands and their inhabitants continued to fight the Poles. In 1672 Hetman Doroshenko asked for Turkish help. The Sultan then attempted to gain possession of both the Polish and Russian Ukrainian territories. In 1681 Moscow recognized Turkey's right to the western bank of the Dnieper, excluding the city of Kiev.

In 1656–9 Alexis was forced to wage war against Sweden, which had intervened in Polish affairs, but he gained no significant success. In Siberia expansion eastward continued. The Russians had reached the Pacific during the reign of Tsar Mikhail. In 1648 the Cossack Dezhnev fixed as a limit between Asia and America the area known today as the Bering Straits. In 1649 Cossacks led by Khabarov reached the river Amur and came into contact with the Chinese, with whom, after a series of collisions, a frontier was established (in the Treaty of Nerchinsk, 1689). Simultaneously, western Siberia was being colonized by migrating peasants who there found themselves free and prosperous. A basis was thus built up for the subsequent assimilation by the Russians of this enormous and potentially rich land.

Fyodor III (1676–82) was fourteen years old at his accession. He was Alexis' eldest surviving son by his first wife Maria Miloslavsky, who had borne him a second son, Ivan. By Alexis' second marriage, to Natalia Naryshkin, he had had another son, Peter, with whom the new young tsar was on friendly terms. Immediately after Alexis' death the two groups of his kinsmen fell out. Closest to Tsar Fyodor were Yazykov and Likhachev (belonging to the upper-class gentry) and the young Prince Vasily Golitsyn. Their influence was constructive: they sought to raise the efficiency of the administration, to carry out the tracing of boundaries of estates and hereditary lands, and to reorganize the fiscal system by unifying the different tax-collecting agencies. The question of the modernization of the army was also raised. At the request of the nobility the *mestnichestvo* was solemnly abolished by a special assembly of boyars and church dignitaries, the *mestnicheskiye knigi* (registers of precedence) being burned (to the subsequent annoyance of historians).

The foundation in Moscow of a Graeco–Latin–Slavonic academy was decided upon and a project was under consideration for the opening of a school for the children of the poorer classes, similar to those existing in the West. Had Tsar Fyodor lived longer, quite a few aspects of life in Russia would probably have been modified in line with European models, though by other methods than those later adopted by Peter the Great. But Fyodor died without heirs. He married twice: his first wife, Agatha Gruszecka, was of Polish origin and died together with her infant son in 1681; he only lived two months after his marriage to his second wife, Marfa Apraksina, and was succeeded jointly by his brother Ivan V (1682–1696) and Peter.

The reigns of the Tsars Alexis and Fyodor occurred in times of far-reaching cultural changes. The influence of Europe was directly and indirectly felt in many domains, a great role being played by Ukrainian savants, and two trends developed – one based on Greek and the other on Latin scholarship. The first translations of scientific works appeared and the first plays were staged in spite of sharp opposition from the church. Even that epitome of Russian culture, icon painting, began to show new traits hitherto unknown. Via the Ukraine and White Russia the influence of western baroque penetrated into Muscovy. Church music passed gradually from unisonal modulations to polyphony. All this would seem to prove that Muscovite Russia after four long centuries of alienation had outgrown exclusively traditional forms and was ripe for her next period when her indigenous culture, the fruits of the creative efforts of all her sons, would assimilate what was offered by the West.

GUIDE TO FURTHER READING

Dictionaries

Dictionary of Russian Historical Terms, from the Eleventh Century to 1917, comp. by S. G. Pushkarev, G. Vernadsky and R. T. Fisher, jun., eds. (New Haven, 1970); R. A. French and R. E. F. Smith, *The Terminology of Settlements and their Lands in Late Medieval Russia* (series no. 7, Centre for Russian and East European Studies, Birmingham, 1970); I. I. Sreznevsky, *Materialy dlya Slovarya drevnerusskogo yazyka* (3 vols., St Petersburg, 1893–1912, repr. Moscow, 1958); G. E. Kochin, *Materialy dlya terminologicheskogo slovarya Drevney Rossii* (Moscow–Leningrad, 1937).

Bibliographies

Bibliografiya russkogo letopisaniya, comp. by R. P. Dmitriyeva (Moscow–Leningrad, 1962). Although there are some lacunae as far as Muscovite Russia is concerned, *A Bibliography of Works in English on Early Russian History to 1800*, comp. by P. A. Crowther (Oxford, 1969) is nevertheless a useful handbook. Also see J. S. G. Simmons, *Russian Bibliography, Libraries and Archives* (Twickenham, 1973).

Original sources

It would be impossible to list them all but the following are certainly useful. V. S. Ikonnikov, *Opyt russkoy istoriografii* (2 vols. in 4 pts., Kiev, 1891–1908); M. N. Tikhomirov, *Istochnikovedeniye istorii SSSR s drevneyshikh vremyon do kontsa XVIII v.* (Moscow, 1962). D. S. Likhachev, *Russkiye letopisi* (Moscow–Leningrad, 1947) provides an elucidation of the development of Russian chronicle writing, which is extremely useful for an understanding of the historical events of this period; pp. 173ff are pertinent to this chapter. The texts of the chronicles themselves are to be found in the relevant volumes of *Polnoye sobraniye russkikh letopisey*, of which thirty-one have so far appeared. State papers and legal documents are usually beyond the scope of university courses but these sources are available, and full reference to them can be found in both Ikonnikov's and Tikhomirov's books. *Muscovite Judicial Texts, 1488–1556* (Ann Arbor, 1966) contains English translations by H. W. Dewey of the texts of the Russian laws; the originals (thirteenth–seventeenth centuries) are to be found in *Pamyatniki russkogo prava*, vols. II–VI (Moscow, 1955–9). The following are useful commentaries: M. Szeftel's 'The Sudebnik of 1497', in *For Roman Jakobson* (The Hague, 1956), 547–52; his 'Le "Justicier" (Sudebnik) du Grand Prince Ivan III', *Revue Historique du droit français et étranger*, 4 (Paris, 1956), 531–68; and H. W. Dewey, 'The 1497 Sudebnik', *ASEER*, 15 (1956). S. I. Shtamm, *Sudebnik 1497 g.* (Moscow, 1955) contains a useful bibliography and explains certain contemporary legal terms. Although perhaps a little beyond the normal student's scope, L. V. Cherepnin, *Russkiye feodal'nyye arkhivy XIV–XV vekov* (Moscow–Leningrad, vol. I, 1948, vol. II, 1951) throws light on many of the legal and political problems of this period.

I. P. Yeryomin, ed., *Poslaniya Iosifa Volotskogo* (Moscow–Leningrad, 1959) deals with problems facing the Russian Church. In N. A. Kazakova and Y. S. Lur'e,

Antifeodal'nyye dvizheniya na Rusi (Moscow–Leningrad, 1955) there is a useful section, 'Istochniki po istorii yereticheskikh dvizheniy XIV – nachala XVI veka', 227–523. Also see *Le Stoglav ou Les Cent Chapitres*, trans. by E. Duchesne (Paris, 1920), or *Stoglav* (in Russian; Kazan', 1862, and D. E. Kozhanchikov, ed., St Petersburg, 1863). For the best analysis, see D. Stefanovich, *O stoglave* (St Petersburg, 1909); W. Palmer, *The Patriarch and the Tsar* (6 vols., London, 1871–6); Ya. L. Barskov, ed., *Pamyatniki istorii staroobryadchestva XVII veka*, vol. I, fasc. 1 (Leningrad, 1927); 'Pamyatniki pervykh let russkogo staroobryadchestva', in Ya. L. Barskov, ed., *Letopis' zanyatiy Arkheograficheskoy kommissii*, vol. 24 (St Petersburg, 1911); and *Patriarch Nikon on Church and State, Nikon's Refutation Text*, ed. with an introd. and notes by G. V. Vernadsky and V. A. Tumins (The Hague, 1974).

It can also be of interest to see Russia as she appeared to foreigners in the sixteenth and seventeenth centuries; see Siegmund von Herberstein, *Description of Moscow and Muscovy*, B. Picard, ed. (London, 1969); Heinrich von Staden, *Aufzeichnungen über den Moskauer Staat*, 2nd edn, F. T. Epstein, ed. (Hamburg, 1964); Giles Fletcher, *Of the Rus Commonwealth*, A. J. Schmidt, ed. (New York, 1966); L. E. Berry, ed., *The English Works of Giles Fletcher the Elder* (Madison, 1964); *The Travels of Olearius in 17th century Russia*, trans. and ed. by S. H. Baron (Stanford, 1967); and A. G. Man'kov, ed., *Zapiski inostrantsev o vosstanii Stepana Razina* (Leningrad, 1968).

Anthologies

By far the best anthology is G. V. Vernadsky, R. T. Fisher, A. D. Ferguson, A. Lossky, and S. Pushkarev, eds. and comps., *A Source Book for Russian History from Early Times to 1917*, vol. I (London, 1972); chs. 3ff. contain a most useful selection of documents on the thirteenth to seventeenth centuries. Also see M. N. Tikhomirov, ed., *Khrestomatiya po istorii SSSR s drevneyshikh vremyon do kontsa XV v.* (Moscow, 1952); and A. A. Zimin, ed., *Khrestomatiya po istorii SSSR XVI–XVII veka* (Moscow, 1962).

General Histories

Undoubtedly the best and most objective of these is G. V. Vernadsky, *A History of Russia* (New Haven); pertaining to this period are vol. III, *The Mongols and Russia* (1953); vol. IV, *Russia at the Dawn of the Modern Age* (1959), and pts. 1 and 2 of vol. V, *The Tsardom of Moscow* (1969). The most recent exposition of Soviet views on Muscovite Russia is *Istoriya SSSR*, 1st series, vols. II, III, B. A. Rybakov, ed. (Moscow, 1966). There are a mass of facts and many interesting maps in *Ocherki istorii SSSR* (Moscow), of which the following sections are relevant: B. D. Grekov, ed., *Period feodalizma, IX–XV vv.* (2 pts., 1953); A. N. Nasonov, L. V. Cherepnin, and A. A. Zimin, ed., *Period feodalizma, konets XV v. – nachalo XVII v.* (1955); and A. A. Novosel'sky and N. V. Ustyugov, eds., *Period feodalizma, XVII v.* (1955). A. E. Presnyakov, *Lektsii po russkoy istorii*, vol. II, pt. 1, *Zapadnaya Rus' i Litovsko–Russkoye gosudarstvo* (Moscow, 1939) gives an extremely clear and factual exposition of often very complicated historical events. A. I. Kopanev, A. G. Man'kov, and N. E. Nosov, *Ocherki istorii SSSR (konets XV – nachalo XVII v.)* (Leningrad, 1957) includes a mass of details.

Of the shorter general histories the following may be found useful: S. F. Platonov, *Lektsii po Russkoy istorii*, 7th rev. edn (St Petersburg, 1910), or the same author's *Uchebnik russkoy istorii*, various editions – its English translation is F. A. Golder, ed., *A History of Russia*, trans. by E. Aronsberg (New York, 1925). N. V. Riasanovsky, *A History of Russia* (New York, 1963), pt. 3, 'Appanage Russia', 69–156, and pt. 4, 'Muscovite Russia', 157–231, give the best account in English of this period to be found in general surveys.

Slavonic migrations in the Muscovite state

S. M. Seredonin, *Russkaya istoricheskaya geografiya* (Petrograd, 1916); P. N. Milyukov, *Ocherki po istorii russkoy kul'tury*, vol. I pt. 2, N. Andreyev, ed. (The Hague, 1964), which provides a new picture of population movements; M. K. Lyubavsky, *Obrazovaniye osnovnoy gosudarstvennoy territorii Velikorusskoy narodnisti: zaseleniye i obyedineniye tsentra* (Leningrad, 1929); D. I. Bagalev, *Ocherki po istorii kolonizatsii i byta stepnoy okrayny Moskovskogo gosudarstva* (Moscow, 1887); D. M. Lebedev, *Ocherki po istorii geografii v Rossii XV i XVII vv.* (Moscow, 1956); the same author's *Geografiya v Rossii XVII veka (dopetrovskoy epokhi)* (Moscow–Leningrad, 1949); M. P. Alekseyev, *Sibir' v izvestiyakh zapadnoyevropeyskikh puteshestvennikov i pisateley XIII–XVIII vv.*, 2nd edn (Irkutsk, 1941); A. I. Andreyev, *Ocherki po istochnikovedenii Sibiri*, vol. I (Moscow–Leningrad, 1960); and G. V. Lantzeff, *Siberia in the Seventeenth Century* (Berkeley–Los Angeles, 1943).

Cultural development in Muscovy

P. N. Milyukov, *Ocherki po istorii russkoy kul'tury*, Jubilee edn (Paris, vol. II, pts. 1 & 2, 1931, vol. III, 1930); this edition was revised by the author and is the one to use. There is a most useful summing-up in chs. 3–6 in V. A. Riasanovsky, *Obzor russkoy kul'tury*, pt. I (New York, 1947), and there is also a particularly interesting chapter 'Vopros o Mongol'skom vliyanii na russkuyu kul'turu', 381–411. D. S. Likhachev, *Kul'tura Russkogo Naroda, X–XVII vv.* (Moscow–Leningrad, 1961) is extremely valuable. A. V. Artsikhovsky, ed., *Ocherki russkoy kul'tury XIII–XV vekov*, vol. I, *Material'naya kul'tura*, vol. II, *Dukhovnaya kul'tura* (Moscow, 1970), contains a mass of new facts. Some interesting articles that are pertinent to this period can be found in M. N. Tikhomirov, *Russkaya kul'tura X–XVIII vv.* (Moscow, 1968). The history of the Russian Church is best dealt with by A. V. Kartashov, *Ocherki po istorii russkoy tserkvi* (2 vols., Paris, 1959); a bibliography is included.

History of Russian art

I. E. Grabar', V. S. Kemenov, V. N. Lazarev, eds., *Istoriya russkogo iskusstva* (Moscow, vol. II, 1954, vol. III, 1955, vol. IV, 1959); M. V. Alpatov, *Russkoye iskusstvo s drevneyshikh vremyon do nachala XVIII veka*, vol. III in the series *Vseobshchaya istoriya iskusstv* (Moscow, 1955); N. P. Kondakov, *The Russian Icon*, trans. and ed. by E. H. Minns (Oxford, 1927); G. H. Hamilton, *The Art and Architecture of Russia*, in the series *Pelican History of Art* (Harmondsworth, 1954), esp. pts. 2 and 3; M. Alpatov, *Andrey Rublyov* (Moscow, 1959); and V. N. Lazarev, *Andrey Rublyov i yego shkola* (Moscow, 1966). M. N. Tikhomirov, 'Andrey Rublyov i yego epokha', in *Voprosy istorii*, no. 1 (Moscow, 1961), 3–17, depicts the cultural development of the period. An interesting appreciation is D. S. Likhachev, *Kul'tura Rusi vremeni Andreya Rublyova i Yepifaniya Premudrogo* (Moscow–Leningrad, 1962). V. D. Likhacheva and D. S. Likhachev, *Khudozhest-*

vennoye naslediye Drevney Rusi i sovremennost' (Leningrad, 1971) contains some stimulating observations. O. I. Podobedova, *Moskovskaya shkola zhivopisi pri Ivane IV* (Moscow, 1972) provides a clear picture of the trends in the field of Russian painting in the sixteenth century. N. Andreyev, 'Nikon and Avvakum on Icon Painting', *Revue des Études Slaves*, XXXVIII, 37–44, in *Mélanges Pierre Pascal* (Paris, 1961) points out – very concisely – some of the more important features of Russian painting in the seventeenth century. L. V. Cherepnin, *Russkaya paleografiya* (Moscow, 1956) provides a useful exposition of the subject and is good for reference. A bibliography on the question of western influence on Russian art is included in V. N. Lazarev, *Iskusstvo srednevekovoy Rusi i Zapad v XI–XV vv.* (Moscow, 1970); this and the work of S. F. Platonov, *Moskva i Zapad v XVI–XVII vv.* (Leningrad, 1925) are two very useful books on this aspect of Russian cultural history. [See also 'Guides to further reading' in vol. 3 of this work, *Introduction to Russian Art and Architecture*.]

Specific problems of Muscovite history

Many of the points are touched on in general histories of the period but the following books treat these questions in detail. V. T. Pashuto, *Geroicheskaya bor'ba russkogo naroda za nezavisimost', XIII vek* (Moscow, 1956) – esp. pt. 3, pp. 199–259; the author stresses the military and organizational roles of Alexander Nevsky and Daniil of Galich. There is a great deal of material treated in a strictly Marxist way in V. T. Pashuto, *Ocherki po istorii Galitsko–Volynskoy Rusi* (Moscow, 1950). A different view of the events of the thirteenth century is advanced by N. A. Klepinin, *Svyatoy i blagovernyy velikiy knyaz' Aleksandr Nevsky* (Paris, n.d.) which stresses the religious significance of the prince's rule.

Further light is thrown on the events of the fourteenth century by J. L. I. Fennell, *The Emergence of Moscow, 1304–1359* (London, 1968); L. V. Cherepnin, *Obrazovaniye Russkogo tsentralizovannogo gosudarstva v XIV–XV vekakh* (Moscow, 1960) – not a very readable book but one that contains a mass of economic and social facts, although it should be realized that the author unjustly denigrates the importance of the Russian Church at this time; and B. D. Grekov and A. Yu. Yakubovsky, *Zolotaya Orda i yeyo padeniye* (Moscow, 1950), which is the best account in Russian. The most detailed account of the political events of Ivan III's reign is J. L. I. Fennell, *Ivan the Great of Moscow* (London, 1961). Useful for the general picture of events is Ian Grey's *Ivan III and the Unification of Russia* (London, 1964). K. V. Bazilevich, *Vneshnyaya politika Russkogo tsentralizovannogo gosudarstva, vtoraya polovina XV v.* (Moscow, 1952) is a detailed analysis of fifteenth-century political events. The fullest account of the reign of Vasily III is A. A. Zimin's *Rossiya na poroge novogo vremeni* (*Ocherki politicheskoy istorii Rossii pervoy treti XVI v.*) (Moscow, 1972). I. I. Smirnov, *Ocherki politicheskoy istorii Russkogo gosudarstva 30kh–50kh godov XVI veka* (Moscow–Leningrad, 1968) is a series of monographs dealing with the activities of various individuals in the 1550s. The same subject is dealt with in A. A. Zimin, *Reformy Ivana Groznogo* (Moscow, 1960). S. F. Platonov, *Ivan Grozny (1530–84)* (Petrograd, 1923) is the most careful and accurate account of the rule and personality of this tsar. The following four books are all investigations designed primarily for scholars: S. B. Veselovsky, *Issledovaniya po istorii oprichniny* (Moscow, 1963); A. A. Zimin, *Oprichnina Ivana Groznogo* (Moscow, 1964); R. G. Skrynnikov, *Nachalo oprichniny* (Leningrad, 1966); and the same author's *Oprichnyy terror* (Leningrad, 1969). For the more general reader P. A. Sadikov, *Ocherki po istorii oprichniny* (Moscow–Leningrad, 1950) is adequate.

APPANAGE AND MUSCOVITE RUSSIA

W. Kirchner, *The Rise of the Baltic Question* (Newark, Del., 1954); ch. 4, on the Livonian war, is of particular interest. V. D. Korolyuk, *Livonskaya voyna* (Moscow, 1954) is a useful account of historical events. Of particular importance is B. Nolde, *La Formation de l'Empire Russe* (2 vols., Paris, 1952-3); the author considers that the creation of the Russian empire dates from the reign of Ivan IV. S. F. Platonov, *Boris Godunov* (Petrograd, 1921) is a helpful book and gives the best account of the reign of Boris. G. V. Vernadsky, 'The Death of the Tsarevich Dimitry', *Oxford Slavonic Papers*, v (1954), 1-19, gives a clear account of this strange happening. S. F. Platonov, *Smutnoye vremya* (Prague, 1924) and Yu. V. Got'ye, *Smutnoye vremya, Ocherki istorii revolyutsionnykh dvizheniy nachala XVII stoletiya* (Moscow, 1921) are the best analyses of the 'Time of Troubles'. An important study elucidating the events of the Romanov dynasty's acceptance of power is P. G. Lyubomirov, *Ocherk istorii Nizhegorodskogo opolcheniya 1611–1613 gg.* (1917; repr. Moscow, 1939). Two parts of J. Blum, *Lord and Peasant in Russia from the Ninth to the Nineteenth century* (Princeton, 1961) merit special attention: 'The Mongol Era' and the section on the sixteenth–seventeenth centuries. B. D. Grekov, *Krest'yane na Rusi s drevneyshikh vremyon do XVIII v.* (Moscow, vol. I, 1952, vol. II, 1954) provides the most complete account of this subject. A. A. Vvedensky, *Dom Stroganovykh v XVI–XVII vekakh* (Moscow, 1962) explains clearly many of the economic problems of the period.

A. A. Novosel'sky, *Bor'ba Moskovskogo gosudarstva s tatarami v pervoy polovine XVII v.* (Moscow–Leningrad, 1948) gives a clear account of the struggle to defend the Russian frontier lands. W. E. D. Allen, *The Ukraine* (Cambridge, 1940) is an objective and valuable survey. A survey of the differing opinions held by historians on the question of the incorporation of the Ukraine into the Muscovite state is to be found in N. Andreyev, *'Pereyaslavskiy dogovor'*, repr. in his *Studies in Muscovy* (London, 1970). V. N. Latkin, *Zemskiye Sobory Drevney Rusi* (St Petersburg, 1885) is the best account of this subject. J. L. H. Keep, 'The Decline of the Zemsky Sobor', *Slavonic and East European Review*, XXXVI, 86 (1957), 100-22, contains some interesting observations. L. V. Cherepnin, 'Zemskiye Sobory i utverzhdeniye absolyutizma v Rossii' in the collection *Absolyutizm v Rossii XVII–XVIII vv.* (Moscow, 1964), 92-133, gives the Soviet viewpoint on this problem.

4

IMPERIAL RUSSIA
PETER I TO NICHOLAS I

MARC RAEFF

INTRODUCTION

The reign of Peter the Great (1682(9)–1725) not only opens the period covered in this chapter, but determines its character and confers on it unity (Map 17). Peter's reforms broke with the policies of the preceding Muscovite period, while in the reign of Nicholas I (1825–55) one can see the culmination and last stage of the basic trends that Peter had introduced. Rooted though they were in the preceding period, however, the reforms of the 1860s and 1870s opened a new period in Russian history characterized by a steadily increasing urbanization and industrialization. If Muscovy was the 'Middle Ages' for Russia, then the century and a half between the accession of Peter I and the death of Nicholas I may be compared to the transitional period of the sixteenth and seventeenth centuries in western Europe.

The reign of Peter I marks a sharp historical cleavage. It is perfectly true, of course, as many historians have pointed out, that his achievements in foreign policy crowned with success efforts initiated in the past, that the westernization of Russian life (of the upper classes at any rate) had begun to be felt in the reign of Tsar Alexis, and that even some of his institutional innovations derived from earlier practices. Yet Peter imparted to the transformation such a dynamic power that it changed its very tone and quality. Furthermore, his relentless drive for rapid westernization seemed like an irresistible force of nature, an impression confirmed by the ruthlessness with which he broke any opposition. His contemporaries, and the generations immediately following, felt that they were living in a time of revolutionary transformation and radical change. This subjective feeling itself became an important factor in shaping the institutions, society, and culture of Russia in the period.

The sharpest break with Muscovite traditions was in the goals and methods of state action; Peter introduced the concept of the active, creative, goal-directed state. As had been the case for the centralized absolute monarchies of western Europe, the machinery of government

121

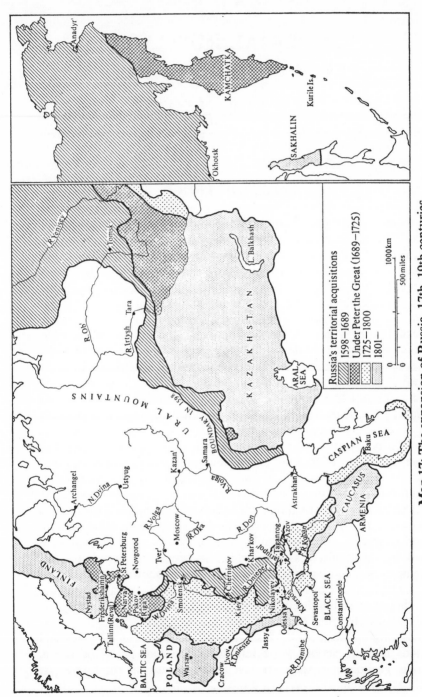

Map 17: The expansion of Russia, 17th–19th centuries

General pattern of Russian expansion, with towns and settlements important
during the periods covered

Russia's territorial acquisitions
1598–1689
Under Peter the Great (1689–1725)
1725–1800
1801–

fashioned by Peter had to perform positive functions in the country's life: to lead in organizing the exploitation of its natural resources, to play an active international role, and to this end to maintain an effective military establishment and develop foreign trade. The goal was to maximize the power of the state, which in turn was to enhance the welfare of the nation. In the particular case of Russia there was the additional aim of introducing and firmly rooting western culture and civilization, which also meant what – for want of a better term – is called the 'modernization' of Russian society. These openly avowed aims of the Petrine government transformed the methods of administration: in Muscovy the functions of government had consisted mainly in the maintenance of law and order and defence against external enemies. These tasks had been performed within the framework of traditional customs and ways which left many areas of private and national life outside the purview of the state (in spite of a relatively high degree of political centralization). The machinery of government that was established by Peter the Great, on the other hand, aimed at reaching the state's goals in rational fashion. The central institutions of the state were assigned positive tasks and given the monopoly of authority in practically all areas of Russian life. Little was left to the autonomous initiative and action of individuals and of constituted groups.

The consequence was not only a high degree of centralization – as well as the extension and strengthening of the ruler's autocratic power – but also a drive for institutional control and uniformity over the whole empire. In addition, the new role in European politics played by the Petrine state resulted in Russia's territorial expansion even beyond the limits set by traditional historical claims or national, linguistic, and religious criteria. Russia became a truly multinational empire, with the status and functions of a world power, involved in diplomatic and military imbroglios and open to influences from the West. The final result of the new direction given by Peter I to the Russian polity, therefore, was to set the country firmly and actively on the road of cultural and material westernization. In the period covered by this chapter the effects of westernization were assimilated only by a select part of the population – mainly the upper classes – but the problems they created affected the entire society. The new political goals and methods required large expenditures and to this end the state became actively involved in the economic transformation of the country as well.

The institutions – either newly created or derived from existing ones – that emerged as a consequence of Peter's reforms used people and country as means for the achievement of the state's goals, not as objects of the government's concern. For this reason the social framework was left much as it had been in the seventeenth century, although an effort was made to bend the people's traditional routine to the will and purpose of the Petrine state. As social realities and traditional patterns of a people's life and thought change slowly and are not easily transformed by government decree, the new administrative institutions and the cultural pattern of the ruling class found themselves out of tune with the people's ways. This is what caused the disharmony between the old and the new, the people and the élite, the traditional and the rational elements in Russian life, that is so characteristic of the approximately one hundred and fifty years between the accession of Peter I and the death of Nicholas I. Russia's performance in the Crimean War dramatically illustrated this disharmony and convinced even the dullest government officials that its continued existence threatened the very survival of the state.

As a consequence of the divergence between the economic–political–cultural life of the élite and the traditional ways of the people, tensions and conflicts punctuated the history of Russia in this period. First were those created by the discrepancy between the old social framework and the new dynamics of the state. In addition new tensions arose as a direct result of the new orientation taken by the government and the importation of western ideas and ways. Paradoxically, in the long run the Petrine state created the very forces which were to undermine and to destroy the imperial regime. This happened largely because the reign of Peter the Great introduced a fundamental discrepancy between ends and means into the Russian body politic. Of course, there had been discrepancies between social ends and political means before; no social body that is alive may be ever completely devoid of them, for various elements of society change their ways of thought and action at different times and rates. But in the case of modern Russia the discrepancy w..s much more blatant, and pregnant with serious troubles because of the onrushing nature of Peter's reforms.

CENTRALIZATION AND INSTITUTIONS

Some of the ambiguities and discrepancies may serve as guidelines in describing the principal features and main institutions in Russia between 1689 and 1855. In the first place, a major and dramatic lack of harmony arose and maintained itself between the drive for centralization and uniformity, on the one hand, and the needs and demands for independent action and autonomy at the level of the individual, the group, or the locality, on the other. On the political plane the opposition between the reliance on centralization and uniformity and the requirements for auto-nomous action provided the main dynamic of the administrative history of the empire. Peter had been so preoccupied with marshalling all the means available to pursue the state's new military and political aims that

124

he had paid attention only to the fashioning of the central administration. He postponed the reform of the local administration necessary to make it consonant with the pattern and demands of the new central institutions; when he did eventually act, it was in a haphazard, experimental, and temporary way, as a sort of afterthought. The empire was thus saddled with a major administrative weakness: an inefficient local administration incapable of adequately performing the ever more numerous tasks demanded of it by the central government.

Peter's successors inherited his centralistic outlook and his lack of concern for local needs, so that his haphazard scheme had to make do for over half a century, giving rise to practices of abuse, inefficiency, corruption, and passivity that proved impossible to eradicate. Catherine II (1762–96) undertook to give local administration some shape, and made serious efforts at delegating to it enough autonomous authority and power of decision to relieve the central institutions. But the practices that had developed could not be overcome. Besides, since Catherine herself did not want to give up the leadership functions of the state, she implemented the reforms only half-heartedly. Her successors proved even less interested in promoting local administrative initiative and they again concentrated their attention on the central institutions. Alexander I did almost nothing, although he did allow some experimental schemes (e.g. the vicegerencies of General Balashov) to be tried. Nicholas I believed that the problem would best be solved through his personal supervision of all facets of life in the empire. To this effect he established the 'Third Section' (of His Imperial Majesty's Own Chancery) and the Corps of Gendarmes, who were to act as *missi dominici* and right any wrongs in the name of the sovereign emperor. This throwback to an essentially medieval conception of kingship was woefully anachronistic in the second quarter of the nineteenth century and failed dismally, as the masterpieces of the great Russian novelists – Gogol, Turgenev, Saltykov-Shchedrin – abundantly illustrate.

Another facet of the political–administrative picture was the ambivalence stemming from the conception of Russia as a united state and the hard fact of its being a multinational empire composed of very diverse regions, acquired at various times and under different circumstances. Although Muscovy had pushed beyond the ethnic confines of the Russian people, this expansion had not much impinged on its life and structure, partly because the newly conquered territories were sparsely populated and were rapidly settled by Russians. Peter the Great, however, acquired completely alien provinces and allowed them to retain their particular laws and institutions. Catherine II later incorporated still more lands whose people had a sophisticated social organization, a high culture of their own, and a lively political tradition. The Russian government was

125

interested in eroding the differences between the political traditions and the administrative and legal structures of these new provinces and those of Russia's heartland. Needless to say, such a policy became a source of friction and tension between the Russian administration and the local population, foreshadowing the still greater conflicts produced by the policy of active Russification in the second half of the nineteenth century. Alexander I had hoped to resolve the difficulty by means of a personal union that would make the Emperor of Russia King of Poland and Grand Duke of Finland. But the solution that worked fairly well for Finland failed in the case of Poland, where national fervour and the demands for constitutional liberties led to an open revolt that was harshly suppressed by Nicholas I.

In the south and in the east, the great territorial expansion of the empire led to the conquest of a large number of non-European and non-Christian peoples. Here the pursuit of centralization and administrative uniformity was paralleled by measures encouraging the social and political Russification of native leadership groups. Although these efforts were on the whole successful, in the long run the government's refusal to permit an administration genuinely adapted to regional needs and conditions lay as a heavy burden not only on the local population but on the empire as a whole, severely handicapping the economic development of the far-flung provinces. In the first quarter of the nineteenth century greater recognition was given to local peculiarity and more administrative flexibility was allowed – in Siberia, for example. Yet even these reforms had as their ultimate goal the promotion of social and administrative uniformity throughout the empire. Local autonomous forces were never given a fair chance. At the death of Nicholas I an impasse had been reached: administrative uniformity fettered social and economic progress and in so doing undermined the military and political strength of the empire.

There was a similar conflict between the government's policy of promoting and directing economic development and its desire to stimulate private enterprise for the exploitation of all potential resources. Peter actively pursued the economic exploitation of the country's resources, to meet the needs of the military and naval establishments, along the lines of the then prevailing principles of mercantilism. Not only did the government provide most of the purchasing power and investment capital, but it also set rigid standards of production, dictated methods of manufacturing, and made available a good part of the labour force by attaching serfs to mines and factories. Catherine II, however, wanted to reverse the pattern of state domination in economic life in favour of private initiative, and her legislation aimed at protecting personal property rights and the exploitation of all the mineral resources of the subsoil as well.

She hoped to create a class of active entrepreneurs, primarily among the landowning nobility. But again the tradition of state control and leadership proved hard to break, the more so since townspeople were not given adequate corporate autonomy and freedom of action, while the nobility's attention continued to be focused on state service. Besides, most of the latter were unable to raise sufficient capital from their estates to invest in industrial and commercial ventures. Alexander I took further steps in the direction pointed by Catherine II. Yet it remained necessary for the government to show the way, to provide much of the capital, or give special privileges to make any large-scale economic endeavour worthwhile. In the field of economic life, too, the heavy hand of the central government's supervision and leadership kept autonomous enterprise in check. A major factor in this situation was, of course, the continuing existence of serfdom: it limited the labour available for non-agricultural pursuits, tied up most of the wealth in land and serfs, and restricted entrepreneurial activities to a tiny fraction of the population. The mounting need for a stronger economic foundation eventually made it necessary, in the first half of the nineteenth century, for the government to acquiesce in the *de facto* existence of some serf enterprises, which gave the impetus to new industrial developments (e.g. textiles).

The condition of the estates (*sosloviya, Stände*) was closely bound up with the opposition between economic *dirigisme* and autonomous entrepreneurship. Indeed, as long as the legal and social status of associations capable of protecting the individual and locality from overbearing control by the government remained inadequate, it was difficult for Russia to emulate the social, economic, and political civilization of western Europe. Yet in the eighteenth and early nineteenth centuries the idea of Russian estates – in the sense of corporations with particular rights and privileges, as well as duties and functions – ran counter to national historical tradition. In particular, they were believed to be contrary to the unity of political sovereignty, which preceding generations had secured at such high price. The preservation of the tsar's autocratic power alongside the state's reliance on centralization and uniformity created conditions unfavourable to the development of estates. Peter the Great had given new form to the pattern of universal service obligations: by instituting the Table of Ranks (1722) he made everyone's status dependent on their position and function in the service of the state, regardless of family background and local ties. Catherine II thought of reversing this tradition by permitting the formation of legally recognized estates of nobility and townspeople, but her reluctance to delegate any effective authority or functions on the local level to these estates resulted in the forms remaining empty shells. Nicholas I reinforced the traditional anti-estate orientation by stressing the autocratic and bureaucratic nature of power

127

in Russia and closely supervising all facets of national life with the help of the Third Section.

WESTERNIZATION AND RUSSIAN SOCIETY

If opposition between the requirements of centralization and autonomy marked the institutional life of Russia, opposition between cultural westernization and institutional traditionalism was characteristic of the social and intellectual scenes. The traditional class structure, such as it was, had been preserved by Peter the Great. But as a result of the changes he wrought a new type of man was emerging within the old class framework. This was particularly true of the upper classes, of course, but it affected the life of the lower ones as well. It is important to note that Peter's rule brought to completion – and then froze – the process by which the traditional peasant bondsman (attached to the land) was changed into a serf (attached to an owner), who in fact – if not quite in law – was merely human chattel. This development not only meant the economic, legal, and physical degradation of the large majority of the Russian people, but it also carried in its wake serious spiritual consequences. The peasant was threatened with becoming dehumanized and transformed into an object; at the same time, the hallowed pattern of communal relationships – in the family or village – was undermined and threatened with extinction. The peasant found himself cast adrift, isolated, at the mercy of landlords and government institutions whose motives he could not understand, whose behaviour he feared, and whose language he had ceased to speak. His alienation from the prevailing institutional pattern and from the culture of the upper classes was complete.

At the other end of the social scale the nobility and state servants – i.e. the educated – were kept in their primary service function and dependence on the state. But to this end they were forced into an education focused on the acquisition of the knowledge and culture of contemporary western Europe. The educated Russian thus was inculcated with a set of values quite different from those of his Muscovite forbears, and developed into a new kind of man, proud of his achievement in acquiring a western culture, conscious of his dignity as an enlightened individual, and resentful of the controls over his life and thought to which a narrow-minded bureaucracy and rigid autocracy subjected him. Eventually, this 'true son of the fatherland' drew apart from the state in whose service he had been fashioned. This alienation produced a tension that briefly broke into open conflict in the Decembrist Revolt of 1825.

At the same time this enlightened and sensitive individual was becoming increasingly conscious of his being cut off from the ways and thought of the common people, whose culture had not shared the westernization that Peter imposed on the upper classes. This awareness, along with his newly acquired western ideals of humanity and social justice, made him want to be useful to his fellow men and to help them overcome what he regarded as being their cultural alienation. Thus the more progressive and enlightened members of the upper class set themselves off from their serf-owning brethren and formed a separate social group which soon became virtually a class of its own: the intelligentsia. In the forefront of the creation of modern Russian civilization, the intelligentsia found its highest expression in the literature of the 1820s and 1830s and set the tone and ideals for all educated Russians in the reign of Nicholas I and thereafter. But in so doing it completely cut itself off from the establishment and broke with the state and the existing social system. Unable to find a meaningful active role in Russian society, persecuted by the government and constricted by censorship, the members of the intelligentsia were finally driven into revolutionary action.

In Muscovite Russia the sentiment of national identity, to the extent that one may speak of it at that early period, had been closely bound up with religion – participation in the Russian Orthodox Church – and with an historical memory that established a connection between a man and the sovereign power of his ruler. The new Petrine state, however, was essentially secular, despite some external trappings of religion. This only deepened the gulf between the common people who clung to the old religious conception of national identity and the more western, secular government and educated classes. For the latter, the triumphs of foreign policy and imperial expansion, the pride in Russia's having joined the western European comity of states and culture, generated a new national consciousness that was no longer defined in traditional terms. In a sense it was something of an artificial creation, restricted to the educated élite and largely based on an attitude of dependence toward the West and an evaluation of national worth in western terms. The government of Nicholas I endeavoured to devise a formula for Russian nationalism by artificially combining the western heritage of Peter with a medieval and religious 'tradition' of their own invention – the so-called 'trinity' of Count S. S. Uvarov: orthodoxy, autocracy, nationality. The intelligentsia answered this official effort with scorn and drew further away from the establishment; both Slavophils and Westerners based their theories and arguments on its complete rejection.

The relationship between the people and the sovereign ruler, the source of political authority, changed too, and became rather confusing to contemporaries. From Peter's time the ruler cut himself off from the people by a wall of new, complicated bureaucratic institutions of foreign inspiration. Throughout his regime these institutions, created supposedly for the sake of greater efficiency, acted as a barrier between the ruler and the ruled. Communication and the passage of information between them were nearly impossible, and this led to mutual ignorance, suspicion, and eventually to a dramatic break. The relationship between ruler and ruled was equally unsatisfactory with respect to the upper classes. Peter the Great and his successors aimed at making the state the object of loyalty for the élite. But it was hard to give up the traditional personal relations between the sovereign and his servicemen, the more so since the autocracy neither disappeared nor ceased to be the dispenser of rewards and bounties. In the final analysis, the source of all authority and of all favours remained the arbitrary and unchallengeable personal power of the autocrat. Such a situation served to undermine the very *raison d'être* of legal and bureaucratic order. It also was at the root of the failures of many attempts at fundamental political reform and of the search for a *Rechtsstaat*.

Finally, a last paradox should be noted before passing to a description of the main features of the period. The reign of Peter the Great had oriented the Russian state and Russian society (at least its conscious elements) toward the development of material resources and power. In the political, economic, as well as cultural domains, it implied a strictly pragmatic and materialistic outlook. Yet this very search for material progress and power was intimately linked to the development of new intellectual and psychological attitudes. The new Russian man, in particular the member of the élite, had to find new ideals and evolve a system of values that stressed service to the country, dedication to the raising of the people's economic and cultural level, and a genuine assimilation of the best that western Europe had to offer at the time. At the end of the eighteenth and in the first decades of the nineteenth centuries, however, the prevailing intellectual fashion in the West was to stress spiritual, idealistic, and fundamentally anti-materialistic values, in open contradiction to the economic development of England and France. This contradiction between idealistic values and the striving for material progress was heightened by the fact that those very qualities that could foster material progress were contrary to the notions of state leadership and the static outlook of the bureaucracy.

THE EMPIRE

Apart from the sixteenth century, the period from 1689 to 1855 witnessed Russia's greatest territorial expansion. Symbolically, it opens with the treaty of Nerchinsk (1689), which stabilized Muscovite conquests in Siberia, and ends with the treaty of Aigun (1858), which laid the foundations of the economic exploitation of the regions in the Far East. In the

West, the expansion started only a few years earlier with Moscow's assumption of the protectorate over the Zaporozhian Cossack Host (1654), and culminated in the partitions of Poland. The greatest territorial advances took place in two stages, in the first and last quarters of the eighteenth century. The nineteenth century brought a general stabilization in the West, the consolidation of Russian domination in the Caucasus, and the first steps in securing the open steppe east of the Caspian Sea. The Peace of Paris (1856), a blow as it was to Russian pride, did not entail any significant territorial losses, but established the borders of the empire that remained roughly to the end of the regime, the only significant exception being the occupation of Central Asia in the second half of the century.

In the south and southeast the expansion was definitely of an aggressive nature (although it may have had its origin in a defensive stance): in the south it was aimed at the promotion of Russian agricultural settlement; in the southeast rather at the acquisition of colonies for exploitation, although Russian settlement eventually followed too, albeit largely in conjunction with the industrialization of the second half of the nineteenth century. But, if these events were shaped largely by domestic factors and concerns, the expansion westward depended on prevailing diplomatic needs and possibilities. Naturally, the style of acquisition varied from case to case, as well as the nature of the problems involved in the integration of the newly acquired areas into the empire. No doubt these differences also accounted for the differences in the psychological reaction to the expansion on the part of Russian society.

EXPANSION TOWARD THE BALTIC

This period begins with Peter's shift from the traditional southward direction of Russian expansion, even though he captured Azov in 1696 and retained it until 1711. Circumstances turned his attention and energies to a new direction in which he was dramatically successful, giving his country a completely new international, military, and naval posture. The Great Northern War, concluded in 1721 by the Treaty of Nystad, firmly established Russia on the eastern shores of the Baltic. Russia thus became a Baltic state, a naval power, the predominant force in northern Europe. Peter dramatically symbolized the shift of the empire's political centre by moving his capital to the newly founded (1703) St Petersburg on the Gulf of Finland. More significant still were the consequences for the domestic organization and life of the empire. For the first time in its history, several provinces with long-standing legal, political, and social privileges, preserved and guaranteed by the acts of incorporation, came under the rule of the Russian autocracy. Their political and social élite not only had a culture, language, and religion different from those of the Russians, but they were also on a superior level of cultural, political, and economic sophistication. In short, as the Russians themselves expressed it, the Baltic provinces were 'Europe' – and it was this parcel of Europe that had been incorporated; how could this territory and its population be integrated, they wondered, into the Petrine empire?

The Russian government made no effort to change the social and political system that prevailed in the Baltic provinces: the German nobility found there were left in control of the local administration as well as of the agricultural resources through serfdom, while the German burghers retained their command over the cities, especially the vital Riga and Reval (Tallinn). In this way a social and administrative order shaped by the heritage of German colonization, feudalism, and Protestantism became a component part of Russian reality. The imperial government endeavoured to enlist the German Baltic nobility for service in the armed forces as well as in administration, and many took advantage of the opportunity offered and had distinguished careers, although it is not true that they had a disproportionately high share of the top positions, as was sometimes alleged. There was thus formed a group of energetic and competent officers and officials loyal to the empire who, however, retained their religion, language, and special corporate rights in their native provinces. In due course, as modern Russian culture took shape, these men became 'bicultural' as well as bilingual. In the eighteenth century they were a link with the West, especially Germany, and served as the link with western European civilization and knowledge. In the economic domain, too, the same was true of the merchants in Riga and other Baltic towns: their trade was rapidly integrated into the Russian economy, a vast market for western goods as well as a valuable source of exportable raw materials. The government, it is true, favoured St Petersburg, but until the middle of the nineteenth century the share of the Baltic ports was large enough to satisfy their traders.

The relation of the imperial administration to the corporate customs and the traditions of local self-government of the German nobles was somewhat complicated and uneven. Throughout the eighteenth century, by and large, the main concern of the Baltic nobility was to preserve their privileged position (mainly with respect to their absolute control over their serfs). But their local power was gradually whittled down. There was no interference in the management of their estates, brutal as it often seemed even to the serf-owning Russians, nor was there practically any interference in affairs relating to the *Kirchspiel*, the lowest level of the territorial subdivision. But the Russian government extended the power of their governors to affect the administration of the districts (*Kreis*) and provinces, as well as appellate justice, and restricted the nobility's rights of self-government until they became largely nominal. In this way the Baltic provinces became assimilated to the regular Russian provincial administration by the end of the eighteenth century.

The Russian government, it is true, paid a price for this administrative uniformity, that of agreeing to respect the economic interests of the Baltic nobility. This led to the emancipation of their serfs without land in 1816–1819. A rural proletariat came into being that was as much at the mercy of the noble landowners as the serfs had been. This in turn generated a policy of Russifying the local population and of converting them to Orthodoxy; an open conflict between the Baltic upper classes and the Russian government was its natural outcome in the 1860s.

EXPANSION IN THE SOUTH

Quite different from those of the expansion toward the Baltic were the aims and results of the Russian advance in the south. There were two stages in this extension – military control and agrarian settlement – and two areas specifically involved – the Ukraine and the Black Sea coast. The area known as 'Little Russia' or the Ukraine had become a part of the Russian state in the seventeenth century through Moscow's assumption of a protectorate (1654) over the Zaporog Cossack Host (*Sich*) and acquisition of Kiev by treaty with Poland (1667, 1686). But the genuine absorption of this territory took place only in the eighteenth century, and was primarily a matter of agrarian and military settlement in which the lead was taken by the governments of Elizabeth (1741–62) and Catherine II. The first movement toward this was the repetition, with some qualifications, of the pattern provided by the Cossack frontier settlements – the creation of military units whose members would be engaged in agriculture (and permitted to employ additional labour for that purpose) on condition that they held themselves in military readiness at all times. Their administrative organization also followed military lines. It was in this manner that various Orthodox and Slavonic-speaking peoples from the Austrian and Turkish empires – the so-called Serbians – were settled in the Ukraine. Their regiments formed the nuclei of new provinces centred on Yelizavetgrad and helped to develop the agricultural resources of the area. In truth, however, this arrangement proved very costly, especially since both the military and economic performances of these settlers turned out to be quite mediocre. The more prosperous officers among them obtained permission to use native labour on their estates and thus were instrumental in the enserfment of the local population. The social conditions in the Ukraine became more like those in the central provinces and the new men who had benefited most from this trend felt a particular loyalty to the empire.

133

In a sense these 'Serbian' settlers experienced the same evolution as had the elected Cossack officers (*starshiny*) after the annexation of the Host's territory to Muscovy. They were absorbed into the service of Moscow and gradually became Russified; they turned into regular men of service and became the owners of estates and serfs, like the average Russian nobleman. Eventually, Russian nobles themselves were given or acquired estates alongside those of the foreign settlers, bringing their own serfs or attaching the local peasants. This contributed to the social Russification of the region, which in the final analysis made possible in the nineteenth century large-scale agrarian enterprises for export markets. The Ukraine thus became a favoured area of economic expansion and peasant resettlement. In addition, the imperial government promoted settlement by any individual or group believed capable of furthering the economic development of the region. Communities of Germans, Swedes, various categories of Russians, and even Jews, were induced to come and settle in the Ukraine.

Naturally the limits of the area of settlement remained ill-defined as long as the southern edge of the steppe was a no-man's-land, open to raids by dissident Cossacks, *haidumaks*, nomadic tribes, and Tatars based on the Crimea. It was natural, too, that the Russian state wished to make this southern frontier secure and to open up the remaining fertile lands to agricultural settlement. This was the primary aim of the wars against Turkey in the eighteenth century, and the goal was achieved by the treaty of Kuchuk Kainardji (1774), consolidated by the annexation of the Crimea (1783), and confirmed by the treaties of Jassy (1791 o.s.) and Adrianople (1829). But to obtain internationally recognized political sovereignty was but the first step; the more important task was to incorporate these empty lands into the economy of the empire.

The rapid and, on the whole, successful incorporation of the southern Ukraine was the work of G. A. Potemkin (1739–91). Taking advantage of the authority that his special relationship with the empress conferred upon him, and making use of traditional Muscovite practices, Potemkin not only firmly established the central government's authority over the new territories but gave the initial impetus to their economic development by integrating into Russian society groups and peoples who previously had been only loosely connected with it. The area of the Don Cossack Host was made into a province within the *guberniya* of Taganrog under the governor-general of this 'New Russia'. Yet on the lowest level of *stanitsa* (camp or village) the rank-and-file Cossacks were allowed to preserve their traditional customs and elect their officials and judges. The officers, on the other hand, by having had their ranks assimilated to those of the regular Russian army and the Table of Ranks system (established in a decree of 24 January 1722), were integrated with the nobility of the empire. This made it possible for them to acquire new estates and settle peasants and serfs on them. Thus the territory of the Don Cossacks was opened up to agricultural pursuits while remaining a source for well-trained cavalry and a military base against Russia's neighbours to the south and east. The Cossacks of the Black Sea and later still of the Kuban' and Terek were organized along similar lines. In this fashion they could spearhead Russian penetration and acquisition of the Caucasus.

In the case of the Crimea, Potemkin first used the old method of sapping the enemy's strength by luring away their most active and useful population. He induced the Greeks, Armenians, and Georgians living in the Crimea to migrate and settle in the recently acquired littoral of the Black Sea and newly created harbours and towns (Taganrog, Mariupol', Kherson, Odessa). The immediate success of the migration was perhaps questionable, although in the long run the Greeks did help to develop the chief urban centres on the Black Sea. But the Crimea's capacity to resist had been undermined and the Russians occupied the peninsula without difficulty in 1783. Potemkin's administration endeavoured to draw into the Russian orbit native leaders by inducing them, through the award of economic privileges and ranks, to Russify their public life and to participate in the local administration. The lands abandoned by those Christians who had gone to Russia earlier, and by those Moslems who had preferred to leave at the time of the conquest, were granted to Russian officers and officials. In this way Russian landowners came to the Crimea and later brought their own Russian serfs and peasant labour. Within a short time the peninsula became an integral part of the empire.

At the turn of the eighteenth century and in the first decades of the nineteenth the agricultural and urban settlement of the southern steppe and the creation of harbours, naval yards, and commercial ports (Nikolaev, Kherson, Odessa, Sevastopol') continued rapidly under the dynamic direction of Potemkin and his assistants and successors. Foreigners were attracted, especially from the Balkans and Mediterranean, to the ports and trading centres. Peasants from central Russia, Poland, the Baltic provinces, as well as from central Europe and the Balkans, were brought in and settled on advantageous terms. In a short time, despite setbacks, 'New Russia' had become part and parcel of the empire. The south became the producer of an exportable surplus of grain, which was shipped through the straits to western Europe. This in turn made for Russia's active diplomatic and military involvement in the 'Eastern Question', and helped to create a new antagonism toward England in the nineteenth century. It should be added that the large number of Greeks who settled in south Russia also played a most active role in the neo-Hellenic cultural revival and in preparing the struggle for the national independence of their homeland. Their activities directly involved the Russian government in the international repercussions of the national and religious struggles of the Balkan peoples.

CONQUEST OF THE CAUCASUS

In the east of the country the newly acquired territories of south Russia bordered directly on the Caucasus, an area in which Russia had been actively involved since the seventeenth century. There had been wars with Persia and its Caucasian tributaries over the security and control of the lower Volga and the north and west shores of the Caspian Sea, and with Russia's emergence as a major power it became the focus for the interests and hopes of various Christian nations – in particular, Georgia and Armenia – who were hard pressed by their Islamic neighbours, Persia and Turkey. In the eighteenth century the Georgians had requested the protection of Russia, but it was only in 1801 that Alexander I finally annexed Georgia. The Caucasus thus ceased to be merely of peripheral concern, best left to the enterprise and skill of the Cossack military and agrarian settlements (which had resulted in Russian control over the northern foothills and slopes of the Caucasian chain). The need to protect the new acquisition led to constant involvement in tribal fights and to regular warfare against Persia and Turkey. After the end of the Napoleonic Wars the Russian government finally decided to impose absolute control and to incorporate the region into the empire. This active policy, at first ably implemented by General A. P. Yermolov, provoked a religious and national reaction – Muridism – which found in Shamil a gifted and determined leader. The war for the pacification and establishment of Russian authority in the Caucasus lasted until the middle of the century, ending with Shamil's surrender in 1859. Alongside military conquest the Russians promoted agrarian settlement in the Caucasus, bringing Russian peasants and other national groups to develop the valley regions. The Cossacks continued to be settled in strategic localities where they combined agriculture with military duties.

As in all conquests of colonial type, which that of the Caucasus clearly was, the Russians exploited national and tribal rivalries. They made efforts to attract native leaders into their service by rewarding them with gifts, rank, and eventual membership in the Russian nobility. But the Russians' basic religious and ethnic tolerance made for relatively mild treatment of religious and national minorities. And thus, with the exception of Shamil's mountain stronghold, the empire's control over the Caucasus was secured rather easily. By the middle of the nineteenth century the economic development of the areas under Russian administration was moving forward; it was given new impetus a few years later by the discovery of rich oil deposits.

SIBERIA

There was no significant expansion in the Far East until Count N. N. Murav'yov-Amursky (1809–80) became governor in eastern Siberia. There had been some border adjustments, especially along the hazy line that separated Siberia from the nomadic peoples roaming the steppes of Kazakhstan. Such 'adjustments' usually took the form of attracting the nearest nomadic clans into the empire by conferring special distinctions on their chieftains and by promising protection and economic benefits to the clan. Russian possessions on the Pacific Ocean were rounded off by the exploration and control of Kamchatka. This was followed by the push into the Aleutians, and across the Bering Straits into Alaska. The initiative for this expansion was taken by the navy as part of its exploration of the northeast passage around Eurasia. In the wake of the naval exploration came Siberian merchants to exploit the local population for their wealth in seals, walrus tusks, and fish. Eventually the Russian–American Company was established to further the economic development – mainly trade – of Russian America and the Pacific coast, and to serve some administrative functions. Its administration, however, proved ruinous to the natives; their extremely high mortality rate reflects the real threat posed to the very existence of entire nationality groups. To protect the natives, as well as their own military and commercial interests, the government had to step in and put the navy in charge of the administration of Kamchatka and the neighbouring islands and coast, under the general supervision of the governor-general of Siberia.

This period also witnessed the setting up of a more effective administration for the far-flung provinces of Siberia. The main problem there had been the need for effectively supervising the local authorities and taking into account the special conditions and needs of the huge subcontinent. Since Peter's time Siberia had been treated as if it were a part of Russia proper; thus Catherine II did not hesitate to extend the terms of the Act on the Provinces of 1775 to Siberia. No account, however, had been taken of the fact that even the Russian population of Siberia had their own social structure: specifically, as there was no serfdom, there was no local nobility. The merchants, therefore, constituted the social élite, while the tasks of administration had to be performed by officials appointed from St Petersburg. Naturally, in view of the sparsity of the population and the length and difficulties of transportation and communication, the imposition of a Russian social pattern resulted in a top-heavy and cumbersome administrative machine whose high cost was disproportionate to its benefits.

In the absence of effective controls on the Siberian administration, abuses and exactions were ubiquitous, weighing most heavily on the merchants and peasants. The economic development of the vast region was stunted and the efforts at promoting agriculture and attracting nomadic natives to its settled ways could not be successful. During his governor-generalship (1819–22) M. M. Speransky, the former state secretary of Alexander I, reorganized the administration to eliminate the abuses and provide a firm basis for Siberia's progress. His reforms did not succeed completely, largely because he still relied too much on the leadership role of the bureaucracy. In the main, however, Speransky succeeded in establishing more effective supervision of the local adminis- tration and in organizing its tasks along clearly defined functional lines. He also relieved the administration from the direct supervision of and interference in the economic activities of the local population. The peasants thus gained some freedom of action and a degree of protection from exactions; the merchants could enjoy freedom in trading, and the natives were freed from constant bureaucratic supervision and interfer- ence, which were usually pretexts for exactions and exploitation. The administrative framework that was created by Speransky permitted the full development of local economic resources and the easy integration of newcomers into Siberia, and protected the interests of natives and peasants. In short, it provided a foundation on which Siberian society and economy could mature, paving the way for Siberia's complete inte- gration with Russia at the end of the century.

POLAND, FINLAND, BESSARABIA

There were three regions that became part of the empire but were never fully integrated into it: Poland, Finland, and Bessarabia. The weakness of the Polish Commonwealth led to its partition. Russia received the eastern part (mainly lands of the former Grand Duchy of Lithuania), which she claimed on grounds of history and the linguistic and religious similarity to Russia of the major part of the population. In 1815, at the Congress of Vienna, Russia also received the former Grand Duchy of Warsaw. With the exception of the eastern provinces, which were merged with Russian provinces, the remaining Polish territories formed the King- dom of Poland (the so-called 'Congress Poland'). This kingdom was bound to the empire in the person of the Russian tsar – who was also King of Poland. Alexander I granted the country a constitution and until 1830 Poland's separate regime was allowed to function more or less independently, but the revolt of 1830 destroyed this special arrangement. Poland lost its constitutional privileges, but remained a separate entity, and was not fused with the regular provinces of the empire until after the revolt of 1863. The eastern parts, however, those annexed under the terms of the first two partitions (1772 and 1793), were treated like old Russian territory which had been returned to the mother country and were given the same organization and institutions as were the other regular provinces of the empire. It is true that some particular local features were retained – for example, the juridical norms of the Lithuanian Statute and of the Magdeburg Law; but in the course of their codification in the 1820s and 1830s they too were Russified.

Yet in truth, these former Lithuanian lands were not Russian. The upper classes were Polonized, at least half of the population was Roman Catholic, and there was a very large Jewish minority. Integration and efforts at Russification led to hostility and resistance and fed the flames of incipient nationalism. Moreover, the genuinely Polish lands, annexed under the terms of the third partition (1795) and the treaty of the Congress of Vienna, definitely could not be Russified. The alien element introduced into the Russian body politic could not and refused to be absorbed. Moreover, the fate of Poland – because of the treaties of partition – made it an international diplomatic concern, and its annexation thus saddled the government with many undesirable and unwanted tasks which the Russian bureaucracy proved incapable of solving. It was a source of constant tension and conflict, which in turn served to justify the continuation of repressive police measures everywhere in the empire, especially with respect to the intelligentsia.

In 1809 Russia also acquired the Grand Duchy of Finland in the form of a personal union, the Russian monarch becoming Grand Duke of Finland. Under provisions of the treaty of Frederikshamn and an imperial grant, the duchy was to retain its traditional institutions, including a representative assembly, and to preserve its laws and internal autonomy, a settlement largely respected up to the latter part of the nineteenth century.

Finally, in 1812, Russia annexed Bessarabia. It too was given a special administration and statute, and a liberal settlement was worked out that paved the way for the integration of the province into the empire – completed without any outward signs of resistance by the middle of the nineteenth century.

In the context of gradual Russification, which has been noted in all the territorial acquisitions of the empire, one must clarify two basic assumptions of the Russian government. It shared with most western European absolute monarchies of the eighteenth century a lack of understanding of nationalism. It also believed that uniformity was the key to administrative efficiency and economic progress. This explains its total ignorance of and disregard for national differences and feelings. This disregard may seem callous and incomprehensible to us only because we are the heirs of the great national movements and revivals of the nineteenth century which – almost all of them – came after the policy of expansion and integration pursued by the Russian government had reached its conclusion.

THE MILITARY IN THE RUSSIAN EMPIRE

Both as instruments and results of the empire's expansion and successes in the field of foreign affairs, the modern Russian army and navy were major elements in the imperial establishment from the reign of Peter the Great. Those created by Peter demonstrated their competence at Poltava (1709) and in naval battles on the Baltic. The high quality of the military establishment did not vary significantly in the years between Poltava and the Crimean War. During the latter the military abilities themselves remained at a high level; what was lacking – and what led to defeat – was the required level of administrative competence and economic mobilization. It was the substructure, the social, economic, and administrative framework, that was wanting. It was to remain a lasting and in the long run fatal burden, which helped to bring about the events of 1905 and 1917. More than anywhere else in contemporary Europe, the military establishment became the leading 'rational' institution in Russia. It served both as model and as training ground for a modern, westernized, and reasonable pattern of behaviour and social organization. During his military service the Russian nobleman (and to a lesser extent the common soldier as well) became familiar with these new western concepts, and later transferred these to the other areas of endeavour in which he might be involved in civilian life. The Russian civil administration, for instance, owed many of its features to military models and personnel. It is true, however, that there was also a reverse side to this picture. The maintenance of such a high-quality military establishment, which was ahead of the country in terms of its modernity and rationality, required considerable resources. The lion's share of the state budget and of the country's industrial production and economic potential went into supplying the army and navy. Sometimes this provided a stimulus for more modern and more intensive productivity, but on the whole this was not very much in evidence in the eighteenth century or even in the second quarter of the nineteenth, and it did not make up for the drain on Russia's limited actual resources. Furthermore, in many instances – e.g. in the newly acquired southern territories in the late eighteenth century – military considerations and preconceptions proved the decisive elements in shaping the sometimes disastrous administrative policy. They fostered a scorn for particular local needs and conditions, a readiness to sacrifice the people's welfare to the fancied requirements of the military alone. This attitude provoked criticism and opposition, even on the part of members of the military establishment such as the Decembrists.

140

THE GOVERNMENT

Early in its history Muscovy became a unitary state with a high degree of centralization. But it was rather a centralization of political authority than of administrative functions. The institutional form of the central political authority was the tsar, assisted by his boyar duma. The increasing complexity of government in the seventeenth century found expression in the growing number of executive departments, the *prikazy*, and their gradual specialization, primarily in the domains of defence, foreign affairs, and fiscal administration. But this development had not gone far in Muscovy because the function of government was conceived to be primarily a negative one: to defend against external enemies and safeguard domestic law and order.

This picture changed radically when Peter the Great gave a positive role to government. This consisted, first of all, of the rapid modernization of the military and naval establishments, for which new institutions had to be created and novel tasks defined for them. This was not done without trial and error, of course, but the end result was radically different from the Muscovite pattern. Peter made use of the existing framework, so that in the first decade of his reign as sole monarch (after the downfall of the regent, his sister Sophia, in 1689) no radically new institutions had been organized, and even at the time of his death some practices and offices were still those carried over from Muscovite times. But the magnitude of the new tasks, especially in military and foreign policy, involving the modernization of the economy and the westernization of the country, rendered the Muscovite traditions obsolete.

The tasks of government were apportioned along quite functional lines among ten 'colleges' (eventually increased to sixteen by the end of the eighteenth century), whose comprehensive functions were spelled out in a *general'nyy reglament* ('general instruction') issued 28 February 1720. Essentially, their purpose was to take care of the enlarged functions of government resulting from military needs, active participation in world affairs, and rapid westernization. The collegiate principle introduced by Peter points to another aspect of his administrative policy. Whatever its origins and justification in the West, it was adopted in Russia largely to make sure that the numerous new administrative tasks really would be carried out. Furthermore, Peter thought in this way to limit the danger of the abuse of authority by having the chief officials keep an eye on each other and thus increase the channels of information available to the monarch. This explains the detailed and rigid rules worked out for the conduct of public affairs, the insistence on having all business transacted only in the proper offices and under constant supervision.

141

At the time of their establishment the colleges performed their task as well as could be expected under the circumstances. But from the very beginning there arose a major problem. The system required effective supervision and co-ordination, and, as long as he ruled, Peter did much of the co-ordinating himself. But even his unbounded energy could not cope with the enormous task of supervision. In Muscovy a similar role, albeit on a more modest scale, had been performed by the whole boyar duma; but Peter had jettisoned the traditional boyar group. True, many boyars and numerous descendants of old noble families were serving Peter loyally and at times very successfully, but they did so as individuals, by virtue of their merit and not by right of birth. At the end of the seventeenth century the boyar duma faded out of existence, although formal legislation to this effect was never enacted.

In 1711, before he left the capital to join the army on the Prut, Peter instituted the Russian Senate, with nine members. This body of high officials was to act collectively as his lieutenant, taking routine policy decisions and supervising the organs of executive administration. But its competence had been neither clearly defined nor permitted to develop naturally out of the needs of the situation. In the beginning, when it was composed of Peter's chief trusted assistants, the Senate acted as an advisory body in reaching policy decisions; but its advisory and co-ordinating role was effectively blocked by the creation of the office of Procurator General of the Senate. At first the office was held by a simple officer of the guards, whose function was to see that the senators met regularly and dispatched business speedily and in orderly fashion. In these circumstances the Senate naturally could not develop into an effective and authoritative organ of the state, and eventually the procurator alone became the supervisory functionary, a task that exceeded the capabilities of one individual. Not unexpectedly this evolution robbed the Senate of much of its prestige.

As the state's need for revenue grew and the government's participation in economic activities increased, the lack of honesty on the part of the officials became a critical problem. Peter regarded himself as the first servant of the state, personally responsible for everything, and thus wanted to supervise and control all officials and institutions directly. The procurator was to assist him with the central institutions, but for the local administration Peter created the corps of *fiskaly* (fiscals). Their special task was to find out, report, and eliminate malpractices and corruption. The fiscals became a corps of government spies and agents with a well defined position in the official hierarchy, and yet outside the regular chain of command, being subject only to the Chief Fiscal and to the Senate. For the purpose of the general control and supervision of the nation, the *Preobrazhenskiy Prikaz* was set up as a political police and

142

tribunal to ferret out, prosecute, and punish all those suspected of political subversion. It became notorious for its ruthlessness and brutality, and lay like a heavy hand on the country. The *Preobrazhenskiy Prikaz* did not survive its founder, although its functions were continued by similar offices under different names (e.g. *Taynaya ekspeditsiya, Taynaya kantselyariya*); the Third Section and the Corps of Gendarmes of Nicholas I had in a sense a similar function.

AFTER PETER THE GREAT

Peter the Great had formally abrogated the traditional custom regulating inheritance to the throne. By a statute of 5 February 1722, he had provided that the succession would be determined by the sovereign choice of each ruler. He himself died without making his will known, and in 1725 Prince A. D. Men'shikov, with the help of the guard regiments, imposed a solution in favour of Peter's widow, Catherine I. Two years later the same group chose Peter's son by his first marriage, the child Peter II. This period was one of frequent palace revolutions, carried out with the help of the guards, and did not close until 1762 with the accession of Catherine II. It was not until 1797 that Tsar Paul (Catherine's son) issued the 'Statute on the Imperial Family and Succession to the Throne', which regularized the order of succession and defined the status of members of the imperial family. In so doing the statute made it clear that the state was no longer the property or patrimony of any one person or family; it gave legal sanction to what had been Peter's goal a century earlier.

After the death of Peter the Great the need for a co-ordinating mechanism grew stronger, since his successors were anything but competent rulers. At first, partly to reduce the influence of Men'shikov, the *Verkhovnyy Taynyy Sovet* (Supreme Privy Council) was established in 1726, and became the focal point for all political and administrative decisions: it also managed to do a fairly good job at supervising the execution of its policies by means of direct contacts with subordinate officials. The personal character of political authority not having been completely eliminated by Peter's reforms, the council acted very much as a collective sovereign. But it did bring about the decline of the Senate to a mere secondary bureaucratic institution that helped to process administrative decisions and reports but had no power of its own.

The accession of Anna (1730–40) did not change the basic character of Russia's administrative and political life. She governed largely through her favourite, Ernst Biron (Bühren), whom she made Duke of Courland, and through a few other Baltic intimates. Biron was not so incompetent or brutally tyrannical as is sometimes depicted, and the function of policy co-ordination was shouldered by the Cabinet of Ministers, consisting of three persons (Osterman, Cherkassky, A. Volynsky) working closely with Biron. But when Volynsky wanted to turn it into a really effective instrument of power, a permanent imperial council with wide advisory and executive authority, he was disgraced and executed (1740). The Cabinet of Ministers faded out of the picture with the death of Empress Anna and the dethronement of her nephew and infant successor, Ivan VI (1740–1).

Empress Elizabeth (1741–62), keen on reviving the system of her father, Peter the Great, tried to give back to the Senate its original authority and power, but the task proved impossible. Not only did her own favourites interfere and prevent a regularization of administrative practice, but the Senate itself was in no position to justify the high hopes placed upon it. Its members were undistinguished and, most important of all, it had no official connection with the colleges. Its inadequacy became manifest at the time of the Seven Years War, when a special conference had to be instituted to plan, co-ordinate, and supervise decisions related to the prosecution of the war. Later, Catherine II resorted to the same device of using an imperial council, on an *ad hoc* basis, to help formulate and co-ordinate decisions in time of war.

If the Senate failed as a co-ordinating body, its Procurator General did perform some functions of supervision. Most legislative drafts and executive papers were sent to the Senate for editing, discussion, or filing in its archives. As chief of the Chancery of the Senate – and with the help of his local agents – the procurator was well placed to supervise and control the routine operations of the administration. If the procurator was energetic, capable, and had the full confidence of the sovereign, he could become the principal executive minister in all but name. This was the case of Prince A. A. Vyazemsky in the reign of Catherine II. But as the empress jealously guarded her own power, he could not become a genuine prime minister who formulated policy as well. This was a role Catherine allowed only to her favourite, G. A. Potemkin. At the beginning of her reign, her influential adviser, Count N. I. Panin, tried to give institutional form to the monarch's advisers in order to prevent interference by favourites, and to this end he submitted a project for an imperial council. It was rejected by Catherine because she was loath to give up any authority and because courtiers and high officials did not want to be cut off from direct access to the monarch by a permanent institution. The ruler's personal autocratic power had to be preserved in order to maintain the effectiveness of the bureaucracy.

The danger inherent in this failure to give solid institutional form to the bureaucracy became painfully clear in the reign of Catherine's son, Paul I (1796–1801). Indeed, Paul reverted to the high-handed, personal way of governing which in Peter's case had benefited the country so much. But unlike his great predecessor, Paul was capricious and unstable; his personal rule degenerated into one of abusive treatment and insecurity of the service nobility, and the legal guarantees of person and property that Catherine II had tried to anchor in Russian life went by the board. Whatever Paul's good intentions, they were brought to nought by his arbitrariness, brutality, and caprice. His reign demonstrated Russia's crying need for security of person and property, as well as stability and continuity in administrative policy. His murder gave Russian society new hope that this need would be satisfied. Indeed the new tsar, his son Alexander I (1801–25), could hardly disregard completely sentiments that coincided so neatly with the country's objective material needs. He knew that it was impossible to preserve Russia's military power and further its economic development as long as there was neither *esprit de suite* in government nor security for members of the leading class.

The collegiate principle introduced by Peter I was manifestly no longer satisfactory, for executive departments had to direct, control, and supervise broad areas of national life in a vast empire. The problem had been made more acute by Catherine's reforms of local government, which had given to the relevant colleges – rather than to the Senate – direct responsibility for the various facets of provincial administration. One should also remember that in the West the monocratic pattern of ministerial government had become the rule at the end of the eighteenth century. In 1802, on the advice of his collaborators on the so-called 'Unofficial Committee', Alexander I abolished the remaining colleges and established monocratic ministries in their stead. A few years later, at the suggestion of M. M. Speransky, the ministries were organized with the minister in complete charge and the advisory functions of his council defined clearly. In particular, the ministers were given effective means for co-ordinating and supervising the activities of subordinate parallel authorities on the local level.

The problem of policy co-ordination and planning on a long-term basis was not resolved simply by the creation of ministries. Not only was each minister appointed by the tsar and responsible only to him, but he also worked with him alone; Alexander I made no attempt to bring together in a regular cabinet or council individuals with broadly similar ideas and goals. He went only as far as establishing the Committee of Ministers, an *ad hoc* meeting of a few ministers to discuss matters overlapping the respective jurisdiction of each. But even this committee did not evolve into a regular institution. In his 1809 comprehensive plan of reform Speransky proposed a solution in the form of a 'council of state'; while the plan as a whole was not implemented, such a council was established in 1810. Designed to act as a central planning board and editorial committee, co-ordinating all important new legislation and

145

advising the tsar on it, it unfortunately was not given the full organizational scope proposed by Speransky. For example, ministers did not become members *ex officio*, although the major administrative areas (armed services, interior, economy, codification) were represented. Under an energetic chief, especially if he enjoyed the confidence of the tsar (as A. Arakcheyev did in military affairs), a department could effectively co-ordinate, plan, and supervise policy for a major sector of national public life. But such a welcome situation was more an accident of personality than an integral feature of the institution. And, in a short time, the council slipped to the status of a mere editorial board and drafting committee for important legislation, occasionally also functioning as an administrative court of appeal. In the meantime the Senate had turned essentially into a judiciary board of review. The reign of Alexander I completed this evolution, although there were attempts at restoring some of its previous governmental powers: for instance, the decree of 8 September 1802 seemed to confer on the Senate a limited *droit de remonstrance*; but as the first practical test proved, the tsar did not allow a meaningful exercise of this right.

The kind of central administrative institutions that took shape in the reign of Alexander I survived until 1905, and with some modifications until 1917. For routine administration the system worked fairly well, but the lack of adequate co-ordination and of a regularized form for planning was a handicap. An energetic individual who had the trust of his monarch could do a great deal toward carrying out a policy, and it was natural, therefore, for the ruler to bring together trusted officers, usually in private, when a specific problem needed a broad and comprehensive solution. Alexander I inaugurated this procedure, but it was his brother Nicholas I who made use of it most consistently and widely. It fitted well with his belief that the personal character of political authority had to be restored to a central role in Russian public life. This attitude, so reminiscent of Peter the Great, could not be easily reconciled with the level of maturity attained by the Russian élite and the social requirements of the country.

To give body to his conception of the autocratic ruler, Nicholas I created two types of institution. The first consisted of new sections of the tsar's own chancery, established to supervise important areas of governmental activity such as codification. The best known and most important of them was the Third Section (and the Corps of Gendarmes attached to it); it was to act as the embodiment of the tsar's ubiquitous personal presence – to gather information, receive complaints and requests, and act as his personal political police and intelligence. But soon it became a state within the state, interfering in the normal administrative process. Whatever Nicholas's good intentions, its appearance in the midst of a well-developed bureaucratic system created havoc. Far from improving the system's efficiency by giving the tsar new information and occasions for direct intervention, the Third Section served to erect new barriers between the ruler and ruled.

The second type of institution created by Nicholas was the secret committee appointed *ad hoc* to investigate conditions and work out plans for specific reforms. Such committees were set up to take testimony from the Decembrists, prepare reforms for the state peasants, discuss the emancipation of serfs, reorganize the municipal government, build railroads, and the like. Most of them worked conscientiously and at length, but in vain. They were overwhelmed by red tape and unreliable information, and they were unable to get their recommendations adopted by the tsar and implemented effectively. But the experience of these committees did also have some positive effects: it accumulated much needed information and brought together institutions that would not have cooperated otherwise. Finally, in a few cases, in spite of their secret character the committees could bring in for consultation men outside the official establishment; in this way a few weak and tenuous – but necessary – bridges were built between the increasingly more active and restless elements of society and the government bureaucracy.

CHURCH AND STATE

The secularization of the Russian state was accompanied by Peter's transformation of the institutional form of the relationship between church and state. Peter inaugurated a radical change in the organization of the church when he failed to appoint, or permit election of, a successor after the death of Patriarch Adrian in 1700. Eventually, in 1721, the church received a collegiate administration, the Holy Synod, similar to that of other major areas of state administration. Consisting of a board of bishops, abbots, and monks, it had also, like the Senate, a High Procurator, a layman who eventually became the virtual head of the ecclesiastical administration. It is therefore fair to say that not only nominally but also in fact the church was put under lay control: that of the tsar and his appointed agent, the High Procurator. The concept of the church as primarily an organ of the state for the purpose of policing the people's conduct and of educating them to be obedient subjects was set forth in the *Dukhovnyy reglament* ('spiritual regulation') on 25 January 1721, the basic constitution of church and clergy, which remained in force until the fall of the empire.

The economic independence of the church also came to an end in the eighteenth century. A series of limited decrees culminated in the secularization of monastic and church lands in the Manifesto of 26 February 1764. Actually the church did not lose all its property – it retained some

147

private donations and the revenue of a few ecclesiastical institutions – but this was far from adequate for the support of regular church activities. The clergy became the salaried employees of the state, on whose financial support all their spiritual and educational activities had to depend. Naturally, this led to a further decline in the position of the clergy. The government used them as instruments of political repression and control, which undermined the moral and spiritual function of the priests. Their meagre salaries and small fees for the performance of rituals condemned them to poverty and relative ignorance. Their moral and spiritual authority were thereby reduced, and not surprisingly they were often ineffective in coping with dissent and heresy. Religious life, therefore, frequently developed along personal, mystical lines. Russia witnessed a powerful revival of religious feeling at the end of the eighteenth century, but it took place largely outside the framework of the church. Even Alexander I, when he turned to religion, did so within the framework of groups and organizations that stood outside the church establishment (the Bible Society, various mystical circles). This also helps explain the sympathetic reception given in Russia to Freemasonry, the Jesuits, and to various pietist sects.

The church hierarchy – bishops, abbots, theologians – became doubly alienated from their flocks. In the first place this was because bishops traditionally were recruited among the monks, and were thus removed from the practical concerns of society and at times quite ignorant of its needs. Moreover, to keep the cost of ecclesiastical administration low, the government divided Russia into very large dioceses, whose area and population were too large for effective pastoral supervision by the bishop. To supervise the hierarchs closely, the government (i.e. the High Procurator of the Holy Synod) shifted them from one diocese to another with great frequency, so that they never learned to know their flocks and their needs well. In the second place, the kind of ecclesiastical education that was provided removed its graduates from genuine understanding of and participation in the people's life. Continuing a trend initiated in the seventeenth century under the strong influence of the Kievan Academy, the better ecclesiastical schools had a 'western' curriculum which emphasized those subjects that were necessary for scholarship but had little relevance to the ministry of souls. The graduates from these schools were learned individuals, capable of writing stylized sermons in Latin, Church Slavonic, or even Greek, but often uninterested in active ministry. They also found themselves under heavy pressure to take monastic vows, in order to be eligible for higher posts in the ecclesiastical hierarchy. In addition, for the successful graduate, there was the temptation to enter government service where his training and talents could find wider scope still. Many of those who could have become successful administrators in the church rose to high bureaucratic positions instead. Finally, in the nineteenth century, many promising graduates turned to secular scholarly and scientific careers, for which ecclesiastical schools offered the best preparation available in Russia at the time. This left the less desirable and able *bursaki* (seminary students) to swell the ranks of the parish clergy.

LOCAL GOVERNMENT

The high degree of centralization and the broadened range of responsibilities of his government explain the low order of priority given to local administration by Peter the Great. He abandoned the old territorial divisions, a product of history, in favour of a mechanical system based on population figures related to the capitation tax system and resulting in large and cumbersome geographic units. The purpose of local administration became essentially that of collecting and securing revenue, the maintenance of order and law being subordinated to this task. The traditional communal participation in local government could not be preserved under this system; in its place, Peter tried to erect a set of institutions with a local base able to secure the co-operation and participation of the population in carrying out orders received from St Petersburg. As local government ceased to exist merely for the preservation of law and order (however inadequately this may have been done in fact) and became a tool in the hands of the central authorities for achieving the political, cultural, and economic goals of the modern state, its day-to-day functions had to be performed by some other arrangement. But to whom were these tasks to be delegated? To the local nobility? But its members were compelled to enter state service and were thus effectively removed from their home provinces. To the merchant and burgher class, the better educated free peasants, and prosperous communes of state peasants? But there were so few of them and their activities would need to be closely supervised, for it was doubted that they had understood or accepted the new orientation of the state. The only solution was to send an official from the capital and invest him with broad powers. But even here there were problems: left to himself, could this official be trusted? The example of Prince Gagarin as Governor-General of Siberia, who was hanged for abuse of power and corruption, showed how unsatisfactory that solution was. In any event, supervision, co-ordination, and control were essential. But the empire was large, communications poor, and adequate personnel scarce. Herein lay Peter's dilemma and that of his successors. The available qualified personnel had first to be used in the military establishment and in the capital. Only those not fit for either (or no longer fit) could be assigned to local administration. The results of this policy took the form of chaos, abuses, incompetence, corruption. Without either backing or checks by locally rooted and influential groups of gentry and burghers, these less than second-rate bureaucrats and short-term governors were completely inadequate to their task.

After the abolition in 1762 of compulsory state service for the nobility and the securing of their property rights, it had been expected that many noblemen would return to their estates and create local corps whose participation in provincial administration might be enlisted. It also had become quite obvious that some kind of parallelism had to exist between the central and local institutions. This new awareness, heightened by the dismal failure of the existing system in dealing with the early stages of the Pugachev rebellion, led on 7 November 1775 to the 'Act on the Provinces'. Essentially the Act – which was to remain the framework of Russian provincial life until the introduction of the *zemstva* in 1864 – provided for several principal reforms. The size of the basic administrative unit, *guberniya*, was set to take into account both population and distances, although little attention was paid to trade patterns, economic ties, history, and ethnic composition. The central colleges and bureaux were given local agents and offices with whom they corresponded directly, without needing to go through the Senate. A valiant effort was made to separate justice from administration, although it was not entirely successful because of the absence of a comprehensive code of laws and the basic defects of Russian judiciary procedure. Finally, governor-generals were appointed to supervise several *gubernii*, or one very large one, as the personal representatives of the monarch, and thus were in direct correspondence with him. They could take necessary steps quickly and on their own make representations directly to the sovereign. As they were supervisors rather than administrators, they were not bogged down with trivia and had time and energy for more essential tasks.

The 'Charters to the Nobility and to the Towns' of 1785 provided for a measure of participation in local affairs by the upper classes through their assemblies and elected marshals or city dumas. The judiciary was also improved: many cases could now be brought before a court in equity, and if the latter's arbitration was accepted by both parties the case was removed from the regular judiciary hierarchy.

The major cause for the failure of these reforms was the inadequacy of the elected officials; the nobility remained service-oriented, and only the poor and less successful nobles were candidates for these offices. In addition, the vast amount of paperwork and the rigid centralization of the system prevented information from flowing freely both up and downward. Co-ordinated supervision and direction remained inadequate, especially after the creation of ministries had eliminated the Senate as a link.

After the ministries had proven their worth, the central government felt that co-ordination and supervision of local administration should be at a higher level than the province, in order not to infringe on the competence of the local ministry agents. This was the origin in the reign of Alexander I of several proposals to establish *namestnichestva* (vicegerencies) comprising several *gubernii*, whose head would receive broad powers of *nadzor* (supervision). (Such a plan was tried in one instance, with General A. D. Balashov as Governor-General of Novgorod, Tver', and Yaroslavl', but the experiment was not successful.) The tsar also feared that vicegerencies could become a threat to his own authority and the unity of the empire. Only in the case of the remote and vast territories of Siberia – as reorganized by Speransky in 1822 – did the system of a governor-general with broad powers prove viable and efficient, and even there quite stringent bureaucratic safeguards and controls were maintained.

Essentially, the basic cause for the government's failure to resolve the problem of local administration was the tsar's fear of delegating authority and responsibility outside the regular bureaucratic framework. Thus the government did not permit adequate participation of elected officials and did nothing to help develop a class of responsible and competent local administrators, either appointed or elected. The autocracy – and public opinion also – was too much concerned with preserving the unity of its sovereign authority, with preventing the formation of viable *corps intermédiaires*, and with maintaining the leadership function of the state. The result was an inert and passive society; initiative and enterprise were stifled and constructive criticism foreclosed. The Crimean War demonstrated clearly the threat to the most elementary needs of military preparedness and national defence implicit in such a situation.

PERSONNEL

So far I have suggested that at the core of the difficulties that beset the Russian administration, both central and local, lay the problem of adequate communications between the various levels and areas of government on the one hand and between the population and the tsar on the other. In large part this failure was due to the nature of the personnel with which the Russian government had to work. The Petrine state required public servants capable of conducting business according to principles of rationality and efficiency; unfortunately, Russia was woefully short of educated and trained men.

In the second quarter of the nineteenth century, however, there could be detected signs of a new trend which held out the promise of a radical improvement in the bureaucracy. For reasons which fall outside the limits of this chapter, this development ultimately was cut short and failed to change the basic nature of the Russian administration; but hope did seem to be offered in the emergence of a genuine professionally committed bureaucracy on the level of the highly specialized institutions of the central government (finances, economy, peasant affairs). This group of high officials, among whom Nicholas Milyutin was the most typical as well as the most distinguished representative, felt called upon to transform Russian social and economic life without violent upheavals, to enable the people to share fully in the benefits of westernization and modernization. They were dedicated to the welfare of the country and no longer to the glory of the tsar. Their high level of education and long administrative experience in their specialized areas made them real experts as well as seasoned politicians. They aimed at bringing to bear on government affairs a more reliable body of information and the participation of loyal and informed members of the élite. In this manner they hoped to bridge the gap that separated public opinion from the establishment. Their most significant – and short-lived – triumph came with the series of reforms that accompanied the emancipation of the serfs. But even prior to that they managed to achieve several technical improvements of the Russian polity, in matters concerning state peasants, municipal administration, finances, and tariffs.

PROBLEMS OF CODIFICATION

The absence of an adequate code or even compilation of laws in force was also a factor in the inadequacy of governmental administration. The reign of Peter the Great had introduced new norms and ideas and flooded the country with countless decrees and laws; his successors were no less prolific in this respect. These new laws and norms were not systematized or brought into concordance with the most recently compiled code, that of 1649, and often administrators and judges did not know which laws to apply. The government was well aware of this situation and in the course of the eighteenth century there were at least ten attempts at codification, of which the best known (but not the most productive) was Catherine's commission in 1767; the effort was continued by four more commissions in the first quarter of the nineteenth century.

Eventually a solution was devised by Speransky. He proceeded in several steps. First he had all the recent relevant legislation collected, and published a virtually complete collection of the legislative acts since 1649. He then made an abstract or digest of the laws actually in force at the time. The last stage, the drafting of a comprehensive new code, was not undertaken, as Nicholas I feared it might be an act directed at forming a constitution in disguise. Despite its many defects, Speransky's codification (1830–3) was a great step forward; this *svod* (collection and digest) clarified the juridical norms in force and paved the way for their orderly and open application. At the same time, in composing the abstracts and digests of existing laws, Speransky and his collaborators introduced new norms (especially in the areas of private and contract law) which were necessary for the development of modern economic relationships. A body of trained jurists was also brought into existence in the course of the codification work. These efforts prepared the ground for the successful judiciary reforms of Alexander II.

THE ECONOMY

One of the major goals of Peter's reforms, directly related to the prevailing conception of the nature of the modern state, was to give maximum development to the economic potential of the country. In so doing, it was hoped, the power of the state would be increased and the welfare and happiness of the population secured. As in everything else, Peter expected quick results, the more so since he felt hard pressed for military supplies in his war with Sweden. Turning to western Europe for guidance and inspiration, Peter found that the prevailing economic ideas and policies were those of mercantilism. The tenets of mercantilism fitted well into the Muscovite heritage of state supervision of at least some aspects of the national economy (e.g. foreign trade, exploitation of Siberia).

The Petrine state thus took the initiative in Russia's economic development. Industries were created, supported, and developed with the help of the state; in some cases the government itself took over their organization and management, in others they started them with state help and eventually took them over. The government also strictly regulated the standards of production; the negative effect of this policy was that it undermined, and in some cases even destroyed, important crafts that might have served as a solid foundation for new industrial development. The major difficulty encountered in modernizing Russia's economy was a lack of the required capital and labour resources. Capital was short because the major part of wealth was not in liquid form but in land, which yielded very little. There was, it is true, a native merchant class; but its resources, too, were quite limited, especially since the disastrous effects of social unrest and foreign competition in foreign trade had limited the scope of its activities in the seventeenth century. Moreover, many merchants were 'Old Believers' and had little desire to engage in risky enterprises involving dealings with the very state that persecuted them. There were no other sources of capital or enterprise, since the peasant class was fettered by serfdom and could not freely dispose of its own labour. As there was practically no free labour market in Russia, Peter had to allow the use of serfs in industry. This was the origin of the *pripisnyye* or ascribed serfs (especially in the Urals), i.e. peasants attached to factories and mines.

The drawbacks of a system dependent on serf labour and with limited private entrepreneurship made themselves felt more and more as time went on. Peter's regulations, which at first had given an impetus to the economy, were proving to be handicaps to further development. Thus in the reign of Elizabeth the government started liberalizing government controls and reducing the state's initiative in economic matters. Internal duties were abolished and trade made free within the entire empire. Catherine II endeavoured to foster private activity still more by giving the landowners absolute rights over whatever was on their estates, above ground or beneath. Easier and more generous credit was made available to the nobility in the hope of encouraging their economic activities. This trend found its culmination under Alexander I. The policy, so well expressed by Speransky in his report on the state of the Russian economy in 1803, of allowing as much scope as possible to private enterprise, and yet recognizing the government's obligation to help out and lead in the newest and most risky projects, remained typical of the Russian economic scene to the middle of the nineteenth century. It was the policy that was followed, for example, in connection with the building of the first Russian railways; not only did the government give permission for their construction, but helped out financially and retained a controlling interest in the subsequent management.

As long as serfdom was the dominant institution, the pool of labour remained small and its efficiency very low. For this reason the iron and smelting industries of the Urals, which in the middle of the eighteenth century had led Europe, slipped to a second-rate position at the end of the same century and still lower in the nineteenth. The failure of the Urals to provide a solid foundation for the industrialization of Russia was made abundantly clear in the 1840s. Russian iron products, e.g. rails (not to speak of machinery), cost immeasurably more than the imports from England or Belgium. Another drawback of serfdom was that it prevented the most enterprising peasants from displaying their talents. It is true that a class of serf entrepreneurs did arise, but they operated on the sufferance of their lords and without any guarantee or security of the enjoyment of the fruits of their labour and initiative. They did help to develop light industries (e.g. textiles), a limited example that clearly demonstrates that an enormous potential of entrepreneurial *savoir-faire* (and perhaps also of capital) lay untapped. Serfdom also promoted the nobleman's lack of initiative, for by having his estate run by serf labour, he developed neither managerial skills nor sound economic attitudes. Moreover, such estates yielded little surplus that could be transformed into capital.

Our knowledge of the operation of the serf economy is still inadequate because of the lack of actual statistics on Russian agriculture at that time. But we do know that Russian agriculture was mainly aimed at satisfying the minimum needs of the peasants and of their lords, and only secondarily did it produce for a market. With a very few exceptions the estates of the nobility were also quite small, and even the large landowners had widely scattered domains whose land was inextricably mingled with that of other owners. Thus each productive unit was very small and could not be managed very efficiently, and it was well nigh impossible to introduce advanced methods of agriculture or machinery on it. This is one reason for the long survival of the three field system. Only in the Ukraine did large-scale farming for a market become a more common occurrence by the beginning of the nineteenth century. It was there, too, that new machinery and techniques were most readily accepted and where the change-over to crops and food industries for industrial ends (sugar-beets, sugar refineries, distilleries) took place in the second quarter of the nineteenth century. The way was paved for the expansion and transformation of the economy in the south.

With the exception of a very few magnates – and even their holdings often were not consolidated – the average nobleman in Russia was far from wealthy. Owners of more than one hundred souls (male serfs), which was considered the minimum for comfortable living, numbered no more than about sixteen per cent of the nobility. The ordinary landlord could not find the necessary capital for improvements and modernization on his estate, let alone for industrial or commercial investment, as the experience of the Free Economic Society showed. He remained, therefore, quite timid in his economic outlook and was content if he made ends meet in traditional fashion. There were two basic systems of organizing the labour of one's serfs for profit. Either the village serfs were put on *corvée, barshchina*, working their lord's lands whenever required (sometimes up to six days a week at the height of the harvest), or they were forced to pay an *obrok* ('quit-rent') which they had earned either by engaging in agriculture for themselves or by obtaining passports and working at some trade away from home. The latter system was particularly widespread in the less fertile regions, whose population filled the trading and industrial centres of European Russia. During the eighteenth century the *obrok* had been steadily increasing (keeping ahead of the capitation tax), so that it was often a very heavy obligation to meet. Actually, as has been shown recently, a good many of the estates of central and southern Russia combined the two systems. But it hardly improved the efficiency or profitableness of the estates. Nor should one forget that in contrast to England and Prussia (and the Baltic provinces) the Russian nobleman was an absentee landlord: he was first of all a state servant and his interests – psychological and economic – were focused primarily on his service career. He took little direct part in the management of his estate, and before 1762 he had little occasion to do so. His methods of accounting were often primitive and misled him into believing that he was making ends meet when, in fact, he was slowly but surely bankrupting himself. He usually left his estate to the care of a steward or manager. If the latter was a serf, he knew only customary and sometimes primitive agricultural methods; if he was an outsider (frequently a foreigner) his main concern was to get quick returns for himself. He therefore often mercilessly exploited the land and the peasants with no regard to their owner's long-range interests. The situation created a mental climate in which the Russian nobleman and later the intelligentsia remained indifferent, and even opposed, to economic efficiency and progress.

The lot of the peasant was hard, not least because of his great tax burdens – the result of Peter's fiscal measures. The modernization and maintenance of a large military establishment, the country's involvement in numerous wars, the expenses of the most lavish and spendthrift court in Europe, the huge largesses dispensed to the guard regiments and the courtiers – all these made for an ever-growing budget. It in turn required a constant rise in direct taxes, especially the capitation tax that fell heavily (if not quite exclusively) on the peasantry. The fiscal burden was draining away whatever little cash surplus there might have been left from the wasteful and primitive methods of cultivation. In addition to the direct taxes payable in cash, the peasants – the state peasants in particular – had to perform various services (*zemskiye povinnosti*) which at times could be very onerous and impoverishing. (For example, the obligation to furnish postal relays and supplies to travelling officials and dignitaries could, as in the case of the embassy to China in 1804, ruin hundreds of peasant communes and households.) Another burdensome service the peasant had to perform was the upkeep of roads, riverways, and bridges – sometimes quite a distance from home.

Similar obligations weighed down the townspeople, craftsmen, labourers, and artisans. The *posad* (urban communal unit) dues and services, for things such as upkeep, police, and collection of taxes, left most towns with little labour, enterprise, or money resources for expansion and building. Again the burden of expanding urban facilities had to be assumed by the government to meet the needs of the administration and of the few wealthy nobles living in towns. In the nineteenth century the situation improved in a few particularly active trade centres where the merchants had acquired enough wealth to spread its benefits. The fact that so many of the merchants engaged in domestic trade were 'Old Believers' proved a hindrance to further urban development, especially after Nicholas I resumed persecutions against them and confiscated their assets.

Like most of Europe at the time, the Russian government also relied heavily on indirect and excise taxes, as well as state monopolies. The latter included such vital items as salt, alcoholic spirits, and (in Siberia) gunpowder. The state relinquished its monopoly on most of these in the second half of the eighteenth century, but retained some control by granting excise rights and restricting their sale and commerce to a few tax farmers. In fact, those who owned the spirit and salt monopolies were the only ones who could accumulate large liquid capital for investment. However, as this new wealth was largely the result of abusive and corrupt practices, it was always threatened with confiscation by the government. Few farmers managed to preserve their acquired wealth to invest later in more secure and long-range enterprises.

In spite of the numerous taxes, tariffs, and dues, the state remained in chronic financial difficulties. The governments of Elizabeth and Catherine II had to borrow heavily from abroad, mainly from Dutch bankers, and Alexander I continued the practice until the Dutch money-market was closed to him. He had to rely on British subsidies to keep his armies in the field after his break with Napoleon. As well as foreign loans the government also borrowed from its own citizens and resorted to printing paper money, the *assignaty*. Started by Catherine II as a temporary emergency measure, the issue of *assignaty* became a regular expedient to raise money. The amount in circulation grew to such an extent that after the Napoleonic Wars silver was worth about fifteen times as much as its nominal paper equivalent. Naturally, the impoverished landlords, heavily in debt to the state bank, were not averse to the situation, but it was hardly conducive to industrial and commercial progress. It took two decades of great caution and hard work by Nicholas I's finance minister, Count E. F. Kankrin, to stabilize Russian currency – which, for a while, made it a reliable instrument of exchange.

One final word remains to be said on the change in the pattern of foreign trade. Imports from western Europe were constantly on the increase: at first luxury items predominated, but early in the nineteenth century industrial goods took the lead. France was the main supplier of the former and England of the latter, followed, toward the middle of the century, by Germany and Belgium. There was also a clear change in the pattern of exports. At first Russia was an exporter of raw materials – mainly timber, naval stores, hemp, and crude iron – through the Baltic; the main buyer was England. In the third quarter of the eighteenth

157

century there was a shift to exporting grain, mainly through Black Sea ports. This created a tension between the big agrarian producers and the struggling pioneers of industrialization. The government followed a protectionist tariff policy in spite of the prevalence of free trade in the West, and both foreign and domestic trade remained handicapped in their development because of inadequate transportation, an inadequacy that was to be overcome only partially through the building of railways.

The Russian economy during the period 1689–1855, then, remained underdeveloped. It was not completely stagnant and was sufficient for the minimum requirements of Russian society, but it must be viewed against the background of the extraordinary economic expansion in the western world. In comparison Russia lagged behind, and this lag helped to undermine its political and social progress as well.

THE SOCIAL CLASSES

It is always difficult to apply social categories developed in one historical and geographic setting to a society with a different experience; the usual western categories fit Russia only with many qualifications. In the eighteenth and first half of the nineteenth centuries Russian society was very fragmented and stratified, but its groupings were not at all clear and rigid. Two main elements went into the definition of any social status or function: relation to the state in terms of service obligations, and way of life.

RURAL POPULATION

The overwhelming majority of the Russian people during the period under discussion were peasants, who were, however, far from a homogeneous or even clearly defined class. In principle 'peasants' included most of those who were subject to the *podushnaya* (capitation tax) introduced by Peter the Great; essentially, however, working the land and being connected with a village made one a peasant. There were two main categories: state peasants, and serfs belonging to individual owners. (After 1764 serfs who had belonged to monasteries were considered to be state peasants.)

The state peasants were settled on and worked land belonging to the state. They were tied to the land and the community where they lived and worked and were subject to peasant dues and services, but the administrative system under which they lived was a combination of some village self-government and supervision by national government officials. While they were the victims of the exactions and corruption of these officials, they did not have to suffer from the whims of a single owner. Throughout the eighteenth century, however, their status was far from secure, for along with the land they worked, they could be the objects of the ruler's gift or loan to a private individual, and hundreds of thousands of state peasants became private serfs in this manner, especially in the reigns of Elizabeth, Catherine II, and Paul I, before Alexander I put an end to the practice. At the end of his reign the first steps were taken that culminated in Count P. D. Kiselyov's reform measures of 1837–41: a Ministry of State Domains was created, the state peasants were removed from direct interference by petty local officials, and their administration was turned over to special officials and institutions, which secured a larger participation to elected village bodies. The better conditions of state peasants after these reforms was demonstrated by the desire of all private serfs to become state peasants. Many contemporary writers on the subject of serfdom, in suggesting the gradual emancipation of serfs, proposed that all serfs be first turned into state peasants, removing them from the arbitrary power of their masters.

A little over half the peasants belonged to private owners. While there was no legal or perhaps even social difference between village serfs and household or domestic serfs, a practical and psychological distinction between them must be made. For the government the principal characteristic of the serf was his being subject to the capitation tax. By shifting the unit of taxation from the peasant household to the individual (male) worker, Peter effectively loosened the legal relation between serf and land. When in addition the landlord was made responsible for the payment of the capitation tax, the serfs became personally dependent on their master and, in everything but name, his chattels. This accounts for the feeling of alienation from the state and the nation which the serfs had and which was intensified by the cultural split (see pp. 176 ff). In the course of the eighteenth century the landlord was given the right to punish his serfs as he saw fit (short of putting them to death), to banish them for settlement in Siberia, or to enrol them in the army. Finally, Catherine II forbade the serfs to petition the monarch (or his agents) against their landlords. The serf could now be, and was, sold, exchanged, pawned, and disposed of at will by his master. He was accepted as security for state loans (cf. *Dead Souls*), he could be transferred and resettled wherever his master wished (in this way large estates arose in the Ukraine), and he could be trained and ordered to perform any task or craft, only to be returned to the most menial duties in the house. In short, little distinguished his fate from that of the American Negro slave, and no appreciable change occurred in his condition until Emancipation in 1861.

What helped to make the situation somewhat bearable for the average village serf was his lord's non-interference in the daily routine of village life. Thus in some areas of central Russia the peasant commune continued to perform many supervisory, judiciary, and administrative functions on the level of the estate. The domestic serf, however, was subject to his master's caprices and, often, tyranny. Of course, the state itself was interested in preserving the productive value of the serfs and in maintaining peace and order in the countryside, and in extreme cases of abuse the administration and judiciary did interfere, albeit hesitatingly, to protect the serfs. Such an intervention was usually prompted by neighbours who feared that the serfs' discontent and anger might lead to rebellion. Rare and inadequate as the state's interventions were, they helped to preserve the illusion among the peasants that the tsar was their protector and kept alive the serfs' loyalty to the monarch.

There were quite a few other classes of peasants with varying obligations to either the state or to individuals. In addition to the serfs attached to factories (see p. 154), another important group was the *yamshchiki*, the peasant keepers and drivers of postal horses. They were free peasants who enjoyed a number of tax exemptions and other privileges in return for the obligation to provide horses, conductors, and maintain relay stations for imperial couriers and those travelling on official business. They were concentrated, naturally, along the major imperial highways connecting the capital with the principal provincial centres. Another group of serfs were the so-called *odnodvortsy*, 'single homesteaders': originally petty nobles in the military service who had become impoverished and ceased to serve in the army, they had retained only their personal freedom, and in terms of their obligations in taxes and services they were equivalent to state peasants. They were to be found in former frontier areas – in the Ukraine, on the Volga. The *pantsyrnyye boyare* and other groups of former military servicemen in the frontier provinces of the empire were virtually identical with the *odnodvortsy*, as were the Tatars under the jurisdiction of the Russian Admiralty on the Volga, whose principal obligation had been to provide lumber for Peter's navy yards.

These small groups, historical anachronisms in this period, illustrate the close relation of social status and service obligations, which determined membership not only in the nobility but in the lower classes as well. This very fact made for some degree of social fluidity, however, and is the reason the Cossacks were in a class somewhere between peasantry and nobility. Muscovy had extended its protectorate over the oldest of the Cossack organizations, the Dnieper Host, in the seventeenth century. Other Cossack units that emerged in the late sixteenth and early seventeenth centuries (Yaik–Ural, Don) or splintered off from the original Dnieper and Don Hosts (Black Sea and Kuban') were formally organized in the second half of the eighteenth century. Originally, the Cossack Hosts had been military democracies with *starshiny* (elected officers) and a *hetman* or *ataman* (chief). Since their coming under Muscovite rule, however, a process had begun that was to bring the Cossack units in line with the social pattern prevailing in the Russian heartlands.

Fundamentally, the process was one of economic and cultural differentiation, the latter having social and political implications. Economic differentiation first undermined and then destroyed the equality that – in principle at least – had prevailed among all members of the Host. The rich Cossacks became an exclusive group from whose ranks officers and *hetmans* were selected. At the same time, since they were in close contact with the Russian administration, the members of this oligarchy gravitated toward Russian service and Russian culture. The rewards for good service were lavish, but at the price of cultural Russification. Eventually, the *starshiny* became assimilated into the Russian service nobility, received a Russian education, and obtained ranks and titles. The latter allowed them to acquire greater prestige and wealth, and, particularly important, to become owners of populated estates and serfs. By the end of the eighteenth century, the *starshiny* had become virtually indistinguishable from Russian noblemen.

In their original territory the Cossacks ceased to play their traditional military role in the first half of the eighteenth century (Mazepa's siding with Charles XII of Sweden proved to be the last serious attempt at independent action) and their headquarters, the Zaporozhian *Sich*, was destroyed (1775). The rank-and-file Cossacks became peasants and many of them were eventually enserfed. In the nineteenth century traces of Cossack traditions survived in local customs and some special groups of free peasants directly stemmed from the Cossack units. Along the Ural, Don, Kuban', and Black Sea (later also on the Terek and the Amur), the Cossack hosts of more recent formation continued to perform a vital military function defending the eastern frontiers of the empire. The officers, usually sons of *starshiny* themselves, became members of the Russian nobility. The most successful among them also served in the capitals, acquired family connections and property, and became serf owners in other provinces in their own right; on occasion, they managed their lands in Cossack territories along capitalist lines. Spiritually, they doubtless belonged to the realm of Russian culture. As members of the nobility they were eligible to attend provincial noble assemblies, and they participated in local government institutions as elected representatives of the Cossack units.

The rank-and-file Cossacks, meanwhile, tilled the soil, but they were free peasants. They owned their land and had a larger share than ordinary state peasants in the *stanitsa* (village administration). In return for their extensive land holdings and the preservation of their traditional organization and customs, the Cossacks had to train for military service, equip themselves at their own expense, and keep in readiness. They constituted the crack cavalry regiments of the imperial army, and were very useful as long as their territory was close to the ill-defined borders of the empire, and they fought constantly against neighbouring nomads. With the latter's pacification and the expansion of the empire, the Cossacks either moved to the new frontier (Siberia, the Amur) or took on police and security duties. In the latter case their traditions and way of life declined and they turned into full-time peasants. As they enjoyed a privileged status in comparison to that of the regular peasantry, they were quite loyal to the regime. In the latter part of the nineteenth century Cossack units were mostly used as a mobile police force and became the main instrument in quelling peasant unrest, strikes and demonstrations.

URBAN POPULATION

The urban population of Russia presents an equally complicated picture. Genuine 'townspeople' (excluding peasants, noblemen, and foreigners who resided in towns more or less permanently) were relatively few. Peter the Great had tried to modernize urban organization by encouraging the development of a prosperous and active merchant class with its own guilds, to protect and enhance its interests. In addition he had wanted to delegate to this urban élite as much of the municipal administration as possible by establishing *magistraty* and *ratushi* in all major cities. Unfortunately, fiscal considerations again played the determining role, and urban self-administration was turned by the government into a tool for the repartition and collection of the many taxes and services that were imposed on the towns. The wealthy members of the first guilds were little interested in their status, for it merely imposed onerous duties and made them legally and financially responsible for their poorer comrades; membership in the guilds was debased into a tax category. The more successful townspeople directed their efforts at obtaining places in the official Table of Ranks by virtue of their public obligations, thus escaping the financial burdens of town membership. The main burden of municipal duties and taxes fell on the poor rank and file, the members of the *posad* (urban community) who performed a plethora of services (sanitation, defence, police, upkeep of streets and buildings, etc.) that kept them from their work and in bondage to the administration.

This state of affairs was the principal cause for the stagnation of Russian urban life throughout the eighteenth century. With an eye on the modernization of the country's economy, Catherine II, continuing various economic measures begun by Elizabeth to free domestic trade, reformed the administrative and social pattern of the towns. The Charter to the Towns was promulgated in 1785 (at the same time as was the Charter to the Nobility). Under it, membership in the guilds remained based on the amount of capital one declared, and continued to be associated with fiscal obligations and specific levels of taxation; elections for representation on the towns' assemblies and councils were conducted on the basis of curias, and members of the two most important guilds received the larger share of responsibility.

Again old customs and traditions kept local participation in urban administration to a minimum. The towns' police remained in the hands of appointed officials, and the ordinary townspeople remained saddled with many onerous obligations and duties so that it was difficult, if not practically impossible, for them to constitute responsible autonomous corporations. Under Alexander I and Nicholas I, furthermore, many of the privileges granted in 1785 were revoked and the towns reverted to having close supervision by government bureaucracies. Only in the special case of St Petersburg was an important reform carried out by N. Milyutin in the 1840s, when the capital's new municipal administration gave a large share of authority and responsibility in the economic life of the metropolis to representatives of their élite. An important reason for the failure of the Charter to the Towns to be of greater benefit to the urban population was that its terms did not clearly define membership in urban 'society'. Indeed, the criterion that was used was ownership of real estate, which meant that noblemen and officials owning houses or land within the confines of a town were entitled to participate – both actively and passively – in municipal elections.

To keep the active and successful merchants within the economically useful municipal 'societies' and also to safeguard the service nobility from being diluted by a new aristocracy of wealth, the special status of *imenityy grazhdanin* ('honoured citizen') was created. At first the category represented someone half-way between the nobility and the upper ranks of the merchant class, but under Nicholas I it no longer served, except in very special circumstances, as an entrée to membership of the nobility. The need to create a bridge between the upper and lower classes by means of some kind of middle class was recognized by most progressive Russians, but the survival of serfdom, and the primacy of state service in determining status, effectively barred the realization of any firm proposals.

OTHER SOCIAL CLASSES

There were many other social classes and status groups. The clergy (see pp. 147 ff) was one. The children of parish clergy who were unable or unwilling to find a place in the church were listed among the *raznochintsy* ('men of various rank'). Many of them became peasants, which meant virtual enserfment. Others joined the government as subaltern officials in local institutions. A few of the better educated, especially in the nineteenth century, joined the university and free professions. Children of soldiers, too, formed a special category within the *raznochintsy* class. Those born after their fathers had become soldiers were free men, and could be enrolled – and under Nicholas I this was automatic – in special schools (garrison and regimental). They could join the army, where they usually became non-commissioned officers or clerks, or they could settle in towns and take up a trade.

To the commoners' class, finally, belonged the bulk of the 'natives' – *inovertsy* ('those of another faith') as they were officially called in the eighteenth century, or *inorodtsy* ('those of another clan') as they subsequently became known. This extremely variegated group consisted of several hundred different peoples and languages. Basically, their treatment and social status depended on their way of life. Indeed, both the Russian government and public opinion categorized them on the basis of a cultural standard: those engaged in hunting, fishing, and trapping were considered the most inferior; then came nomadic cattle raisers; and finally, permanent settlers and those who tilled the soil (especially the grain-growers) were accorded the highest status. From a religious point of view not much distinction was made between primitive Shamanism, paganism, and Buddhism; Islam on the other hand was considered to be a somewhat higher form of religion.

The primitive peoples, especially those living far from any agrarian or urban centres, were left alone by the government, on condition that they paid a *yasak* (tribute in kind). However tolerant this may sound, the policy had its negative side: it facilitated exploitation and oppression by individual entrepreneurs and administrators. The government interfered only when such abuses threatened either the treasury's interests or peace and order. The aim of the policy, however, was to associate these peoples with those of a higher status, and to push them into settling down to agricultural pursuits – an aim which produced no significant results.

The nomadic cattle raisers created two problems: it was necessary to preserve peace and order on the frontiers where they roamed, since they could easily embroil the empire in military conflicts over border and trade questions; more importantly, the agricultural migration and settlement of Russian (including Ukrainian and White Russian) peasants or noble landlords resulted in the nomads being pushed out of their traditional grazing lands. Naturally, this was the source of numerous and bitter conflicts, such as the revolts of Bashkirs in the eighteenth century. Not only did the government favour the Russian colonists in the nomads' lands, but it encouraged the settlement of the nomads and their transformation into soil-tilling peasants. Various enticements, such as gifts and distinctions, were offered to nomad chieftains, or long-term exemption from dues and taxation to all those taking up agriculture. For the natives who remained nomads, the government preferred an indirect system of administration: tribal or clan structures and institutions were preserved, and Russia recognized the internal authority of native chieftains or princelings who served as intermediaries between the Russian administration and their people. Native customary law was applied in all cases, except for a few specific major crimes (rebellion, highway robbery, and murder) and when Russians were involved, in which case Russian law took precedence. As long as contacts between Russians and natives were few and superficial, all was well; but increased contacts, economic and political, created friction.

Whenever the nomads were persuaded or pressured into settling they were assimilated to state peasants, and given the same administrative supervision as the regular state peasants of Russia, except that the nomads' village elders could be drawn on a hereditary basis from among the traditional ruling families, and native customary law remained in force whenever possible. Naturally, it was expected, such a change in their way of life would eventually also lead to their gradual Russification. In the areas closest to the central Russian provinces (e.g. along the Volga and the western slopes of the Urals) this process often culminated in the natives becoming private serfs, if their land was granted to or seized by an individual Russian noble, although this was not the general rule. However, the government did not interfere if natives became the serfs of their own chieftains. The only prohibition that applied throughout the empire was that non-Christians could not own Christian serfs.

The small groups of urban 'natives', mainly traders and craftsmen in cities along the Volga and in western Siberia (and later in the Caucasus), enjoyed a special status only exceptionally. In most cases they belonged to a *posad* run along the same lines as the Russian ones. Only a few select groups of foreign native merchants (from Central Asia for example, the so-called *Bukhartsy*) had the right to form separate corporations and take care of their internal affairs outside the framework of the Russian administration and courts.

Two trends may be distinguished in the history and treatment of the 'natives'. In the first place, a high economic and administrative premium was set on bringing them to a settled agricultural way of life. As soon as this occurred they were assimilated – administratively speaking – into the more privileged categories of the Russian peasantry. Linguistic and religious Russification was a subordinate concern to the authorities, although no special effort was made to guarantee the use of the native language in official business or to preserve customary laws. Administrative practices that put the natives at the mercy of unscrupulous

Russian merchants and officials and kept them in their primitive condition had to be eliminated. The state was supposed to deal with the native peoples or clans directly through special officials (and in the case of the most primitive tribes, to restrict these dealings to occasional contacts). The relations between the Russian 'sector' and the natives had to be properly regulated. The natives had to be helped to clarify and stabilize their customs and laws, to facilitate orderly and consistent administrative and judiciary decisions. In the process, it is true, Russification was pushed a step further, since gaps were filled and doubts resolved by referring to Russian norms and practices. Such were the principles of the reform in native administration carried out by Speransky in Siberia in 1822, a reform that served as model and inspiration for other areas whose conditions resembled those of Siberia.

The second trend was that this policy encouraged the Russification of the native leadership. Local chieftains were given distinctions and decorations and their children were drawn into the orbit of Russian language, schools, and culture. The ultimate reward was assimilation into the nobility of the empire. This could be obtained by providing regular positions in the Table of Ranks for the administrative participation of these native leaders, by attracting them – or their children – into regular Russian military service, or by offering their children the opportunity of attending various military cadet schools. In this way the traditional leadership often became the most aggressive and effective agent of the Russification of the natives and of the transformation of their way of life.

THE NOBILITY

Membership of the nobility was a coveted goal in Russia for both rich merchants and native leaders. As everywhere in Europe at the time, the nobility constituted the élite in terms of wealth, prestige, authority, and education; in Russia it was the only privileged class. But what was the nobility? The answer is not a simple one: there was no clear legal definition; nor were the privileges and rights of its members spelled out. True enough, as the eighteenth century progressed, some order and clarity were introduced, primarily in a negative way, by the precise statement of who was excluded from certain privileges, rights, and benefits. The Charter of 1785 was supposed to have made this clear, but it had not. Throughout this period the Table of Ranks was the basis and framework of noble status; unlike the western nobilities of feudal origin, the Russian had no other source of prestige and power than this connection with the apparatus of the state.

The Table of Ranks not only implied that every nobleman had to serve the state, but it also provided that in order to reach a high rank the nobleman had to go through the lower ranks first. Peter the Great even toyed with the idea of not recognizing the noble status of sons of noblemen until they had reached, by dint of service, the rank at which nobility was conferred upon a commoner. But he did decree that without education a nobleman was to remain a minor in the legal sense, with the upper positions closed to him. The corollary was that if a commoner in state service reached a specified rank in the table (eighth at first, later fifth) he was to be ennobled. Providing for fourteen grades or *chiny* (ranks) for each of the main state service functions, the table originally had tied rank to office, i.e. certain offices carried a specified rank (the names of *chiny*, taken from the German, indicated function). For special distinction of a purely honorary character, not related to service functions and not tied to rank, Peter created the titles of count and baron. Since the traditional custom that all members of a family inherited a title was preserved, the number of titled individuals increased (although remaining always a small minority).

The Table of Ranks became the criterion for and the path to position, status, and indirectly wealth as well. While the legislator's original intention had been to have one's function in service confer rank, very soon the reverse became the practice. Certain offices could be held only by persons of a specified level of rank. The efforts of the nobility were directed at preventing commoners from reaching the higher levels of rank in any large numbers. Thus in the eighteenth century certain offices (secretaries of the colleges, for example) could not be held by commoners, since they required a rank that was not readily granted to the latter. Subsequent legislation was aimed at preventing rapid promotions and automatic ennoblement by setting longevity qualifications for promotions and by raising the rank level at which hereditary nobility was conferred. In spite of these restrictions, access to the hierarchy of the Table of Ranks was never closed and perforce the nobility remained a relatively open – and hence insecure – class.

What were the privileges or rewards associated with rank, besides the right to outward display of luxury and those privileges connected with an official service function? Theoretically only one – exemption from the capitation tax. In other respects, such as personal and property rights, the nobleman had no particular privileges in law. Naturally, throughout the eighteenth century and even later the efforts of the nobility as a class were bent on the acquisition of such guarantees and rights. The efforts did not end with the accession of Alexander, although other considerations, constitutional and political rather than social, then became prevalent.

Their first demand was to be treated like noblemen and not put on the same footing as commoners, even while serving in the lower ranks: noblemen should be exempted from corporal punishment, for instance.

Indirectly, the nobility gained satisfaction on this point by having its children assigned to special schools or cadet units from which they were directly promoted to full officer rank. Another method of avoiding the period of service in lower ranks was to enrol the noble child in a regiment at birth, so that when he was ready to enter active service he had been promoted to officer rank on the basis of longevity. The second demand of the nobility was that of security of person and property: that is, a guarantee against arbitrary confiscation, arrest, exile, and even worse. Security of property became assured rather rapidly by the general social and economic progress of Russia in the eighteenth century and the state's recognition that its own advantage would be served by an economically secure and prosperous nobility. Legal sanction of this security was given by Catherine II, as we have seen, as one aspect of her promotion of the development of all economic resources. Security of person, however, was not to be achieved fully. Of course the growing sophistication of Russian government and society contributed to making crying abuses rare, if not impossible, but the reign of Paul I served as a grim reminder that a capricious and tyrannical monarch could still dispose of his nobles at will. The treatment given the Decembrists, although clad in regular legal form, was construed to be a threat to personal security, and so were the activities of the ubiquitous Third Section and of the Corps of Gendarmes in the reign of Nicholas I. The minor nobleman was not fully secure even from the caprices of the local officials; in remote provinces a governor or land captain could keep a noble in prison or exile him to remote districts, and it sometimes took years to obtain redress from superior authorities.

Nobles were owners of populated estates – i.e. of serfs – and the nobility, for whom the revenue from their estates was essential to keep up a western-style way of life, endeavoured to secure the monopoly over the ownership of serfs. This they had in fact obtained by the time of Catherine II, although it proved to be a short-term victory, since Alexander I eliminated the monopoly in 1802 in the hope of initiating the process of gradual emancipation. Although the nobles secured complete control over their own property they never succeeded in making any one type of property their exclusive monopoly and a criterion of noble status.

As a matter of fact, as has been seen in another connection, the nobility's economic position was far from brilliant. The custom of splitting an inheritance among all the deceased's children meant that even a large estate would, within only a few generations, have to support a large number of impoverished noblemen at a very low standard. It also made for the scattering of an individual's property over several districts or provinces in many small parcels; it was difficult to manage these dispersed fragments and often each one of them was barely profitable. For the ordinary nobleman the revenue from his estates was hardly adequate to keep him going and he had to supplement it with the salary and gifts he received while in service. One form this took was that, for good services or as compensation for unforeseen losses (in war, for example), the government freely granted lifelong or temporary usufruct of *arendy* (state domains). The state also helped out by establishing loan banks on which the nobility drew heavily, putting up their serfs and land as security.

The search for personal security was closely bound up with demands for some kind of corporate organization to protect the interests of the nobility. In their political form these demands have been noted in connection with the proposals for better communication between ruler and ruled and the creation of a consultative mechanism. They were also the burden of the political programme of the Decembrists, whose failure precluded further efforts in this direction during the reign of Nicholas I, although it may be argued that the codification of Russian law greatly enhanced the security of property and person by providing for orderly legal procedures and standards.

The Charter to the Nobility of 1785 was to have given the nobility corporate status and organization and full security, as well as a truly privileged position in Russian society. It did all of these things partially, but none completely. Corporate status was not fully achieved because there was no clear, unambiguous definition of 'the nobility'. The charter repeated the old phrase about it being an honorific title bestowed for outstanding services. In addition, several of its provisions made possession of a rank a prerequisite for participation in noble assemblies and local institutions. Thus the system of the Table of Ranks remained the primary criterion of nobility. The charter did nothing to help the individual nobleman overcome the geographic dispersion of his interests and his lack of regional loyalty, and while it freed him from corporal punishment and promised him trial by a jury of his peers, in practice these provisions were frequently violated by the bureaucracy.

The most prominent and rich dignitaries of the eighteenth century seemed on their way to forming an aristocracy that aspired to permanent and legally guaranteed participation in the affairs of the state (cf. 1730, the Panin proposal, the Senatorial party). They failed, as we have seen. Largely this was because they could not enlist the support of the lesser nobility, and also because in the final analysis they themselves were entirely dependent on the state. They had to rely on its economic support and serve in the military and administration.

WESTERNIZATION

The century following the accession of Peter the Great was one of westernization; Peter aimed at making Russia into a European power and society. Of course, Russia had been working toward some degree of westernization ever since the sixteenth century, but until the reign of Peter it had had very definite limits. It had allowed the introduction only of what was immediately useful and entertaining, of that which did not affect the essence of Russian life and its traditions; basic religious notions and values, in particular, remained untouched.

Not so with Peter. Westernization for him meant the transformation of all facets of Russian life, if possible affecting all classes of society. While his primary interest lay in technology and military matters, he was also concerned to westernize the administration and to introduce the useful sciences, learning, and arts from the West. The outward way of life of at least the upper classes had to be made to conform as much and as rapidly as possible to that of western European societies. In this sense, with respect to the upper classes, his goal was achieved in the first quarter of the nineteenth century, when modern Russian culture – a lively and creative blend of western European and native elements – came into being. But the conscious striving for westernization continued to be a foremost concern of the Russian élite.

State service was both the cause and the purpose of westernization under Peter and his immediate successors. Peter had ordered physical westernization by requiring that servicemen, nobles, and the educated dress in 'German' fashion, shave their beards, and behave in a 'civilized' manner in public. Within one generation the upper class had become quite westernized in outward appearance – so much so that even the provincial nobleman wore the 'German' garb of his service when he retired to his estate. Of course, the western style of social life took somewhat longer to spread and become rooted: while St Petersburg became a western city immediately upon its foundation and while its court and social life was a brilliant copy of the European *salons* and courts, the rest of the country followed suit very slowly. Throughout the eighteenth century even Moscow preserved the traditional Russian family pattern, and in the provinces westernization was quite superficial and frequently very comical.

More significant than the externals of dress and social intercourse was the intellectual and cultural westernization of the upper classes. The main agent in this respect was the technical training required of the service nobility by Peter the Great. He established secular schools and tried to develop a network of preparatory and secondary schools – the so-called 'cypher' schools – staffed mostly by the clergy, but under government supervision. These schools were not successful and did not last for long, because the clergy were reluctant to participate in secular institutions and the nobility objected to their children's being put on a level of equality with those of other classes, and so special schools – Corps of Cadets and its imitators – were set up that led to appointment at officer rank upon graduation. From the very start, technical training alone was felt to be inadequate, and dancing, deportment, etiquette, riding, foreign languages – in short all the social graces – were included in the curriculum. Naturally, private schools and private tutors followed suit.

The amount of western science and scholarship known in Muscovy at the time of Peter's accession was negligible. The Russians therefore had to learn everything *ab initio*, and they needed books on all subjects. Translation was the obvious answer, but the Russian language lacked the vocabulary and flexibility that would make for readable translations, and a great deal of time and energy were needed to make the large corpus of western literature available in Russian. So it became imperative for the Russian élite to learn foreign languages. At first the most popular and widely known language was German, although French and Italian were recognized media for the *salon* and the arts. French, whose scientific literature was less well known to the teachers in Russia, only became popular among the court nobility in the reign of Catherine II.

Peter's concern for the rapid westernization of Russian cultural life led him – probably under the influence of Leibniz – to lay plans for an academy of sciences. He did not live to see its inauguration, which took place in the reign of his successor, Catherine I, in 1725. Significantly, the academy was designed for the double purpose of promoting scholarly and scientific research and of giving high-level instruction to new cadres of technically competent state servants. At first all of its members were foreigners, and Russians were not in a majority until the end of the eighteenth century. Similar technological and intellectual needs of westernization resulted in the founding of the first university in Moscow in 1755. The needs of state service, which had helped to bring this about, also kept its student body small, since the nobility was not attracted by lengthy studies, and little use could be made of such advanced learning outside state service. In time, of course, the need for highly professionalized state servants and intellectuals came to be acutely felt, and in 1805 it was decided to create new or renovate existing universities (e.g. Kazan', Khar'kov, Dorpat, Vil'na (Wilno), St Petersburg). From then on their number grew, accompanied by the extension of the network of secondary schools in the chief provincial towns. Specialized and professional schools were also created at an ever-increasing rate (the *lycée* at Tsarskoye Selo, the Juridical Institute, the Military Surgical–Medical Academy, schools of engineering, transportation, and mining). By 1855 Russian education had attained equality with the technical and scholarly training offered in western Europe.

Concurrently, however, the areas of friction between the government and intellectual Russia had also increased. The disastrous effects on Russian technical and intellectual progress of bigoted and rigid constraints made themselves felt particularly on two occasions. In the heyday of Alexander I's mysticism (in the late 1810s and early 1820s), the development of the Universities of Kazan' and St Petersburg was halted and largely ruined by controls imposed by the government on both faculty and students. The second instance was in the reign of Nicholas I, when the humanities and legal studies were much handicapped by ideological controls, and the progress of university education was stymied by the drastic reduction and restriction of enrolments. A police-inspired 'university statute' (1835), combined with severe censorship regulations (1828), undermined the morale and effectiveness of academic life, and contributed to the widening of the gulf separating the educated élites from the state. The needs of service had helped bring into being the very group that was to fight the establishment most consistently and violently.

The nobility was not the only class to participate through the schools in the process of cultural westernization. While the church had balked at implementing Peter's plan of providing elementary secular technical education through the 'cypher' schools, it worked for westernization through its seminaries and theological academies. Even before Peter's accession the church had been under the strong influence of the progressive Kiev Theological Academy, and during his reign Feofan Prokopovich (1681–1736) expanded the ecclesiastical school system. The ecclesiastical schools provided a solid background in Latin and Greek, western philosophy, history, and theology. More important still, they imparted the powerful skills of rhetoric and argument, and – after Speransky's reforms, which modernized the administration and curriculum – the best of them also offered a solid grounding in mathematics and the natural sciences.

It is of course impossible to follow with precision the westernization of the common people, especially the peasants. In general, it would seem that western ways failed to make a significant impact on them before the end of the eighteenth century. Yet one can say that quite obviously the new interests and needs of the serf-owners must have affected the lives of their serfs.

Westernization not only set new goals but also introduced new ways into the intellectual and social life of the country. The new goals were those of rationalism, enlightenment, material welfare and progress, concern for the individual, and the spiritual and economic welfare of the lower classes. The new ways of behaviour were closely tied to these goals: a product of the scientific and intellectual revolutions of the seventeenth and eighteenth centuries in the West, they stressed rationality and efficiency and the creative role of the energetic and conscious individual, in contrast to the traditionalism and passivity of the community. Yet Russia's social structure did not change in any significant way during this period. Little wonder that the elements of westernization that I have described found themselves in artificial, uncongenial surroundings. They thus generated opposing forces, threatening the social and political stability of the establishment. In turn the government developed an ambivalent attitude toward westernization: it welcomed it to enhance the military and economic power of the state; it opposed it and endeavoured to suppress it in most other cases.

TENSIONS

THE SERVICE NOBILITY

Although Soviet and Marxist historians have dubbed this period 'dvoryanskaya imperiya' ('the nobility's empire'), it was far from being a time of halcyon friendship between the state and the service nobility. Tension between them arose partly from the compulsory, permanent, and pedagogical aspects of state service imposed by Peter the Great. While a few enthusiastically supported him, the ordinary noblemen had a hard time breaking with the customs and traditions that had been developed by several generations of their ancestors. Their discontent was deepened because the new service practices eroded the old local and family solidarities; since assignments were made on an individual basis, the connections which in the seventeenth century had begun to bind together nobles from the same region, families, or service units were disregarded (perhaps deliberately so). The nobleman felt lost, at the mercy of an impersonal force that made his life difficult, scorning as it did his needs and interests. The permanent character of his service obligation meant that he had almost no occasion to stay on his estate with his family.

Avoidance of service and efforts to retire early and hide from further calls characterized the relationship between Peter's government and the nobility. The war and the driving energy of Peter prevented an open break. Yet we know from the records of the *Preobrazhensky Prikaz* that disaffection was widespread and involved the ordinary nobility as well as disgraced members of old boyar families. One cause around which these malcontents could rally was that of the Tsarevich Alexis. The affair surrounding him was very complicated and has not been fully disentangled by historians even to this day. Suffice it to say here that, besides the personal clash between Alexis and Peter, it involved a general dissatisfaction with Peter's brusque turning from the old path, his enforced westernization, and the hardships that they brought in their wake.

This particular aspect of the noblemen's discontent did not end with Peter's death; the nobleman in service remained very much at the mercy of the state machine and could be used and abused by the ruler and his favourites. The nobles who were serving in the capital and at court bore the brunt of their capriciousness, and it is little wonder that conflicts between them and the monarch ended in palace *coups*. Such was the fate, in 1741, of the infant Ivan VI and his mother, Anna Leopol'dovna, the regent; it was also the end of Peter III, whose diplomatic volte-face and decision to send the guard regiments to fight on the side of Frederick II of Prussia led to his wife Catherine's successful *coup* in 1762. The capriciousness of Tsar Paul I and his reviving of the Petrine service practices produced a sense of insecurity and dissatisfaction among the nobles in the capital that cost him both his throne and life.

The high dignitaries of the Supreme Privy Council who in fact had ruled in the reigns of Catherine I and Peter II understood the connection between the service pattern, economic decline, and the disaffection of the nobility. They searched for means of changing the service rules without, however, changing the nature, purpose, and methods of the new Petrine state. Rules for leave and retirement were eased; a plan was worked out for rotating tours of duty in such a way that the nobleman could spend one year out of three on his estate. But the practical results were not very impressive and the discontent remained acute. The succession crisis following the death of Tsar Peter II provided an opportunity for this discontent to be brought out into the open.

The demands presented by the nobility in 1730 were aimed at safeguarding their status and at eliminating the most burdensome features of the lifelong service pattern. They demanded that there be established special regiments or units, special schools for the nobility in which they could earn their first grades and then be assigned to regular regiments or offices with officer rank. The lifelong service term should be replaced, they said, by a period of approximately twenty-five years. No objection in principle was raised to the notion of compulsory service, and only a lessening of its burdens was sought, but the state succeeded in resisting even these modest demands. True, the Corps of Cadets was established for children of the nobility, and the custom developed of giving nobles privileged treatment while they were in subaltern grades, but it did not completely protect them from abuse or from the brutal treatment that was the lot of the commoner. Some years later, the required length of service was cut to thirty years, and under Elizabeth to twenty-five, and then twenty, but this was granted as a favour and not all dared to take undue advantage of it.

The nobility's lack of success in gaining their demands was due to their inability to offer a united front to the autocracy. Faced with the choice between greater privileges and freedoms under an oligarchy and the maintenance of the autocracy, most members of the service nobility preferred the latter, since they believed that their interests would be better safeguarded if the country avoided a splintering of political authority. In due course the hardships of service decreased, and eventually (1762) the service noble was given the right to serve or not to serve. How real the option was may be questioned, for there was still little that the nobleman could effectively and profitably do outside state service. One may even argue that the granting of freedom from service resulted in a new form of tension between the state and the service nobles. Indeed, the decree of 19 February 1762 made it quite clear that the government no longer depended on the nobility to perform its tasks; or, alternatively, the nobility had no choice but to serve the state. In any case, the noble-man felt that he was threatened with the loss of his special ties to the monarch and the government. This feeling was strengthened by the belief that court favourites kept the tsar from contact with and knowledge of the condition of the nation.

The desire to have some competent spokesmen with regular access to the autocracy was thus given new impetus. It was proposed by Count N. I. Panin in 1762 that a sort of council to assist the ruler be established, composed of high dignitaries and officials sitting together with a few selected spokesmen for the provincial nobles. An alternative institutional framework for such an arrangement seemed to be the Senate, provided it were modified to admit representatives of the provincial nobility and given a limited *droit de remonstrance*. This point of view was most actively propounded at the beginning of the reign of Tsar Alexander I by spokesmen of the 'Senatorial party'. At the beginning of the nineteenth century the tension between nobility and state focused on the nobility's rights to security of person, property, and especially the safeguarding of the individual's dignity and worth. One solution was to devise procedural safeguards that would force the actions of officials and institutions into clearly prescribed rules and regulations, supervised by special bodies of officials. This programme found its most vocal advocates following the death of Paul I, whose capricious reign had shown the importance of securing procedural protection. It was a strictly bureaucratic approach, which provided little or no direct communication between the state and the nation, on the Petrine premiss that the state was best qualified to guide and lead in the modernization of the country. This point of view was advocated energetically by Tsar Alexander I's 'Unofficial

Committee', and then repeatedly favoured by progressive bureaucrats, especially Speransky. Well-intentioned as they may have been, the high officials were not in a position to exact such a great concession. That is why the bureaucratic reformism of the early nineteenth century proved to be stillborn.

The experiences of the noble servicemen during the wars against Napoleon exacerbated the friction between the educated élite and the state. The successful defence of the fatherland against the French, the participation in the liberation of Europe from Napoleon's yoke, the role played by the Russian government in establishing moderate constitutional regimes in the liberated, and even in the defeated, countries, and finally, the personal experience of life abroad – all contributed to raising the expectation of the young enlightened members of the nobility that upon the conclusion of peace Alexander I would take the initiative in bringing about a constitutional arrangement. There was a feeling that the purpose of government was no longer to ensure the power of the Russian state (which already had been achieved) but rather the welfare of the Russian people, in particular its most downtrodden and oppressed group, the serfs. Such was the origin of the Decembrist movement, whose attempt at seizing power on 14 December 1825 was, as we know, a failure. But it clearly demonstrated the alienation of the enlightened and educated nobility from the autocratic state. The class whose development had been the aim of Peter the Great came to break openly with the state that had brought it into being. Nicholas I drew the conclusion that the educated nobility could not be trusted, and reinforced the rigid bureaucratic and narrow police elements of the imperial government. This did not eradicate alienation and opposition, but on the contrary reinforced them: the intelligentsia came into being, as matters rapidly passed from searching and discussion of *Weltanschauungen* to organized efforts at bringing about a radical transformation of the country's social and political structure.

THE PEASANTS

The tension and conflicts that marked the peasants' relation to the state and to other classes of society were much more acute and profound, but also less complex. The complete alienation of serf and lord was influenced, essentially, firstly by the absolute insecurity in which the serf found himself: he was virtually the plaything of his master and hence always uncertain of his own and his family's future. Secondly, the lord's culture and way of life were becoming increasingly different from that of his serfs; the lord tried to live in a 'European' manner, introducing these new ways into the village and into the management of his estates. The serf was almost completely left out of this new way of life.

176

Deep hatred and helpless anger were accumulating in the minds of the peasants; contained as long as the nobles interfered little in the peasant routine, they threatened explosion at the least provocation. When the compulsory service obligation of the nobles was abolished in 1762 and there was no sign of a corresponding liberation of the serfs, rumours that there had been an emancipation charter that the nobles had suppressed could not be quashed. The serfs' anger and despair turned to revolts directed at the nobility rather than the state.

The close connection between peasant unrest and the increasing burden of serfdom should not surprise us; the evidence for it had been accumulating since the middle of the seventeenth century. The revolts were growing in number and violence, and often took on the character of regular peasant wars, especially in the remote areas of the empire, along the Volga, where national, religious, and special social grievances (e.g. of the Cossacks) provided additional fuel. Such a peasant war took place in the reign of Peter the Great on the lower Volga under the leadership of Bulavin. But the most serious of all of the peasant rebellions, in which their passionate hatred of the nobles' way of life came to the fore with particular force, was the war led by E. Pugachev in the region of the middle Volga and the Urals in 1773-5. The savagery of the peasants' upsurge sowed panic and deep fear in the ranks of the nobility and of the government, which was not forgotten for a long time after the bloody suppression of Pugachev's revolt. This helps to explain the local nobility's feeling of hopeless weakness and their dependence on the state as their only protector. Among the more enlightened members of the educated classes the uprising aroused compassion and indignation at the condition of the peasantry. It had become obvious that serfdom as it existed, in destroying the humanity of the peasant, threatened the moral integrity of the élite as well. Bulavin's and Pugachev's rebellions were by no means the only ones. It is not possible to give a full and accurate account of every instance of peasant revolt, for the line is hard to draw between a minor localized grievance leading to open discontent and a real rebellion with ominous implications, but the incidence of peasant unrest did not abate, and it reached an almost endemic character in the first half of the nineteenth century.

The government could not remain indifferent to the condition of 80 per cent of the population for long. Until the end of the eighteenth century the state had made the individual nobleman perform all the necessary police and administrative functions on his estate. The acts of 1775 and 1785 may be considered the high points of this system, as they gave the nobles a regular place in local administration and secured their rights over the serfs. The reign of Tsar Paul I, however, marked the beginning of a change. By limiting the corvée obligations to three days a week Paul tried to bring some balance and order into the peasants' obligations. He seems to have believed that the system should neither completely destroy the productive elements of the population nor permit the nobility to behave in tyrannical and arbitrary fashion (Paul distrusted and disliked the nobility, especially those living on their estates). The measure was not enforced, nor was it enforceable under Russian conditions; and Paul did not live long enough to make a serious attempt. His son, Tsar Alexander I, perhaps out of more philosophic and humanitarian considerations, also felt it necessary to start turning Russia away from serfdom, and toyed with several approaches to restrict and eventually abolish it. He may not have considered the latter to be a real possibility in his own lifetime, but he would have welcomed it. Meaningless perhaps from a practical point of view, but characteristic of the changed atmosphere, was the prohibition to advertise the sale of serfs in the official press. More significant was the legislation concerning the Free Agriculturists (1803) and the emancipation of the serfs in the Baltic provinces (1816–19). But the latter were emancipated without land, and this created a landless proletariat whose economic condition was not much better than that of serfs. To enlightened Russians it served as a warning.

The creation of military colonies in the second half of Alexander's reign aimed not merely at ushering in a gradual change in serf status, but also at creating a better managed agriculture to serve the needs of the army. State peasants were forcibly settled in these colonies and their lives were organized along military lines. They were to combine military drill and preparedness with rationally and efficiently organized agricultural labour. The scheme was implemented with unbending rigour and brutality by Count A. A. Arakcheyev and his staff. The forced, rigid, militaristic organization of their lives aroused the bitter resentment and anger of the peasants impressed into the colonies, even though there were rewards in better material conditions and education for their children. The peasants revolted, their rebellion had to be drowned in blood, and eventually Nicholas gave up the struggle and abolished the colonies.

At Speransky's suggestion the government tried to tackle the problem of serfdom by first improving the lot of the state peasants, over which it had direct control, in preparation for a change in the status of private serfs to that of state peasants. This reform was eventually carried out by Count P. D. Kiselyov (1837–41), and it put the regular administration of the state peasants into the hands of a separate Ministry of State Domains. A wider range of peasant participation in local affairs was provided for, and wherever it existed the peasant commune became the institutional framework for the new system. This approach foreshadowed the emancipation settlement of 1861.

RELIGIOUS DISSENTERS

Closely related to the tension between the peasants and the empire's ruling classes was the antagonism between groups of religious dissenters – many of them peasants – and the state. The conflict that involved the greatest number of people (and antedated Peter I's accession) was that between the 'Old Believers' (and their various offshoots) and the official church supported by the government. The Old Believers' opposition to the establishment deepened as the purpose of Peter's policy became apparent. Their belief that the government had become the instrument of Antichrist was confirmed by Peter's introduction of western dress and manners, the further secularization of public life, and the imposition of new heavy economic burdens. The rumour that Peter was not the rightful tsar originated among the Old Believers and then spread among the common people who resented his harsh policies and innovations. Ironically, Peter's enlightened and secular reign was a period of the most ferocious persecution of religious dissent.

The Petrine policy of persecution was continued by his successors. The Old Believers were discriminated against socially, legally, and administratively, and they were subjected to double taxation. Energetic and brutal reconversion campaigns were countenanced by the state. The Old Believers themselves were rent by dissensions over the vexing matter of ordination. Many new radical sects (sometimes influenced by foreign ideas) sprang up, so that the religious picture in Russia was quite varied, even within the framework of the Orthodox faith. Empress Elizabeth began to relax the legislation against the Old Believers and Catherine II, more concerned with economic progress, followed a tolerant policy, provided the dissenters did not disturb the peace and quietly bore additional fiscal burdens imposed on them. She only continued to persecute the most extreme sects which engaged, in her opinion, in practices that 'went against nature'. As a matter of fact, to further the agricultural development of southern Russia she called back from Poland Old Believers who had fled there in Peter's and Anna's times. She also settled German pietists (Mennonites), who became an influence in the emergence of new sects. The policy of toleration was continued in the reign of Alexander I, when it reached its high point. The attitude that went into the establishment of the Bible Society in Russia made for an acceptance of religious dissent. The latter even came to be seen as a positive manifestation of genuine Christian religious feeling and a potential tool of popular enlightenment.

Nicholas I, however, returned to more repressive policies. The Old Believers were outside the purview of state control, from both a religious

179

and socio-economic point of view, living as they did in closely knit communities that played a very significant role in Russian trade and small industry. Nicholas ordered the destruction of the most important Old Believer communities, the dispersal of their members, and the confiscation of their at times large commercial holdings. Discriminatory legislation was introduced and a harsh programme of forced conversion put into motion. The expectation of cowing the Old Believers into submission failed to materialize. On the contrary the disaffection of this very numerous group was intensified and their alienation from official Russia became virtually complete.

A major problem was created by the admission of many Roman Catholics to Russia as a result of the partitions of Poland.[1] The government's attitude to the problem was ambivalent: it hoped to conciliate the Catholics, but on condition that their church be loyal and subservient to the Russian state. To this end Catherine admitted the Jesuits when their order was disbanded by the Pope, and she promoted an autonomous Catholic ecclesiastical administration under Archbishop S. Siestrzeńcewicz-Bohusz of Mogilyov in the western provinces. As the success of Jesuit schools and Catholic influence became noticeable among the upper classes of Russian society Alexander I grew afraid of the role that Catholics might play in Russian public and cultural life. Besides, after 1812 Catholicism went against his own mysticism and pietism. But the decisive element in the government's relation to Catholicism was, of course, the close connection between it and the Polish question: it was firmly believed that a consistently liberal and tolerant policy toward the Catholic Church would enhance and strengthen nationalism and threaten Russia's political security in the Polish provinces and its diplomatic position in Europe. The Polish revolt of 1830 sounded the death knell of any efforts at toleration and accommodation with the Catholic Church. Nicholas I embarked on a course of repression and suspicious discrimination which set the Catholic population, as well as clergy, against the state for generations to come.

NON-RUSSIAN NATIONALITIES

The policies of the government toward non-Christian religions are hard to distinguish from its attitude toward non-Russian nationalities, for as late as the middle of the nineteenth century religion and nationality were considered to be almost inseparable. Essentially the state's intolerant attitude, shared by most absolute monarchies of the seventeenth and eighteenth centuries, rested on the belief that religious, cultural – i.e.

[1] Protestantism (mainly Lutheranism in the Baltic provinces) enjoyed favourable treatment and impinged little on Russian life, and can therefore be excluded.

national – uniformity was an essential ingredient of political stability. In Russia there was in addition the lingering belief that it was the ruler's duty to spread Orthodoxy, although this belief only intermittently had impelled tsars to practical action. Its revival in the reign of Nicholas I . had a distinctly political and cultural aspect.

There was no general repression of Moslems and little missionary effort toward their conversion, mainly out of considerations of political and administrative expediency, reinforced by the desire not to alienate possible dissenting elements in the Turkish Empire at the time of the conquests of the Crimea and Caucasus. But this policy of toleration was not always enforceable on the local level, since it was not easy to separate cultural and political disaffection among Moslem Tatars from the religious element that lay at the root of their national consciousness. Discriminatory taxation and, more important still, administrative difficulties and abuses arising out of differences in legal norms and language created a source of constant tension and potential conflict. Again the traditional policy of toleration was reversed in the reign of Tsar Nicholas I, the government turning to active proselytizing and the suppression of linguistic and religious expressions of national identity.

The Russian government had always been highly inimical to the Jews and for centuries kept them out of the empire altogether. Ironically, it was the partition of Poland that resulted in Russia's acquiring one of the largest European areas of Jewish settlement. At first the policy remained rather passive; the Jews were allowed to retain their own communal organization and rabbinical courts, but settlement outside the newly acquired provinces was restricted or prohibited altogether. This prohibition to settle in certain regions of the empire proved to be the most important and oppressive discriminatory measure. In the reign of Alexander I a reasonable statute for the Jews was promulgated, but as it was based on the belief and hope that the Jewish élite, like that of other nationalities, might become Russified in due course, it failed to improve the lot of the Jews significantly. The desire to break down Jewish 'exclusiveness' lay at the heart of all the government measures that were enacted in response to Jewish pleas to be admitted into the mainstream of the empire's economic and public life. In this case, too, Tsar Nicholas I followed a simple-minded and ruthless policy, using the army and the military orphanages as vehicles for the Russification of the Jews, or at least of their children. The psychological and moral horrors that accompanied this practice only served to confirm the Jews in their own ways and to instil in them an unreconcilable opposition to the Russian establishment.

The conquest of the Caucasus and Finland and the partitions of Poland brought under Russian rule advanced peoples with a developed sense of national identity and cultural pride, who could not be absorbed as easily as had the more primitive nomadic tribes of the eastern frontier. They remained alien bodies in the empire and in the process of dealing with them administratively the Russians were fated to arouse conflicts and enmities. The government knew only force and repression as measures for keeping these nations in obedience – with fatal results, as the twentieth century was to show.

In the Baltic provinces the conflict was primarily between the German ruling classes and the Russian government. The downtrodden and exploited native Baltic peasants were not involved, except in cases of serf rebellions; these, however, were in all respects identical to those in Russia proper. The conflict between Germans and the Russian state was primarily a legal one (see pp. 132–3), the government gradually whittling down the Baltic provinces' special privileges, not only by overpowering political force, but also through the increasing integration of the Baltic economy into that of the empire and by the Russification of those Baltic Germans who entered the imperial state service. They rose to high positions, earned privileged Russian status in their own right, and often lost interest in their medieval local privileges.

In the case of the more 'primitive' nationalities it is difficult to separate the economic from the social and national factors that caused conflict. Thus the many Bashkir rebellions in the eighteenth century were as much due to Russian agricultural expansion as to the efforts of the government to put the nomadic Bashkirs under firm control and to subject them to the regular Russian provincial administration. Similarly the conflicts with the Tatars were due not only to religious and national causes, but also to the state's policy of eliminating privileges and autonomies granted to the Tatars at the time of their conquest, in order to bring about administrative uniformity and to further the economic development of their territory. The same could be said of the more numerous and sophisticated Siberian native peoples (the Buriat Mongols and the Kazakhs, for example).

The tension and conflicts which had existed since the time of Tsar Peter I had been the direct consequence of the new direction he gave to Russia and to the policies of the state. But the full extent of the consequences became apparent only in the reign of Nicholas I, who sought to apply, with inexorable logic and little imagination, the standards of political control, government leadership, and administrative uniformity he had inherited from Peter. But operating in a much more developed and complex situation than his forebear, he met with greater resistance. His efforts at breaking the opposition paved the way to open conflict and led to a dramatic break between the various elements of Russian society and the state.

GUIDE TO FURTHER READING

This selective list is arranged to supplement the major themes of the text, with the emphasis on recent works, particularly those in western European languages. In the great majority of cases the items cited contain detailed bibliographical references for further study.

Bibliographies

The most comprehensive and up-to-date bibliographical introduction to the subject now available is J. S. G. Simmons, ed., *Russian Bibliography, Libraries and Archives (A Selective List of Bibliographical References for Students of Russian History, Literature, Political, Social and Philosophical Thought, Theology and Linguistics)* (Oxford, 1973). See also P. L. Horecky, ed., *Basic Russian Publications – An Annotated Bibliography on Russia and the Soviet Union* (Chicago, 1962); D. Shapiro, *A Select Bibliography of Works in English on Russian History 1801–1917* (Oxford, 1962); P. A. Crowther, ed., *A Bibliography of Works in English on Early Russian History to 1800* (Oxford, 1969); M. Hellmann, ed., *Osteuropa in der historischen Forschung der D. D. R.* (2 vols., Düsseldorf, 1972); K. Meyer, *Bibliographie der Arbeiten zur osteuropäischen Geschichte aus den deutschsprachigen Fachzeitschriften 1858–1964* (Wiesbaden, 1966); the same author's *Bibliographie zur osteuropäischen Geschichte (Verzeichnis der zwischen 1939 und 1964 veröffentlichten Literatur in westeuropäischen Sprachen zur osteuropäischen Geschichte bis 1945)* (Wiesbaden, 1972). Also useful are: E. M. Zhukov, ed., *Sovetskaya istoricheskaya entsiklopediya* (Moscow, 1961) – so far 14 vols. have been published, 16 announced; *Istoriya SSSR – Annotirovannyy perechen' Russkikh bibliografiy, izdannykh do 1965 goda,* 2nd edn (Moscow, 1966); *Bibliografiya Russkoy bibliografii po istorii SSSR (Annotirovannyy perechen' bibliograficheskikh ukazateley izdannykh do 1917 goda)* (Moscow, 1957); *Istoriya SSSR – Ukazatel' Sovetskoy literatury za 1917–1952 gg.* (2 vols. and 2 vols. of indexes, Moscow, 1956–8); K. D. Muratova, ed., *Istoriya Russkoy literatury XIX veka – Bibliograficheskiy ukazatel'* (Moscow, 1962); I. V. Vladislavlev, *Russkiye pisateli XIX–XX st.,* 2nd edn (Moscow, 1913); *Istoriya istoricheskoy nauki v SSSR – Dooktyabr'skiy period – Bibliografiya* (Moscow, 1965); M. N. Tikhomirov, *Istochnikovedeniye istorii SSSR* (2 vols., Moscow, 1940; 2nd edn, vol. I only, Moscow, 1962); S. N. Valk, *Sovetskaya arkheografiya* (Moscow–Leningrad, 1948).

More specialized but extremely valuable bibliographical tools are P. A. Zayonchkovsky, ed., *Spravochniki po istorii dorevolyutsionnoy Rossii – Bibliografiya* (Moscow, 1971); and P. K. Grimsted, *Archives and Manuscript Repositories in the USSR – Moscow and Leningrad* (Princeton, 1972). Of general value to the student and scholar is G. Vernadsky and R. T. Fisher, jun., eds., *Dictionary of Russian Historical Terms from the Eleventh Century to 1917,* comp. by S. G. Pushkarev (New Haven, 1970).

General histories

H. Seton-Watson, *The Russian Empire, 1801–1917* (Oxford, 1967); A. Kornilov, *Modern Russian History* (New York, 1943); P. Milioukov, C. Seignobos, and

L. Eisenmann, *Histoire de Russie* (3 vols., Paris, 1935), English trans. by C. L. Markmann (3 vols., New York, 1968); M. Raeff, *Imperial Russia 1662–1825: The Coming of Age of Imperial Russia* (New York, 1970), which includes a comprehensive bibliographical essay; K. Stählin, *Geschichte Russlands von den Anfängen bis zur Gegenwart* (4 vols., Berlin, 1930–9); V. O. Klyuchevsky, *Kurs Russkoy istorii* (many edns, the latest in vols. 1–5 of collected works, Moscow, from 1956) – there exists a very poor English translation by C. J. Hogarth, *A History of Russia* (5 vols., London, 1911–31); *Ocherki istorii SSSR* (3 vols., Moscow, 1954–6), dealing with the eighteenth century; S. M. Solov'yov, *Istoriya Rossii s drevneyshikh vremyon* (St Petersburg, n.d.; a new Soviet edn in 15 vols., Moscow, 1959–66), books XIV to XXIX covering the period relevant to this chapter, reaching the beginning of the reign of Catherine II; *Istoriya Rossii v XIX veke* (9 vols., St Petersburg; 1907–11); M. Cherniavsky, ed., *The Structure of Russian History – Interpretive Essays* (New York, 1970), which reprints valuable articles that have appeared in periodical literature. *Canadian–American Slavic Studies* (previously *Canadian Slavic Studies*) devoted special issues to Catherine II (IV, 3, Fall 1970) and Paul I (VII, 1, Spring 1973) that have some recent monographic scholarship in article form; similar special numbers on the reigns of Peter I and Alexander I are in press and planned. The more important facts of Catherine II's life and reign are illuminated in articles collected in M. Raeff, *Catherine the Great – A Profile* (London, 1972), with an historiographical–bibliographical essay. Recently Soviet scholars have resumed active publication of Festschriften that contain extremely valuable studies and comprehensive historiographical and bibliographical information; among these, volumes dedicated to the following scholars may be mentioned as being particularly useful: B. D. Grekov (1952), N. M. Druzhinin (1961, 1971), B. B. Kafengauz (1964), N. V. Ustyugov (1966), I. I. Smirnov (1967), L. G. Beskrovny (1969), V. V. Mavrodin (1971), M. V. Nechkina (1971), B. A. Romanov (1971), and L. V. Cherepnin (1972). On Russian political and cultural relations with foreign countries one may profitably consult the collections published in the Soviet Union under various similar titles, such as 'Russko-frantsuzskiye svyazi'. See *Russkaya periodicheskaya pechat'* (*1702–1894*) – *Spravochnik* (Moscow, 1959); N. Smirnov-Sokol'sky, *Russkiye literaturnyye al'manakhi i sborniki XVIII–XIX vv.* (Moscow, 1965).

The reign of Peter the Great

See S. F. Platonov, *Lektsii po Russkoy istorii* (St Petersburg, 1904); V. Klyuchevsky, *Peter the Great*, trans. by L. Archibald (New York, 1961); *Rossiya v period reform Petra I* (Moscow, 1973); M. Raeff, ed., *Peter the Great – Reformer or Revolutionary?* (Boston, 1963); 2nd rev. edn, *Peter the Great Changes Russia* (Boston, 1972).

Peter the Great and the expansion of Russia

General

For a general discussion of Russian political and military involvement with other powers, see the following standard works: P. Renouvin, ed., *Histoire des Relations Internationales* (several vols., Paris, 1953ff); *Istoriya Diplomatii* (Moscow, 1941–62); E. Bourgeois, *Manuel Historique de Politique Étrangère* (4 vols., Paris, 1897–1926); also the relevant vols. of the *Cambridge Modern History;* and of *Peuples et Civilisations* (Paris, 1926ff). See also N. E. Saul, *Russia* and the Mediterranean, 1797–1807 (Chicago, 1970), and P. K. Grimsted, *The Foreign Ministers of Alexander I – Political Attitudes and the Conduct of Russian Diplomacy 1801–1825* (Berkeley, 1969).

Petrine diplomacy and foreign policy

The most comprehensive and best up-to-date treatment of the entire reign, particularly good on foreign affairs, is R. Wittram, *Peter I – Czar und Kaiser (Peter der Grosse in Seiner Zeit)* (2 vols., Göttingen, 1964); an excellent concise survey is B. H. Sumner, *Peter the Great and the Emergence of Russia* (London, 1950), and his *Peter the Great and the Ottoman Empire* (Oxford, 1950). More detailed treatments of particular aspects of Petrine diplomacy can be found in the following: S. A. Feygina, *Alandskiy Kongress (Vneshnyaya politika Rossii v kontse Severnoy voyny)* (Moscow, 1959); L. A. Nikiforov, *Russko-angliyskiye otnosheniya pri Petre I* (Moscow, 1950), the same author's *Vneshnyaya politika Rossii v posledniye gody Severnoy voyny i Nishtadtskiy mir* (Moscow, 1959); W. Mediger, *Moskaus Weg nach Europa* (Braunschweig, 1952), which transcends the chronological limits of Peter's reign. For general characterization of the Russian imperial policy see M. Raeff, 'Patterns of Russian Imperial Policy Toward the Nationalities', in E. Allworth, ed., *Soviet Nationality Problems* (New York, 1971), esp. pp. 22–42 and the bibliography.

Baltic expansion

Apart from the general works already noted, useful studies are: I. Zutis, *Ostzeyskiy vopros v XVIII veke* (Riga, 1946); R. Wittram, *Baltische Geschichte – Grundzüge und Durchblicke* (Darmstadt, 1973); and G. von Rauch, *Russland – Staatliche Einheit und nationale Vielfalt* (Munich, 1953).

Expansion into the Ukraine

W. E. D. Allen, *The Ukraine: A History* (Cambridge, 1940); M. Hrushevsky, *A History of the Ukraine* (New Haven, 1941); for the Soviet viewpoint, *Istoriya Ukrainskoy SSR* (2 vols., Kiev, 1956). The best treatment of social trends is V. A. Myakotin, *Ocherki sotsial'noy istorii Ukrainy XVII–XVIII vv.* (3 vols., Prague, 1926). On agrarian settlement in the region in the eighteenth century see N. D. Polons'ka–Vasylenko, 'The Settlement of the Southern Ukraine', *Annals of the Ukrainian Academy of Arts and Sciences in the U.S.*, IV, V (Summer–Fall, 1955); and H. Auerbach, *Die Besiedelung der Südukraine in den Jahren 1774–1787* (wiesbaden, 1965).

Expansion to the Crimea and the Black Sea

M. Raeff, 'The Style of Russia's Imperial Policy and Prince G. A. Potemkin', in G. N. Grob, ed., *Statesmen and Statescraft of the Modern West* (Barrie, Mass., 1967), 1–51 which cites the relevant literature. Also see T. Adamczyk, *Fürst G. A. Potemkin (Untersuchungen zu seiner Lebensgeschichte* (Emsdetten, 1936). On the incorporation of south Russia see the very important, although incomplete magisterial study of B. Nolde, *La Formation de l'Empire Russe – Études, Notes, Documents* (2 vols., Paris, 1952–3) – the second vol. is relevant in this context; also see E. I. Druzhinina, *Severnoye Prichernomor'e v 1775–1800 gg.* (Moscow, 1959); and *Yuzhnaya Ukraina v 1800–1825 gg.* (Moscow, 1970). For the political background of the incorporation, see E. I. Druzhinina, *Kyuchuk-Kainardzhiyskiy mir 1774 (yego podgotovka i zaklyucheniye)* (Moscow, 1955). For a comprehensive history of the Don Cossacks, see S. G. Svatikov, *Rossiya i*

Don, 1549–1917 (Belgrade, 1924); the economic and social picture is stressed by V. A. Golobutsky, *Zaporozhskoye kazachestvo* (Kiev, 1957), and his *Chernomorskoye kazachestvo* (Kiev, 1956). A detailed study is to be found in A. W. Fisher, *The Russian Annexation of the Crimea, 1772–1783* (Cambridge, 1970).

Russian involvement in the Balkans

For a bibliography and general introduction to the field, see L. S. Stavrianos, *The Balkans Since 1453* (New York, 1958); and the older work by E. Driault, *La question d'Orient depuis ses origines jusqu'à nos jours* (Paris, 1914); briefer treatments are to be found in the standard works listed under 'General' in this section.

Penetration of the Caucasus

A good introduction to the history of this period is D. M. Lang, *The Last Years of the Georgian Monarchy, 1658–1832* (New York, 1957); the military side is well described by J. F. Baddeley, *The Russian Conquest of the Caucasus* (London, 1908); economic and social aspects are emphasized by A. V. Fadeyev, *Rossiya i Kavkaz v pervoy treti XIX v.* (Moscow, 1960).

Expansion into Siberia and the Far East

Bibliographical guidance is given by R. J. Kerner, *North-Eastern Asia: A Selected Bibliography* (Berkeley, 1939); a general, if dated survey is F. A. Golder, *Russian Expansion in the Pacific, 1641–1850* (Cleveland, 1914); for the history of Russian geographic explorations in the north-eastern Pacific see the useful introductory sketch by A. V. Yefimov, *Iz istorii Russkikh ekspeditsiy na Tikhom okeane* (Moscow, 1948); and the very suggestive study that has more implications than its title suggests, J. R. Gibson, *Feeding the Russian Fur Trade – Provisionment of the Okhotsk Seaboard and the Kamchatka Peninsula 1639–1856* (Madison, 1969); also the works of the historical geographer L. S. Berg. The standard history of the Russo-American Company is available in English: S. Okun', *The American–Russian Company* (Cambridge, Mass., 1951); the official biography by I. Barsukov, *Graf Nikolay Nikolayevich Murav'yov-Amursky* (2 vols., Moscow, 1891) has not been superseded and contains much documentary material. The establishment of an administrative structure for the area is discussed in M. Raeff, *Siberia and the Reforms of 1822* (Seattle, 1956). For the smaller nationality groups on the eastern frontier and in Siberia consult the Soviet histories of the relevant Soviet republics and autonomous regions, e.g. *Kazakhsko-russkiye otnosheniya v XVIII–XIX vekakh* (Alma Ata, 1964); *Istoriya Yakutskoy ASSR* (Moscow, 1957–63); *Materialy po istorii Bashkirskoy ASSR* (Moscow, 1955–6); and the vols. of the series *Sibir' perioda feodalizma – Materialy po istorii Sibiri* (Novosibirsk, 1962ff).

Russia and Poland

The best overall introduction to all problems of Polish history is the *Cambridge History of Poland* (2 vols., Cambridge, 1941–50); see also A. Gieysztor, S. Kieniewicz, E. Rostworowski, J. Tazbir, and H. Wereszycki, *History of Poland* (Warsaw, 1968). The diplomacy of the partitions is best described in H. Kaplan, *The First Partition of Poland* (New York, 1961) and R. H. Lord, *The Second Partition of Poland* (Cambridge, Mass., 1915).

GUIDE TO FURTHER READING

Finland

The primary document is available in French: *La Constitution du Grand Duché de Finlande* (Paris, 1900) and discussed by Wol'f von der Osten Sacken, *The Legal Position of the Grand Duchy of Finland in the Russian Empire* (London, 1912), and P. Scheibert, 'Die Anfänge der finnischen Staatswerdung unter Alexander I', *Jahrbücher für Geschichte Osteuropas*, IV, 3–4 (1939). The history of Finland under Russian rule is best summarized in M. G. Schybergson, *Politische Geschichte Finnlands 1809–1919* (Gotha–Stuttgart, 1925).

The Modernization of the military and its role in foreign affairs

The overall history of the military establishment in the eighteenth century is well presented in L. G. Beskrovny, *Russkaya armiya i flot v XVIII veke (ocherki)* (Moscow, 1958); and *Russkaya armiya i flot v XIX veke* (Moscow, 1973); further guidance to the literature on military matters is to be found in L. G. Beskrovny, *Ocherki po istochnikovedeniyu voyennoy istorii Rossii* (Moscow, 1957), his *Ocherki voyennoy istoriografii Rossii* (Moscow, 1962); see also *Russkaya voyennaya periodicheskaya pechat' (1702–1916) – Bibliograficheskiy ukazatel'* (Moscow, 1959); M. Lyons, *The Russian Imperial Army – A Bibliography of Regimental Histories and Related Works*, in the *Hoover Institution Bibliographical Series*, XXXV (Stanford, 1968). The main military figures of the eighteenth and early nineteenth centuries have been the subject of multi-volume collections of documents in recent years. For the War of 1812, whose anniversary celebrations gave rise to much valuable literature (with references to previous sources and studies), see M. Raeff, 'The 150th Anniversary of the Campaign of 1812 in Soviet Historical Writing', *Jahrbücher für Geschichte Osteuropas*, XII, 2 (1964). For the military as a 'rational' institution, see M. Raeff, 'L'État, le gouvernement et la tradition politique en Russie impériale avant 1861', *Revue d'Histoire Moderne et Contemporaine*, Oct.–Dec. 1962, and, by the same author, *Origins of the Russian Intelligentsia: The 18th Century Nobility* (New York, 1966).

Peter the Great and the modernization of government

B. I. Syromyatnikov, *'Regulyarnoye' gosudarstvo Petra Pervogo i yego ideologiya*, I (Moscow–Leningrad, 1943) is the fullest account of foreign intellectual influences. The best general statement is to be found in the first section of the first chapter of M. Bogoslovsky, *Oblastnaya reforma Petra Velikogo: provintsiya 1719–1727 goda* (Moscow, 1902); a more cursory survey from the Soviet point of view is in N. F. Demidova, 'Byurokratizatsiya gosudarstvennogo apparata absolyutizma v XVII–XVIII vv.', in *Absolyutizm v Rossii (XVII–XVIII vv.)* (Moscow, 1964). See also Wittram, *Peter I – Czar und Kaiser* and V. Klyuchevsky, *Peter the Great* (New York, 1961). For the implications in economic life, and a somewhat dissenting opinion, see P. N. Milyukov, *Gosudarstvennoye khozyaystvo v Rossii v pervoy chetverti XVIII stoletiya i reforma Petra Velikogo*, 2nd edn (St Petersburg, 1905). The documentation for the history of several seminal acts is well traced in N. Voskresensky, ed., *Zakonodatel'nyye akty Petra I*, vol. I, *Akty o vysshikh gosudarstvennykh ustanovleniyakh* (Moscow–Leningrad, 1945); also K. A. Sofronenko, ed., *Pamyatniki Russkogo prava*, vol. VIII (Moscow, 1961). A repertory guide for the evolution of the main government institutions in

187

the eighteenth century is provided by A. V. Chernov, ed., *Gosudarstvennyye uchrezhdeniya Rossii v XVIII veke (zakonodatel'nyye materialy)* – *Spravochnoye posobiye* (Moscow, 1960); see also E. Amburger, *Geschichte der Behördenorganisation Russlands von Peter dem Grossen bis 1917*, vol. x of *Studien zur Geschichte Osteuropas* (Leiden, 1966). An historical treatment may also be found in the most important and best histories of Russian public law: N. M. Korkunov, *Russkoye gosudarstvennoye pravo*, 4th edn (2 vols., St Petersburg, 1901); G. V. Vernadsky, *Ocherk istorii prava Russkogo gosudarstva XVIII–XIX vv.* (Prague, 1924); the Soviet approach is in S. V. Yushkov, *Istoriya gosudarstva i prava SSSR*, vol. I (Moscow, 1950); and N. Yeroshkin, *Istoriya gosudarstvennykh uchrezhdeniy dorevolyutsionnoy Rossii* (Moscow, 1968). A succinct summary can be found in S. Blanc 'La Pratique de l'administration russe dans la première moitié du XVIIIe siècle', *Revue d'Histoire Moderne et Contemporaine*, 1961.

The Senate has been the subject of a large history published on the occasion of its second centenary: S. F. Platonov, ed., *Istoriya Pravitel'stvuyushchego Senata za dvesti let* (St Petersburg, 1901). For the Senate's fate immediately after Peter's death, see A. N. Filippov, *Pravitel'stvuyushchiy Senat pri Petre Velikom i yego blizhayshikh preyemnikakh 1711–1741* (St Petersburg, 1911). For details of the political police established by Peter, see N. B. Golikova, 'Organy politicheskogo syska i ikh razvitiy v XXVII–XVIII vv.', in *Absolyutizm v Rossii* (Moscow, 1964), which refers to much of the earlier literature. For the Third Section of Nicholas I, see S. Monas, *The Third Section: Police and Society in Russia under Nicholas I* (Cambridge, Mass., 1961); also P. Squire, *The Third Department* (Cambridge, 1968); and L. Luig, *Zur Geschichte des russischen Innenministeriums unter Nikolaus I, Veröffentl. des Osteuropa-Instituts-München*, no. 32 (Wiesbaden, 1968). The history of the palace *coups* is best summarized in K. Stählin, *Geschichte Russlands*, vol. II (Berlin, 1930).

Administration and politics after the death of Peter the Great

The history of the Supreme Privy Council is summarized topical.· by B. L. Vyazemsky, *Verkhovnyy Taynyy Sovet* (St Petersburg, 1909), and the minutes of its meetings are published in the *Sbornik Imperatorskogo Russkogo Istoricheskogo Obshchestva*, vols. 55, 56, 63, 69, 79, 84, 94, 101. See also W. Slany, 'Russian Central Government Institutions, 1725–41' (unpubl. Ph.D. diss., Cornell Univ., 1958). The reign of Anna has been 'rehabilitated' somewhat by A. Lipski, 'A Re-examination of the "Dark Era" of Anna Ioannovna', *American Slavic and East European Review*, xv (Dec. 1956); a more thorough study of the reign and its institutions is to be found in V. Stroyev, *Bironovshchina i kabinet ministrov* (St Petersburg, 1909–10), and the minutes of the cabinet are in *Sbornik Imperatorskogo Russkogo Istoricheskogo Obshchestva*, vols. 104, 106, 108, 111, 114, 117, 120, 124, 126, 130, 138, 146. The supervisory functions of the procurator general are examined in several works: A. D. Gradovsky, 'Vysshaya administratsiya Rossii XVIII stoletiya i General Prokurory', in *Sobraniye sochineniy A. D. Gradovskogo*, vol. I (St Petersburg, 1899) is a classic. A more recent account is in V. I. Veretennikov, *Ocherki istorii General Prokuratury v Rossii do-Yekaterininskogo vremeni* (Khar'kov, 1915). From a narrow juridical point of view the whole question has been dealt with by S. A. Korf, *Administrativnaya yustitsiya v Rossii*, book I (St Petersburg, 1910). A useful introduction, with good bibliography, is Friedhelm B. Kaiser, *Die russische Justizreform von 1864*, vol. XIV of *Studien zur Geschichte*

GUIDE TO FURTHER READING

Osteuropas (Leiden, 1972); and the idiosyncratic interpretation of G. L. Yaney, *The Systematization of Russian Government – Social Evolution in the Domestic Administration of Imperial Russia, 1711–1905* (Urbana, 1973).

Institutional reforms and the development of a bureaucracy

A useful introduction to the question of the imperial council is to be found in S. O. Schmidt, 'La politique du tsarisme au milieu du XVIII° siècle', *Annales: Economies, Sociétés, Civilisations*, XXI, I (Jan.–Feb. 1966). The project of Panin (and general discussion of the problem of communications in the imperial administration) are discussed in M. Raeff, *Plans for Political Reforms in Imperial Russia 1730–1905* (Englewood Cliffs, 1966). For a positive assessment of Paul's reign, see M. V. Klochkov, *Ocherki pravitel'stvennoy deyatel'nosti vremeni Pavla I* (Petrograd, 1916), and the special issue on Paul I, *Canadian–American Slavic Studies*, VII, 1 (Spring 1973). For changes in administrative policy, see M. Raeff, 'Le Climat politique et les projets de réforme dans les premières années du règne d'Alexander I°ʳ', *Cahiers du Monde russe et soviétique*, II (Oct.–Dec. 1961). For a general interpretative survey of the reign of Alexander I, see A. McConnell, *Tsar Alexander I – Paternalistic Reformer* (New York, 1970), with an excellent critical biography. The abolition of the colleges and the establishment of monocratic ministries are discussed in more detail in M. Raeff, *M. M. Speransky – Statesman of Imperial Russia*, 2nd edn (The Hague, 1968), where further bibliographical indications may be found. Most of the ministries had a history of their activities published on the occasion of the centenary of their organization in 1902. The text of Speransky's reform plan of 1809 is included in S. N. Valk, ed., *M. M. Speransky – Proyekty i zapiski* (Moscow–Leningrad, 1961); an analysis of the proposals can be found in M. Raeff, *M. M. Speransky* (The Hague, 1968).

The reign of Nicholas

The reign of Nicholas I has been the subject of several recent studies. See N. V. Riasanovsky, *Nicholas I and Official Nationality in Russia 1825–55* (Berkeley, 1959); C. de Grünwald, *Tsar Nicholas I* (London, 1954), which gives the portrait of the man; S. Monas, *The Third Section: Police and Society in Russia under Nicholas I* (Cambridge, Mass., 1961); the best short account is still M. Polievktov, *Nikolay I – Biografiya i obzor tsarstvovaniya* (Moscow, 1918); see also P. Squire, *The Third Department* (Cambridge, 1968).

Church and state

The most comprehensive account of the Russian Church since Peter the Great is I. Smolitsch, *Geschichte der russischen Kirche* (vol. I, Leiden, 1964, no more published), which has the most comprehensive and useful bibliography on the question. A briefer survey covering the entire history of the Russian Church is A. M. Ammann, *Abriss der ostslawischen Kirchengeschichte* (Vienna, 1950). An original interpretation is by A. V. Kartashov, *Ocherki po istorii Russkoy tserkvi* (2 vols., Paris, 1959), which, however, only covers the period up to 1800. Peter's administrative innovations are described and summarized in James Cracraft, *The Church Reform of Peter the Great* (Stanford, 1971), and the text of the Spiritual Regulation is now available in English: A. V. Muller, *The*

Spiritual Regulation of Peter the Great, Publications on Russia and Eastern Europe of the Institute for Comparative and Foreign Area Studies, no. 3 (Seattle, 1972).

Provincial and local government and administration

There is very little available, apart from the following two weighty monographs for eighteenth-century developments: M. Bogoslovsky, *Oblastnaya reforma Petra Velikogo: Provintsiya 1719–1727 goda* (Moscow, 1902); Yu. V. Got'e, *Istoriya oblastnogo upravleniya ot Petra I do Yekateriny II* (2 vols., Moscow, 1913, 1941). The reforms of Catherine II are sketchily treated by V. A. Grigor'yev, *Reformy oblastnogo upravleniya pri Yekaterine II* (St Petersburg, 1910). The office of governor is discussed by I. Blinov, *Gubernatory – Istoriko-yuridicheskiy ocherk* (St Petersburg, 1905). A most important contribution to the history of Russian local administration is the study by S. F. Starr, *Decentralization and Self-Government in Russia, 1830–1870* (Princeton, 1972). Yaney, *Systematization of Russian Government*, makes some useful and suggestive observations. The monograph by S. A. Korf, *Dvoryanstvo i yego soslovnoye upravleniye za stoletiye 1762–1855* (St Petersburg, 1906) treats in detail the institutions of the nobility and their elected officials in the provinces. From the point of view of the nobility as a class, the matter is discussed in detail on the basis of the legislation by A. Romanovich-Slavatinsky, *Dvoryanstvo v Rossii ot nachala XVIII veka do otmeny krepostnogo prava*, 2nd edn (Kiev, 1912); and on the implication of the statutes of 1775 and 1785 for the nobility see R. E. Jones, *The Emancipation of the Russian Nobility 1762–1785* (Princeton, 1973). See also the relevant sections in P. Dukes, *Catherine the Great and the Russian Nobility* (Cambridge, 1967). Proposals for administrative reform in the time of Alexander I are dealt with by M. Raeff, *Plans for Political Reform in Imperial Russia 1730–1905* (Englewood Cliffs, 1966); and G. Vernadsky, *La charte constitutionnelle de l'empire russe de l'an 1820* (Paris, 1933).

A comprehensive survey of the bureaucracy in the first half of the nineteenth century, which also sheds light on the preceding period, is to be found in H.-J. Torke, *Das russische Beamtentum in der ersten Hälfte des 19. Jahrhunderts*, vol. 13 of *Forschungen zur osteuropäischen Geschichte* (Berlin, 1967), 7–345. See also an interpretative essay by M. Raeff, 'The Russian Autocracy and its Officials', *Harvard Slavic Studies*, IV (1957). A Soviet summary interpretation is to be found in N. F. Demidova, 'Byurokratizatsiya gosudarstvennogo apparata absolyutizma v XVII–XVIII vv.', in *Absolyutizm v Rossii (XVII–XVIII vv.)* (Moscow, 1964). Early nineteenth-century attempts at improvements in the bureaucracy are dealt with in H.-J. Torke, *Das russische Beamtentum*, and B. Lincoln, 'N. Miliutin and the Reform of the Municipal Government of St Petersburg' (unpubl. Ph.D. diss., Univ. Chicago, 1966).

Codification of the laws

For the codification commissions in the eighteenth century, see V. N. Latkin, *Zakonodatel'nyye kommissii v Rossii v XVIII v.* (St Petersburg, 1887). Catherine's commission is discussed from the point of view of the urban population in a significant little study by Fr.-X. Coquin, *La Grande Commission législative (1767–1768) – les cahiers de doléances urbains (Province de Moscou)*, Publications de la Faculté des Lettres et Sciences Humaines de Paris–Sorbonne, série 'Recherches', no. 67 (Paris–Louvain, 1972). A fuller bibliography on the question is to be found in M. Raeff, *M. M. Speransky – Statesman of Imperial Russia* (The Hague, 1968); see also P. Dukes, *Catherine the Great and the Russian Nobility* (Cambridge, 1967).

Economic reforms

The standard survey of the subject is P. I. Lyashchenko, *Istoriya narodnogo khozyaystva SSSR* (2 vols., Moscow, 1947–8), which is also available in English, *History of the National Economy of Russia to the 1917 Revolution* (New York, 1949); A. I. Pashkov, ed., *Istoriya Russkoy ekonomicheskoy mysli* (2 vols. in 4 pts., Moscow, 1955–9), also available in English as *A History of Russian Economic Thought: Ninth through Eighteenth Centuries* (Berkeley, 1964). See also the articles contained in S. G. Strumilin, *Ocherki ekonomicheskoy istorii Rossii i SSSR* (Moscow, 1966) and in the very handy volume W. L. Blackwell, ed., *Russian Economic Development from Peter the Great to Stalin* (New York, 1974). A very good summary of Peter's policies and ideas is to be found in S. Blanc, 'La politique économique de Pierre le Grand', *Cahiers du Monde russe et soviétique*, III (Jan.–Mar. 1962), where the relevant recent Soviet literature is cited. Also, of course, P. N. Milyukov, *Gosudarstvennoye khozyaystvo v Rossii v pervoy chetverti XVIII stoletiya i reforma Petra Velikogo* (St Petersburg, 1905). State initiatives in economic development are dealt with in M. Tugan-Baranovsky, *Russkaya fabrika v proshlom i nastoyashchem*, vol. 1, 7th edn (Moscow, 1938), of which a German translation is also available; P. Lyubomirov, *Ocherki po istorii russkoy promyshlennosti* (Moscow, 1947); A. Kahan, 'Continuity in Economic Activity and Policy during the Post Petrine Period in Russia', *Journal of Economic History*, XXV (1965), 61–85. A Gerschenkron, *Europe in the Russian Mirror. Four Lectures in Economic History* (Cambridge, 1970) presents a stimulating and informative discussion on the role of mercantilist state policies in the development and modernization of Russia's economy. Russian policy of encouraging private enterprise, while taking the lead in the newest projects, is dealt with in W. M. Pintner, 'Government and Industry during the Ministry of Count Kankrin, 1823–44', *American Quarterly of Soviet and East European Studies* XXIII, I (Mar. 1964). The unpublished dissertations by R. Haywood (on railway construction) and H. Repczuk (on Count Mordvinov) at Columbia Univ. are relevant in this connection. See also W. L. Blackwell, *The Beginnings of Russian Industrialization, 1800–1860* (Princeton, 1968). The decline of the iron industry is analysed in R. Portal, *L'Oural au XVIIIe siècle* (Paris, 1950).

Peasant economy and society

For a general introduction see J. Blum, *Lord and Peasant in Russia from the Ninth to the Nineteenth Century* (Princeton, 1961). The most perceptive analysis of the lord–serf relationship, as well as of the mentality of the Russian serf-owner, is by M. Confino, *Domaines et seigneurs en Russie vers la fin du XVIIIe siècle* (Paris, 1963), where one will also find references to articles by the same author on particular aspects of the subject. The Russian classic is by V. Semevsky, *Krest'yane v tsarstvovaniye Imperatritsy Yekateriny II* (2 vols., St Petersburg, 1901–3), while the most recent and best Soviet study is N. L. Rubinshteyn, *Sel'skoe khozyaystvo Rossii vo vtoroy polovine XVIII v.* (Moscow, 1957). A survey of recent discussions and literature is contained in M. Laran, 'Nobles et paysans en Russie, de l'age d'or du servage à son abolition 1762–1861', *Annales: Economies, Sociétés, Civilisations*, XXI, I (Jan.–Feb. 1966); also I. D. Koval'chenko, *Russkoye krepostnoye krest'yanstvo v pervoy polovine XIX v.* (Moscow, 1967). Much valuable material and many suggestive observations on the peasantry in general are to be culled from the impressive monograph by Fr.-X. Coquin, *La Sibérie – Peuplement et immigration paysanne au XIXe siècle* (Paris, 1969). The impact of the landlord–serf relationship on contemporary attitudes to economic efficiency and progress is examined in A. Gerschenkron, 'The Problem of Economic Development in Russian Intellectual History of the 19th Century', in E. J. Simmons, ed., *Continuity and Change in Russian and Soviet Thought* (Cambridge, Mass., 1955). M. Confino, *Systèmes agraires et progrès agricole. L'assolement triennal en Russie aux XVIIIe–XIXe siècles*, vol. XIV of *Études sur l'histoire, l'économie et la sociologie des pays slaves* (Paris–The Hague, 1969) discusses the implication of agricultural techniques for social configurations and resistance to economic modernization. For the peasantry as a social class, see P. K. Alefirenko, *Krest'yanskoye dvizheniye i krest'yanskiy vopros v Rossii v 30–50kh godakh XVIII veka* (Moscow, 1958); N. M. Druzhinin, *Gosudarstvennyye krest'yane i reforma P. D. Kiselyova* (2 vols., Moscow–Leningrad, 1946–58); see also the very informative work of G. T. Robinson, *Rural Russia under the Old Regime* (New York, 1949), which, although focusing on a different period, also throws considerable light on the period under review.

Fiscal policy and trade

The literature on this question is somewhat dated: see I. S. Blyokh, *Finansy Rossii XIX stoletiya* (St Petersburg, 1899); N. Brzhesky, *Gosudarstvennyye dolgi Rossii* (St Petersburg, 1884). Some useful information is in P. A. Khromov, *Ekonomicheskoye razvitiye Rossii v XIX–XX vekakh* (Moscow, 1956); P. I. Lyashchenko, *Istoriya narodnogo khozyaystva SSSR* (Moscow, 1947–8); S. M. Troitsky, *Finansovaya politika Russkogo absolyutizma v XVIII veke* (Moscow, 1966); W. M. Pintner, *Russian Economic Policy under Nicholas I* (Ithaca, 1967). Taxes on the urban sector have recently been summarized by Yu. R. Klokman, 'Gorod v zakonodatel'stve Russkogo absolyutizma vo vtoroy polovine XVII–XVIII vv.', in *Absolyutizm v Rossii* (Moscow, 1964). The standard monograph is A. A. Kizevetter, *Posadskaya obshchina v Rossii XVIII st.* (Moscow, 1903); see also W. L. Blackwell, *The Beginnings of Russian Industrialization 1800–1860* (Princeton, 1968).

For an overall survey of the history of Russian trade see I. M. Kulisher, *Istoriya Russkoy torgovli do devyatnadtsatogo veka vklyuchitel'no* (St Petersburg, 1923); and the classic N. N. Firsov, *Pravitel'stvo i obshchestvo v ikh otnosheniyakh k vneshney torgovle Rossii v tsarstvovaniye imperatritsy Yekateriny II. Ocherki iz istorii torgovoy politiki* (Kazan', 1902, repr. Cambridge, 1972). Much useful material on the subject is in C. Foust. *Russians and Manchurians* (Durham, N.C. 1972). For attempts at currency stabilization see W. M. Pintner, *Russian Economic Policy under Nicholas I* (Ithaca, 1967). The change in trade patterns as a factor in the diplomatic relationship between Russia and the European powers has been most suggestively worked out by D. Gerhard, *England und der Aufstieg Russlands* (Munich–Berlin, 1933). With reference to specific developments in the Black Sea, see the three works by H. Halm, *Donauschiffahrt und -Handel nach dem Südosten* (Breslau, 1943); *Habsburgischer Osthandel im 18. Jahrh.* (Munich, 1954); *Gründung und erstes Jahrzehnt von Festung und Stadt Cherson* (Wiesbaden, 1961).

GUIDE TO FURTHER READING

Social classes

Population growth and social classes

For general demographic information for the period see V. E. Den, *Naseleniye Rossii po pyatoy revizii. Podushnaya podat' v XVIII v. i statistika naseleniya v kontse XVIII v.* (Moscow, 1902); V. M. Kabuzan, *Narodonaseleniye Rossii v XVIII – pervoy polovine XIX v. (po materialam revizii)* (Moscow, 1963), and his essential *Izmeneniya v razmeshchenii naseleniya Rossii v XVIII – pervoy polovine XIX v. (po materialam revizii)* (Moscow, 1971).

The urban classes

A general survey is by P. G. Ryndzyunsky, *Gorodskoye grazhdanstvo doreformennoy Rossii* (Moscow, 1958); A. A. Kizevetter, *Posadskaya obshchina v Rossii XVIII st.* (Moscow, 1903) is also relevant here, as is Coquin, *La Grande Commission législative*. The Charter to the Towns has been thoroughly analysed and its sources traced by A. A. Kizevetter, *Gorodovoye polozheniye Yekateriny II 1785 goda* (Moscow, 1909). For more popular, general accounts, see P. A. Berlin, *Russkaya burzhuaziya v staroye i novoye vremya* (Moscow, 1922); and V. Bill, *The Forgotten Class: The Russian Bourgeoisie from the Earliest Beginnings to 1900* (New York, 1959). On the demographic side, the complexities (as well as the evidence) are illustrated by V. M. Kabuzan, *Narodonaseleniye Rossii v XVIII – pervoy polovine XIX v.* (Moscow, 1963); and the more recent *Izmeneniya v razmeshchenii naseleniya Rossii* (Moscow, 1971).

The church as a social class

The definition of the *raznochintsy*, and its evolution, have been well stated by C. Becker, '*Raznochintsy*: The Development of the Word and of the Concept', *American Slavic and East European Review*, XVIII, 1 (Feb. 1959). Also see the original analysis of the clergy as a social class by G. L. Freeze, 'The Russian Parish Clergy: Vladimir Province in the 18th Century (unpubl. Ph.D. diss., Columbia Univ., 1972).

Social class among the minority ethnic groups

For general accounts see B. Nolde, *La Formation de l'empire russe* (Paris, 1952–3); M. Raeff, *Siberia and the Reforms of 1882* (Seattle, 1956); and the now very numerous Soviet histories of the constituent republics and their peoples.

Education – the westernization of the Russian nobility

The general histories in English on Russian education should be used with caution: N. Hans, *History of Russian Educational Policy* (London. 1931); W. H. E. Johnson, *Russia's Educational Heritage* (Pittsburgh, 1950). The most complete monographic treatment is S. Rozhdestvensky, *Ocherki po istorii sistem narodnogo prosveshcheniya v Rossii v XVIII–XIX vv.* (St Petersburg, 1912); for a treatment within a broader cultural and social framework, see P. Milyukov, *Ocherki po istorii Russkoy kul'tury* (3 vols., Paris, 1937), esp. vol. II, pt. 2, and vol. III. An extension of the treatment presented in the text is to be found in M. Raeff, *Origins of the Russian Intelligentsia* (New York, 1966); also M. Raeff, 'Les slaves, les allemands et les "lumières" ', *Revue Canadienne d'Études Slaves*, I, 4 (Winter 1967). Peter's plans for the westernization of cultural life in Russia receive their most recent treatment in English in A. Vucinich, *Science in Russian Culture - A History to 1860* (Stanford, 1963). See also, more specifically, *Istoriya Akademii nauk SSSR* (3 vols., Moscow–Leningrad, 1958–64 – the 3rd vol. on the Soviet period has not yet appeared); M. N. Tikhomirov, ed., *Istoriya Moskovskogo universiteta* (Moscow, 1955); M. J. Okenfuss, 'The Jesuit Origins of Petrine Education', and 'Russian Students in Europe in the Age of Peter the Great', in J. Garrard, ed., *The Eighteenth Century in Russia* (Oxford, 1973); J. T. Flynn, 'The Universities in the Russia of Alexander I' (unpubl. Ph.D. diss., Clark Univ., 1964). For church involvement in the process of cultural westernization, see I. Smolitsch, *Geschichte der russischen Kirche* (Leiden, 1964), which gives all the relevant bibliography; a shorter list is included in Raeff, *M. M. Speransky*. Modernization of the ecclesiastical system of education is dealt with in G. Bissonnette, 'Pufendorf and the Church Reforms of Peter the Great' (unpubl. Ph.D. diss., Columbia Univ., 1962). For related questions, see also J. Cohen Zacek, 'The Russian Bible Society' (unpubl. Ph.D. diss., Columbia Univ., 1964).

Conflict between the state and the nobility

E. F. Shmurlo, *Pyotr Velikiy v otsenke sovremennikov i potomstva* (St Petersburg, 1912) gives examples, as well as a bibliography, of the literature in the eighteenth century. Wittram, *Peter I - Czar und Kaiser* presents a thoughtful and balanced discussion of the Alexis affair. The 1730 demands of the nobility, together with documents and a full bibliography, are included in M. Raeff, *Plans for Political Reform in Imperial Russia 1730–1905* (Englewood Cliffs, 1966). Nineteenth-century tensions between nobility and state are treated in some detail in Raeff, *Plans for Political Reform* and in his 'Le climat politique et les projets de réforme dans les premières années du règne d'Alexandre Ier', and his *M. M. Speransky*. In English there is a summary history of the Decembrist episode in A. G. Mazour, *The First Russian Revolution 1825 - The Decembrist Movement, its Origins, Development and Significance* (Berkeley, 1937; repr. 1962 and 1966). For excerpts of documents and further bibliographical references, see M. Raeff, *The Decembrist Movement* (Englewood Cliffs, 1966); and for the cultural and psychological framework of noble oppositionist attitudes see M. Raeff, 'Russian Youth on the Eve of Romanticism: Andrei I. Turgenev and His Circle', in A. and J. Rabinowitch, eds., *Revolution and Politics in Russia - Essays in Memory of B. I. Nicolaevsky* (Bloomington, 1972).

The state and the peasantry

See P. K. Alefirenko, *Krest'yanskoe dvizheniye i krest'yanskiy vopros v Rossii v 30–50kh godakh XVIII veka* (Moscow, 1958); documents on the Bulavin rebellion are in *Bulavinskoye vosstaniye 1707–1708* (Moscow, 1935); the Pugachev rebellion is the subject of a monumental monograph by V. V. Mavrodin, *Krest'yanskaya voyna v Rossii v 1773–75 godakh - Vosstaniye Pugachova* (3 vols., Leningrad, 1961–70); D. Peters, *Politische und gesellschaftliche Vorstellungen in der Aufstandsbewegung unter Pugačev (1773–1775)* (Wiesbaden, 1973); J. T. Alexander, *Autocratic Politics in a National Crisis. The Imperial Russian Government and Pugachev's Revolt 1773–1775, Russian and East European Series*, no. 38 (Bloomington, 1969); M. Raeff, 'Pugachev's Rebellion', in R. Foster and J. P. Greene, eds., *Preconditions of Revolution in Early Modern Europe* (Baltimore, 1970); documents and a calendar of peasant unrest are contained in N. M. Druzhinin, ed., *Krest'yanskoye dvizheniye v Rossii v XIX – nachale XX veka* (Moscow, 1961).

For state concern over the plight of the peasantry, see the classic monograph by V. I. Semevsky, *Krest'yanskiy vopros v Rossii v XVIII i pervoy polovine XIX veka* (2 vols., St Petersburg, 1888). A useful summary is in vol. I of *Velikaya reforma* (Moscow, 1911). For a positive revision of Paul I's reign, see M. V. Klochkov, *Ocherki pravitel'stvennoy deyatel'nosti vremeni Pavla I* (Petrograd, 1916).

The creation of the military colonies during the reign of Alexander I is dealt with in R. Pipes, 'The Russian Military Colonies, 1810–31', *Journal of Modern History*, XXII, 3 (Sept. 1950); A. D. Ferguson, 'The Russian Military Settlements 1810–1866' (unpubl. Ph.D. diss., Yale Univ., 1954). Reforms in the administration of the state peasants are most comprehensively treated in N. M. Druzhinin, *Gosudarstvennyye krest'yane i reforma P. D. Kiselyova* (Moscow–Leningrad, 1945–58).

The state and religious dissent

The relationship between social tensions amongst the peasantry and religious dissension is discussed in P. Milyukov, *Ocherki po istorii Russkoy kul'tury* (Paris, 1937), particularly vol. II, pt. 1; E. F. Shmurlo, *Pyotr Velikiy v otsenke sovremennikov i potomstva* (St Petersburg, 1912). The most recent histories of dissent and sectarianism are by A. I. Klibanov, *Istoriya religioznogo sektanstva v Rossii* (Moscow, 1965), and R. O. Crummey, *The Old Believers and the World of Anti-Christ, The Vyg Community and the Russian State* (Madison, 1970). A. M. Ammann, *Abriss der ostslawischen Kirchengeschichte* (Vienna, 1950) provides useful bibliographical guidance. For an interesting and perceptive picture of the Catholic influence in the reign of Alexander I, see M. J. Rouët de Journel, *Un collège de Jésuites à Saint-Petersbourg 1800–1816*, 2nd edn (Paris, 1922); also his *Une Russe catholique – la vie de Madame Swetchine 1782–1857* (Paris, 1953). The classic account of the Jews is S. M. Dubnow, *History of the Jews in Russia and Poland* (3 vols., Phila., 1920), particularly vol. I and the first part of vol. II.

Conflicts between the state and minority groups

For details of the Bashkir rebellions, see R. Portal, 'Les Bachkirs et le gouvernement russe au XVIIIe siècle', *Revue des Études Slaves*, XXII (1946); also B. Nolde, *La Formation de l'empire russe – études, notes, documents* (Paris, 1952–3); and N. V. Ustyugov, *Bashkirskoye vosstaniye 1737–1739 gg.* (Moscow–Leningrad, 1950); and the Soviet histories of union republics and autonomous republics, as well as – for broader context and bibliography – the volume edited by E. Allworth, *Soviet Nationality Problems* (New York, 1971).

5

IMPERIAL RUSSIA
ALEXANDER II TO THE REVOLUTION

JOHN KEEP

Russia's defeat in the Crimean War ushered in a period of rapid change that affected profoundly every area of national life. Within a mere sixty years much was done to overcome the country's historic legacy of backwardness – to modernize its economy and to encourage at least some elements in Russian society to take an active part in public affairs. In retrospect, however, it is clear that insufficient action was taken to relieve the serious underlying tensions which afflicted the body politic. The consequence was that, when Russia suffered a major military débâcle during the First World War, the imperial regime collapsed.

The cataclysmic events that followed have naturally influenced historians' judgement on the period. Some have assumed that violent revolution was inevitable, and have taken as their leitmotiv the struggle between the 'reactionary' forces and their 'progressive' opponents, particularly those on the extreme left. Others have emphasized the role of fortuitous factors and claimed that, at least after the constitutional reforms of 1905–6, Russia had taken the road of peaceful evolution toward western European democracy: according to this analysis, only the war placed revolution on the agenda. Both views are exaggerated, but on a long-term view the latter probably comes nearer the truth. The historian can usefully distinguish those phenomena in the period 1855–1917 that affected the shape of the revolution when it came – remembering that Russia's development was complex and contradictory, and that the pace of advance was quicker in some fields than others. The following discussion assumes familiarity with basic chronology and considers in turn the principal problems that faced Russia during the reigns of her last three tsars.

THE BURDENS OF EMPIRE

The international balance of power prevented Russia from making any significant territorial gains in Europe in this era; nor did her leaders actively seek to expand the empire's limits westward. They sought no more than political influence, i.e. to establish 'client states' whose governments would at critical junctures align their foreign policy with that of Russia. This was straightforward nineteenth-century imperialism, much like that practised by other Great Powers. It did, of course, permit her to acquire territory in Asia, to the extent compatible with the colonial ambitions of her rivals. This forward drive owed much to the desire for prestige of rulers, bureaucrats, and particularly military leaders, but it was rationalized by the argument that the empire needed 'firm frontiers' to safeguard its security as well as by appeals to economic interest. Although these views found some eloquent advocates, Russian society generally never developed an elaborate, well-articulated 'imperialist ethos' comparable to that in Great Britain, the power most alarmed by Russian expansion.

Problems of foreign policy can be considered here only in relation to colonial conquests or the development of national movements within the empire or on its perimeter.

Contemporaries were slow to perceive that the wave of nationalist feeling that surged eastward through Europe during the nineteenth century posed a mortal threat to the integrity of an empire in which, by 1914, the dominant 'Great Russian' element comprised a mere 45 per cent of the population. Official *narodnost'* or Great Russian nationalism (see p. 129) was both an exemplar for this movement and a reaction to it. It was a vaguely defined creed, at first respectably camouflaged as Slavophilism or Panslavism, and confined mainly to official circles – although after 1908, as the European diplomatic scene darkened, it won more support from the educated public. The liberal and radical intelligentsia (see pp. 244 ff) was by tradition internationalist in outlook, stoutly opposed to chauvinism, racism, and militarism. Its members rather naïvely assumed that such phenomena were the artefacts of an ill-willed autocratic regime and overlooked their very real *potential* appeal to the masses, once they had been drawn into political activity. Popular nationalism was to become a feature of the post-revolutionary era, and only its first fruits were apparent during this period. If for the Great Russians nationalism was thus above all an 'Establishment doctrine', often tied up with sectional vested interests, the situation was very different in the minority regions. Here nationalist-minded élites arose strong enough to

197

lead their peoples in the struggle for independence and force the imperial officials on the defensive.

RISKS AND OPPORTUNITIES IN EASTERN EUROPE

In south-east Europe the Russians' sentimental interest in their Orthodox and Slav kinsmen, actively promoted by the Panslavs, was on balance less important than their government's concern for political, strategic, and economic advantage. The naval clauses of the Treaty of Paris exposed the Black Sea littoral to the risk of foreign (especially British) attack; and this threat was only partially lessened by the unilateral denunciation of these clauses, effected in 1870 with German diplomatic support. In January 1878, when a British fleet passed through the Dardanelles, danger seemed imminent, but once again Bismarck's intervention proved decisive. Russia's new battleships could dominate the Black Sea, but egress from it depended on Turkey, and thus indirectly on Great Britain. The Straits also were important as a commercial outlet for Russia's grain exports. The idea of bringing them under direct Russian control, however attractive emotionally, was impracticable in view of Russia's strategic inferiority *vis-à-vis* the maritime powers. It was considered, but rejected, by Nicholas II and his advisers in 1896. A more moderate aim was to secure international agreement to a revision of the Straits Convention in Russia's favour. This appeared feasible momentarily in 1908, but was frustrated by Great Power rivalries. It was doubly ironic that in 1915 Russia should have obtained satisfaction of her maximum goal – on paper – from Great Britain, her wartime ally but traditional adversary at the Straits, and that this gain should almost immediately have been nullified by the revolution. This eliminated the commercial motive, since Russia ceased to be a major grain exporter, and caused Britain to reverse her attitude. The strategic importance of the Straits was much attenuated by the development of air transport.

In the Balkans Russian influence, both political and cultural, was strongest among the Bulgarians and Serbs. It was limited by their natural fear of Russia's autocratic government and by her economic backwardness in comparison to the West. Ideologically, western liberalism and democracy had far greater appeal to them than did Panslavism or anything else Russia could offer. On the other hand, ease of linguistic communication made Russia a bridge between Balkan intellectuals and European left-wing thinkers, and in the process their ideas sometimes acquired a distinctive Russian flavour. Socialists such as S. Marković in Serbia, L. Karavelov in Bulgaria, and C. Dobrogeanu-Gherea in Roumania were all to some extent influenced by the Russian revolutionary tradition. A number of Balkan intellectuals obtained their education in Russia, some with the aid of the 'Slavonic Benevolent Committees' set up in four Russian cities between 1858 and 1870, although these bodies were politically conservative. Panslavism, enunciated most clearly by such writers as N. Ya. Danilevsky and General R. A. Fadeyev, exerted some influence on government policy in the 1870s. Individual activists in high places, notably N. P. Ignat'yev, the ambassador in Constantinople, helped to involve Russia in the war with Turkey of 1877–8. But the movement's insubstantiality was demonstrated by its evanescence after the Congress of Berlin, which crushed its adherents' initial high hopes. The crude, egotistical brand of nationalism professed by such publicists as M. N. Katkov or I. S. Aksakov found little public support, and Alexander III's government reverted to a conventional pro-German foreign policy.

In part this was a natural corollary of Russia's setbacks in the independent Balkan states, where her relations with local nationalists took a chequered course. The Roumanians, who had loyally supported her in the Russo-Turkish War, did not relish the loss of territory to their ally, and looked to Vienna and Berlin rather than to St Petersburg. The Bulgarians, who owed their statehood to Russian armed intervention, were unenthusiastic about the military occupation that followed, particularly when Alexander II, who had granted them a liberal constitution, was succeeded by his son. The latter first backed their prince, Alexander of Battenberg, against his subjects and then, when he resisted Russian pressure, intrigued to bring about his overthrow (1886). Diplomatic relations were broken off until the mid 1890s, when Nicholas II's accession helped to effect a reconciliation.

Thereupon Russia sought to ease tensions in the area by collaborating with her chief rival, Austria–Hungary. This policy was somewhat strained by troubles in Macedonia and by the advent to power in Serbia of the Karageorgević dynasty (1903). Events in the Far East temporarily diverted Russia's energies, but in 1908 the problem was forced upon her attention by Austria's annexation of Bosnia and Herzegovina. This was a direct challenge to the national aspirations of the Serbs, who looked to Russia for protection. Nicholas, however, was obliged to yield, for Russia was still too weak, militarily and diplomatically, to face a confrontation with the Central Powers. The most he could do was to strengthen Russian influence in Serbia, Montenegro, and Bulgaria (as well as Greece), and to encourage these states to co-operate politically and militarily. This aim was impeded by their contradictory ambitions. When the bloc was finally formed (1912), Russia soon lost control: it led its member states into war, not with Austria, but with the Turks and later with each other. Neither Russia nor her clients could derive much satisfaction from this experience, and the settlement painfully reached at Bucharest (1913) involved them in further concessions. Bulgaria drifted once again into the orbit of the

Central Powers; even Serbia began to look westward for support rather than to Russia.

All this changed after Sarajevo, when the Central Powers threatened Serbia's very existence as an independent state. This was a challenge that in the existing climate of opinion no Russian government could ignore, even though the empire was unprepared for a major war and was hard pressed to defend itself, let alone its Balkan protégés. Germanophil elements at court warned that the war might lead to the collapse of the monarchy and social revolution. Their advice was reasonable – but unrealistic. The alternative policy, to accept a status of permanent inferiority in a German-dominated Europe, seemed to most Russians unthinkable. Few of them appreciated the catastrophic social impact of twentieth-century warfare; the only honourable course, it seemed, was 'to pick up the gauntlet'. In 1914 such views were common in the ruling circles of all belligerent nations, but Russia was to pay for them more heavily than most.

THE NATIONALIST UPSURGE IN EUROPEAN RUSSIA

Once traditional legitimist notions had been undermined, the autocracy had no creed that could compete with the romantic appeal of nationalism. The fact that many of the subject minorities, for historical reasons, were culturally and politically more advanced than the Great Russians, made the problem of controlling them more difficult. So did their geographical location in border areas that were of potential strategic importance. The imperial authorities were too conventional and unsophisticated to apply the methods of modern dictatorships, involving the systematic mobilization and manipulation of opinion, and when on occasion subordinate officials tried to exploit inter-group tensions they usually failed. The regime had in fact no consistent policy or machinery for dealing with the 'nationalities problem', whose very existence was barely recognized. Efforts at political or religious indoctrination in schools were ridiculously amateur. The police took the over-simple view that any insubordination should be punished, by violence where necessary. This only added to the feeling among the minority peoples that their legitimate basic human rights were endangered by the very existence of the autocratic imperial system.

This was particularly true of the Poles, a nation that had once known independent statehood and possessed a strong sense of ethnic and religious identity. The Polish cause enjoyed the sympathy of liberals and democrats in the West, but the governments of these countries were loath to give the Poles effective material support. The Central Powers, on the other hand, who had Polish minorities of their own to contend with, tended to co-operate with Russia on this question. Symptomatic was the 'Alvensleben Convention', a Russo–Prussian agreement concluded in February 1863 providing for joint action by frontier officials against nationalist guerrillas. This was of some assistance in quelling the insurrection that broke out in that year, although the principal reasons for its defeat lay elsewhere – in the overwhelming military preponderance of the Russians and factionalism among the rebel leaders.

For all its desperate heroism the revolt probably harmed Polish interests. It halted Alexander II's sincere, if clumsy efforts to work out some kind of constitutional compromise. His plan had been to create autonomous central and local government bodies, partly elected and staffed by Poles, under a Russian viceroy, the liberal-minded Grand Duke Constantine. These relatively generous terms did not satisfy even the moderate landowner party, led by A. Zamoyski; the radicals, who drew their support from the urban intelligentsia, wanted an independent sovereign Poland, to include some territory taken from Russia, a widening of the franchise, and far-reaching agrarian reform. These demands were scarcely practicable at the time. Under the repressive military regime imposed after the rising, educated Poles had to abandon such aims and a new mood of 'realism' prevailed. The peasants benefited by a fairly generous land reform (1864) whose object was political: to win their sympathies for Russia and autocracy. In this it failed, since possession of the land helped to strengthen the Polish peasants' national consciousness.

No better success attended the authorities' efforts to Russify the Poles by curtailing their linguistic rights, aligning the educational and judicial systems with those in the rest of the empire, and introducing more Russian officials in the administration, railways, or banks. From the 1870s onward the Polish provinces participated energetically in the development of industry and commerce (see pp. 216 ff). New social classes emerged that could provide a broader base for political opposition movements. The most influential of these now adopted a socialist colouring. The Polish Socialist Party (PPS), founded abroad in 1892, placed national independence in the forefront of its programme. Among its leaders were J. Piłsudski and S. Wojciechowski, who were to achieve prominence when the new Polish state was eventually born. To the left of the PPS stood the followers of Rosa Luxemburg, who in 1899 took the name 'Social Democratic Party of the Kingdom of Poland–Lithuania' (SDKPL). A doctrinaire interpretation of Marxism led them to oppose the slogan of national independence in the interests of rapid economic development and eventual revolution. They also urged close collaboration with Russian socialists. On the right the National Democratic Party of R. Dmowski, founded in 1895, likewise inclined toward Russia, but for a different reason: the belief, by no means ill founded, that repression in Prussian Poland represented a greater

201

threat to the nation's survival than that carried on by officials of the tsar, who were less sophisticated and efficient than either Germans or Poles.

The National Democrats put to good practical use the relative freedom that existed in Austrian Poland (Galicia), which served them (and some other groups) as an operational headquarters. But the Austrians gave them no diplomatic aid, even in 1905 when the tsarist empire was gripped by revolution. Forced to rely mainly on their own resources, all the Polish parties moved to the left, and violence erupted on a major scale. Once again, as in 1863, political differences often impaired collaboration, but there was general agreement on the need for autonomy, even if the detailed provisions aroused controversy. The National Democrats loudly asserted this claim in the first two dumas (see pp. 242–3), where they were able to enlist the sympathies of many Russian liberals; but Stolypin's electoral reform of 1907 muted their voices, and soon reaction set in. Russian Poland had secured a little more freedom in the cultural sphere, and could reasonably hope for further gains in future, since tsarist policy was clearly ineffective. This policy fell between two stools: it was neither conciliatory enough to appeal to the moderates nor firm enough to suppress opposition entirely. Even so national independence and unity for all Poles seemed a far-off dream in 1914. It could be accomplished only if all three partitioning powers obligingly allowed themselves to be defeated in war. This, fortunately for the Poles, they did.

If in Poland the autocracy faced an inherited problem, scarcely soluble by the means at its disposal, in Finland the problem was largely of its own creation. The Finns were fairly content with the autonomous status granted by the settlement of 1809, which offered them safeguards against Swedish domination, and their pro-Russian orientation was strengthened by several wise measures of Alexander II. In 1863 he convened the diet and in 1878 conceded to the Finns an independent national army; economic development and education were promoted with vigour; and use of the Finnish language increased, which encouraged national feeling. Alexander III, however, became alarmed at 'separatist' tendencies, and his successor embarked upon a systematic programme to bolster Russia's supposed imperial interests. A conscription law (1898) imposed upon Finns the same obligations as upon the tsar's Russian subjects, and in the following year the powers of the diet were significantly curtailed. The Finns defended their autonomous status with impressive unanimity. The government replied by suspending the constitution (1903) and ruling the country directly from St Petersburg, whereupon Finnish opposition merged into the general stream of revolutionary unrest. The chief parties were the moderate constitutionalist 'Young Finns' and the Social Democrats. The latter formed the strongest group in the reformed diet that Nicholas II reluctantly conceded in November 1905. Finland now had an institution denied to the rest of the empire: a house of representatives elected on a broad democratic suffrage. But the new arrangements did not work well. The diet's legislative acts required the assent of the more conservative Finnish Senate and, after 1908, of the Russian government as well. The latter dissolved the diet three times in the hope of securing the election of more amenable deputies, and finally suspended it altogether (1910). In these moves the administration had support from Russian nationalist opinion. The Finns concluded that they could win only by adopting more militant policies, and some of them looked for aid to Germany. The outbreak of war distracted the government's attention and placed national independence on the agenda.

South of the Gulf of Finland the pattern was similar in so far as two indigenous Baltic peoples, the Estonians and Latvians, eventually won independence only because Russia and Germany fell out; it differed in that the resident German minority played a much greater part in this area's history than the Swedes did in Finland. The struggle here was consequently a three-cornered one. Traditionally, the German nobles had collaborated closely with the imperial authorities; indeed, they provided a conspicuously large share of the governing class. In the 1860s Yu. F. Samarin, the Slavophil writer, strongly criticized their influence, but his views were repudiated by the tsar. Alexander II pursued an equivocal policy that facilitated educational and cultural progress among the Baltic peoples, whose leaders at this stage looked to St Petersburg to defend them against German predominance. But in the 1880s Alexander III's government embarked upon a policy of deliberate Russification. Measures were taken against local Lutheran churches and schools; the Russian language was made obligatory in most public institutions; the administrative system was centralized. By these steps the government short-sightedly alienated its German supporters without, however, winning sympathy from the native Balts, who were suffering widespread social distress as a consequence of rapid industrialization. Particularly in Latvia a strong socialist movement developed, and in 1905 there was a general insurrection, led by workers and landless peasants. It was brutally repressed by German nobles and Russian troops. The government, greatly alarmed, sought to revive the old alliance, but found that the Baltic Germans now looked to Berlin rather than St Petersburg. Thus by 1914 Russian imperial authority in the area had been gravely weakened. Yet for all their disappointments the native peoples still preferred Russian rule to German, and fought with rare determination against the invaders. The Latvians were allowed to form military units of their own. These played a prominent part in the bitter civil war that began in 1917 and led eventually to the eclipse of both German and Russian influence.

The Lithuanians' experience was less traumatic, for theirs was a more agrarian society, constrained by a Catholic priesthood and relatively slow to develop an articulate national movement. Some violence occurred in 1905, but subsequently the political élite was by and large content to co-operate with the government. One reason for this was an undercurrent of antagonism toward Poles and Jews. Similar considerations operated in the case of the White Russians (Belorussians), although they of course were a Slav and predominantly Orthodox group. Their history may be regarded as a pale reflection of that of the Ukrainians further south.

A much more numerous people, the Ukrainians had a better chance to develop a consciousness of their linguistic and cultural identity, although the process was delayed by the lack of a native upper class. Most leading positions in the administration were held by Russians or Poles, and those in business by Jews. The eastern Ukraine, with its nascent industry (see p. 217), was naturally more 'assimilationist', whereas the less urbanized western districts were more sympathetic to the nationalist ideas that could be ventilated freely across the Austrian border. Galicia, where the so-called 'Ruthenians' enjoyed political rights, played much the same role for Ukrainians as it did for Poles, although little love was lost between these two peoples. Within Russia's borders the Ukrainians at first aspired to autonomy within a democratic federal union; they also sympathized with the Russian Populists' (see p. 245) demands for radical agrarian reform. The main spokesman for this tendency was M. P. Drahomaniv (Dragomanov). In 1876 the government embarked upon a repressive policy, closing down Ukrainian cultural organizations and severely restricting use of the vernacular. As a result, after a period of enforced quiescence, opposition took a more radical form. When political parties appeared in the Ukraine, the constitutional reformists (Radical Democrats) spoke less loudly than did the revolutionary socialists. The latter were divided between pro-Russian 'integrationists' and a larger group which, like the Polish PPS, laid more emphasis upon national demands. There was also a small but vociferous right-wing nationalist group. These parties were led by intellectuals and had no strong mass following, although after 1907 the nationalists did gain a foothold in the farm co-operatives. Most Ukrainians were more interested in social advancement than in politics. It was the First World War that really laid the basis for independence. The hardships it imposed, especially upon the inhabitants of Galicia when it was temporarily under Russian military occupation, strengthened nationalist and pro-German sentiment. Anti-Semitism, too, flourished on this embittered soil.

The people that suffered most from tsarist nationalities policy were the Jews, whose very existence as a nation was still in doubt, and who were victims of religious as well as political prejudice. In 1897 they numbered some five million. The overwhelming majority were obliged to dwell in certain urban areas of western and southern Russia (the 'pale of settlement'), where they were subject to humiliating occupational and other restrictions. Such segregation, in conditions of acute overcrowding and poverty, naturally aggravated local ethnic tension. The few educated Jews whom Alexander II's government permitted to reside in other towns soon had their privileges curtailed, and in the 1880s a systematic policy of discrimination was enforced. Jews were forbidden to hold certain posts and a *numerus clausus* was instituted in schools and universities. In the 'pale' several outbreaks of mob violence – *pogroms* – were tolerated and even abetted by certain officials as a means of deflecting revolutionary unrest. Alexander III disapproved of such malpractices, which ceased after 1882, but his successor was less squeamish. Serious *pogroms* recurred at Kishinev in 1903 and in many other towns in 1905–6; the worst, at Odessa, claimed 400 Jewish lives.

The 'assimilationist' tendencies prevalent among Jewish intellectuals in the 1860s and 1870s were now discredited. Some escaped by emigrating: during the 1880s the Jewish exodus to the United States proceeded at an average rate of one thousand a month. Subsequently many Jews who remained turned either to Zionism or to revolutionary socialism. The Jewish 'Bund', formed in 1895–7, was the first Marxist organization in Russia to strike root in the working class, but its activities were hampered by differences with non-Jewish socialists as well as by the police. In 1905 a Jewish civil rights movement also developed, which enjoyed the support of Russian liberal opinion. Even Prime Minister P. A. Stolypin (see p. 235) favoured toleration, if only for *raisons d'État*; but Nicholas II decided that concessions would affront his Christian conscience. Instead he extended his personal patronage to extreme right-wing organizations that sought to stir up hatred against Jews – and socialists – as scapegoats for all Russia's troubles. Their propaganda foreshadowed that of later fascist parties elsewhere in Europe, but as popular movements they were ineffective. Traditional loyalty to absolutist principles was incompatible with an outright racist ideology. Mass anti-Semitism was a latent force in Russian society, but it was as yet scarcely politicized. This was at least one positive by-product of the regime's failure to evolve a realistic programme for dealing with the minorities, which otherwise did such harm – not least to the monarchy itself.

THE EMPIRE IN THE EAST

Russian imperialism rested on a firmer footing, and had a more plausible *raison d'être*, in Asia than in Europe. In many regions the initial tasks of colonization had only just been broached, and as yet few indigenous peoples had acquired the prerequisites of nationhood. To most of them religious (or even tribal) affinities counted for more than did ethnic ties – although the problems of Asia in the mid twentieth century were already present in embryonic form. (Two important exceptions were the Georgians and Armenians, whose political development paralleled that of the European minorities: no summary could do their complex history justice.)

Of the Muslim peoples under Russian rule, the most advanced were the Tatars of the middle Volga, who at the turn of the century numbered more than 3 million. From the 1870s onward efforts were made to spread education and Orthodox Christianity among them, but with somewhat paradoxical results. Missionary activity helped to stimulate national feeling, the very phenomenon the Russifiers hoped to prevent. Muslim intellectuals appeared who sought to modernize and secularize their society. This movement spread to the Tatars of the Crimea and of Azerbaijan in the Caucasus. Some enthusiasts, notably Ismail Bey Gaspirali, developed a consciousness of allegiance to a wider community embracing all Turkic peoples. Pan-Turkism, misnamed 'Pan-Islamism', was deemed by some officials a threat to the empire's security, but when Russia found herself at war with Turkey in 1914 these groups gave little trouble. They were too weak to bridge the deep cultural divisions among the various Muslim peoples of the empire.

In the event the socially more backward, but geographically more compact natives of Central Asia posed a more immediate challenge to Russia's authority in the East. In 1916 they arose in an ill-organized revolt, which was suppressed with great ferocity. Hundreds of thousands perished or emigrated. Russian power was first imposed on this area by force of arms between 1864 and 1881. After a period of direct military rule the administration of Turkestan was partially civilianized, the khanates of Bukhara and Khiva being granted autonomous status as Russian protectorates. By comparison with their British counterparts in India, the Russian colonial officials interfered less in the pattern of native life, either for the worse or for the better (e.g. by spreading education). The Muslim masses initially benefited by the elimination of slavery and some other medieval survivals. Subsequently their position deteriorated as the area was opened up to cotton-growing. This provided a new source of income, but earnings were abysmally low. In the Steppe area (modern Kazakhstan) the nomads were hard pressed by Russian peasant colonists, who by 1911 comprised forty per cent of the population; and from 1910 settlers were also allowed into the more fertile province of Turkestan. The local peoples (especially the Kazakhs and Kirghiz) had good reason to doubt their capacity to survive this influx. The final straw was a decree mobilizing able-bodied males for labour services behind the front lines (1916), which in their eyes amounted to conscription in the armies of the infidel, and touched off the revolt.

Preoccupation with Central Asia at first deflected the Russian government's attention from the Far East. After the treaties of Aigun and Peking (1858, 1860), whereby China was forced to yield the Amur and Ussuri districts, Alexander II sensibly adopted a policy of consolidation and retrenchment. In 1867 the Russian possessions in North America were sold to the United States. This decision, sometimes criticized by nationalist and communist historians, was reasonable, since Russia lacked sufficient capital to make the colony pay. In 1874 Russia surrendered the Kurile Islands to Japan in exchange for full sovereign rights in Sakhalin, hitherto administered jointly by the two powers. This too was a good bargain, even though the island was later used mainly as a penal settlement. The principal reason why so little was done to promote settlement and economic progress in the Pacific territories – and, indeed, in Siberia generally – was the lack of adequate communication facilities. Only in the 1890s, with the building of the Trans-Siberian railway (see p. 218), was a real start made and migration positively encouraged. The European population of Siberia, which numbered 2.3 million in 1858, had by 1911 reached 8.3 million; meanwhile the native population grew more slowly, to less than 1 million.

The growing Russian 'presence' in Siberia facilitated further encroachment upon Chinese territory, as well as upon Korea, where Chinese and Japanese interests conflicted. Russian ambitions in Korea first made themselves felt in 1884, when naval chiefs sought to obtain an ice-free port in the peninsula, but were frustrated by Japanese and British opposition. After the Sino-Japanese war of 1894–5 Russia secured an influence upon Korean internal affairs, but within a year her protégés were dislodged by pro-Japanese elements. Nicholas II refused to accept this defeat, and rejected Japanese suggestions for an agreement on respective spheres of influence, whereby Russia was to have a free hand in China and Japan in Korea. Instead he acquired, upon the advice of the irresponsible A. M. Bezobrazov, a personal interest in certain forest land across the river Yalu. Although this scheme never bore fruit, Russian designs upon northern Korea were an important contributory cause of the war with Japan that broke out in February 1904.

Meanwhile Russia had acquired a strong position in parts of China. An agreement of May 1896 allowed her to build through northern Manchuria a direct rail link to Vladivostok, and to maintain paramilitary units there. Two years later she forced China to lease the Liaotung peninsula, where she constructed the stronghold of Port Arthur; this, too, was linked to Russia by rail. All Manchuria seemed about to fall under Russian control. But in April 1902, under Japanese and British pressure, Russia was obliged to consent to a phased withdrawal of her troops. These terms were never fully carried out, and Russia was therefore fairly well placed to withstand the offensive launched in Manchuria by the Japanese (1904–5). Her defeat – at sea as well as on land – by another Asian power made a considerable impact upon international opinion.

Yet prestige is one thing, physical power another: if Russia lost the war, she certainly won the peace. True, she ceded to Japan her recent acquisitions in southern Manchuria, as well as southern Sakhalin. But these territorial losses were more than offset by Japanese acquiescence in her control of northern Manchuria, in which the other powers concurred. This *de facto* partition was affirmed in three secret treaties with Japan (1907, 1910, 1912). The last of these agreements extended the line between the two powers' spheres of influence westward to Mongolia. When the Mongols rebelled against China in 1911, they received military and diplomatic support from Russia, and the nominally independent regime established in the following year was in effect a Russian protectorate, even though it formally remained under Chinese sovereignty.

Some zealous imperialists, such as E. E. Ukhtomsky, dreamed of acquiring for Russia a position of hegemony in Asia; but although Nicholas II found these ideas attractive they were not practicable. There was a little room left for encroachment upon Chinese Turkestan (Sinkiang), but apart from this remote area the Russian empire had reached the maximum territorial limits compatible with the international balance of power and the nature of tsarist imperialism itself. Great Britain opposed any extension of Russian influence into Tibet or Afghanistan – or Persia, although there British policy was modified in 1907, when by the Anglo-Russian convention Russia was given a foothold in the northern third of that country. But every display of Russian power in this area led to friction with Great Britain, who was determined to prevent Russia from gaining access to the Persian Gulf – had she actively sought to pursue such aims, which she did not. (The 'Russian threat to India' was a myth without substance.) The imperialists in St Petersburg were wise enough to limit their commitments. This was partly because they had to bear in mind Russia's relative strategic and economic weakness; partly because they were themselves divided between 'doves' and 'hawks' (most obviously in the conflict between Witte and his rivals in the period 1897–1903); but basically because their imperialism was of the old-fashioned nineteenth-century variety. It relied upon infiltration from above rather than revolution from below. Pressure was applied to the élite groups in the target area, not to the populace. But in twentieth-century conditions imperial ambitions could be sustained only by mass-mobilization techniques that were alien to the tsars, but were to be perfected by their successors.

THE EFFLORESCENCE OF SECULAR CULTURE

Russia's impact upon the world owed less to her imperial expansion or prowess at arms than to her attainments in the arts of civilization. The history of literature is discussed in vol. 2 of this work, but some consideration of Russia's cultural development in general is essential. Two rather obvious points stand out: firstly, that her accomplishments were unevenly distributed between different realms of endeavour or inquiry; secondly, that they were the work of a relatively small élite, although toward the end of the period this abnormal 'intensivity' of Russian culture was being rectified by progress in popular education.

THE ARTS AND SCIENCES

The 'realistic' tradition in the arts in nineteenth-century Russia was an expression of that elusive phenomenon, the 'Russian spirit'; it was also the product of specific historical circumstances. Among sensitive intellectuals political frustration encouraged civic-mindedness and ideological commitment. They were particularly responsive to the needs of the oppressed, and entertained an idealistic, sometimes even Messianic desire to affirm the place of the Russian people in the forward march of civilization. It was often difficult to give these ideas concrete shape, and many intellectuals preferred to engage in quasi-philosophical speculation, questing after ultimate, absolute truths in all domains of the spirit – a tendency manifest in the work of Dostoyevsky and Tolstoy as well as in that of many lesser nineteenth-century writers.

From the 1890s onward, in what has been called the 'silver age' of Russian culture, a contrary trend developed in the direction of aesthetic values, individualism, and creative experimentation. This 'revolt of feeling, taste and imagination' owed much to the Symbolist movement. One of its main tenets was the existence of a close relationship among all the arts, and in the new intellectual climate painting, drama, and the ballet flourished as they seldom had before.

The government subsidized some cultural ventures on a lavish scale, and although independent-minded artists were prone to grumble about bureaucratic interference they enjoyed a wide measure of freedom as well as high social prestige. A large and appreciative public attended theatrical and musical events, even in small provincial towns. The bass voice of Fyodor Shalyapin (Chaliapine) could be heard in 'people's houses' as well as in aristocratic *salons*. There was a powerful movement for 'democratization of the arts' that owed much to private patrons, among them the Moscow entrepreneurs Savva Mamontov and Pavel Tret'yakov. In 1898 the former founded a private opera company that could call on Mikhail Vrubel' to design its scenery and Sergey Rachmaninov to conduct its orchestra. The outstanding features of Russian cultural life before 1914 were rich diversity, a readiness to pursue novel lines of approach, and careful attention to aesthetic standards. The picture is one of energy, colour, and movement.

Nor should this efflorescence be dismissed as simply 'an exotic flower blossoming upon a stagnant pool of ignorance'. Russia produced many eminent scholars in various fields, whose relations with their western colleagues became closer as time went by. In such politically sensitive fields as economics, sociology, and law the climate of opinion was not favourable to independent thought, and some of the best men chose to work abroad. Maxim Kovalevsky, a professor of jurisprudence at Moscow University, was obliged to resign his chair in 1887 and subsequently lectured at Oxford; he devoted himself to the study of democratic institutions and on his return to Russia in 1905 entered politics as a liberal. The economist M. I. Tugan-Baranovsky, whose work on business cycles earned international recognition, was a *Kathedersozialist* who likewise found his academic career obstructed. Characteristically, the first department of economics in any Russian institution of higher learning was set up, not in one of the universities, but in the St Petersburg Polytechnic Institute (1903).

It is therefore understandable that many scholars preferred to study the past rather than the present. As a result Russia developed a fine tradition in historiography. Much excellent work was also done by archaeologists and ethnographers. The first professional historian to adopt a sound methodological approach was S. M. Solov'yov (1820–79). A moderate conservative and nationalist, he was much influenced by Hegelian thought, as were many of his contemporaries. The 'juridical' (or 'state') school that he helped to found was toward the end of the century displaced by the 'sociological' school, whose leading luminary was V. O. Klyuchevsky (1841–1911). He was the last to formulate a comprehensive theory of Russian history; subsequently, as in other countries, the specialists took over – until in 1917 the revolution intervened.

Geography was another field in which Russian scholars did first-class work. Numerous expeditions of discovery were sent out. Large areas of Asia that at mid-century had still been *terra incognita* were charted and investigated. N. M. Przhevalsky (Przewalski), an adventurous army officer, spent nine years from 1871 exploring inner Asia, whence he returned with thousands of zoological and botanical specimens, including the wild horse since named after him. The Arctic regions were somewhat neglected, so that a foreigner, the Swede Adolf Nordenskjöld, became the first to navigate the Northeast Passage (1878–9); nevertheless, a Russian hydrographic expedition traversed it from east to west in 1914–15. Between 1899 and 1914 Russia's leading geographer, P. P. Semyonov, published in nineteen volumes a detailed description of the empire's natural resources. Of particular value, in view of the urgent agrarian problem, was the work done by V. V. Dokuchayev (1846–1903) on soil analysis and distribution.

Russian scientists were hampered by lack of funds for research and the country's technological lag. It was sadly characteristic that the experiments made in the 1870s by P. N. Yablochkov and A. N. Lodygin with the use of electricity for street lighting should have been followed up abroad rather than in Russia. Similarly, the naval engineer A. S. Popov's successful experiments in radio signalling (1895) did not win him immediate international recognition. In fairness it should be added that professional and academic exchanges with other countries proceeded normally. Russia sent strong delegations to many international congresses, and her industrial development benefited greatly from the work of foreign scientists and engineers.

In no sphere was the practical application of scientific discoveries more urgent – or more striking in its effects – than in medicine. At first standards of public health were deplorably low and epidemics frequent. Such improvements as took place were the work of dedicated individuals, pitifully few in number, some of them officials and others private citizens. The cities of Moscow and St Petersburg owed their modern systems of water supply and drainage to a Swiss, F. F. Erismann, and a Russian, A. P. Dobroslavin. The latter was a pioneer in nutritional research and set up a municipal laboratory for the public analysis of foodstuffs. The first modern medical clinic was founded by Dr S. P. Botkin (1832–84), who became immensely popular: 'His unaffected goodness and humanity, free from all sentimentality, had a marvellous educational effect upon his students.' An elected member of the St Petersburg municipal council, he set up a free hospital and a subsidized service for domiciliary medical care. It was a model emulated by some of the more enlightened provincial authorities (see p. 239). Yet progress in this field was dauntingly slow. The mortality rate, which in the 1860s was 37 per thousand, in 1913 still stood at 30, higher than most other European countries.

EDUCATIONAL PROGRESS

The need to bestow the benefits of education upon the mass of the population was appreciated by everyone in Russia, at least in theory. In practice much of the effort expended to this end by enlightened individuals and public bodies met with obstruction by arch-conservative elements. Some officials and landowners feared that too rapid an advance would spread egalitarian democratic ideas and threaten the existing order. The risk was indeed present; but to delay was riskier still. As time would show, in a moment of crisis an ill-educated populace was far more likely to respond to revolutionary agitation, and radicalism had a natural appeal for intellectuals and others who felt alienated from a society that offered educated men so little opportunity to apply their talents.

In fairness to the conservatives three points may be noted. Firstly, radical critics of the administration often failed to recognize that Russia's slender economic resources limited the amounts available for educational purposes. Secondly, they themselves did not seriously contest the system of centralized control, which introduced a valuable element of homogeneity into the educational system: had they been in charge, there would probably have been less tolerance of diversity (particularly in regard to church and private schools). Thus what at the time seemed to be a struggle of principle between 'reactionary' centralizers and 'progressive' advocates of local autonomy was in effect a struggle for power between different groups with different social and educational philosophies. Thirdly, the clumsy efforts of the more reactionary ministers, notably I. D. Delyanov (1882–97), to encourage social segregation *inter alia* by allowing university entrance to *gimnaziya* (grammar school) children but denying it to candidates from *realshuly* (modern secondary schools), failed to achieve the results intended. Among university students the proportion of *meshchane* (burghers) and peasants rose from 16 per cent in 1880 to 39 per cent in 1914; among *gimnaziya* pupils their share increased from about one-quarter to one-half. Moreover, the spirit in Russian schools and colleges was generally more 'democratic' (i.e. socially inclusive) than it was in many equivalent western institutions. Female education also made significant progress.

In numerical terms the expansion was impressive, particularly in the relatively more enlightened periods before 1880 and after 1905, and at the upper levels of the educational system. The number of university students multiplied tenfold, from 3,700 in 1855 to 35,700 in 1916. Many more attended various specialized institutes, so that the total of those receiving higher education in 1916 exceeded 100,000. The number of secondary-school pupils quintupled during Alexander II's reign; thereafter the rate slackened, but between 1900 and 1914 enrolment increased from 217,000 to about 700,000. In elementary education the big push did not come until the twentieth century. The number of pupils doubled, from four to eight million, between 1900 and 1916, when over half the children aged eight to eleven attended school. The Education Act of 1908 aimed to make primary education universal and compulsory within fourteen years. This goal was not unrealistic, to judge by the appropriations made by central and local authorities in the pre-war years. One effect was a rapid rise in the rate of literacy. The 1897 census showed that only one Russian citizen in five could read and write. In 1914 the proportion is estimated to have been 44 per cent.

If Imperial Russia's achievements seem modest in international perspective (particularly in comparison to Japan), one should remember that no other country had yet tackled a problem of such magnitude. The challenge was taken up by several distinguished pedagogues, such as K. D. Ushinsky and P. F. Lesgaft, whose theories were advanced for their time. Attempts to implement them, however, often ran into the sand. The ministry closely supervised curricula and similar details. The regimented atmosphere caused widespread disaffection among teachers, students, and even schoolchildren, which had important political consequences. The universities in particular became seedbeds of radicalism. The student disorders in St Petersburg and Kazan' in 1861 set a pattern for many subsequent protests against professional and political injustice. After the last of these disturbances (1910–11) 6,000 students were expelled. University autonomy, granted in 1863, was suspended from 1884 to 1906, and even when in force was often infringed by narrow-minded and security-conscious administrators.

RELIGION AND THE SPIRITUAL CRISIS

Conditions were no better in the ecclesiastical seminaries, whose pupils sometimes forsook the church for the revolutionary movement; the latter may itself be seen (in part) as a secular perversion of spiritual impulses frustrated by the clerical establishment. The Orthodox Church was slow to enter the field of popular education. When, after 1880, it did so, prodded by the reactionary ideologue K. P. Pobedonostsev, its achievements scarcely justified the effort. The parochial schools, staffed by inadequately trained 'supernumerary priests', with a limited, archaic curriculum, were opposed by enlightened public opinion on educational grounds and by lay officials who objected to their maladministration. Russia experienced a muted version of the laicization controversy. As in France, it was decided in favour of the secularists. After 1905 the Holy Synod's influence upon educational policy was much reduced.

The Orthodox Church was sadly ill equipped to cope with the problems of a secularizing society. This inadequacy was the result partly of its pre-Petrine ascetic, unworldly outlook and partly of its post-Petrine bureaucratic institutional structure. The former successfully withstood the challenge of modernizing intellectual tendencies; the latter was actually reinforced by Pobedonostsev, who as Chief Procurator of the

213

Holy Synod from 1880 to 1905 ruled the church with an iron hand. A layman, he was a protagonist of the state's claims to paramountcy over the church, for whose dignitaries he had little respect ('dull and stupid people, scattered about the snowy wastes', as he once called them privately). He restricted the scope of discussion among churchmen and bolstered the authority of those bishops – and they were the majority – who accepted and loyally enforced his narrow disciplinarian ideas. The parish priests, appointed arbitrarily from above, ill-educated and badly paid, could seldom claim much moral authority over their flocks. Some men of exceptional quality, such as John of Kronstadt, won wide popular acclaim, but they stood somewhat apart from the institutional hierarchy.

In such circumstances a movement for reform naturally made itself felt, particularly among lower clergy, theologians, and a few interested laymen. This gained strength under the impact of the 1905 revolution. Nicholas II reluctantly agreed to summon a commission to conduct preliminaries for a *sobor* (church council). At this meeting the reformers had a majority, but were divided between the moderates, who wished to strengthen the church *vis-à-vis* the state by reviving the patriarchate, and those who sought a wider devolution of authority and other far-reaching reforms that they deemed essential if the church was to regain its proper status in the eyes of believers. The split helped the reactionary group, who with the tsar's aid succeeded in thwarting the movement for reform. Liberal churchmen were harassed, while such unscrupulous individuals as the *starets* Rasputin, the tsar's favourite, and the monk Iliodor, a fanatical demagogue, wielded considerable power. In the last years of the old regime the corruption within the church became a public scandal.

Attempts to fill the resultant spiritual void took two principal forms. The populace was attracted to various movements of religious dissent, the intellectuals (and educated persons generally) to scepticism, atheism, and secular 'substitute religions'. Of the dissenter communities the most important were the Old Believers, who numbered some 20 million at the turn of the century. In western and southern districts certain rationalistic sects (*shtundisty*, *molokane*, *dukhobory*) secured many converts, despite bitter persecution by the state authorities. The juridical position of dissenters was somewhat improved by an edict (1905) promising religious toleration, but this principle was never legally formalized; they therefore continued to feel insecure and had few ties to the existing order. Some of them developed a chiliastic *Weltanschauung* that made them susceptible to influence by revolutionary intellectuals, whose atheism, however, they stoutly rejected.

Materialist doctrines, inspired by the West, obtained a following among Russian students in the 1860s. They could not be freely expounded, but this merely enhanced their appeal. The Populist movement (see

p. 245) contained a strong ethical, salvationist, and missionary streak that could not readily be reconciled with its adherents' declared hostility to religion. This contradiction became still more acute when the Russian socialists were converted to Marxism. This doctrine soon came to acquire strong fideistic overtones, even though its leaders, among them G. V. Plekhanov and V. I. Ul'yanov (Lenin), proclaimed themselves materialists and militant atheists. A group of Bolshevik intellectuals (Maksim Gor'ky, A. V. Lunacharsky, V. A. Bazarov) attempted to reconcile the contradiction, but were denounced by their comrades as 'God-seekers'. The problem was eventually to be 'resolved' in the most drastic fashion: Russian Marxism was transformed into a 'state' ideology, whose devotees launched a terrorist assault upon all transcendental religion, as well as upon all rival secular creeds.

Long before 1917 Fyodor Dostoyevsky had prophesied that Russia's spiritual crisis would have a tragic dénouement, and religious philosophers had vainly sought to avert it. In 1901–3 D. S. Merezhkovsky organized 'religious–philosophical discussions' in St Petersburg at which speakers invited the intelligentsia to embark upon 'a new course'. In 1909 a volume of essays, *Vekhi* ('Signposts'), was published, the leitmotiv of which was that educated Russians should abandon their traditional shallow positivism and atheism, and instead embrace religion, 'the basic prerequisite for any consistent philosophy of life' (S. L. Frank). Such thinkers as S. N. Bulgakov and N. A. Berdyaev, who had at first been attracted to Marxism, came to perceive its latent totalitarian features and rebelled in favour of a forward-looking, if somewhat mystical Christianity. Their ideas had some success within a small coterie (including the 'God-seekers'). If they did not appeal to a broader segment of educated opinion, this was principally because they lacked an adequate institutional base. The official church took no interest in such movements, and had in any case long since lost the capacity to guide Russia's spiritual and intellectual development.

ECONOMIC AND SOCIAL CHANGE

The 'great reforms' of the 1860s, by eliminating serfdom and other archaic restraints upon production, paved the way for an upsurge of entrepreneurial activity. This gathered momentum slowly and reached its peak in the two 'boom' eras of 1893–1900 and 1908–13. Russian 'capitalism' (as many contemporaries called it) differed in several essentials from the western European prototype, and had features that anticipated those found in many 'developing' countries today. Growth was uneven, with agriculture lagging behind industry (some sectors of which were particularly favoured); foreign investment played a key role; so too did the state, most obviously in its capacity as creditor and tax-gatherer, but also as proprietor of a sizeable share of the nation's resources; last but not least, the 'revolution of rising expectations' created bitterness and social tension. The producers themselves, whether workers or peasants, enjoyed few of the immediate advantages that industrialization brought, yet had to bear most of the burden. It was also characteristic that their instinctively hostile reaction to the harsh new industrial world, with its commercial materialist values, should strike a sympathetic echo among the educated élite. Few intellectuals inquired realistically how the human cost of economic progress could be minimized; many took refuge in vague romantic ideas of a social utopia, in the past or in the future. Nor did the country's leaders, with the shining exception of S. Yu. Witte, minister of finance from 1892 to 1903, realize how urgent it was to develop the country's productive resources.

INDUSTRIALIZATION AND ITS PROBLEMS

The rate of industrial growth over the period 1860–1913 has been estimated at $5\frac{1}{4}$–$5\frac{1}{2}$ per cent per annum (slightly less if craft industries are included); in the good years 1888–1900 it was in the region of 7 per cent. These are creditable figures, although they are less striking when seen in international perspective. By 1913 industry still contributed only one-fifth of the national income and employed about 5 per cent of the total labour force. Meanwhile the population was expanding rapidly. In 1858 the empire had some 74 million inhabitants; by 1897, when the first modern census was taken, the number had risen to 128.9 million; by 1916 it had reached some 170 million – an average annual increase of 1.5 per cent. This was the result of medical progress and higher living standards. Overall output (including agriculture) rose more rapidly than the population. The per capita growth rate has been estimated at $\frac{3}{4}$ per cent per annum in the period 1860–85 and $1\frac{1}{4}$ per cent in the period 1885–1913. This was about half that of Sweden, two-fifths that of Japan.

Industrial growth was most marked in mining and metallurgy, then in textiles and food processing. It lagged in the more sophisticated products, such as machinery, which often had to be imported. Engineering expanded rapidly, but in 1913 employed only 14 per cent of the industrial labour force and accounted for 11 per cent of total industrial output. Of Russia's three motor-car plants, the largest (at Riga) had by 1916 produced a derisory 450 vehicles. Yet during the First World War, by some economic miracle, several thousand home-built aeroplanes appeared in the skies.

Considered geographically, the most advanced regions were in Russian Poland and the St Petersburg area. However, the most significant development was undoubtedly the emergence of a new fast-growing industrial centre in the Ukraine, based on the coal and iron-ore resources of the Donets valley. By 1913 this region was producing 64 per cent of the nation's iron and steel and 70 per cent of its coal. Its value was vividly demonstrated during the First World War, when the Polish provinces came under enemy occupation: despite appalling difficulties output was sustained remarkably well until the revolution broke. Another key expanding area was Transcaucasia. In 1913 the oilfields of Baku, first worked in the 1870s, produced over 7 million tons of petroleum, four-fifths of the country's output. The old-established industrial region in the Moscow and Vladimir provinces remained the principal area for the manufacture of textiles. In its competition with the cheaper fabrics produced in Poland it was assisted by easier access to the raw cotton now being grown in Central Asia; some surplus was available for export. In 1913 this central region accounted for over one-third of the empire's manufacturing output and for two-fifths of its industrial labour force. The mining and metallurgical industry of the Urals long suffered from remoteness and lack of capital for technical improvements.

A similar unevenness may be noted in the organizational structure of industry. At one pole were the peasant handicrafts, which put up stiff resistance to pressure from the mechanized factories; at the other were giant enterprises with many thousands of employees. Statistics show that Russia had an exceptionally high density of industrial concentration (see pp. 228–9) yet these large factories were but tiny islands amidst a sea of small-scale entrepreneurship. After 1902 many firms set up syndicates or cartels that endeavoured to corner the market in particular products and maintain price levels. But these associations were unpopular with consumers and in practice their influence was limited. The modern business corporation was only just emerging in Russia toward the end of this period. It is true that banks were coming to take a leading part in industrial development, as owners as well as creditors, and this raised the bogy of 'finance capitalism'. Far more significant, however, was the continuing pre-eminence of the state. Officials maintained close ties with the business community, but it was the former that determined the general tone and direction of economic life. This became particularly evident during the First World War, even though Russia experienced less state regulation than did other belligerents. As a force independent of the government, Russian 'capitalism' never really got off the ground; many features of the 'planned economy' instituted after 1917 had pre-revolutionary antecedents.

The reason for this was that in nineteenth-century Russia any independent entrepreneur faced many formidable obstacles which he could overcome only with extensive state support. Chief among these were:

poor communications, shortage of capital, uncertain markets, and lack of skilled labour. Another factor was the general *kosnost'* ('inertia') noted by many contemporaries, a legacy of Russia's authoritarian tradition, which encouraged corruption and hindered the growth of a modern 'business ethos'. The latter phenomenon cannot easily be documented and must be omitted from this discussion.

Historically, the medium of communication in Russia had been river transport. This was inadequate to the needs of a developing economy, although some progress was registered with the introduction of steam-powered vessels. Since the roads remained in a state of serious neglect, one may readily appreciate the significance of the railway, a veritable symbol of modernity. Witte likened it to 'a leaven which stimulates cultural ferment among the population'. Its economic (as distinct from social and psychological) effect was immense. It enabled farmers to sell their crops in distant cities and ports at reasonably uniform prices; it made possible the exploitation of untapped mineral wealth; and it served as a 'pump-primer', by creating a market for rails and rolling-stock; these industries needed others to supply them. This function was of particular importance in the last quarter of the century.

Much railway-building had strategic implications. The construction programme of the 1860s was stimulated by the knowledge that lack of any rail communication from Moscow to the Crimea had contributed to military defeat in 1855. The Russo-Turkish War highlighted certain defects in railway management and led the state to take over many private lines. Strategic and political motives were uppermost in the final decision (1892) to build the great Trans-Siberian railway (completed in 1904) and two other important lines in Asia: the Trans-Caspian from Krasnovodsk to Samarkand (1880–96), and that from Orenburg to Tashkent (1900–6). Before the First World War the government, with French aid, was actively intensifying the network of strategic railways on the western border and in 1916 a line was built to Murmansk, in the face of immense difficulties, to speed the flow of Allied war supplies. These enterprises were not expected to be commercially successful.

In most cases, however, economic considerations were paramount, and it was the prospect of quick profits that attracted Russian and foreign entrepreneurs. There were two main phases in the railway boom, *c.* 1866–1879 and *c.* 1891–1902. At first promoters and investors were loath to risk their money and the government had to grant them advantageous privileges – such as guaranteed interest rates – which led to unhealthy speculation. Some state-owned railways were sold to private companies on terms highly favourable to the latter, and when this policy was reversed it was the least profitable lines that the government repurchased first, so that vested interests again profited. By 1890 one-quarter, and by 1914 over two-thirds of total track mileage were publicly owned; the government also had a considerable stake in the private sector. Much was done, especially after 1908, to encourage amalgamations, reduce overstaffing, and improve operating standards. The annual number of passenger journeys rose from 34 million in 1881 to 244 million in 1913, but freight was naturally the main consideration. In the 1870s this consisted largely of grain, but eventually it gave place to coal, timber, and industrial products. Average traffic density, the best indicator of efficiency, was higher in Russia than in Great Britain (although lower than in Germany or the USA). This was no mean achievement. The sheer scale of the construction programme was impressive: total track length, a bare 1,000 miles in 1860, exceeded 13,000 miles by 1880, 33,000 miles by 1900, and 45,000 miles by 1917. This was, however, insufficient to meet the empire's needs. In the First World War the transport system broke down under the heavy strains imposed upon it, with catastrophic results.

Much of the capital required for the development of communications, as for industry generally, was provided by the state, especially in the earlier years. In 1860 a state bank replaced various earlier central credit institutions; its funds came mainly from the treasury. By the end of the century its 104 branches were financing projects worth 145 million roubles, ten times the scale of its operations in 1861. From the late 1880s onward it was overtaken as the chief supplier of credit by commercial joint-stock banks, of which there were several dozen; by 1914, after a series of mergers, the six largest joint-stock banks had a capital of 400 million roubles. The pace of expansion can be gauged from the fact that fourteen years earlier *all* these banks had held only 275 million roubles. Equally noteworthy was the development of post office and other savings banks. In 1890 these held 139 million roubles, invested by 800,000 persons. By 1913 the figures were 1.7 milliard roubles and 8.9 million depositors.

The savings accumulated in this way, impressive testimonials as they were to financial stabilization and rising prosperity, were insufficient to support large-scale economic development. Accordingly a vital role was played by foreign credit, in the form both of inter-governmental loans and direct investment in industry. Russia borrowed more heavily than any other European state. Alexander II's finance minister, M. K. von Reutern, an internationalist and advocate of *laissez-faire*, sought to encourage investors by bringing order into the country's finances, which had been undermined by the Crimean War. His chief task was to control the circulation and stabilize the exchange rate of the paper 'credit rouble'. Its metallic cover, which in 1864 fell as low as 10.6 per cent, gradually improved until in 1876 it reached 29 per cent; but the outbreak of the Russo-Turkish War, which Reutern stoutly opposed, played havoc with his recovery programme, and this figure was not surpassed until 1893. Reutern also improved the treasury's housekeeping machinery: the annual budget was published (from 1863) and efforts made to balance revenue and expenditure by tightening controls over departmental commitments; malpractices continued, however, especially over the award of state contracts.

When the next industrial spurt began the finance ministry took a more active initiating and supervisory role. I. A. Vyshnegradsky (1887–92) improved Russia's standing on the international exchanges by converting earlier loan agreements on better terms; it was now that France replaced Germany as Russia's chief creditor. His successor, Witte, was an energetic and capable organizer who believed in state-guided national economic development. He built up for himself a strong position as virtual economic overlord. His career reached its climax in 1897 when Russia adopted the gold standard: bank-notes in circulation were devalued by one-third and became freely convertible. This reform, by a characteristic paradox, was opposed by contemporary Russian public opinion and was forced through only on the tsar's authority. It proved a complete success: as Witte had predicted, foreign investors' confidence in the Russian economy was enhanced and much-needed capital flowed in. In 1860 foreign capital had not exceeded 10 million, twenty years later not 100 million roubles; but by 1900 the figure was between 700 and 900 million and by 1914 some 1,750 million roubles. Over half of it was in mining and metallurgy, and the rest in textiles, municipal utilities, and banking.

The significance of foreign capital in the Russian economy before 1914 is difficult to assess, since much depends on the criterion applied. In terms of managerial power, appearances can mislead: firms with Russian directors might be under alien control; conversely, in a foreign-owned enterprise real authority might well rest with a local man. In terms of company assets, the non-Russian share was probably about one-third. In mining it reached 90 per cent, in metallurgy over 40 per cent, in textiles 28 per cent; in the eighteen largest commercial banks the proportion was 43 per cent.

Was Russia therefore a 'foreign colony'? Contemporaries, from conservative agrarians and nationalists to revolutionaries, lamented her ever-mounting foreign debt, which between 1861 and 1914 increased from 1¼ to about 8 milliard roubles, of which 2.6 milliard were due on intergovernmental loans. The large obligations entered into with Allied governments during the war, totalling some 6 milliard roubles by February 1917, raised the figure almost to the equivalent of the annual pre-war national income (16.4 milliard roubles); some estimates are higher. Had this debt not eventually been repudiated, one may doubt whether it could have been paid. At the turn of the century about one-fifth of budgetary expenditure was devoted to amortization of the foreign debt – ten times as much as was spent by the ministry of education. The political implications are evident from the fact that the 850 million roubles borrowed in 1906 from an international (mainly French) bankers' consortium greatly strengthened the government's domestic position at a critical hour, enabling it to prevail over its constitutional opponents (see p. 243). On the other side of the coin, Russia's creditors took care not to infringe her prerogatives as a sovereign state. Foreign-owned firms were often technological leaders. Nor does it appear that foreign investors derived unduly large profits from the enterprises they owned, considering the high risks involved. One historian of anti-capitalist sympathies estimates the average annual return in the boom years 1894–1900 at between 4.8 per cent and 8.9 per cent. Dividends fluctuated sharply from year to year. Working conditions in foreign-owned factories were not generally worse, and were often much better than those in Russian-owned concerns. Native employees were given technical training and dormant native capital resources mobilized for productive investment. Certainly many abuses could have been avoided, but on balance the verdict must be favourable. The alternatives to the 'Witte system' of industrialization were utter stagnation or an advance at breakneck speed sustained solely by the savings of the poor, under a still more authoritarian regime – as Russia was to experience after 1928.

Another obstacle that nineteenth-century entrepreneurs faced, in Russia as in other developing countries, was the lack of a reliable, buoyant domestic market for their goods. Some socialists thought that this would fatally stunt the growth of 'capitalism' (see p. 246). However, this view underrated the flexibility possible in a free-enterprise economy. It was broadly true that industrial expansion was hampered by rural poverty, but the effect of this could be offset to some extent by state intervention. In the first place the government provided an ersatz market by concluding long-term fixed-price purchase agreements for certain commodities it needed (e.g. defence equipment, steel rails), which was profitable to producers. Secondly, it assisted entrepreneurs by adopting a protectionist tariff policy. Initially, when industry was still very weak, Russia had stood to gain more by a policy of free trade, reflected in the liberal tariffs of 1857 and 1868. The protectionists argued that high tariffs would safeguard domestic producers against competition from more advanced countries, especially Great Britain, and that the consumer would benefit ultimately from cheaper goods made at home, even if he now had to pay more. The government was less concerned with long-term economic strategy than with obtaining an immediate growth of customs receipts. These rose by 25–30 per cent when, in 1877, such dues were made payable in gold. Several further tariff increases were authorized during the 1880s, culminating in a new general tariff of June 1891, which led to tension with Germany, Russia's principal trading partner. The Russian government thereafter adopted a differential system based on country of origin, from which Germany was the principal gainer: in 1913 she supplied 53 per cent of Russia's imports and took 32 per cent of her exports. The two countries' economies were in many ways complementary. In a rational world this would have aided co-operation; as it happened, fear of economic penetration by Russia's more advanced neighbour served to aggravate nationalist passions that had their source elsewhere.

A further problem that faced industrialists was the provision of an adequate labour supply. There was no lack of peasants forced from their villages by poverty, but from their employers' viewpoint such men were unpromising material: addicted to the traditional rhythm of country life, they could not easily adjust to industrial conditions and changed jobs frequently. As late as 1913 the overwhelming majority of Donets miners returned home in summer to help with the harvest – and this was one of the most advanced industrial areas. Labour productivity in the pre-war years was $2\frac{1}{2}$ to 3 times greater than it had been in the 1860s, and grew by some 45 per cent between 1900 and 1913. Yet at the latter date the Russian factory worker produced only one-quarter as much as his American counterpart. Employers tried to compensate for these defects by imposing harsh discipline in the factory. Not enough was done to train men to hold positions of responsibility as managers or engineers, or to improve working conditions. The paternalistic attitudes affected by some employers all too often concealed a callous indifference to the human aspects of the industrial system: for example, the company housing provided in most newly developed areas was woefully primitive. Indeed, the industrialists of the Moscow region, fearing any deterioration in their competitive position, opposed and obstructed the modest labour protection measures enacted in 1882–5, which covered women workers and juveniles. They made life difficult for the officials of the factory inspectorate, established in 1882. The first real improvements came in 1897, when under pressure from striking textile workers Witte sanctioned an $11\frac{1}{2}$-hour working day for male adults. The employees' attitude to the 'labour question' is discussed below.

In the last years of peace problems of industrialization received increasing attention in high places, but an attitude of complacency was all too common. It is difficult to accept the proposition that Imperial Russia had reached what is today called 'the take-off point for self-sustained economic growth'. Her very backwardness acted as a drag upon development. The economy was disfigured by the legacy of the authoritarian pre-reform order as well as by many irrationalities characteristic of the more advanced entrepreneurial systems of the West. The First World

War confronted Russia's nascent industry with a severe challenge that, not unexpectedly, it failed to meet.

THE EVOLUTION OF AGRICULTURE

The agricultural sector of the economy was naturally slower to adapt itself to the demands of the modern age. For the bulk of the peasantry living conditions during this period improved only slightly; food consumption per head may even have declined. The basic reason for rural poverty was rapid population growth, coupled with inadequate capital investment in agriculture and (until 1906 at least) a failure to provide enough incentive to farmers to raise productivity.

These deficiencies were in part the result of the circumstances in which the Acts of Emancipation (1861–6) were promulgated. Under their terms the former state and crown peasants, and also those living in the western borderlands (see p. 201), obtained better treatment than the unfortunate serfs of private landlords, who on the eve of the reform numbered some 23½ million, or 46 per cent of the total peasant population. Even worse was the condition of the former domestic serfs and 'possessional' peasants, and of those in certain minority areas such as Georgia. The ex-serfs, whose fate was determined mainly by the principal edict of 19 February 1861, found that 'liberation' cost them dear. This was the greatest single act of social legislation in European history to date; nevertheless it was the product of a compromise between enlightened officials, who sought to ensure that the peasants should at least be able to meet their obligations to the state, and conservative landowners, who sought to perpetuate their power over their former 'subjects' indirectly, as their economic interests dictated. Where land was valuable, as in the fertile south, they cut down the size of peasant allotments, in some cases below the minimum needed for subsistence at current levels of farming technique. In the north, where peasants earned their livelihood largely by non-agricultural labour, they demanded redemption payments at a high rate unrelated to the land's market value or its potential yield, but based on the previous rate of *obrok* (quit-rent). The ex-serfs thus had in effect to provide their own ransom. They were often allotted poor-quality arable land and deprived of access to vital pastures, meadows, and forests; since their lands continued to be intermingled with those of the proprietor, this could lead them into economic subjection. But it would be truer to say that these provisions condemned both landlords and peasants to a relationship of frustrating *interdependence*. The psychological climate in the post-reform village was embittered by countless petty jealousies. The real case against the settlement was not that it 'took the land from the toiling *muzhik* [peasant]', as was widely thought at the time, especially by the peasants themselves, but rather that it tied them to their villages by a host of obligations and placed them under the 'tutelage' of a hierarchy of authorities. These controls rendered nugatory much of the liberty nominally granted them.

Of the institutions tying the peasant to his village the most important was the ancient *mir* (commune). It was retained partly as a convenient administrative and fiscal instrument, partly in the belief that it would hinder the emergence of a depressed rural proletariat. But its advocates overlooked the economically restrictive effects of the three-field system, which communal ownership perpetuated, and of the custom whereby (in Great Russia, at least) the scattered strips were periodically redistributed to ensure some rough correlation between the resources and obligations of each household. The more enterprising members had no incentive to improve land that they might lose at any time, and their natural acquisitive instincts were either crushed or diverted into unhealthy speculative channels. Collective responsibility for payment of taxes and other debts had the effect of binding the individual peasant to his community. He needed its permission to dispose of his plot, and even to travel outside the locality in search of employment. Such journeys also required the approval of the head of the household, the patriarchal figure whose word was law among members of the traditional 'extended family' still extant in many parts of Russia. Higher up the pyramid of authority were justices of the peace and local commissions for peasant affairs, replaced in 1889 by land captains (see p. 238).

The peasants responded to the reform with acts of passive protest that in some cases led to violence. Yet they had no real choice but to submit and to conclude, with the aid of specially appointed 'arbitrators', agreements with their former owners in respect of land allotments and redemption dues, as the law prescribed. Pending such local settlements they remained tenants in 'temporary bondage'. To some peasants this status seemed preferable to the uncertainties that awaited them as nominally free citizens, and in 1881 over a million householders, still serfs in all but name, had to be 'compulsorily liberated' by decree. In theory, once the peasant had paid his redemption dues (which might take up to forty-nine years), he was to become a full-fledged proprietor. But as time passed this principle sank into oblivion. An edict of 1893 actually encouraged communes to repartition the land. Alexander III's ministers, particularly D. A. Tolstoy, were more concerned to tighten rural security than to better the peasants' economic status. True, some attempt to alleviate their lot was made by N. Kh. Bunge during his tenure of the finance ministry (1881–6): redemption dues were reduced (1882) and three years later the archaic poll tax was finally abolished. But these were palliatives, which left the basic problems untouched; moreover, the treasury offset its losses by almost doubling the rents paid by former state peasants and raising rates of indirect taxation. These taxes, imposed on mass consumption goods, fell most heavily upon the rural population. In the 1890s the fiscal load was further increased as part of the price of industrialization. State regulation of sugar-beet production, introduced in 1895, kept prices artificially high and made this commodity more of a luxury than ever at the peasant's table. Another revenue-raising move was the introduction of a state monopoly on alcoholic spirits (1893/6–1914), which proved immensely successful: by 1913 it provided 28 per cent of the treasury's receipts. It could fairly be said that the government had a vested interest in promoting intemperance, the chief scourge of Russian village life.

The impact of this economic pressure was apparent in the steadily mounting sum owed in arrears of taxes and redemption dues. In the late 1890s, despite various local cancellations or deferments, these exceeded by one-fifth the average annual assessment. There were other warning signs. One-fifth of all army recruits had to be rejected as physically unfit. Famines, which at first afflicted relatively limited areas (e.g. the Samara province, 1873), became more widespread. In 1891–2 the whole black-earth belt suffered and some half-million persons died of hunger or disease. Even so officials were slow to grasp the seriousness of the problem.

Obscuring all public discussion of the 'agrarian question' was the myth that the trouble was rooted in unequal distribution of land resources. In fact rural population density in European Russia was considerably below that in more advanced countries, and the Ukraine had exceptionally fertile soil. Under the emancipation settlement the average allotment of former privately-owned peasants was 8.9 acres, of state peasants 16–18 acres. They could buy more land, through the government-sponsored Peasant Land Bank (founded in 1882) or other credit institutions, and between 1861 and 1905 some 43 million acres passed into the hands of peasants actually engaged in farming. In 1905 peasants held 375 million acres as allotment land and 67 million as private property; nobles owned 144 million acres (of which about 80 million were leased to peasants), merchants and burghers 64 million, and the state and other public bodies 418 million (most of it unsuitable for agriculture). Thus the problem was not shortage of land but the low productivity of small-scale peasant farming. In 1869 experiments showed that metal ploughs could improve crop yields by as much as 28 per cent; yet the ancient wooden *sokha* remained in general use, even on landowners' estates, until the end of the period. Introduction of imported agricultural machinery was hindered by tariff restrictions and, much more significantly, by the conservatism of the farmers themselves. Livestock was relatively scarce on peasant land (the total number of cattle rose by only 40 per cent between 1864 and 1914), so that little natural fertilizer was available. Crop yields in Russia were about one-quarter of those obtained in England, two-fifths of those in Germany. Between the 1860s and 1900s average grain yields per acre on peasant plots rose from 385 to 573 lb.; the figures for manorial land were somewhat better, but showed the extent to which the two types of property were interrelated. Everyone was subject to the village's seasonal routine. Yet it was precisely this egalitarian atmosphere that made social conflicts so bitter. Antagonism developed over pasturage and timber rights, rates of pay for working manorial land, and especially tenancy arrangements. In the poorest parts of rural Russia, as in Ireland, a peasant might pay more in rent for a patch of land than he could earn by selling its produce.

There were two possible ways out of the impasse: revolutionary violence from below or radical reform from above. The anarchic *jacquerie* movement, which began in the Poltava province in 1902 and spread to most of Russia in 1905-6 (see p. 246), lent a sense of urgency to the government's deliberations. From 1898 onward Witte belatedly tried to curb the excesses of communalism but was thwarted by his colleagues. In 1902 he set up a special committee that collected much material, focused public attention on the problem, and prepared the ground for the reforms launched in 1906 by his rival P. A. Stolypin. These represented a major breakthrough in official thinking, even though Stolypin's approach was more narrowly political than that of his predecessor. His main objective was to build up a strong class of independent peasant farmers, such as Russia had hitherto conspicuously lacked, and so to reinforce the conservative landowning gentry, now clearly in decline. Stolypin realized that time was not on his side and that success would require a generation of peaceful organic development. Yet even had Russia been granted this happy fate, one may doubt whether his reform would have accomplished its purposes.

Its main feature was the dissolution of the commune. This process had two phases: first, the conversion of communal to individual property by the issue of appropriation certificates; second, the physical separation and consolidation of the land, where possible as a *khutor*, a self-contained farm on the western European model. The first operation was administratively simpler. By January 1915 some 2 million householders in repartitional communes had been granted title-deeds, as had another half-million persons in those communes that no longer practised repartition; some historians would add to these another 1.7 million householders who were converted to individual tenure automatically,[1] but this is misleading. It is estimated that the 2.5 million householders whose

---

[1] This resulted from the law of 14 June 1910, which ruled that an entire non-repartitional commune could be broken up at the request of even a single member wishing to separate, with the authorities' approval.

lands were so appropriated comprised between 20 and 24 per cent of all peasant householders and owned approximately 29 per cent of the former communal land. The second operation was much more difficult. By January 1916 only 1.3 million consolidated farms had been set up, comprising 10.3 per cent of all peasant households with 8.8 per cent of all peasant land; of these a mere 22 per cent were *khutora*. For obvious historical and geographical reasons the reform was more successful in the more individualistic west and south than it was in Great Russia. Communal feeling made itself felt strongly in 1917, when the new petty proprietors were swept away, along with the landowners, in another wave of violence.

It would be unfair to judge the Stolypin reform solely by these modest achievements. During the pre-war years the condition of the peasantry improved in many important respects. The fiscal burden was reduced by the abolition (from 1907) of the ill-fated redemption payments; much money was invested in amelioration schemes; the number of agronomists, veterinary surgeons, and teachers in rural areas greatly increased; and peasants were encouraged to diversify their crops. In 1905 the Peasant Land Bank was allowed to extend the scope of its operations and some crown holdings were distributed. Between 1905 and 1914 another 25 million acres are thought to have passed into peasant hands. The government also speeded up its programme to settle thinly populated regions of Siberia and Central Asia by encouraging peasant migration. In the peak year 1908 some 750,000 pioneers crossed the Urals, but subsequently the rate declined; many of them returned in dismay at the hardships they encountered. This mass movement, significant as it was, could do no more than absorb the natural increase of the rural population. The continuing exodus to the cities and factory settlements also helped to mop up surplus labour in the countryside.

Stolypin's bold attempt at social engineering came too late to be effective. Nor was individual ownership the panacea that his supporters believed. The successes achieved before 1914 by the co-operative movement, a spontaneously growing phenomenon that received only lukewarm official support, suggest that there was a more democratic – and economically rational – alternative to the extremes of individualism and collectivism.

MASS AND ÉLITE IN RUSSIAN SOCIETY

The 'great reforms' did something to soften the rigidities of the empire's social structure. The power of the landowning nobility declined and new groups emerged with aspirations to leadership. The legal impediments to upward social mobility could in practice be bypassed fairly easily, so that classification according to *sosloviya* (estates), although still officially adhered to, became more anachronistic than ever. To an increasing extent it was neither hereditary rights nor service to the state that determined an individual's social status, but rather his good fortune in obtaining an education, accumulating wealth, or distinguishing himself in a particular field of endeavour. This development was naturally more marked in the cities than in the countryside, and took effect more slowly than in the contemporary West. Until the First World War Russian society was characterized by a high degree of inequality. There was a deep chasm between the relatively small élite and the underprivileged. A legacy of the age of serfdom, it made tension and conflict endemic. The cohesion of Russian society was strained still further by the very real cultural and psychological divide that persisted between the upper classes and the common people. In a period of crisis the tenuous and somewhat artificial bonds that held the nation together were likely to snap, so creating the preconditions for violent revolution.

The peasants and workers

The peasants constituted the lowest tier in the social pyramid and the largest group in the population. According to the census of 1897, which understated the facts, 93.4 million persons (including dependents), or nearly three-quarters of the total population, earned their livelihood from agriculture or kindred pursuits. By the terms of the emancipation settlement the peasants comprised a kind of separate caste, distinct from the rest of the nation, with its own institutions and laws. Not until 1905 did they secure juridical equality with other Russian citizens. Shortly before this their legal status had been improved by abolition of collective responsibility for debts (1903) and of liability to corporal punishment (1904). Subsequently the Stolypin reform helped to enhance the peasant's consciousness of his rights and obligations as an individual. Yet these measures came too late to break the hold of traditional collectivist and egalitarian thinking upon the peasant's mind – at least in Great-Russian areas. He was deeply conservative, yet readily accepted the idea of revolutionary violence. The view that the land belonged rightfully to those who worked it was widespread.

To some extent this outlook was undermined by social differentiation within the village, the natural consequence of exposure to market forces. The emergence within the commune of a well-to-do group, comprising those who employed hired labour and owned more horses or cattle than their neighbours, was a subject keenly debated by contemporary Russian radicals. Marxist writers tended to overstate the significance of this phenomenon, and argued that the Russian peasantry was becoming polarized into two classes, bourgeois and proletarian, analogous to those supposedly existing in the capitalist West. They seized eagerly upon any evidence of class antagonism and sought to stimulate it in the interests of revolution (see p. 245). The Populists criticized this view as unduly schematic: it failed to take due account of the natural inertia of traditional peasant society, the psychological legacy of serfdom, or the balancing normative role played by the middle peasant. They could show, for example, that social stratification within the commune was governed by demographic as well as economic factors: peasants with large families had both the incentive and the means to expand their farms and so increase their wealth. Thus the natural trend of social development was not necessarily linear, toward an accentuated contrast between extremes, but might rather be cyclical, with wealthier and poorer families rising and falling in turn. Modern studies of peasant society in other countries have borne out many of the Populists' ideas. The Marxists were correct in pointing to the anachronistic and reactionary features of the commune, which the early Populists were prone to idealize, and in predicting its decay. However, in the disturbances of 1905–6 and 1917–18 the peasants gave little sign of Marxist 'class consciousness'; on the contrary, they rallied in a common front against all alien groups – not only the landowners but the whole urban élite – in a movement basically egalitarian, anarchic, and (in socio-economic terms) retrograde.

A related issue, likewise vigorously discussed by contemporary students of Russian society, was the size and significance of the industrial working class. For Marxists the emergence of a 'proletariat' was an ideological necessity, for this was *ex hypothesi* the most progressive class and the agent of socialist revolution. They therefore inclined to exaggerate the degree to which such workers had broken away from their peasant roots. The Populists countered by stressing the political and psychological affinities between all 'toilers', whether in field or factory. Again, there was merit in both doctrines. The Marxists rightly appreciated that industrial workers were more likely than peasants to initiate revolutionary action, particularly where they were concentrated in large concerns or industrial settlements. In 1913, according to one (probably exaggerated) estimate, about 44 per cent of Russian workers were employed in enterprises with a labour force of 1,000 or more. Such men tended to develop feelings of loyalty toward their comrades, or to the radical intelligentsia, which superseded old ties to the village. On the other hand, poverty and depressed social conditions limited workers' opportunities to enjoy a normal family life, and so hindered the emergence of a 'hereditary proletariat'. Many men had to leave their families in their villages, which enhanced their interest in maintaining their rural connections. Some habitually returned in summer to help with the harvest; many more retained a claim to a share in communal land. Until 1912, when a rudimentary form of social insurance was introduced for industrial workers, they had to depend on the village for a modicum of social security if they should become unemployed or sick. There was a constant influx of young recruits to industry who found the harsh discipline little to their taste. This element, militant by nature, helped to keep much of the working class in an alienated, rebellious frame of mind. This factor, and the natural affinity between industrial labourers and the peasant milieu whence they had so recently sprung, proved significant in 1905 and 1917. Paradoxically, the 'socialist revolution' succeeded because Russia *lacked* a proletariat in the western sense, i.e. a sizeable segment of the work force reconciled to the factory system, with an interest in its perpetuation, and anxious to better their lot by winning reforms. The regime first forbade, and after 1906 harassed trade unions and other working-class bodies; this too strengthened the tendency to radicalism among industrial labour.

The privileged groups

Once the powerful social forces latent in this multimillion-person worker–peasant mass had been mobilized, the privileged groups could offer little effective resistance. Traditionally, their hegemony had rested upon popular inertia, reinforced by the myth of a God-given autocracy; but this belief was losing force and there was no easy alternative means of legitimizing the social order.

The élite consisted of three main groups (four if the clergy (see p. 214) are included). As they overlapped, any attempt at characterization is naturally somewhat hazardous. The best criterion is an occupational one.

The most important element in the élite may be termed the 'service class'. It comprised those who held posts in the administration and armed forces, as well as a sizeable element of the landowning nobility. The gentry had traditionally been more interested in pursuing careers in the official world of the capital than in playing a leading economic or cultural role in the countryside. For a few aristocrats education in the exclusive Corps of Pages might open the way to service at court, while one or other of the scarcely less exclusive cadet corps gave entrée to a guards regiment. The cavalry enjoyed higher social prestige than the infantry; both these fighting arms stood above the more technical ones (artillery, engineers). Similarly, in the fleet there was a sharp distinction between aristocratic line officers and naval engineers. The armed forces generally were more favoured than the civil service. In gaining admission to the officer corps or the upper reaches of the bureaucracy, academic or professional excellence was generally less important than *svyazi* (personal and family connections). Likewise, promotion did not depend wholly upon merit, but for some came automatically after they had occupied for a given period a particular grade in the Petrine Table of Ranks, which had long since tended to obstruct rather than facilitate social mobility within the official service hierarchy. This often had harmful effects, encouraging bureaucratic formalism and pettifogging regimentation, disregard for the law or considerations of common humanity, careerism and obsequiousness – vices satirized by many literary critics of the 'realist' school. In fairness it should be added that these intellectuals had a political axe to grind and that many problems facing Russian administrators would have taxed a Solon.

Of special significance was the growth among the service class of a more professional spirit. In the 1890s Witte's Ministry of Finance was more efficient than was the Ministry of Internal Affairs, and the conflict between new ways and old took the form of a bitter inter-departmental conflict (see p. 237). Later the Ministry of Agriculture built up a bureaucratic 'empire' that was likewise distinguished for its more modern and technical approach to social policy. In the army this process was still more marked. Defeat in the Crimean War stimulated the reforms of D. A. Milyutin, who introduced compulsory (but selective) universal military service (1874) and also improved the army's educational establishments. Subsequently there was a reaction toward a more rigid caste spirit, typified by Alexander III's announcement (1885) that he desired 'the Russian nobles to preserve a dominant place in the military leadership'. The effects of this policy were apparent in the Russo-Japanese War. After 1905 defeat once again prompted reform. Imperial patronage within the high command was reduced and greater attention given to the support troops. In 1913 military schools were opened to all qualified applicants regardless of birth. These measures were, however, resisted by the more conservative elements in the officer corps, who feared and scorned the professionals with technical training. Yet the First World War was soon to demonstrate tragically their vital importance. The 'old guard' officers suffered heavy losses during the first months of the fighting, and commissions were granted to men from more humble social strata, often with democratic political sympathies. When the imperial regime collapsed, the officer corps was grievously split. It could provide no effective leadership able to act as counterweight to the forces of revolution.

The second element within the élite comprised the commercial and industrial groups, together with such large-scale agricultural producers as succeeded in adapting themselves to the demands of a market economy. Nineteenth-century Russia conspicuously lacked an urban bourgeoisie of the western type. Her great merchant families, descended in many cases from peasants who had prospered under serfdom, were inward-looking and tradition-bound. In their way of life they preserved and embodied the values of the old patriarchal society whence they had sprung. This was particularly the case in Moscow and other Great-Russian centres, such as Nizhny-Novgorod, whose ancient fair continued to attract a larger share of the country's internal trade until the First World War. Some leading merchants belonged to Old Believer communities, and strongly emphasized the simple puritan virtues of piety, thrift, caution, and modesty in the display of wealth. The acquisitive and avaricious *kuptsy* (merchants) portrayed in the plays of Aleksandr Ostrovsky were literary fictions; nevertheless the fact remains that this milieu produced few men fitted to provide the civil leadership that the country so desperately required.

Nor could the gap be filled by the more modern-minded, cosmopolitan industrialists and bankers who appeared toward the end of the period, the creatures of westernization and economic expansion. They were too few in number and bound by ties of material interest to the state. They often favoured authoritarian policies in the hope of checking turbulence among their employees. In 1905, carried forward by the general mood, they adopted a more liberal stance, but were soon appeased by limited constitutional concessions. The partnership between government and industry, effected by such organizations as the Congress of Representatives of Industry and Trade (founded in 1906), reached its climax in the last years of peace. In 1915–16 private businessmen were active in the Zemgor movement which, although highly critical of the empire's supreme leadership, worked closely with the defence ministries to bolster the war effort.

This collaboration helps to explain why public life in nineteenth-century Russia should for so long have been dominated, first by members of the gentry, and then by the intelligentsia that sprang from it. Relatively few noble entrepreneurs had the resources or skill to refashion their estates on capitalist lines. Most of the successful farms were located in the deep south (cereals) or south-west (sugar-beet, distilling); a few reached a high level of mechanization and technical efficiency. In 1913 Russia had some 110,000 large farms, which covered only 10 per cent of the sown area but accounted for about one-third of marketed produce. The landowners' contribution to agricultural output was thus very significant, but the agrarian system as such suffered from fundamental defects. The average estate faced well-nigh insoluble problems, not only economic (lack of skilled personnel, credit, and transport facilities) but also 'socio-psychological': the survival of the 'service-oriented' attitude that had been general under serfdom, which led so many landowners to neglect their properties and waste their assets. It was these difficulties, together with the latent threat of peasant revolt, that caused them to sell their land and to seek a new career in the cities, either in the state service or in the free professions. In doing so, it might be said, they were 'reverting to type'.

The aristocratic (and clerical) origins of the intelligentsia, the third element in the social élite, left a decisive imprint upon its ideas – and it was these ideas, rather than any precise occupational function, that served to distinguish it from other social groups. It comprised those who, having received a modern education, felt alienated from the existing political and social order. They might earn their living as professional men, *zemstvo* employees, or even (paradoxical as this may seem) civil servants and landowners; indeed, the figure of the 'repentant nobleman' stands at the cradle of Russian intellectual history.

The ideologies propounded by the Russian intelligentsia tended to be socially radical, democratic, and cosmopolitan, although they might have a concealed élitist, authoritarian, or nationalist streak. These theories, derived from the advanced thought of contemporary Europe, often bore little relevance to the immediate problems confronting Russian society, but this seldom detracted from their appeal. Intellectuals were acknowledged to be their mentors by nearly all educated Russians, i.e. by everyone not closely identified with the autocratic regime. Their leadership was in normal times implicit, but in periods of crisis (1877–81, 1901–7) it became overt and decisive (see pp. 240, 247). Before the First World War their hegemony began to wane, partly for political but mainly for sociological reasons – the long-delayed emergence of a genuine modern 'middle class' of the western European type, a leadership group with firm roots in society and experience of a pluralistic political system. Before it could reach maturity, alas, war and revolution supervened. In the upsurge of mass violence the intellectuals were swept away, along with the rest of the social élite. There was a tragic irony in their fate: it might be said of them that they had sown the wind but reaped the whirlwind.

GOVERNMENT AND OPPOSITION

THE CENTRAL EXECUTIVE

It was remarkable that, in an age of rapid modernization, the autocratic regime should withstand every challenge until 1905, and even more remarkable that the semi-constitutional system then established should allow the monarchy to preserve intact the greater part of its ancient prerogatives until the final collapse came in 1917. This achievement – for such it was – cannot really be attributed to the political talents of the last three tsars, each of whom, though for different reasons, was tragically ill-fitted for the task of governing Russia. The primary reason lies in the relative inertia of a polity in which the ruler's authority retained more than a shadow of its former 'divine' aura, and supernatural sanctions could readily be invoked to legitimize and buttress it. To this task the established church devoted itself with almost excessive zeal (see p. 213). Secondly, the regime had at its command very potent instruments of coercion. There was an outwardly impressive hierarchy of administrative institutions; and wherever this civilian apparatus of control proved defective, and opposition assumed a menacing character, the armed forces could be brought in to maintain order. The most striking instances of this occurred in 1906–7, when there was a virtual 'white terror' in certain parts of the empire afflicted by revolutionary outbreaks; the fate of the Turkestan rebels in 1916 (see p. 206) may also be recalled in this context.

The central government, for all its power, was notoriously slow-moving and inefficient. This was partly due to the élitist, non-professional principles adopted in the selection of personnel; partly to the persistence of the traditional notion that the main tasks of an administrator were to keep the peace and limit public expenditure, rather than to promote purposive social change; and partly to the lack of any adequate institutional machinery for co-ordinating executive decisions. This latter 'technical' deficiency had a political cause, in the fear felt by the most zealous defenders of autocracy lest such a body infringe the sovereign's prerogatives. Thus the State Council, composed (to 1906) of appointed elder statesmen, restricted itself to scrutinizing draft bills put forward either by the tsar (and his unofficial advisers) or by the various ministries (and other official bodies). It had no power of legislative initiative. It met in private and until 1893 even kept its agenda confidential. The tsar was free to disregard majority opinion among his counsellors, and to issue laws without consulting them at all – as he quite frequently did.

The Committee of Ministers met regularly but concerned itself mainly with routine matters, since individual ministers could decide whether to submit their proposals to it or to approach the tsar directly. Once the latter had made his resolution, the matter could not be re-examined in the committee, since the sovereign's word was law. No clear distinction was drawn between executive orders binding upon officials and legislative acts applicable to all subjects. The result was administrative chaos: decisions might be taken that contradicted one another or the law as it stood. Real power lay with those ministers who managed, for a time, to secure the tsar's ear and could thus exercise an informal authority over their colleagues. Factional conflicts over policy and inter-departmental intrigues were rife, particularly in the period 1894–1906. Alexander II, however, allowed competent and broad-minded ministers such as Milyutin or Reutern to hold office for lengthy periods. This made for continuity, and a recognizable liberal faction emerged within the government; but it could not consolidate its power institutionally and its members were forced out of office singly in 1881–3. Alexander III harnessed together a team of consistently conservative ministers, but this homogeneity ended in 1893 with the rise of Witte, who for a decade enjoyed a bitterly contested pre-eminence. His 'overlordship' was not entirely unprecedented. In 1880–1 General M. T. Loris-Melikov headed an emergency 'supreme administrative commission' to maintain internal security and subsequently became interior minister. In a less formal way Pobedonostsev was virtual prime minister to Alexander III, but his influence over day-to-day policy-making was less than is generally assumed.

The constitutional settlement of October 1905 brought into being a cabinet, the Council of Ministers, with Witte as chairman. But the new government lacked cohesion or public support; Nicholas II feared his new premier, and took the first opportunity to dismiss him (April 1906). Two months later his place was filled by another strong-willed personality, Stolypin, who held office for five years. Although he showed himself an effective (if brutal) leader and was irreproachably loyal to the tsar, he did not enjoy the latter's complete confidence. After Stolypin's assassination (September 1911), right-wing extremists who desired a return to untrammelled autocracy regained influence and the government began to disintegrate. One premier succeeded another with increasing rapidity, and the same occurred at ministerial level. From 1915 onward a number of senior appointments were made informally by the Empress Aleksandra Fyodorovna, advised by her favourite, Rasputin. With this the imperial regime entered upon its death agony. In the middle of a critical war the empire found itself worse governed than at any time since the eighteenth century.

Right up to 1917 the monarchical regime had a bad reputation for arbitrary rule and neglect of legal norms. Personal rights and civil liberties, supposedly safeguarded by the revised fundamental laws of 1906, remained precarious. Junior officials often ignored the law when it was administratively convenient, assuming that their actions would be condoned by their superiors. Admittedly, this was to some extent a 'backlash phenomenon', a despairing response to the growth of violent opposition, which caused the regime to retract measures that had implied self-limitation of the supreme power, i.e. acknowledgment of prescriptive, even if informal, limitations upon its freedom. It is also true that juridical consciousness was weak in Russian society generally, not merely among the ruling élite. Nevertheless on balance the monarchy deserves the historian's censure, if only for its lack of political rationality. Most members of the dynasty and their associates were devoted to preserving the principle of personal autocracy at a time when it had long since become anachronistic, and had value only as a 'social myth' that could disguise the realities of the modern bureaucratic state. In their effort to implement goals that were essentially Utopian, the right-wing extremists helped to destroy both the image and the substance of the imperial regime.

Turning to the lower echelons of the executive, the discussion will be confined to the most important institution, the Ministry of the Interior. It was this body that set the *tone* of official policy, and in practice the tone might well be more significant than any formal legislative enactments. As in all authoritarian regimes, there were alternating periods of 'freeze' and 'thaw'. The relationship between government and society – in contemporary parlance, *vlast'* and *obshchestvo* – was determined by subtle variations in the climate of official opinion, which the public, from long experience, was quick to detect. The interior ministry interpreted its functions broadly, to include political guidance and supervision of popular morale, in addition to normal police activities such as the apprehension of lawbreakers. Its aim was to crush subversion before it could manifest itself. This involved press censorship and the covert subsidizing of 'reliable' publications, the employment of spies and *agents-provocateurs* to penetrate clandestine organizations, and the use of crude physical violence against suspected enemies.

The 'great reforms' of the 1860s led to a relative de-emphasis of police activity, at least in the cities. The easing of censorship restrictions after 1855 permitted a rapid rise in the number and circulation rates of periodicals, and the 'provisional regulations' issued in 1863 were comparatively liberal. A large segment of the educated public took part in an initially fairly free discussion of serf emancipation, and expert opinion was consulted in the preparation of the judicial and other reforms. After an attempt on the tsar's life in April 1866, security measures were tightened. Of P. A. Shuvalov, who headed the Third Section and *gendarmerie* from 1866 to 1873, a colleague observed that 'he interferes in everything, under the pretext of protecting the emperor's person and the monarchy, and all matters are decided in accordance with his whisperings'. The repression was particularly severe in the universities. But the authorities could not understand the reasons for the mounting opposition or devise effective measures to control it. Several individuals were punished severely, and even executed, for relatively minor offences. This led to further assassination attempts, which claimed the lives of several prominent officials, including Shuvalov's successor, General N. V. Mezentsev (August 1878). The government now lost the initiative and blew hot and cold in turns. Only after Alexander II's assassination (1 March 1881) were more rigorous security methods enforced. At the interior ministry D. A. Tolstoy (1882–9) and I. N. Durnovo (1889–95) greatly improved police efficiency, although at the cost of alienating public opinion. The *gendarmerie*, which employed some 50,000 men, was

236

administratively streamlined; regulations were introduced giving certain provincial governors wide emergency powers and press freedom was curbed.

The accession of Nicholas II in 1894 brought a less certain hand to the helm. It was becoming increasingly apparent that the problems facing the regime were too formidable to be solved by conventional security measures; yet the obvious alternative, timely constitutional reform, was ruled out by the tsar's own prejudices and his need to placate highly-placed reactionaries – men who, paradoxically, derived their power chiefly from their official position, yet limited the government's freedom of action. One novel venture by the interior ministry was to set up (from 1901) trade unions under camouflaged police control, in the hope of weaning workers away from socialism. The scheme, devised by S. V. Zubatov, a police official who combined considerable professional skill with political opportunism, at first worked well; but soon some of his followers threw off the reins and in 1903 he was repudiated. His techniques, however, continued to command respect in police circles. V. K. Plehve, Minister of the Interior in 1902–4, used methods of 'provocation' on a nationwide scale, but with insufficient sophistication, and fell victim to his own intrigues: among those responsible for his assassination was a treacherous police agent, E. F. Azev.

During the revolution of 1905 the Ministry of the Interior pursued an erratic course and its control apparatus temporarily disintegrated. Several leading police officials were assassinated; another, A. A. Lopukhin, betrayed its secrets to the opposition; and some junior men, carried away by the spirit of the times, even thought of forming their own trade union. Yet the crisis passed. Under Stolypin's firm hand the security services were reorganized, expanded, and refined. Particularly successful were their efforts to infiltrate illegal revolutionary parties and sow distrust among their leaders. R. V. Malinovsky, an *agent-provocateur* who in 1912 became chief Bolshevik spokesman in the duma, helped to bring about the final breach within the Social Democratic party; he was, however, exposed shortly afterward. Neither constitutional formalities nor the outbreak of war seriously inhibited the political police from continuing their work. It was, for example, an agent's denunciation that led to the arrest of the labour group on the War Industries Committee (January 1917), an incident that helped to provoke revolution a few weeks later. Naturally, *gendarmes* were among the prime targets for popular wrath after the overthrow of the regime they had served so well; the institution itself, however, was to survive in a new form.

THE PREREQUISITES OF POLITICAL MATURITY

Judged by the standards of later totalitarian dictatorships, tsarist rule must be adjudged to have been fairly mild. The brutalities inseparable from any authoritarian regime were in practice often tempered by respect for considerations of morality or expediency. But arbitrary police power, with all that it implied in terms of human suffering, created a deep reservoir of bitterness and hatred. Its most harmful consequence was that it undermined respect for law (of which the police were ostensibly the guardians) among the population at large. Yet a juridical consciousness did grow among an important segment of the public, and this represented an important step forward to political maturity. Another progressive development was the emergence of autonomous public bodies, particularly in the field of local government. Both these were basic prerequisites for any constitutional advance.

The reform of November 1864 introduced radical changes in the administration of justice. Modelled in part on contemporary French practice, it prescribed that judges should be properly trained and paid, and enjoy security of tenure. Cases were to be heard in open court before a jury; the accused had the right to counsel, and provision was made for a bar of professional advocates. Most old class barriers were swept away, although lawsuits between peasants were dealt with by *volost'* (cantonal) courts under customary, not statutory law. Minor cases between peasants and members of other classes were heard by locally elected justices of the peace, who soon earned a high reputation for their impartiality. Their powers were subsequently (1889) limited in favour of appointed officials called *zemskiye nachal'niki* ('land captains'), and not until 1912 were they restored. Conservatives also campaigned against the jury system and the independence of the judiciary. As opposition mounted, they sought to have political offences tried by administrative tribunals, which generally passed sentence of banishment or exile. Members of the Russian bar resisted strongly all efforts by the executive to bend the law to suit its purposes. Some made a point of defending political prisoners without expectation of reward. In the courtroom free speech was tolerated, and trials were reported in the press; thus advocates found themselves in the van of the struggle for liberty and civil rights. Many entered the political arena, where their mature experience served the opposition parties well. One should in fairness add that not all self-styled democrats who loudly endorsed the rule of law fully appreciated its implications; this was an unfortunate by-product of the bitter political struggle.

No less important as nurseries of civic leadership were the many autonomous organizations, serving a variety of public purposes, that

238

sprang up after 1862, when the laws of association were liberalized. The existence of such bodies still required ministerial approval, but in 1906 this was whittled down to formal registration (except for political organizations and trade unions, which suffered much police harassment). Of professional associations the most important was the medical society named after the surgeon N. I. Pirogov, whose national congresses attracted wide public attention. Similar societies existed for teachers, statisticians, and other groups. Each province had numerous voluntary bodies engaged in various kinds of welfare work. The control that officialdom sought to exercise over their affairs often led to friction.

Tension between government and society reached its highest pitch in the struggle over the *zemstva*, the elected organs of rural self-government introduced in 1864. From their earliest days these institutions, and the municipal councils established in 1870, constituted a potential threat to the autocratic–bureaucratic state. Their representative character made them, as it were, 'foreign bodies'. As Witte argued in an ambiguous memorandum to the tsar (1899), unless they were either absorbed into the official institutional hierarchy or suppressed, they would serve as the nucleus of a constitutional system. Conversely, it was precisely the hope that the edifice of local self-government would eventually be 'crowned' by a national representative assembly that made the zemstva attractive to liberal opinion. They were elected by indirect suffrage, with gentry, peasants, and townspeople meeting separately to choose deputies to the council, which in turn appointed its executive board. This system was scarcely democratic, but did at least ensure that peasants could take part in the work and negotiate with their former masters around a common table. The most active members, naturally enough, were landowners, many of whom were keenly interested in improving local conditions. The emphasis in zemstvo activity at first lay mainly upon relieving social distress and developing communications (including railways); but in the 1880s, as cadres of professional men became available, they concerned themselves more with public health and education. Annual zemstvo expenditure on health per head of population, which in 1871 stood at 4.5 kopecks, reached 20 kopecks in 1890 and 38 kopecks in 1900, by which date most districts had one doctor for every 20,000–40,000 inhabitants. This was, of course, pathetically little; nevertheless, a number of hospitals were built, and the zemstvo employees were pioneers in the fight against disease and ignorance. They did not always receive adequate backing from their executive boards, still less from the central government. A particularly long and bitter conflict developed over control of rural schools, which were managed by the Ministry of Education (through school boards) but were financed largely by the zemstva and local communities. Officials in the capital saw the zemstva as their rivals for popular favour and hampered them in various ways. As early as 1867 their tax-raising powers were curtailed and governors given the right to censor their official papers. They were forbidden to communicate with each other even on technical matters. Such unreasonable restrictions naturally provoked the very movement of opposition they were designed to forestall.

THE MODERATE OPPOSITION

Russian liberalism first emerged as a significant force in 1857–62, during the public debate on serf emancipation. It had two strains, oligarchic and democratic. The former group (Yu. F. Samarin, V. A. Cherkassky), which was the stronger, emphasized the progressive role of the enlightened nobility, whose social position it hoped to safeguard; the latter (A. M. Unkovsky, A. I. Koshelyov) was ready to forswear all class privileges as a gesture of appeasement to the *narod* (people). The Slavophil elements wished to move gradually toward a constitutional order, and suggested reviving the consultative *zemskiy sobor* or convoking a chamber of notables. The 'westerners' wanted the immediate summons of a national legislative assembly, elected without regard for class differences. In 1862 Unkovsky and his friends were arrested, and the liberal *fronde* collapsed. The Polish insurrection eased the transition to a more conservative and nationalistic viewpoint. Many moderates devoted themselves to practical work in the new zemstva. Liberalism revived during the Russo-Turkish war, which revealed the shortcomings of the regime – as did the successes of the revolutionary terrorists. Both emboldened and alarmed by this movement, some zemstvo assemblies adopted 'loyal addresses' to the tsar in which they hinted at the need for constitutional reform (1878–9). I. I. Petrunkevich and others established contact with the revolutionaries and founded the politically motivated Zemstvo Union; but this organization was soon destroyed by police infiltration. Loris-Melikov allowed several new opposition newspapers to appear.

The pressure from society evoked a favourable response among some officials. Already in 1863 P. A. Valuyev, then interior minister, had devised a plan for drawing elected representatives of society into the work of the State Council. It was rejected by Alexander II, but in 1880 his modest ideas again served as a basis for discussion in bureaucratic circles. The war minister, D. A. Milyutin, suggested that half the state councillors might be elected by the provincial zemstva. He did not mention the autocracy itself, but apparently envisaged curtailing the imperial prerogative. The terrorist *coup* of February 1880 made these ideas *mal à propos*. A few months later Milyutin inspired the complicated and cautious project submitted to the tsar by Loris-Melikov on 28 January

1881,[2] which he approved on 17 February. However, before it could be published Alexander II was assassinated.

It has often been argued that this reform, although not in itself a constitution, might have served as a basis from which further progress in this direction could have been made, and that the liberal cause was frustrated by the extremists. There is much truth in this view. On the other hand, the existence of a revolutionary threat strengthened the moderates' bargaining power. Conceivably, if the proposed commissions had met and clashed with entrenched conservative forces, the liberal elements in government and society might have succumbed without revolutionary support. In any event, Alexander III's accession dealt a blow to all hopes of early constitutional reform. He was a convinced partisan of firm government, and his views were fortified by his father's untimely death.

Once again the liberals withdrew to unspectacular 'small deeds' in the zemstva, business, or education. This practical work was of considerable importance, in that it created the infrastructure of the much more solidly based movement that reappeared when circumstances permitted. Official efforts to buttress the gentry's position in the zemstva by tampering with the electoral system (June 1890) and by introducing the land captains (1889) did not have the political results anticipated, since the country landowners now responded quite readily to western liberal ideas. Their reformist attitudes were strengthened by the famine of 1891–2, when the public, not the government, took the lead in organizing relief.

After Nicholas II's accession the intellectual ferment grew apace. In Moscow D. N. Shipov, a zemstvo leader in the oligarchic and Slavophil tradition, skilfully exploited the more fluid political situation and managed to establish contact with colleagues in other towns. Simultaneously a more radical activist trend emerged, with its roots in the new urban professional classes. Its spokesmen included the historian P. N. Milyukov and the economist P. B. Struve. The former was a convinced admirer of western European parliamentary democracy, the latter a convert from Marxism who combined social reformism with belief in free enterprise. These elements were prominent in the programme of the Liberation League, a small pressure group that emerged in 1902–4 around the clandestine newspaper *Osvobozhdeniye* ('Liberation'). As the internal crisis deepened, the radical intellectuals won increasing influence

[2] Two 'provisional preparatory commissions', composed of 'reliable specialists' appointed by the tsar, were to draft bills on 'economic–administrative' and financial questions; these were to be considered by a 'general commission', whose members would include some men elected by the zemstva and municipalities; bills which this body approved were then to go before the State Council, to which would be attached 10–15 'representatives of public institutions', whose nature was not clearly specified.

over the moderate zemstvo men. Their hour of triumph came in November 1904, when the first national zemstvo congress passed a resolution calling for full civil rights and the immediate convocation of a constituent assembly, which most delegates wished to be elected by universal, direct, equal, and secret suffrage. During the turbulent months that followed, these demands were strongly endorsed by all articulate opinion – a development that came as a surprise to the liberals themselves, since their organizations were still weaker than those of the socialists.

The government, isolated and discredited at home and abroad, had no alternative but to compromise. Nicholas II tried vainly to gain time by making various minor concessions while clinging to his prerogatives as autocrat, and was saved at the eleventh hour by the indefatigable Witte. The imperial manifesto of 17 October 1905 was Witte's handiwork, in which Nicholas concurred reluctantly. It promised that no law should take effect without the consent of the Imperial Duma, the new legislative chamber. In theory Russia now became a constitutional state with an autocratic tsar – a contradiction that only time could resolve.

The liberals' hopes could scarcely be realized so long as massive revolutionary violence continued. On the other hand, as order was gradually restored the government's willingness to abide by its constitutional undertakings evaporated. Many officials found it difficult to shake off so suddenly their accustomed arbitrary ways. Moreover, most liberals were dissatisfied with the concessions granted, and regarded the Imperial Duma simply as a stepping-stone to a fully democratic sovereign parliament. This was the viewpoint of Milyukov and other leaders of the Kadet (Constitutional–Democratic) party, which in October 1905 superseded the Liberation League. Those who adhered to the old gradualist traditions, notably Shipov and A. I. Guchkov, broke away to form the Union of 17 October ('Octobrists'). The re-emergence at this critical hour of the historic schism within Russian liberalism was a source of weakness that the administration could exploit, just as it exploited the more fundamental division between liberals and socialists.

The omens for Russia's experiment in parliamentary government were thus not bright. New fundamental laws, promulgated on 20 February 1906, limited narrowly the Duma's right to control government policy or expenditure, and even to question ministers, who were still responsible solely to the tsar. The State Council, expanded to include some elected representatives, became the upper chamber of the legislature; the assent of both houses and the tsar was required for a bill to become law. The procedure for emergency legislation (Article 87) gave the executive a means of bypassing the assembly. The franchise remained limited and indirect, but, as in the zemstva, this did at least mean that some peasants were elected as deputies, and an edict of December 1905 extended the suffrage to certain working-class groups as well.

In the first Duma (April–July 1906) the Kadets had a majority and provided vigorous leadership. Their demands for greater freedom and a thorough-going agrarian reform brought the assembly into direct confrontation with the government, which would not entertain the idea of compulsory expropriation of landed property. Stolypin and Milyukov met privately to explore the possibility of compromise, but the gap between them could not be bridged, and shortly thereafter the assembly was prematurely dissolved. The second Duma (February–June 1907), however, proved more radical than the first, and it overwhelmingly opposed Stolypin's agrarian policy. The Kadets tried to hold the balance, but their strength had waned, and the premier wanted a more pliant assembly that would co-operate with the government on its own terms. Once again the Duma was dissolved, but this time the electoral law was revised to favour upper-class and Great-Russian voters. This act (3 June 1907) was a flagrant breach of the constitution that failed to produce the results intended, since the opportunity to effect a *modus vivendi* with the opposition was thrown away.

In the third Duma (1907–12) the moderate Octobrists formed the strongest party. They were willing to collaborate with the government provided that it respected the law. But this Stolypin would not always do. He accepted the new order in principle, but was easily irritated by criticism and treated the Duma in arrogant fashion. There were frequent conflicts over administrative abuses. In 1910, disappointed by the Octobrists' insubordination, the premier transferred his patronage to the right-wing Nationalists, but they proved to be a broken reed. Disillusionment was general when in March 1911 Stolypin provoked a serious crisis by pushing through an unpopular measure (the Western Zemstva Bill) under Article 87, for which purpose he temporarily suspended the sittings of the legislature. Such blatant manipulation outraged public opinion, and Stolypin's assassination a few months later did nothing to relieve the tension. The opposition justifiably took strong exception to heavy-handed official gerrymandering in the 1912 election campaign and to the Rasputin affair.

These problems were greatly intensified when war broke out. The fourth Duma at first supported the government but turned against it in 1915, when its gross shortcomings became apparent. Despite its unrepresentative character the assembly became a focal point for resistance to the court camarilla. The opposition parties united in the Progressive Bloc, led by Milyukov. The Kadet spokesmen had now moved to the right and, while not averse to criticizing those in authority, sought to avoid any precipitate action that might weaken national unity in wartime. This patriotic 'defencist' stance, reasonable in a democratic western state, was unsuited to Russian conditions. It condemned the moderates to sit by idly while the country drifted into anarchy and revolution. Not until the monarchy had fallen did they form an alternative government, by which time the political initiative had passed into the hands of men whose commitment to liberal democratic values was uncertain.

The cause of constitutional government in Russia was not foredoomed from the outset. It failed principally because essential reforms were delayed for too long. This created an unbridgeable chasm of mistrust between the administration and its opponents, which offered ample scope to revolutionary extremists.

THE RADICAL OPPOSITION

Russian socialism was a product of the intelligentsia – for the most part idealistic men and women who were profoundly shocked by the backward, impoverished state of the Russian people and believed that radical improvements could come about only by violent revolution. It was characteristic that they should absolutize their hatred of oppression and love of equality and liberty, so that an apocalyptic striving for the total regeneration of society came to be regarded as a hallmark of Russian radicalism. It presupposed contempt for 'bourgeois liberalism' and the values it was believed to embody (formalism, legalism, gradualism), and a hypertrophied moralistic approach to politics. This could lead to acts of great courage and heroic self-sacrifice – but also to dogmatism, self-righteousness, intolerance of criticism, and (in the most extreme cases) the subordination of all ideas and actions to the single test of their political expediency. This attitude was the seedbed of modern totalitarianism.

These less attractive features of the radical intellectuals' *Weltanschauung* were aggravated by the difficulties that confronted those who sought to struggle actively against the autocratic regime. Obliged to operate underground, they had to adopt the methods and outlook of conspirators. They were subject to immense psychological strain: extravagant hopes mingled with deep uncertainties; they were the vanguard of the *narod*, yet were denied the means to test or demonstrate their claims. In normal times authority seemed omnipotent and all-pervasive; it was extremely difficult to maintain a clandestine organization in being, let alone spread subversive ideas among the population at large. Only when the state's power was weakened, by external wars and internal dissension, did opportunities arise to win mass support.

Radical circles appeared among students in Moscow and Khar'kov as early as 1855–6, but they first became significant in 1861, when the defects of the peasant reform aroused widespread indignation. Protest leaflets were distributed and disturbances broke out at several universities. N. A. Serno-Solov'yevich founded an organization that claimed to embrace adherents in several cities, but it was soon broken up by the police (July 1862). The suppression of the leading radical journal, *Sovremennik* ('The Contemporary'), whose widely respected editor, N. G. Chernyshevsky, was exiled to Siberia, temporarily caused the movement to lose its way. Some members took to individual terrorism (among them the student D. V. Karakozov, who in April 1866 made a vain attempt on the tsar's life); others were attracted to the egotistical utilitarian doctrines of D. I. Pisarev (sometimes miscalled 'nihilism'); many more succumbed to the appeal of the revolutionary anarchism taught by M. A. Bakunin.

Another voice was that of P. L. Lavrov, who took a more ethical stand. His followers began to form discussion circles that soon attempted to spread the socialist gospel more widely. In 1874–5 some 2,000 young radicals 'went to the people', but with disappointing results: they found the peasants largely indifferent to their message, and several hundred propagandists were arrested. The *narodniki* (Populists), as they came to be called, learned their lesson and adopted more sophisticated tactics, setting up small groups of resident agents and founding (1876) a new potentially national organization, which like its predecessor took the name *Zemlya i Volya* ('Land and Liberty'). Its leaders, notably A. D. Mikhailov, were skilled conspirators and insisted on the need for discipline, but they soon quarrelled over questions of tactics. The more experienced and reflective Populists emphasized the need for steady propaganda work (particularly among factory workers, who were more responsive to socialist teaching) and for collaboration with liberal 'society' for constitutional ends. The zealots, however, wanted to bring about immediate reforms, and even revolution, by terrorist methods. In 1879 this group prevailed and set up a new clandestine organization, *Narodnaya Volya* ('The People's Will'), which concentrated its energies on attempts to assassinate prominent officials, and ultimately the tsar himself. Its dramatic *coup* of 1 March 1881 was a technical success but politically a confession of bankruptcy (see p. 241): neither a constitution nor a revolution ensued, and the surviving terrorists, lacking any significant popular support, were easily mopped up by Alexander III's revitalized police.

This defeat enhanced the intellectual appeal of Marxist 'proletarian socialism' *vis-à-vis* the agrarian variety propagated by the Populists. Marx's ideas had been familiar to the 'men of the '70s', but only during the next two decades did they gain a firm following in clandestine discussion circles. Ideological differences were less clearly defined at the grass-roots level than was thought desirable by such *émigré* leaders as G. V. Plekhanov, a convert from Populism who gave the new doctrine an intolerant slant. He formed in Geneva a Labour Liberation Group (1883) that tried to infiltrate propaganda literature into Russia, with intermittent success. The 'thaw' on Nicholas II's accession benefited the Marxists, who were regarded by the police as being less dangerous than their Populist rivals. They could publish some books and journals openly and engage in public discussions. Many intellectuals were impressed by their seemingly more 'scientific' *Weltanschauung* and their self-identification with the triumphs of social democracy in western Europe; the progress of industrialization in Russia also made their theories more plausible. But some radicals objected to their doctrinaire proletarian bias and castigated them for their moral relativism, as evidenced by the equanimity with which they seemed to regard the peasants' fate under 'capitalism'. In the late 1890s, as in the late 1860s, this idealistic mood brought about a renascence of Populism.

The Socialist Revolutionary party, led by V. M. Chernov, became the first radical organization to win any significant degree of popular support (outside minority regions). It turned to good account the peasant disturbances that broke out in 1902, and also took up again the weapon of terrorism, this time to greater effect. From 1901 onward attempts on the lives of ministers and other officials aggravated the confusion in government policy.

Meanwhile the Social Democrats (as the Marxists now called themselves) were also strengthening their mass base. The most advanced groups were located in minority regions (Poland, Latvia, the Jewish 'pale'), where economic and cultural standards were higher among the workers and western European patterns of labour organization could strike root more easily. The Jewish 'Bund' (see p. 205) passed from surreptitious propaganda to the bolder tactics of mass agitation in the factories. Its example was followed by organizations in St Petersburg and other centres in Great Russia and the Ukraine. In 1898 the Social Democrats tried to merge several Jewish and Russian organizations of local significance into a party with nationwide connections, but the attempt was premature. Such a party came into existence only in 1903, when it was created, not by the workers' leaders themselves, but by a group of *émigré* intellectuals, led by V. I. Ul'yanov (Lenin). The new party, a somewhat artificial construction, immediately split into rival factions. The differences between Bolsheviks and Mensheviks, partly personal and partly political, were reminiscent of those among the Populists of the 1870s.[3] Their arguments were conducted on ideological lines, each invoking the authority of Marx and accusing the other of heresy.

[3] The Mensheviks wanted a measure of democracy in party organization and stressed the need to work in trade unions and other mass bodies to create a 'class-conscious proletariat' in the Marxist sense; they welcomed as allies anyone,

The largely spontaneous mass upsurge of 1905 brought the socialist parties great opportunities but also spotlighted their organizational weakness. Flexibility was at a premium, and they were swept away from their doctrinal moorings. The Mensheviks won a hold in many trade unions and could claim much of the credit for founding and leading the St Petersburg *soviet* (council), which for six weeks challenged the government's authority in the capital. The Bolsheviks inspired and headed several attempts at armed insurrection, notably in Moscow, where for ten days in December a few hundred guerrillas held out against troops and police. Of particular significance were the mutinies that broke out in the army and navy, which anticipated the events of 1917. Menshevik influence predominated in most cities of the west and south, Bolshevik influence in those of the north and east. The Socialist Revolutionaries' supporters were more numerous, but were located mainly in rural areas.

Despite widespread violence and some local successes, especially in the minority regions, the revolutionary movement did not prevail. This was partly because the socialist (and nationalist) leaders failed to co-ordinate their actions and wasted much energy in factional disputes, but chiefly because the government concluded a timely peace with Japan and did not lose control of the armed forces, which it used extensively as police auxiliaries. The socialists had insufficient opportunity to institutionalize their hold over their followers or to adjust themselves ideologically to the prospect of constitutional opposition. If they participated in the duma, they did so solely for purposes of agitation.

After 1907 their support soon evaporated. The party leaders were jailed or forced to emigrate to the West, where they resumed their theoretical wrangling. While the Mensheviks moved hesitantly toward reformist socialism, Lenin refined further his notion of the party as a militant revolutionary élite. Though few in numbers, the Bolsheviks could take advantage of the government's failure to tackle the sources of labour unrest. True, industrial earnings rose slightly, and in 1912 a contributory pensions scheme was introduced; but these were small gains. The workers remained in sullen mood, deprived of adequate channels through which to ventilate their grievances. A massacre in the Lena goldfields (1912) touched off a new wave of strikes, which was halted only by the outbreak of war. Whether this movement augured a repetition of the events of 1905 is arguable; nevertheless the urban scene in these years was characterized by conflict rather than stability. Taking into account the government's

including bourgeois liberals, willing to fight autocracy. The Bolsheviks advocated an authoritarian conspiratorial party as a political 'vanguard' to lead the workers and peasants in speeding up the revolutionary process, which was to pass rapidly from its 'bourgeois democratic' to its 'proletarian socialist' phase, the latter characterized by a 'dictatorship of the proletariat' (i.e. the party).

failure to appease the moderates, it may be said that in the Russia of 1914 the chances of revolution were once again in the ascendant. Her involvement in the First World War tilted the balance of probabilities much further in this direction.

Why then was revolution nevertheless delayed for two-and-a-half years? Three main reasons may be given: firstly, the general conviction that the war had been forced upon Russia by the enemy, which created (initially, at least) a mood of patriotic euphoria; secondly, the continued strict police surveillance, which all but ruled out organized subversive activity; thirdly, the deep chasm between those in educated 'society' who opposed the government for its lethargic or inefficient prosecution of the war, and the populace, who were by and large apathetic about the war, if not overtly hostile to it. All these factors helped to make the explosion more powerful when it came.

The tensions that had disfigured the Russian body politic and Russian society before 1914 were immeasurably aggravated by the burdens of war. Underprivileged civilians, especially in the towns, resented the unequal distribution of its hardships. The morale of the troops, particularly in the rear, was gradually undermined by military defeat, shortage of essential supplies, and rumours of corruption in high places. The distrust that developed between officers and men reflected the profound divisions in the country as a whole. Public confidence in the traditional authorities was seriously undermined, and a political climate created that encouraged apocalyptic expectations and limitless ambitions – for peace, social justice, rapid material progress, and, last but not least, an intoxicating and all-encompassing liberty. This spirit could not be contained within Russia's existing political and social institutions. It led, inevitably, to cataclysmic revolution and to a new authoritarianism built upon the ruins of the old.

GUIDE TO FURTHER READING

Abbreviations

AHR	*American Historical Review*, Washington
ASEER	*American Slavic and East European Review* (now *SR*), Seattle
CMRS	*Cahiers du monde russe et soviétique*, Paris
CSP	*Canadian Slavonic Papers*, Ottawa
CSS	*Canadian Slavic Studies*, Montreal (now *Canadian–American Slavic Studies*, Philadelphia)
CSSH	*Comparative Studies in Society and History*, The Hague
EHR	*Economic History Review*, London
FOEG	*Forschungen zur osteuropäischen Geschichte*, Berlin
IRSH	*International Review of Social History*, Amsterdam

GUIDE TO FURTHER READING

JCEA	*Journal of Central European Affairs*, Boulder
JEH	*Journal of Economic History*, New York
JGOE	*Jahrbücher für Geschichte Osteuropas*, Stuttgart, etc.
JMH	*Journal of Modern History*, Chicago
RR	*Russian Review*, Stanford
SEER	*Slavonic and East European Review*, London
SR	*Slavic Review*, Seattle
SS	*Soviet Studies*, Glasgow

1: General

Bibliographies.

A handy guide is *A Select Bibliography of Works in English on Russian History*, D. Shapiro, comp. (Oxford, 1962). Cf. also the relevant sections of K. Meyer, *Bibliographie zur osteuropäischen Geschichte* (Berlin, 1972), which contains works in west European languages published between 1939 and 1964.

Surveys

The standard history is H. Seton-Watson, *The Russian Empire, 1801–1917* (Oxford, 1967); cf. by the same author, *The Decline of Imperial Russia, 1855–1914* (London, 1952, repr. 1966). Other useful works of similar scope are S. Harcave, *Years of the Golden Cockerel: the Last Romanov Tsars, 1814–1917* (New York, 1968), and S. Pushkarev, *The Emergence of Modern Russia, 1801–1917* (trans.; London, 1963). One may also consult with profit the relevant chapters in such general histories as M. T. Florinsky, *Russia: a History and an Interpretation*, vol. II (London, 1953, 8th impress. 1963), and N. V. Riasanovsky, *A History of Russia* (New York, 1963, 2nd edn 1969).

Specific periods

A good introduction to Alexander II's reign, with emphasis on the reforms, is W. E. Mosse, *Alexander II and the Modernization of Russia* (London, 1958). Nicholas II's reign is surveyed by R. Charques, *The Twilight of Imperial Russia* (London, 1958). Fuller but now rather dated is S. S. Oldenburg, *Tsarstvovaniye Imperatora Nikolaya II* (2 vols., Belgrade–Munich, 1939, 1949). There are two useful recent collections of essays on this period: G. Katkov *et al.*, eds., *Russia Enters the Twentieth Century, 1894–1917* (London, 1971), and T. G. Stavrou, ed., *Russia under the Last Tsar* (Minneapolis, 1969). For the last years of Nicholas II's reign see also M. T. Florinsky, *The End of the Russian Empire* (New Haven, 1931, repr. New York, 1961). There is no comparable general treatment in English of the reign of Alexander III. R. Hare, *Portraits of Russian Personalities between Reform and Revolution* (London, 1959) provides fifteen biographical sketches of individuals active in political and intellectual life; that of Count S. Yu. Witte should be supplemented by T. H. von Laue, *Sergei Witte and the Industrialization of Russia* (New York, 1963); and that of K. P. Pobedonostsev by R. Byrnes, *Pobedonostsev: His Life and Thought* (Bloomington, 1968). An interesting debate by C. E. Black and others on 'The Nature of Imperial Russian Society', in *SR*, 20 (1961), 565–600, is reprinted in D. W. Treadgold, ed., *The Development of the USSR: an Exchange of Views* (Seattle, 1964), 173–210. For contemporary impressions by an acute foreign observer, see D. M. Wallace, *Russia* (2 vols., London, 1877, repr. in an abridged edition with a foreword by C. E. Black, New York, 1961).

2: Imperialism and nationalism

G. von Rauch, *Russland: staatliche Einheit und nationale Vielfalt* (Munich, 1953); cf. also L. I. Strakhovsky, 'Constitutional Aspects of the Imperial Russian Government's Policy towards National Minorities', *JMH*, 13 (1941), 467–92. A useful survey of the nationalities problem is contained in ch. I of R. Pipes, *The Formation of the Soviet Union: Communism and Nationalism, 1917–23*, 2nd edn (London, 1964, repr. New York, 1968). Still stimulating is the lecture by B. H. Sumner, *Tsardom and Imperialism in the Far East and Middle East, 1880–1914* (London, 1942).

3: Foreign policy

An introductory outline is given by B. Jelavich, *St Petersburg and Moscow: Tsarist and Soviet Foreign Policy, 1814–1974* (Bloomington, 1974), which replaces this author's *Russian Foreign Policy, 1814–1914* (Philadelphia–New York, 1964); see also G. H. Bolsover, 'Aspects of Russian Foreign Policy, 1815–1914', in R. Pares and A. J. P. Taylor, eds., *Essays Presented to Sir Lewis Namier* (London, 1956), 320–56. Of the many studies of European diplomatic history in this period, one that pays due attention to Russia is A. J. P. Taylor, *The Struggle for Mastery in Europe, 1848–1918* (London, 1954). For Russo-German relations under Alexander II, see especially W. E. Mosse, *The European Powers and the German Question, 1848–1871* (Cambridge, 1958) and, for a Soviet view, L. I. Narochnitskaya, *Rossiya i voyny Prussii v 60kh gg. XIX v.: bor'ba za obyedineniye Germanii 'sverkhu'* (Moscow, 1960). The attitude of Russian public opinion to foreign policy questions during the Duma period is considered by H. Jablonowski, 'Die Stellungnahme der russischen Parteien zur Aussenpolitik der Regierung von der russisch–englischen Verständigung bis zum I. Weltkriege', *FOEG*, 5 (1957), 60–92, and at greater length by M. Wolters, *Aussenpolitische Fragen vor der IV. Duma*...(Hamburg, 1969); in English, see J. F. Hutchinson, 'The Octobrists and the Future of Imperial Russia as a Great Power', *SEER*, 50 (1972), 220–37.

4: Official nationalism; Panslavism; conservatism

E. C. Thaden, *Conservative Nationalism in 19th-Century Russia* (Seattle, 1964) provides a general account; see also H. Rogger, 'Reflections on Russian Conservatism, 1861–1905', *JGOE*, 14 (1966), 195–212. On the Panslavs, see H. Kohn, *Panslavism: its History and Ideology* (Notre Dame, Ind., 1953, 2nd rev. edn New York, 1960); and M. B. Petrovich, *The Emergence of Russian Panslavism, 1856–1870* (New York, 1956), which may be compared with the Soviet account by A. Nikitin, *Slavyanskiye komitety v Rossii v 1858–1876 gg.* (Moscow, 1960). A. Ulam, 'Nationalism, Panslavism, Communism', in I. J. Lederer, ed., *Russian Foreign Policy: Essays in Historical Perspective* (London, 1962), 39–68, is wide-ranging and lively. Among recent biographies of conservative and nationalist thinkers are: S. Lukashevich, *Konstantin Leontyev, 1831–1891: a Study in Russian 'Heroic Vitalism'* (New York, 1967), and the same author's *Ivan Aksakov, 1823–1886: a Study in Russian Thought and Politics* (London, 1965) – the latter is the better work; R. E. MacMaster, *Danilevsky: a Russian Totalitarian Philosopher* (London, 1967); M. Katz, *M. N. Katkov: a Political Biography* (The Hague–Paris, 1966) – neither is wholly satisfactory. For Samarin, see G. Hucke, *Yu. F. Samarin: seine geistesgeschichtliche Position und politische Bedeutung*

(Munich, 1970). The career of an influential right-wing journalist is studied by E. Ambler, *Russian Journalism and Politics, 1861–1881: the Career of A. S. Suvorin* (Detroit, 1972). Danilevsky's tract *Rossiya i Yevropa* has been republished with a brief foreword (in Russian) by G. Ivask (New York, 1965), and the same editor has also made a selection from Leont'yev's works under the title *Against the Current* (New York, 1969). Useful articles on individual thinkers include: J. D. Morison, 'Katkov and Panslavism', *SEER*, 107 (1968), 422–41; H. Kohn, 'Dostoyevsky and Danilevsky: National Messianism', in E. J. Simmons, ed., *Continuity and Change in Russian and Soviet Thought* (Cambridge, Mass., 1955), 500–15; H. Kohn, 'Dostoyevsky's Nationalism', *Journal of the History of Ideas*, 6 (1945), 385–414; and H. H. Cloutier, 'Leontyev on Nationalism', *Review of Politics*, 17 (1955), 262–72.

5: The Straits

See the relevant chapters in M. S. Anderson, *The Eastern Question, 1774–1923: a Study in International Relations* (London, 1966), which replaces an earlier classic, Sir J. A. R. Marriott, *The Eastern Question*...(1917, 4th edn, Oxford, 1940). J. Hoffmann, 'Das Problem einer Seeblockade Kaukasiens nach dem Pariser Frieden von 1856', *FOEG*, 11 (1966), 130–75 deals with the 1850s; B. Jelavich, *The Ottoman Empire, the Great Powers and the Straits Question, 1870–1887* (Bloomington, 1973) examines the most critical years in the evolution of this problem; and E. C. Thaden, 'Charykov and Russian Foreign Policy at Constantinople in 1911', *JCEA*, 16 (1956), 25–44, treats the final period; see also the same author's *Russia and the Balkan Alliance* [see sec. 6]. On diplomatic developments during the First World War see W. A. Renzi, 'Great Britain, Russia and the Straits, 1914–1915', *JMH*, 42 (1970), 1–20.

6: Russian influence in the Balkans

The classic study by B. H. Sumner, *Russia and the Balkans, 1870–1880* (London, 1937) may be supplemented by several monographs and articles from the pens of B. Jelavich, *Russia and the Rumanian National Cause, 1858–1859* (Bloomington, 1959); C. Jelavich, ed., *Russia in the East, 1876–1880* (Leiden, 1959); and C. Jelavich, *Tsarist Russia and Balkan Nationalism: Russian Influence in the Internal Affairs of Bulgaria and Serbia, 1879–1886* (Berkeley–Los Angeles, 1958). For a favourable view of Ignat'yev's activities, see G. Hünigen, *N. P. Ignat'ev und die russische Balkanpolitik, 1875–1878* (Göttingen, 1968). The leading Soviet specialist in this area, S. A. Nikitin, chief editor of the collective work *Osvobozhdeniye Bolgarii ot turetskogo iga* (3 vols., Moscow, 1961–), has assembled several of his articles in *Ocherki po istorii yuzhnykh slavyan i russko-balkanskikh svyazey v 50–70kh gg. XIX v.* (Moscow, 1970). For the Serbs' role, see also D. Mackenzie, *The Serbs and Russian Pan-Slavism, 1875–1878* (London, 1967), and W. S. Vucinich, *Serbia between East and West: the Events of 1903–1908* (Stanford, 1954). The later stages of Russia's involvement in Balkan affairs are traced by E. C. Thaden, *Russia and the Balkan Alliance of 1912* (University Park, Pa., 1965), and several contributors to the volume *Russian Diplomacy in Eastern Europe, 1914–1917*, with an introduction by H. L. Roberts (New York, 1963). Among the most useful articles are: I. J. Lederer, 'Russia and the Balkans', in Lederer, ed., *Russian Foreign Policy* [see sec. 4], 417–52; C. E. Black, 'Russia and the Modernization of the Balkans', in C. and B. Jelavich, eds., *The Balkans in Transition: Essays*...(Berkeley–Los Angeles, 1963), 145–83; C. and B. Jelavich, 'The Danubian Principalities and Bulgaria under Russian Protectorship', *JGOE*, 9 (1961), 349–66; C. Jelavich, 'Russo-Bulgarian Relations, 1892–6...', *JMH*, 24 (1952), 341–51; and M. D. Sturdza, 'La Russie et la désunion des Principautés roumaines, 1864–1866', *CMRS*, 12 (1971), 247–85.

7: Poland

R. F. Leslie, *Reform and Insurrection in Russian Poland, 1856–1865* (London, 1963) is a standard work on its subject; see also I. M. Roseveare, 'Wielopolski's Reforms and their Failure before the Uprising of 1863', *Antemurale* (Rome), 15 (1971), 87–215; S. Kieniewicz, 'Polish Society and the Insurrection of 1863', *Past and Present*, no. 37 (July 1967), 130–48; S. J. Zyzniewski, 'The Futile Compromise Reconsidered: Wielopolski and Russian Policy in the Congress Kingdom, 1861–1863', *AHR*, 70 (1965), 395–412. Two Soviet documentary collections that stress the sympathy for the insurgents in Russian society are V. A. D'yakov *et al.*, eds., *Russko-pol'skiye revolyutsionnyye svyazi 60kh godov: vosstaniye 1863 goda* (Moscow, 1962), and V. D. Korolyuk and J. S. Miller, eds., *Vosstaniye 1863 g. i russko-pol'skiye revolyutsionnyye svyazi 60kh gg.* (Moscow, 1960). On the peasant reform in Russian Poland see chs. 11–14 and 17–18 of S. Kieniewicz, *The Emancipation of the Polish Peasantry* (London, 1969); for a Soviet view cf. I. I. Kostyushko, *Krest'yanskaya reforma 1864 g. v tsarstve Pol'skom* (Moscow, 1962).

On the evolution of political ideas after 1863, the relevant chapters of the early study by J. Feldman, *Geschichte der politischen Ideen in Polen seit dessen Teilungen* (trans. from Polish; Munich, 1917) may still be consulted with profit. More recent are U. Haustein, 'Sozialismus und nationale Frage in Kongresspolen', ...*JGOE*, 10 (1962), 513–62, and L. Blit, *The Origins of Polish Socialism, 1878–1886* (Cambridge, 1971). For documents, cf. G. W. Strobel, *Quellen zur Geschichte des Kommunismus in Polen 1878–1918: Programme und Statuten* (Cologne, 1968). Also useful are the first chapters in M. K. Dziewanowski, *The Communist Party of Poland: an Outline of History* (Cambridge, Mass., 1959); cf. by the same author, 'The Making of a Federalist [Pilsudski]', *JGOE*, 11 (1963), 543–60. On the Polish question, during the last years of tsarism: E. Chmielewski, *The Polish Question in the Russian State Duma* (Knoxville, Tenn., 1970).

8: Finland

E. Jutikkala, *A History of Finland* (London, 1962) is a more reliable survey than the somewhat nationalistic J. H. Wuorinen, *A History of Finland* (London, 1965); an older (but still useful) study is M. G. Schybergson, *Politische Geschichte Finnlands* (trans.; Halle, 1925). Two useful articles are: J. H. Hodgson, 'Finland's Position in the Russian Empire, 1905–1910', *JCEA*, 20 (1960), 158–73; and L. Krusius-Ahrenberg, 'Finnischer Separatismus und russischer Imperialismus im vorigen Jahrhundert', *Historische Zeitschrift*, 187 (1959), 249–88. The economic aspects of the 'Finnish question' are examined by G. D. Kornilov, *Russko-finlyandskiye tamozhennyye otnosheniya v kontse XIX – nachale XX v.* (Leningrad, 1971).

9: Baltic provinces

Three unsatisfactory popular works on Estonia are: E. Nodel, *Estonia: Nation on the Anvil* (New York, 1964); E. Uustalu, *A History of the Estonian People* (London, 1952); and E. Uustalu, ed., *Aspects of Estonian Culture* (London, 1961). The first concentrates on the German minority, the second and third on the Estonians. Of the following two histories of Latvia, the former is to be preferred: A. Bilmanis, *A History of Latvia* (Princeton, 1951); A. Spekke, *A History of Latvia* (Stockholm, 1951). Cf. also A. Schwabe, *Grundriss der Agrargeschichte Lettlands* (Riga, 1928). On the Baltic Germans, see E. C. Thaden, 'N. A. Manaseins Senatorenrevision in Livland und Kurland während der Zeit von 1882 bis 1883', *JGOE*, 17 (1969), 45–58, and G. H. Schlingensiepen, *Der Strukturwandel des baltischen Adels in der Zeit vor dem ersten Weltkrieg* (Marburg, 1959); in English, see C. L. Lundin, 'The Road from Tsar to Kaiser: Changing Loyalties of the Baltic Germans, 1905–1914', *JCEA*, 10 (1950), 223–55.

10: Lithuania and White Russia

A. E. Senn, *The Emergence of Modern Lithuania* (New York, 1959) is a standard work, preferable to J. J. Stukas, *Awakening Lithuania* (Madison, N.J., 1966); see also M. Hellmann, *Grundzüge der Geschichte Litauens und des litauischen Volkes* (Darmstadt, 1966), and, on the First World War period, A. E. Senn, 'Garlawa: a Study in Emigré Intrigue, 1915–1917', *SEER*, 45 (1967), 411–24. On White Russia, see N. P. Vakar, *Belorussia: the Making of a Nation: a Case Study* (Cambridge, Mass., 1956); V. N. Pertsev *et al.*, eds., *Istoriya Belorusskoy SSR*, vol. I (Minsk, 1954), which may be supplemented by T. N. Fyodorova, *Obshchestvenno-politicheskaya mysl' v Belorussii i 'Minskiy Listok', 1886–1902 gg.* (Minsk, 1966). On Russian policy in the region after 1907, see E. Chmielewski, 'Stolypin's Last Crisis', *California Slavic Studies*, 3 (1964), 95–126.

11: Ukraine

Surveys include M. Hrushevsky, *A History of Ukraine* (trans.; New Haven, 1941), and B. Krupnyckyj, *Geschichte der Ukraine von den Anfängen bis zum Jahre 1917*, 3rd rev. edn (Wiesbaden, 1963). See also I. L. Rudnytsky, 'The Role of the Ukraine in Modern History', with discussion, in *SR*, 22 (1963), 199–262, repr. in D. W. Treadgold, ed., *The Development of the USSR: an Exchange of Views* (Seattle, 1964), 211–74. For political developments see the first chapters of J. S. Reshetar, *The Ukrainian Revolution, 1917–1920* (Princeton, 1952). A selection from the writings of I. Franko has been edited by E. Winter and P. Kirchner, *Beiträge zur Geschichte und Kultur der Ukraine. Ausgewählte deutsche Schriften des revolutionären Demokraten, 1882–1915* ([East] Berlin, 1963).

12: Jews, anti-Semitism

The standard history (albeit unfinished) is L. S. Greenberg, *The Jews in Russia* (2 vols., New Haven, 1944–51, repr. 1966), which supplements a previous classic, S. M. Dubnow, *History of the Jews in Russia and Poland* (trans.; 3 vols., Philadelphia, 1916–20, repr. 1946). J. Frumkin and others have edited a volume of essays entitled *Russian Jewry, 1860–1917* (London, 1966). On anti-Semitism, see H. Rogger, 'Was there a Russian Fascism? The Union of Russian People', *JMH*, 36 (1964), 398–415; the same author's 'The Formation of the Russian Right, 1900–1906', *California Slavic Studies*, 3 (1964), 66–94; H. Jablonowski, 'Die russischen Rechtsparteien, 1905–1917', in *Russland-Studien: Gedenkschrift für*

Otto Hötzsch (Stuttgart, 1957), 43–55; and literature cited in sec. 4. N. Cohen, *Warrant for Genocide* (London, 1967) has a chapter on Russian anti-semitism. On the celebrated Beilis trial, see H. Rogger, 'The Beilis Case: Anti-Semitism and Politics in the Reign of Nicholas II', *SR*, 25 (1966), 615–29; more detailed is M. Samuel, *Blood Accusation: the Strange History of the Beiliss Case* (New York, 1966). I. L. Rudnytsky examines a different angle of the problem in 'M. Drahomanov and the Problem of Ukrainian–Jewish Relations', *CSP*, 11 (1969), 182–98. One phase in the struggle against anti-Semitism waged by Russian liberals is briefly examined by M. F. Hamm, 'Liberalism and the Jewish Question: the Progressive Bloc', *RR*, 31 (1972), 163–74; the author is preparing a monograph to be entitled *Liberals and Urban Russia, 1906–1917*. On the general subject of political activity by Russian Jews, see L. B. Schapiro, 'The Role of the Jews in the Russian Revolutionary Movement', *SEER*, 40 (1961–2), 148–67. The emergence of the Bund is examined in two works, of which the former is more sociological, the latter more political in approach. E. Mendelsohn, *Class Struggle in the Pale: the Formative Years of the Jewish Workers' Movement in Tsarist Russia* (Cambridge, 1970), and H. J. Tobias, *The Jewish Bund in Russia from its Origins to 1905* (Stanford, 1972); these replace A. L. Patkin, *The Origins of the Russian–Jewish Labour Movement* (Melbourne–New York, 1947). See also S. Harcave, 'The Jews and the First Russian National Election' [1906], *ASEER*, 9 (1950), 33–41.

13: Transcaucasia

There are no surveys of the region as a whole, but see J. P. Le Donne, 'La Réforme de 1883 au Caucase', *CMRS*, 8 (1967), 21–35, which stresses the significance of this measure in the development of administrative centralization. On Georgia an admirable introduction is provided by D. M. Lang, *A Modern History of Georgia* (London, 1962), which may be supplemented by two volumes of memoirs published under the auspices of the *Inter-University Project on the History of the Menshevik Movement*, the first of which is more informative: G. Uratadze, *Reminiscences of a Georgian Democrat* and N. Zhordania, *My Life* (both Stanford, 1968). R. G. Hovannisian, the historian of the Armenian revolution, reviews the western and Soviet literature on the preceding period in 'Russian Armenia: a Century of Tsarist Rule', *JGOE*, 19 (1971), 31–48; the best monograph is L. Nalbandian, *The Armenian Revolutionary Movement*...(Berkeley–Los Angeles, 1963).

14: Moslem peoples

A useful bibliography is A. Bennigsen and C. Lemercier-Quelquejay, 'Musulmans et Missions Orthodoxes en Russie Orientale avant 1917. Essai de bibliographie critique', *CMRS*, 13 (1972), 57–113. These authors have also conducted two studies of the rise of nationalism among the Moslem peoples: *Les Mouvements nationaux chez les musulmans de Russie* (Paris–The Hague, 1960) and *La Presse et le mouvement national chez les musulmans de Russie avant 1920* (Paris–The Hague, 1964). Cf. also J. Saussay, 'Ilminsky et la politique de russification des Tatars, 1865–1891', *CMRS*, 8 (1967), 404–26. In English, see S. A. Zenkovsky, *Pan-Turkism and Islam in Russia* (Cambridge, Mass., 1960).

15: Central Asia

M. Beard, 'European Travellers in the Trans-Caspian before 1917', *CMRS*, 13

(1972), 590–6. Two contemporary travellers' accounts that still preserve their interest are G. N. [later Lord] Curzon, *Russia in Central Asia in 1889*...(1889, repr. London, 1967), and E. Schuyler, *Turkestan: Notes of a Journey*...(1873, repr. London, 1966, G. Wheeler, ed.). Other reprints as well as recent monographs are reviewed by D. MacKenzie, 'Russian Expansion in Central Asia, 1864–1885: Brutal Conquest or Voluntary Incorporation?' *CSS*, 4 (1970), 721–35. MacKenzie has also studied the initial period of Russian rule in 'Kaufman of Turkestan: an Assessment of his Administration, 1867–1881', *SR*, 26 (1967), 265–85. For a Soviet account of the conquest, see N. A. Khalfin, *Russia's Policy in Central Asia, 1857–1868* (trans.; London, 1964). An important source is K. K. Pahlen, *Mission to Turkestan*, ed. and trans. by R. A. Pierce (London, 1964), being the memoirs of an official who reviewed the workings of the colonial administration in 1908–9. Pierce is the author of an excellent study of the colonial regime: *Russian Central Asia, 1867–1917: a Study in Colonial Rule* (Berkeley–Los Angeles, 1960). Briefer is G. Wheeler, *The Modern History of Soviet Central Asia* (London, 1964), which covers the post-1917 period as well; so too does E. Allworth, ed., *Central Asia: a Century of Russian Rule* (New York, 1967). For the Steppe region in particular, consult G. J. Demko, *The Russian Colonization of Kazakhstan, 1896–1916* (The Hague, 1969); cf. also D. S. M. Williams, 'Land Reform in Turkestan', *SEER*, 51 (1973), 428–38. Strongly nationalist in tone are the works by B. Hayit, which include *Turkestan im XX. Jahrhundert* (Darmstadt, 1956), and *Turkestan zwischen Russland und China* (Amsterdam, 1971).

On cultural policy, see H. Carrère d'Encausse, 'La Politique culturelle du pouvoir tsariste au Turkestan, 1867–1917', *CMRS*, 3 (1962), 374–407. The impact of Russian activities in Central Asia on relations with China is examined by I. C. Hsü, *The Ili Crisis: a Study of Sino-Russian Diplomacy, 1871–1881* (London, 1965). For the rebellion of 1916, see E. D. Sokol, *The Revolt of 1916 in Russian Central Asia* (Baltimore, 1954); much new information has, however, since become available. See in particular A. V. Pyaskovsky *et al.*, eds., *Vosstaniye 1916 g. v Sredney Azii i Kazakhstane: sbornik dokumentov* (Moscow, 1960). Two works dealing specifically with Russian protectorates are: S. Becker, *Russia's Protectorates in Central Asia: Bukhara and Khiva, 1865–1924* (Cambridge, Mass., 1968), and H. Carrère d'Encausse, *Réforme et révolution chez les musulmans de l'empire russe: Bukhara, 1867–1924* (Paris, 1966).

16: Siberia and the Far East

On Russian settlement of Siberia, see the works quoted in sec. 40. On the penal aspects of the problem, a famous contemporary account is G. Kennan, *Siberia and the Exile System* (2 vols., London, 1891, repr. – but abridged – Chicago, 1958). A general account of Russia's expansion is D. J. Dallin, *The Rise of Russia in Asia* (London, 1950); cf. also A. Lobanov-Rostovsky, *Russia and Asia* (New York, 1933, repr. Ann Arbor, 1951), and D. W. Treadgold, 'Russia and the Far East', in Lederer, ed., *Russian Foreign Policy* [see sec. 4], 531–74. On the initial acquisitions, see R. K. I. Quested, *The Expansion of Russia in East Asia, 1857–1860* (Kuala Lumpur, 1968). A standard work on Russo-Japanese relations is: G. A. Lensen, *The Russian Push towards Japan: Russo-Japanese Relations, 1697–1875* (Princeton, 1959); cf. for the later period, by the same author, 'Japan and Tsarist Russia: Changing Relationships, 1875–1917', *JGOE*, 10 (1962), pp. 337–48.

An authoritative study of its subject is J. A. White, *The Diplomacy of the*

Russo-Japanese War (London, 1964): For a revisionist view of Japanese policy, see S. Okamoto, *The Japanese Oligarchy and the Russo-Japanese War* (London, 1970). The diplomatic antecedents of the war have been thoroughly studied in several earlier works, notably: B. A. Romanov, *Russia in Manchuria, 1892–1906* (trans.; Ann Arbor, 1952), by an early Soviet historian; A. Malozemoff, *Russian Far Eastern Policy, 1881–1904*...(Berkeley–Los Angeles, 1958); E. H. Zabriskie, *American–Russian Rivalry in the Far East...*, *1895–1914* (Philadelphia, 1946). A contemporary view is available in G. A. Lensen, ed., *Korea and Manchuria between Russia and Japan, 1895–1904. The Observations of Sir Ernest Satow, British Minister Plenipotentiary to Japan (1895–1900) and China (1900–1906)* (Tallahassee, Fla., 1966). On Mongolia, see P. S. H. Tang, *Russian and Soviet Policy in Manchuria and Outer Mongolia, 1911–1931* (Durham, N.C. 1959); E. B. Price, *The Russo-Japanese Treaties of 1907–1916 Concerning Manchuria and Mongolia* (Baltimore, 1933). A general work on Russia's relations with China during this period is M. N. Pavlovsky, *Chinese–Russian Relations* (trans.; New York, 1949); cf. also Hsü, *The Ili Crisis* [see sec. 15].

17: Inner Asia; Persia

O. Lattimore, *The Inner Asian Frontiers of China*, 2nd edn (New York, 1951). F. Kazemzadeh, *Russia and Britain in Persia, 1864–1914: a Study in Imperialism* (London, 1968), which incorporates the gist of several earlier articles; cf. also *Tsardom and Imperialism* [see sec. 2]. The broader international implications of Russian expansion in this region are examined by R. P. Churchill, *The Anglo-Russian Convention of 1907* (Cedar Rapids, Iowa, 1939); W. Habberton, *Anglo-Russian Relations Concerning Afghanistan, 1837–1907* (Urbana, 1937); and E. W. Edwards, 'The Far Eastern Agreement of 1907', *JMH*, 26 (1954), 340–55.

18: Culture (General)

Among general textbooks [see also sec. 1], those by Harcave and Pushkarev give most attention to this aspect of Russian history. See also the earlier work of P. N. Milyukov, available in a much abridged English translation: *Outlines of Russian Culture*, vol. III (Philadelphia, 1942) (the whole work has also been reprinted in one volume). Stimulating is the general survey by W. Weidlé, *Russia Absent and Present* (trans.; London, 1952, repr. New York, 1961).

19: The Arts

On the fine arts, see C. Gray, *The Great Experiment: Russian Art, 1863–1922* (London, 1962), and relevant sections of such general histories as G. H. Hamilton, *The Art and Architecture of Russia* (London, 1949). A. N. Benois has given his own account of the *Mir iskusstva* group in *Vozniknoveniye 'Mira iskusstva'* (Leningrad, 1928); see also S. Makovsky, *Na parnase 'serebryanogo veka'* (Munich, 1962). On the theatre the standard work is S. S. Danilov, *Ocherki po istorii russkogo dramaticheskogo teatra* (Moscow–Leningrad, 1948). Works in English include S. Lifar, *A History of the Russian Ballet from its Origins to the Present Day* (London, 1954); S. C. Grigoriev, *The Diaghilev Ballet, 1909–1929* (trans.; London, 1953); F. I. Shalyapin, *Pages from My Life: an Autobiography* (trans.; London, 1927); V. I. Nemirovich-Danchenko, *My Life in the Russian Theatre* (London, 1937). [See also vols. 2 (*Introduction to Russian Language and Literature*) and 3 (*Introduction to Russian Art and Architecture*) of this work.]

20: Scholarship

A sadly neglected field. See D. N. Anuchin, *O lyudyakh russkoy nauki i kul'tury* (Moscow, 1952); G. A. Knyazev, *Kratkiy ocherk istorii Akademii nauk SSSR* (Moscow–Leningrad, 1945). The fate of Russian scholars who emigrated is discussed in R. C. Williams, *Culture in Exile: Russian Emigrés in Germany, 1881–1941* (Ithaca, N.Y., 1972).

21: Historiography

A survey is to be found in the relevant chapters of A. G. Mazour, *Modern Russian Historiography* (Princeton, 1958). S. M. Solov'yov's career is studied in K.-D. Grothusen, *Die historische Rechtsschule Russlands* (Giessen, 1962); cf. also, by the same author, 'Die russische Geschichtswissenschaft des 19. Jhd. als Forschungsaufgabe', *JGOE*, 8 (1960), 32–61. The liberal historian Klyuchevsky has recently been the object of intense interest among Soviet scholars. See particularly V. O. Klyuchevsky, *Pis'ma. Dnevniki. Aforizmy i mysli ob istorii* (Moscow, 1968); R. A. Kireyeva, *V. O. Klyuchevsky kak istorik russkoy istoricheskoy nauki* (Moscow, 1966); E. G. Chumachenko, *V. O. Klyuchevsky – istochnikoved* (Moscow, 1970); and M. V. Nechkina, *Vasily Osipovich Klyuchevsky: istoriya zhizni i tvorchestva* (Moscow, 1974). On the sociologist and historian Kovalevsky, see V. G. Safronov, *M. M. Kovalevsky kak sotsiolog* (Moscow, 1960).

22: Geography, Anthropology

L. S. Berg, *Ocherki istorii russkoy geograficheskoy nauki* (Leningrad, 1929); *Vsesoyuznoye Geograficheskoye Obshchestvo za 100 let* (Moscow–Leningrad, 1946); S. A. Tokarev, *Istoriya russkoy etnografii: dooktyabr'skiy period* (Moscow, 1966). On Arctic exploration see T. E. Armstrong, *Russian Settlement in the North* (Cambridge, 1965).

23: Science

The fundamental work in English is A. Vucinich, *Science in Russian Culture, 1861–1917* (Stanford, 1970). See also N. A. Figurovsky *et al.*, eds., *Istoriya yestestvoznaniya v Rossii*, vol. 2 (Moscow, 1960). A popular biography of Mendeleyev is V. Stankevich, *D. I. Mendeleyev: velikiy russkiy khimik* (Prague, 1923); cf. also P. P. Ionidi, *Mirovozzreniye D. I. Mendeleyeva* (Moscow, 1959).

24: Medicine

The whole field of philanthropic activity has been unjustly ignored. On Botkin see N. A. Belogolovy, *Vospominaniya i drugiye stat'i*, 3rd edn (Moscow, 1898); V. B. Farber, *S. P. Botkin* (Leningrad, 1948).

25: Education

The basic work is P. L. Alston, *Education and the State in Tsarist Russia* (Stanford, 1969). Also useful are W. H. E. Johnson, *Russia's Educational Heritage* (Pittsburgh, 1950), repr. New York, 1969), and N. A. Hans, *The Russian Tradition in Education* (London, 1963); the latter adopts a somewhat old-fashioned approach. An early official account is S. V. Rozhdestvensky, *Istoricheskiy obzor deyatel'nosti Ministerstva Narodnogo Prosveshcheniya, 1802–1902* (St Petersburg, 1902). A brief sketch of school policy is given by O. Anweiler in Katkov *et al.*, *Russia Enters* [see sec. 1], 287–313. Other useful recent articles on the schools are: A. Sinel, 'Educating the Russian Peasantry: the Elementary School Reforms of Count D. Tolstoy', *SR*, 27 (1968), 49–70; and J. Saussay, 'La Vie scolaire des campagnes à l'époque des réformes d'Alexandre II', *CMRS*, 10 (1969), 392–413. For a Soviet account, see N. A. Konstantinov and V. Ya. Struminsky, *Ocherki po istorii nachal'nogo obrazovaniya v Rossii*, 2nd edn (Moscow, 1953).

The St Petersburg Polytechnic Institute is discussed briefly by G. Guroff, 'The Legacy of Pre-Revolutionary Economic Education: St Petersburg Polytechnic Institute', *RR*, 31 (1972), 272–81. The university reforms of the 1860s have been studied in English by W. L. Mathes, 'N. I. Pirogov and the Reform of University Government, 1856–1866', *SR*, 31 (1972), 29–51; cf. also the articles by R. G. Eymontova and G. I. Shchetinina in vols. 70 and 84, respectively, of *Istoricheskiye zapiski* (Moscow, 1961, 1969). For the impact of the events of 1905 on higher education, consult A. E. Ivanov, 'Universitety Rossii v 1905 g.', *Istoricheskiye zapiski*, 88 (1971), 114–49. On university policy in the empire's last years see D. M. Odinets and P. J. Novgorodtsev, *Russian Schools and Universities in the World War* (New Haven, 1929), which may be supplemented by L. I. Strakhovsky, 'Count P. N. Ignatyev: Reformer of Russian Education', *SEER*, 36 (1957–8), 1–26.

26: The Church

An indispensable guide is I. Smolitsch, *Geschichte der russischen Kirche, 1700–1917*, vol. I (no more published; Leiden, 1964), which treats the subject thematically rather than chronologically. G. Simon, *K. P. Pobedonostsev und die Kirchenpolitik des Heiligen Sinod, 1880–1905* (Göttingen, 1969) gives a broad picture of church life during that period. On the reform efforts of 1906 see I. Smolitsch, 'Der Konzilsvorbereitungsausschuss des Jahres 1906...', *Kirche im Osten*, 7 (1964), 53–93. J. S. Curtiss, *Church and State in Russia: the Last Years of Empire, 1900–1917* (New York, 1940) is critical of the 'establishment'; for a contrary view, see Metropolitan Yevlogy, *Put' moyey zhizni* (Paris, 1947). [See also 'Guide to further reading' for Ch. 7, this vol.]

27: Religious Dissent

E. Amburger, *Geschichte des Protestantismus in Russland* (Stuttgart, 1961) in large measure replaces F. C. Conybeare, *Russian Dissenters* (Cambridge, Mass., 1921). See also E. Heier, *Religious Schism in the Russian Aristocracy: Radstockism and Pashkovism* (The Hague, 1970). The study by A. I. Klibanov, *Istoriya religioznogo sektantstva v Rossii: 60-ye gody XIX v. – 1917 g.* (Moscow, 1965) contains much useful material but is vitiated by anti-religious bias. On the Tolstoyans, see E. Oberländer, *Tolstoj und die revolutionäre Bewegung* (Munich–Salzburg, 1965); and on the Dukhobors, G. Woodcock and I. Avakumovic, *The Doukhobors* (Toronto–New York, 1968).

28: Atheism; the Spiritual Crisis

E. T. Weiant, *Sources of Modern Mass Atheism in Russia* (Newark, Ohio, 1953). N. Zernov, *The Russian Religious Renaissance of the Twentieth Century* (London, 1963) covers a subject hitherto little explored in English. P. Scheibert, 'Die Petersburger religiös-philosophischen Zusammenkünfte von 1902 und 1903', *JGOE*,

12 (1964), 513–60, has now been superseded by J. Scherrer, 'Die Petersburger religiös-philosophischen Vereinigungen. Die Entwicklung des religiösen Selbst-verständnisses ihrer Intelligencija-Mitglieder (1901–17)', *FOEG*, 19 (1973), a work of some 400 pages abstracted in *FOEG*, 20 (1973), 57–75. An interesting account by a participant in this movement is F. Stepun, *Byvsheye i nebyvsheye*, vol. I (New York, 1956). On the philosophical founder of the movement, see W. G. Moss, *Vladimir Soloviev and the Russophils* (Georgetown, 1968). *Vekhi: sbornik statey o russkoy intelligentsii*, 2nd edn (Moscow, 1909), a seminal work, has now been translated into English: *CSS*, 2–4 (1968–70). On this controversy see L. B. Schapiro, 'The Vekhi Dispute and the Mystique of Revolution', *SEER*, 34 (1955), 56–76, and N. P. Poltoratzky, 'The Vekhi Dispute and the Significance of Vekhi', *CSP*, 9 (1967), 86–106. The latter author also discusses Berdyaev's ideas in 'N. Berdyaev's Interpretation of Russia's Historical Mission', *SEER*, 45 (1967), 193–207; cf. also G. Putnam, 'Russian Liberalism Challenged from Within: Bulgakov and Berdyaev in 1904–1905', *SEER*, 43 (1964–5), 335–53. There is a biography of this thinker by M. A. Vallon, *An Apostle of Freedom: Life and Teachings of N. Berdyaev* (London, 1960).

On Rozanov, see the brief article by H. A. Stammler, 'Conservatism and Dissent: V. V. Rozanov's Political Philosophy', *RR*, 32 (1973), 241–53; for more thorough treatment see the study by R. Poggioli, *Rozanov* (New York, 1962); a selection from Rozanov's writings, translated by H. Stammler, is available in German: *Ausgewählte Schriften* (Munich, 1963). A somewhat uncritical life of Gippius has been contributed by T. Pachmuss, *Zinaida Hippius* (Carbondale, Ill., 1971); on Merezhkovsky there is a large literature, of which C. H. Bedford, 'Dmitry Merezhkovsky, the Intelligentsia, and the Revolution of 1905', *CSP*, 3 (1958), 27–42 is the most relevant here. The biography of Struve by R. Pipes, *Struve: Liberal on the Left, 1870–1905* (Cambridge, Mass., 1970), of which the first of two volumes has so far appeared, promises to be a classic. [See also sec. 52.]

29: Economics, General

A standard general Soviet textbook is P. I. Lyashchenko, *History of the National Economy of Russia to the 1917 Revolution* (trans.; New York, 1949). More up to date, particularly as regards statistical material, are two monographs by P. A. Khromov: *Ekonomika Rossii perioda promyshlennogo kapitalizma* (i.e. *c.* 1860–1900; Moscow, 1963), and *Ocherki ekonomiki Rossii perioda monopolist-icheskogo kapitalizma* (i.e. *c.* 1900–17; Moscow, 1960). A good general western survey, highly concentrated, is B. Gille, *Histoire économique et sociale de la Russie* (Paris, 1949). Another approach is taken by B. Brutkus, 'The Historical Peculiarities of the Social and Economic Development of Russia' in R. Bendix and S. M. Lipset, eds., *Class, Status and Power* (London, 1954), 517–40. Both these works should, however, be supplemented by the more recent analytical studies [quoted in sec. 30]. On population, see A. G. Rashin, *Naseleniye Rossii za 100 let* (Moscow, 1956); W. W. Eason, 'Population Changes', in C. E. Black, ed., *The Transformation of Russian Society. Aspects of Social Change since 1861* (Cambridge, Mass., 1960), 72–90; L. S. Gaponenko *et al.*, 'O chislennosti i sostave naseleniya Rossii nakanune velikoy oktyabr'skoy revolyutsii', *Istoricheskiy arkhiv*, no. 5 (1962), 57–82. A. Kahan, 'Natural Calamities and their Effect upon the Food Supply in Russia...', *JGOE*, 16 (1968), 353–77, breaks fresh ground.

30: Industrialization

On growth rates, R. W. Goldsmith, 'The Economic Growth of Tsarist Russia, 1860–1913', *Economic Development and Cultural Change* (Chicago), 9 (1960–1), 441–75, supplements A. Gerschenkron, 'The Rate of Industrial Growth in Russia since 1885', *JEH*, 7 (1947), Supplement, 144–74; see also P. Gregory, 'Economic Growth and Structural Change in Tsarist Russia: a Case of Modern Economic Growth', *SS*, 23 (1972), 418–34. On the general problem of industrialization, see the important studies by A. Gerschenkron, 'Economic Backwardness in Historical Perspective' (1952; repr. in a book with the same title, Cambridge, Mass., 1962, 5–30), and 'Problems and Patterns of Russian Economic Development', in Black, ed., *Transformation of Russian Society* [see sec. 29], 42–71; see also Gerschenkron, 'Agrarian Policies' [see sec. 36]. For different approaches to this question, see A. Kahan, 'Government Policies and the Industrialization of Russia', *JEH*, 27 (1967), 460–77; and R. Portal, 'The Industrialization of Russia', in *Cambridge Economic History of Europe*, vol. 6, pt. 2 (Cambridge, 1965), 801–72; cf. also H. J. Ellison, 'Economic Modernization in Imperial Russia. Purposes and Achievements', *JEH*, 25 (1965), 523–40; and an earlier study by M. Miller, *The Economic Development of Russia, 1905–1914* (London, 1926, repr. 1967).

T. H. von Laue's studies of industrialization in Russia have led him to formulate an original and stimulating theory of the historical process in modern Russia as a whole; in addition to his biography of Witte [see sec. 1], see especially 'Die Revolution von aussen als erste Phase der russischen Revolution 1917', *JGOE*, 4 (1956), 138–58, and his *Why Lenin, why Stalin?: a Reappraisal of the Russian Revolution, 1900–1930* (London, 1965); the same author's 'The State and the Economy', in Black, ed., *Transformation of Russian Society* [see sec. 29], 209–25; 'Imperial Russia at the Turn of the Century: the Cultural Slope and the Revolution from Without', *CSSH*, 3 (1961), 353–67; and 'Of the Crises in the Russian Polity', in J. S. Curtiss, ed., *Essays in Honor of G. T. Robinson* (New York, 1963), 303–322. Yet another original approach to the basic questions of industrialization and economic progress is J. Nötzold, *Wirtschaftspolitische Alternativen der Entwicklung Russlands in der Ära Witte und Stolypin* (Berlin, 1966).

31: Communications

A relatively neglected field. The popular study by J. N. Westwood, *A History of Russian Railways* (London, 1964) contains a bibliography; cf. also his article on the Vladikavkaz railway in *SR*, 25 (1966), 669–75.

32: Finance, Banking

The chief Soviet authority is I. F. Gindin: see his *Banki i promyshlennost' v Rossii* (Moscow, 1927); *Gosudarstvennyy Bank i ekonomicheskaya politika tsarskogo pravitel'stva, 1861–1892 gg.* (Moscow, 1960); *Russkiye kommercheskiye banki* (Moscow, 1948); 'K voprosu ob ekonomicheskoy politike tsarskogo pravitel'stva v 60-kh – 80-kh godakh XIX v.', *Voprosy istorii*, no. 5 (1959), 63–82; 'Gosudarstvennyy kapitalizm v Rossii domonopolisticheskogo perioda', *ibid.* no. 9 (1964), 72–95. The chief western authority is O. Crisp: see her 'Russia, 1860–1914' in R. Cameron, ed., *Banking in the Early Stages of Industrialization* (New York, 1967), 183–238; 'Russian Financial Policy and the Gold Standard at the End of the Nineteenth Century', *EHR*, 6 (1953), 156–72 [and the works cited in sec. 33]. Cf. also H. Barkai, 'The Macro-Economics of Tsarist Russia in the Industrialization Era: Monetary Developments, the Balance of Payments and the Gold Standard', *JEH*, 33 (1973), 339–71.

33: Foreign credit and investment

A pioneering study is J. P. McKay, *Pioneers for Profit: Foreign Entrepreneurship and Russian Industrialization, 1885–1913* (London, 1970); it is based largely on French and Belgian materials. Of similar scope is R. Girault, *Emprunts russes et investissements français en Russie, 1887–1914* (Paris, 1973). Earlier works include L. Pasvolsky and H. G. Moulton, *Russian Debts and Russian Reconstruction* (London, 1924), and A. Crihan, *Le Capital étranger en Russie* (Paris, 1934). Three useful studies by O. Crisp are: 'Some Problems of French Investment in Russian Joint-Stock Companies', *SEER*, 35 (1956–7), 223–40; 'French Investment in Russian Joint-Stock Companies', *Business History* (Liverpool), 2 (1960), 75–90; 'The Russian Liberals and the 1906 Anglo-French Loan to Russia', *SEER*, 39 (1960–1), 497–512; on the latter subject, see J. W. Long, 'Organized Protest against the 1906 Russian Loan', *CMRS*, 13 (1972), 24–39. Two recent Soviet studies, both richer in factual information than in originality of treatment, are B. V. Anan'ich, *Rossiya i mezhdunarodnyy kapital, 1897–1914: ocherk istorii finansovykh otnosheniy* (Leningrad, 1970), and V. S. Dyakin, *Germanskiye kapitaly v Rossii: elektroindustriya i elektricheskiy transport* (Leningrad, 1971). Another senior Soviet economic historian, A. L. Sidorov, in his fundamental study *Finansovaya politika Rossii v gody I-oy mirovoy voyny* (Moscow, 1960), argues that Russia's foreign indebtedness played a major part in the tsarist regime's collapse.

34: Trade, tariffs

A neglected field; see the works cited in secs. 29, 44. There is an early study by M. N. Sobolev, *Tamozhennaya politika Rossii vo vtoroy polovine XIX v.* (Tomsk, 1911). On foreign trade policies after 1900, see J. P. Sontag, 'Tsarist Debts and Tsarist Foreign Policy', *SR*, 27 (1968), 529–41.

35: Labour

On the demographic aspects the useful work by A. G. Rashin, *Formirovaniye rabochego klassa Rossii* (Moscow, 1958) should be supplemented by the first chapters of L. S. Gaponenko, *Rabochiy klass v Rossii v 1917 g.* (Moscow, 1970), which is, however, more dogmatic. A relatively sophisticated interpretation of government policy is offered by V. Ya. Laverychev, *Tsarizm i rabochiy vopros* (Moscow, 1972). Two early studies that have not lost their value are G. von Schulze-Gävernitz, *Volkswirtschaftliche Studien aus Russland* (Leipzig, 1899), and M. I. Tugan-Baranovsky, *Russkaya fabrika v proshlom i nastoyashchem* (1898; 7th edn, Moscow, 1938); the latter has been translated into English by A. and C. S. Levin under the title *The Russian Factory in the Nineteenth Century* (Homewood, Ill., 1970).

The leading western students of labour problems are G. V. Rimlinger and T. H. von Laue. Among articles by the former are 'The Expansion of the Labor Market in Capitalist Russia, 1861–1917', *JEH*, 21 (1961), 208–15; 'The Management of Labor Protest in Tsarist Russia, 1870–1905', *IRSH*, 5 (1960), 226–48; 'Autocracy and the Factory Order in Early Russian Industrialization', *JEH*, 20

(1960), 67–92; 'Herrschaft und Fabriksordnung in der russischen Industrialisierung', in W. Fischer and G. Bajor, eds., *Die soziale Frage* (Stuttgart, 1967), 253–83. Among articles by von Laue are 'Russian Peasants in the Factory, 1892–1904', *JEH*, 21 (1961), 61–80; 'Factory Inspection under the "Witte System", 1892–1903', *ASEER*, 19 (1960), 347–62; and 'Tsarist Labor Policy, 1895–1903', *JMH*, 34 (1962), 135–45. A thorough study of the earliest phase in the 'labour question' is R. E. Zelnik, *Labor and Society in Tsarist Russia: the Factory Workers of St Petersburg, 1855–1870* (Stanford, 1971). For later phases, in addition to the works already noted see the two articles on the factory inspectorate by F. C. Giffin in *SR*, 25 (1966), 641–50, and *SEER*, 49 (1971), 80–91; and for the period of the 1905 revolution, G. E. Snow, 'The Kokovtsov Commission: an Abortive Attempt at Labor Reform in Russia in 1905', *SR*, 31 (1972), 780–96. On the Zubatov episode of 1902–3, see now D. Pospielovsky, *Russian Police Trade Unionism: Experiment or Provocation?* (London, 1971).

36: Agriculture, general

The following are useful surveys. A. Gerschenkron, 'Agrarian Policies and Industrialization: Russia, 1861–1917', in *Cambridge Economic History of Europe*, vol. 6, pt. 2 (Cambridge, 1965), 706–800; the first chapters of L. Volin, *A Century of Russian Agriculture: from Alexander II to Khrushchev* (Cambridge, Mass., 1970); H. Willetts, 'The Agrarian Question' in Katkov *et al.*, *Russia Enters* [see sec. 1], 111–37. Two valuable earlier general studies are: G. T. Robinson, *Rural Russia under the Old Régime* (1932, 3rd edn New York, 1957), and G. Pavlovsky, *Agricultural Russia on the Eve of Revolution* (London, 1930, repr. New York, 1968); the former adopts a more social, the latter a more economic approach. Of pre-revolutionary works, the most useful for the modern student is A. A. Kaufman, *Agrarnyy vopros v Rossii* (Moscow, 1908); see the ample bibliography in Robinson.

37: Peasant commune

The workings of the three-field system of tillage are explored at length in M. Confino, *L'assolement triennial en Russie au XVIIIe–XIXe siècles* (The Hague, 1969). For peasant industries, see P. G. Ryndzyunsky, *Krest'yanskaya promyshlennost' v poreformennoy Rossii* (Moscow, 1966). Two contemporary works are: A. A. Kachorovsky, *Russkaya obshchina*, 2nd edn (Moscow, 1906); A. A. Kaufman, *Russkaya obshchina v protsesse yeyo zarozhdeniya i rosta* (Moscow, 1908). In English, M. M. Kovalevsky, *Modern Customs and Ancient Laws of Russia* (London, 1912) is illuminating on the patriarchal household. Of the more recent literature, see especially D. Atkinson, 'The Statistics on the Russian Land Commune, 1905–1917', *SR*, 32 (1973), 773–87, which emphasizes its vitality, and W. T. Shinn, 'The Law of the Russian Peasant Household', *ASEER*, 20 (1961), 601–21, which also covers the post-revolutionary period. For the attitudes of the intelligentsia to the commune, see C. Goehrke, *Die Theorien über die Entstehung und Entwicklung des 'Mir'* (Wiesbaden, 1964).

38: Emancipation and after

For the discussions preceding the emancipation, see T. Emmons, *The Russian Landed Gentry and the Peasant Emancipation of 1861* (Cambridge, 1968), and

A. A. Skerpan, 'The Russian National Economy and Emancipation', in A. D. Ferguson and A. Levin, eds., *Essays in Russian History: a Collection Dedicated to George Vernadsky* (Hamden, Conn., 1964), 161–229. Centennial reappraisals are offered by R. Portal, ed., *Le Statut des paysans libérés du servage, 1861–1961: Recueil d'articles et de documents*...(Paris–The Hague, 1963), and S. A. Zenkovsky, 'The Emancipation of the Serfs in Retrospect', *RR*, 20 (1961), 280–93; cf. also S. Pushkarev, 'The Russian Peasants' Reaction to the Emancipation of 1861', *RR*, 27 (1968), 199–214. The vacillations in government policy before the reform are brought out in C. A. Ruud, 'Censorship and the Peasant Question: the Contingencies of Reform under Alexander II, 1855–1859', *California Slavic Studies*, 5 (1970), 137–67; while W. B. Lincoln, in 'The Karlovka Reform', *SR*, 28 (1969), 463–70, and 'The Circle of the Grand Duchess Yelena Pavlovna, 1847–1861', *SEER*, 48 (1970), 373–87, stresses the role of liberal elements at court. A selection of readings on the subject (from secondary sources) has been prepared by T. Emmons, *Emancipation of the Russian Serfs* (New York, 1970).

The leading Soviet authority is P. A. Zayonchkovsky, whose two monographs *Otmena krepostnogo prava v Rossii* (Moscow, 1954), and *Provedeniye v zhizn' krest'yanskoy reformy 1861 g.* (Moscow, 1958) are essential reading for the specialist. He reviews the Soviet literature on the question in 'Sovetskaya istoriografiya reformy 1861 g.', *Voprosy istorii*, no. 2 (1961), 85–104. In the series entitled *Krest'yanskoye dvizheniye v Rossii v XIX – nachale XX v.* (Moscow, 1959–68), S. V. Okun' has edited a selection of archival materials on peasant disturbances during this period: vol. 2, *1857–may 1861 gg* (1963), and vol. 3, *1861–9 gg.* (1964). Soviet historians stress the importance of these disturbances. For a recent review of this question, see A. M. Anfimov, 'Krest'yanskoye dvizheniye v Rossii vo vtoroy polovine XIX v.', *Voprosy istorii*, no. 5 (1973), 15–31. Two recent Soviet articles on the government's peasant policy in the post-emancipation period are N. M. Druzhinin, 'Likvidatsiya feodal'noy sistemy v russkoy pomeshchich'yey derevne, 1862–1882 gg.', *ibid.* no. 12 (1968), 3–34; and E. M. Brusnikin, 'Krest'yanskiy vopros v Rossii v period politicheskoy reaktsii' [i.e. the 1880s], *ibid.* no. 2 (1970), 34–47.

39: Stolypin reform

The massive volume by S. Dubrovsky, *Stolypinskaya zemel'naya reforma* (Moscow, 1963), a revised edition of a work published in 1925, is somewhat disappointing but contains valuable statistical tables. In addition to Pavlovsky, *Agricultural Russia*, and Robinson, *Rural Russia* [see sec. 36], see the following articles: D. W. Treadgold, 'Was Stolypin in Favor of Kulaks?' *ASEER*, 14 (1955), 1–14; W. E. Mosse, 'Stolypin's Villages', *SEER*, 43 (1964–5), 257–74; G. L. Yaney, 'The Concept of the Stolypin Land Reform', *SR*, 23 (1964), 257–93; G. Tokmakoff, 'Stolypin's Agrarian Reform: an Appraisal', *RR*, 30 (1971), 124–38. All but the second of these studies arrive at positive conclusions.

40: Migration and resettlement

On the migration aspect of the Stolypin reform, see D. W. Treadgold, *The Great Siberian Migration: Government and Peasant in Resettlement*...(Princeton, 1957), and Fr.-X. Coquin, *La Sibérie. Peuplement et immigration paysanne au XIXe siècle* (Paris, 1969). The latter author studies peasant settlement in the Ukraine in

IMPERIAL RUSSIA: ALEXANDER II TO THE REVOLUTION

'Faim et migrations paysannes en Russie au XIXe siècle', *Revue d'Histoire Moderne et Contemporaine, II* (1964), 127–44; on the same subject, cf. J. W. Leasure and R. A. Lewis, 'Internal Migration in Russia in the Late Nineteenth Century', *SR*, 27 (1968), 375–94. On the peasant *jacquerie* of 1905 (and 1917–18) see L. A. Owen, *The Russian Peasant Movement, 1906–1917* (London, 1937, repr. New York, 1963); it is, however, to be used with caution.

41: Peasantry: sociological works

See T. Shanin, *The Awkward Class. Political Sociology of Peasantry in a Developing Society: Russia 1910–1925* (London, 1972); also L. Volin, *Century of Russian Agriculture* [see sec. 36], and his 'The Russian Peasant from Emancipation to Kolkhoz', in Black, ed., *Transformation of Russian Society* [see sec. 29], 293–311. A valuable collection of essays is W. S. Vucinich, ed., *The Peasant in Nineteenth-Century Russia* (Stanford, 1968); note in particular M. Matossian, 'The Peasant Way of Life', 1–40. An anthropological approach is also taken by the contributors to V. A. Aleksandrova *et al.*, eds., *Russkiye: istoriko-etnograficheskiy atlas. Zemledeliye. Krest'yanskaya odezhda. Seredina XIX v. – nachalo XX v.* (Moscow, 1967). On peasant housing, see B. Kerblay, 'L'Evolution de l'isba aux XIXe et XXe siècles...', *CMRS*, 13 (1972), 114–39. The Marxist–Populist controversy over the peasantry is ably treated in Mendel, *Dilemmas*, and in Baron, *Plekhanov* [see sec. 55]. See also the stimulating work by D. Mitrany, *Marx against the Peasant: a Study in Social Dogmatism* (London, 1951).

42: Industrial workers

Rashin, in *Formirovaniye rabochego* [see sec. 35], estimates the number of those employed in industry, building, transport and distribution at 1.3 million in 1860 and 5.3 million in 1913. Two western studies should be noted here: J. G. Gliksman, 'The Russian Urban Worker: from Serf to Proletarian', in Black, ed., *Transformation* [see sec. 29], 311–23; L. A. Haimson, 'The Problem of Social Stability in Urban Russia, 1905–1917', *SR*, 23 (1964), 619–42; 24 (1965), 1–22; and the discussions *ibid.* 23–56, 561–7, and 25 (1966), 149–54.

43: The 'service class'

Study of the increasing professionalism in Russian society is still in its infancy; but see the articles by R. A. Feldmesser, 'Social Classes and Political Structure', and R. L. Garthoff, 'The Military as a Social Force', in Black, ed., *Transformation* [see sec. 29], 235–52 and 323–38. J. A. Armstrong has made a statistical study of some 1,400 senior office-holders in 'Old Régime Governors: Bureaucratic and Patrimonial Attributes', *CSSH*, 14 (1972), 2–29; see also his comparison with their Soviet equivalents in *SR*, 31 (1972), 1–28. D. K. Rowney attempts a similar operation in 'Higher Civil Servants in the Russian Ministry of Internal Affairs: Some Demographic and Career Characteristics, 1905–1916', *SR*, 31 (1972), 101–10. E. Amburger has compiled an authoritative index of bureaucratic offices and their holders: *Geschichte der Behördenorganisation Russlands von Peter dem Grossen bis 1917* (Leiden, 1966), which contains an appendix on the 'ruling élite', 502–19. He also provides a brief note on social mobility within the bureaucracy in 'Behördendienst und sozialer Aufstieg in Russland um 1900', *JGOE*, 18 (1970),

127–34. On the army as a social force, consult H.-P. Stein, 'Der Offizier des russischen Heeres...zwischen Reform und Revolution, 1861–1905', *FOEG*, 13 (1967), 346–507; and in English P. Kenez, 'Changes in the Social Composition of the Officer Corps during World War I', *RR*, 31 (1972), 369–75, which relates to this author's work on the Volunteer Army of 1918.

Much information on the *mores* of the official world is to be found in memoir literature, of which only the most important are listed here: S. Yu. Witte, *Vospominaniya* (3 vols., Moscow, 1960) – to be preferred to the abridged English edition, *The Memoirs of Count Witte* (Garden City, N.Y., 1921); P. A. Valuyev, *Dnevnik*, P. A. Zayonchkovsky, ed., vol. I, 1861–4, vol. II, 1865–76 (Moscow, 1961); D. A. Milyutin, *Dnevnik, 1873–1882 gg.*, P. A. Zayonchkovsky, ed (4 vols., Moscow, 1947–50); A. A. Polovtsov, *Dnevnik gosudarstvennogo sekretarya...* [1883–92] (2 vols., Moscow, 1966); V. I. Gurko, *Features and Figures of the Past: Government and Opinion in the Reign of Nicholas II* (trans.; Stanford, 1939); V. N. Kokovtsov, *Out of My Past: the Memoirs...*(trans.; Stanford, 1935); B. N. Chicherin, *Vospominaniya* (4 vols, in 2 pts. Moscow, 1929–34, repr. Cambridge, 1973, with foreword by D. P. Hammer); A. A. Polivanov, *Iz dnevnikov i vospominaniy po dolzhnosti voyennogo ministra...1907–16 gg.* (Moscow, 1924); A. I. Denikin, *Put' russkogo ofitsera* (New York, 1953).

44: Merchants and 'bourgeoisie'

A difficult subject, dealt with unsatisfactorily by P. A. Berlin, *Russkaya burzhuaziya v staroye i novoye vremya* (Moscow, 1922) and V. T. Bill, *The Forgotten Class: the Russian Bourgeoisie from the Earliest Beginnings to 1900* (New York, 1959). More profitable, although covering a shorter period, is R. A. Roosa, 'Russian Industrialists Look to the Future: Thoughts on Economic Development, 1906–1917', in Curtiss, ed., *Essays* [see sec. 30], 198–220; cf. by the same author, 'Russian Industrialists and "State Socialism", 1906–1917', *SS*, 23 (1971–2), 395–417. R. Portal studies one constituent element in 'Industriels moscovites: le secteur cotonnier (1861–1914)' *CMRS*, 4 (1963), 5–47; and A. Gerschenkron offers two stimulating lectures on entrepreneurship among the Old Believers (mainly anterior to this period) in *Europe in the Russian Mirror. Four Lectures in Economic History* (London, 1970). The relations between the entrepreneurs and the government have received much attention from Soviet historians. See in particular A. P. Pogrebinsky, *Gosudarstvenno-monopolisticheskiy kapitalizm v Rossii: ocherk istorii* (Moscow, 1959), and V. S. Dyakin, *Russkaya burzhuaziya i tsarizm v gody I-oy mirovoy voyny, 1914–1917* (Leningrad, 1967); the latter also covers the political history of these years. One of many functionaries with commercial interests was A. A. Polovtsov [see his *Dnevnik...*, sec. 43]; the connection is examined by E. Amburger, 'Der Reichssekretär A. A. Polovtsov als Privatunternehmer', *JGOE*, 18 (1970), 426–38. Internal trade has been little studied. See P. Herliby, 'Odessa: Staple Trade and Urbanization in New Russia', *JGOE*, 21 (1973), 184–95. An early study of one still important aspect of the commercial scene is I. Kandelaki, *Rol' yarmarok v russkoy torgovle* (St Petersburg, 1914).

45: Gentry

The dominant group in Russian society has yet to receive due scholarly attention. For a Soviet view, see A. P. Korelin, 'Dvoryanstvo v poreformennoy Rossii

(1861–1904 gg.)', *Istoricheskiye zapiski*, 87 (1971), 91–173. For one landowner's description of his problems, see N. A. Pavlov, *Zapiski zemlevladel'tsa* (Petrograd, 1915). See also Pavlovsky, *Agricultural Russia* [see sec. 36], and A. M. Anfimov, *Rossiyskaya derevnya v gody I-oy mirovoy voyny, 1914 – fevral' 1917* (Moscow, 1962), which, however, suffers from bias.

46: Intelligentsia

On the sociology of the intelligentsia, O. W. Müller, *Intelligencija: Untersuchungen zur Geschichte eines politischen Schlagwortes* (Frankfurt, 1971) is fundamental; in English, see *The Russian Intelligentsia* (New York, 1961), repr. from *Daedalus: Journal of the American Academy of Arts and Sciences*, vol. 89, no. 3 (1960), 437–690, with a foreword by R. Pipes; C. Becker, 'Raznochintsy: the Development of the Word and the Concept', *ASEER*, 18 (1959), 63–74; A. P. Pollard, 'The Russian Intelligentsia...', *California Slavic Studies*, 3 (1964), 1–32; D. R. Brower, 'The Problem of the Russian Intelligentsia', *SR*, 26 (1967), 638–47; and, by the same author, 'Fathers, Sons and Grandfathers: Social Origins of Radical Intellectuals in Nineteenth-Century Russia', *Journal of Social'History*, 2 (1969), 333–55.

47: Central government

G. L. Yaney, *The Systematization of Russian Government* (London, 1973) provides a wealth of data but the interpretation is most idiosyncratic; cf. also, by the same author, 'Some Aspects of the Imperial Russian Government on the Eve of the First World War', *SEER*, 43 (1964–5), 68–90. G. B. Sliozberg, *Dorevolyutsionnyy stroy Rossii* (Paris, 1933) is a reliable introduction to Russian governmental institutions in general. For earlier works, see Yaney's excellent bibliography. Four articles by M. Szeftel should be noted: 'The Form of Government of the Russian Empire prior to the Constitutional Reforms of 1905–1906', in Curtiss, ed., *Essays* [see sec. 30], 105–19; 'Personal Inviolability in the Legislation of the Russian Absolute Monarchy', *ASEER*, 17 (1958), pp. 1–24; 'The Legislative Reform of August 6, 1905', in A. Marongiu, ed., *Mélanges: Études presentées à la Commission Internationale pour l'Histoire des Assemblées d'États* (Palermo, 1967); 'Nicholas II's Constitutional Decisions of October 17–19, 1905 and Sergius Witte's Role', in *Album J. Balon* (Namur, 1968). For a thorough study of the central government's response to the events of 1905, see H. D. Mehlinger and J. M. Thompson, *Count Witte and the Tsarist Government in the 1905 Revolution* (London 1972). On government in the empire's last years, see secs. 53, 56.

48: Ministry of Interior; police

A first step in modern scholarly investigation into this field is R. J. Abbott, 'Police Reform in the Province of Yaroslavl', 1856–1876', *SR*, 32 (1973), 292–302. The early official account, *Ministerstvo Vnutrennikh Del: istoricheskiy ocherk, 1802–1905* (3 vols., St Petersburg, 1902), is naturally enough not very informative on the security aspects of the ministry's activities. See S. Monas, 'The Political Police: the Dream of a Beautiful Autocracy', in Black, ed., *Transformation* [see sec. 29], 164–90, and the memoirs of Gurko, *Features and Figures*, and Witte, *Memoirs* [see sec. 43]. Some suggestive points are contained in A. A. Lopukhin, *Otryvki iz vospominaniy* (Moscow–Petrograd, 1923); P. P. Zavarzin, *Rabota*

GUIDE TO FURTHER READING

taynoy politsii (Paris, 1924); A. T. Vasilev, *The Ochrana* (London, 1930); B. Nikolaevsky, *Aseff* [Azev]: *the Russian Judas* (trans.; London, 1934), despite the melodramatic title (US title: *Azeff the Spy*). On the press and censorship, see *Iz istorii russkoy zhurnalistiki II-oy poloviny XIX v.: stat'i, materialy i bibliografiya* (Moscow, 1964); D. Balmuth, 'Origins of the Russian Press Reform of 1865', *SEER*, 47 (1969), 369–88; C. A. Ruud, 'A. V. Golovnin and Liberal Russian Censorship, January–June 1862', *SEER*, 50 (1972), 198–219 [see also sec. 38]; and three articles by B. Rigberg dealing with the later period, in *JGOE*, 13 (1965), 331–43; 14 (1966), 327–46; and 17 (1969), 59–76.

49: Justice

A thorough account of the 1864 reform is F. B. Kaiser, *Die russische Justizreform von 1864: zur Geschichte der russischen Justiz von Katharina II bis 1917* (Leiden, 1972). The first major Soviet work on the subject is B. V. Vilensky, *Sudebnaya reforma i kontrreforma v Rossii* (Saratov, 1969), which also covers later developments. In English see S. Kucherov, *Courts, Lawyers and Trials under the Last Three Tsars* (New York, 1953), a good popular account; and for an area that the reformers largely neglected, P. Czap, 'Peasant-Class Courts and Peasant Customary Justice in Russia, 1861–1912', *Journal of Social History, 1* (1967), 149–78. The speeches of the liberal lawyer A. F. Koni are republished in his *Izbrannyye proizvedeniya* (2 vols., Moscow, 1959); see also V. A. Maklakov, *Rechi* (Paris, 1949). On the intellectuals' ambiguous attitude to law, see L. B. Schapiro, 'The Intelligentsia and the Legal Order', in *The Russian Intelligentsia* [see sec. 46], 459–71.

50: Local government

On autonomous institutions generally, see the popular work by J. Walkin, *The Rise of Democracy in Pre-Revolutionary Russia...*(New York, 1962). More thorough, but covering an earlier time-span, is S. F. Starr, *Decentralization and Self-Government in Russia, 1830–1870* (Princeton, 1972). An important source on the institution and practice of the zemstva is S. B. Veselovsky, *Istoriya zemstva za 40 let* (4 vols., St Petersburg, 1911). Two Soviet studies are V. V. Garmiza, *Podgotovka zemskoy reformy 1864 g.* (Moscow, 1957), and L. G. Zakharova, *Zemskaya kontrreforma 1890 g.* (Moscow, 1968). The latter was edited by P. A. Zayonchkovsky, who has also written a monograph on the relations between government and 'society' during Alexander III's reign: *Rossiyskoye samoderzhaviye v kontse XIX stoletiya: politicheskaya reaktsiya 80-kh – nachala 90-kh gg.* (Moscow, 1970). The fate of the zemstva after 1907 is examined by M. S. Conroy, 'Stolypin's Attitude towards Local Self-Government', *SEER*, 46 (1968), 446–62. On their role after 1914, see T. Polner *et al.*, *Russian Local Government during the War and the Union of Zemstvos* (New Haven, 1930).

51: Liberalism: to 1881

An introduction, of indifferent quality, is G. Fischer, *Russian Liberalism: from Gentry to Intelligentsia* (Cambridge, Mass., 1958); it should be read in conjunction with V. Leontovitsch, *Geschichte des Liberalismus in Russland* (Frankfurt, 1957), which directs more attention to liberal reformers in official circles. See also P. Scheibert, 'Über den Liberalismus in Russland', *JGOE* 7, (1959), 34–48 and M. Raeff, 'Some Reflections on Russian Liberalism', *RR*, 18 (1959), 218–30. An early classic on the era of the 'great reforms' is A. A. Kornilov, *Obshchestvennoye dvizheniye pri Aleksandre II* (Moscow, 1909). A fresh sceptical view of the government's 'liberalism' during the period is offered by A. J. Rieber, 'Alexander II: a Revisionist View', *JMH*, 43 (1971), 42–58; cf. his *The Politics of Autocracy. Letters of Alexander II to Prince A. I. Baryatinsky, 1857–1864* (Paris–The Hague, 1966), which has an important lengthy introduction (pp. 15–93). For gentry liberalism in the pre-emancipation discussions, see Emmons, *Russian Landed Gentry* [see sec. 38], and I. P. Popov, 'Liberal'noye dvizheniye provintsial'nogo dvoryanstva v period podgotovki i provedeniya reformy 1861 g.', *Voprosy istorii*, no. 3 (1973), 36–50 – in essence, a reply to Emmons. See also H. Neubauer, 'Die Bauernreform Alexanders II. als Ausgangspunkt adeliger Konstitutionsbestrebungen', *JGOE*, 4 (1956), 105–37. One important early episode in government–society relations is explored by J. A. Malloy, jun., 'Russian Liberalism and the Closing of the 1867 St Petersburg Zemstvo', *CSS*, 4 (1970), 653–70.

On K. D. Kavelin, see D. Field, 'Kavelin and Russian Liberalism', *SR*, 32 (1973), 59–78; on A. I. Koshelyov, consult M. Raeff, 'Russia after the Emancipation: Views of a Gentleman Farmer', *SEER*, 29 (1950–1), 470–86; on one of the first liberal émigrés, see B. Hollingsworth, 'The "Republican Prince", the Reform Projects of Prince P. V. Dolgorukov', *SEER*, 47 (1969), 447–68; on Gradovsky, see B. Dilger, 'Die politischen Anschauungen A. D. Gradovskijs', *FOEG*, 15 (1970), 145–306. On Milyutin, there is a biography by F. A. Miller, *Dmitry Milyutin and the Reform Era in Russia* (Nashville, Tenn., 1968), but it concentrates on the military aspects of his career; cf. by the same author, 'Dmitry Milyutin: Liberal or Conservative?' *JGOE*, 13 (1965), 192–8. For the text of Milyutin's constitutional project, see P. A. Zayonchkovsky, *Krizis samoderzhaviya na rubezhe 1870–1880kh gg.* (Moscow, 1964), 138ff; the text of Valuyev's project is available in English in M. Raeff, *Plans for Political Reform in Imperial Russia, 1730–1905* (London, 1966), 121–31. On the crisis of 1878–81, see also Milyutin's *Dnevnik* [see sec. 43], and E. A. Peretts, *Dnevnik*, A. E. Presnyakov, ed. (Moscow, 1927). The text of Loris-Melikov's project is translated by Raeff in *Plans* [see this sec.], 132–40; see also H. Heilbronner, 'Alexander III and the Reform Plan of Loris-Melikov', *JMH*, 33 (1961), 384–97. On the constitutional problems of this period some stimulating views are advanced by L. B. Schapiro, *Rationalism and Nationalism in Russian Nineteenth-Century Political Thought* (London, 1969).

52: Liberalism after 1881 the birth of constitutional government

A collection of conference papers edited by C. Timberlake, *Essays on Russian Liberalism* (Columbia, Miss., 1972) contains an essay by the editor on I. I. Petrunkevich, founder of the radical constitutionalist trend; see also the latter's memoirs *Iz zapisok obshchestvennogo deyatelya: vospominaniya*, A. A. Kizevetter, ed. (Berlin, 1934). Kizevetter's own memoirs, *Na rubezhe dvukh stoletiy* (Prague, 1929) are illuminating on the 1880s and the 1890s, and for the following years D. N. Shipov, *Vospominaniya i dumy* (Moscow, 1918) is an important source. Shipov's moderate views are defended by L. B. Schapiro, *Rationalism and Nationalism* [see sec. 51]. For another moderate, V. A. Maklakov, see M. Karpovich, 'Two Types of Russian Revolution: Maklakov and Milyukov', in Simmons, ed., *Continuity and Change* [see sec. 4], 129–43; an essay by D. A. Davies in Timberlake, ed., *Essays* [see this sec.], 78–89; and Maklakov's semi-autobiographical studies: *Vlast' i obshchestvennost' na zakate staroy Rossii* (Paris, 1936): *Pervaya Gosudarstvennaya Duma* (Paris, 1939) – indifferently translated as *The First*

State Duma (Bloomington, 1964); and *Vtoraya Gosudarstvennaya Duma* (Paris, 1946).

The hitherto obscure group in which many of these men first met is scrutinized by T. Emmons, 'The Beseda Circle, 1899–1905', *SR*, 32 (1973), 461–90; cf. also the same author's 'The Statutes of the Union of Liberation', *RR*, 33 (1974), 80–5. The Union of Liberation itself is the object of a monograph by S. Galai, *The Liberation Movement in Russia, 1900–1905* (Cambridge, 1973). Cf. also G. L. Freeze, 'A National Liberation Movement and the Shift in Russian Liberalism, 1901–1903', *SR*, 28 (1969), 81–91, and the biography by Pipes, *Struve* [see sec. 28]. P. N. Milyukov's memoirs, *Vospominaniya* (2 vols., New York, 1955) are a *tour de force* considering the difficult circumstances in which they were written; they have been translated (but abridged) as *Political Memoirs, 1905–1917* A. P. Mendel, ed. (Ann Arbor, 1967). For his biography, see T. Riha, *A Russian European: Paul Milyukov in Russian Politics* (London, 1969), which includes material previously published in *JMH*, 32 (1960), 16–24. Cf. also R. L. Tuck, 'P. Milyukov and the Negotiations for a Duma Ministry, 1906', *ASEER*, 10 (1951), 117–29.

On the Duma as an institution, see W. B. Walsh, 'Political Parties in the Russian Dumas', *JMH*, 22 (1950), 144–50; S. L. Levitsky, 'Legislative Initiative in the Russian Duma', *ASEER*, 15 (1956), 313–24 – and rather more fully as 'Interpellation und Verfahrensfragen in der russischen Duma', *FOEG*, 6 (1958), 170–207; M. Szeftel, 'The Representatives and their Powers in the Russian Legislative Chambers', in *Liber Memorialis Sir Maurice Powicke...*(Louvain–Paris, 1965), 221–57; M. Szeftel, 'The Reform of the Electoral Law to the State Duma on 3rd June 1907', in *Liber Memorialis G. de Lagarde* (London, 1968), 321–67. Some of the relevant constitutional documents are conveniently reproduced in F. I. Kalinychev, ed., *Gosudarstvennaya Duma Rossii v dokumentakh i materialakh* (Moscow, 1957).

53: Constitutional politics, 1907–14

G. A. Hosking, *The Russian Constitutional Experiment. Government and Duma 1907–1914* (London, 1973) is likely to prove a standard work. There is a large secondary literature on Stolypin. See especially A. Levin, 'P. A. Stolypin: a Political Appraisal', *JMH*, 37 (1965), 445–63, and 'Russian Bureaucratic Opinion in the Wake of the 1905 Revolution', *JGOE*, 11 (1963), 1–12; L. I. Strakhovsky, 'The Statesmanship of Peter Stolypin: a Reappraisal', *SEER*, 37 (1958–9), 348–70, and the same author's 'Stolypin and the Second Duma', *CSP*, 6 (1964), 3–17; G. Tokmakoff, 'P. A. Stolypin and the Second Duma', *SEER*, 50 (1972), 49–62; E. Chmielewski, 'Stolypin and the Russian Ministerial Crisis of 1909', *California Slavic Studies*, 4 (1967), 1–38. A. Levin, *The Second Duma: a Study of the Social-Democratic Party and the Russian Constitutional Experiment* (New Haven, 1940, repr. New York, 1960) is a thorough work on a limited period; cf. by the same author, 'The Russian Voter in the Elections to the Third Duma', *SR*, 21 (1962), 660–77. The account by the Soviet historian A. Ya. Avrekh, *Stolypin i tret'ya Duma* (Moscow, 1968) is valuable on many points although it lacks focus. On the right-wing parties, see Jablonowski, 'Die russischen Rechtsparteien' [see sec. 12], and see also sec. 4. On Kadet policy before and after 1907, see the articles by J. E. Zimmerman and W. G. Rosenberg in Timberlake, ed., *Essays* [see sec. 52], 119–63; for the Constitutional-Democratic party see W. G. Rosenberg, *Liberals in the Russian Revolution: the Constitutional Democratic Party, 1917–1921* (Princeton, 1974).

54: Radicalism to 1881

For a popular general account see A. Yarmolinsky, *The Road to Revolution: a Century of Radicalism* (New York, 1959). F. Venturi, *Roots of Revolution. . .* (trans.; London, 1960, paperback edn, New York, 1968) is a comprehensive study of Populism to 1881. The biographical sketch of Chernyshevsky in R. Hare, *Pioneers of Russian Social Thought* (London, 1951) should be supplemented by W. F. Woehrlin, *Chernyshevsky, the Man and the Journalist* (Cambridge, Mass., 1971). Bakunin, Mikhaylovsky, and Lavrov are discussed in Hare, *Portraits* [see sec. 1], to which add the following biographies: E. H. Carr, *Michael Bakunin* (London, 1937, rev. edn London, 1961) – see also new material in A. Lehning, ed., *Archives Bakounine* (4 vols., Leyden, 1961–71); J. H. Billington, *Mikhailovsky and Russian Populism* (Oxford, 1958); P. Pomper, *Peter Lavrov and the Russian Revolutionary Movement* (London, 1972). There is also an indifferent life of the 'jacobin' Tkachov: A. L. Weeks, *The First Bolshevik: a Political Biography of Peter Tkachev* (New York, 1968). Lavrov's *Historical Essays* [1869] have been edited with an introduction by J. P. Scanlan (London, 1967). R. Wortman, *The Crisis of Russian Populism* (Cambridge, 1967) breaks fresh ground by investigating the psychological dilemmas of three less familiar figures: V. P. Vorontsov, G. I. Uspensky, and N. N. Zlatovratsky. Less ponderous and most enjoyable is D. Footman's brief biography of the terrorist leader A. I. Zhelyabov: *Red Prelude. . .* (London, 1944, 2nd edn London, 1968). Some extracts from the writings of these men is available in vol. II of J. M. Edie *et al.*, eds., *Russian Philosophy* (London, 1965).

The vast western periodical literature cannot be discussed here. Of Soviet writers, B. P. Koz'min is the most prolific; see especially his *Nechayev i nechayevtsy; sbornik materialov* (Moscow–Leningrad, 1931), and (with B. Gorev), *Revolyutsionnoye dvizheniye 60kh gg.* (Moscow, 1932); published more recently are his essays entitled *Iz istorii revolyutsionnoy mysli v Rossii: izbrannyye trudy* (Moscow, 1961). The latest study of the 'movement "to the people" ', B. S. Itenberg, *Dvizheniye revolyutsionnogo narodnichestva. . .*(Moscow, 1965), rests on a wide range of sources, as does S. S. Volk, *Narodnaya Volya, 1879–1882* (Moscow, 1966).

55: Radicalism, 1881–1900

S. H. Baron, *Plekhanov. Father of Russian Marxism* (London, 1963) is an excellent biography. The career of Plekhanov's closest colleague is treated by A. Ascher, *Pavel Axelrod and the Development of Menshevism* (Cambridge, Mass., 1972). A. P. Mendel, *Dilemmas of Progress in Tsarist Russia. . .*(Cambridge, Mass., 1962) is a thoughtful study of the debate between Populists and Marxists in the 1890s. On the 'legal Marxists', see R. Kindersley, *The First Russian Revisionists: a Study of 'Legal Marxism' in Russia* (Oxford, 1962). One of the better Soviet studies of this period is Yu. Z. Polevoy, *Zarozhdeniye marksizma v Rossii, 1883–94 gg.* (Moscow, 1959).

56: Revolutionary politics, 1901–17

On the Socialist Revolutionaries see the relevant chapters in D. W. Treadgold, *Lenin and his Rivals: the Struggle for Russia's Future, 1898–1906* (London, 1955), and the first chapters of O. H. Radkey, *The Agrarian Foes of Bolshevism. . .*(New York, 1958). On the Social Democrats, see J. L. H. Keep, *The Rise of Social*

Democracy in Russia (Oxford, 1963), which examines the Party's history to 1907, and (from a Menshevik standpoint) F. I. Dan, *The Origins of Bolshevism* (trans.; London, 1964). On the first revolutionary circles, see R. Pipes, *Social Democracy and the St. Petersburg Labor Movement, 1885–1897* (Cambridge, Mass., 1963), and A. K. Wildman, *The Making of a Workers' Revolution*...(London, 1967). For lives of the new generation of Social-Democratic party leaders, see I. Getzler, *Martov: a Political Biography* (London, 1967); I. Deutscher, *The Prophet Armed: Trotsky, 1879–1921* (Oxford, 1954, repr. New York, 1965). The best biography of Lenin is now A. B. Ulam, *Lenin and the Bolsheviks*...(London, 1966) – US title: *The Bolsheviks*...(New York, 1965). N. Valentinov, *Encounters with Lenin* (trans.; London, 1968) is by one of the Bolshevik leader's early critics.

A. Fischer has studied the Social Democrats' experience in 1905 in *Russische Sozialdemokratie und bewaffneter Aufstand im Jahre 1905* (Wiesbaden, 1967). For the 1905 revolution in general, see the outline sketch by O. Anweiler, 'Die russische Revolution von 1905', *JGOE*, 3 (1955), 161–93. The popular account in English by S. Harcave, *First Blood*...(New York, 1964) is fuller but less reliable. On the soviets, see O. Anweiler, *The Soviets*...*1905–1921* (trans.; New York, 1974). For the government's response to the revolution, see sec. 47. On the anarchist tendency in Russian radicalism, see P. H. Avrich, *The Russian Anarchists* (London, 1967). P. A. Kropotkin's *Memoirs of a Revolutionist* have been edited with an introduction by N. Walter (New York, 1971); cf. also his *Selected Writings on Anarchism and Revolution*, M. A. Miller, ed. (Cambridge, Mass., 1971). On the revolutionary movement during the war, see A. E. Senn, *The Russian Revolution in Switzerland, 1914–1917* (London, 1971). The work by A. Badayev, *The Bolsheviks in the Tsarist Duma* (trans.; London, 1932) is strongly partisan. O. H. Gankin and H. H. Fisher, eds., *The Bolsheviks and the World War* (Stanford, 1940) includes many documents.

The background to the collapse of the monarchy in 1917 may be studied in the volumes prepared under the aegis of the *Carnegie History of the Economic and Social Consequences of the War* (*Russian Series*), which *inter alia* include Florinsky, *Russia* [see sec. 1]; Odinets and Novgorodtsev, *Russian Schools* [see sec. 25]; Polner *et al.*, *Russian Local Government* [see sec. 50]; and P. P. Gronsky and N. J. Astrov, *The War and the Russian Government*...(New Haven, 1929). Two general accounts are B. Pares, *The Fall of the Russian Monarchy* (London, 1939) and G. Katkov, *Russia, 1917: the February Revolution* (London, 1967): the former relies too heavily upon contemporary political rumour, but the interpretation is more plausible than that offered in the latter work. The Soviet literature on this topic is generally unreliable, but see Dyakin, *Russkaya burzhuaziya i tsarizm* [see sec. 44]. The proceedings of the crucial 1915 meeting of the Committee of Ministers have been translated and edited by M. Cherniavsky under the title *Prologue to Revolution* (London, 1967). On Russia's internal state in 1914 and the prospects of reform versus revolution, see Haimson's 'Problem of Social Stability' and the discussions of it cited in sec. 42; and H. Rogger, 'Russia in 1914', *Journal of Contemporary History*, 1 (1966), 95–119.

6

SOVIET RUSSIA

H. T. WILLETTS

THE FEBRUARY REVOLUTION

In the third year of the First World War disturbances in Petrograd, caused by exaggerated rumours of impending food shortages and by the disaffection of battle-shy troops, prompted a handful of liberal politicians to overthrow the tsar and declare themselves the 'Provisional Government'. The 'February Revolution' was accomplished with remarkable ease: Russia shrugged off an autocracy which commanded neither the affection of the people at large, nor the confidence of the educated middle class, nor yet – and this was decisive – the loyalty of its generals. The tsar had fatally weakened his position by assuming personally the command of the armies in the field, thus simultaneously identifying himself with Russia's defeats, putting himself in the hands of the generals, and depriving his ministers in Petrograd of effective authority. The belief of the liberal politicians and the generals that with the tsar out of the way Russia would prosecute the war more efficiently was shared by her western allies. And so, in February 1917, Nicholas II found himself completely isolated, and renounced the throne for himself and for his invalid son.

The fall of the tsar left three potential centres of authority: the military high command, the Provisional Government, and the Petrograd Soviet of Workers' and Soldiers' Deputies. The generals, preoccupied with the war, at first looked to the liberal politicians to stabilize the home front, but the task was to prove beyond their powers: they had been thrust into prominence by an electoral system that disfranchised wide sections of the population, and their names held no magic for the masses. They had acquired some administrative experience in wartime committees that had made a useful contribution to the organization of industry and medical services – the first Prime Minister of the Provisional Government, Prince L'vov, owed his position to his record in this sphere of activity – but had never shared governmental power. A still more serious weakness was their determination to continue the war 'to decisive victory', and to postpone major social changes in the meantime, whereas the people at large longed for peace and immediate reforms. The authority both of the Provisional Government and of the high command was seriously undermined by 'Order No. 1' of the Executive Committee of the Petrograd Soviet, which urged the army to obey the government's orders only if they did not conflict with instructions from the soviet, and called for the election in every unit of committees which would co-operate with the soviet. Order No. 1 accelerated the erosion of discipline in the army and the effective striking force at the disposal of the generals steadily shrank.

Late in April the soviet forced the resignation of Milyukov, Minister of Foreign Affairs, and Guchkov, Minister of War, perhaps the ablest members of the government. Milyukov, in notes to the Allies, had defined Russian war aims in terms of which the soviets disapproved, envisaging Russian annexation of Constantinople (to which the desperate Allies had already secretly agreed) and 'war to final victory'. Here again, the soviet showed both its strength and the weakness of the Provisional Government. There existed in the capital what Trotsky characterized as 'a duality of power'. The soviet, dominated by Mensheviks (right-wing socialists) and Socialist Revolutionaries (a party of radical agrarian reform), swayed the masses, and could impede or overrule ministers who had little popular support, but refused to take over governmental functions. The Mensheviks had a Marxist explanation for their apparently inconsequential behaviour, which the Socialist Revolutionaries (SRs) did not contradict: the people could not take power in backward Russia until a period of bourgeois democracy had laid the foundations for popular rule. But ideological inhibitions were certainly reinforced by reluctance to take full responsibility for the conduct of affairs while the war lasted, and particularly for the unpopular measures that it might make necessary. To act as the conscience of the revolution and as arbiters of the government's performance was a more satisfying and apparently safer role. It was, however, one which many workers and soldiers found difficult to understand. Their growing exasperation was pithily expressed in July by a demonstrator who demanded of the SR leader Chernov: 'Why won't you take power when it's offered to you, you son of a bitch?' This incomprehension was aggravated by the inconsistent behaviour of the socialists themselves. One of them, A. F. Kerensky, had broken ranks in March and entered the coalition government, representing himself as the soviet's watchdog in ministerial circles. In May he became Minister of War, and thereafter dominated the government, which other socialists now joined. The effect of this *rapprochement* was to reduce friction between the Petrograd Soviet and the government, but it also meant that the turbulent masses began to look for leaders outside the soviets.

The Provisional Government and the soviet majority leaders, as temporary custodians of power, postponed all major political and social legislation, including land reform, until the election of a constituent assembly. It is hardly surprising that they were in no hurry to convene an assembly until the situation at the front improved and the country was more settled. Kerensky staked everything on a successful summer campaign, but an initial Russian advance on the Galician front in July was halted and turned into a rout – partly because of the confusion caused by the soldiers' committees, which debated every stage in the army's progress.

Rioting in Petrograd on 16 and 17 July, provoked by the Galician débâcle, gave the Bolsheviks their first chance to take the lead in a mass protest. In March the senior Bolsheviks present in Petrograd had behaved very much like the Mensheviks and SRs, calling not for the overthrow of the Provisional Government, but for pressure on it to negotiate peace. In mid April the policy of the Bolshevik Party was transformed overnight by the arrival of Lenin, whose return from Switzerland amongst other left-wing émigrés was arranged by the Germans, on the calculation that they would further damage Russia's military capacity. Lenin lived up to their expectations. In Petrograd he rebuked his temporizing colleagues, called for the withdrawal of support from the Provisional Government, the transfer of power to the soviets, the overthrow of capitalism, and a speedy end to the 'imperialistic' war. Lenin's 'April Theses' were greeted with derision by the larger socialist parties, and made little impact to begin with on the population of Petrograd. Many of his supporters saw no great advantage in presenting power to Mensheviks and Socialist Revolutionaries: but Lenin had no doubt that the 'petty bourgeois socialists' would fail to satisfy the demands of the masses, and rapidly lose ground to his own party. Before July the Bolsheviks seemed to have made little headway. The Party had grown, it is true, but was still minuscule in comparison with its rivals, and its position in the soviets was not significantly stronger. In July, however, Bolshevik banners dominated some of the street demonstrations, and the slogan 'all power to the soviets' was taken up on the morrow of the Galician débâcle by mutinous garrison troops. The soviet leaders not only refused the power that the Bolsheviks pressed on them in order to submerge them, but turned the tables on Lenin. The Minister of Justice, a Socialist Revolutionary, circulated allegations, which were widely believed, that Lenin had long been in the pay of the German government. On 18 July the Bolshevik newspaper *Pravda* was suppressed, and two Bolshevik leaders were arrested. Lenin shaved off his beard, went into hiding, and whiled away his time by composing a Utopian pamphlet on proletarian democracy.

A trivial dispute in the cabinet led on 21 July to the replacement of Prince L'vov by Kerensky. His assets included a patent devotion to democratic ideals and a tireless voice, but not political foresight or a cool head. He made some attempt to restore order in the army by appointing a popular and efficient commander-in-chief, General Kornilov, and to relax the stranglehold of the soviets by convening in Moscow a more broadly representative State Conference. Kerensky and Kornilov discussed, through a confused and confusing intermediary, joint action to reinforce the government, but when Kornilov sent troops to Petrograd in September with ambiguous intentions Kerensky thought his own position was endangered and rallied the left to repel a 'Bonapartist counter-revolutionary threat'. In doing so he conjured up a more menacing foe, for at the height of the crisis the Bolsheviks were authorized to form a 'Red Guard', which later became the main striking force in their seizure of power.

THE OCTOBER REVOLUTION

The Sixth Congress of the Bolshevik Party had already, in August, declared the slogan 'all power to the soviets' obsolete, and resolved on preparations for the assumption of power by the revolutionary classes. Some delegates felt that Lenin, who spoke from his refuge through Stalin and others, was dangerously forcing the pace. His impatience, and his habit of identifying the will of the masses with his own, were still strange to many of his followers. Even when, in the autumn, control of the soviets in several important centres including Moscow passed to the Bolsheviks, it was widely understood in the Party that the swing reflected growing hostility to the Provisional Government, and impatience with Menshevik and SR inertia, rather than enthusiasm for a Bolshevik dictatorship. When on 10 October the Bolshevik Central Committee resolved that 'armed uprising is inevitable and the time is ripe' two of its members, Zinoviev and Kamenev, made their disagreement public. And many of those who accepted Lenin's view did so in the expectation that the victorious Bolsheviks would form a coalition of the left.

The uprising was timed for the eve of the Second All-Russian Congress of Soviets, in which the Bolsheviks and their allies held 380 out of 650 seats. On the night of 24–5 October (6–7 November, New Style) Red Guards and pro-Bolshevik troops, organized by Trotsky from his office as chairman of the Military Revolutionary Committee of the Petrograd Soviet, seized key points in the city. Kerensky had belatedly announced plans for the election of a constituent assembly, and convened a preparatory 'pre-parliament', but, obstinate to the last, resisted advice from this body that he should seek an early peace and speed up preparations for land reform. When the Bolsheviks struck he fled from the capital, and his colleagues were arrested by the insurgents in the Winter Palace. His attempt to lead loyal troops against the capital was repulsed, and a revolt of military cadets and a strike of civil servants in Petrograd both proved ineffectual. The Bolsheviks themselves felt their position to be precarious, but their discipline and energy and Lenin's boldness in political manoeuvre gave them an enormous advantage over their opponents. The unwillingness of Kerensky and the old soviet leaders alike to restore order in the capital while there was still time, by bringing in loyal troops, or yet to woo the masses with immediate reforms, had delivered them into Lenin's hands.

Lenin now established what was at first a military dictatorship, exercised through the Red Guard and the pro-Bolshevik garrison troops, but another miscalculation on the part of his opponents enabled him to represent his *coup* as a transfer of power to the soviets. When the Second All-Russian Congress met on 26 October the Mensheviks and right-wing SRs walked out in protest against the *coup*, leaving the Bolsheviks and their new left-wing SR allies unopposed. The congress approved the composition of an all-Bolshevik government, the 'Council of People's Commissars', of which Lenin was chairman, and voted for a 'peace without annexations and indemnities' and for immediate land reform. These first 'Leninist decrees' were of decisive significance. The Bolshevik policy on peace differed from that of the old soviet leaders only in that the former proceeded to put it into effect. When the commander-in-chief refused to obey orders to open negotiations with the Germans, he was murdered by his troops and replaced by a Bolshevik barrack-room lawyer. A preliminary armistice was concluded at Brest-Litovsk on 15 December. The 'Decree on Land' abolished private ownership and authorized local committees and soviets to distribute all private and church lands to the peasants according to 'labour norms'. Here, as in the peace decree, the Bolsheviks were merely recognizing facts. The demoralized and undisciplined army was incapable of mounting another campaign against the Germans or sustaining a heavy German attack. And its disintegration had been accelerated by the desertion of peasant soldiers, which had begun as early as March, to take part in the spontaneous seizures of gentry estates. The terms of the land decree, and the 'Instruction on the Socialization of Land' attached to it, were as Lenin readily admitted based on decisions of the SR-dominated Congress of Peasant Soviets in May/June, and were incompatible with traditional Marxist agrarian policy or the earlier agrarian programme of the Bolshevik Party. Lenin saw the Decree on Land as a means of sealing a temporary alliance between the proletariat and the peasantry at large. Their experience as struggling smallholders would soon disillusion the poorer peasants, and they would join with the workers against their more prosperous fellows to impose a socialist pattern on agriculture. In 1917, these ominous sophistries were above the heads of the Russian masses who saw in Lenin only the landgiver, and indeed were so confused when his agrarian policy hardened that they often thought of 'Bolsheviks' and 'communists' as being distinct and mutually inimical groups.

The land decree also enabled Lenin to broaden his government. Since he had adopted the central item in the SR programme, a splinter party of left SRs supported him, and by December members of this group held six commissariats in a coalition government of seventeen commissars. The most important was the Commissariat of Agriculture, with which went Lenin's assurance that although in a minority the SRs would not be overruled on agrarian questions. This alliance in turn salved the conscience of those leading Bolsheviks who had stood out for a socialist coalition, and they returned to office. The authority of the new government had already been extended, after fierce fighting in some places, to most Russian urban centres, though the non-Russian periphery of the former empire remained for the most part outside the control of Petrograd. Bolshevik power rested on widespread support amongst the industrial population, who were authorized to establish workers' control in factories, and amongst troops who enjoyed their role of crushing the bourgeoisie at home as much as they had loathed the prospect of fighting at the front. There was as yet little organized support in the countryside, but there was also for the time being nothing for the Bolsheviks to fear from the peasantry. In December 1917, as a precaution against any attempt to overthrow them, the government established a political police, the Cheka ('Extraordinary Commission for Combating Counter-Revolution'). They also sought to forestall any danger from the old generals by hasty demobilization.

The Bolsheviks did not feel secure enough in November to cancel elections to the constituent assembly. The elections gave them a majority in many urban centres, but in the countryside they were swamped by the SRs. Of the delegates who met on 18 January 1918 over one-half were right-wing SRs, while the Bolsheviks and their left SR allies accounted for fewer than one-third. Lenin claimed that rapid political changes since November had made the assembly unrepresentative before it met, and saw nothing for it to do but hail the new regime and gracefully retire. The assembly in its one lengthy session directly challenged Bolshevik policy only by calling for an international socialist conference to discuss peace instead of the German–Soviet negotiations in progress at Brest-Litovsk. At 5 a.m. the guard commander said that his men were tired and sent the delegates home. Later in the day, this first semblance of a democratically elected parliament in Russia's history was not allowed to reassemble, and troops opened fire on protesting crowds.

Lenin's most pressing need was peace with Germany, which would give him a 'breathing space' to begin the reconstruction of his war-shattered and disorganized country. He was willing to pay a heavy price for it, hoping that the war would ultimately provoke a revolution in Germany, and that the final settlement would be between fraternal proletarian governments. The negotiations that began on 22 December 1917, and ended only on 3 March 1918 with the signature of the Brest-Litovsk Treaty, brought Lenin into conflict for a time with the majority of Bolshevik leaders. He was for quick acceptance of the German terms, which stiffened as the Bolsheviks temporized, but a powerful leftist faction wanted revolutionary war, for which Russia had no forces, while a group around Trotsky favoured 'neither peace nor war', which would have been a reasonable policy if the Germans had been unable to fight on. An admonitory German offensive in mid February helped Lenin to win his argument in the Central Committee by one vote. Under the Brest-Litovsk Treaty, the Soviet government renounced broad territories already in fact outside its control, including Finland, Poland, the Baltic provinces, the Ukraine, and parts of White Russia. For safety's sake the government removed to Moscow, and the capital founded, like the Russian Empire itself, by Peter the Great became merely the most magnificent of provincial cities. The left-wing SRs choked on the humiliating peace and left the Bolsheviks to rule alone. In the summer of 1918, further exacerbated by harsh Bolshevik measures in the countryside, they reverted to their parent party's old bad habits. SR terrorists assassinated the German ambassador and two important Bolsheviks, and gravely wounded Lenin himself. These outrages, and peasant unrest in many places, were the signal for a 'Red Terror'. Amongst the victims of Bolshevik fury were the deposed tsar and his family, murdered in Ekaterinburg in July on orders from Moscow.

CIVIL WAR AND FOREIGN INTERVENTION

The sudden collapse of the Central Powers in November 1918 filled the Bolsheviks with conflicting fears and hopes. They feared that the Allied Powers would convert their limited military intervention (originally undertaken to prevent the Germans from seizing arms depots and bases in Russia and if possible to reconstitute an eastern front against Germany) into a crusade against the Soviet regime and in support of its enemies, who had entrenched themselves in the north-west, the north, the south Russian steppes and seaboard, and in Siberia. They hoped that revolutions in the Baltic states as the Germans withdrew, in the newly independent and still unstable Poland, and above all in tottering Germany and the disintegrating Habsburg Empire, would establish fraternal governments in a number of states, deliver the Soviet regime from its dangerous isolation, and help it to solve its terrifying economic problems. Neither their fears nor their hopes were to be realized.

The Bolsheviks had hastened to demobilize the unruly and ramshackle army and immediately begun building up their own defences by decreeing on 12 February 1918 the establishment of a 'Workers' and Peasants' Red Army'. The boldness, energy, and superb organizing talent of Trotsky, who moved to the Commissariat of War in April and throughout the civil war had Lenin's confidence in military matters, determined its character and its quality. He created not the people's militia that socialists had traditionally demanded, but a rigidly disciplined conscript army. The election of officers, and the soldiers' committees that had done so much to weaken the old army, had no place in Trotsky's scheme. In spite of misgivings in the Party, some 50,000 former professional officers were drawn or pressed into the new army during the civil war. To ensure their reliability, Bolshevik political commissars were attached to military commanders. The death penalty was reintroduced to strengthen discipline. Within two years the Red Army enrolled 5 million men, though it remained so short of weapons that it could never field more than 700,000 'bayonets and sabres'. In 1918 about three-quarters of the country that they claimed to rule was outside Bolshevik control, but this enabled the Soviet government to concentrate its efforts. The compact central area was converted into an armed camp, and the whole economy geared to military needs. Industry and transport were nationalized, and a piecework and bonus system helped to stimulate production. The middle classes, debarred by their class origin (except for professional soldiers) from the armed forces, were liable to conscription for labour service. A state grain monopoly was set up, and the peasants' surplus production requisitioned at a risible fixed price. The 'village poor' were organized to confiscate, in co-operation with 'provisioning squads' from the towns, what they identified as 'surplus' to the requirements of their neighbours. Food was strictly rationed, and differential norms fixed for various occupational groups. These drastic, and on the whole effective, emergency measures were dignified with the name of 'war communism'.

The Bolsheviks were greatly helped by the heterogeneity and incoherence of the forces arrayed against them. The anti-Bolshevik politicians could never agree on a positive programme of reforms which might win mass support. The nationalists in the Ukraine, the Caucasus, and Central Asia, though anti-Bolshevik, were also reluctant to support White generals who if victorious might try to restore the empire. The generals, though not all of them reactionary, showed no flair for political warfare. Worse still, strategic co-ordination between the White forces based in

279

Siberia, south Russia, Archangel, and (after the German withdrawal) Estonia was never achieved, and attempts to link up these widely separated armies failed. They had no industrial base, and were chronically short of ammunition. Political divisions and popular discontent at home limited the material support which Britain, France, and the USA gave to the White armies, and their troops, like those of the Japanese (who were interested only in territorial gains in the Far East), fought no major battle with the Bolsheviks.

Thus handicapped, the White generals were unable to consolidate their successive advances into Soviet territory. The armies organized by Admiral Kolchak from Siberia in the summer of 1919 were prevented from linking up with General Miller's forces around Archangel, or those of General Denikin in south-east Russia, and were driven back beyond the Urals. In October of that year the Soviet regime momentarily seemed close to extinction as simultaneous offensives from Estonia and the southern steppes brought White armies to the outskirts of Petrograd and within striking distance of Moscow. But these deep thrusts over-extended their supply lines and dangerously exposed them. General Yudenich gave up the struggle after his failure against Petrograd, and General Denikin's forces were slowly rolled back to their southern bases. Kolchak, recognized by other commanders as 'supreme ruler', fell into Bolshevik hands at Irkutsk in January 1920 and was executed. General Miller was overthrown at Archangel in February. By March the remnants of Denikin's army, in the Crimean peninsula, were the only sizeable White force still intact.

In the spring of 1920 Poland entered the lists against the Soviet regime. The Polish Head of State and Commander-in-Chief, Józef Pilsudski, disliked patriotic White generals almost as much as he did the Bolsheviks, and had refused Denikin's proposals for military co-operation. He saw in the civil war an opportunity to regain for newly independent Poland the eastern frontier of 1772. As a first step he allied himself with the fugitive Ukrainian nationalist leader Petlyura, invaded the Ukraine, and in May captured Kiev. An unexpectedly swift and heavy Soviet counter-attack drove the Poles back into their own territory, split their forces, and by August opened the way to an apparently defenceless Warsaw. This success inflamed the hopes of the Bolshevik leaders. In January 1919 and again in March 1920 they had seen badly planned and feebly supported communist risings suppressed in Germany. Eagerness to shatter barriers between themselves and the puny Soviet regimes in Budapest and Munich had exacerbated their onslaught on Denikin in the summer of 1919. Now, in Trotsky's words, they were 'rushing westward to meet the European proletariat. . .over the corpse of White Guard Poland, in a free and independent workers' and peasants' Poland'. A Polish communist 'government' in Białystok awaited the summons of their worker and peasant compatriots. It never came. Instead in October, to the relief of the Polish people at large, a hastily mustered and ill-equipped Polish force confronted and routed the Red Army on the approaches to Warsaw. This 'miracle on the Vistula' and the Treaty of Riga (March 21), under which Soviet Russia abandoned parts of White Russia and the Ukraine to Poland, checked the westward advance of communism until September 1939.

While the main forces of the Red Army were engaged in the west, General Wrangel began in June 1920 a vigorous northward dash described by Lenin as 'enormously dangerous'. It was only in November, after the armistice with Poland, that the Red Army succeeded in penning him once again in the Crimea. Allied vessels were used to evacuate 150,000 of Wrangel's supporters, but many thousands of those who listened to promises of amnesty were executed by the punitive squads of Cheka. Having defeated the last of the White generals the Red Army could turn to tidying-up operations on the non-Russian periphery – the liquidation of nationalist and anarchist bands in the Ukraine, the suppression of native independence movements in Central Asia (where sporadic fighting continued until 1926), and the annexation in March 1921 of independent socialist Georgia. By the spring of 1921 the Soviet regime had reassembled almost all the territories of the former Russian Empire, except Poland, Finland, the Baltic States, and Bessarabia (returned to Roumania by the Allied Powers). The only foreign forces left on Soviet territory were the Japanese, based in Vladivostok, who finally withdrew under US pressure in 1922.

The civil war inflicted immense human and material losses on a country already severely damaged by the war with Germany. The Red Army alone lost 1 million men, and total mortality as a result of military action, famine, and epidemics was estimated at 8 million. In the central regions held by the Bolsheviks and effectively cut off throughout the war from the main sources of fuel and raw material, industrial production sank to a small fraction of its pre-war volume. Occasional strikes were put down by troops. In the outlying regions scoured by the foraging parties of Whites and Reds, and in the Soviet heartlands, picked bare by Soviet requisitioning squads, the sown area shrank until the country faced the worst famine in its history. Slogans, party labels, and programmes lost all meaning for a people brutalized by the struggle to survive. Banditry was rife. Both Red and White armies were plagued by desertion – thousands of men abandoned Denikin in his hour of defeat and joined in the Red campaign against Poland, while the Soviet countryside teemed with Red Army conscripts in hiding. Peasant risings broke out in the province of Tambov and elsewhere in the autumn of 1920.

Worse still, troops clashed with hungry workers in Petrograd early in 1921, and on 2 March the sailors at Kronstadt, a naval base seventeen miles away and a former Bolshevik stronghold, set up a 'Provisional Revolutionary Committee' and called for the election of soviets without Bolsheviks. The mutiny, put down with savage reprisals after fifteen days, was a warning signal that Lenin could not ignore.

He had justified the Bolshevik dictatorship with assurances that it would quickly win wide popularity and mass support, and that revolutions abroad would deliver it from isolation. As the civil war ended it was clear that he had been overly optimistic. The masses were resentful and restive, while in the West it was the revolutionaries who found themselves isolated. Lenin had to plan for the survival of his regime in an alien and uncongenial domestic and international environment. His immediate objectives were the 'preservation of the worker–peasant alliance' at home, and 'peaceful coexistence with capitalism' abroad. These policies involved compromises with hostile forces at home and abroad, but Lenin saw them as mere tactical manoeuvres. At home, the Party would conciliate the peasantry by concessions to its petty bourgeois instincts, and prepare for the socialization of agriculture at a pace tolerable to the peasants themselves. Abroad, the Soviet state would seek recognition by bourgeois states, strengthen itself by trading with them, defend itself by playing on their differences, but would not abandon its work for world revolution through the Communist International (set up in March 1919), nor forget that 'final victory' would be preceded by a series of 'frightful clashes' between communism and capitalism. The years 1921–2 saw the introduction of the 'New Economic Policy' (NEP), an intensified drive for the normalization of international relations, and an apparent diminution of Comintern militancy.

THE NEP

The foundations of the NEP were laid at the Tenth Party Congress, which met in March 1921 while Kronstadt was still up in arms. The requisitioning of grain was abandoned in favour of a tax in kind, set later at not more than 10 per cent, and the peasants were allowed to sell their produce freely in local markets. Subsequent decrees allowed peasants to hire labour and lease land. So long as the 'commanding heights' of the economy – heavy industry, mineral extraction, banking, foreign trade – remained state monopolies Lenin thought it safe to permit a measure of private enterprise in light industry, consumer services, and trade, and even to lease previously nationalized enterprises to small businessmen. These 'Nepmen', heavily taxed, without electoral rights, lampooned in the Party press and in literature, by definition a regrettable and ephemeral anomaly, flourished until 1928 and helped greatly to make life more tolerable.

What many Russian *émigrés* and foreign politicians greeted as a 'change of signposts' – the triumph of realistic nationalism over communist illusions – was bitterly deplored by some of Lenin's followers as a capitulation to capitalism. One prominent critic interpreted NEP to mean 'new exploitation of the proletariat'. Thousands left the Party in despair, and some committed suicide. Revulsion from Lenin's version of proletarian dictatorship had already found expression at Party congresses. There were two main types of criticism. Some communists, of whom the so-called 'Workers' Opposition' were the most articulate, thought that dictatorial power should be vested not in the Party but in the working class at large, and that logically the trade unions should take over the management of industry. Others, for whom the 'Democratic Centralists' spoke, were perturbed by the authoritarianism of the Party leaders, and pleaded for a democratization of the Party itself. Both groups could defy charges of heresy: the directing role of the trade unions in industry was envisaged by the Party programme, and the tightly disciplined Party whose leading organs were democratically elected and accountable was a Leninist fantasy. Lenin, however, was intent on concentrating control of all other administrative and public duties within the Party, and control over the Party itself within the leading organs. Unity and firm leadership were still as necessary as they had been in the civil war: for NEP was a continuation of the struggle by other means, a tactical retreat in preparation for a new offensive, which in the meantime carried risks of disarray within the ruling Party. At the Tenth Party Congress, therefore, Lenin completed the discomfiture of his critics and legislated against future opposition in the fateful resolution 'On Party Unity'. This condemned factionalism, which, since the highest Party organs by definition represented the will of the majority, came to mean any attempt from below to open a discussion of their policies or administrative decisions. The Party thereupon reduced its numbers from some 700,000 to about half a million by purging itself of persons identified as 'political undesirables, careerists, criminals, or degenerates'.

Within the next few years the leadership completed the task of centralizing power. In December 1922 the four major territorial divisions (the Russian Federation, the Ukraine, White Russia, and the Transcaucasian Federation) were formally joined in a 'Union of Soviet Socialist Republics' – a name chosen to conceal the reality of Russian dominance, and to facilitate the adherence of future proletarian states. The constitution of the new union, finally ratified in January 1924, guaranteed the constituent republics the right of secession, which was meaningless since their communist parties enjoyed no similar right within the All-Union Party, and reserved the most important governmental functions to the central government. The constitution also preserved the fiction of proletarian supremacy by weighting representation in the soviets in favour of the workers. Since, however, candidates for election were selected by the Party, and the soviets at all levels were now firmly under the control of Party organs, the worker gained little by having a vote worth that of five peasants.

The Party command had also asserted its right to determine the composition of the trade union leadership, and had brought the Party network in the forces and in transport, which had enjoyed some independence, under control. The extension and centralization of Party control had made necessary a large and functionally diversified Party apparatus. Stalin, General Secretary of the Central Committee from 1922, played a large part in building it up, and made it his own power base. Lenin, who ceased to take any active part in government from April 1922, became increasingly alarmed by Stalin's aggrandizement. As Commissar for Nationalities Stalin was largely responsible for the peremptory annexation and assimilation of Georgia, and for the embarrassingly frank curtailment of republican rights under the new constitution. At the Commissariat for Workers' and Peasants' Inspection, intended to curb bureaucratic tendencies in government and economic agencies (which greatly exercised Lenin), Stalin had emerged as the most high-handed of bureaucrats. Worst of all, Stalin late in 1922 obstructed the incapacitated leader's contacts with the Central Committee, and was unforgivably rude to Lenin's wife, Krupskaya, in the process. In a document that came to be known as his 'testament' Lenin discussed his possible successors, giving none of them his unqualified approval, but speaking out strongly against Stalin, who had concentrated great power in his hands, did not always use it wisely, and should be transferred to other work. The contents of the document were made known to the inner Party circle shortly after Lenin's death in January 1924, but for tactical reasons Stalin's rivals did not press the charge against him.

In the years 1922–8 Stalin patiently built up a position of unassailable strength. He was careful, to begin with, not to play a particularly aggressive part in the struggles within the top leadership which began even before Lenin's death. Nor did he put himself forward until 1928 as the main author of policy. Compared with other leaders he often spoke the language of conciliation and moderation. His speeches in Party assemblies were as a rule no more than clear and careful formulations of policies devised by others. He joined with Zinoviev and Kamenev to undermine Trotsky, whose chances of succeeding Lenin were scotched in January 1925. At the same time, he quietly reinforced the central Party organs with his own clients, manoeuvred Zinoviev and Kamenev into a minority position, captured their Party fiefs of Leningrad and Moscow and, in alliance with Bukharin and the party 'right', pushed them out of the Politburo (1925–6). Finally he turned against his 'rightist' allies, and used what was now an irresistible preponderance in the Party to demote Bukharin (1929), Rykov (1930), and Tomsky (1930). Stalin had exploited with impressive political skill a uniquely influential position: he alone held office in all four main central Party organs – the Politburo (responsible for making policy), the Orgburo (concerned with organizational measures to implement policy), the Control Commission (empowered to check on the performance and behaviour of all communists), and the Secretariat (which came to control information and largely determine the agenda of other high Party bodies). He was strategically well placed to pack central and local Party agencies with his own men, and so largely to determine the composition of Party congresses, and the Central Committee which they elected.

After Lenin's death the 'first triumvirate' (Zinoviev, Kamenev, and Stalin) thought it politic to capitalize on Lenin's prestige, which far transcended that of his surviving colleagues or of the Party itself. They initiated a cult of the dead leader, renaming Petrograd in his honour, and housing his embalmed remains in a sumptuous mausoleum. Stalin outdid his colleagues with an emotional speech, calling for pledges of loyalty to Lenin's cause, followed this up with a course of public lectures on 'Foundations of Leninism', and launched a recruiting drive (the 'Lenin call-up') to the Party, which incidentally enabled him to expand the Party apparatus under his control. Five years later, during celebrations of his fiftieth birthday, Stalin was hailed as 'Lenin today'. His vainglorious modesty and political shrewdness kept him throughout his life in the role that he tentatively claimed in 1924 and firmly annexed in 1929. He discouraged, for instance, suggestions that an '-ism' of his own should be tacked on to Marxism–Leninism. He was merely the humble (but only true) interpreter of Lenin, the loyal 'continuator' (however alarmingly novel his actions might seem) of Lenin's policy. And this ideological monopoly as much as his overriding organizational authority raised him to a pinnacle of dictatorial power that Lenin had never aspired to occupy.

The Party leadership in the 1920s was divided and reshaped not merely by personal rivalries but by fierce disagreements on policy. The NEP was intended to create the economic and social conditions for a fresh advance toward socialism, but the ailing Lenin offered only the sketchiest guidance to those who would have to execute this manoeuvre. They faced two main problems: how to extract capital for the development of industry from a backward agrarian country, and how to change the mentality of the petty bourgeois peasant. The second question was the subject of Lenin's articles 'On Co-operation' – the last of those upsurges of Utopian euphoria which carried him through every ideological impasse in his career. The peasant would be drawn into an expanding network of interconnected consumer and producer co-operatives, and his own growing prosperity would convert him from private enterprise to socialism. This policy obviously was feasible only if Soviet industry could produce the machinery and consumer goods that would make integrated co-operatives advantageous to the peasantry. In 1923 the Soviet leaders were confronted with what Trotsky defined as being a 'scissors crisis': a widening divergence between the prices of industrial and agricultural goods, which made the peasant reluctant to trade. The short-term remedy was to depress industrial prices, but this inevitably slowed down industrial growth. Those who, like Trotsky and the economist Preobrazhensky, favoured the rapid development of heavy industry, to be paid for by 'socialist accumulation' at the expense of the peasantry, could not explain how this was to be done without coercion. Those who, like Bukharin, relied on growing peasant prosperity and a concomitant expansion of light industry to provide eventually a base for heavy industrial development could offer no convincing safeguards against the reinforcement of peasant 'capitalism'. As the peasant grew more prosperous he looked not for an end to NEP but for further concessions to private enterprise. At the same time industry grew slowly, unemployment was widespread, and there were murmurings that the 'dictatorship of the proletariat' was building a peasant paradise at the workers' cost.

STALIN'S RISE TO POWER

Stalin, in opposition to Trotsky, had asserted the possibility of building socialism in one country, and in 1925–7 identified himself with Bukharin's policies, though he deprecated the latter's tactless exhortation to the peasants to 'enrich yourselves'. But by 1927 NEP was judged to have served one of its purposes in raising industrial and agricultural production to their pre-war level. There was a general feeling, which Bukharin shared, that the tempo of economic development should now be stepped up. The intricate discussion among the economists of the targets to be set and the means of attaining them must have aggravated the feeling of many Party men that they were at the mercy of forces beyond their control or comprehension. The Party's natural inclination, as Stalin had shrewdly hinted in a speech supporting Bukharin's gradualism, was to force the pace excessively. In the winter of 1927–8 he found an opportunity of gratifying the pent-up longing for drastic action. Unattractive prices had sharply reduced the supply of grain to the towns; local Party organizations were authorized to collect grain forcibly, and communists who showed too little energy and enthusiasm were purged. Denials that these emergency measures foreshadowed the end of NEP were overtaken by Stalin's declaration in May 1928 that the alternative to collectivization of agriculture and the rapid development of heavy industry was suicide. The State Planning Commission had been at work on a 'Five-Year Plan' (and also a 'Fifteen-Year Plan') since 1926. Impatience with what Stalin's associate Kuybyshev called 'the learned pessimism of economists' inspired the highest economic–administrative body (Supreme Economic Council) to propose in May 1928 an overall economic expansion of 140 per cent in the five-year period. The argument between those who exaggerated and those who underestimated the possibilities of accelerating economic growth by administrative pressures continued for many months, but the plan as approved by the Sixteenth Party Congress in April 1929 envisaged an expansion of industrial production by 180 per cent (including a particularly rapid increase in the means of production – 230 per cent) and of agricultural production by 55 per cent.

Stalin's change of course provoked furious debate within the Politburo. The 'rightists' led by Bukharin desperately tried to patch up a compromise, or to upset Stalin's majority – and two of his supporters indeed momentarily wavered. Early in 1929 the right wing even appealed to their old leftist opponents to sink ideological differences and rally in defence of the Party against its general secretary, whom Bukharin described to Kamenev as a 'Genghis Khan'. But Stalin's opponents were heavily outnumbered. The leaders of the right – Bukharin, Rykov (Chairman of the Council of People's Commissars since Lenin's death), and Tomsky (head of the trade unions) – admitted to the Central Committee in November that their views had 'proved erroneous'. No doubt they hoped to keep their footing until they could reopen the fight, but they were summarily dismissed from the Politburo. When Rykov was replaced by Molotov in 1930 no 'right deviationist' remained in any high office.

COLLECTIVIZATION

In December 1929 Stalin announced that the Party had begun 'the liquidation of the *kulaks* [rich peasants] as a class', and in January 1930 the Central Committee resolved to collectivize by 1933 the great majority of peasant households instead of the 20 per cent recommended by the Sixteenth Party Congress.

Stalin sought to justify this 'Great Change' by arguing that rapid industrialization was essential to the defence of the country and for the mechanization of agriculture, without which no great increase in productivity could be expected. As for collectivization, it was by now, according to Stalin, fervently desired by the mass of small and middle peasants, and opposed only by kulaks. In fact, what he himself called a 'second revolution' and a 'revolution from above' was carried through against massive peasant resistance, with the help of specially recruited squads of urban communists and the active participation of the OGPU (formerly Cheka). Millions of recalcitrants were uprooted and deported. In the words of a Soviet novelist, 'the countryside stank of roast meat' as the peasants slaughtered and ate livestock rather than surrender it to the *kolkhoz* (collective). Wild rumours swept through the uncomprehending peasant mass – one was that women were to be gathered into collectivized herds.

By March 1930 over half the peasant smallholdings had been collectivized, but at such a price in material damage that Stalin was compelled to slacken the pace. In his article 'Giddiness from Success' he blamed over-zealous local officials for excesses, in particular for interpreting the term 'kulak' much too widely, and deprecated the use of force. The shakier collectives were allowed to fall apart, and by the autumn the percentage of collectivized households had sunk from 58 to 21. To help reconcile the peasant to his lot – and give the state a freer hand in disposing of the collective produce – each collectivized household was permitted to retain a private plot and some livestock. The campaign was shortly resumed. By 1934 almost 75 per cent of peasant households were grouped in collective farms, and by 1937 the figure was 93.4 per cent.

Soviet agriculture recovered very slowly from the damage inflicted by forced collectivization. In spite of mechanization food production failed to keep up with the growth in population, and livestock figures in particular were lower in the late 1930s than in 1928 or 1913. But collectivization enabled the state to dispose freely of agricultural production, to export grain, and to feed the expanding industrial population. Collective farms were required to deliver produce to the state in quantities determined in advance and at low fixed prices. The peasant's income was a share in the residue of produce and revenue, after the farm had met its obligations to all state agencies. In practice, this came to mean that the peasantry depended heavily on the private plot for subsistence and especially for ready cash. Although the collective farm was nominally a self-governing producer co-operative, its management and its operations were minutely controlled by the 'Machine and Tractor Stations', which combined the functions of a machine hiring agency and political–economic supervision, and which were regarded as outposts of socialism by local Party officials and in the incompletely socialized countryside. A discriminatory passport regime tied the peasant to the land, except when he was transferred to industry by the labour recruitment agencies. Stalin persisted in representing mass collectivization as the implementation of Lenin's co-operative plan. Bukharin's description – a system of military feudal exploitation – was in the short term at least more accurate.

Soviet figures for economic growth in the 1930s were distorted by dubious statistical procedures, but that Stalin's methods created a powerful heavy industrial base there is no doubt. The claims that in 1940 the Soviet Union produced 166 million tons of coal, 31 million tons of oil, 18.3 million tons of steel, and 48.3 kWh of electric power were probably near the mark. (The figures for Russian output of these items in 1913 were 29.1, 9.2, 4.2, and 1.9, respectively.) These successes were won at the cost of great hardship to the industrial worker. Real wages fell sharply in the First Five-Year Plan period, and did not regain the 1928 level until the 1950s. The disorganization and the sag in agricultural production caused by collectivization made it necessary to ration food-stuffs. Though rationing was formally abolished in 1935 the special shops reserved to particular occupational categories were always better stocked than those open to the general public. Industrial plans always presupposed a quick rise in labour productivity, and workers were incessantly bullied to increase their output. Resentment sometimes drove them to sabotage, or even to murdering the 'Stakhanovites', whose feats of labour heroism were used as an excuse for raising production norms. The trade unions had some responsibilities for administering social insurance and welfare amenities, but their main function was to assist managements in carrying out the plan, and enforcing severe disciplinary rules. None the less, in spite of low wages, harsh working conditions, persistent shortages of some foodstuffs and all consumer goods, the lot of the industrial workers was generally felt to be lighter than that of the peasant.

After the expulsion of the rightists the Party apparatus appeared to be solidly packed with loyal Stalinists. The Seventeenth Party Congress in 1934 was spoken of as 'the congress of victors'. Ostensibly, the successes celebrated were those of collectivization and the First Five-Year Plan, but these were at the same time a personal victory for Stalin over all his rivals. Zinoviev, Kamenev, and Bukharin were allowed to speak at the congress, and there was apparently some reason to hope that old quarrels would now be forgotten. The growing menace of Nazi Germany, on which Bukharin dwelt in his congress speech, seemed to make harmony within the Soviet leadership imperative. But the façade of unity was deceptive. The mass expulsion of rightists in 1929 (which reduced

289

the Party's numbers by 11 per cent) was followed from year to year by the systematic weeding-out of members declared unreliable or inefficient. In many cases 'unreliability' had meant undisguised revulsion from the brutalities of forcible collectivization. The waste and bungling inseparable from a crash programme of industrialization in a backward country provoked hysterical accusations of 'wrecking', and in 1928-9 the first of several groups of managers and experts was tried for sabotage. Some of Stalin's closest associates seem to have felt the need for normalization and especially for conciliatory policies toward the peasantry, and to have watched uneasily his brusqueness toward colleagues, his readiness to blame subordinates for 'excesses' that he had demanded, his obsessional search for hidden enemies, his gross appetite for flattery.

THE PURGES

Soviet accounts of the period published since Stalin's death support the view long held by some western scholars that in 1934 an attempt was made to curb Stalin (the only public indication at the time was his unexplained election no longer as 'General Secretary' but merely as 'Secretary' of the Central Committee). But in December 1934 S. M. Kirov, Secretary of the Party in Leningrad and a fast-rising star in the Party firmament, was murdered. The assassin, Nikolayev, and thirteen others executed with him, were described as 'Zinovievites', but Khrushchev in his 'secret speech' and some recent Soviet works on Party history hint strongly that Stalin engineered the crime. However this may be, he used it as an excuse for launching the 'Great Purge', in which former rivals, colleagues who had shown or might show some independence of mind, office-holders who were not his creatures, tens of thousands of minor Party men, and countless politically insignificant citizens perished together. The first sign that a protracted screening of Party members was about to degenerate into a witch-hunt came in January 1935, when Zinoviev, Kamenev, and others were tried *in camera* and imprisoned, on the grounds that they had organized a secret centre of opposition, deceived the Party with hypocritical recantations, and indirectly inspired Kirov's assassin. The purge gathered momentum with two Central Committee directives in January and July 1936, the first ordering a general expulsion of all unworthy members from the Party, the second urging greater efforts to unmask the 'terrorist' and 'counter-revolutionary' 'Trotskyite–Zinovievite counter-revolutionary bloc'. In September 1936, in a telegram from his summer villa at Sochi, Stalin grumbled that the political police were four years behind in their work and ordered the appointment of N. I. Yezhov to the Commissariat for Internal Affairs (NKVD – which had absorbed the OGPU in 1934). The new commissar's name is unenviably immortalized in the word 'Yezhovshchina', used to describe the bloodbath of 1936–8.

To lend a semblance of truth to the story of a treasonable and murderous conspiracy manipulated by the exiled Trotsky and reaching into every corner of Soviet life a series of public trials was staged, at which the 'conscience of Bolshevism' – or at least the voice of Stalin – spoke through Public Prosecutor Vyshinsky. Sixteen former leftists, including Zinoviev and Kamenev, were tried and executed in August 1936. Seventeen other Bolshevik notables stood trial in January 1937, thirteen of whom were shot, while four were sent to a slower death in labour camps. At this trial it was alleged that the conspirators were in the service of Germany and Japan. In June the Red Army Commander-in-Chief, Tukhachevsky, and seven other senior commanders were tried secretly and executed as spies and traitors, while Gamarnik, head of the Political Directorate of the Army, committed suicide. In March 1938 twenty-one members of what was now called the 'anti-Soviet bloc of rightists and Trotskyites', including Bukharin, Rykov, and the laggardly ex-Commissar for Internal Affairs, were tried, and the eighteen major offenders executed. At each of the public trials the defendants were allowed only to confirm confessions previously extracted by the NKVD, whose methods, as Khrushchev much later admitted, included torture.

The vast majority of those purged were tried clandestinely by tribunals that included subordinates of Vyshinsky and Yezhov, which had powers of summary sentence. A wave of destructive hysteria swept the country. Party and police officials, fearing for their own skins, vied with each other in a macabre competition to unmask more and more cunningly disguised traitors and saboteurs. Human sacrifice was exacted from every institution and organization. Everywhere the cowardly and the ambitious joined in denouncing colleagues. Their anxious or hopeful slanders did not always save them from sharing the fate of their victims and of those who spoke up in protest. The Great Purge served its purpose. The absurd fable of a multi-tentaculate conspiracy served as a warning that all opponents of Stalin past, present, or future were traitors and deserving of death. Stalin had shown that high military posts carried no political weight. More important, he had, with little difficulty, struggled free of the Party, from which his authority nominally derived, and shown that on the contrary the Party was one lever of power amongst others which he could manipulate. The secret police was now seen to be a more important instrument of rule, but also one which he had firmly in hand, as he demonstrated by dismissing Yezhov and replacing him by a fellow-Georgian, L. P. Beria, in December 1938. Many suspects were immediately released, the witch-hunt was called off, and recent excesses were laid, inevitably, at the door of subversives in the security organs. There would, Stalin told the Eighteenth Party Congress in March 1939, be no further need of mass purges, and his prediction was accurate. Thereafter endemic terror, the fear of sudden arrest and consignment without trial to the ever more swollen labour camps, sufficed to keep the country in thrall.

From 1 January 1935 the rationing of bread and some other foodstuffs ended. In November, Stalin had encouraged expectations of better times ahead with the words 'life has become better, life has become happier'. He was simultaneously planning the Great Purge. In 1936, as it gathered momentum, he promulgated a new constitution, since the building of socialism was nearing completion. The constitution contained an impeccable list of civil rights, with no guarantee that they would be respected. It included a clause formalizing the leading role of the Party, whose powers were by now subsumed in Stalin's personal dictatorship. It removed the electoral disabilities of the peasantry, which, like the representative bodies themselves, were now of less significance than ever. It reconstructed the organs of Soviet rule, and confirmed the right of Union Republics (now eleven in number) to secede. As Stalin said in another context, 'paper will stand anything'. The constitution was a useful document for propaganda purposes abroad, and seems to have been accepted by many Soviet citizens as a blueprint for the future. If indeed the Soviet Union was, as the promoters of the constitution said, a family of fraternal peoples and without class antagonisms, there was no obvious reason why the regime should not have relaxed its rigours. But Stalin himself in 1937, by way of ideological explanation of the purge, advanced the novel idea that the class enemy grew more active and dangerous as the country neared its socialist goal. At the Eighteenth Party Congress he removed any lingering hope of greater freedom in the foreseeable future by declaring that the state would continue to exist even under communism in conditions of capitalist encirclement. Since it was not Marx, nor even Lenin, but Stalin who had decreed the possibility of building socialism and even communism in a single country, his latest glaring heterodoxy was no more than a logically necessary footnote.

SOVIET FOREIGN POLICY BETWEEN THE WARS

The victory of the Entente had saved Lenin's regime and enabled him to scrap the Brest-Litovsk Treaty. But in the 1920s memories of the Intervention, communist agitation in Europe and Asia, and the Soviet refusal to pay Imperial Russia's debts soured Anglo-Soviet and Franco-Soviet relations. The Soviet government condemned the 'robber treaty' of Versailles and that 'instrument of French and British imperialism', the League of Nations. The USSR naturally drew closer to their main 'victim', Germany, and in 1922 the Rapallo Treaty ushered in a period of co-operation between the two countries which among other things facilitated German evasion of the military restrictions imposed at Versailles. It was moreover easier for the Soviet government to pursue its dual policy – 'normal' inter-governmental relations and the promotion of communist revolution – in weakened Germany than elsewhere. A third abortive communist rising in 1923, and the activities of a party that stubbornly challenged Germany's democratic institutions until Hitler destroyed it and them together, did not much disturb the course of Soviet–German relations, whereas Anglo-Soviet relations were troubled and for a time disrupted by the Comintern's interference in Britain and in Asia. When Stalin's propagandists at the end of the 1920s looked for a military threat to underline the urgency of industrialization they named Britain and France as the most likely aggressors.

The Soviet leaders (unlike the exiled Trotsky) underestimated the dangers of Nazism until it was far too late. Fascism, in their view, was an alternative method of rule to which capitalists resorted in desperate crises, when bourgeois democracy could no longer control the masses. In other words, the rise of fascism showed that a revolutionary situation was ripening. In Germany, Nazism was not a serious threat to the communists, but rather an assurance of their imminent triumph. Their immediate task was not to oppose the Nazis but to break the hold of the reformist social democrats – or 'social fascists' as Soviet propaganda ludicrously called them – on the masses. The struggle between communism and fascism would follow and arise out of the assault of both extreme parties on the social-democratic middle, in the course of which, it was assumed, the communists would win over the masses to their side. This policy effectively precluded joint resistance by communists and social democrats to Nazism, and indeed there were instances of Nazi–communist collaboration against social democrats.

It was of course axiomatic that the local interests of communist parties were subordinate to the global strategy of communism, the first object of which was to preserve and strengthen the Soviet base. Lenin himself was ready to sacrifice foreign communists to the needs of Soviet foreign policy – as when he connived at the suppression of communism in Turkey to purchase the goodwill of Kemal Ataturk. Doggedly clinging to the line laid down in 1923, Stalin had insisted that the Chinese communists should continue to operate within the broad nationalist movement (Kuomintang), until Chiang Kai-shek destroyed his Trojan horse in 1927. Stalin took this gamble because he was primarily interested in undermining the position of imperialism in China. The left turn in international communism in 1929 was yet another, and highly peculiar application of the principle that Soviet needs must determine communist action everywhere, peculiar because in this instance the needs were Stalin's own. The new policy was a projection into international communism of Stalin's 'second revolution' at home. Comintern's slogan 'class against class' echoed Stalin's slogan 'liquidation of the kulaks as a class'. Comintern's war on social democracy and reformism paralleled Stalin's fight against 'rightism'. Internationally, as well as in the Soviet Union, communism seemed to have resumed the offensive after a long period of stagnation and to be in sight of tremendous victories. The new course demanded stricter discipline, fresh proofs of loyalty, the elimination of doubters and waverers. In 1929–33 the foreign communist parties were converted from merely Bolshevik into Stalinist agencies.

Soviet policy changed sharply in the middle 1930s. Border conflicts with Japan, Hitler's violent denunciations of Bolshevism, and the conclusion of the anti-Comintern pact (1936) made necessary a *rapprochement* with the western democracies. The Soviet Union joined the much-abused League of Nations (1934), concluded defensive pacts with Czechoslovakia and France (1935), and became, in words at least, the main protagonist of collective security against fascist aggression. In 1935 Comintern abandoned its war on social democracy and called for a 'Popular Front' of all anti-fascist forces. At the same time Stalin hedged his bets. In 1937, while Germany and the Soviet Union were intervening on opposite sides in the Spanish Civil War, Soviet emissaries in Berlin began exploring the possibility of an understanding between the two countries. Stalin feared that the western democracies were planning to divert German aggression eastward, and that even if he allied himself with them the Soviet Union would be left to 'pull the chestnuts out of the fire' in the event of war. He was not reassured by discussions with Britain and France in 1939, and in August the Soviet Union and Germany signed the Non-Aggression Pact, which gave Hitler a free hand in the West. The two countries partitioned Poland between them, and Molotov, then Chairman of the Council of People's Commissars, publicly rejoiced in the destruction of 'the freakish creation of Versailles'. While Germany was at war with France and Britain, the Soviet Union attacked Finland and annexed the Baltic states of Estonia, Latvia, and Lithuania. Communists in the western democracies received orders, which not all of them obeyed, to condemn the imperialist war, work to end it speedily, and refrain from supporting their governments against Germany. Though relations between the two countries were not easy, the Soviet Union gave considerable material assistance to Germany. Stalin's hope seems to have been for a stalemate in the West and a peace settlement that would leave the Soviet Union in possession of its new territories. However this may be, he avoided provoking Germany by rapidly reinforcing his forward defences, and ignored western warnings of an imminent German attack.

THE SOVIET UNION IN THE SECOND WORLD WAR

Hitler's invasion in June 1941 converted the 'imperialist war' at once into a 'war of the peoples against fascism'. Britain offered alliance and the United States extended its 'lend–lease' operation to the Soviet Union. The anti-Hitler alliance held firmly throughout the war, in spite of Stalin's real or pretended suspicions that the western powers might conclude a separate peace with Germany, and that they deliberately delayed opening a second front in order to weaken the Soviet Union. Grudging Soviet acknowledgment of western aid and of western military successes always contrasted strangely with frank western admiration for the tremendous Soviet contribution to allied victory over Germany.

If Stalin was ill prepared in June 1941, Hitler greatly underestimated Soviet military capacity. He expected another lightning victory, and his troops entered Russia unprepared for a winter campaign. But his own error in diverting tanks from the Central Army Group in late summer, when it was fast approaching Moscow, gave the Soviet Union an opportunity to regroup its forces and to launch a winter counter-offensive. Though the Germans in the first few months of war occupied White Russia and the Ukraine and invested Leningrad, the Soviet government had succeeded in evacuating some 1,500 industrial enterprises to the rear, and quickly reconstructed a formidable industrial base. In 1942, Hitler's drive toward Baku in the hope of cutting off Soviet oil supplies was checked, and he made his second mistake by concentrating his main effort on an objective of greater symbolic than strategic importance – the city of Stalingrad on the Volga. The defeat and capture of Field Marshal von Paulus's huge army at Stalingrad in January 1943, after four months of furious fighting, marked the turning point in the war. The Soviet armies in the next eighteen months fought their way back to the 1939 frontier on most sectors of the front. Between August 1944 and May 1945 they rolled on westward and southward, occupying Roumania, Bulgaria, the Baltic states, Poland, Hungary, Austria, Czechoslovakia. On 25 April 1945 Soviet troops surrounded Berlin, and linked up with American troops on the Elbe. Germany unconditionally surrendered to the Allies on 7 May. To make good its claim to territorial adjustments to which the western powers had already agreed, the Soviet Union declared war on Japan on 8 August (two days after the dropping of the atomic bomb on Hiroshima) and, in the remaining weeks before the Japanese surrendered to General MacArthur, mopped up the Japanese forces in Manchuria.

These Soviet victories would have been impossible without western aid, without the impact of western bombing on Germany, and without the western campaigns in Africa, Italy, Western Europe, and the Far East. It is none the less true that the scale of the achievement took the world by surprise. The Soviet Union had withstood the onslaught of the largest German land forces, and had shattered them. Soviet losses, human and material, were enormous: 20 million killed (half of them civilians or prisoners), 1,710 urban centres destroyed, 25 million people left homeless, thousands of enterprises and thousands of kilometres of railway put out of action. Through it all, the Soviet armies fought with unsurpassed heroism and endurance. Their patriotism, and that of the Soviet people at large, was stiffened by barbaric German treatment of prisoners and the inhabitants of occupied territories. Soviet industry was sufficiently developed to equip its army, with western help, for a modern war. Stalin's efforts as a strategist have often been disparaged in the Soviet Union since his death, but it must be said that after the first Soviet setbacks he promoted a galaxy of brilliant commanders and rarely hampered them. In one sense at least he deserved the title that he liked so much to hear – 'organizer of our victories'. The administrative machine which he built and controlled proved remarkably efficient in gearing the country's human and material resources to the needs of war. He also showed great psychological skill in his handling of the population. He called for the defence not of communism but of 'the Fatherland', and held up as examples the Russian warrior heroes of earlier centuries – Alexander Nevsky, Dimitri Donskoy, Suvorov, Kutuzov. He enlisted the help of the long-persecuted (and traditionally nationalistic) Orthodox Church by permitting the re-establishment of the patriarchate (1943) and the re-opening of churches. The most incongruous of his patriotic declarations greeted the surrender of Japan. Russians, he said, had awaited that moment since their defeat by Japan in 1905 – a defeat that the Bolsheviks in fact had ardently desired.

STALIN'S LAST YEARS

The outcome of the war seemed to many both a vindication of Stalin's course since 1928 and an assurance of milder policies for the future. Their hopes were soon dashed. Relations between the Soviet Union and its wartime allies deteriorated rapidly as communist regimes were installed by force and fraud in countries under Soviet military control.

Soviet propagandists and a new international communist organization called Cominform (established in September 1947) declared the world 'divided into two camps – the camp of socialism and peace' (headed by the Soviet Union) and 'the camp of imperialism and war' (headed by the United States). In 1946 Stalin had already committed the Soviet Union to a new series of five-year plans in which the main aim would be to treble pre-war industrial output and so 'to guarantee our motherland against all eventualities'. By 1948 the country had basically reconstructed its war-damaged industries, and heavy industry began to expand rapidly. Where the Germans had left a desolation of rubble new cities began to rise, many of them well planned and pleasant, marred only by tastelessly ornate public buildings that were severely criticized after Stalin's death. Progress in other sectors of the economy was unimpressive. Agriculture, starved of capital, languished. There were frequent shortages of meat, fats, and sugar outside the big towns, and flour was issued only on special occasions. Clothing and footwear were always in short supply. In the cities that war had not destroyed the residents were more and more tightly packed in decaying dwellings. Open discontent and indiscipline were punishable as before by imprisonment, and the teeming camps were themselves an economic institution of great importance, especially in concentrating very cheap labour in remote and primitive mining and timbering areas.

The ever-present danger of an imperialist attack was invoked to justify the Soviet government's heavy demands on its people, and during the Soviet blockade of Berlin (June 1948–May 1949) or the first year of fighting between North and South Korea (1950–1) a third world war seemed only too likely. To strengthen his forward positions and make possible defence of the Soviet Union in depth Stalin tightened his grip on his east European satellites. In 1948 Yugoslavia, the only European country apart from the Soviet Union in which communists had won power by their own efforts, rebelled against Soviet interference in its affairs, and was outlawed by the international communist movement. To discourage any would-be emulator of Marshal Tito, the communist parties in each of the satellites were purged, leaders suspected of nationalist leanings or merely of having minds of their own were dismissed, and in some countries (Bulgaria, Hungary, Czechoslovakia) show trials were staged on the 1936–8 Soviet model and communists of the highest standing executed or sent to prison camps. It was much later revealed that the Soviet secret police directly supervised these terrorist operations in the fraternal 'people's democracies'. As a safeguard against 'ideological subversion' Stalin stringently limited travel and cultural contacts. After the war, as in the 1930s, Soviet writers, artists, scientists, and scholars were jealously scrutinized for signs of foreign contamination or spontaneous degeneration, and Stalin's personal tastes and prejudices set a rigid official line in various fields of cultural and academic endeavour.

In his last years Stalin was something of a recluse. His life was bounded by the Kremlin and his villa near Moscow. He seldom received diplomats or visitors from non-communist countries. His knowledge of the Soviet Union and of the world beyond was derived from men who feared and flattered. Many of his decisions on home and foreign policy were later admitted to have been ill-informed and erratic. But there is no evidence to suggest that his hold on power grew feebler. He treated his closest colleagues with contemptuous irony – and they, as one of them later said, never knew whether after an interview with him they would be going home or to a prison camp. For reasons still obscure he authorized in 1949 the arrest and execution of several senior Party men, including Voznesensky, who was a member of the Politburo and head of the State Planning Commission. Full meetings of the Politburo were rarely held, and policy was delegated to *ad hoc* subcommittees. Since 1940 Stalin had been head of the government (renamed Council of Ministers in 1946) as well as of the Central Committee, and he used this position to dilute the authority of the high Party officials. He seems also to have played off the weightiest members of the Politburo against each other, giving greater prominence in turn to Malenkov and Zhdanov until the latter's death in 1948, and allowing differences on agricultural policy between Malenkov and Khrushchev to come into the open in 1950–2. After the Nineteenth Party Congress in October 1952 the Politburo was renamed the Presidium and greatly enlarged. Stalin's next step, as Khrushchev later told the Party, would have been to eliminate older leaders and 'bring in less experienced persons'. Khrushchev also hinted that 'elimination' would not have meant comfortable retirement, and indeed it seemed clear in January 1953 that Stalin was meditating bloodshed. *Pravda* announced that a terrorist group of nine doctors had confessed to the murder of Zhdanov, and to plotting against a number of leading military figures, on the orders of the US intelligence service. The scope of the intended purge was still unknown when Stalin died on 5 March. A month later it was admitted that the doctors had 'confessed' under torture, and the charges against them were dropped. In 1954 a high security official was executed for having organized the operation.

THE ASCENDANCY OF KHRUSHCHEV

There was and could be no heir apparent to Stalin. A lieutenant powerful enough to step into his shoes when he died might not have waited so long.

He had lent authority, but never beyond recall, and had carefully trimmed the balance between his nearest colleagues, thus making a contest for power inevitable after his death. In March 1953 government leaders exhorted their countrymen not to fall into 'disarray', but nowhere was this danger more real than within the inner leadership. They made a show of unity by reducing the Presidium to the size of the old Politburo and distributing responsibility for the main branches of administration among its members. Behind this façade a struggle was in progress. G. M. Malenkov, the senior surviving Secretary of the Central Committee, also became Chairman of the Council of Ministers, and newspaper readers saw for the first time a photograph intended to suggest that Stalin and Mao Tse-tung had accepted him as their peer. A few days later, however, Stalin's mantle was rent in two, and Malenkov resigned his Party secretaryship to concentrate on his work as head of government. A second Stalin would have needed the personal allegiance of the secret police or the exclusive support of their overlord. It was no doubt with this in mind that some of his colleagues brought about the fall of L. P. Beria, quaintly described as being an agent of British intelligence, and his execution – either at the moment of arrest, as rumour had it, or after trial by a military tribunal in December, as *Pravda* reported. Thereafter the security services were probably collectively supervised by a group within the Party leadership.

In September 1953 N. S. Khrushchev was elected First Secretary of the Central Committee, and soon established himself as the dominant figure in the new Presidium. His rapid rise is explained by the pattern of his previous career and by his personal qualities. The decapitation and taming of the secret police greatly enhanced the role of that other all-embracing system of controls – the Party network. Khrushchev had worked in the Party apparatus, with only short breaks, for twenty-five years, and had for many years directed two of the most important Party organizations – that of the Ukraine and that of Moscow. He had wide contacts with the provincial Party secretaries who now carried great political weight, and was their natural leader in any conflict with the ministerial bureaucracy. During the war, while most other Politburo members had remained at the centre, he had served as senior Party representative at Stalingrad and elsewhere in the front line, and his comradely relations with some of the generals were now to prove an asset. He was by temperament and training a politician rather than a bureaucrat, more at home on the platform or even among the crowd than behind a desk, boisterous in manner, rough and racy in speech, quick-witted and quick-tempered. For eleven years he towered above his colleagues, and more powerfully than any other individual he influenced the pace and direction of the remarkable changes in Soviet policy after Stalin.

That many of Stalin's ideas and methods were obsolete and damaging seems to have been generally accepted. If only for their own safety, his successors set their faces against individual dictatorship and proclaimed the principle of collective leadership. They renounced police terror on the Stalinist scale, and began to liquidate the worst of the prison camps. They set about correcting imbalances in the economy which Stalin's inflexibility had aggravated: in particular they saw the need to shift more of their heavy industrial investment to sectors in which Soviet technology was falling behind, to pump capital into their chronically neglected agriculture, to produce more consumer goods, to build more houses. In international relations they sought at once to reduce tension, and at the Geneva summit meeting of 1955 showed themselves more flexible than their late leader. Khrushchev to begin with devoted himself to the revival of agriculture, largely by the novel means of offering incentives to the peasant. His sphere of activity, however, broadened rapidly after February 1955, when Malenkov was forced to resign. The main complaint against Malenkov was one that Khrushchev's military friends would have regarded as being very grave: he was said to favour an excessive diversion of resources to light industry. He himself explained his political weakness in his speech of resignation when he confessed to a lack of local experience, which was of course the great strength of Khrushchev and the Party *apparatchiki*. Malenkov's successor, N. A. Bulganin, had worked closely with Khrushchev in the past, and for the time being assiduously played second fiddle. From now on and until his dismissal in October 1964, Khrushchev was the main architect of Soviet domestic and foreign policy. Though he started from the generally agreed principles of the post-Stalin reform he elaborated them with a demagogic *panache* which even his supporters sometimes found embarrassing, showed a restless and sometimes reckless passion for organizational innovation against which more cautious minds rebelled, was endlessly prolific in good and less good recipes for quick economic and social progress. The list of his failures is long, but it is doubtful whether a more circumspect man could have supplied, as Khrushchev did, what after the grim reign of Stalin the country most urgently needed – the sense of renewal, the hope of a healthier relationship between governors and governed, an earnest of prosperous times to come.

At the Twentieth Party Congress in February 1956 Khrushchev dramatically contradicted Stalin's (and Lenin's) darkest idea. War, he said, was not 'fatally inevitable', because the might of the Soviet Union and its allies could deter any would-be aggressor. Moreover in the world at large the forces of communism were growing so fast that they might come to power in some countries by peaceful means. These reassurances were addressed as much to the Soviet people, who had lived so long with the prospect of an eventual thermonuclear conflict, as to the outside world. A weightier pledge was given in the 'secret speech', which was quickly imparted to all sections of the population. In this Khrushchev rehearsed some of Stalin's crimes, particularly those against the Party, and condemned the 'personality cult' which had sanctified a murderous and in many respects inept tyranny. The speech was generally taken to mean that the new rulers renounced the use of terror against their own people. The ubiquitous portraits and images of Stalin, and all the paraphernalia of the cult, were called in. Places named after him gradually resumed their former appellations or found inoffensive and eminently forgettable new ones. Thousands of his surviving victims received some compensation, and many thousands more were posthumously rehabilitated. The great deviationists, however, although absolved of the most absurd charges against them, were still politically anathematized. In the following years Stalin's official reputation fluctuated. In his running fight with other old Politburo members in 1957–8 Khrushchev accused them of encouraging and abetting Stalin, while implicitly including himself in a salutary 'Leninist nucleus' within the old leadership; but he was less eager than some of his younger supporters for open and thorough examination of the record. And when critics of Stalinism in effect questioned the very foundations of the regime, Khrushchev himself remembered virtues in the master whom he had renounced.

Khrushchev applied himself energetically to some of the gravest problems bequeathed by Stalin: the inertia of an overgrown and over-centralized bureaucracy, the stagnation of the countryside, the lawlessness of the law-enforcers, the widening gap between the privileged and the masses. The solutions that he offered were also those that would help a man of his special talents and limitations to stay in power. He liked to appear to be the champion of the Party against the ministerial bureaucracy, of the provinces against the centre, of the common man against stick-in-the-mud officialdom, highfalutin intellectuals, foolish experts. In the last resort he could not of course and would not have wished to weaken central authority. Nor could he seriously modify the bureaucratic habits of mind which the Party *apparatchik* fully shared with his governmental colleagues. What he tried to do, by repeated reorganizations, was to break up strong concentrations of power not directly subordinate to himself, to spread operative authority more broadly and at lower levels, always under the co-ordinating control of his own central Party machine, to jolt desk-bound officials into vigorous action. He could, to begin with, rely on the eager response of ambitious men, especially in the provinces and the middle ranks of the Party, to whom he offered greater scope for action and better chances of promotion. But each of his organizational upheavals swelled the numbers of demoted and displaced persons, and when, having apparently subdued the ministerial bureaucracy, he began drastically restructuring the provincial Party apparatus, he overtaxed the loyalty of his own clients.

The first measures of administrative decentralization in 1955–6, which enhanced especially the powers of the republican governments, and of course the parallel Party organizations, provoked no visible resistance, but at the end of 1956 some of the economic overlords in Moscow made common cause with the precarious *fronde* in the Presidium against Khrushchev. His standing was temporarily weakened by the recent crisis in Poland, the uprising in Hungary, and unrest amongst Soviet students, all of which took their impulse from the Twentieth Congress. In December control of the economy was concentrated in a powerful new body, the State Economic Commission, which would plainly limit Khrushchev's encroachment in this sphere. His retort, in February 1957, was a proposal to curtail the functions of industrial ministries and abolish many of them, to establish a network of 'economic councils' for regional co-ordination of industry, and to increase the powers of plant managers. This measure was passed into law in May, significantly without the fiat of the Presidium. At the end of June an emergency meeting of the Central Committee defeated an attempt to unseat Khrushchev. His supporte·s condemned the 'anti-Party group', naming Molotov, Malenkov, anu Kaganovich, together with Khrushchev's renegade protégé Shepilov, and expelled them. Of the two chief economic overlords in the Presidium one (Saburov) was quietly dropped and the other (Pervukhin) demoted. It was only gradually revealed that Khrushchev's opponents in the Presidium had in fact been in the majority, and that they included Bulganin. The Presidium and the Secretariat were enlarged by the promotion of Khrushchev's supporters. One of them, Marshal Zhukov, who was said to have helped Khrushchev by arranging for scattered Central Committee men to be flown in for the emergency meeting, enjoyed his new position only briefly. In October he came back from a visit to Yugoslavia to find that he was no longer Minister of Defence, and a week later he was formally removed from the Presidium. The most serious charge against him was that he had sought to eliminate the control of Party and government over the armed forces. However that may be, it is understandable that Khrushchev did not relish the presence within the supreme Party organ of a defence minister who was also the Soviet Union's most distinguished soldier and a popular hero.

The resuscitation of agriculture was perhaps the most urgent of tasks, and for Khrushchev the most congenial. It had a moral as well as a practical aspect. Educated Soviet citizens were well aware that Stalinism had matured in the social and political climate created by collectivization, that the peasants had paid dearly for the country's industrial successes, that they were still downtrodden, ill-paid, second-class citizens. The 'kolkhoz literature', which flourished under Khrushchev and which was often hauntingly reminiscent of the old Populist writers, insinuated that the masters must make amends for the peasant's historic woes and wrongs, and even at times that the countryside was after all wiser, more virtuous, more 'Russian' than the town. Khrushchev of course did not say such things, but he tolerated searching criticism of past errors in the treatment of the peasantry. The new Party programme of 1961 declared that the 'dictatorship of the proletariat' was quickly changing into a 'state of the whole people'. This crabbed formula was a promise of equality to the peasant. More tangible improvements in his lot came from fairer prices for his produce, advance payments for work in the collective sector, and bigger investments in rural housing and amenities, as well as in mechanization, fertilizers, and farm buildings, and, by no means least important, the abolition of the bloodsucking Machine and Tractor Stations and the transference of powered machinery to the farms. Khrushchev's impatient mind was not content with these obvious measures. He expected an enormous increase in grain production from new crops, new methods of cultivation, new lands – and here he showed a disastrous tendency to overdo good ideas. In the popular memory Khrushchev, unfairly, is above all the *kukuruznik*, who absurdly insisted on the sowing of *kukuruza* (maize) in all soils and climates, and to make room for it allowed established grasslands to be destroyed. Just as rashly he pushed through an over-ambitious scheme for ploughing up some 70 million acres of virgin and idle land, most of it in arid Central Asia, and mainly with the labour of youthful volunteers. Precautions against erosion were neglected, arrangements for storing and shifting the crops were wastefully inefficient, and intolerable living conditions drove many of the volunteers home again. It was doubtful whether in the end the new lands would repay the cost of maintaining them. But they contributed to the record harvests which in the short run justified Khrushchev's agricultural policies. The year 1958, however, proved to be the high point of his achievement, and in subsequent years the Soviet Union sometimes had to supplement its grain crop by imports.

Under Khrushchev the Soviet citizen had less reason than ever before to fear arbitrary arrest, summary condemnation, and indefinite confinement. Open trial, a measure of public supervision over prisons and camps exercised through local soviets, and an amended criminal code gave some safeguards against 'infringements of socialist legality'. Khrushchev boasted that there were no political prisoners in the Soviet Union, and it is at least incontestable that he carried out no terrorist operations. Even his political enemies were punished only by derisory appointments. He was however not averse to harsh penalties, and in 1961 for instance certain categories of 'economic crime' (forgery, currency speculation, embezzlement of state property) became punishable by execution. Nor was he pedantically attached to formal processes of law. Parasites, idlers, and hooligans could be hauled before street courts and comrades' courts in enterprises and summarily expelled from their communities. In the most elaborate anti-religious campaign since the 1920s the line between persuasion and brutal harassment was far too easily crossed, and the civil rights of believers most inadequately protected.

Informal courts, volunteer brigades for assisting the police, and production conferences with worker participation in enterprises were intended partly to involve wider sections of the public in the activities of the regime, and so to narrow the gap between rulers and ruled. These policies were an aspect of what Khrushchev now called 'the all-out construction of communism', and he claimed that the transference of state functions to the public was already proceeding. Similarly, he did something to mitigate the inequalities of what purported to be a society 'without antagonistic classes', not only raising the lowest wages but also slightly reducing inflated bureaucratic salaries. His egalitarianism was seen at its boldest in his original proposals on educational reform, which made a period of service in industry, agriculture, or the armed services a condition of admission to higher education. The scheme was primarily intended to overcome a labour shortage caused by the wartime birth deficiency, but Khrushchev seized on it to spread educational opportunity more evenly and stimulate social mobility. Similarly, he increased the vocational content of school curricula, partly for purely practical reasons, but also to reduce the differences between administrators and professional men on the one hand and the working masses on the other.

These policies are more interesting as a recognition of social problems than for their effects. Public participation in administration and law enforcement was inevitably cramped within a rigid framework of Party control. A hierarchic structure of authority inevitably limited the reduction of class differences. Khrushchev's educational ideas clashed not only with the interests of a self-perpetuating upper class but with the needs of the economy, and anxious educationists, scientists, and planners succeeded eventually in emasculating them.

In foreign as in domestic policy Khrushchev's initiatives showed a strange mixture of rationality and impetuosity. No previous Soviet leader had travelled so widely, and no Russian ruler since Peter the Great was so uninhibited in his dealings with foreigners. Everywhere he gratified his appetite for the dramatic gesture – hurrying to Belgrade in 1955 for what some of his colleagues thought an over-demonstrative reconciliation with Tito, haranguing huge crowds in the same year on his visit to India, permitting himself a hot exchange with an equally emotional Labour politician during his visit to Britain in 1956, banging the table with his shoe in the General Assembly of the United Nations in 1959, stalking out of a summit meeting in Paris in 1960. Many of his fellow country-men deplored his behaviour, but abroad he was a popular figure, at once comic, formidable, and reassuring. He successfully for a time conveyed the idea that the Soviet Union was intent on avoiding war, but equally on asserting its strength to obtain quick and favourable settlements of major international problems. He began to lose credibility when he resorted too frequently to bluff, as in his attempt to force revision of the Berlin regime (1958) or during the Lebanese crisis (1960).

When in November 1962 he ended the acutest of all crises in Soviet–American relations by withdrawing Soviet missile installations from Cuba, few can have been persuaded by his claim to have scored a diplomatic victory. For the greatest Soviet setback during his period of office Khrushchev probably bears no personal responsibility. This was the deterioration of relations with China to the point at which each regime could condemn the other as degenerate, un-communist, and imperialistic. Mao Tse-tung was presumably angered by the inadequacy of Soviet economic and technical assistance, the lukewarmness of Soviet support for Chinese efforts to recover Taiwan, and the obvious Soviet reluctance to accept China as an equal partner in the leadership of the world communist movement. The quarrel came into the open in 1960, and grew fiercer after the Soviet Union leaned to the Indian side during the Sino-Indian border dispute of 1962.

THE FALL OF KHRUSHCHEV

Khrushchev's position grew steadily weaker from 1960. His agricultural policies, after initial good results, promised no further rapid gains. His system of economic management was modified by the resurrection of some previously dismantled ministries, and in 1963 by the creation of the Supreme Economic Council, visibly intended to limit Party influence in this sphere. International setbacks, diminishing returns from the Soviet Union's efforts to win firm friends in the Third World, the decline of Soviet influence over foreign communist parties, especially as a result of the quarrel with China, helped to aggravate dissatisfaction with Khrushchev. In 1962 he divided the Party at the regional level into separate industrial and agricultural organizations. Here he succeeded not only in further exasperating governmental and economic bureaucrats, since his object was to intensify Party control of their activities, but also in alienating large numbers of Party officials whose scope and

305

status were diminished. In 1964 he gave offence to immediate colleagues by sending his son-in-law on missions to West Germany and the Vatican. Unwisely, he spent more than four months of that year in travelling. In October, while on holiday in the Crimea, he exchanged greetings with the commander of a spaceship in orbit, and looked forward to welcoming the victorious astronauts in Moscow. The ceremonial reception party was, however, headed by his successors. An economical announcement in *Pravda* stated that in view of his advanced age and deteriorating health Khrushchev had been relieved of his duties. L. I. Brezhnev replaced him as First Secretary of the Central Committee and A. N. Kosygin as Chairman of the Council of Ministers. The new leaders, without mentioning Khrushchev, repudiated his methods and his style of leadership. The regional Party organizations were reunified, and the central ministries re-established or reinforced. Party officials were warned for the future against 'petty surveillance' of economic organs and 'incompetent meddling' in their work. The party of Lenin, *Pravda*'s readers were told, was the enemy of 'subjectivism and drift', 'project-mongering', 'hasty decisions and aims divorced from reality', 'boastfulness and empty prating'. Khrushchev had deserved a kinder political obituary.

After the excitements and upheavals of Khrushchev's reign, his successors insisted on the need for more conventional, cautious, and businesslike ways. They presented to the country and the world faces of a studied and enigmatic blankness. They set out to readjust the balance between Party and government, and the Central Committee declared it undesirable that the same person should hold the highest offices in both. It was, however, made clear that the highest Party organ was still the seat of final authority when in 1966 the Presidium resumed its former name of Politburo and Brezhnev took the title of General Secretary, previously held by Stalin but not by Khrushchev. Although his 'mistakes' were not forgotten Stalin's official reputation steadily improved. The charge of military incompetence made against him by Khrushchev and by some of the generals was rejected by the Party press. Agrarian historians were warned against over-critical examination of the collectivization process. The revised edition of the one-volume Party history (1969) even described the Great Purge as having been necessary to protect the Party against alien elements and to 'forestall actions hostile to socialism and the interests of the Soviet state'. In the same year, on the ninetieth anniversary of his birth, *Pravda* described Stalin as a 'great theoretician', while also mentioning 'errors which became serious during the latter period of his life'. The effect of these changes was to suggest that Khrushchev rather more than Stalin had interrupted the smooth course of Soviet history. They were also intended to stifle nonconformity among the intelligentsia, and practical measures for this purpose included promulgation of a menacingly elastic law against utterances and writings slandering the Soviet state or social order. Dissident writers, awkward religious groups, audacious campaigners for civil rights or for greater independence in non-Russian areas, were sternly repressed, with or without trial.

In foreign policy the present rulers have adhered firmly to the line of peaceful coexistence, and have dealt skilfully with some long-standing problems. In particular, they have contributed to an improvement in Soviet, Polish, and East German relations with the German Federal Republic, and have joined in promising talks on strategic arms limitation. They carefully limited their involvement in the Vietnamese war. In the Middle East the Soviet Union has asserted an interest equal to that of the western powers, and has given extensive diplomatic and military assistance to Egypt, so far without serious risk of broadening the Arab–Israeli conflict. The most impressive demonstration of ever-increasing Soviet might has been the building of a huge ocean-going fleet. The events most damaging to Soviet prestige have occurred in relations with other communist countries. In particular, fresh efforts towards a *modus vivendi* with China have so far been unsuccessful; and in August 1968 Soviet troops invaded Czechoslovakia to replace a reforming government which seemed likely to escape from Soviet control and perhaps itself lose control of its people.

For the present leaders economic problems overshadow all others. The Soviet Union is a 'superpower', comparable in terms of military strength only to the United States. Soviet technical advances in certain fields, notably in space exploration, are again equalled only by those of the United States. But the maintenance of this position places a disproportionate burden on Soviet resources. Though the Soviet economy is highly developed, the ambition to 'overtake and surpass' the United States is still far from realization. Indeed, at present relative rates of growth the gap between the two countries will widen in the next decade or so, and Japan will achieve a gross national product equal to that of the Soviet Union. Economic overstrain has generated disagreements on investment priorities within the leadership, clearly reflected in the Soviet press. In particular, there were conspicuous differences of emphasis in the years 1965–7 in speeches by Brezhnev, who seemed to favour heavier investment in defence and capital goods industries, and Kosygin, who seemed more concerned with the expansion of light industry. A portion of the surprisingly large allocation to agriculture for 1966–70 was in the event diverted to heavy industry, but this trend was partly corrected in 1968 by plans for a greater expansion of chemical fertilizer production. The Soviet Union's interest in arms limitation, and a more discriminating overseas aid policy, are no doubt partly explained by a desire to free funds for other purposes. At the same time, the present leaders are keenly aware of the need to increase productivity. Proposals to stimulate the economy by more flexible planning methods, by adapting to Soviet circumstances western methods of business training, and by allowing market forces freer play, have been eagerly canvassed, and of course jealously scrutinized by bureaucrats and *apparatchiki* fearing some diminution of central control.

The period since the fall of Khrushchev can be seen as having been a pause for retrenchment. His successors, preoccupied with immediate foreign and economic problems, have, perhaps gladly, passed to a future generation of leaders those larger and more intractable questions which Khrushchev so boldly opened. Brezhnev and Kosygin, both about seventy, must soon give way to younger men, who must if they are to maintain and raise the standing of the Soviet Union in the world find ways of adapting a rigid dictatorial regime, born of backwardness and effective for limited purposes but now obsolete, to the needs of a relatively highly developed, well-educated and increasingly dissatisfied society.

GUIDE TO FURTHER READING

General histories

Soviet general histories of the period are significant political documents in their own right, but seldom impressive as works of scholarship. They paraphrase and cautiously elaborate the currently valid official history of the CPSU. *Istoriya kommunisticheskoy partii Sovetskogo Soyuza (bol'shevikov) – kratkiy kurs*, approved by the Central Committee in 1938, and subsequently attributed to Stalin personally, was the master text until his death. This was superseded in 1959 by another single volume, *Istoriya kommunisticheskoy partii Sovetskogo Soyuza* (supervised by B. N. Ponomaryov), revised editions of which appeared in 1962 and 1971. Publication of a six-volume work of the same title, under the imprint of the Institute of Marxism–Leninism, began in 1964 and is still in progress. It is equally remarkable for its wealth of otiose detail and its bland evasion of awkward subjects.

Published Soviet documentary material is much fuller and more varied for the years 1917–30 than for the following decades. This literature provided the basis for the most ambitious general history of the Soviet Union in its formative period, E. H. Carr's *History of Soviet Russia*, of which the following volumes have appeared: *The Bolshevik Revolution, 1917–1923* (3 vols., London, 1952–4); *The Interregnum, 1923–1924* (London, 1954); *Socialism in One Country, 1924–1926* (3 vols., London, 1958–64); and *Foundations of a Planned Economy, 1926–1929* (2 vols., vol. I in collaboration with R. W. Davies; London, 1969–71). Open at times to the criticism that it is too narrowly concerned with the rulers and somewhat neglects the ruled, this is none the less a work of the greatest value for its masterly ordering and analysis of official documentation, and its

308

unfailing clarity and readability. The sections on Soviet relations with the outside world are superbly organized and written.

Two other works in English are of fundamental importance. L. Schapiro's *The Communist Party of the Soviet Union*, 2nd edn (London, 1970) is unrivalled as an account of the ideological, political, and organizational history of the Party from its beginnings until 1969. As a study of the ruling Party it also of course provides an outline history of the Soviet state and its policies. M. Fainsod's *How Russia is Ruled*, 2nd edn (London, 1963) is the most authoritative work on the evolution of the Soviet political and administrative system. See also G. von Rauch, *A History of Soviet Russia*, 5th edn, trans. from the German by P. and A. Jacobsohn (New York, 1957); and D. W. Treadgold, *Twentieth Century Russia* (Chicago, 1964).

The revolutions of 1917

The basic documentary publications are *Arkhiv russkoy revolyutsii* (22 vols., Berlin, 1921–37); *Krasnyy arkhiv* (106 vols., Moscow, 1922–41); M. N. Pokrovsky and Y. A. Yakovlev, eds., *Arkhiv oktyabr'skoy revolyutsii 1917* (10 vols., Moscow, 1925–39); *Padeniye tsarskogo rezhima* (7 vols., Leningrad, 1924–7). See also J. Bunyan and H. H. Fisher, *The Bolshevik Revolution 1917–1918 – Documents and Materials* (Stanford, 1934).

Works of special interest by participants or eyewitnesses include V. Chernov, *The Great Russian Revolution* (New Haven, 1936); A. F. Kerensky, *The Catastrophe* (New York, 1927); P. N. Milyukov, *Istoriya vtoroy revolyutsii* (3 vols., Sofia, 1921); J. Reed, *Ten Days that Shook the World*, 3rd edn (London, 1934); J. Sadoul, *Notes sur la révolution bolchévique* (Paris, 1919); A. Shlyapnikov, *Semnadtsatyy god* (3 vols., Moscow, 1923–7); N. Sukhanov, *Zapiski o revolyutsii* (7 vols., Berlin, 1920) – for extracts in English see *The Russian Revolution, 1917 – A Personal Record by N. N. Sukhanov*, ed., abr., and trans. by J. Carmichael (London, 1955); L. Trotsky, *History of the Russian Revolution*, trans. by M. Eastman (3 vols., London, 1932–3; reissued in single vol. 1934, 1965); and I. Tsereteli, *Vospominaniya o russkoy revolyutsii* (Paris, 1963–4). The most valuable of these are the works of Sukhanov (once an SR, later a Menshevik), Trotsky (writing in exile), and Tsereteli (a Menshevik).

Amongst the profusion of secondary works, W. H. Chamberlin's *The Russian Revolution 1917–1921* (2 vols., New York. 1952) is a classic, and the best introduction for students. See also Carr's *Bolshevik Revolution*. G. Katkov's *Russia 1917: the February Revolution* (London, 1967) is an eloquent and erudite, deliberately controversial account of the background to the establishment of the Provisional Government. E. N. Burdzhalov, *Vtoraya russkaya revolyutsiya* (Moscow, 1967) is the most scholarly survey of the same subject from the Soviet viewpoint. Marc Ferro's *La révolution de 1917 – la chute du tsarisme et les origines d'octobre* (Paris, 1967) is a very useful detailed treatment of the period between February and June. G. Walter's *Histoire de la révolution russe* (Paris, 1953) includes an excellent bibliography. Useful monographs on particular aspects include O. Anweiler, *Die Rätebewegung in Russland 1905–1921* (Leiden, 1958), on the origins and evolution of the Soviets; E. N. Burdzhalov, 'Taktika bol'shevikov v burzhuazno-demokraticheskoy revolyutsii', in *Voprosy Istorii*, nos. 4 and 8 (1956), on the differences between Lenin and Stalin in April 1917; K. Gusev, *Krakh partii levykh eserov* (Moscow, 1963), on the formation and collapse of the Bolshevik-Left SR alliance; A. Rabinowitch, *Prelude to Revolution:*

the Petrograd Bolsheviks and the July 1917 Uprising (Bloomington, 1968); and O. Radkey, *The Election to the Russian Constituent Assembly of 1917* (Cambridge, Mass., 1950).

Civil war and intervention

The most useful Soviet publications date from the twenties. See especially *Grazhdanskaya voyna 1918–1921* (3 vols., Moscow, 1928–30), and *Bor'ba za Ural i Sibir'* (Moscow–Leningrad, 1926). *Istoriya grazhdanskoy voyny v SSSR* (5 vols., Moscow, 1936–60) is more ambitious, but see G. F. Kennan's comments in *American Historical Review*, January 1960. See also J. Bunyan, ed., *Intervention, Civil War and Communism in Russia, April–December 1918, Documents and Materials* (Baltimore, 1936); and G. Varneck and H. H. Fisher, *The Testimony of Kolchak and other Siberian Materials* (Stanford, 1935).

The following works by Bolshevik military leaders are particularly important: V. A. Antonov-Ovseyenko, *Zapiski o grazhdanskoy voyne* (4 vols., Moscow, 1924–33); M. V. Frunze, *Izbrannyye proizvedeniya* (2 vols., Moscow, 1957); L. Trotsky, *Kak vooruzhalas' revolyutsiya* (Moscow, 1924); and M. N. Tukhachevsky, *Voyna klassov* (Moscow, 1921). The most substantial work by a White general in emigration is A. I. Denikin, *Ocherki russkoy smuty* (5 vols., Paris, 1921–6). Pokrovsky and Yakovlev, *Arkhiv russkoy revolyutsii* should also be consulted, as should *Beloye delo – Letopis' beloy bor'by*, vols. 1–7 (Berlin, 1926–33), and *Belyy arkhiv*, vols. 1–3 (Paris, 1926–8).

Chamberlin's *Russian Revolution* is essential reading, and D. J. Footman's *Civil War in Russia* (London, 1961) is an excellent account of certain major episodes. On the Allied intervention in Russia see especially G. F. Kennan, *Soviet–American Relations 1917–20*, vol. II, *The Decision to Intervene* (Princeton, 1958); and R. H. Ullman, *Anglo-Soviet Relations 1917–21*, vol. I, *Intervention and the War* (Princeton, 1961), and vol. II, *Britain and the Russian Civil War* (Princeton, 1968).

Lenin, Trotsky, Stalin

B. Wolfe's *Three who Made a Revolution* (New York, 1948), on Lenin, Trotsky, and Stalin, is indispensable to students of the political background to the October Revolution.

Lenin's collected works, *Polnoye sobraniye sochineniy*, 5th edn (55 vols., Moscow, 1958–65) are a vivid self-portrait of Lenin the politician, but remarkably bare of information on his personal life. The best biography is A. Ulam, *Lenin and the Bolsheviks* (London, 1966). A. G. Meyer's *Leninism* (Cambridge, Mass., 1957) usefully analyses his political philosophy. Interesting first-hand impressions are given by L. A. Fotiyeva, *Iz vospominaniy o Lenine* (Moscow, 1964) and *Iz zhizni V. I. Lenina* (Moscow, 1967); M. Gorky, *Days with Lenin* (London, 1931); N. K. Krupskaya (his wife), *Memories of Lenin* (London, 1942); A. Lunacharsky, *Revolyutsionnyye siluety* (Moscow, 1923); and N. Valentinov (a critical Menshevik journalist), *Vstrechi s Leninym* (New York, 1953).

Unlike Lenin, Trotsky produced an autobiography, *Moya zhizn'* (2 vols., Berlin, 1930). I. Deutscher's three volumes, *The Prophet Armed: Trotsky 1879–1921* (London, 1954), *The Prophet Unarmed: Trotsky 1921–1929* (London, 1959), and *The Prophet Outcast: Trotsky 1929–1940* (London, 1963), are immensely readable, and generally reliable, though coloured by the author's own revolutionary romanticism. Two studies of Trotsky from the early twenties retain their interest – Lunacharsky's chapter in his *Revolyutsionnyye siluety*, and G. A. Ziv's *Trotsky, kharakteristika po lichnym vospominaniyam* (New York, 1921).

Stalin's own writings and occasional utterances will be found in *Voprosy Leninizma*, 11th edn (Moscow, 1945), and his *Sochineniya* (13 vols., Moscow, 1946–51), supplemented by R. H. McNeal, ed., *Stalin: Sochineniya*, vols. 14–16 (1–3) (Stanford, 1967). Of the older biographies B. Souvarine, *Stalin: a Critical Survey of Bolshevism*, trans. by C. L. R. James (London, 1939) is a sharply perceptive polemical work. I. Deutscher, *Stalin: A Political Biography* (London, 1949) is a brilliant critical apologia which places Stalin among the 'great revolutionary despots', beside 'Cromwell, Robespierre and Napoleon'. R. Hingley's *Joseph Stalin: Man and Legend* (London, 1974), R. C. Tucker's *Stalin as Revolutionary, 1879–1929* (New York, 1973), and A. Ulam's *Stalin: the Man and his Era* (New York, 1973) embody information unavailable to Deutscher. All three are works of serious scholarship.

Evolution of the Soviet polity and economy, 1917–53

The major general histories have already been mentioned. On the evolution of the Party and the Soviet system readers should also consult J. L. Armstrong, *The Politics of Totalitarianism* (London, 1961); P. Avrich, *Kronstadt 1921* (Princeton, 1970); W. Batsell, *Soviet Rule in Russia* (New York, 1929); R. V. Daniels, *The Conscience of the Revolution – Communist Opposition in Soviet Russia* (Cambridge, Mass., 1960); R. Pipes, *The Formation of the Soviet Union – Communism and Nationalism* (Cambridge, Mass., 1954); N. N. Popov, *Outline History of the Communist Party of the Soviet Union* (New York, 1934); L. Schapiro, *The Origin of the Communist Autocracy* (London, 1955); J. Towster, *Political Power in the USSR, 1917–1947* (New York, 1948); and E. Yaroslavsky, ed., *Istoriya VKP(b)* (4 vols., Moscow–Leningrad, 1926–30).

The background to the 'revolution from above' in the late 1920s is most conveniently studied in Carr and Davies, *Foundations of a Planned Economy*; A. Erlich, *The Soviet Industrialisation Debate, 1924–1928* (Cambridge, Mass., 1960); N. Jasny, *The Socialised Agriculture of the USSR* (Stanford, 1949) – a gloomy account, relying when written on ingenious statistical conjecture, but substantially confirmed by Soviet data after Stalin's death; N. Jasny, *Soviet Industrialisation 1928–1952* (Chicago, 1961); M. P. Kim, senior ed., *Istoriya Sovetskogo krest'yanstva i kolkhoznogo stroitel'stva v SSSR* (Moscow, 1963); and M. Lewin, *Russian Peasants and Soviet Power* (London, 1968).

Useful general works on the development of the Soviet economy include M. Dobb, *Soviet Economic Development since 1917* (London, 1948); P. I. Lyashchenko, *Istoriya narodnogo khozyaystva SSSR*, vol. III (Moscow, 1956); H. Schwartz, *Russia's Soviet Economy*, 2nd edn (New York, 1954); S. N. Prokopovich, *Histoire économique de l'URSS* (Paris, 1952).

M. Fainsod's *Smolensk under Soviet Rule* (Cambridge, Mass., 1958) draws on a provincial Party archive captured by the Germans, and is a unique source of information on local conditions and attitudes. Amongst the welter of books on the secret police, the Great Purge, and the labour camps, the following are of special importance: P. Barton, *L'Institution concentrationnaire en Russie, 1930–1957* (Paris, 1959); Z. K. Brzezinski, *The Permanent Purge: Politics in Soviet Totalitarianism* (Cambridge, Mass., 1956); R. Conquest, *The Great Terror – Stalin's Purge of the Thirties* (London, 1968); Dewey Commission, *Not Guilty –*

the Case of Leon Trotsky (London, 1937); D. J. Dallin and B. I. Nicolaevsky, *Forced Labour in Soviet Russia* (New Haven, 1947); B. Lewytzkyj, *Die rote Inquisition: die Geschichte der sowjetischen Sicherheitsdienste* (Frankfurt, 1967); R. C. Tucker and S. F. Cohen, eds., *The Great Purge Trial* (documents; New York, 1965); S. Swianiewicz, *Forced Labour and Economic Development* (London, 1965); S. Wolin and R. M. Slusser, *The Soviet Secret Police* (New York, 1957). Political control of the armed forces is dealt with by R. Kolkowicz, *Army–Party Relations in the Soviet Union* (Chicago, 1967), and by Yu. P. Petrov, *Partiynoye stroitel'stvo v sovetskoy armii i flote* (Moscow, 1964). J. Erickson's *The Soviet High Command* (London, 1962) is as important to the political as to the military historian.

The Second World War

The official Soviet history is the collective work of a commission under P. N. Pospelov, *Istoriya Velikoy Otechestvennoy voyny Sovetskogo Soyuza, 1941–1945* (Moscow, 1960–5). Several senior Soviet commanders have published memoirs. The most interesting are both available in English translations: V. I. Chuikov, *The End of the Third Reich* (London, 1967); and G. Zhukov, *The Memoirs of Marshal Zhukov* (London, 1971).

Albert Seaton, *The Russo-German War, 1941–1945* (London, 1971) is a clear and scholarly survey of military operations. See also A. Guillaume, *La Guerre germano-soviétique* (Paris, 1949). A. Werth, *Russia at War, 1941–1945* (London, 1965) is a vivid impressionistic account by a journalist who spent the war years in the Soviet Union. Relations between the Soviet population and the German invaders in occupied areas are examined by A. Dallin, *German Rule in Russia, 1941–45* (London, 1957). On the diplomatic history of the war see especially H. Feis, *Churchill–Roosevelt–Stalin* (Princeton, 1957); G. Hilger and A. G. Meyer, *The Incompatible Allies – a Memoir–History of German–Soviet Relations 1918–1941* (New York, 1953); and V. L. Izraelyan, *Diplomaticheskaya istoriya Velikoy Otechestvennoy voyny* (Moscow, 1959).

Foreign policy

The official Stalinist history was V. P. Potemkin, ed., *Istoriya diplomatii*, vol. III (Moscow, 1945), and since this is the most sluggish sector of Soviet historiography few of its judgements on the period covered have subsequently been modified. An equally official but far more scholarly work on the post-war period is I. I. Inozemtsev, chief ed., *Mezhdunarodnyye otnosheniya posle vtoroy mirovoy voyny* (3 vols., Moscow, 1962–5), which includes a copious bibliography of western as well as Soviet literature on the subject.

The Ministry of Foreign Affairs in 1957 began slow but systematic publication of documents on foreign policy from November 1917. The most important events are admirably covered by J. Degras, ed., *Soviet Documents on Foreign Policy*, vol. I, 1917–24, vol. II, 1924–32, vol. III, 1933–41 (London, 1951–3). See also the same editor's *Calendar of Documents on Soviet Foreign Policy* (London, 1948), and *The Communist International 1919–1943, Documents* (3 vols., Oxford, 1956–65). Other useful documentary surveys are X. J. Eudin and R. C. North, *Soviet Russia and the East, 1920–1927* (Stanford, 1957); X. J. Eudin and H. H. Fisher, *Soviet Russia and the West, 1920–1927* (Stanford, 1957); and A. Z. Rubinstein, *The Foreign Policy of the Soviet Union* (New York, 1960). The

GUIDE TO FURTHER READING

standard history of early Soviet foreign policy is L. Fischer, *The Soviets in World Affairs, 1917–29* (2 vols., London, 1930; 2nd edn, Princeton, 1951). For an admirably clear and accurate survey of foreign policy from the 'Great Turn' to the German invasion, see M. Beloff, *The Foreign Policy of Soviet Russia* (Oxford), vol. I, 1929–36 (1947), vol. II, 1936–41 (1949).

Since the USSR has achieved 'superpower' status its interests have become so diverse, and Soviet policy so intricate and flexible, that there is, and perhaps can be, no general survey for any of the post-war decades as thorough and authoritative as that of Beloff for the earlier period. A student who took care to seek the necessary correctives in western literature on particular subjects might profitably use Inozemtsev's *Mezhdunarodnyye otnosheniya* as his starting point. Useful general works include M. E. Airapetyan and G. A. Deborin, *Etapy vneshney politiki SSSR* (Moscow, 1961); V. Aspaturian, *Process and Power in Soviet Foreign Policy* (Boston, 1971); D. J. Dallin, *Soviet Foreign Policy after Stalin* (London, 1962); H. L. Dinerstein, *War and the Soviet Union – Nuclear War and the Revolution in Soviet Military and Political Thinking* (London, 1959); R. L. Garthoff, *Soviet Strategy in the Nuclear Age* (New York, 1958); H. Kissinger, *The Troubled Partnership* (New York, 1966); J. A. Lukács, *A New History of the Cold War*, 3rd edn (New York, 1966); J. M. Mackintosh, *Strategy and Tactics of Soviet Foreign Policy* (London, 1962); P. Moseley, *The Kremlin and World Politics* (New York, 1960); H. Seton-Watson, *Neither War nor Peace* (London, 1961); M. D. Shulman, *Stalin's Foreign Policy Reappraised* (Cambridge, Mass., 1963); and A. Ulam, *Expansion and Coexistence – a History of Soviet Foreign Policy, 1917–1967* (Cambridge, Mass., 1968).

On Soviet relations with other communist countries and parties, see especially G. Altman *et al.*, *Moscou au tournant* (Paris, 1957); G. Boffa, *Inside the Khrushchev Era*, (New York, 1959); H. L. Boorman *et al.*, *The Moscow–Peking Axis* (New York, 1957); F. Borkenau, *The Communist International* (London, 1938) and *European Communism* (London, 1953); J. F. Brown, *The New Eastern Europe* (London, 1967); Z. Brzezinski, *The Soviet Bloc – Unity and Conflict* (Cambridge, Mass., 1960); V. Dedijer, *Tito* (New York, 1953); W. E. Griffiths, *The Sino-Soviet Rift* (Cambridge, Mass., 1964) and *Sino-Soviet Relations* (Cambridge, Mass., 1967); G. Ionescu, *The Break-Up of the Soviet Empire in Eastern Europe* (Harmondsworth, 1965); L. Labedz, ed., *International Communism after Khrushchev* (London, 1965); M. J. Lasky, ed., *The Hungarian Revolution* (London, 1957); H. G. Skilling, *Communism National and International* (New York, 1964); M. Tatu, *L'hérésie impossible – chronique du drame tchécoslovaque* (Paris, 1968); P. Windsor and A. Roberts, *Czechoslovakia 1968 – Reform, Repression and Resistance* (London, 1969); P. E. Zinner, ed., *National Communism and Popular Revolt in Eastern Europe* (New York, 1956); and the same author's *Revolution in Hungary* (New York, 1962).

Evolution of the Soviet polity since the death of Stalin

A number of relevant works have been listed above. The student of very recent history must rely to a great extent on periodical publications. In this context, the *Current Digest of the Soviet Press*, published by the American Association for the Advancement of Slavic Studies, is invaluable. Important western periodicals devoted partly to Soviet affairs are *Osteuropa* (Stuttgart), *Problems of Communism* (Washington), *Soviet Studies* (Glasgow), *Survey* (London).

Khrushchev expounds his policies in *Stroitel'stvo kommunizma i razvitiye*

313

SOVIET RUSSIA

sel'skogo khozyaystva (8 vols., Moscow, 1962–4). The text of Khrushchev's 'secret speech' with commentary will be found in B. Wolfe, *Khrushchev and Stalin's Ghost* (New York, 1957). B. Meissner, in *Russland unter Chruschtschow* (Munich, 1960), presents many important documents for the years 1956–9, which he regards as the decisive period for the post-war development of Bolshevism. The second (Khrushchevian) programme of the CPSU is analysed in L. Schapiro, *The USSR and the Future* (London, 1962). Among 'kremlinological' writings on the Khrushchev era M. Rush's *Rise of Khrushchev* (Washington, 1958), and the same author's *Political Succession in the USSR* (New York, 1965) are good. See also A. Dallin and T. B. Larson, eds., *Soviet Politics since Khrushchev* (particularly C. Linden's essay 'Khrushchev and the Soviet Leadership 1957–64'), and J. W. Strong, ed., *The Soviet Union under Brezhnev and Kosygin – the Transitional Years* (New York, 1971). Of Brezhnev's collected speeches, under the admonitory title *Leninskim kursom*, vols. I and II appeared in 1970, and vol. III in 1972. The most useful general works on economic development are M. Kaser, *Soviet Economics* (London, 1970), and A. Nove, *The Soviet Economy*, 3rd edn (London, 1969).

Influential works by Soviet dissidents published abroad are A. Amalrik's 'Will the USSR Survive to 1984?', *Survey*, Autumn 1969; R. A. Medvedev's *Let History Judge – the Origins and Consequences of Stalinism* (London, 1971); Z. A. Medvedev's *The Medvedev Papers* (London, 1971); A. D. Sakharov's *Progress, Coexistence and Intellectual Freedom* (London, 1969); and A. Solzhenitsyn's *Arkhipelag Gulag* – English trans. of vols. I and II is *Gulag Archipelago* (London, 1974–5). See also P. Reddaway, *Uncensored Russia: the Human Rights Movement in the Soviet Union* (London, 1972). Among journalistic writers on the Soviet Union, R. Conquest, E. Crankshaw, W. Leonhard, H. Salisbury, and M. Tatu are outstandingly good. Leonhard's *The Kremlin since Stalin* (New York, 1962), and Tatu's *Power in the Kremlin* (London, 1969) are particularly informative and perceptive.

In recent years several scholars have attempted to apply the techniques and categories of western political science to the study of contemporary Soviet society. The value of their work is inevitably affected by the deficiencies of the data and the obstacles to fieldwork, but some interesting results have been achieved. A. H. Brown's *Soviet Politics and Political Science* (London, 1974) is an excellent critical survey of work along these lines to date. A. Inkeles, ed., *Social Change in the Soviet Union* (Cambridge, Mass., 1968); B. Meissner, ed., *Social Change in the Soviet Union* (Notre Dame, 1972); M. Matthews, *Class and Society in Soviet Russia* (London, 1972); and H. G. Skilling and F. Griffiths, *Interest Groups in Soviet Politics* (Princeton, 1971), are all useful.

314

7

THE CHURCH

JOHN MEYENDORFF

It was by adopting the Christian faith from Byzantium that Russia found a place among the 'civilized' nations of the early Middle Ages. And since 988 the history of the Orthodox Church in Russia is inseparable from the history of Russia itself.[1] Until 1917, and throughout an otherwise turbulent history, the Russian Church represented a solid element of continuity and stability. Eastern Orthodoxy has known none of those ultimate crises, such as the Renaissance or the Reformation, which disrupted the history of western Christianity. In Russia modern secularism of the nineteenth and twentieth centuries was confronted directly, almost without preparatory stages, with a form of religion which had been evolving organically since early Christianity and throughout the Middle Ages: this encounter is still taking place today and only the future will show the ultimate results.

DOCTRINE, LITURGY, SPIRITUALITY, AND MISSIONS

Even if the schism between East and West was not yet officially consummated when Russians accepted the Christian faith, their affiliation with the eastern, Byzantine tradition of Christianity had a decisive effect upon their entire religious destiny. One of the main points of disagreement between the Greek and the Latin Churches concerned the question of authority. While in the West it was widely accepted that the pronouncements of the Bishop of Rome were final in matters of faith, the East stood on the assumption that the highest doctrinal authority was the ecumenical council, and that even such a council – normally convened by the East Roman Emperor and consisting of all the bishops of Christendom – could eventually prove to be a 'pseudo-council' and needed,

[1] This explains the absence, in this chapter, of a separate account of the history of the Russian Church before 1917.

therefore, to be 'received' by the consciousness of the whole church in order to be recognized as the truthful expression of divine will. In fact the conflict between East and West was on the issue of whether or not there existed a God-established external and juridically-defined criterion of Christian truth: whereas in the West the emphasis was laid upon obedience to Rome, the East emphasized a corporate, mutually checked, but still personal vision of the Divine, to which the councils were the most authoritative witnesses, without being themselves the source, of Christian truth.

It was, in this writer's opinion, this conception of Christianity which enabled the Russians, during the darkest periods of political despotism, to discover in their Orthodox faith the ultimate refuge of human freedom, responsibility, and dignity. Christianity always appeared to them not as imposed by authority, but something expressing their own personal relation to God. The 'mystical' character of this faith should not, however, be identified with relativism, individualism, or emotionalism: in Orthodoxy the foundation of every form of religious life and vision lies in participation in the sacramental life of the church, and this in turn implies the acceptance of an authoritative and authenticated hierarchy and the preservation of an uninterrupted organic tradition going back to the Apostles. In fact the eastern Christians, and particularly the Russians, have always seen in the liturgy their main contact with God. The *Primary Chronicle* reported that it was the beauty of the liturgy celebrated in the church of Saint Sophia of Constantinople that convinced the envoys of Vladimir – who did not know any more 'whether they were in heaven or on earth'[2] – of the truth of the Greeks' faith.

It is impossible to appreciate the significance of this legendary account of the medieval chronicler without an understanding of the variety and wealth of liturgical worship in Byzantine Christianity. While the sacraments were the same as in Roman Catholicism, their actual impact on the faithful was made more real by the use of a comprehensible language, and also by the ancient Christian realism which marks their celebration: baptism by immersion, the solemnity and corporate character of the Eucharist, the cosmic character of certain rites, such as the 'Blessing of Water' on Epiphany. The liturgical life of the church suggests and realizes the notion that man's true destiny lies in participating in God's life. Just as Christian truth is not determined by any external criterion, so is salvation nothing else than participation and communion in God's life, for which man was created, against which he has rebelled and continually rebels, but which has been restored in Jesus Christ. The

[2] English translation by S. H. Cross, *The Russian Primary Chronicle* (Cambridge, Mass., 1953), p. 111.

sacraments of the church, its entire liturgical life, make life in God available to men.

This understanding of Christianity, which was already expressed in its essentials by the early church fathers, has inspired the Russian spiritual tradition, and in particular the teachers of monasticism. At the beginning of the nineteenth century the greatest of modern Russian saints, Seraphim of Sarov (d. 1833), would amaze his disciples by appearing to them with a shining face and would tell them: 'Fear nothing. You too have become as radiant as I. You yourself are now in the fullness of the Divine Spirit, or else you could not see me as I appear to you. . .God is with us.'[3] The goal of Christian life was to achieve a new, transfigured state of humanity, the one which was originally created and which appeared in the risen Jesus: this humanity was made accessible in the church.

Such also was the message conveyed by the eastern Christian iconographers: an Orthodox Church building decorated with mosaics, or more frequently with frescoes and portative icons, suggested that the entire Communion of Saints constantly took part in the worship of the congregation. Man is never alone when he partakes of the transfigured, deified humanity of Christ: this humanity shines on the faces of his friends and brothers, Mary, the Mother of God, the Apostles, the saints of all ages.

This conception of the Christian faith explains why eastern Christianity – in the Balkans, the Middle East, and in the Slav countries – has survived centuries of cultural and educational decay so successfully: the educational power of the liturgy, enhanced by the theological and artistic contribution of Christian hymnography and religious art, temporarily succeeded in replacing sermons, schools, and universities.

This vitality of the Orthodox Church was also manifested in its missionary expansion. Patterned on the example of Saints Cyril and Methodius (the apostles of the Slavs, who began their missionary work in Moravia by translating scripture and liturgy into the vernacular language of their prospective converts), Orthodox missions, interrupted in the Middle East by the Moslem conquest, continued to advance in eastern Europe and in Asia. Already in the fourteenth century, Stephen of Perm' translated some of the scriptures into the language of the Zyrians (Komi), and his tradition has continued almost to our own time. In 1903, in the region of Kazan' alone, the Orthodox Byzantine liturgy was celebrated in more than twenty languages or dialects. Russian missions penetrated to Alaska and other parts of the American continent, and later established a native church in Japan.

---

[3] G. Fedotov, ed., *A Treasury of Russian Spirituality* (London, 1964), p. 274.

INTELLECTUAL TRENDS

The Byzantine Christian tradition not only brought forth fruits on Russian soil; it also created problems which led to conflicts and, often, to tragedies and failures. Early in the sixteenth century this tradition provoked in the Russian Church a deep crisis which was to determine the later destiny of Russian Christianity. The clash between the 'Possessors' and the 'Non-Possessors' has been described in Chapter 3 (p. 95). It may be noted here, however, that despite the victory of the 'Possessors' in the beginning of the century, the Muscovite state, later in the century, rapidly evolved towards secularism. Against the wishes of the 'Josephites', who dreamed of a church using its wealth for the betterment of a Christian society, ecclesiastical lands were confiscated and the church moved a step further on the way to becoming a department of state. The Josephite victory thus deprived the church of the means of resisting a government in which it had placed a premature confidence.

Another problem was posed by the reforms of Peter the Great. One of their positive results was that, by entering the family of western European nations and following their pattern of social organization, Russian society also adopted their educational standards. Thus, during its synodal period, the Russian Church developed an elaborate system of theological schools. The teachers came mainly from the Ukraine where western systems of education prevailed under the rule of Poland. The results of this importation, however, were somewhat peculiar: a church with a Greek Byzantine tradition and a Slavonic liturgy was sponsoring schools where teaching was given in Latin according to western Roman Catholic standards and books. Russian theology of the eighteenth century was passing through a stage which G. Florovsky has aptly called 'western captivity'. Not all of these theologians, in fact, followed Latin patterns of thought: some, like Feofan Prokopovich, Peter's main adviser on ecclesiastical affairs, reacted against the Latin training he himself had received by falling under the influence of Protestantism. It was not uncommon, in Russian theological literature of that time, to see Protestant arguments used against Roman Catholicism and Roman Catholic arguments against Protestantism.

However, the Russian Church soon produced spiritual writers and theologians who, while remaining under western influence, were not prisoners of western categories of thought. Thus, St Tikhon Zadonsky, bishop and hermit (1724–83), could happily combine a strong influence of German pietism with Orthodox monastic spirituality. This spirituality remained a living force and even found new strength with the translation into Slavonic, by Paisy Velichkovsky (1722–94) in Moldavia, of the famous Greek collection of patristic writings on spiritual life known as the *Philokalia* (Slav *Dobrotolyubiye*), whose influence was of incalculable importance in Russia.

The system of schools created in the eighteenth century led to the emergence in nineteenth-century Russia of independent historical and biblical scholarship. Gradually liberated from the strictest forms of Latin formalism, the four ecclesiastical 'academies' – those of Moscow, St Petersburg, Kiev, and Kazan' – provided the Russian Church with theologians and scholars. Under the guidance of Filaret Drozdov (1783–1867), Metropolitan of Moscow, the Bible was translated into modern Russian; many patristic writings were also made available in Russian. Scholarly monographs appeared in numerous fields and, just before the First World War, the names of such scholars as V. V. Bolotov, E. E. Golubinsky, V. O. Klyuchevsky – all trained in ecclesiastical 'academies' – deservedly acquired fame.

Although the rigidity of the Petrine legislation was gradually softened toward the end of the nineteenth century, the church was still largely divorced from society and especially from the intelligentsia. However, a religious revival did take place in some lay circles. It was channelled not through the official clerical bureaucracy, nor even through the theological schools, but through monastic spiritual centres, such as Sarov and Optino. The *startsy* ('elders', or spiritual advisers) of these centres exerted a personal influence on leading writers, such as Gogol, Dostoyevsky, and even Tolstoy. The Slavophil movement called for a return to patristic Orthodoxy. A. S. Khomyakov (1804–60), a remarkable amateur theologian, after being obliged to publish his theological pamphlets abroad, was later widely accepted in Russia as a prophet of *sobornost'* ('conciliarity'), a term which came to express the Orthodox understanding of the church as opposed to western legalism and 'juridicism'. Another intellectual trend, connected with less Orthodox sources, is represented by Vladimir Solov'yov (1853–1900), the distinguished philosopher. Indebted to German idealism, Origenism, and Gnosticism, Solov'yov's views led him to consider the schism between East and West to be essentially non-existent and Christianity to be spiritually transcending both Orthodoxy and Roman Catholicism. Solov'yov gained among the Russian intelligentsia a group of disciples who, even when they did not follow all of his metaphysics, were led by him 'from Marxism to idealism': P. B. Struve, S. N. Bulgakov, N. S. Berdyaev, S. L. Frank, and several others were among them. Expelled from Russia after the communist Revolution, they contributed greatly to making Orthodoxy known in the West and continued the tradition of modern Russian religious thought abroad.

SCHISMS AND SECTS

The triumph of the 'Third Rome' ideology led, early in the sixteenth century, to the forceful suppression of the Judaizers, adherents of a Russian sect connected perhaps – directly or indirectly – with the dualist movement of the Bogomils: the followers of Joseph of Volotsk could not tolerate any dissenters in the unified and monolithic society of their dreams. However, the causes of a major split, which shook the entire Russian Church a century later, were contained in the very nature of this 'Josephite' reaction.

In adopting Byzantine Christianity, the Russians also received, in a Slavonic translation, the whole corpus of Byzantine liturgical books, as well as theological literature, canon law, and even secular writings – the fruits of the old and sophisticated Christian civilization of Byzantium. The young Russian nation was far from capable of comprehending and digesting all this material at once: much of its liturgical life amounted, at first, to a mechanical reproduction of incomprehensible rites; many translations were done both hastily and mechanically, reproducing complicated Greek syntax word for word; scribes copied these translations more or less faithfully, sometimes adding their own conjectures to texts which they were unable to understand. The result of this process was often distressing and confusing. Attempts to correct the 'books' were made in the sixteenth century by Maximus the Greek, a learned Athonite monk who was invited to Moscow as a scholarly expert. His critical approach to Russian ecclesiastical ways and his solidarity with the 'Trans-Volga Elders' led by Nil Sorsky led to his condemnation (1525, 1531) and imprisonment by the Josephites. About the middle of the seventeenth century, however, the need for liturgical reforms was recognized by the leading Muscovite churchmen; the obscurity of some texts and practices was obvious to all. While it was admitted that corrections were necessary, it was far from clear what pattern or criterion was to be followed. The liturgical books were translated from the Greek; but were the contemporary Greeks – punished by God for their betrayal in Florence and controlled by an infidel Turkish sultan – the right authorities to teach the Russians how to pray to God? Was Moscow, the 'Third Rome', to abdicate its providential election as the last pillar of Orthodoxy? The 'Third Rome' ideology had come to a tragic impasse.

In the end, Patriarch Nikon (1652–8) decided that the Russian Church was to adapt its liturgy and practices to those of the contemporary Greeks; the sign of the cross was to be made with three fingers, not with two as the Russians were accustomed to make it; all liturgical books were to be corrected to conform to the modern Greek pattern. These measures proved highly controversial: some of the old Russian practices were closer to the Byzantine original than were those of the contemporary Greeks; moreover, the sudden and authoritarian character of Nikon's reform made it highly unpopular among Russian conservatives. Millions of Russian Christians seceded from the official church, creating the *Raskol* (schism); these were the 'Old Believers'. Their greatest leader was Archpriest Avvakum, who was martyred for 'the old faith' in 1682.

The leaders of the Old Believers were exiled and sometimes executed by the government, but repression only strengthened the movement's popular appeal. Unable to gain the support of any bishop, however, they were soon deprived of validly ordained clergy and, therefore, of all sacraments – except baptism, which could be administered by laymen. In 1847 in Bila Krynytsya, on Austrian territory, a retired Greek bishop consecrated two bishops for the Old Believers; only some of the Old Believers followed these bishops, however, and they were not recognized by the Orthodox Church. Since 1800 the official Orthodox Church has admitted parishes using the old pre-Nikonian liturgical books: this group, in full communion with Orthodoxy, are the *Yedinovertsy* ('people one in faith').

The history of the *Raskol* and the issues which were involved in this tragic schism obviously involve more than the disagreements about ritual between the Nikonians and the Old Believers; in giving an absolute validity to the local Russian traditions of Orthodoxy, the *Raskol* illustrates the impasse to which the Russian Church was led by the triumph of the Josephites. On the other hand, the Old Believers' protest against an Establishment that under Peter the Great had become not only reformative but also aggressively secular enjoyed popular support. A similar protest was also at the root of the other Russian sectarian movements.

The personalistic and mystical trend which permeated eastern Christian spirituality found, in the Russian sects, a peculiar and sometimes perverted expression. As has been noted already, religion, for an eastern Christian, was not equated with authority. So, in the case of Russia, the extraordinary degree of political submissiveness which the Russian people have shown in their history did not prevent them from tending, almost naturally, toward religious non-conformity. The movement of the Trans-Volga Elders, the popularity of peculiar types of sanctity (e.g. *yurodivyye*, 'fools for Christ's sake'), the almost 'underground' character of monastic spirituality which remained alive during the period of secularization in the eighteenth century, constituted the Orthodox forms of this non-conformity. The sects flourished side by side with expressions of genuine Orthodox spirituality, especially since the official church had been brought into an inconsistent and oppressive alliance with the secularized empire of Peter and his successors. The simple souls of the eternal wanderers, the seekers after spiritual freedom and emotional religious experience, found their way into the sects.

It seems that the most important of the genuinely Russian sects, the *khlysty*, appeared within the framework of the *Raskol*: late in the seventeenth century, in the Trans-Volga region – an ancient refuge of nonconformity – groups of Old Believers became convinced that they were living the 'last days'; they renounced all discussions about 'books', and proclaimed that only one book was essential: 'the golden book, the book of life, the book of the Dove – the Holy Ghost'.[4] The Holy Spirit was invoked in collective vigils, which included chanting and dancing, and sometimes eventually led to hysterical paroxysms and sexual orgies, justified by the idea that the actual presence of the Spirit suppressed the regular norms of social ethics. The sect's leaders were often considered to be incarnations of the Holy Spirit and were called 'Christs' and 'Mothers of God'. As a reaction against the sexual attitudes of the *khlysty*, the eighteenth century saw the appearance of another sect, the *skoptsy* ('the castrated'), which found the most radical way of escaping the temptations of the flesh. Collective hysteria preparing for the 'coming of the Spirit' remained a characteristic of the sect.

Other sects were more rationalistic. The *dukhobory* ('wrestlers by the Spirit') seem to have originated in the preaching of Quakerism by a Prussian corporal in the region of Khar'kov in 1740–50. A connection, however, between their doctrine and that of the Ukrainian philosopher Gregory Skovoroda (1722–84) can also be traced. Non-dogmatic, moralistic, and socially non-conformist, the *dukhobory* considered any recognition of the law of the state to be a compromise with the 'world'. Persecuted in Russia, some of them (1898–9) found refuge in Canada, under the sponsorship of Leo Tolstoy, who admired their teaching of non-resistance to evil. A more moderate group seceded from the *dukhobory* late in the eighteenth century: known as the *molokane*, it designated itself 'spiritual Christianity'. Opposed to hierarchy and sacraments, the group preserved a doctrine similar to Protestant pietism, and enjoyed official patronage in the early days of Alexander I.

In the second part of the nineteenth century the impact of Protestantism became even stronger in Russia; *stundism* had its origin in the missionary zeal of German Mennonites and Nazarenes, who came as colonists to Russia. A Russian aristocrat, V. A. Pashkov, inspired by the revivalism of Lord Redstock, founded his own group, 'Reformed Christianity' (after 1874). The origin of the Baptist movement in Russia is usually connected with the preaching of the German colonist Unger

---

[4] Quoted in P. Milyukov, 'Religion and the Church', pt. I of his *Outlines of Russian Culture* (Philadelphia, 1943), p. 89.

(after 1869). It soon came to dominate all the other forms of Russian 'evangelical' and 'spiritual' Christianity. The Baptists enjoyed a period of relative freedom after 1906 and of short but vigorous growth in the first years after the Revolution.

THE RUSSIAN CHURCH AND THE SOVIET STATE

The Orthodox Church of Russia and the other religions represented in the Soviet Union since 1918 have been facing the challenge of a militantly anti-religious state. The decree 'on the separation of the Church from the State, and of the School from the Church', issued by the Soviet government on 23 January 1918, reflects a philosophy and an attitude radically different from those which prevail in western democracies where church and state are separated. While proclaiming freedom of conscience, the decree refused to religious associations the right of property (§12), nationalized all buildings belonging to the church, and stipulated that any building necessary for a 'religious cult' could be lent to the faithful only by special state decision (§13). Public worship was permitted on the condition that it would not disturb 'public order', and state authorities were alone to judge what this expression meant (§5). In fact the church was deprived of all rights. Later Soviet legislation – especially Stalin's Constitution of 1936 (§124) – proclaimed 'freedom of cult and of anti-religious propaganda'. The church was by law restricted to a purely passive function, while the Party and the state promoted the ideological battle against religion in which the faithful were deprived of the opportunity to answer or counter-attack. In addition to administrative and constitutional measures, the church was subjected to violent repressions, mainly carried out by local authorities, and thousands of bishops, priests, and laymen were either killed or exiled.

The attitude of the church toward the fateful events that marked the end of the old regime has been, and still is, a debated issue. Some observers – and this is also the official Communist Party interpretation of events – consider that the church had been, before the Revolution, a close ally and an instrument of the regime, and that the reaction of the Soviet government could not have been different. Is this charge, however, historically justified? Since Peter's reforms, the state, while often using the church as an ally, was not favourably disposed to the Orthodox clergy. On the contrary, deprived since the eighteenth century of its lands, the clergy, especially the parish priests, were a poor and socially despised caste. The Marxist analysis, which determined the Soviet government's attitude toward religion, was based upon nineteenth-century conditions in western Europe, where churchmen were socially and economically part of the ruling classes. The Russian priest, however, was not necessarily an ally of the old regime: indeed he was often, in the eyes of the people, the reviled underdog. In fact the Marxist forecast was proved wrong: the church did not disappear with the elimination of the social and economic conditions that were supposed to have been its basis.

This remarkable survival was partially prepared for by the intense intellectual and spiritual ferment which took place in Russian Orthodoxy between 1906 and 1917. Under the constitutional regime resulting from the 1905 Revolution, with an almost total freedom of speech and publication, the Russian Church had undertaken what its most enlightened members had been seeking throughout the nineteenth century – a reform of its internal structure and of its attitude toward society. The result was the Church Council of 1917–18, which not only restored the office of the Patriarch of All Russia and elected Tikhon to it, but also introduced many reforms: for instance, it gave laymen responsibilities at various levels of church life.

Faced by a communist state violently hostile to religion, the new patriarch, the council – which continued its work until August 1918 – and other leaders of the church did not refrain from explicit political declarations: they condemned the measures banning religion from the schools, as well as the new government's decision to make peace with Germany, regardless of the cost. This attitude of the church is, even today, used to explain – if not to justify – the violent persecution directed against it by the government.[5] It should be pointed out, however, that the Russian Church, while condemning the policy, the excesses, and the crimes of the new regime, never called for the restoration of the old order.

A more decisive blow was dealt to the church in February 1922, when the government required the confiscation of church valuables in order to raise funds to deal with a devastating famine on the Volga. The patriarch agreed to the government's request subject to certain conditions, but a group of clergy decided to break with him while he was temporarily under arrest: this was the beginning of a lengthy schism in the church. Alongside the 'patriarchal' church, a 'renovated', or 'living' church came into existence and soon obtained from the government the use of most of the church buildings. The split provoked violent reprisals against the leaders of the clergy who remained faithful to the patriarch: the Metropolitan of Petrograd, Benjamin, was publicly tried and shot; hundreds of other Russian Christians died as martyrs to the faith. However, the 'renovated' church, which at first was supported by many members of the educated clergy and by some prominent intellectuals,

[5] Milyukov, op. cit. pp. 163–4, 166–7.

compromised itself not only by the support it received from the Soviet authorities, but also by uncanonical reforms, such as the admission of married priests to the episcopate and the permission given to widowed priests to remarry. Its membership dwindled, and its last adherents joined the 'patriarchal' church in 1943.

Meanwhile Patriarch Tikhon was set free in June 1923. He formally condemned the schismatics, and also undertook to secure the position of the Orthodox Church under the new regime. The civil war was over, and he realized that the Soviet government was not likely to disappear quickly. He therefore published a declaration retracting his previous political statements and concluded with these words: 'Let the monarchists, abroad and at home, know that I am not an enemy of the Soviet Government.'[6] He died suddenly on 7 April 1925, and after his death the newspapers published his will, in which he called the faithful to recognize the Soviet government and expressed the hope that, in return, the regime would again permit religious instruction for children, the re-establishment of theological schools, and the publication of religious books and periodicals.[7]

His hopes proved to be vain. The policy of the Soviet government toward the church remained fully consistent with the original decree of January 1918: religious activities were to be limited to those of a 'cult', and were never to include 'religious propaganda', i.e. education of youth or the right to publish. Ideological and administrative persecution of religion continued.

After Tikhon's death, as the government forbade the election of a new patriarch, the leadership of the church fell briefly into the hands of Metropolitan Peter of Krutitsy and, following his arrest and exile, into those of Metropolitan Sergius of Nizhny-Novgorod. Sergius was arrested in December 1926, and, after his release on 30 March 1927, he published a declaration which pledged, much more explicitly that had any previous statement of the church, 'loyalty' to the Soviet government: 'We want to be Orthodox', the declaration read, 'while recognizing in the Soviet Union our civil country; we want its joys and achievements to become our joys and our achievements, and its failures – our failures.'[8] Sergius also successfully petitioned the government to grant 'legalization' to the patriarchal administration in Moscow.

These steps taken by Sergius were considered to be dangerous to the independence of the church by many Russian churchmen in the Soviet Union and abroad. A group of bishops exiled on Solovki, in the White

---

[6] *Izvestiya*, no. 149 (6 July 1923).
[7] Ibid. (15 Apr. 1925).
[8] English translation of the declaration in W. F. Emhardt, *Religion in Soviet Russia* (Milwaukee, Wisconsin, 1929), pp. 145–50.

Sea, sent an unsuccessful but dignified and eloquent letter of protest, which approved the church's policy of according recognition to the government, but objected to the request for 'legalization', which in their view implied state control.[9] Despite its having been 'legalized', the situation of the church remained catastrophic. After Stalin's purges of 1936–7, which decimated the church leadership, there were barely three or four bishops at liberty, and only a few hundred churches remained open. The church in the Soviet Union seemed doomed to disappear. However, in response to the patriotic appeal made by Metropolitan Sergius on the first day of the German invasion in June 1941, Stalin, on 4 September 1943, received a group of bishops and encouraged them to re-establish the patriarchate, to rebuild the administrative structure of the church, and to open theological schools. The change was so sudden that the church leaders themselves were long hesitant about the attitude to adopt to these suggestions. In the event Sergius was elected patriarch. He died in 1944 and was succeeded by Alexis, who remained patriarch until his death in 1970.

The rapid growth of the church which followed these events reached its peak in 1958, when it was reckoned that there were 25,000 parishes, 33,000 priests, 70 dioceses, two theological academies (graduate schools), and eight seminaries with almost 2,000 students. Several monasteries were also in existence, the majority of them in western areas which had been under German control during the war. The church in all its official statements always followed the policies of the Soviet government, for 'loyalty' excluded the right of criticism or disagreement.

In 1959, however, the religious policy of the government changed dramatically once again. Trials of clergymen, crippling taxation, the closing of churches under the flimsiest administrative pretexts were resumed, this time by Khrushchev's government. As a result, more than half of the churches were closed; of the eight seminaries only three remained open; and the number of students admitted to seminaries and academies was drastically reduced. Anti-religious propaganda, which in practice had been stopped during the last ten years of Stalin's rule, acquired a new vigour in the press and in specialized periodicals (such as *Nauka i religiya*), as well as in numerous pamphlets and books. This development, which was strangely combined with a relative liberalization of the political regime, was probably due to a reversal to doctrinal rigidity by a leadership whose Marxist orthodoxy was being widely challenged.

After the 1959–64 anti-religious campaign, the Orthodox Church stood again much diminished in its outward structure. It has continued, however, to play a role in Soviet foreign policy and to take part in various

[9] Text in Milyukov, op. cit. pp. 193–4.

international gatherings, e.g. those of the World Council of Churches. This activity is seen by the church leadership to be a means of proving the church's usefulness to the government, and thus avoiding its total strangulation. However, it also allows the Soviet Union to project abroad an image of liberalism, which, in the field of religion, is certainly not justified. Thus the position of the church toward the Soviet government remains ambiguous.

During the past decade (1964–74), this ambiguity has been criticized openly, not only abroad but also inside the Soviet Union. Letters of protest have come from the Archbishop of Kaluga, Germogen, from individual priests, and, also, from Alexander Solzhenitsyn (in his 'Lenten Letter' to Patriarch Pimen, 1973). These beginnings of a free debate over church–state relations are a sign of a new vitality in Russian Christianity.

Today there is no doubt that the vast majority of Soviet youth are ignorant of religion. The total absence of religious literature and the constant impact of anti-religious propaganda have had their effect. Regular participation in church worship can be detrimental to a professional career, and Soviet citizens normally tend to hide any religious convictions, especially when they are of working age. But it is certain that the impact of religion goes much beyond the crowds that can be seen in the very few churches that remain open. Reliable information shows that a sizeable minority of intellectuals, as well as of the younger generation, remain faithful to the church. The revival in interest in religion among the young has become particularly apparent in 1970–5.

Finally, an important feature of the religious situation in the USSR is the growth of the Baptist movement. Its missionary zeal, its less formal organization and, also, the disappearance in many areas of the traditional structures of the Orthodox Church, have worked to the advantage of the Baptists. Alongside the Orthodox Church, there exists the 'Union of Baptists and Evangelical Christians', in which a number of older Russian Protestant groups (*pashkovtsy*, *molokane*, *shtundisty*) have merged. The union is a duly legalized institution and falls, as such, under government supervision. An important and vocal segment of the Baptist movement has seceded from the Union, considering that government control is incompatible with Christian mission: the separatists (*initsiativki*) are, of course, severely persecuted by the authorities. The Soviet press also frequently mentions a number of other sectarian groups, illegal and persecuted: Old Believers of various persuasions, 'True Orthodox Christians' refusing to acknowledge the patriarch's co-operation with the government, *khlysty*, Jehovah's Witnesses, and many others.

GUIDE TO FURTHER READING

History

The history of the Russian Orthodox Church is treated in detail in the classic works of Metropolitan Makary, *Istoriya Russkoy tserkvi*, 3rd edn (12 vols., St Petersburg, 1889), and E. Golubinsky, *Istoriya Russkoy tserkvi* (4 vols., and an atlas, Moscow, 1901–4). These two fundamental works are, however, both incomplete: Makary ends his narrative in the middle of the seventeenth century, and Golubinsky in the sixteenth. More recently, A. V. Kartashov published his *Ocherki po istorii Russkoy tserkvi* (2 vols., Paris, 1959), covering, in addition to the medieval period, the entire eighteenth century. Kartashov's work is especially valuable for his brilliant interpretation of the *Raskol* and his characterization of the Petrine reforms. A well-documented study on the last two centuries of Russian Christianity has been written by Igor Smolitsch, *Geschichte der russischen Kirche, 1700–1917* (vol. I, Lieden, 1964).

For a Roman Catholic view on the development of Russian church history see A. M. Ammann, *Abriss der ostslawischen Kirchengeschichte* (Vienna, 1950). The English reader will find useful general introductions in A. N. Mouravieff, *A History of the Church of Russia*, trans. by R. W. Blackmore (Oxford, 1842); H. Y. Rayburn, *The Story of the Russian Church* (London, 1924); and N. Zernov, *The Russians and Their Church* (London, 1964). For a very perceptive view of the religious dimensions of Russian social and intellectual history, see also J. H. Billington, *The Icon and the Axe. An Interpretive History of Russian Culture* (New York, 1966).

Doctrine, liturgy, spirituality, and missions

A full understanding of Russian religious history requires some acquaintance with the doctrine and tradition of the Orthodox Church. Several general introductions to Orthodoxy exist in English; the following are recommended: S. Bulgakov, *The Orthodox Church*, rev. edn (New York, 1963); J. Meyendorff, *The Orthodox Church* (London, 1965); T. Ware, *The Orthodox Church* (London, 1964). For further familiarity with Orthodox theology, see V. Lossky, *The Mystical Theology of the Eastern Church* (Napierville, Ill., 1957) and the same author's *Vision of God* (London, 1964); on Russian monasticism, see I. Smolitsch, *Russisches Mönchtum, Entstehung, Entwicklung und Wesen* (Würzburg, 1953). For the position of the Orthodox Church vis-à-vis the Christian West, see J. Meyendorff, N. Afanassieff, A. Schmemann, and N. Koulomzine, *The Primacy of Peter in the Orthodox Church* (London, 1963); J. Meyendorff, *Orthodoxy and Catholicity* (New York, 1965). For a general appreciation of the history of the Christian East, see A. Schmemann, *The Historical Road of Eastern Orthodoxy* (London, 1965).

The best general introduction to Russian spirituality in English is by G. Fedotov, *The Russian Religious Mind* (2 vols., Cambridge, Mass., 1966); the same author has also compiled the extremely useful *Treasury of Russian Spirituality* (New York, 1961), containing valuable source material, both medieval and modern. For an English translation of the classic collection of patristic texts on prayer, see K. Kadloubovsky and G. E. H. Palmer, *Early*

Fathers from the Philokalia (London, n.d.). On individual Russian saints see N. Zernov, *St Sergius, Builder of Russia* (London, n.d.), and N. Gorodetzky, *St Tikhon Zadonsky, Inspirer of Dostoyevsky* (London, 1951); cf. also E. Behr-Siegel, *Prière et sainteté dans l'Eglise russe* (Paris, 1950); for the connection between the Russian and the Byzantine spiritual traditions, see J. Meyendorff, *A Study on Gregory Palamas* (London, 1963) and *St Gregory Palamas and Orthodox Spirituality* (New York, 1974). There are numerous translations of the Orthodox Eucharistic liturgy in English; other liturgical texts (for sacraments, feasts, special services), translated from the Church Slavonic, can be found in the *Service Book of the Holy Orthodox Catholic. Apostolic Church*, 3rd edn, comp., trans., and arranged by I. F. Hapgood (Brooklyn, 1965); cf. also N. Cabasilas, *A Commentary on the Divine Liturgy*, trans. by J. M. Hussey and P. A. McNulty (London, 1960), and *The Festal Menaion*, trans. by Mother Mary and K. Ware (London, 1969).

There are numerous publications on religious art in Russia; an excellent introduction to it and its spiritual significance can be found in L. Ouspensky and V. Lossky, *The Meaning of Icons* (Olten, 1952). On the missionary activity of Byzantium among the Slavs and on the origins of Slavonic Christianity, see F. Dvornik, *Les Légendes de Constantin et de Méthode vues de Byzance* (Prague, 1933) and his *Byzantine Missions to the Slavs* (New Brunswick, 1970); and F. Grivec, *Konstantin und Method, Lehrer der Slaven* (Wiesbaden, 1962). A good survey in English of the Cyrillo-Methodian mission and its significance is found in a special issue of *St Vladimir's Seminary Quarterly* (vol. 7, no. 1, New York, 1963), with articles by D. Obolensky, R. Jakobson, F. Dvornik, and N. Struve. On modern Russian missions, the studies by J. Glazik, *Die russisch-orthodoxe Heidenmission seit Peter dem Grossem* (Münster, Westphalia, 1954) and *Die Islammission der russisch-orthodoxen Kirche* (Münster, Westphalia, 1959), make use of the very rich Russian bibliography on the subject; for a brief survey of Russian missions in English, consult E. Smirnoff, *Russian Orthodox Missions* (London, 1903), and S. Bolshakoff, *The Foreign Missions of the Russian Orthodox Church* (London, 1943).

Intellectual trends

The most authoritative study of the history of Russian religious thought is by G. Florovsky, *Puti russkogo bogosloviya* (Belgrade, 1937); it contains a mine of bibliographical references. Scholarly literature on the sixteenth-century debate between the 'Possessors' and the 'Trans-Volga Elders' is abundant; the basic monograph on Nil Sorsky is by A. S. Arkhangel'sky, *Nil Sorsky i Vassian Patrikeyev, ikh literaturnyye trudy i idei v Drevney Rusi* (St Petersburg, 1882). The debate has aroused interest both abroad and in Russia: see J. Meyendorff, 'Une controverse sur le rôle social de l'Eglise', *Irénikon*, XXVIII–XXIX (1955–6); F. von Lilienfeld, *Nil Sorskij und seine Schriften* (Berlin, 1963). Contemporary Soviet scholars, while emphasizing the social aspects of the controversy, provide a great deal of new material: see, in particular, N. A. Kazakova and Ya. S. Lur'e, *Antifeodal'nyye yereticheskiye dvizheniya na Rusi XIV – nachala XVI veka* (Moscow–Leningrad, 1955); a new edition of the letters of Joseph of Volotsk, ed. by A. A. Zimin and Ya. S. Lur'e, *Poslaniya Iosifa Volotskogo* (Moscow–Leningrad, 1959), established his connection with the aristocracy.

On the development and significance of the ideology of 'Moscow, the Third Rome', see V. Malinin, *Starets Eleazarova monastyrya Filofey i yego sochineniya*

THE CHURCH

(Kiev, 1901); W. K. Medlin, *Moscow and East Rome, A Political Study of the Relations of Church and State in Muscovite Russia* (Geneva, 1952); H. Schaeder, *Moskau das dritte Rom*, 2nd edn (Darmstadt, 1957). For the modern period of Russian religious thought, completely ignored in Soviet publications, see V. Zenkovsky, *A History of Russian Philosophy* (2 vols., New York, 1953), essential; N. O. Lossky, *History of Russian Philosophy* (London, 1951); N. Gorodetzky, *The Humiliated Christ in Modern Russian Thought* (London, 1938); and N. Zernov, *The Russian Religious Renaissance* (London, 1963). The works of several authors, especially V. Solov'yov, N. Berdyaev, and S. L. Frank, are easily accessible in English. A convenient anthology of little-known extracts by several Russian religious thinkers has recently been published by A. Schmemann, *Ultimate Questions* (New York, 1965).

Schisms and sects

On the origins and the history of the *Raskol*, see above all P. Pascal's *Avvakum et les débuts du Raskol*, 2nd edn (Paris, 1963); the work by W. Palmer, *The Patriarch and the Tsar* (7 vols., London, 1871–6), has not lost its importance. On the history of modern Russian sects, see S. Bolshakov, *Russian Non-Conformity* (Philadelphia, n.d.), F. C. Conybeare, *Russian Dissenters* (New York, 1962), and P. N. Milyukov, 'Religion and the Church', pt. I of his *Outlines of Russian Culture* (3 vols., Philadelphia, 1943).

The Russian Church and the Soviet state

The literature on the subject is abundant; only the main publications in English are cited here. In Milyukov's *Outlines*, the view of a Russian liberal, slightly anti-clerical, is brilliantly and competently expressed; among the other books on the subject, the most important are W. S. Emhardt, *Religion in Soviet Russia* (London, 1929), including an English translation of the very important 'Essay on the Living Church' by S. Troitsky; P. A. Anderson, *People, Church, and State in Modern Russia* (New York, 1944); J. S. Curtiss, *The Russian Church and the Soviet State, 1917–1950* (Boston, 1953). For an evaluation of the crucial role of the locumtenens Sergius, see particularly W. C. Fletcher, *A Study in Survival: The Church in Russia, 1927–1943* (New York, 1965).

A large number of documents on the religious policy of the Soviet government and the internal church controversies have been published, in an English translation, by B. Szczesniak: *The Russian Revolution and Religion* (Notre Dame, Ind., 1959). For a perceptive analysis of the anti-religious campaign under Khrushchev, see N. Struve, *Christians in Contemporary Russia* (New York, 1967), and the anthology of recent texts, reflecting the reaction of Russian Christians, in M. Bourdeaux, *Patriarch and Prophets: Persecution of the Russian Orthodox Church Today* (London, 1969); cf. also, by the same author, *Religious Ferment in Russia* (New York, 1968). For an overall view of the various religious groups in the USSR see R. H. Marshall, jun., ed., *Aspects of Religion in the Soviet Union, 1917–67* (London, 1971).

THE STRUCTURE OF THE SOVIET STATE

GOVERNMENT AND POLITICS

L. B. SCHAPIRO

HISTORICAL FACTORS

Three major historical factors are reflected in the Soviet political system. The first is the role which Lenin attached to the Communist Party as leader of the proletariat. He had elaborated his doctrine very largely for the purposes of making a revolution. But it soon became plain – after the seizure of power by the Bolsheviks on 7 November 1917, and indeed before – that he envisaged a similar leading role for the Communist Party after the revolution had been accomplished. Lenin's theory of leadership, first formulated in 1902, that the proletariat as a class could never accomplish its historic mission of seizing power without being led and inspired 'from outside', logically entailed certain other consequences. One was the rejection by Lenin of what he called 'spontaneity'; that is to say, the unguided, as distinct from the guided, activity of any mass. Numerical majority as such was not something that Lenin regarded as being decisive. What was important was that all decisions should be taken in accordance with the scientific principles of doctrine; once these principles had been explained to the popular masses by the leaders, the masses would ordinarily accept them. This view was applied by Lenin in practice to his leadership of his party. Hence, in the last resort, if a decision had to be taken, and if it could not be taken by the counting of heads, then logically it had to be taken by one man imposing his authority over the others. It was true that in Lenin's lifetime his great moral authority, his intellectual superiority to most (if not all) of his companions in the Party leadership, and indeed his modest personality as contrasted with his essentially authoritarian behaviour, made it possible for decisions to be taken in accordance with Lenin's wishes without much use of violence. Another consequence of Lenin's doctrine was that there could be no room for other parties, since the proletariat could only have one party and that was the party led by him – the Party of the Bolsheviks, or 'Communists' after 1918.

The second historical factor that must still be borne in mind is the way in which the Bolsheviks came to power in 1917. They enjoyed no majority in the country, though of course they had one at the key points in the capital and in a number of major towns. But, as the elections to the constituent assembly held immediately after their seizure of power showed, their total support in the country was no more than one quarter. During the civil war the Bolsheviks had vacillated between compromise on the one hand and fraud or violence on the other in order to prevent the socialist parties – the Social Democrats, or Mensheviks, and the Socialist Revolutionaries – from asserting what they regarded as being their obvious right to participate in government. They failed to prevent this during the civil war, and by the spring of 1921 Lenin was faced with two alternatives: either he had to accept the continual participation in government of socialists, or else he had to reconstruct his as yet undisciplined party in such a way as to ensure the elimination once and for all of all rivals. At the Tenth Congress of the Communist Party in 1921 he chose the latter alternative: not only were the socialist parties thereafter physically restrained or eliminated, but criticism was severely restricted even inside the Communist Party and the forming of factions or groups was prohibited. It is from this congress that the so-called 'monolithic' character of the Party dates.

The third historical influence is the period of the predominance of Stalin. The circumstance in which Stalin forced collectivization on the peasants, the breakneck speed with which he industrialized the country, and the elimination of all his opponents, both of the left and of the right, which this process entailed, all left their mark on Soviet society. By 1936 when total terror was unleashed on both the Party and the country as a whole, totalitarian rule had already been established. The process of terrorization was completed by 1938. Equally important was the undoing of Stalin's reputation, principally in February 1956 by his successor, the First Secretary of the Party, N. S. Khrushchev. The public unmasking of someone who had been above criticism, the open ventilation of horrors which, although known to be true, had never in fact been publicly mentioned, shattered all the 'monolithic' unity of the system, which had only been preserved by terror. In spite of all the efforts of the leaders to minimize the shock, the challenging of the legitimacy of Stalin the man necessarily entailed in the eyes of many a challenge to the legitimacy of the Party itself. The Twentieth Party Congress thus marked the beginning of a process in the history of Soviet politics that was far from exhausted nineteen years later.

THE COMMUNIST PARTY OF THE SOVIET UNION

Although it is necessary to look separately at the two parallel sets of political institutions in the Soviet Union, the Party institutions and the government, or state institutions, there is no doubt that the predominant element in this dyarchy is the Party. All policy emanates from the Party and at the top levels Party and government are intertwined. The relation between them is the key to Soviet political order.

The Communist Party of the Soviet Union has, of course, undergone very substantial changes since the Revolution. Barely a quarter of a million strong at the time when the Bolsheviks seized power, it numbered nearly fourteen and a half million by April 1971, still predominantly urban and predominantly male. On the other hand, the stress that was laid in the early days of the Party's growth on proletarian composition has ceased to play so significant a part. The Party now recruits among all sectors of life, principally in those where most influence can be exercised. According to official figures, slightly more than half of the Party (55 per cent in 1969) consists of workers and peasants. The white collar element is probably a good deal higher in fact, because many of those classified as being workers or peasants are in positions of authority. With the passage of time and as the result of successive purges the older Bolsheviks have virtually disappeared. In 1967 only 5 per cent had spent more than twenty-five years in the Party; and 52 per cent of all Party members were forty years old or younger. The instrument which the leaders use in order to exercise control is probably most accurately described as the 'apparatus' of the Party – that is to say, those who are in full- or part-time paid employment of the Party, or at all events those who are active on Party committees and other organs. If full-time paid Party officials alone are considered their number is probably less than a quarter of a million, while if the term 'apparatus' is used in its wider sense, the number may be as high as half a million. The rank and file of the Party, although of course under Party discipline, play a relatively unimportant part in the carrying out of policy. The question of the extent to which they can influence policy will be considered later.

As conceived by Lenin, the Party's function was to act as the motive element not only of control, but also of stimulus and leadership in all branches of life. This conception of a ruling élite has remained the ideal in spite of the very substantial departures from it which took place under Stalin. By the time Stalin had established his rule, the Party had become only one of several instruments which he used for the purpose of maintaining his power, the others being the police, the army, and the state bureaucracy. It cannot be said that during the years of Stalin's rule the

Party really predominated over any of these, because he used now one and now the other in order to carry out his aims. The police arm was used against the Party quite as much as it was against other sections of society. The real instrument of control, certainly after 1934, was Stalin's private secretariat, or the 'secret department' of the central Party secretariat – the two were apparently identical – through which, with the aid of a number of chosen henchmen, he operated what in effect was a purely personal despotism.

One of the features of Stalin's reign was the atrophy of the normal operation of the Party organs. Between 1939 and 1952 no congress met; the Central Committee hardly ever met, and even the Political Bureau of the Party (or Politburo) hardly met as a whole, but only in select combinations of those whom Stalin chose to invite.

After Stalin's death it became possible once again to speak of Party constitutional practice. At the same time his successors endeavoured to make the Party once again into the kind of ruling élite that Lenin had in his time intended it to be. The Party, though of course much more of a mass party than it had ever been under Lenin, became with the aid of its 'apparatus' once again the leading organ in every sphere of life. Its influence extended even into the collective farms, where, during Stalin's lifetime, it had very largely failed to penetrate. At any rate during the period of Khrushchev's dominance, from 1952 until 1964, the Party was beyond any question the leading and authoritative element in the whole social and state machinery. The complete interpenetration of party and state which he had achieved was symbolized by the fact that after 1958 the First Secretary of the Party and the Chairman of the Council of Ministers, or Prime Minister, were one and the same person. After Khrushchev's fall in October 1964 this no longer was the case. The First, or General Secretary of the Party (Brezhnev) and the Chairman of the Council of Ministers (Kosygin), appeared to be maintaining something in the nature of separate domains of influence; and the prime minister's domain had in many ways succeeded in emancipating itself from the constant Party control and interference which characterized the period of Khrushchev's rule – in particular in the sphere of planning and the control of industry. It is true that by 1975 the Party was showing signs of asserting itself more in this sphere, too. At the highest level of decision-making, the Politburo, a system called 'collective leadership' prevailed. This appeared to mean that no one member predominated, and that decisions were taken after consultation among the most influential members at least – the General Secretary of the Party, the Chairman of the Council of Ministers, and the Chairman of the Presidium of the Supreme Soviet.

THE PARTY MACHINERY

According to the Party rules or statute, the highest authority in the Party is the Party Congress; it is required to meet every five years, and in practice this requirement has been, more or less, observed. The congress decides the programme of the Party and approves the rules; the latest programme and rules date from 1961, but some amendments to the rules were adopted at the Twenty-fourth Congress in 1971. The congress also elects the Party organs, namely the Political Bureau (Politburo, known as the Presidium between 1952 and 1966) and the Central Committee; and appoints the members of the Party Secretariat. Congress proceedings tend to follow a very formal pattern, and its decisions are always unanimous. It cannot in any real sense be said to formulate or even to debate Party policy. It does, however, serve two important purposes: firstly, it lays down publicly for all subordinate Party organs and for the country as a whole the policy directives for some time to come; and secondly, it does in the course of its debates, however formalized, sometimes reveal a great deal of information on the past history of Party in-fighting, and on the current state of society generally.

The Politburo, which at present (1975) consists of fifteen full members and seven candidate (alternate) members, is the policy-making organ of the country. Its meetings are invariably secret and even the fact that it has met is not usually made public. Its discussions, if only because they are secret, are real, and supply the means by which conflicting opinions at the top level of the Party leadership are resolved. The First Secretary of the Party was chairman of the Presidium so long as Khrushchev occupied this post, and after October 1964 Khrushchev's successor as First Secretary (later 'General Secretary'), Brezhnev, became chairman. The Central Committee of the Party elected in 1971 consisted of 241 full members and 155 candidate members. The main function of the Central Committee is the formal one of approving policy laid before it by the First (or General) Secretary in the name of the Politburo (or Presidium). The Politburo is technically a subcommittee of the Central Committee, which must formally approve its actions. Indeed it is in the name of the Central Committee, which under the Party rules has the right to lay down policy between congresses, that all Party instructions and decisions are promulgated. When Khrushchev became First Secretary of the Party he not only revived the long-disused practice of summoning regular meetings of the Central Committee, but started the innovation of publicizing its proceedings. Moreover, while he held his office the Central Committee became a kind of lesser congress, often meeting in conjunction with representatives of agriculture or industry or other

335

persons appropriate to the subject matter of the discussion. The public debates of the Central Committee thus became almost as formal as those of the Party congresses, though less formal discussions continued to take place in secret. Although some of the proceedings of the Central Committee are still published, the practice of using it as a wider forum was discontinued after Khrushchev fell. It is possible that, with the diminution of the authority of any one man after Stalin's death, the Central Committee became for a time the forum to which appeal could be made in the event of disagreement among the top leaders. Such questions as the defeat by Khrushchev in June 1957 of the considerable majority which had formed against him in the Presidium, and the decision to remove Khrushchev from his post as First Secretary in October 1964, were both resolved in the Central Committee. To what extent these decisions were the result of genuine debate as distinct from manoeuvre is a matter of conjecture.

The most important organ of the party is the central Secretariat. There were in 1975 nine secretaries, of whom one was officially known as General Secretary. The Secretariat employs an administrative staff believed to number about a thousand. It is charged under the Party rules both with the selection of 'cadres' and with the supervision of the carrying out of party decisions. Its staff provides the Politburo with the expert information for policy decisions. The Secretariat also exercises general supervisory control over the Party apparatus and its network, and hence over the whole life of the country. Secretaries differ in seniority and are responsible for groups of subjects, or for single subjects, and these subjects are in turn administered through a number of departments of whom the heads are very influential officials. These departments are mostly of a specialized nature – such as those for heavy industry, agriculture, or propaganda. But two departments are of particular importance: one is the Department of Organizational Party Work, which is in effect the department which deals with the selection of persons to fill all appointments throughout the country both in the Party apparatus and in the Party delegations and committees. The other is the Department for Administrative Organs, which deals, among other things, with the army, with the law courts, and with the security service. The central Secretariat is assisted in its work by secretariats in the union republics and by the subordinate administrative organizations throughout the territorial network of the Party.

The organization of the Party throughout the country is based upon two principles: the territorial and the functional. Territorially this is exemplified by the Party organizations which exist at all administrative levels of the country – in the union republics (except for the largest and most important RSFSR), in administrative divisions such as the circuits and regions, in the districts, both urban and rural, and in the cities. The functional Party organizations, on the other hand, are based in the place of work or employment and consist of the primary Party organizations, of which there were about 370,000 in 1971. These are formed in the great majority of farms, factories, enterprises, public institutions, and government departments. The primary Party organization is the centre to which the individual Party member is most closely attached. It deals both with recruiting and with discipline, including expulsion (though subject to appeal). The primary organizations are hierarchically subordinate to the nearest district Party organization in the territorial network. It must be recalled that the basic principle in the practice of the Soviet Communist Party is strict centralization, even if in theory this is described as 'democratic centralism'. No organization is autonomous in any sense, and each is always subordinate to the next in the hierarchy. This makes the combination of the central organs in Moscow, the territorial organs throughout the country, and the primary organizations throughout the social and industrial life of the country a very powerful instrument of control in the hands of the leader or leaders who at any time are masters of the central organization.

PARTY DEMOCRACY

Compared to most of the period during which Stalin was in control, there is somewhat more democracy in the Party now. But so far as policy-making by the Politburo is concerned, it is very difficult to see how rank-and-file members of the Party can exercise any control. They do not elect the Politburo, and they have no say at all in removing it. Decisions of policy, like decisions on questions of personal power at the top, take place at many removes and are quite beyond their influence. What is occasionally possible to discern is a sign of some kind of 'participatory democracy' taking place inside the Party. Discussion in Party organs at lower levels has become less inhibited by fear both at meetings and in the press. This at any rate enables the Party authorities at the top to sense, in a way which was not possible under Stalin, the state of opinion in the Party and at times to pay more heed to it. Some observers have claimed that vital policy changes, such as the dismantling in turn of the reputations of Stalin and Khrushchev or reform of economic policy, have been the result of pressure from broader sections of the Party, but the evidence for this is inconclusive. On the other hand it is, no doubt, the case that in formulating policy the Politburo and the Secretariat which advises it take full account of the views of powerful interests like those of the military, the planners, the managers, and probably others.

Although elections inside the Party are nominally free, they are in practice very strictly controlled by the Department of Organizational Party Work of the Secretariat (and its subordinate organizations) in order to ensure that only approved candidates are 'elected'. A representative of the next organization in the hierarchy is always present at elections at lower levels; and in many cases the Party rules, by such devices as providing for voting by show of hands or for the approval by higher authorities of certain elections, enable the centre effectively to control virtually all Party posts. Nevertheless, cases have occasionally occurred since 1954 of refusal by a lower Party organization to have someone foisted upon it as a candidate for 'election', or to have someone whom it wished to elect kept out of office. The tradition of hierarchy and discipline is very strong, however, and the uncertainty within the Party about the reactions of the authorities to such behaviour is still very great. One big move which could substantially alter the nature of the Party would be the setting up of an independent organ of a judicial nature to deal with cases of discipline over Party members. So far there have been no signs even of any proposal to establish such an organ.

THE CONSTITUTION OF 1936

The constitution at present in force was adopted on 5 December 1936. It has frequently been amended, but its main features remain substantially the same. The constitution is in the form of that of a federal union stated to be founded on the basis of the voluntary union of fifteen equal 'soviet socialist republics'. The voluntary nature of the union is further underlined by a provision, unique in federal constitutions, that every union republic has the free right of secession. In practice the enforced adherence of some at least of the union republics is not open to doubt; control by the Party can effectively prevent any one of them from exercising its formal right to secede, and such a move would beyond question be treated now, as it has been in the past, as counter-revolutionary rebellion.

The second chapter of the Soviet Constitution enumerates the powers of the all-union government which are exclusive to it. These powers may be divided under three main headings: 'external political matters', such as treaties, war and peace, and foreign trade; 'internal political matters', which include state security and establish what are called the 'basic principles' governing education, public health, civil, family, and criminal legislation, and legislation on nationality; and a third category embracing the most extensive powers, which include the laying down of the all-union economic plan and control over transport and communications, the money system, loans, labour legislation, economic statistics, and, most important of all, the power of 'approval of the consolidated state budget' of the USSR, and the determination of the taxes and revenue which go respectively to the all-union, the union-republican, and the local budgets. When it so wishes the union can enjoy almost complete control over the union republics. Yet the rights of the union republics are limited quite as much by the nature of the Soviet political system as by the terms of the constitution. The centralized party ensures control over general policy. Centralized security and finance ensure complete control in all other respects. Moreover, the provisions of the constitution are of little use to the union republics in so far as they have no means, such as are available for example to the states of the United States, to challenge all-union legislation in the courts. However, all this does not mean that the union republics are devoid of all autonomy. In practice since 1957 they have been allowed by the centre increasing rights, although of late years some of the autonomy conceded after 1957 has once again been withdrawn. The union republics, however, are still represented at all levels of union government and their needs are to a large extent taken into account; there are also certain minor spheres in which their autonomy is tolerated. It should, however, be emphasized that this is *tolerated* autonomy, which depends upon the decision of the centre, and can be (and often is) withdrawn as easily as it can be conferred.

Quite apart from legal and political considerations, the disparity in size and influence between the RSFSR, on the one hand, and the remaining union republics on the other, renders effective federalism in the Soviet Union a matter of great practical difficulty.

THE SUPREME SOVIET

According to chapter three of the Soviet Constitution, supreme power in the USSR is vested in the Supreme Soviet of the USSR. It possesses the exclusive power of legislation and the exercise of all state powers enjoyed by the government of the USSR, in so far as they are not vested in either the Presidium of the Supreme Soviet or in the Council of Ministers or Ministries of the USSR. The Supreme Soviet is bicameral, consisting of the Soviet (council) of the Union in which each delegate represents three hundred thousand inhabitants; and the Soviet of Nationalities, in which the union republics and the autonomous republics as well as autonomous regions are represented, irrespective of their size, by fixed numbers of deputies. The two chambers have equal rights. Each Supreme Soviet is elected for four years and is required to meet twice a year: extraordinary sessions may be summoned by the Presidium. Only a simple majority of each chamber is required to pass a valid law and there is elaborate provision for cases of disagreement between the two chambers. In practice, since the first Supreme Soviet met in 1937 under the provisions of the present constitution, there has been no recorded instance in which any decision of the Supreme Soviet has been reached otherwise than by a unanimous vote of both chambers. The Supreme Soviet meets usually for only a few days and it follows that even the formal work of legislation, let alone debate and discussion, must take place somewhere else.

The Presidium of the Supreme Soviet, which in 1975 consisted of a chairman, fifteen deputy chairmen (one from each republic), and seventeen other members, is one place where the formal work of legislation can, and probably does, take place. It performs the titular functions which are usually exercised by a president in a republic, but it also has very considerable legislative powers, though in theory the legislative functions require formal approval by the Supreme Soviet. The Presidium also exercises considerable executive powers. Some legislative activities also take place in the commissions of the Supreme Soviet. These meet more frequently and sit for longer periods, and their activities are not public. There are eleven such commissions in all, in each of the two chambers. There is some evidence that these commissions play a real part at times in shaping the legislative activity of the Supreme Soviet when this body meets for its short sessions formally to adopt a number of major laws. The deputies of the Supreme Soviet enjoy certain immunities and privileges and, apart from their formal functions in the Supreme Soviet sessions and their somewhat less formal duties in the commissions, they also perform a valuable service behind the scenes in acting as intermediaries between their constituents and the central government.

The system of soviets is not, however, confined to the centre. There are Supreme Soviets in the republics and there are soviets in all administrative divisions throughout the country, right down to the villages.

The Soviet Constitution also lays down the main principles of the electoral system. All Soviet citizens who have reached the age of eighteen are entitled to vote without distinction of race, sex, ethnic or social origin, past or present activity, or the extent of their property, and any citizen of twenty-three and over can be elected a deputy; only the insane are denied the vote. Candidates are nominated by constituencies. The right to nominate candidates for election is reserved to the Communist Party organizations, the trade unions, co-operatives, youth organizations, and cultural societies. In theory, contested elections are possible. The regulations for the Supreme Soviet elections provide that the voter should cross out all names on the ballot paper except the name of the one candidate for whom he desires to vote. In practice there has been no single instance in which more than one candidate has been put forward in any constituency in any Supreme Soviet election or, so far as is known, in any election to a lower soviet. This unanimity is achieved through the influence of the Party at all levels on the nominations.

Considerable propaganda is devoted to ensuring that everyone participates in the election. It is under the control of an electoral commission which acts through local commissions in every constituency and in every polling district. These commissions are not elected but 'composed', and in practice invariably include the most important local Party members. The local polling districts are fairly small, the maximum size being about three thousand voters, and the voting on polling day is under the supervision of the local electoral commission. The voter on arrival is presented with a ballot paper on which one single name appears. He can either drop the paper unmarked into the voting box, or else enter a booth which is provided. Since the purpose of entering the booth can only be to mark the paper in some way other than to express approval for the single name upon it, and since this act has to take place in the full view of the Party representative on the local electoral commission, it is perhaps not surprising that not many avail themselves of this privilege. The result is that in practice over 99 per cent of the electorate usually go to the polls and over 99 per cent of all votes are normally cast for the official candidates of the Party and non-Party bloc.

THE EXECUTIVE

Chapter five of the Soviet Constitution deals in detail with the All-Union Council of Ministers, which is described as 'the Supreme Executive and directing organ of state power'. It is in theory not empowered to legislate and is subordinate to the Supreme Soviet and its Presidium, but in practice its directives, ostensibly issued in amplification of existing legislation, undoubtedly effect changes in the law. Since there is no judicial review in the USSR, the council enjoys legislative power in practice, and its ordinances are never challenged. The All-Union Council of Ministers has at many periods of Soviet history issued its directives jointly with the Central Committee of the Party. The council is a very large body: its composition frequently varies and the constitution is then amended accordingly. Broadly speaking certain of its features may be said to be constant. It appears to act through a kind of inner cabinet, or presidium, which consists of the chairman and the first deputy and deputy chairmen. All the ministers are of course members of the council as are also a number of other persons, such as the chairmen of state committees and of certain other important state bodies, such as the State Bank.

Ministries at the union level are either all-union or union-republican ministries. All-union ministries have sole charge of the sphere of administration entrusted to them, while union-republican ministries are central

341

bodies which have a corresponding ministry in the union republics. There is therefore that much less centralization in the case of a branch of administration entrusted to a union-republican ministry. In addition there are ministries in the union republics which have no counterpart at the central level. It will be obvious from this that the degree of autonomy which a union republic is allowed to exercise at any time will to some extent depend on the subdivision of administrative functions between these various types of ministry. The subdivision has varied a great deal in the course of Soviet history. Certain matters are invariably controlled at the all-union level: security, foreign trade, and national transport. On the other hand such matters as agriculture, defence, finance, foreign affairs, and health are now normally dealt with by union-republican ministries. There have been various changes in the course of Soviet history which have broadly reflected different views of the character that central ministerial supervision should assume. One view is that as far as possible each branch of industry should be centralized. When this view prevails the number of ministries in the All-Union Council of Ministers tends to grow. On the other hand, experiments have been made with types of decentralization to areas or regions. A bold attempt in this respect was made by Khrushchev in May 1957, when he divided the country into about one hundred industrial regions and placed the entire industry of each region under the 'Council of National Economy'. Centralized control of policy was maintained under this system not so much by the All-Union Council of Ministers as by the Party organs both in the regions and at the centre. This system was abandoned in October 1965 when the Soviet Union reverted to the system of an extensive number of all-union and union-republican ministries, each dealing with one branch of the national economy. Over and above the specialized ministries there are a number of state committees for various forms of co-ordination and for planning – for example, Gosplan, or the State Planning Commission.

During the period when Khrushchev was First Secretary of the Party he either dominated the office of Chairman of the Council of Ministers through a subordinate nominee (Bulganin) or, after 1958, occupied it himself. This ensured complete co-ordination but at the price of Party domination over all affairs of government. After Khrushchev was overthrown these offices became separate; even so, there is a very high degree of integration. The Chairman of the Council of Ministers is a member of the Politburo, and a number of the other important ministers are also leading members of the Party. The departments of the Secretariat of the Party provide an indispensable expert staff for all questions of policy. There can, therefore, be no question of any real separation between the Party and government machines, although under the system of 'collective leadership' after 1964 there was certainly a great deal more autonomy than before conceded by the Party to the sphere for which the government was primarily responsible. The extent of state–Party co-operation, and the degree to which the government machine may attempt to assert its independence in policy-making, have at all periods posed a very important political question in the USSR. But it is not one that can be resolved by looking at the formal machine of government and Party, but only by an assessment of the relative influence of the key personalities concerned at any one time.

For the implementation of its executive policy at all levels the Soviet system relies once again on the twin machines: on the one hand the administrative officials, on the other the corresponding Party organ officials, at all territorial levels. If one looks purely at the administrative machine, it is highly centralized in the sense that the local Soviet authorities and officials, from the union republics downward, are in terms of the constitution in one way or another subordinate to the orders of the authority next highest in the hierarchy. The constitution of the union and the constitution of the union republics certainly provide for a considerable subdivision of functions. But the extensive overlapping, the duplication of functions, together with the long-established tradition of centralization, about which Soviet commentators have been complaining almost since the inception of the regime, all lead to the result that the administrative machine is an unwieldy one and very hard to operate smoothly or quickly. There have been attempts made at various times to ensure greater decentralization of administrative responsibilities. But the tradition of overcentralization has proved too strong, and the attempts have failed. In some ways also the strength of the Party lies in the fact that it is not in practice bound by the complicated rules of hierarchy and bureaucracy which affect the civilian authorities, and can therefore cut through difficulties and resolve deadlocks by the simple expedient of using its own network in order to get straight to the authorities in Moscow. This privilege, which the Party has enjoyed for so many years, together with its tradition of 'running' the country whatever the constitution and the law may say, are the main strengths of the Party. In periods of crisis in Soviet history the pre-eminence of the Party in administrative talent and freedom of action has been particularly evident.

CIVIL RIGHTS

One of the features of the 1936 Soviet Constitution is a chapter which deals specifically with the rights and duties of citizens. So far as the rights are concerned, there are extensive guarantees of basic civil freedoms – freedom of speech, freedom of assembly, freedom of association, and the like. However, the existence of formal guarantees of civil freedom in any constitution does not necessarily mean that these rights are safeguarded in practice. The 1936 Soviet Constitution was already in force at the height of the 'great terror', when millions of people were being sent to their death or to concentration camps without trial. Moreover, the language of the safeguards is such as to leave a very considerable degree of discretion. Freedom of speech is guaranteed 'with the aim of strengthening the socialist system' – a phrase that obviously can be interpreted very widely. Similarly, the guarantee of freedom of 'religious worship', as contrasted with the guarantee of freedom of 'anti-religious propaganda', plainly means, and is in practice so interpreted, that religious instruction can be severely restricted. However, the weakest feature of the Soviet system is the lack of any right possessed by the citizen to enforce the guarantees written into the constitution. He cannot have recourse to the courts in order to challenge legislation on the grounds that it is inconsistent with the constitution; nor can he seek redress in the courts against any official whom he wishes to charge with having violated the provisions of the constitution. He can only complain to the government or to Party authorities, and is therefore at the mercy of the various categories of officials. It is for this reason that the sphere of civil liberties has had so chequered a record in the history of the USSR. Since the death of Stalin the position of the individual has indeed improved; the authorities are still guilty of serious irregularities and violations of the law when they find it necessary, but the number and frequency of such violations has been reduced. The large and arbitrary powers of the police have also to some extent been curbed. But this process has not taken place through the activities of the courts, but by a change in policy from above, and in particular by a change in the policy relating to those numerous organs of control which the Soviet Union employs for the supervision of the vast and cumbersome system of its government and administration.

ORGANS OF CONTROL

One such organ is the Committee of State Security, known by its initials as the KGB, which is the successor of the MVD, NKVD, OGPU, GPU, and Cheka. This security system is completely centralized at the all-union level. The chairman of the Committee of State Security operates through a large network of subordinates. He is responsible not only for internal security but also for external espionage. He has at his disposal a very considerable armed force which can be swiftly moved from one part of the country to another in case of need, and which is also used for guarding the borders of the Soviet Union. Next in importance is the system of the 'procurators', also a highly centralized method of control. Procurators are judicial officials in the sense that they also exercise general supervision over the courts. They act as prosecutors in criminal cases and they supervise, indeed themselves undertake, the preliminary investigations into criminal charges. The procurators have very considerable powers at their disposal in order to investigate whether or not the law has been violated. There is one very severe limitation on their powers: they cannot investigate the legality of the conduct of the higher legislative organs or of the All-Union Council of Ministers, nor can they challenge decisions of the Central Committee or Politburo of the Party. They are indeed in practice Party members and wholly under the control of the Party. This said, it is certainly also true that the procurators can play, and in latter years have often played, an important role in safeguarding the rights of the individual. The procurators are also the guardians of proper procedure in the courts. Thus, it is as much the duty of the procurator as prosecutor in a criminal case to appeal a verdict which goes in his favour as it is to appeal one which goes against him, and it may be said that this is a duty which he often fulfils in practice.

Apart from the procurators and the KGB there exist a number of other instruments of control. One such is the State Bank, which exercises a very stringent financial control over all enterprises. It has indeed the power to deny an enterprise the right to use the credit of the bank and can thereby declare it bankrupt. In conjunction with other departments the bank exercises control over personnel and pay in the administrative service. Another important organization of control is a body which is at present known as the 'People's Control', which has at various stages been either a ministry, commission, or committee of overall control. The function of all these organizations has been to investigate and to bring to justice cases of corruption and dishonesty throughout the economic and administrative life of the country.

CONCLUSION AND PROSPECTS

During its fifty-eight years of existence the Soviet regime has undergone frequent changes. However, fundamentally the system has remained the same in the sense that there has at all periods been one element in the state which has been able to act arbitrarily and to cut across any kind of barriers the rulers may have set themselves in the shape of legal rules or constitutional provisions. This has usually been the Party, though for much of the period during which Stalin was in control it was often rather Stalin's personal secretariat than the actual Party organization.

The arbitrary power of the Party and of its main executive arm, the KGB, still remains to this day, even though it may have been hemmed in with some limitations. There is one limitation the Soviet system has obdurately refused to tolerate: the existence of any form of appeal to an independent judiciary. In so far as the observance of legal rules has improved – and it has improved, though neither uniformly nor consistently, in the last twenty years – this has been by way of 'tolerated legality' only. It may be that tolerated legality is not legality at all because the essence of law is certainty and predictability. Nevertheless, even tolerated legality is better, while it lasts, than total absence of any legal restraints, although it is somewhat pointless to apply such terms as 'the rule of law' to the conditions which obtain in the Soviet Union. It is impossible to predict whether this situation will necessarily remain in the future. In one country, at any rate, which was originally closely modelled on the Soviet Union – namely, Yugoslavia – there has been some modest progress toward real rule of law, in spite of the continuing predominance of the Communist Party. Whether the Soviet Union will evolve in the same direction it is impossible to predict.

One reason which has led some observers to predict with some degree of optimism a likelihood of progress in the Soviet Union in the direction of legality is based on the continuing economic development which is taking place in the country. The administration of any complicated economy requires for its effective running a number of qualities which a legal system can provide – predictability, certainty, reliability. The Party, with its tradition for disregard of the law, for arbitrary action, and for cutting across all established rules, is at variance with this necessary requirement. Therefore, it is argued that the future is on the side of predictability and certainty – in other words, of law – and that this trend must necessarily lead to a reduction in the influence of the Party in most spheres of life and to a strengthening both of legality and of the administrative machine. Only time can tell. But it can be stated confidently that evolution along the lines of legality would have to begin with the development within the Soviet governmental system of institutions and organs completely independent of the Party, of institutions which could operate without any fear of interference from the Party and its apparatus at all levels. Such independent institutions would have to be able to protect themselves, against the Party as much as against all else, in courts which were not dominated, as the Soviet courts are at present, by the Party. There were no signs in 1975 of such a momentous change in the Soviet political system.

GUIDE TO FURTHER READING

This list of selected books for further study relates mainly to the institutions of government and to the Communist Party of the Soviet Union. Reference should also be made to the 'Guide' for Ch. 5, pp. 248ff, and Ch. 6, pp. 308ff, especially for works on the intellectual origins of Bolshevism and the revolutionary movements.

Collections of documents

M. Matthews, ed., *Soviet Government: A Selection of Official Documents on Internal Policies* (London, 1974) is a very well edited selection. Parts 1 and 2 deal, respectively, with 'Government and Administration' and with 'The Party'. Serious students of the subject will need to consult the numerous Soviet collections of government and CPSU documents published since 1917, which are too numerous to be listed. R. H. McNeal, ed., *Guide to the Decisions of the Communist Party of the Soviet Union 1917–1967* (in Russian; Toronto, 1972) is a very useful hand-list of the official resolutions of the CPSU which are available in many Soviet editions.

Periodicals

The following are the periodicals in which articles on Soviet Party and government questions are most frequently published: *Problems of Communism* (Washington, every 2 months); *Soviet Studies* (Glasgow, quarterly); *Survey* (formerly *Soviet Survey*, London, quarterly); a weekly *Current Digest of the Soviet Press* appears in New York.

Text books on Soviet government

J. Armstrong, *Ideology, Politics, and Government in the Soviet Union*, rev. edn (New York, 1968), an excellent, very short introduction to the subject; F. C. Barghoorn, *Politics in the Soviet Union*, 2nd edn (Boston, 1972), a good introduction, with a sociological approach; L. G. Churchward, *Contemporary Soviet Government* (London, 1968), which contains a much fuller treatment than is usual on Soviet local government; M. Fainsod, *How Russia is Ruled*, 2nd edn (Cambridge, Mass., 1964), far and away the best study of Soviet government up to 1963; D. Lane, *Politics and Society in the USSR* (London, 1970), a sociological study of Soviet government; A. G. Meyer, *The Soviet Political System: An Interpretation* (New York, 1965), a somewhat idiosyncratic theory on the nature of modern Soviet government; L. Schapiro, *The Government and Politics of the Soviet Union*, 5th edn (London, 1974), a short study with both an historical and a descriptive approach; and D. J. R. Scott, *Russian Political Institutions*, 4th edn (London, 1969), a more detailed study than the last, but mainly descriptive.

The Communist Party of the Soviet Union (CPSU)

J. Armstrong, *The Politics of Totalitarianism* (New York, 1961), a detailed study of the history of the CPSU from 1934–60; P. Broué, *Le Parti bolchévique* (Paris, 1963), a fairly detailed and documented history of the CPSU; R. Conquest, *The*

Great Terror (London, 1968), a detailed and documented study of Stalin's assault on the Party and the country, 1934–8; M. Fainsod, *Smolensk under Soviet Rule* (Cambridge, Mass., 1958), a digest of the archives of the Smolensk Party organization captured during the Second World War – unique source material, very well edited; J. F. Hough, *The Soviet Prefects* (Cambridge, Mass., 1969), a valuable study of the local Party organs in action in the industrial field; J. S. Reshetar, jun., *A Concise History of the Communist Party* (New York, 1960), much shorter than the other general histories listed; T. H. Rigby, *Communist Party Membership in the USSR, 1917–1967* (Princeton, 1968), the most detailed study of all aspects of the composition of the CPSU; L. Schapiro, *The Origin of the Communist Autocracy* (London, 1955), and the same author's *The Communist Party of the Soviet Union*, 2nd edn (London, 1970), both detailed studies of the history of the CPSU.

There are also available in Russian both short and long histories of the CPSU, of greater interest for their reflection of officially approved interpretations of the past than for scholarship. The short version is entitled *Istoriya Kommunisticheskoy Partii Sovetskogo Soyuza*. There have been several editions since 1959, each successive edition revised to correspond to changes in the CPSU official version of the past. The long version has the same title but is in six volumes, several of them in two parts. It has an editorial board of leading party officials, headed by P. N. Pospelov. Both versions are published in Moscow.

Monographs on particular topics

KGB

See R. Hingley, *The Russian Secret Police* (London, 1970), and S. Wolin and R. Slusser, eds., *The Soviet Secret Police* (New York, 1957).

Pressure groups

H. G. Skilling and F. Griffiths, eds., *Interest Groups in Soviet Politics* (Princeton, 1971) is a collection of essays, with summaries of the conclusions by the editors.

Convergence

See Z. Brzezinski and S. P. Huntington, *Political Power: USA/USSR* (London, 1964).

Decision making

W. J. Conyngham, *Industrial Management in the Soviet Union* (Stanford, 1973) describes the role of the CPSU in industrial decision-making, 1917–70.

Social Structure

M. Matthews, *Class and Society in Soviet Russia* (London, 1972) is a sober and scholarly analysis of Soviet society, and is well documented.

Some Selected Biographies of Soviet Leaders

Lenin

L. Fisher, *The Life of Lenin* (New York, 1964), a well-written and scholarly popular biography; L. Schapiro and P. B. Reddaway, eds., *Lenin: the Man, the Theorist, the Leader* (London, 1967), a collection of articles on various aspects of Lenin; R. H. W. Theen, *Lenin* (Philadephia and New York, 1973), the best short study of Lenin, incorporating the results of recent research; A. B. Ulam, *The Bolsheviks* (London, 1966), which, in spite of its title, is mainly devoted to Lenin.

Stalin

There are numerous biographies of Stalin. Far and away the best is B. Souvarine, *Stalin: a Critical Survey of Bolshevism* (London, 1939). More up-to-date biographies are the following: I. Deutscher, *Stalin: a Political Biography*, 2nd edn (London, 1967), very readable, not always reliable in its scholarship; R. Hingley, *Joseph Stalin: Man and Legend* (London, 1974), very readable and reliable; A. B. Ulam, *Stalin: the Man and his Era* (New York, 1973), very detailed and reliable, although sparsely documented.

Bukharin

S. F. Cohen, *Bukharin and the Bolshevik Revolution* (New York, 1973) is an outstanding work of scholarship.

Trotsky

I. Deutscher, *The Prophet Armed: Trotsky 1879–1921* (London, 1954), *The Prophet Unarmed: Trotsky 1921–1929* (London, 1959), and *The Prophet Outcast: Trotsky 1929–1940* (London, 1963) are essential reading on Trotsky. However, they are not reliable on the historical background and not free from political bias.

9

THE STRUCTURE OF THE SOVIET STATE

THE ECONOMY

ALEC NOVE

THE SYSTEM BEFORE 1928

The Bolshevik leaders, when they seized power, had only the vaguest conception of how to run the economy. Conceiving the Russian Revolution to be an integral part of a great European or world cataclysm, Lenin devoted his energies and his talents primarily to the vastly difficult task of seizing and retaining power. Already in December 1917 the 'Supreme Council of the National Economy', usually known by its Russian abbreviation, VSNKh or *Vesenkha*, was set up to run the state sector. But any ideas on the normal functioning of the economy were quickly swept aside by the desperate emergency of civil war and economic chaos. In the period known as 'war communism', the government suppressed all private enterprise in industry and trade, and sought to compel peasants to deliver surpluses against increasingly valueless paper roubles. Many Bolshevik intellectuals believed that they were making a direct leap into socialism. But the system of war communism could not survive the civil war emergency that was its only possible justification. Reluctantly, Lenin and the Party in 1921 adopted a 'New Economic Policy' (NEP), again permitted private enterprise in industry and trade, and allowed the peasants to dispose of their produce freely after payment of a tax in kind.

Throughout the NEP period, the Supreme Council of the National Economy directed the operations of the state sector of industry, working through its own industrial and functional subdivisions, and also through republican and provincial economic *sovnarkhozy* (councils). Above it, co-ordinating economic and military policy, was the *Sovet Truda i Oborony* (Council of Labour and Defence), which in one sense was a committee of the Council of People's Commissars (i.e. of the cabinet), but which issued decrees in its own name and could be regarded as being

350

a part of the highest organs of government. In 1921 Gosplan – the State Planning Commission – was created, which eventually became a key element in Soviet planning, but which at first was a somewhat academic advisory body, serving the Council of People's Commissars and more especially the Council of Labour and Defence. However, there was not yet any pretence that a planning *system* had been established, even within the state sector. Enterprises (i.e. factories, mines, etc.) were, as a rule, grouped into 'trusts', and the trust management had considerable financial and planning independence.

In agriculture the private sector was overwhelmingly predominant at this period. The People's Commissariat for Agriculture did its rather ineffective best to encourage proper agricultural practices and kept a watch on undesirable manifestations of 'capitalism' in the villages, i.e. the excessive growth of so-called *kulaks*. It also fostered the small and weak *kolkhozy* (collective farms), of which several varieties existed in the 1920s but which touched only a tiny proportion of peasant households.

THE STALIN SYSTEM

INDUSTRY

The genesis of the present economic structure must be seen in the ending of NEP in 1928–9. Private enterprise was squeezed out of existence. From then on, the employment of any persons by any private individual for gain, or the earning of a living through trade (save as an employee of the state or a legally recognized co-operative) became illegal. The Soviet regime launched its 'revolution from above', with great new industrial investments and the collectivization of agriculture. This vast effort to lift the nation up by its own bootstraps called for centralized planning of a totally new kind, and set off a whole series of changes in the structure of the economy. (It also led to terror, cruelties, and famine, but that is another story.) The Supreme Council of National Economy was unable to cope with the rapidly growing industries and was abolished in 1932. In its place arose three industrial people's commissariats: for heavy industry, light industry, and for the timber industry; these now controlled all enterprises of all-union significance. Gradually the trusts were either eliminated or reduced in importance, and enterprises acquired the financial and legal position that they now have – a legal personality and their own separate financial accounts, with the right and duty to enter into contracts, to fulfil the plans and orders received from above. In 1931 the State Bank acquired a monopoly of credit, and it was no longer possible for subordinate units of the economy to bypass financial controls by extending credit to one another. At the centre, Gosplan became the co-ordinator-in-chief, under the Council of People's Commissars and the Council of Labour and Defence. The latter was supplanted in 1937 by the 'Economic Council', which was abolished during the war.

Gradually, the number of industrial people's commissariats increased, as groups of industries became too complex to manage as one. By 1939 there were twenty-one of them (e.g. for the textile industry, ferrous metallurgy, etc.). Their numbers and designations varied from year to year, and in 1946 they, along with all other commissariats, became known as 'ministries'. In 1946-8 the number of industrial ministries reached its maximum so far – thirty-two – and the system established at the end of the 1930s lasted in essentials until 1957 (changes during the war and during the immediate aftermath of Stalin's death were followed by a return to the *status quo*). All industrial enterprises of significance were subordinated to a *glavk* (main administration) in an appropriate ministry. Smaller enterprises were sometimes dealt with by an individual republic's ministry, but in most cases this ministry was itself under the command of an identically named one at the all-union level. Powers of appointment and dismissal of management, the confirmation of output and financial plans, and all powers of operational control belonged to the appropriate ministry.[1] The task of Gosplan was to ensure consistency of the separate ministerial 'empires', to plan the general development of the economy, and to allocate the most important commodities among the different areas, ministries, and uses.

AGRICULTURE

One had and has in Soviet agriculture three distinct property forms: collective farms, state farms, and the private sector. Individual peasants, i.e. independent cultivators, were virtually eliminated in the early 1930s, and peasants in territories acquired in 1939-40 were collectivized during 1948-50. However, collectivized peasants and other village inhabitants, and also many town-dwellers, were allowed a small plot of land and the right to keep a limited number of animals, which grazed on collective or state pastures. These part-time 'auxiliary' private holdings were the source of a large part of the peasants' money income and of over half the total output of livestock products and potatoes until the most recent years. This private sector was not provided with any modern implements or machinery. The produce belonged to the peasant household, and, subject to meeting a quota of compulsory deliveries to the state (until 1958), the household could either use it themselves or sell it on a tolerated

---

[1] But note the role of the Party, page 356. There were also some small workshops controlled by local soviets and also producers' co-operatives.

free market at free market prices. This limited and part-time private agriculture has been, for the past thirty years, by far the biggest form of private enterprise in the Soviet Union, and the market in which peasant surpluses are sold has represented by far the largest authorized form of private trade. (Note, however, that the peasants may only sell *their own* produce; if they wish to sell through intermediates, they must use the state's own or the state-controlled 'co-operative' sales network.)

Collective farms were established on a mass scale in 1930–4, largely by force or by threats. They were and are legally co-operatives, cultivating state-owned land, rent free, in perpetuity. They were set up with the aim of ensuring that the state obtained the foodstuffs and raw materials required for its needs and for industrialization at minimum cost to itself. Deliveries to the state became 'the first commandment' – the state took its share at very low prices, while the peasants were residuary legatees; this meant that they were given neither wages nor any minimum payment or prescribed share of revenues or produce. The peasants divided up the money and produce that was left after other needs were met, in proportion to the quantity and quality of their work. This was measured in *trudodni* ('labour-days', or, better, workday units), in terms of which all work was rated. The value of each such unit was not known in advance, and varied greatly from place to place and from year to year. The average was very low during the Stalin period, and particularly after the end of the war. Some farms distributed no cash at all to their members for years on end.[2]

Collective farm management was nominally in the hands of an elected committee with an elected chairman. However, the Communist Party effectively appointed and removed the chairmen. Partly because of the need for control and supervision, partly because of a real shortage of skilled mechanics and workshops, farm machinery (tractors, combines, etc.) was concentrated in the hands of a state agency, the Machine and Tractor Station (MTS), which combined the functions of a machine hiring agency and political–economic supervision. The farms paid for the services of the MTS almost wholly in kind.

State farms are state agricultural enterprises with their own farm machinery. They have shared the characteristics of similar enterprises, paying wages to the workers, having appointed managers, profit-and-loss accounting, and subsidies to cover losses. This was a disadvantage from the point of view of the state, since it was liable to cover any financial deficiency that could arise from paying low prices for deliveries of produce. Therefore, until after Stalin's death, collective farms predominated; in 1952 the total sown area of the USSR was divided as follows:

[2] Khrushchev, *Pravda*, 7 March 1964.

	Millions of hectares[3]
Collective farms	130.6
State farms	17.9
Privately cultivated	5.9

The existence of these different categories of producers led to complications in the structure of planning and control. The actual task of imposing collectivization was placed under the Ministry (then People's Commissariat) of Agriculture, with a central *Kolkhoztsentr* (collective farm administration), later renamed 'Committee for *Kolkhoz* affairs', to supervise collectives. (This was liquidated, revived in 1946, and then again liquidated.) At first the state farms were placed under the same people's commissariat as were collectives, but from 1932 until 1959 (with a short break in 1953) they were under a separate people's commissariat of their own, with its own plans, its own supply arrangements, its own local organs of control. The planning of collective farm production, and also control over the MTS, remained the province of the Ministry of Agriculture. A committee of procurements handled the acquisition of produce from the farms. Because prices were so unattractive, it was deemed necessary to substitute detailed orders for the non-existent incentives. After Stalin's death in 1953, prices were substantially improved, and in 1955 it was decreed that, subject to meeting the delivery quotas, farms were to be free to decide their own production pattern. But the habits of administrative interference survived (a decree discouraging such interference, however, was issued in March 1964).

OTHER SECTORS

Other sectors of the economy can be dealt with more briefly. Transport was and is wholly state run (save the lorries and carts owned by collective farms), though a few individuals do have horses and some owners of private cars run illegal taxi services. The Ministry of Transport has at various times been divided: for example, in some years there have been ministries of automobile transport, seagoing fleet, and river fleet; the Ministry of Transport proper in such years dealt principally with the railways. Nationalized transport undertakings are a commonplace in western Europe, and the Soviet system provides little that is new and unfamiliar in this particular field.

The building industry under Stalin was either in the hands of enterprises created *ad hoc* for some particular project, or run by specialized

---

[3] 1 hectare=2.54 acres. The total of 'state farms' in the table includes many thousands of small auxiliary farms operated by non-agricultural state enterprises (e.g. to supply their own works' canteens), and these add yet another category to the list.

enterprises scattered among the various commissariats. For example, there were building organizations within the Ministry of Coal Mines, which built not only for that ministry but also did work on contract for other ministries, such as building schools and hospitals. There was also a Ministry of Construction, with building enterprises under its control, and some large cities had (and still have) general service construction trusts (e.g. *Lenstroy* in Leningrad). The common problems of the building industry were, from 1950, under the general supervision of *Gosstroy*, the State Committee on Construction, and from 1954 to 1957 a number of construction administrations within industrial ministries (e.g. the electric power, coal, and oil industries) were 'promoted' to separate ministerial status.

Retail trade was, throughout the Stalin period, the primary responsibility of a centralized ministry. Wholesaling of consumer goods was shared between this ministry and the disposals departments of the industrial ministries that manufactured the goods in question. The retail trade network was divided after 1935 between urban ('state') and rural ('co-operative') areas and separately administered at all levels. *Tsentrosoyuz*, the central organization of rural co-operatives, also sold materials and equipment to collective farms. The various offices responsible for supplying state enterprises formed a quite separate system of 'material supplies'.

Trade unions lost such independence as they ever possessed in the early 1930s, and, at any rate under Stalin, remained junior auxiliaries of the Party's economic policy. Their function has been to administer social insurance and help to decide labour disputes at enterprise level, on the basis of government rules and decrees. Wage rates are decided in principle by the government, which, with the participation of top trade-union officials, grades each job and decides on the basic pay for each grade and also determines the salaries of all white-collar workers and officials. Except in the period 1940–56, workers have been free to change their occupation, and consequently supply and demand considerations greatly influence actual pay; this can differ considerably from the basic rate, as it is 'adapted' by management by manoeuvring with piece-rates and bonus schemes. Since 1956, the State Committee on Labour and Wages has had supervisory functions over labour questions, a responsibility dealt with between 1934 and 1956 by the Trade Union Central Council.

The structure outlined above is complicated by the federal organization of the Soviet state. However ephemeral the independence of the various republics of the USSR, some decisions about the economy over the years have been taken in the republican capitals. But the Stalin period was essentially one of strict centralization, top priority for the objectives being decided in Moscow. Republican and other local authorities dealt, as a rule, with minor matters, with small factories and workshops using locally procured materials, or with adapting central orders to the circumstances of the given locality.

The structure is further complicated by the role of the Communist Party. Basic economic policies, as other policies, were and still are decided by the Party leadership, and it is the job of the government to implement Party policy. But the Party does more than merely issue general instructions about general aims; its Central Committee contains economics departments, and it can and does issue binding orders on any topic, bypassing the relevant governmental agency – including, where necessary, the Council of Ministers itself. Some state agencies, notably Gosplan, appear to report directly to the Central Committee and receive instructions from it. In republics, provinces, cities, and rural districts, the first secretary of the Party is the boss, and this includes control over such economic decisions as are taken on his territorial level. Of course, there are limits to the interference of local Party officials: obviously, they cannot countermand a Central Committee planner's order, since this usually reflects the central Party line. However in some spheres, notably in agriculture, the local Party official plays a key role in the mechanism of economic command and control. One weapon in the hands of the Party is the elaborate system of *nomenklatura*, or appointment control: no economic post of any importance, from factory director to minister, can be filled save by a person either nominated or approved by an appropriate Party committee, and the withdrawal of Party confidence equals dismissal. This is true regardless of which state body is formally responsible for appointing or dismissing the economic official in question. The official himself is, at least in recent years, almost invariably a Party member, and is subject to Party discipline. There are also Party groups within enterprises, offices, and ministries, whose duties include checking and inspection, but these seem to have only modest powers in practice.

During the latter part of Stalin's rule, several senior Party leaders played the role of 'overlords', controlling a group of ministries and having the rank of 'deputy premiers'. The economic ministers were gradually relegated to purely technical–executive rather than political functions, and this is still the case today. (It is as if the head of the National Coal Board in Great Britain were a minister.) In a one-party state, it is clearly unnecessary to have both a permanent *and* a political head of a nationalized industry. In the early years of Soviet power, a Party man with little technical knowledge was often in charge of politically unreliable technical experts. This has not been the case for many years; though various kinds of supervision by Party and other organs

356

continue, the head of a department or ministry, as of an enterprise, is now normally a specialist in managing or otherwise running that particular kind of activity. To describe him as a 'politician' in the western sense would be to misunderstand his position.

Banking was and is a state monopoly. Banks act as inspector-controllers of financial enterprises, and are instructed to refuse to honour cheques which do not accord with official plans or price regulations. Foreign trade has also been a state monopoly from the start, controlled by the Ministry of Foreign Trade, which acts through *vneshnetorgovyye obyedineniya* (specialized foreign trade corporations). State enterprises cannot enter into direct commercial relations with any customer or supplier outside the USSR, but must make application through the proper channels, and the deal, if authorized, will form part of the centralized production, supply, and foreign trade plan. It will be incorporated (especially if the deal is with another communist country) in the list of goods to be exchanged between the countries in that year.

Table 1	*Roubles to the US dollar*		
1925–32	1.94	1950	4.00
1933	1.57	1961	0.90
1934	1.16	1971	0.90
1935	1.15	1972	0.82
1936	5.03	1973	0.725
1937–49	5.30	1974	0.746

In terms of currency and finance, the Soviet rouble underwent a drastic inflation and lost virtually all value by 1923. At this date it was stabilized at a new rate of 1.99 roubles to US $1. Since then, its nominal value has been as set out in Table 1. (After 1961, 'new' roubles were worth 10 old roubles internally.) However, one must always distinguish between the internal and external value of the rouble. The latter is purely nominal, in the sense that roubles cannot be bought and sold freely (save for a few limited purposes, such as diplomatic expenditures and tourist 'incidentals'), and the official rate has been little more than a method of accounting used in foreign trade statistics, which has no necessary connection with internal prices. Save in the limited free market, prices within the USSR are fixed by the government. In the Stalin period, the practice was to fix prices of basic industrial materials and fuels as low as possible, and a number of industries (e.g. coal, timber) operated for many years at a loss. The bulk of state revenue was derived from turnover tax on foodstuffs and consumer goods (income taxes were and are very low), and so retail prices were very much higher than the prices charged by state enterprises to transfer goods to one another, relative to production costs.

As must be the case in a country where the bulk of economic activity is conducted by state enterprises, the Soviet budget is closely related to the overall economic plan, and a higher proportion of the national income 'passes through' the state budget than is the case in any western 'capitalist' country. Expenditures include the bulk of investment financing, which was and is made in the form of outright grants, at least within the state sector (collective farms finance their own investments, or borrow from the State Bank and have to pay interest on the loan).

A CENTRALIZED, COMMAND ECONOMY

Stalin's methods of ensuring rapid industrial growth involved stern centralization. Many urgent needs were sacrificed to the build-up of heavy industry, and the central authorities imposed these priorities by denying local officials any effective say over the disposal of resources. As Stalin pointed out in his last published work, *Economic Problems of Socialism*, the priority given to heavy industry could not be justified by the criterion of short-term profitability: of course, he said, consumer goods industries would yield a higher rate of return than steel; yet it was self-evident that investments 'had' to be devoted to steel. For this reason, and also because of an ideological prejudice against the profit motive and for administrative allocation of resources, neither the planners nor the subordinate units of the economy were guided by market or price considerations. Indeed, prices were something changed deliberately to make a given economic policy *appear* profitable. The essential task was to fulfil the plan, this being expressed wherever possible in quantitative terms. The central planners made 'material balances' for the year and for a longer period, with the expected supply on one side and the anticipated utilization requirements of a long list of commodities on the other. They sought to achieve balance – by expanding output, or reducing consumption, or drawing on reserves, or by way of foreign trade. A consolidated and consistent plan, once approved, became mandatory for all subordinate administrators and managers. This was, and still is, a system which merits the description of 'a command economy'; one based, in the words of Kosygin at the 24th Party Congress (1971), on the principle of 'directive planning'. The dominant criterion for all but the topmost leadership has always been obedience to instructions, conveyed in the form of plans.

This does not mean that material inducements are unimportant in the Soviet system. On the contrary, both at managerial level and in the factory they are very important indeed. But the bonuses of management were and are paid to reward plan fulfilment, i.e. for obedience to instructions given. Nor does a 'command economy' imply that the centre ever could or did issue orders covering all circumstances and every eventuality. This would be as impossible as it would be to imagine a code of laws that covered every conceivable case. As the Soviet economy grew in size and complexity, the possibility of deciding everything centrally became ever more remote. But the centre had the power to decide in every individual instance, and the subordinate units take their decisions by reference to central orders, sometimes distorting them in the process. Thus if the planners indicated a planned target for an area or an enterprise that required 200,000 tons of 'metal goods' or 200,000 square metres of 'wool cloth', the men on the spot would tend to produce a variety of metal or cloth products that added up to the required quantity – which only by coincidence could represent the kinds of metal goods or wool cloth actually required by the consumers. A further problem in the Soviet planned economy has been that of unintended inconsistencies, arising from the sheer magnitude of the planners' tasks. Each enterprise of any significance had to be told what to produce, to whom to deliver its products, from whom to receive its raw materials; and its plan indicators had to be decided not only for output but also for costs, investments, wages, labour productivity, material utilization norms, and so on. This task had to be divided among a large number of different plan offices, and it was impossible to ensure complete consistency, especially as plans frequently have to be amended. This has meant that subordinate organs and enterprise management have often had to choose which instructions to obey and which not. The planners also unavoidably depend to a considerable extent on the information supplied to them by businesses, and managers thus have considerable *de facto* influence on the planning process. These very real difficulties of organization have led, especially in recent years, to repeated and confusing changes in the structure of planning.

The Soviet *direktor* (enterprise manager) bears the same sort of relation to his superiors in the planning hierarchy as does a plant manager of a large western corporation to his board of directors. Neither of these men is a capitalist; both are salaried employees, subject to orders from above on any topic. The difference is that the equivalent in the USSR of the managing director of, for example, Imperial Chemical Industries in Britain would have ministerial rank in the Soviet Union.

THE KHRUSHCHEV PERIOD

After a year in which an important role was played by Malenkov, Khrushchev emerged as the dominant character in the first post-Stalin years, and the organizational restructuring of the economy bore the imprint of his ideas and personality. Khrushchev was aware of the inflexibilities and inefficiencies of the system he inherited and tried to set matters right, though he sometimes was unable to identify the real causes of the troubles he was seeking to remedy, and occasionally made the situation worse. At first his agricultural policies showed good results. A series of price increases greatly improved collective farm finances, and therefore both investment and present incomes increased. So did the relative importance of state farms, partly through the setting up of new farms in newly cultivated lands in Asia, partly through the conversion of some collective farms to state farms.[4] The artificial division between the collectives and the machinery they used was eliminated in 1958 by the abolition of the MTS and the sale of the equipment to the farm. However, after 1958 the gap between ambition and agricultural reality increased, and Khrushchev sought to cope with the problems that faced him by repeated reorganization. He strengthened the Party and gravely weakened the Ministry of Agriculture, until the latter became responsible for little more than running advice bureaux. Various state committees were set up with powers over procurement, equipment, and the like. In 1962 an elaborate new hierarchy of agricultural committees was announced, but appears not to have functioned, largely through the obstruction of local officials. Khrushchev even tried to divide the Party itself into agricultural and non-agricultural units. Various ambitious schemes mounted largely through Party channels (e.g. to grow more maize or to overtake the US in meat production within three years) proved disorganizing and counter-productive, as well as interfering with necessary farm autonomy. The farms themselves had been growing steadily in size since 1950 and became difficult to manage: there are serious diseconomies of scale under Soviet conditions.

In industry Khrushchev at first toyed with the idea of increasing managerial autonomy. Then, convinced that ministerial industrial 'empires' stood in the way of proper co-ordination, and also in pursuit of political objectives, he abolished industrial ministries altogether, preferring to base industrial planning on regions. Therefore in 1957 he set up over one hundred *sovnarkhozy* (regional economic councils); their precise number varied and was subsequently reduced by amalgamation to forty-seven. The various industrial enterprises were in theory subordinate to these regional councils. It was claimed that coherent regional planning was thereby facilitated. Within this system the individual union republics exercised a significant role in supervising the plans of 'their' *sovnarkhozy*. In Khrushchev's conception regional plans were to be co-ordinated by Gosplan. However, it is clear that he underestimated the

[4] By 1970, state farms were cultivating more land than were the collectives.

importance and necessity of all-union control under a command economy system in which only the centre has the necessary information to identify needs and to take the necessary production and allocation decisions. It therefore proved necessary to recreate a number of central bodies, most with the designation of State Committees, some covering particular industrial sectors (e.g. State Committee on the Chemical Industry) and some of a more general co-ordinating nature. These various agencies proliferated, until by 1963 it was necessary to co-ordinate the co-ordinators through the State Council for the National Economy. State committees were distinguished from ministries by having no powers to issue direct instructions. It all became bewilderingly complex and illogical. It may be confidently asserted that economic officialdom rejoiced at the fall of Khrushchev in 1964.

STRUCTURE OF THE ECONOMY UNDER BREZHNEV AND KOSYGIN

Khrushchev's successors speedily abandoned these organizational experiments. The Party was reunited and the Ministry of Agriculture restored, as were the functions of local agricultural planning organs (the role of the Party in agriculture remained large, but this had been so ever since collectivization). The *sovnarkhozy* were abandoned and economic ministries re-established (see Table 2). In the process the role of central all-union ministries became actually greater than it had been in the years immediately prior to the setting up of the *sovnarkhozy*, and there is no doubt that the union republics have emerged from the change with fewer economic functions.

In agriculture there was a further increase in prices, incomes, and investment, and the *trudodni* system of paying peasants in collectives was replaced by a guaranteed cash minimum method. There is now not much difference between collective and state farms in this respect, in that both pay what amounts to wages and pay the same prices to the same supply agencies for their raw materials. The important difference is that collectives remain in law co-operatives with elected managements, while state farms are state enterprises with appointed managements. In practice both remain supervised by state and Party organs, and compulsory deliveries to the state have been retained.

The industrial structure was supposed to have been modified by the adoption of economic reform proposals in 1965. Much was said about the importance of profits, of enterprise autonomy, of the gradual replacement of administrative allocation of resources by wholesale trade (i.e. enterprises would be freer to buy from each other and make plans

---

Table 2 *Economic Ministries of the* USSR

Council of Ministers

Chairman	A. N. Kosygin
Deputy Chairman, Chairman of Gosplan	N. K. Baybakov
Deputy Chairman, Chairman of Gossnab (State Committee for Material-Technical Supply)	V. E. Dymshits
Deputy Chairman, Chairman of State Committee for Science and Technology	V. A. Kirillin
Deputy Chairman, Chairman of Gosstroy (State Committee for Construction)	I. T. Novikov

Ministries

Aviation Industry
Motor Industry
Foreign Trade
Gas Industry
Civil Aviation
Engineering
Engineering for light and food industries and service equipment
Medical Industry
Merchant Marine
Oil Industry
Defence Industry
General Engineering
Instrument-making, Automation and Control Systems
Means of Communication
Radio Industry
Medium Engineering
Machine Tool and Instrument Industry
Construction, Road and Communal Engineering
Shipbuilding Industry
Tractor and Agricultural Machinery
Transport Construction
Heavy, Power, and Transport Engineering
Chemical and Oil Engineering
Chemical Industry

Cellulose-paper Industry
Electronic Industry
Electro-technical Industry
Light Industry
Timber and Wood Processing Industry
Land Improvement and Water Installation and Special Construction Work
Meat and Dairy Industry
Oil-processing and Petrochemical Industry
Food Industry
Industrial Construction
Building Materials Industry
Fisheries
Post and Telecommunications
Agricultural Construction
Agriculture
Construction
Construction of Heavy Industrial Enterprise
Trade
Coal Industry
Finance
Non-Ferrous Metallurgy
Ferrous Metallurgy
Power and Electrification

Committees

Committee for People's Control
State Committee for Labour and Wages
State Committee on Prices
State Committee for Forestry

State Committee for Foreign Economic Relations
Soyuz sel'khoztekhnika (Agricultural supply organization)
Gosbank
Central Statistical Administration

362

accordingly). It is true that there has been some reduction in the number of compulsory plan indicators, but the reform was modest in conception and has been implemented half-heartedly. The basic principles of the command economy remain untouched. The task of industrial management is still to fulfil plans that specify details of output and customers. The State Committee on Supply, *Gossnab*, together with Gosplan still allocate administratively all important commodities. The profit motive remains of secondary importance. Prices were revised in 1967, but remain inflexible and unresponsive to fluctuations of demand and supply. The one organizational change about which much is spoken is in the direction of creating industrial associations, i.e. grouping or amalgamating enterprises into larger units – a species of Soviet corporations – but this is proceeding rather slowly. There has been much discussion about computerization, but the more far-reaching proposals of the mathematical economists remain on paper, though steps are being taken greatly to increase the output and utilization of computers.

At the 24th Party Congress (March 1971) a new Five-Year Plan was presented and adopted. Much was said about the need for efficiency and for stimulation of technical progress. However, it is clear that the present leadership imagine that this can be achieved within a largely unaltered system, by such methods as tighter discipline, better calculation, and exhortation. Reformers argue that this is not enough, and that greater efficiency would require the adoption of some elements of market socialism, such as have in fact been put into operation in Hungary. It would seem that this view is rejected by the leadership.

GUIDE TO FURTHER READING

The Soviet Economy

The following provide a comprehensive introduction to the subject: A. Nove, *The Soviet Economy: An Introduction*, 2nd rev. edn (London, 1969); M. Kaser, *Soviet Economics* (London, 1970); P. Wiles, *The Political Economy of Communism* (Oxford, 1968); G. Garvy, *Money, Banking and Credit in Eastern Europe* (New York, 1967); E. Strauss, *Soviet Agriculture in Perspective: A Study of its Successes and Failures* (London, 1969); M. Ellman, *Soviet Planning Today: Proposals for an Optimally Functioning Economic System*, University of Cambridge Department of Applied Economics, *Occasional Papers*, no. 25 (Cambridge, 1971); W. Brus, *The Market in a Socialist Economy* (London, 1972); B. Ward, *The Socialist Economy: A Study in Organizational Alternatives* (New York, 1967); and P. Hanson, *The Consumer in the Soviet Economy* (London, 1968).

Also see: M. I. Goldman, *Soviet Marketing* (New York, 1963); P. J. D. Wiles, *Communist International Economics* (Oxford, 1968); E. Ames, *Soviet Economic Processes* (London, 1967); A. Bergson, *The Economics of Soviet Planning* (New Haven, 1964); R. W. Campbell, *Soviet-type Economies* (London, 1974); and

THE SOVIET STATE: THE ECONOMY

P. Gregory and R. C. Stewart, *Soviet Economic Structure and Performance* (New York, 1974).

The system after the Revolution

On the economic history of the period, the following are useful: A. Nove, *Economic History of the USSR* (London, 1968); E. H. Carr, *A History of Soviet Russia: Socialism in One Country*, vol. I (London, 1958); M. Dobb, *Soviet Economic Development since 1917*, 3rd edn (London, 1966); A. Baykov, *The Development of the Soviet Economic System* (Cambridge, 1947); H. Schwartz, *Russia's Soviet Economy* (London, 1966); N. Spulber, *Soviet Strategy of Economic Growth* (Bloomington, 1964); and E. Zaleski, *La Planification de la croissance économique* (Paris, 1962).

On the relation between Marxism and economic theory in the Soviet Union, see H. Chambre, *Le Marxisme en Union Soviétique* (Paris, 1955); T. J. Hoff, *Economic Calculation in the Socialist Society* (London, 1949); O. Lange, *On the Economic Theory of Socialism* (The Hague, 1938); the same author's *Political Economy* (Warsaw, 1963); J. Robinson, *An Essay on Marxist Economics* (London, 1942); J. Schumpeter, *Capitalism, Socialism and Democracy* (London, 1943); and P. J. D. Wiles, 'Scarcity, Marxism and Gosplan', *Oxford Economic Papers*, September 1953.

The Stalin system

For discussions of the economy during the period of Stalin's leadership see N. Jasny, *Soviet Industrialization 1928–1952* (Chicago, 1961); the same author's *Socialized Agriculture in the USSR* (Stanford, 1949); A. Nove, *Was Stalin Really Necessary?* (London, 1964); A. Erlich, *The Soviet Industrialization Debate* (Cambridge, Mass., 1960); N. A. Voznesensky, *The Economy of the USSR During World War Two* (Washington, 1948); J. Chapman, *Real Wages in Soviet Russia Since 1928* (Cambridge, Mass., 1963); R. Moorsteen, *Prices and Production of Machinery in the Soviet Union, 1928–1958* (Cambridge, Mass., 1962); and M. Levin, *Russian Peasants and Soviet Power* (London, 1968).

A centralized, command economy

On some of the problems presented by the Soviet economy, the following articles are helpful: J. M. Montias, 'Planning with Material Balances in Soviet-type Economies', *American Economic Review*, December 1959; and G. Grossman, 'Notes for a Theory of a Command Economy', *Soviet Studies*, October 1963. On material supply the best article is G. Schroeder, 'The reform of the supply system in Soviet industry', *Soviet Studies*, vol. XXIV, no. 1 (July 1972).

On state enterprise and management, see J. Berliner, *Factory and Manager in the USSR* (Cambridge, Mass., 1957); D. Granick, *Management of the Industrial Firm in the USSR* (New York, 1954); J. Kornai, *Overcentralization in Economic Administration* (London, 1959). On Soviet labour, consult S. Schwarz, *Labour in the Soviet Union* (London, 1953); E. C. Brown, *Soviet Trade Unions and Labour Relations* (Cambridge, Mass., 1966); and M. McAuley, *Labour Disputes in Soviet Russia* (Oxford, 1969).

On prices in the Soviet economy, see M. Bornstein, 'The Soviet Price System', *American Economic Review*, March 1967; M. Dobb, 'Soviet Price Policy', *Soviet*

Studies, July 1960; G. Grossman, 'Industrial Prices in the USSR', *American Economic Review*, May 1959; A. Nove, 'The Changing Role of Soviet Prices', *Economics of Planning*, no. 3 (Oslo, 1963); and N. Jasny, *The Soviet Price System* (Stanford, 1951).

On topics related to various sectors of the economic system, see M. Goldman, *Soviet Marketing* (London, 1963); H. Hunter, *Soviet Transportation Policy* (Cambridge, Mass., 1957); M. Kaser, *Comecon*, 2nd edn (London, 1967); F. Pryor, *The Communist Foreign Trade System* (London, 1963); A. G. Korol, *Soviet Education for Science and Technology* (New York, 1957); and N. de Witt, *Soviet Professional Manpower* (Washington, 1955).

The Khrushchev period

The following books and articles deal with the Soviet economy during Khrushchev's years of leadership: H. R. Swearer, 'Agricultural Administration under Khrushchev', in R. D. Laird, ed., *Soviet Agriculture and Peasant Affairs* (Lawrence, 1964); K. Bush, 'Agricultural Reforms Since Khrushchev', in *New Directions in the Soviet Economy* (U.S. Congress, 1967); J. Karcz, 'The New Soviet Agricultural Programme', *Soviet Studies*, October 1965; and A. Balinsky, A. Bergson, J. N. Hazard, and P. Wiles, *Planning and the Market in the USSR – the 1960s* (New Brunswick, N. J., 1967).

10

THE SOVIET UNION AND ITS NEIGHBOURS

HUGH SETON-WATSON

The neighbours of the Russian people have increased in numbers as the Russian state has expanded from the original nucleus of the principality of Moscow, and as means of communication and weapons of war have caused the world to shrink until it can be said that most large states are neighbours of most others. The nature of the relations between the Russians and their neighbours was also profoundly affected by the Bolshevik Revolution, as a result of which Russia became not only a territorial Great Power but the centre of a world-wide revolutionary movement guided by the principles of Marxism–Leninism. Inevitably, at the three distinct levels of official foreign policy, of communist activity, and of contacts between peoples, Russia's relations with neighbouring countries have been more important than its relations with more distant lands. In the following brief survey an attempt has been made to strike a balance between these various factors.

THE RUSSIANS AND NEIGHBOUR NATIONS

The neighbours with whom the Russians have been for longest in contact in Europe are the Baltic peoples in the north-west, the White Russians in the west, the Ukrainians in the south-west, the Roumanians in the south, the Tatars in the south and south-east, and various Finno-Ugrian peoples in the north-east and in the Volga valley.

The origins and extent of the difference between Russians and Ukrainians are still the subject of controversy among historians. There is no doubt that the difference greatly increased after most of Russia came under Tatar, and most of the Ukraine under Lithuanian and Polish rule; but some would claim that great differences existed even before the Mongol invasion. Whether the differences in social and legal institutions, cultural traditions, and spoken language, which distinguished Russians from Ukrainians at the end of the eighteenth century, when nearly all the Ukraine had been incorporated in the Russian Empire, amounted to a difference between two nations is still a matter for argument. By the end of the nineteenth century, however, Ukrainian national consciousness was a fact, though it was not clear how far down the social pyramid it extended. The failure of the Ukrainian nationalists to establish an independent state between 1917 and 1920 led to the incorporation of most of the Ukraine in the Soviet Union. In 1939 those districts of Galicia (Austrian 1772–1918, Polish since 1918) in which a majority of the population was Ukrainian were annexed by the Soviet Union in agreement with the Third Reich. In 1940 a similar fate befell those districts of Bukovina (Austrian 1776–1918, Roumanian since 1919) together with the whole of 'Bessarabia' (eastern Moldavia), in which Ukrainians formed a minority and Roumanians a majority. In 1945 these territories were reconquered by the Soviet Army, and in the same year Sub-Carpathian Ruthenia (Hungarian until 1919, thereafter part of Czechoslovakia), which had a substantial Ukrainian population, was also annexed. Thus the whole Ukrainian nation has been forcibly incorporated in the Soviet Union, and forms the most numerous immediate neighbour of the Russians in Europe.

The three Baltic peoples – Estonians, Latvians, and Lithuanians – were incorporated in the Russian Empire in the eighteenth century; established independent states in 1919; were annexed by the Soviet Union with the consent of the Third Reich in 1940; and were reconquered by the Soviet Union in 1945. The White Russians, a people whose national identity was less pronounced than that of the Ukrainians in the nineteenth century but which undoubtedly increased during the twentieth, lived under Polish rule until the eighteenth-century partitions; were then incorporated in the Russian Empire; were divided in 1921 between Poland and Russia; were recovered by the Soviet Union with the consent of the Third Reich in 1939; and reconquered in 1945. The majority of the population of Bessarabia – the eastern portion of the historical Principality of Moldavia – have long been Roumanians. This territory was, however, annexed by Russia in 1812, and was united with the Roumanian state only between 1918 and 1940.[1] Its annexation by the Soviet Union with the consent of the Third Reich in 1940, and its reconquest in 1945, brought a large Roumanian population into the Russian state. The small group of Finno-Ugrian peoples were brought under Russian rule at various times from the fourteenth century onward,

---

[1] Bessarabia was divided in 1856 following the Crimean War, its southern portion being transferred from Russia to Moldavia (which united with Wallachia in 1859 to form the Roumanian state). This southern portion was ceded to Russia by Roumania under the Treaty of Berlin in 1878.

and still occupy wide areas of the Soviet Union, particularly near the Gulf of Finland, in the Volga region, and on either side of the Ural range, though always intermingled with Russian populations. The Mordvinians, inhabiting extensive areas in the middle Volga region, are the third largest group of Finno-Ugrian people in the world, numbering over a million and a quarter. The Tatars, who once ruled most of European Russia, were reduced by the early twentieth century to smaller but substantial communities in the Ural area, in the middle and lower Volga valley, and in the Crimea. The Crimean Tatars were deported from their homeland in 1944 as a punishment for alleged collaboration with the German invaders in the Second World War. As of 1975 they had still not been allowed to return, though many of the survivors, living in Central Asia, agitated publicly for this right, and were assisted by a brave Russian, the former Soviet Army General Grigorenko. The Volga and Ural Tatars remain in substantial numbers in their old homelands.

The expansion of Russia eastward, from the sixteenth century onward, led to the conquest and incorporation in the Russian Empire of many smaller groups of Asian peoples. In the Caucasian regions this included a variety of small Moslem groups; about half the Turkish-speaking Shiite Azerbaijanis, divided since 1828 between Russia and Persia; the Christian Georgians; and a portion of the Armenian people, in territory annexed from Persia in 1828. Between 1918 and 1921 the three independent states of Georgia, Armenia, and Azerbaijan were established, but they were reconquered by the Soviet Union with the consent of their southern neighbour Turkey. In Central Asia a number of principalities with Moslem inhabitants, of varying degrees of Turkic speech and Persian culture, were annexed by Russia in the mid nineteenth century. Such efforts as they made to win independence after 1917 were crushed by the Bolshevik government. In the Far East Russian expansion brought numbers of Buddhist Mongols under Russian rule, and in the Far Northeast miscellaneous Eskimo or other Arctic tribes became Russian subjects. The annexation of south Sakhalin and the Kurile Islands in 1945 brought some thousands of Japanese into the Soviet Union.

Thus the Soviet Union, like its predecessor the Russian Empire, was inhabited around its land frontiers by non-Russians. It is only in the two ports of Leningrad and Vladivostok, and in the former German city of Königsberg (annexed in ruins from Germany in 1945, repopulated with Russians, and renamed Kaliningrad) that the Russians are in direct contact with the outer world. In the most literal and narrowest sense, the only neighbours of the Russians are the nations which they have conquered.

If we now consider not nations but states, we find that the neighbours of the Russian Empire for many centuries were Sweden, Poland, and

Turkey. The partitions of Poland made Russia the neighbour of Austria and Prussia. The disintegration of the Ottoman Empire made Roumania a neighbour by land and Bulgaria one by sea. In 1918 the three Baltic states, Finland, and Poland were added to the European neighbours of the Soviet Union. By 1945 the first three had been removed, but Czechoslovakia and Hungary had been added. In Asia both Persia and China, with which contact had been made in the seventeenth century, became important neighbours in the nineteenth, as the economic and strategic importance of both countries to Russia increased. In the mid nineteenth century relations were established with Japan, a neighbour by sea and, after the division of Sakhalin in 1905, by land. From the end of the eighteenth century until 1867, the Russian Empire extended to the North American continent, and was a potential neighbour at various times, in a vast but ill-defined area, of British Canada, the Spanish Empire, Mexico, and the United States. The conquest of Central Asia in the mid nineteenth century brought the Russian Empire into direct contact with Afghanistan, and thus into proximity with British India. The replacement of British rule by the two independent states of India and Pakistan did not increase the number of direct neighbours (both countries are separated from the USSR by Afghan or Chinese territory), but enormously affected the real interests of the Soviet Union in Asia. Mongolia, which became in effect a Russian protectorate in 1914, was transformed in the 1920s into a client state of the Soviet Union, ruled by a Mongolian government controlled by the Communist Party of the Soviet Union.

Since 1945 the Soviet Union has been one of the world's two 'super-powers', concerned with events in every part of the world, eager and able to make itself felt. Thus the whole world is the neighbour of the Soviet Union. This statement is supported by three considerations: the immense industrial and military strength of the USSR; its continued interest in world-wide communist activities; and the fact that, with the development of inter-continental ballistic missiles with nuclear warheads, no power, not even the Soviet Union, can be completely secure as long as even one state independent of its control and possessing these weapons exists in any part of the world. Nevertheless, the affairs of the countries situated nearest to the Soviet Union inevitably bulk largest in Soviet foreign policy, and even more distant Russian historical experience of these countries inevitably influences Soviet attitudes to foreign policy on a world scale. The areas of special importance to the Soviet Union can conveniently be divided into three groups: eastern Europe and Germany; the Middle East; and eastern and southern Asia. Each of these will be considered in turn, but it will first be necessary briefly to survey the main phases in Soviet foreign policy since 1917.

369

PERIODS OF SOVIET FOREIGN POLICY

The first period (1917–23) was one of revolutionary illusions and struggle for survival. The Bolsheviks were fully engaged in three years of civil war followed by an economic crisis and a dangerous cleavage within their own ranks. Meanwhile hopes of revolution in Finland, Poland, Hungary, the Balkans, and above all Germany were disappointed. Capitalist Europe recovered from the aftermath of war, and the rulers of the revolutionary republic had to establish diplomatic relations with states that they regarded as enemies but were not strong enough to destroy.

The second period (1923–35) was one of caution in Europe and of unsuccessful revolution in the Far East. Stalin, who rose to supreme power in the first years of this period, was occupied first with the defeat of his political rivals, then with the destruction of an independent peasantry and the launching of his First Five-Year Plan of forced rapid industrialization. In Europe his main concern was to exploit the conflict of interest between Germany and her victors. In Asia great hopes were placed in the revolutionary movement in China, but this ended in 1927 with crippling defeats for the communists at the hands of General Chiang Kai-shek. The rise to power of Hitler's National Socialists in Germany was indirectly aided by Soviet foreign policy, whose makers regarded the Social Democrats as their main enemy.

The third period, that of the 'Popular Front', was introduced when the Soviet leaders became convinced that Hitler was a more dangerous enemy than were the western powers. At the doctrinal level the new policy was formulated by the Communist International (Comintern) at its Seventh Congress, in 1935, as an alliance of all democratic forces against Fascism: at the diplomatic level it was expressed in the efforts of the Soviet government to establish good relations with the western powers. At first it had some success, symbolized by the Franco–Soviet and Soviet–Czechoslovak alliances and by the advent of Popular Front governments in France and Spain in 1936. However, the outbreak of the Spanish Civil War led to a revival of ideological fanaticism, right and left, throughout Europe, and this was cleverly exploited by Hitler and Mussolini. The Munich agreement of 1938 marked the failure of the Popular Front in Europe. In the Far East Soviet policy vacillated between appeasement of the Japanese invaders of Manchuria and support of the Chinese government. A limited agreement between Chiang Kai-shek and the Chinese communists, essentially an application of the Popular Front in the Far East, was strengthened as a result of the Japanese invasion of China, which began in 1937. Soviet policy now inclined more substantially toward China.

370

The fourth period (1939–41) was initiated by the Soviet–German pact of 23 August 1939. This was in part a reaction against the western powers' contemptuous treatment of Soviet interests at Munich, and in part an attempt to avoid involvement in a major war. But it was also an offensive alliance, and it led to the annexation by the Soviet Union of eastern Poland, the Baltic states, and portions of Finland and Roumania. The alliance with Hitler was complemented by an agreement in 1941 with Japan: the first directed German aggression against western Europe, the second directed Japanese aggression against the possessions of the western maritime powers in the Far East. This period ended when Hitler invaded the Soviet Union, though the agreement with Japan lasted until 1945.

The fifth period (1941–6) was that of the 'Grand Alliance' in the Second World War. At first the Soviet armies suffered terrible losses, but when the tide of war turned, Soviet foreign policy achieved enormous successes. The western powers were extremely unwilling to oppose Soviet wishes, and accepted in effect the control by the Soviet Union of eastern and central Europe, which the Soviet armies entered in the last stages of the war. Soviet policies in these countries, especially in Poland, caused resentment in the US and Britain, but no practical steps were taken by either government to prevent them. A few days before the surrender of Japan the Soviet Army entered Manchuria. North Korea was occupied by Soviet troops, and south Sakhalin and the Kurile Islands were annexed to the Soviet Union.

The sixth period began with the breakdown of co-operation between the Soviet Union and the western powers, which was fairly complete by 1946. From this time until the death of Stalin in 1953, two hostile blocs faced each other along a line that was more or less recognized by both sides. Stalin's attitude was invincibly hostile, but it was also cautious. In 1946 Soviet troops were withdrawn from north-western Iran, and the plan which seemed to be in operation for the annexation of Persian Azerbaijan to the Soviet Union was abandoned. In February 1948 the communists seized power in Czechoslovakia, but when they were defeated in Finland a few months later the Soviet government took no action to help them. The Berlin blockade was abandoned in May 1949 after a year's 'airlift' from the West had proved able to keep the city supplied. The attempt to coerce Yugoslavia into submission to Stalin's will in 1948 was a complete failure, and Stalin did not risk the use of force to achieve his aim. The invasion of southern Korea in July 1950 was presumably approved by Stalin, but the Soviet government never allowed itself to be directly involved.

A seventh discernible period of Soviet foreign policy began with the death of Stalin in March 1953. The hostile blocs continued to exist, but the new rulers showed less caution in two directions. In eastern Europe they pressed for more liberal policies by the communist governments. In 1956 matters got out of control in both Poland and Hungary; Soviet forces invaded Hungary to destroy the revolutionary regime, but a satisfactory bargain was struck between the Soviet and Polish leaders. In the following years all the countries of eastern Europe underwent varying degrees of political and economic evolution, and a looser but mutually acceptable relationship was achieved between their governments and the Soviet Union. The other direction in which experiments were tried was toward the 'Third World' – as the continents of Asia, Africa, and South America came to be called during these years. Whereas Stalin had shown no interest in these countries, Khrushchev became deeply involved in them. Soviet influence was strengthened by vigorous diplomacy, by frequent journeys of Soviet leaders, and by increasing – if comparatively small – Soviet financial contributions to their economic projects and their military establishments. It was also helped by the growing unpopularity of the western powers, due not only to their actions in Egypt and the Congo, or to the policies of white minorities in South Africa, but also to deeper resentments of longer standing, which Soviet policy did its best to exploit.

An eighth period began around 1960, when it became unmistakably clear that there was profound hostility, due to a number of causes, between the Soviet Union and China. Sino–Soviet hostility deeply affected the political situation in all parts of the world, and in particular the Soviet Union's relations with eastern Europe, with India, and with the United States. By 1974 it was clear that the Soviet Union's main enemy was China, not the US. Whether one should reckon that yet another period in Soviet policy was introduced by the Chinese–American *rapprochement* of 1972, symbolized by President Nixon's visit to China, it is too early to say. Another plausible view would be that a ninth period of Soviet foreign policy was introduced by the American–Soviet confrontation in Cuba in October 1962, which appeared to produce serious new thinking in the Soviet Union about the nature of the Soviet–American relationship.

GERMANY AND EASTERN EUROPE

Relations with Germany were the key to Soviet policy in Europe from 1917 onward. The strange love–hate relationship between German and Russian culture, immensely complicated, goes back at least two centuries.[2] In the nineteenth century an important factor in Russia's relations

[2] For an unusually sensitive modern study of this relationship, see Walter Laqueur. *Russia and Germany: A Century of Conflict* (London, 1965).

with Prussia, which later became the German Empire, was a common interest in the repression of Polish aspirations to national independence.[3] Nevertheless the conflicting aims of German and Russian imperialism, backed by the ideological passions of Pan-Germanism and Russo-Panslavism, brought the two empires into conflict and led them to a common ruin. In the 1920s defeated Germany and Bolshevik Russia, the two outcasts from the respectable society of the European states, were united in at least a negative solidarity, which found expression in the Rapallo Treaty of 1922, whose political importance diplomatic historians have tended to overrate. More important was the secret co-operation between the German and Soviet military general staffs: in return for some valuable German expert advice to its young army, the Soviet government gave the Germans an opportunity to evade the disarmament provisions of the 1919 peace settlement by trying out weapons on Soviet soil.

The Soviet government in the 1920s was haunted by the fear that all 'capitalist' governments must inevitably tend to combine in order to attack the Soviet republic. It was therefore essential for Soviet diplomacy to maintain the breach between Germany and the western powers, and to give at least moral support to any German opposition to French or British demands. The advent of Stresemann to power in 1923, and the adoption of a policy of co-operation with the West, was a blow to Soviet diplomacy. The Locarno Treaty of 1925 was interpreted in Moscow as a preparation for a common onslaught on the Soviet Union. The German Social Democrats, with their preference for the western democracies, were considered to be dangerous enemies of the Soviet Union and tools of 'imperialism'. The advent to power of Hitler, who was unquestionably determined to undo the 1919 peace settlement, was viewed with equanimity, if not with actual satisfaction, by the Soviet leaders. Only in 1934, when Hitler sought the co-operation of Poland and began to talk of Germany's need for the natural wealth of the Ukraine, did Stalin change his course, and seek an alliance with the West against the Third Reich. This policy suffered a fatal reverse at Munich. In 1939 Stalin moved once more toward co-operation with Hitler. The agreement of August 1939 led to the fifth partition of Poland.[4] For nearly two years the two totalitarian regimes co-operated. However, it proved impossible to settle amicably the conflicting interests arising from Hitler's domination of central Europe and the Balkans, and Hitler also had both economic and ideological reasons for attacking Russia. The German–Soviet war began, without formal declaration, on 22 June 1941.

[3] This common hostility to the Poles was shared at times by Austria, the third power that had participated in the eighteenth-century partitions of Poland. But after 1867 Austria treated her Polish subjects with tact, and the solidarity with Russia in this matter came to an end.

[4] The first four were in 1772, 1793, 1795, and 1815.

The relations of the Russians with the smaller peoples of eastern Europe in modern times have been largely determined by Russian–German relations. This was especially true between the world wars. In general the Czechs, Serbs, and Bulgarians were pro-Russian, the Hungarians and Roumanians anti-Russian. The governments of eastern Europe, with the partial exception of Czechoslovakia under President Beneš, were hostile to the Soviet Union, chiefly because of their fear of the effects of communist propaganda among their own peoples, who suffered both from poverty and from repressive administrations. Czechoslovakia and Poland were destroyed by Hitler, and the other governments in the late 1930s appeared willing to become satellites of Germany. When Yugoslavia and Greece opposed German and Italian aims in 1940–1, they too were conquered.

During the Second World War resistance movements developed in some of the east European occupied countries. The Polish movement was democratic and nationalist, hostile to both the powers that had partitioned Poland. Therefore, when the Soviet Army entered Poland in 1944–5, orders were given from Moscow to destroy the movement and arrest its leaders. In Yugoslavia, Czechoslovakia, and Bulgaria the resistance movements (very strong in the first, weak in the other two) were led by communists, and so were favoured by the Soviet government.

In 1945 the Soviet Army was in occupation of all of the east European countries except Yugoslavia, Albania, and Greece. Communist governments were placed in power by direct Soviet intervention in Poland, Hungary, Roumania, and Bulgaria. In Czechoslovakia Soviet intervention was indirect, but undoubtedly decisive, in the communists' rise to power in 1948. Soviet troops occupied the eastern part of Austria, surrounding Vienna on all sides. But a single Austrian government was recognized by all the victor powers in 1945, the Soviet forces on the whole respected its authority, and in 1955 all occupation forces were removed in return for the undertaking by the Austrian government to pursue a foreign policy of permanent neutrality. In Germany, however, no central government was set up in 1945, and it proved impossible for the victor powers to achieve an agreed policy in the defeated and occupied country. Consequently, by 1949 two German states were formed. The western 'Federal Republic' became an independent ally of the western powers, the eastern 'Democratic Republic' was a communist dictatorship entirely dependent on Soviet military support. In 1953 this dictatorship was nearly overthrown by a workers' rising in Berlin and other industrial centres: it was saved by the Soviet Army. During the 1950s various schemes were discussed for the creation of a neutralized, reunified Germany, but all were unacceptable to the Soviet government.

By the 1960s it became clear that Soviet policy was committed to the maintenance of a divided Germany.

An important factor in Soviet–German relations since 1945 has been the Polish problem, but its role is not the same as it was in the nineteenth century. In 1945 the Soviet Union retained the eastern Polish provinces that it had taken in the fifth partition of 1939, but compensated Poland by giving it the eastern German provinces of Pomerania, Silesia, and most of East Prussia.[5] The western frontier of Poland lay along the Oder and western Neisse rivers. This created a community of interests between Poland and the Soviet Union, of which any Polish government, whether communist or not, would have to take account. In 1956 relations between Poland and the Soviet Union became seriously strained, as a result of a working-class revolt in the city of Poznań and an increasingly nationalist attitude to Russia on the part of the leaders of the Polish Communist Party. The crisis was, however, overcome: the Soviet leaders agreed to place their relations with Poland on a new basis. Soviet supervision of the Polish army and police ended. Soviet exploitation of Polish economic resources (especially of the coal industry) diminished. The trend of the previous years toward collectivization of Polish agriculture was reversed. In return for this more liberal attitude by the Soviet government, the Polish leader Gomułka committed himself to close co-operation in foreign policy with the Soviet Union, especially in regard to Germany. In the 1960s, as the Polish government adopted increasingly repressive internal policies, and increasingly lost the popularity which it had won among its citizens by its resistance to Soviet pressure in 1956, it felt more and more obliged to exploit the one asset which it still had – the widespread Polish fear of Germany. Thus hate propaganda against the Germans in Poland became equally essential to the Polish and Soviet governments. One may indeed say that the situation of the nineteenth century had become reversed: the Russo–German common interest in the partition of Poland had been replaced by a Russo–Polish common interest in the partition of Germany. Though this remained a basic fact, Soviet tactics changed in the 1970s. Mainly because it needed economic co-operation with West Germany, the Soviet government decided to call off its anti-German hate campaign, and obliged the Polish government to do likewise. For its part the West German government adopted a much more conciliatory attitude toward both the Soviet Union and Poland. The new *Ostpolitik* of Chancellor Willy Brandt led not only to the recognition of Poland's western frontier on the Oder and western Neisse

---

[5] A strip of East Prussian territory, including Königsberg, was annexed directly to the Soviet Union, and Königsberg was renamed Kaliningrad, in honour of the titular president of the USSR.

rivers but also to the establishment of official relations between the two German states in 1972.

Soviet domination of the rest of eastern Europe was first challenged by the successful Yugoslav defiance of Stalin's will in 1948. The expulsion of Yugoslavia from the Soviet bloc (or 'socialist camp') led to more severe totalitarian methods of government in the other communist states. After the death of Stalin in 1953 these were appreciably relaxed. Still greater 'liberalization' followed the Twentieth Party Congress of the CPSU in February 1956. The movement, however, got out of control in the Hungarian Revolution of October 1956. The Communist Party was driven from power, and it had to be reimposed by large-scale Soviet military intervention. In the next two years there was a certain consolidation of Soviet authority in eastern Europe. However, in the 1960s the growing conflict between the Soviet Union and China strengthened the bargaining power of the east European governments. As a price for their support of the Soviet Union in the conflict, they demanded greater sovereignty within their own countries. In a different class was Roumania, which from 1962 onward pursued a strikingly independent policy, not only maintaining a neutral posture between Moscow and Peking, but establishing increasingly close economic and cultural relations with west European states. The Soviet leaders tolerated the reassertion by the Roumanian government of the independence of Roumanian national culture, and the claim that the country's economic policy should be determined by its national interests. They could console themselves by the reflection that the Roumanian government had the merit of maintaining strong internal control by the Communist Party. This was not the case in 1968 in Czechoslovakia: Antonín Novotný, for many years unchallenged boss of the Communist Party of Czechoslovakia, was dismissed from his posts in the Party and in the government. Under new leadership, the Communist Party permitted an unparalleled degree of civil and political liberty. 'Socialism with a human face' was the slogan. Party branches all over the country elected new men to lead them. The Party appeared rapidly to be turning itself into a social-democratic party of the western type. Censorship was abolished; victims of the purges of 1949–52 were released; and demands were loudly advanced for the punishment of those responsible for judicial murders and torture. This was more than the leaders of the Soviet Union could stomach: they themselves had risen to power in the 1930s by massive denunciation of innocent men whose places they had taken. The possible contagion from Czechoslovakia could not be tolerated. On 21 August 1968 Soviet forces numbering several hundred thousand invaded Czechoslovakia, accompanied by small contingents from Poland, East Germany, Hungary, and Bulgaria. This action was retrospectively justified by the Brezhnev doctrine of 'limited sovereignty'. If 'socialism' were endangered in any 'socialist state', the other 'socialist states' had the duty to send 'help', whether or not the government of the state in question asked for help: whether or not there was a threat to 'socialism' was something to be decided by the leaders of the 'socialist camp' – that is to say, by the Soviet leaders.

One argument used in defence of the Soviet action was that Czecho-slovakia's position on the border of West Germany made it particularly dangerous to allow greater political freedom there. It was even asserted by Soviet or pro-Soviet propagandists that West German 'revanchists' had been behind the whole movement in Czechoslovakia. It was there-fore to be expected that the reconquest of Czechoslovakia would be followed by an intensification of anti-German hate propaganda. This expectation was, however, belied by events. The Soviet government decided, as noted above, to sign a treaty with the government of Willy Brandt, which also recognized the Oder–Neisse frontier. As a result, the position of the arch German-hater Gomułka was inevitably weakened. At the end of the year there were massive strikes in the Polish Baltic ports, and after shootings by the police had failed to crush the workers' movement, Gomułka resigned, being replaced as Party leader by the more conciliatory Edward Gierek. In April 1971 another symbolic event seemed to mark the end of an era: Walther Ulbricht, the leader of the East German communist regime for more than twenty years, resigned on grounds of old age and ill health. There was, however, little sign in the following years that his successors intended significantly to change his policies, or were under Soviet pressure to do so.

THE MIDDLE EAST

The area which in recent years has come to be called the 'Middle East' lies to the south of Russia, beyond the Black Sea, the Caucasus, and the Caspian. This region was of interest to the great powers before 1914 from two points of view. For Britain, France, and Germany, it was a land bridge between Europe and India, a sphere of intense rivalries in the heyday of colonial expansion. For Russia it was a land barrier cut-ting her off from access to warm waters. The two key positions were the straits of the Black Sea, controlled by Turkey, and the Persian Gulf, at the head of which were Persia and Turkey, later Iraq. Between the world wars the Soviet government was interested in both these areas but was unable to do much about them. In 1940 they formed an object of Nazi–Soviet conflict. The Germans offered their support for Soviet expansion toward the Persian Gulf. This offer was not rejected by the

Russians, but they asked for more – above all, for control of the Turkish Straits. This Hitler could not conceivably grant: if he had until that moment hesitated about his attack on Russia, this presumptuous Soviet demand removed his doubts.

After the Second World War, Stalin attempted to frighten Turkey into giving him bases in the Straits, and also seems to have toyed with the idea of annexing some Turkish territory in eastern Asia Minor.[6] But Turkey refused to yield, and from 1947 onward it received US economic and military support. In 1941 Soviet troops occupied northern Iran, in agreement with the British government, and when the time came to evacuate Iran after the war, the Soviet government delayed. For a time it looked as if it intended to annex Persian Azerbaijan; however, a combination of American political pressure and promises – later unfulfilled – by the Iranian government brought about Soviet evacuation in 1946. For the rest of Stalin's lifetime Soviet policy in the Middle East was quite inactive.

Already between the world wars the Middle East had acquired a new significance for international politics, as the world's main source of supply of oil. After the Second World War the growth of Arab nationalism, and the instability of the individual Arab states, made the Middle East one of the main areas of international tension. The regime established by Colonel Nasser after 1952, and the failure of the Anglo–French expedition to Port Said in 1956, increased the importance of Egypt. Beyond Egypt lay tropical Africa, in which nationalist movements rapidly developed in the 1960s, and in which Egypt had its own imperial ambitions.

These new forces offered a challenge to Soviet policy. Stalin had ignored the Arab world and Africa. He had not even tried to exploit the internal crisis in Iran under the nationalist government of Mosaddeq, nor had he encouraged the Iranian communists to act. His successors, however, were more willing to take risks. In 1955 the Soviet government offered arms to Egypt: this was one of the causes of the Anglo–Franco–Egyptian crisis of the following year. The crisis was followed by Soviet financial support for the Aswan Dam project, vital to Egyptian plans of economic development. During the following decade Soviet–Egyptian relations grew closer, and the Soviet government decided not only to support the Arab countries against the western 'imperialists' but definitely to commit itself to back the Arabs against Israel. In the 1967 war in Sinai, the Israelis quickly defeated the Soviet-equipped Egyptians. However, the Soviet leaders decided to arm Egypt once more, and to

---

[6] This was not an official Soviet demand: it was expressed in the 'unofficial' form of articles by Georgian and Armenian intellectuals in the Soviet press. These of course must have been authorized by the Soviet government.

incite hatred of Israel all over the Arab world. In the early 1970s the Soviet leaders seemed a little frightened by the passions that they had encouraged, and there were some signs that they might be willing to consider co-operation with the United States for a peaceful settlement. The paradoxical situation had been reached that the blocking of the Suez Canal was now a threat to Soviet rather than to western interests, since once the canal was opened it could be expected that it would be used to the advantage of the Soviet Union, which had replaced the British Empire as the master of Egypt. In 1972 President Sadat of Egypt obtained the departure of many of his Soviet advisers. This brought a certain coolness in Soviet–Egyptian relations, which was however partly compensated for by growing Soviet influence in Iraq. The Egyptian Army still obtained valuable equipment from the Soviet Union, and launched, together with its Syrian ally, a new attack on Israel in October 1973. To what extent the Soviet Union was informed beforehand was a matter of dispute among commentators at the time. As long as the war went well for the Egyptians and Syrians the Soviet government took no action; but as soon as the Israeli counter-offensive made progress, Moscow urged the United Nations to call for a cease-fire. Early in 1975 the prospects of reopening the Suez Canal, or of establishing an Arab–Israeli peace – and the Soviet attitude to these prospects – still remained obscure.

Soviet policy toward the new states of Africa also had its successes and failures. In the Congo in 1960 too much was attempted too quickly, and the result was defeat. Sympathy was expressed for the Algerian insurgents, but Khrushchev took care to avoid irreparably antagonizing General de Gaulle, whose disagreements with the United States he hoped to exploit. Soviet influence in Ghana and Guinea had its successes and its setbacks. Nevertheless during the 1960s the independent African states came to regard the Soviet Union as an important potential source of economic aid and diplomatic support. The Soviet presence in Africa was a fact.

In the early 1960s Soviet–Iranian relations were extremely bad, and internal revolutionary pressures, derived from social and political discontent, made Iran one of the principal danger-points of world politics. But the Shah of Iran survived, by a combination of US economic aid, police repression, and social reforms. In 1965 Soviet policy toward both Turkey and Iran changed: friendly declarations and offers of economic aid took the place of propaganda campaigns and threats. One reason for the change was the disillusionment of Turkey with the West because of Cyprus. Another was a certain growth of neutralism in Iranian government circles. Neutrality seemed to have served both Afghanistan and India well, while Pakistan appeared to have gained nothing from her membership of the American-sponsored CENTO and SEATO systems of alliances. The attitude of the Soviet Union to Pakistan and India, however, cannot be considered without reference to Soviet–Chinese relations.

CHINA AND THE FAR EAST

Before the Revolution, Russia had been the most active of all the imperialist powers in intervention and domination in China. In 1860, by the Treaty of Peking, Russia had annexed from China the long strip of Pacific coastline between Korea and the mouth of the Amur. At the end of the century it had built up a sort of empire, based on control of the railways, in Manchuria. Defeat by Japan in 1905 had compelled the Russian government to cede southern Manchuria to its victor, but in 1912 Russian encroachment on China had been continued, with the consent of the Japanese, by the establishment of a Russian protectorate in Outer Mongolia. During the Russian civil war Japanese troops occupied the Russian Pacific provinces, but in 1922 they were withdrawn. The Russian protectorate over Outer Mongolia was reasserted in a new form in the 1920s, with the establishment of a communist-controlled Mongolian People's Republic. In the 1920s the Soviet government, and the Communist International, supported the Chinese nationalist movement based on Canton, and the Chinese Communist Party acted accordingly. In 1927 however the nationalists, who had extended their authority over central China, broke with the communists, and massacred many of them in Shanghai. This disaster to Chinese communism was widely regarded as the result of bad advice given them from Moscow, and from Stalin personally.

Relations between the Soviet government and the Chinese nationalist government were at first bad. In 1929 Soviet and Chinese troops were engaged in fighting on a considerable scale on the Manchurian border. When the Japanese conquered Manchuria in 1931 the Soviet government accepted the new situation. In 1935 it sold to the Japanese government its share in the Chinese Eastern Railway through Manchuria, the last remaining asset from the pre-revolutionary Russian domination of northern China. In 1937, as part of the world-wide communist strategy of the Popular Front, the Chinese communists adopted a policy of co-operation with the nationalists, and both resisted the Japanese invasion of China. The Soviet Union sympathized with their struggle, but gave them little material help. In April 1941 the Soviet government signed a treaty of non-aggression with Japan, whose purpose was to safeguard the Soviet Union in the East in case it should be attacked in Europe, and to divert Japanese aggression to the south and east, against the British and Dutch colonies in Asia and against the United States. This agreement precluded Soviet aid to China, and in any case from June 1941 onward the Soviet government was fully occupied in resisting the German invasion. During the Second World War co-operation between Chinese communists and nationalists broke down, and after the defeat of Japan a civil war developed, which ended with the victory of the communists in 1949. During the civil war the Soviet government seems to have given little aid to the communists. Supplies of surrendered Japanese weapons in Manchuria were allowed to pass into Chinese communist hands; but, on the other hand, the Soviet authorities removed industrial equipment from Manchurian factories on a massive scale. The Soviet government recognized the government of Chiang Kai-shek for the first years after the war. In 1945 it signed a treaty with it, by which the Soviet Union was given rights over Manchurian railways and a base at Port Arthur. Essentially, the Chinese were being forced to restore to the Soviet Union the privileges which Imperial Russia had enjoyed until it had been defeated by Japan. This was a gesture of revenge against defeated Japan, but the victim, as in the nineteenth century, was China.

Inevitably the events of these twenty years had created in the minds of the Chinese communists resentment against the Soviet leaders. The bad advice of 1927 and consequent disaster to the Chinese communist cause, and the preference of the Comintern leaders during the subsequent decade for the rivals of Mao Tse-tung within the Chinese Communist Party, had been neither forgotten nor forgiven by the victorious Mao. Already in the 1940s Chinese communist propaganda was building up Mao as one of the great prophets of communism, on a level with Marx and Lenin and superior to Stalin. When Stalin died and was succeeded by lesser men, the claim of Mao to be the greatest thinker and leader of world communism was still more insistent.

Another very important issue in Soviet–Chinese relations was economic aid. Admittedly the Soviet Union emerged from four years of war terribly devastated, and was obliged to devote its resources to its own reconstruction. Yet China's needs were even greater. Not only had years of war devastated the country, but the whole economy was much more backward than Russia's, and needed a tremendous investment of resources and manpower in order to launch it on the path of modernization. The Soviet Union made only very small contributions. It did not even give up the Manchurian railway until 1952, Port Arthur until 1955. Chinese bitterness was increased in the mid-1950s when the Soviet government began to dispense comparatively large sums in economic aid to various countries of Asia and Africa which, in the Chinese view, had much less right than 'socialist' China to expect 'comradely' assistance. Evidence on Soviet–Chinese economic negotiations is extremely sparse, but it is a reasonable assumption that already in Stalin's lifetime disappointments in this field had affected the relations between the two governments.

At the end of the 1950s the fact of Soviet–Chinese tension could no longer be concealed. It was first expressed in theoretical arguments in the Chinese press, whose tone gradually grew more angry and the contents of which took ideological form. At the end of 1958, with the announcement of the 'great leap forward' in Chinese industrialization and the introduction of 'peoples communes', the extraordinary claim was made that China (in which communists had attained power thirty years later than they had in Russia) was approaching the stage of 'full communism'. The claim was later modified, but it had certainly been intended by the Chinese, and felt by the Russians, to be an insult to the Soviet Union. There were also theoretical arguments about the 'correct' strategy for communist parties and 'socialist' states to adopt in relation to nationalist movements and 'the national bourgeoisie' in Asia and Africa, which were unmistakable criticisms of Soviet practice. That the Chinese and Soviet communists felt strongly about these ideological issues, and that the Russians resented Mao's assumption of supreme pontifical status, need not be doubted. But as the quarrel developed, it became increasingly clear that it was being transformed into a profound overall hostility between two power systems, between two great states. The factors of ideological, political, economic, and strategic conflict were being fused into a mutually hostile mentality that was more important than its original causes. Two aspects of this must be briefly mentioned here.

First was the interconnection between Soviet–Chinese and Soviet–American relations. The Chinese communists since 1940 had resented with special bitterness the fact that Formosa (Taiwan), which they regarded as being an integral part of China, was ruled by Chiang Kai-shek and enjoyed the protection of the US Navy and Air Force. But the Soviet government refused to give them any support in their efforts to reconquer Formosa, or even the offshore islands that were controlled by the Formosa government. The Chinese maintained that the United States was a 'paper tiger', and that if the military threat were increased the nationalists would eventually surrender. The Soviet government refused to help, or even to go through the motions of threatening the US with nuclear weapons. In addition, in 1959 Khrushchev went out of his way to seek better relations with the United States. The Soviet government, moreover, refused to share its nuclear armoury with China. In the 1960s the Soviet and Chinese leaders accused each other, with repetitive ritual rhetoric, of betraying Vietnam to the United States.

The second aspect is the increasing conflict between Soviet and

Chinese aims in Asia. The Soviet Union in the 1960s gave economic aid to Indonesia and large supplies of arms to the Indonesian Army, while the Indonesian Communist Party took the side of China in the Soviet–Chinese dispute. In 1965 the ill-timed rebellion by the Indonesian communists, which may or may not have been due to Chinese prompting, ended in their defeat and wholesale massacre; both Soviet and Chinese influence ebbed in the new regime.

Even more distasteful to the Chinese was Soviet support to India. This consisted not only of economic aid but of political support at the time of the Indian–Chinese hostilities in 1962. The Chinese attempted to counteract Soviet policy by seeking the friendship of Pakistan. At the time of the Pakistan–Indian war in the autumn of 1965 the Chinese publicly declared their sympathy for Pakistan. This situation was doubly alarming to the Soviet government. Not only was it dangerous to them to have a situation on their southern frontier that was liable to degenerate into war: more specifically, the Chinese–Pakistan combination was a potential threat to the Soviet position in Central Asia. As long as Pakistan was an ally of the western powers, the Soviet government treated it with contempt. The official attitude was that Pakistan was an artificial creation of the British imperialists, and had become a tool of the Americans. But a Moslem country on the borders of Soviet Central Asia, inhabited by peoples closely akin to those of neighbouring Soviet territory, and manipulated by a Chinese communist government fully versed in communist techniques of subversion among national minorities, was a much more formidable phenomenon. The Soviet attitude to Pakistan rapidly changed. Instead of treating it as a western satellite, the Soviet government accepted it as an independent state, equal in status to India. At the Tashkent meeting in January 1966 Kosygin avoided any appearance of partiality to either side. However, the mere fact that the Soviet government was now treating Pakistan as an equal of India was to some extent a defeat for Indian policy.

Nevertheless, the Indian government did not appear to resent the change in Soviet attitude. In particular, when Mrs Indira Gandhi became prime minister, she heaped unctuous praise on the Soviet leaders. India continued to take economic aid principally from the United States, while pouring forth the stream of moralizing denunciation of the sins of America that had begun during the rule of Mrs Gandhi's father, Jawaharlal Nehru. A curious feature of the Indian scene was a sort of negative co-operation between the United States and the Soviet Union. To a historically minded observer, this was bound to recall the situation in Persia in the nineteenth century: then the Shahinshah was at the mercy of the British and Russian ambassadors, who alternately competed with each other for his favours or co-operated at his expense. In 1971, less than a quarter-century after the proud declaration of Indian independence, the ruler of India, moral conscience of world opinion, doling out praise and blame to all humanity, was similarly at the mercy of the US and Russian ambassadors.

The conflict between West Pakistan and Bengal, and the consequent war between India and Pakistan at the end of 1971, presented difficult problems for the United States and Soviet Russia, and perhaps even more for China. If the Chinese supported East Bengal they would antagonize their friends in West Pakistan, whom they hoped to use to make trouble in Soviet Central Asia. If, however, they backed the West Pakistan leaders, they would lose the chance of creating a reunited Bengal, of some 80 million inhabitants, as their own satellite on the borders of India. In the event, the United States antagonized India by refusing wholly to condemn Pakistan; Indian–Soviet relations, already strengthened by a mutual friendship treaty, became still closer; and China gave its support to the residual Pakistan state. Prospects for the future remained extremely uncertain. The relation of Bangladesh to India would depend on internal conditions in the former. The poverty of the peasants, the revolutionary cravings of the intelligentsia, the sense of Bengali nationalism common to many people in Indian West Bengal and in Bangladesh, and suspicions of Delhi politicians with neo-imperialist aims, all offered great opportunities for Chinese political influence among the 100 million Bengalis. Soviet policy had achieved a prestige success by cementing official friendship with India. Whether this would lead the Soviet government to pour resources and specialized manpower down the bottomless pit of India's need remained to be seen.

Another alarming and distant problem was that of the Pacific provinces of the Soviet Union. These of course had in the 1970s a Russian population, after more than a century of Russian colonization. But Chinese statements made it clear that they regarded the Treaty of Peking of 1860 as one of those 'unequal treaties', imposed by European powers on China, whose validity China questioned. The Chinese demand that this nature of the treaties should be admitted on the Soviet side (though *not* that the territories should be returned) met with stony silence in Moscow.

In the mid-1960s the USSR had become a world power in the fullest sense. Theoretically, the Bolshevik Revolution had made her a world power in so far as she had become the centre of the world-wide communist movement. However, for the next three decades her material strength was not sufficient to give her effective world-wide status. Industrial growth, nuclear weapons and rocketry, and further shrinking of world communications gave Soviet Russia this status in the 1970s, at a time when, paradoxically, its earlier claim to world influence was losing its force with the disintegration of the world communist movement.

As a world power in the 1970s, the USSR had two great enemies, the United States and China. Could she afford to be an enemy of both at once? Which was the more dangerous enemy? Was a policy of support for any anti-western revolutionary movement anywhere, of involvement in any crisis of nationalism in Africa or the Arab world or Latin America, worth the risks that were a part of the age of nuclear weapons? Was it still certain that the conflict between 'capitalist' and 'socialist' states was more important than the common interest of the world powers in maintaining peace and in facing the world-wide problems of economic 'underdevelopment', poverty, and overpopulation?

These questions were probably being asked in Moscow already in the 1960s, but no answer had been reached. Until 1972 these questions could be based on the assumption that it was for the Soviet Union alone to decide whether or not it would seek reconciliation with the United States: it was taken for granted that the United States was not on speaking terms with China. After 1972 this assumption could no longer be made. The Soviet Union could no longer choose between the United States and China, since China was its implacable enemy: the United States, however, could choose between the Soviet Union and China, could play each against the other. In the Far East it was no longer even a matter solely of China: Japan also was becoming a giant power. Soviet policy in Europe could not be offensive if the Far Eastern situation was so uncertain. Would a new 'Greater East Asia Co-Prosperity Sphere' grow up, with China and Japan this time equals? Would such a combination receive American support? Or would Soviet diplomacy be able to detach the US and Japan from China, and at the same time benefit the Soviet economy, by inducing American and Japanese business to invest heavily in Siberian oil? Or would inflation, civil strife, and the progressive loss of nerve of the political class in western Europe and North America bring about the collapse of the capitalist West which Soviet prophets had been announcing ever since 1917?

Soviet Russia remained economically weaker than the West and Japan, militarily equal to the United States, and stronger than either in one important respect: in the will to power of its rulers and their relentless determination sooner or later to crush all rivals. In this respect, however, the Chinese rulers were their equals. In this new, precarious, and unfamiliar world situation, it was at least certain that Russia could no longer ignore the responsibilities of world-wide power, and that little enlightenment could be obtained from old slogans.

GUIDE TO FURTHER READING

Relations between Russia and neighbouring peoples

The following works throw light on the history of the relations between Russians and neighbouring nations, in some cases reaching up to present times.

A good introduction to Finnish–Soviet relations, and indirectly to Russia's relations with Scandinavia, is J. H. Wuorinen, *Nationalism in Finland* (New York, 1931). On Polish–Russian relations, R. H. Lord, *The Second Partition of Poland* (Cambridge, Mass., 1915) may be recommended. Also see: R. F. Leslie, *Polish Politics and the Revolution of November 1830* (London, 1956); R. F. Leslie, *Reform and Insurrection in Russian Poland, 1856–65* (London, 1963); W. Lednicki, *Russia, Poland and the West: Essays in Literary and Cultural History* (1954); and J. Feldman, *Geschichte der politischen Ideen in Polen seit dessen Teilungen* (Munich, 1917). The subjects of the first two are evident from their titles. Leslie's second book deals with the events of 1855–64. Lednicki's work is intellectual history, but has some penetrating insights into Polish–Russian relations: it is the work of a brilliant scholar. Feldman's survey of political movements throws much light on Polish attitudes to Russia.

On the Ukraine, the best introduction from a Ukrainian point of view is M. Hrushevsky, *A History of the Ukraine* (New Haven, 1941). On the revolution and civil war in the Ukraine, see J. Reshetar, *The Ukrainian Revolution* (Princeton, 1952). On the later history consult Ya. Bilinsky, *The Second Soviet Republic: the Ukraine after World War II* (Rutgers, 1964). On relations with the Moslem peoples of the Russian Empire, the following are excellent surveys: A. Bennigsen and C. Quelquejay, *La presse et le mouvement national chez les musulmans de Russie avant 1920* (Paris and The Hague, 1964); the same authors' *Les mouvements nationaux chez les musulmans de Russie: le 'Sultangalievisme' au Tatarstan* (Paris and The Hague, 1960); and S. A. Zenkovsky, *Pan-Turkism and Islam in Russia* (Cambridge, Mass., 1960). For Russian contacts with the Far East, G. A. Lensen, *The Russian Push Towards Japan 1697–1875* (Princeton, 1959) may be strongly recommended. This is not a mere diplomatic and military account, but shows sensitive understanding of Russian and Japanese attitudes. The best single work on the aspirations of non-Russian peoples of the former Russian Empire during the Revolution and civil war is R. E. Pipes, *The Formation of the Soviet Union* (Cambridge, Mass., 1954).

On particular problems of Russian foreign relations in the pre-1917 period the following deserve mention. On the Balkans: N. Ya. Danilevsky, *Rossiya i Yevropa* (St Petersburg, 1869); S. Goriainow, *Le Bosphore et les Dardanelles* (Paris, 1910); K. N. Leont'yev, *Vizantizm i slavyanstvo* (Moscow, 1876); M. B. Petrovich, *The Emergence of Russian Panslavism* (New York, 1956); B. H. Sumner, *Russia and the Balkans 1870–1880* (Oxford, 1937). On Russian expansion in the Far East, the best single secondary work seems to me to be A. Malozemoff, *Russian Far Eastern policy 1881–1894* (Berkeley, 1958). Two invaluable Russian studies are B. B. Glinsky, *Prolog russko–yaponskoy voyny* (St Petersburg, 1906), based on Count Witte's papers; and B. D. Romanov, *Rossiya v Man'chzhurii* (Leningrad, 1928).

The foreign relations of the Soviet Union

A number of excellent collections of documents are available in English translation: Jane Degras, ed., *Soviet Documents on Foreign Policy* (3 vols., London, 1951–3); Jane Degras, ed., *The Communist International 1919–1943: Documents* (3 vols., London, 1956–65); H. Hanak, ed., *Soviet Foreign Policy since the Death of Stalin* (London, 1972); S. Clissold, ed., *Soviet relations with Latin America 1918–68: A Documentary Survey* (London, 1970).

The best source for Soviet attitudes are the following periodicals. The appropriate numbers for the date of any important event in international politics should be consulted. *Pravda* (daily organ of the CPSU); *Bol'shevik* (till 1952), then *Kommunist* (since 1952), monthly theoretical organ of the CPSU; *Mirovoye khozyaystvo i mirovaya politika; Mirovaya ekonomika i mezhdunarodnyye otnosheniya; Problemy vostokovedeniya; Narody Azii i Afriki; World Marxist Review*. The appropriate passages in the works of Lenin (numerous Soviet editions, with interesting differences between them) and of Stalin should also be consulted.

Western surveys of Soviet foreign policy, from widely differing points of view, but of high quality, are: E. H. Carr, *The Bolshevik Revolution, 1917–23*, (London, 1953); M. Mackintosh, *Juggernaut: A History of the Soviet Armed Forces* (London, 1967); A. Ulam, *The Rivals: America and Russia Since World War II* (New York, 1967); and the same author's *Expansion and Coexistence: The History of Soviet Foreign Policy, 1917–67* (London, 1968).

On Soviet relations with Eastern Europe, see: *The Soviet–Yugoslav Dispute* (published by RIIA, 1948, consisting of the correspondence between the Soviet and Yugoslav parties up to the breach in 1948); P. Auty, *Tito: A Biography* (London, 1970); J. F. Brown, *The New Eastern Europe* (New York, 1966); V. Dedijer, *Tito Speaks* (London, 1953); G. Golan, *The Czechoslovak Reform Movement* (London, 1971); V. V. Kusin, *Political Groupings in the Czechoslovak Reform Movement* (London, 1972); H. L. Roberts, *Rumania. The Politics of an Agrarian State* (New Haven, 1951); H. Seton-Watson, *The East European Revolution* (London, 1950); H. J. Stehle, *The Independent Satellite: Society and Politics in Poland since 1945* (London, 1965); A. Bromke, *The Communist States at the Cross-Roads* (New York, 1965); S. Fischer-Galati, *The New Rumania* (Cambridge, Mass., 1967); H. Gordon Skilling, *The Governments of Communist East Europe* (New York, 1970). The dates of publication indicate which moments in the history of Soviet–East European relations are stressed.

On Germany and the 'German Question' in European politics, consult the following: E. H. Carr, *German–Soviet Relations Between the Two World Wars 1919–1939* (London, 1952); G. Kennan, *Russia and the West under Lenin and Stalin* (London, 1961); W. Laqueur, *Russia and Germany: A Century of Conflict* (London, 1965); W. Leonhard, *Die Revolution entlässt ihre Kinder* (Cologne, 1950); P. Ludz, *Parteielite im Wandel: Funktionsaufbau, Sozialstruktur und Ideologie der SED-Führung* (Cologne, 1970); P. Windsor, *City on Leave: A History of Berlin 1945–1962* (London, 1963); and E. Wiskemann, *Germany's Eastern Neighbours* (London, 1956). On Soviet relations with Moslem peoples, see: A. Bennigsen and C. Quelquejay, *Islam in the Soviet Union* (London, 1967); W. Laqueur, *Communism and Nationalism in the Middle East* (London, 1956); G. Wheeler, *The Modern History of Soviet Central Asia* (London, 1964). On Soviet–Chinese relations, the following are useful: C. Brandt, *Stalin's Failure in China 1924–1927* (Cambridge, Mass., 1958); W. E. Griffith, *The Sino-Soviet Rift* (London, 1964); H. Isaacs, *The Tragedy of the Chinese Revolution* (London, 1938); B. Schwartz, *Chinese Communism and the Rise of Mao* (Cambridge, Mass., 1950); L. Trotsky, 'Summary and Perspectives of the Chinese Revolution' (1928), in *Selected Works of Trotsky* (New York, 1936); and D. S. Zagoria, *The Sino-Soviet Conflict 1956–1961* (Princeton, 1962).

APPENDIX

GENEALOGICAL TABLES OF
RUSSIAN RULERS

THE KIEVAN LINE

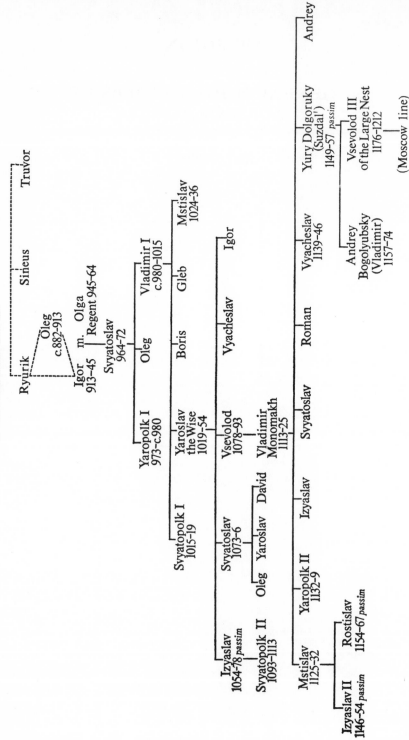

THE MOSCOW LINE

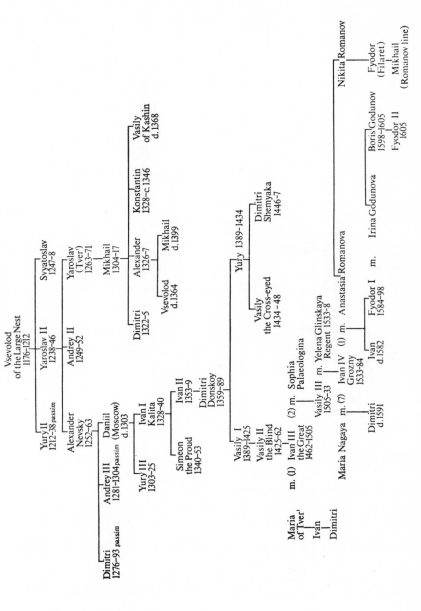

THE ROMANOV LINE

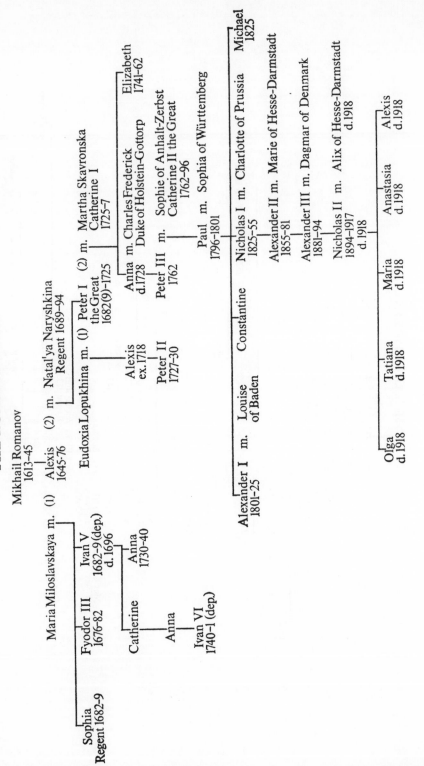

INDEX

Adashev, Aleksey, 100, 102
administration, 74, 124–5, 149–52,
302, 304; under Alexander I, 125,
145–6, 151; under Catherine II,
125, 135, 145, 162–3; central, 124–6,
140, 141, 150–1, 203, 342–3; under
Ivan IV, 100–1, 104; in Kiev, 57,
62, 69–74; local, 124–6, 132, 135,
150, 158–60, 165, 177–8, 238; in
Moscow state, 85, 90, 94, 96, 99–
100, 109; in new territories, 132–3,
135, 137, 139–40, 180–2, 203; under
Peter the Great, 123–6, 132–3, 137,
149–50, 162; under Romanovs, 110,
111–12, 115, 133; urban, 162–3;
see also appanage system; Communist Party; government
Adrian, Patriarch, 147
Adrianople, Treaty, 134
Afghanistan, 208
agriculture, 21–4, 56, 110, 178;
development, 201, 204, 215–16,
223–7, 232, 243; drawbacks, 7, 9, 42;
investment, 21–2, 24, 42, 155, 223,
227, 300, 360–1; productive areas,
11, 13, 14, 23–4, 41, 45–6; regions,
23–4; Soviet: collectivization, 25,
282, 286–90, 297–8, 302–3, 305–7,
332, 351–5, 358, 360–1; private
sector, 352–3, state farms, 352–3,
360–1; and territorial expansion,
131, 133–6, 138, 164, 182; *see also*
grain; livestock farming
Ahmad, Khan, 90, 92–3
Aksakov, I. S., 199
Alaska, 137, 207, 317
Aleksandra Fyodorovna, Empress,
235
Aleksey, Metropolitan, 85–6
Aleutian Islands, 137
Alexander, Grand Prince of
Lithuania, 93
Alexander I, Emperor, 138, 148, 167–
168, 172, 179–81; administrative

reforms, 125, 145–6, 151, 159, 163,
175–6, 178, 322, council of state,
145–6, ministries created, 145–6;
annexed Georgia, 136; and economy, 127, 154, 157; judiciary
reforms, 153; and Poland, 138; state
unification, 126
Alexander II, Emperor, 153, 219, 236,
241; and Baltic peoples, 203; and
education, 212; and Emancipation,
223–4; and Finland, 202; imperialism, 206–7; and Jews, 205; liberal
policies, 199, 201, 234, 240; reforms,
215, 238–40
Alexander, III, Emperor, 224, 231, foreign policy, 199, 202, 203; government, 235, 241, 245; *pogroms*,
205
Alexander Nevsky, Grand Prince, 79–
81, 82, 83, 296
Alexis, Patriarch, 326
Alexis, Tsar, 111–15, 121
Alexis, Tsarevich, 173–4
Amur, 161–2, 207
Anastasia, Tsaritsa, 102, 109
Andrey Bogolyubsky, Grand Prince
of Vladimir and Suzdal', 74–5
Andrey of Polotsk, Prince, 86–7
Andrey Yaroslavich, Grand Prince,
79, 81
Andrusovo, Treaty, 114
Anna, Byzantine Princess, 63
Anna, Empress, 143–4, 179
Antae, 51
appanage system, 81–2, 85, 86, 89–90,
97, 102; abolition, 92
Arabs, 52
Arakcheyev, Count A. A., 146, 178
Archangel, 17, 111
Armenia, 206, 368
Asia; and Russia, 1, 2, 17, 78, 227,
368–9, 383; expansion in, 131, 197,
205–8
Askold, early Russian ruler, 54, 58

393

Astrakhan', 90, 101
Austria, 202, 367, 369, 374; rivalry with, 199; Soviet dominance, 295
autocratic rule, 95, 102, 111, 123, 146, 175, 180–1, 200–1, 233–5, 240–4, 272
Avars, 49, 51
Avvakum, Archpriest, 321
Azerbaijan, 206, 368, 371, 378
Azev, E. F., 237
Azov: fortress, 110, 112; Sea of Azov, 55, 78

Baku, 217
Bakunin, M. A., 245
Balashov, General A. D., 125, 151
Balkans: Russian expansion in, 60–1, 133–6; Russian influence in, 198–200, 370, 373
Baltic coast: importance to Russia, 42, 93, 101; Peter's expansion to, 17, 131–3
Baltic states, 34, 182, 294–5, 366–7, 369, 371; independence, 203–4, 278, 281
banking: and industrial development, 217, 291–20, 232; Peasant Land Bank, 225, 227; State Bank, 341, 345, 351, 357–8; state monopoly, 219, 282
Bashkirs, 164, 182
Basil II, Emperor, 63
Batory, Stefan, King of Poland, 101, 104
Batu, Khan, 79–81
Bel'sky family, 99, 104
Benjamin, Metropolitan, 324
Berdyaev, N. A., 215, 319
Beria, L. P., 291, 299
Bering Straits, 137
Bessarabia, 19; Russian rule, 138–9, 281, 367
Biron, Ernst, 143–4
Bismarck, Prince Otto von, 198
Black Sea, 51, 60, 63
Bogomils, 320
Bolsheviks, 215, 246–7, 274–82, 291, 294, 296, 331–3, 370; leaders, 237, 350; see also Communist Party; Soviet Russia
Boretsky, Martha, 92
Boris, son of Vladimir I, 65
Bosnia and Herzegovina, 199
Botkin, Dr S. P., 211
boyars: of Kiev, 62, 70, 75; of Moscow, 84–5, 91–2, 94, 97–100, 104, 106–8, 111, and government, 141–2, 173; see also government, Duma

Brest-Litovsk, Treaty, 278, 292
Brezhnev, L. I., 306–8, 334–5, 376–7
Bukhara, 206
Bukharin, N. I., 285–6, 287, 289, 291
Bulavin, C., 177
Bulgakov, S. N., 215, 319
Bulganin, N. A., 300, 302, 342
Bulgaria, 51, 57–61, 64, 198–9, 369, 374; Soviet dominance, 295, 297
Bunge, N., 224
bureaucracy, 230–1; emergence, 144, 151–2, 175–6
Buriat Mongols, 182
Byzantium, 51; and Christianity, 58–59, 63–4, 66, 95, 315–17, 320; dominance, 60–4; fall, 91, 104; trade with, 52, 55, 57–8

capitalism, Russian, 215, 217, 221, 232, 246, 274, 283; finance capitalism, 217; peasant capitalism, 286, 351
Casimir IV, King of Poland, 91–2
Caspian, Sea, 7, 43, 55, 112
Catherine I, Empress, 143, 171, 174
Catherine II, Empress, 143, 159, 171, 174, 180; administrative reforms, 125, 144–5, 162–3; and economy, 126–7, 157, 162, 168, 179; and estates, 127, 154; legal commission, 153; territorial expansion, 125, 137, in south, 133–5
Caucasus, 1, 26, 29, 43–4, 87, 165; conquest, 18, 131, 135, 136, 181, 368; nationalism, 206, 279
Chaliapine, see Shalyapin
Charlemagne, 51
Charles, XII, King of Sweden, 161
Chernigov, 57, 65, 69, 72, 74, 83
Chernov, V. M., 246, 273
Chernyshevsky, N. G., 245
Cherson, 63, 64
Chiang Kai-shek, 293, 370, 381–2
China, 207; nationalist movement, 293–4, 380–1; Russian relations with, 20, 44–5, 207–8; Soviet relations with, 305, 307, 369, 370, 372, 376, 380–5
Christianity in Russia, beginnings, 57, 58–9, 60–4, 67; see also Russian Orthodox Church
cities. growth, 35–40, 43
classes, social, see society
climate, 2, 6, 7–9, 14, 20, 40, 41; continentality, 7; dryness, 9; uniformity, 7–9
coal, 26–30, 31, 43, 217, 219, 289, 355
coastline, as barrier, 2, 7

colonization, 14, 17–18, 49–51, 205–6; and expansion, 130–1, 136
commune (peasant), 160, 224, 226–7, 228–9
communism, war, 279, 350
Communist International (Comintern), 282, 293–4, 370, 380–1
Communist Party, 331–2, 333–8, 353, 356; Central Committee, 285, 287, 298–9, 302, 306, 334–6, 339, 345, 356; Congress, 335–6; Constitution (1936), 292, 323, 338–44; Control Commission, 285; Council of Ministers, 298–9, 306, 341–2, 345, 356; and government, 333–4, 338, 342–3, 356; Politburo (Presidium), 285, 287, 298–9, 302, 306, 334–7, 339, 340–2, 345; Secretariat, 285, 302, 334–8, 342; Supreme Soviet, 339–41
Constantine, Grand Duke, 201
Constantine VII Porphyrogenitus, Emperor, 53, 55, 58–9
Constantine IX, Emperor, 66
Constantinople, 58, 59, 63, 64, 66, 73, 91, 316
co-operatives, 227, 286, 288–9, 340, 353, 355; see also agriculture, Soviet
Cossacks, 18, 103, 107–10, 112, 114; revolts, 105, 177; under Russian rule, 131, 133–6, 160–2
Crimea, 63, 87, 92, 96, 104, 134, 181, 206, 218; Crimean War, 124, 140, 151, 196, 218–19, 231
Cyril and Methodius, Sts, 317
Czechoslovakia, Soviet relations with, 294–5, 297, 307, 367, 369–71, 374, 376–7

Daniil, Metropolitan, 98, 99
Daniil, Prince of Moscow, 83
Daniil, Prince of Volhynia and Galicia, 79
Danube, 51, 57
Decembrists, 140, 147, 168–9, 176; Decembrist Revolt (1825), 128, 176
Denikin, General A. I., 280, 281
Dimitri, Prince of Tver', 84
Dimitri, son of Ivan IV, 102, 104, 105–6
Dimitri of Bryansk, Prince, 86–7
Dimitri Donskoy, Grand Prince, 85–7, 89, 90, 99, 296
Dir, early Russian ruler, 54, 58
dissent, religious, 179–80, 214, 321–3; Baptists, 322–3, 327; see also 'Old Believers'

Dmowski, R., 201
Dnieper, 49, 51, 60, 63, 73, 74, 93, 114, 160
Dniester, 51
Don, 51, 52, 87, 103, 112, 134, 160, 161
Donets, 217, 222
Dorpat, see Yur'yev
Dostoyevsky, Fyodor, 209, 215, 319
Durnovo, I. N., 236
Dvina, Northern, 87

economy, 2, 126–7, 153–8, 174, 198, 208, 212; and centralism, 125–7, 140, 355–6, 359; development of new territories, 126, 134, 138, 140, 155, 182, 198; foreign investment, 220; free enterprise, 221; under Ivan IV, 103; mercantilism, 153, 156–7, 162, 231–2; modernization, 196, 215–20, 223, 232; under Peter the Great, 123, 132–3, 141, 153–4; 'planned', 217–18; under Romanovs, 110, 111–12; state-guided, 125–7, 220, 222; western elements in, 132–3
economy, Soviet, 279, 286–7, 289, 297, 300, 302, 304–5, 307–8, 346; before 1928, 350–1; under Brezhnev and Kosygin, 361–3; command economy, 358–9, 361–3; Council of National Economy, 342, 350–1, 361; Five-Year Plans: (1928), 287, 289, 370, (1946), 297, (1971), 363; Gosplan, 342, 350–2, 356, 360, 363; under Khrushchev, 302–5, 342, 359–61; under Stalin, 286–7, 351–9; see also New Economic Policy
Edigey, ruler of Golden Horde, 88, 89
education, 105, 115, 170–2, 175, 209, 211–13, 239; academy of sciences, 171; church, 148–9, 172, 213, 319, 324–6; under Peter the Great, 170–171, 318; Soviet, 304
Ekaterinburg, murder of Imperial family at, 278
Elizabeth, Empress, 133, 159, 175–6, 179; and economy, 157, 162; and government, 144, 154
energy, 26–30, 42, 45, 46; coal, 26–30, 31, 43, 217, 289; gas, 26–30, 31, 42, 44; oil, 26–30, 31, 42, 136, 217, 289, 295, 385; water-power, 26–30, 42–3
England, relations with, 102, 103, 109–10, 135, 157
Ephraim, Metropolitan, 66
estates: and economy, 154–6, 168–9, 228, 232; and government, 127, 132,

133–4, 150, 159, 177–8; *see also* land tenure; serfs
Estonia, 101, 203
Europe: and Russia, 1, 2, 17, 20, 40–1, 78, 123, 176, 369, 371–2, 374; and Peter the Great, 132, 170

Feognost, Metropolitan, 83–4, 85
Filaret, Metropolitan, 319
Filaret (Fyodor Romanov), Patriarch, 105, 107, 109–10, 113
Filofey, Pskovian monk, 91, 92
Finland, 294, 369, 370; autonomy, 19, 202–3, 278, 281; Finns, 66, 74; Russian rule, 126, 138–9, 181, 367–368, 371
First World War, 200, 204, 217, 222, 231; and revolution, 196, 243–4, 248, 272–4, 276–7
Florence, Council of, 95
Florovsky, George, 318
foreign policy, 90–4, 96, 101–2, 197, 273, 366–85; under Peter the Great, 121–2, 129, 131–3, 141; Soviet, 292–298, 300, 304–5, 307–8, 326, 342, 370–2, in Middle East, 307, 368, 377–80; *see also* Khrushchev; Stalin; *and under individual countries*
forests, 6; coniferous (*tayga*), 11, 13, 15, 17, 45; 'mixed', 11, 13, 14–15, 21, 23
Foty, Metropolitan, 89, 95
France: relations with, 66, 157, 176, 218; and Soviet Russia, 280, 292–4, 370, 377–9
Frank, S. L., 215, 319
Frederick II, the Great, King of Prussia, 174
Fyodor I, Tsar, 104–5
Fyodor II, Tsar, 105–6
Fyodor III, Tsar, 115
Fyodor Romanov, *see* Filaret (Fyodor Romanov)

Galicia, 74, 75, 83, 204, 367
Gedimin, Grand Prince of Lithuania, 88, 97
Genghis Khan, 78
Georgia, 94, 206, 223, 368
Germany, 157, 198, 203, 274, 291, 372–7; Brest-Litovsk Treaty, 276–8, 292; Democratic Republic, 307, 374–6; Federal Republic, 306–7, 374–6, 377; hopes for revolution in, 278–9, 293, 370; Soviet–German pact, 294–5, 370–1, 377; Soviet war with, 26, 295–6, 373–4, 381

Germogen, Patriarch, 106, 108
Gleb, son of Vladimir I, 65
Glinsky family, 98–9
Godunov, Boris, Tsar, 104–6
Gogol, N. V., 125, 159, 319
Golden Horde, 78, 81, 85, 87, 89, 90, 92
Golitsyn, Prince Vasily, 115
Gorky, Maxim, 215
Goths, 49, 51
Gotland, 73
government, 233–7; centralization, 123, 141, 146–7, 154, 175–6, 179, 181, 200, 212, 339, 342–3, 358; colleges, 141–2, 144–5, 150; con-stituent assembly, 274–5, 277, 332; Council of Ministers, 234–5, Soviet, 298–9, 306, 341–2, 345, 356; Duma, 94, 104, 107, 141–2, 150, 237, 243, 247, Imperial Duma, 242–3; early forms, 57–8, 62; expenditure, 123, 220–1, 234; ministries, 145–6, 150–1, 234–5, 305–6; opposition, 234–7, 238, 240, moderate, 240–4, radical, 244–8; parliamentary, 242–4, 247, 277; under Peter the Great, 123, 141–2, 144, 179; Procurator General, 142, 144; Senate, 142–6, 147, 150, 175; Soviet state, 331–63; State Council, 234, 240, 242; *see also* Communist Party; nationalism; police systems; Soviet Russia; *and under individual rulers*
grain, 21–4, 42, 219, 303; export, 112, 135, 158, 198, 288; import, 73, 303; state monopoly, 279, 282, 287
Great Britain: rivalry with, 197–8, 207–8, 221; and Soviet Russia, 280, 292–5, 371, 377
Greece, 199
Grekov, B. D., 54, 56
Grigorenko, General P. G., 368
Grigory Otrep'yev, Pretender to throne, 105–6
Guchkov, A. I., 242, 273

Hilarion, Metropolitan, 66
Hitler, Adolf, 293–5, 370–1, 373–4, 378
Holy Roman Empire, and Poland, 89, 93–4, 110
Holy Trinity Monastery, 108
Hungary, 74–5, 93, 363, 369, 370, 372, 374; Hungarian Revolution, 376; relations with, 66, 79, 295, 297, 301
Huns, 49, 51

Ignat'yev, Count Nicholas, 199
Igor, Prince of Kiev, 55, 57–8
imperial expansion, 15–20, 101, 130–140, 197–208, 367–8, 380
India, 208
industrialization, 24–5, 131, 158, 216–223, 225, 246, 332; under Peter the Great, 121, 153–4; under Stalin, 25–26, 370
industry: development in Poland, 201; foreign investment, 216, 219–21; growth, 25–6, 40, 43, 127, 211, 215–223, 230, 358; heavy, development, 17, 29, 287, 358, in Soviet Russia, 281, 285–6, 287–90, 293, 296–7, 302, 307; light, 282–3, 286, 300, 307; location, 26–30, 45; mining, 216–17, 220; nationalization, 279, 350–2; and state, 216–19, 221, 225, 232, 342; in Ukraine, 17, 28, 29, 41–2, 43, 45, 217
intelligentsia, 139, 156, 197, 232, 306; creation, 129, 176, 233; and radicals, 201, 215, 229, 244
Iona, Metropolitan, 95
Iosif Volotsky, see Joseph of Volotsk
Iov, Metropolitan, later Patriarch, 104
Iran, see Persia
iron-mining, 25, 28, 43, 154, 216–17
Isidor, Metropolitan, 95
Ivan III, Grand Prince, 90–4, 95, 96–7, 101
Ivan IV, Tsar, 98–105, 107, 109; expansion policies, 101–2; military organization, 100–1; reforms, 99–101, 102–3
Ivan, son of Ivan IV, 103–4
Ivan V, co-Tsar, 115
Ivan VI, Emperor, 144, 174
Ivan Kalita, Grand Prince, 84–5
Izyaslav, Prince, son of Yaroslav, 68–70

Jadwiga, Queen of Poland, 88
Japan, 216, 291, 307, 317; relations with, 20, 207–8, 247, 294–6, 368–71, 380–1, 385; war with (1904–5), 19, 207–8, 231, 380
Jassy, Treaty, 134
Jeremiah, Patriarch, 104
Jews, position, 181–2, 204–5, 246
John of Kronstadt, 214
Joseph of Volotsk, 95, 318, 320–1
Judaizers, 95, 320
judicial systems, 235–7, 238, 341, 345–6; see also legal codes

Kadet party, 242–3

Kaganovich, L. M., 302
Kaliningrad, see Königsberg
Kalka, battle, 78
Kamchatka, 137
Kamenev, L. B., 275, 284–5, 287, 289–291
Kankrin, Count E. F., 157
Karakozov, D. V., 245
Karamzin, N. M., 82
Kasimov, princedom, 90, 103
Katkov, M. N., 199
Kazakhs, 182, 206
Kazan', 17, 89–90, 92, 96, 101, 171–2, 317, 319
Kerensky, A. F., 273–6
Khar'kov, 170, 244, 322
Khazar empire, 51–2, 55, 60
Khiva, 14, 206
Khmel'nitsky, Bohdan, hetman, 114
Khomyakov, A. S., 319
Khrushchev, N. S., 290–1, 298, 326; ascendancy, 298–305; fall, 305–6, 308, 337; foreign policy, 372, 379, 382; government, 332, 334–6, 342
Kiev, 29, 64, 280, 319; administration, 57, 62, 69–74; decline, 71–5, 81, 86, 93· early development, 15, 42, 49, 62–70; under Lithuania, 86; Mongol sack, 15, 78; under Moscow, 114, 133; origins, 54–8, 59–61; and Slavs, 51–4; see also trade, external; veche
Kirghiz, 206
Kirillo–Belozersky monastery, 95
Kirov, S. M., 290
Kiselyov, Count P. D., 159, 178
Kizevetter, A. A., 82
Klyuchevsky, V. O., 55, 67–8, 72, 82, 87, 210, 319
Kolchak, Admiral A. V., 280
Königsberg, 20, 368, 375
Korea, 207
Kornilov, General L. G., 275
Kosygin, A. N., 306–8, 334, 358, 383
Kovalevsky, Maxim, 210
Kronstadt, mutiny, 282
Krupskaya, N. K., 284
Kuban', 135, 160, 161
Kuchuk Kainardji, Treaty, 134
'kulaks', 287–8, 294, 351
Kulikovo, battle, 87
Kurbsky, Prince Andrey, 102
Kurile Islands, 207, 368, 371
Kutuzov, Prince M. I., General, 296

labour: productivity, 289; shortage, 30, 45, 127, 153–4, 218, 222, 304; unrest, 247, 355 land tenure, 57, 115, 226–7; crown, 102–3, 110; ecclesiastical, 95, 99–100, 103, 111, 276, secularization, 147–8, 318, 323; gentry, 97–8, 100, 104, 110, 227, 230, 232–3; and peasants, 100, 103–4, 111–12, 158–9, 201, 223–7, 228–30, collectivization, 286–7; reform, 274–7

Latvia, 101, 203, 246

Lavrov, P. L., 245

legal codes, 67, 99–100, 150, 152–3, 235, 303; under Ivan III, 94; under Nicholas I, 152–3, 169; under Romanovs, 111–12

Lena, 247

Lenin, V. I., 215, 246–7, 274–9, 281–6, 289; ascendancy, 350; foreign policy, 292–3, 300; government, 331–2, 333–4; industrialization, 24

Leningrad, 2, 42, 368; see also Petrograd; St Petersburg

Leninism, 301, 366

literature, 67, 125, 129

Lithuania, 17, 42, 66, 74–5, 101, 107, 203–4; Russian rivalry with, 79–81, 85–9, 91–3, 96–7, 108–9, 138–9

livestock farming, 22, 23, 42, 225, 288

Livonian Order, 93

Lopukhin, A. A., 237

Loris-Melikov, Count M. T., 235, 240–1

Lunacharsky, A. V., 215

L'vov, Prince G., 272, 274

Lyubavsky, M. K., 82

Lyubech, 69

Magyars, 52

Makary, Metropolitan, 99–100, 102

Malenkov, G. M., 298–300, 302, 359

Mamay, Khan, 86–7

Manchuria, importance, 18–20, 207–8, 371, 380–1

Mao Tse-tung, 299, 305, 381–2

Marxism, 215, 229–30, 245–6, 273, 276, 366; Jews and, 205; Polish, 201

Maxim, Metropolitan, 83

Maximus the Greek, 320

Mazepa, Ivan, hetman, 161

Mengli-Girey, Khan of the Crimea, 93

Mensheviks, 246–7, 273–6, 332

Men'shikov, Prince A. D., 143

Merezhkovsky, D. S., 215

Mikhail Aleksandrovich, Prince of Tver', 86

Mikhail Borisovich, Prince of Tver', 92

Mikhail Romanov, Tsar, 109–11, 114

Mikhail Yaroslavich, Prince of Tver', 83–4, 85

military organization, 97–8, 133, 135, 156, 174–5, 178, 231; under Boris Godunov, 105; and Cossacks, 133, 161–2; under Ivan IV, 100–1; under Peter the Great, 123, 140–1, 149; under Romanovs, 115; Soviet, 279, 295–6

Miller, General E., 280

Miloslavsky, Maria, Tsaritsa, 111

Miloslavsky, Prince Ivan, 102–4

Milyukov, P. N., 82, 241–3, 273

Milyutin, Count D. A., 231, 234, 240

Milyutin, Nicholas, 152, 163

Mindovg, Prince of Lithuania, 79

Minin, Kuz'ma, 108

Mniszek, Marina, 106–7, 108

Molotov, V. M., 287, 294, 302

Monastery of the Caves, near Kiev, 65

Mongolia, 18, 20, 79, 208, 369, 380

Mongols, 61, 64, 78–90, 94–5, 366; end of rule over Russia, 92–3; invasion of Russia, 15, 49, 75; Russian protectorate, 208; see also Tatars

Montenegro, 199

Morozov, Boris, boyar, 111

Moscow: emergence of state, 82–8, 89–90, 141; geographical position, 2, 82; growth, 35–6, 87–8, 93–4, 96–97; as industrial centre, 29, 31, 41, 217, 222; social structure, 97–8, 99–101, 104; supremacy, 6, 15, 17, 90–3, 95–115; see also imperial expansion

Mstislav, Prince, son of Vladimir Monomakh, 71

Mstislav, Prince of Tmutarakan', 65

Murav'yov-Amursky, Count N. N., 137

Murmansk, 7, 218

Nagoy family, 104

Napoleon I, Emperor, 176

Naryshkin, Natalia, Tsaritsa, 115

national debt, 220–1

National Democratic Party, Poland, 201–2

nationalism, 139–40, 197–9, 200–5, 206, 233, 240, 247, 283, 293, 382–5; Baltic, 203–4; Finnish, 202; Great-Russian, 197, 203, 243; and Jews, 204–5; Polish, 126, 139, 180, 200–2, 240, 373–5; Ukrainian, 204, 279–81, 367; see also Panslavism

Nerchinsk, Treaty, 114, 130

Neva, 79
New Economic Policy (NEP), 282–6, 287, 350–1
Nicholas I, Emperor, 121, 124, 164, 178; centralism, 125–8, 163, 181–2; economy, 157; legal codification, 152–3, 169; nationalism, 129; and Poland, 126; political authority, 146, 172, 176; and religion, 157, 179–81; Third Section, 125, 128, 143, 146–7, 168, 236
Nicholas II, Emperor, 199; and church, 214; government, 235, 237, 241–2, 245; imperialism, 207–8; and Jews, 205; and naval power, 198, 207; reforms in Finland, 202
Nikon, Patriarch, 113, 320–1
Nil Sorsky, 95, 320
Nizhny-Novgorod, 83, 85, 87, 108, 232
Normanist controversy, 52–4; see also Varangians
Norway, 66
Novgorod: administration, 74, 91–2; defeat by Moscow, 91–2, 103; early development, 54, 57–8, 60, 61–2, 67, 69; independence, 72–4, 79–81, 90–91; under Muscovy, 109, 112; political and economic centre, 15, 42, 52, 83–5
Nystad, Treaty, 131

Obolensky, Prince Ivan, see Ovchina-Telepnev-Obolensky
Octobrists, 242–3
Odessa, 135, 205
Ohrid, 64
oil. 26–30, 31, 42–3, 136, 217, 289, 295, 355
Oka, 83, 93
'Old Believers', 112–13, 153, 179–80, 214, 232, 321–2, 327
Oleg, Prince, son of Svyatoslav, 60, 61, 72
Oleg, Prince of Kiev, 54–5, 57, 58, 73
Oleg, Prince of Ryazan', 86–7
Olga, ruler of Kiev, 57–9
Olgerd, Grand Prince of Lithuania, 85–6, 88
Oprichnina, 102–3
Ostrovsky, Aleksandr, 232
Otto I, Emperor, 59
Ovchina-Telepnev-Obolensky, Prince Ivan, 98

Panin, N. I., 144, 169, 175
Panslavism, 197–9, 373
Paris, Treaty (1856), 131, 198

Pashkov, V. A., 322
Paul I, Emperor, 143; and nobles, 144–5, 168, 174–5, 177–8; and serfs, 159, 177–8
peasants, see land tenure; 'kulaks'
Pecheneg nomads, 57, 60–1, 62–3, 66
Pereyaslavl', 57, 64, 65, 69, 70, 72, 74
Persia: relations with, 94; rivalry with, 136, 368–9, 371, 377–9
Peter, Metropolitan, 83, 325
Peter I, the Great, 17, 25, 93, 115, 121–43, 152, 167, 173–4, 177, 304; centralization and uniformity, 124–126, 129–30, 133, 141, 146, 179; church and state, 147–8, 318, 321–3; creation of colleges, 141–2, 144–5; creation of Senate, 142–4; economic policy, 142, 149, 153, 156, 158–9, 162; foreign policy, 121–2, 129, 131–3, 141; military organization, 123, 140–1, 149; new capital, 17, 131, 278; Preobrazhensky Prikaz, 142–3, 173; territorial expansion, 125–6, 129, 131–3, 137; westernization, 121–4, 128–30, 141, 170–1; see also administration; economy; serfs; trade, external
Peter II, Emperor, 143, 174
Peter III, Emperor, 174
Petlyura, Symon, 280
Petrograd, 272, 274, 280, 282; see also Leningrad; St Petersburg
Photius, Patriarch, 58
Piłsudski, Józef, 201, 280
Pimen, Patriarch, 327
Plano Carpini, papal envoy, 79
Platonov, S. F., 82
Plehve, V. K., 237
Plekhanov, G. V., 215, 245–6
Pobedonostsev, K. P., 213–14, 235
Pogodin, M. P., 82
Pokrovsky, M. N., 82
Poland, 66, 74–5, 104, 278, 301, 307; dominance, 101, 103, 107–10, 113–114, 366–7; nationalism, 126, 139, 180, 200–2, 240, 373–5; partitions, 131, 138–9, 180–1, 294, 369, 373; rebellions: (1830), 180; (1863), 201, 240; relations with, 66, 79, 88, 91–3, 96, 104, 368, 374, 377; Russian revolutionary movement, 246, 280–281, 370; Russian rule, 126, 138–9, 216–17, 295, 371–2, 375
police systems: tsarist, 102, 142–3, 176, 236–7, 238–9, 245, 248; Soviet, 334, Cheka, 277, 281, 288, KGB, 344–6, MVD, 344, NKVD, 291, 297, 299–

300, 304, OGPU, 288, 291; *see also*
   Nicholas I, Third Section
Polish Socialist Party, 201, 204
Polotsk, 65, 70, 74, 87, 101
Polovtsian nomads, 60–1, 62, 69–75
Poltava, battle, 140
Popov, A. S., 211
population, 1, 28, 34, 82; categories,
   97–8; distribution, 2, 6, 11, 15–20,
   21, 24, 31–40; increases, 32, 41,
   216, 223, 227, 288; rural/urban, 34,
   41–2, 45–6, 228, *see also* society
Populists, 204, 214–15, 229, 245–6, 303
Port Arthur, 207
Possevino, Antonio, papal legate, 101
Potemkin, Prince G. A., 134–5, 144
*Povest' vremennykh let (The Primary
   Chronicle)*, 52–5, 60, 61, 63, 66, 70,
   83, 316
Pozharsky, Prince Dimitri, 108
Pravda russkaya, 67, 70, 73
Preslav, 61
Presnyakov, A. E., 82
Pretenders to throne: Grigory
   Otrep'yev, 105–6; Pseudo-Dimitri II,
   107–8
Prokopovich, Feofan, 172, 318
proletariat, 228–90, 245–6, 331;
   dictatorship, 283–4, 286, 303; rural,
   133, 178, 224
protectionist tariffs, 158, 221–2
Przhevalsky, N. M., 210
Pskov, 79, 81, 84, 90, 101, 112
Pskov-Petseri monastery, 101
Pugachev, E., 150, 177

Rachmaninov, Sergey, 210
railway system, 29, 30–3, 41, 154, 158,
   239, 354, 380; importance to Moscow, 29, 41; and industrial development, 218; Trans-Siberian railway,
   18, 23, 207, 218–19
Rapallo Treaty, 293, 373
Rasputin, Gregory, 214, 235, 243
Razin, Stepan, 112
regions, natural, 2, 6, 9–13, 14, 41–5;
   policies for, 25–6; specialization in,
   20, 23–4, 29–30, 40–5; *see also*
   steppe, wooded; tundra
resources, natural, 20, 28–9, 40, 42, 45;
   exploitation, 123, 126, 130, 218;
   iron ore, 28, 43
Reutern, Count M. K., 219–20, 234
Reval (Tallinn), 132
revolution, 198, 212–13, 226, 234, 240,
   245–8; of 1905, 19, 214, 237, 324;
   of February 1917, 272–3; factors

leading to, 20, 228–30, 237, 243–4;
   October Revolution, 275–6; world
   revolution, 282, 350, 366, 369
Riga, 132; Treaty, 281
rights, civil: under tsars, 200, 235,
   242–3; in Soviet state, 292, 304, 307,
   343–4
river systems, 6–7, 15, 17, 29, 31–3, 41;
   and trade, 52, 218
Roman, Prince of Volhynia, 75
Rostov, 74, 83, 85, 90
Roumania, 199, 281, 366–7, 369, 371,
   374, 376; Soviet dominance, 295
Rozhkov, N. A., 82
Russian Orthodox Church, 63–4, 81–4,
   94–5, 108, 112, 315–27; and
   Catholicism, 79, 93, 95, 107, 180–1,
   315–16, 318–19; and education, 172,
   213; Holy Synod, 147–8, 213–14;
   Ivan IV, 99–100, 102–4; liturgy,
   112–13, 316–17, 320; missionary
   activity, 206, 317; mysticism, 94–5,
   148, 316, 321; 'Possessors' and
   'Non-Possessors', 95, 318; and
   Soviet Russia, 296, 323–7; and state,
   129, 147–8, 172, 214, 234, 318, 321–
   327; *see also* dissent, religious; land
   tenure; 'Old Believers'
Russian state: culture, 209–15;
   emergence, 15, 90, 93–5; expansion,
   101–2, 104, 110, 113–14, 123, 125–6;
   imperialism, 15–20, 130–40, 197–
   208, 367–8, 380; under Peter the
   Great, 121–5, 129–30; *see also*
   Moscow, supremacy; Russian
   Orthodox Church
Ryazan', 83, 86, 89, 90, 96
Rykov, A. I., 285, 287, 291
Ryurik, Varangian ruler, 52, 54, 93,
   97, 104

St Petersburg (Petrograd, 1914–24;
   Leningrad, 1924–), 17, 25, 42, 131–
   132, 163, 170, 171, 319; *see also*
   Leningrad; Petrograd
Sakhalin, 207–8, 368, 369, 371
Saltykov-Shchedrin, M. E., 125
Samarin, Yu. F., 203, 240
Samarkand, 14
Sarajevo, 200
Saray, 78, 81, 87
Sarmatians, 49
Sclaveni, 51
Scythians, 49
Seraphim of Sarov, St, 317
Serbia, 199–200
serfs, 112, 128, 132–4, 147, 158–60,

INDEX

163, 168; and economy, 127, 154–5, 223; emancipation, 18, 152, 159, 176–8, 215, 236, 240; *see also* society
Sergius, Metropolitan, later Patriarch, 325–6
Sergius of Radonezh, St, 94–5
Sevastopol', 135
Shakhmatov, A. A., 53
Shalyapin, Fyodor, 209
Shamil, 136
Shemyaka, Dimitri, 89
Shepilov, D. I., 302
Shipov, D. N., 241–2
Shuvalov, Count Peter, 236
Shuysky, Prince Vasily, later Tsar, 105–7
Siberia, 87, 90, 153; administration, 126, 151, 166, 182; expansion, 17–18, 21, 30–1, 114, 130, 137–8, 162, 207, 227; and industry, 25–9, 43, 45, 157
Sigismund III of Poland, 105, 107–9, 114
Simeon Begbulatovich, Tatar prince, 103
Simeon the Proud, 85
Sineus, 52, 54
Sinkiang, 208
Skopin-Shuysky, Prince Michael, 107
Skovoroda, Gregory, 322
Slavophilism, 129, 197, 319
Slavs, Eastern, 14–15, 34, 49–53, 56, 58, 60–3; *see also* Kiev; Normanist controversy; Varangians
Smolensk, 72, 88, 93, 96, 109, 110
Social Democratic Party, 237, 246, 332
socialism, 221, 237, 242, 245, 247; and Marxism, 215; revolutionary, 204–5, 229–30, 285–6, 288–9, 292, 350; rise, 198, 201, 203–4, 244
Socialist Revolutionary Party, 246, 273–8, 332
society, 158–69, 173, 227–33; clergy, 163–4; *see also* Russian Orthodox Church; of Moscow state, 97–8, 99–101, 104; 'natives', 164–6; in new territories, 132–4, 137–8; nobility, 166–9, 170–2, 173–6, 177, 230–3, 240, *see also* Table of Ranks; nomads, 164–5; under Peter the Great, 123–4, 128, 131–2, 167, 170, 173–4, 182; rural population, 128, 158–62, 172, 176–8, 223–7, 228–9, 238–9; tensions in, 124, 128–9, 140, 165, 173–82, 196, 216, 226, 228, 239, 248; urban population, 162–3, 229–

230; *see also* Cossacks; land tenure; serfs
soil, 6, 9–11, 15, 23, *chernozyom*, 13; *löss*, 6, 13, 18, 44; *podzol*, 11, 21
Solomoniya Saburov, 98
Solovki Monastery, 113
Solov'yov, S. M., 82, 210
Solov'yov, Vladimir, 319
Solzhenitsyn, Alexander, 327
Sophia Palaeologina, 96
Soviet Russia, 272–308; civil war, 20, 203, 278–83, 325, 332, 350, 370, 380; culture, 297–8; Five-Year Plans: (1928), 287, 289, 370, (1946), 297, (1971), 363; Party control, 283–5, 289–92, 299, 301–2, 304–6, 334, 338; Petrograd Soviet, 272–3, 275; Provisional Government, 272–5; purges, 290–2, 298, 306, 326, 332; Red Army, 275–6, 279, 281, 291; Second World War, 295–6; *see also* agriculture; foreign policy; Khrushchev; Lenin; New Economic Policy; Stalin
Speransky, Count M. M., 166, 172, 176, 178; administration, 138, 145–146, 151, 152–4, 172
Stalin, J. V., 275, 300–1, 306, 323; ascendancy, 284–5, 286–7, 298–9, 370; collectivization, 287–90; foreign policy, 293–8, 371–3, 376, 378, 380–382; government, 332, 333–4, 336–7, 345; industrial development, 25–6; purges, 290–2, 326
Stefan Batory, King of Poland, 101, 104
steppe, 6, 13, 17, 21, 42, 49, 134, 206; wooded, 11–13, 15, 18, 21, 42
Steven of Perm', St, 317
Stolbovo, Treaty, 109
Stolypin, P. A., 235, 237; electoral reform, 202, 243; and Jews, 205; land reform, 226–7, 228
Straits, the (Dardanelles and Bosphorus), 198
Strigol'niki, 95
Stroganov family, 103
Struve, P. B., 241, 319
Sub-Carpathian Ruthenia, *see* Transcarpathia
Suleiman I, the Magnificent, Sultan, 96
Suvorov, General A. V., 296
Suzdal', 72, 73, 74, 83, 85, 87
Sveneld, 57
Svyatopolk I, Prince of Kiev, 65, 67
Svyatopolk II, Prince of Kiev, 68–9, 70–1, 73

Svyatoslav I, Prince of Kiev, 55, 57, 59–61
Svyatoslav II, son of Yaroslav the Wise, 68–9
Sweden, 17, 202–3, 216, 368; and early history of Russia, 53, 79, 101, 103; prominent role, 107–9, 112, 114; wars with, 104, 153
Sylvester, priest, 100, 102

Table of Ranks, 127, 134, 162, 166–7, 169, 231
Taganrog, 134, 135
Tallinn, see Reval
Tannenberg, battle (1410), 88
Tatars, 15, 78, 81, 85–6, 182, 366, 368; Crimean, 17–18, 90, 92, 96, 103, 134, 368; national feeling, 206; Russia pays tribute, 78, 84–5; see also Mongols
taxation, 156–7, 162, 224–5; capitation tax, 149, 155–6, 158–9, 167, 224; under Ivan IV, 100; under the first Romanovs, 110, 115
tayga, see forests, coniferous
Terek, 135, 161
Teutonic Knights, 74–5, 79–81, 88
Theopemptus, Metropolitan, 63–4, 66
Tibet, 208
Tikhon, Patriarch, 324–5
Tikhon Zadonsky, St, 318
Timur (Tamerlane), 88
Tito (Josip Broz), Marshal, 297, 304
Tmutarakan', 55, 64
Tokhtamysh, khan of 'White Horde', 87–8, 89
Tolstoy, Count D. A., 224, 236–7
Tolstoy, Count Leo, 209, 319, 322
Tomsky, M. P., 285, 287
trade: external, 42, 51–2, 73, 94, 157–8, 221–2, under Boris Godunov, 105, and early development of Kiev, 54–57, 62, 66, under Ivan IV, 103, under Peter the Great, 123, under the first Romanovs, 110, 111–12, Soviet, 42, 282, 342, 350, 357; internal, 14–15, 56, 154, 158, 162, 221, 232, under Ivan III, 94, Soviet, 352–3, 355
trade unions, 230, 237–8, 247, 283–4, 289, 340, 355
Transcarpathia (Sub-Carpathian Ruthenia), 22, 367
transport system, 30–3, 46, 158; and industry, 29, 218–19; nationalization, 279, 342, 354; see also railway system; river systems

Trotsky, Leon, 275, 278, 284, 286, 290–1, 293; and revolution, 273, 275, 279–80
Truvor, 52, 54
Tsarskoye Selo, 171
Tugan-Baranovsky, M. I., 210
Tukhachevsky, General M. N., 291
Tula, 87, 96
tundra, 6, 11, 13, 45
Turgenev, Ivan, 125
Turkestan, 1, 9, 18, 34, 44, 208; rebellion, 206, 234
Turkey, 90, 94, 96, 114, 198, 293, 368–369, 377–9; wars with, 134, 136, (1855), 218, (1877–8), 199, 219–20, 240, (1914), 206
Tver': importance, 82, 84, 89; rivalry with Moscow, 86–7, 90, 92

Uglich, 104–5, 106
Ugra River, battle, 92–3
Ukhtomsky, Prince E. E., 208
Ukraine, 34, 103, 105, 113–14, 278, 283, 295, 318, 366–7, 373; agriculture, 6, 9, 21, 41–2, 43, 133–4, 155, 160, 225; industry, 17, 26–8, 29, 41–42, 43, 45, 217; nationalism, 204, 279–281, 367
Ul'yanov, V. I., see Lenin
United States: rivalry with, 46, 297, 369; and Soviet Russia, 280, 295, 298, 371–2, 379, 382, 384–5
universities, 171, 172, 212–13
Ural Mountains, 101, 103, 165; Ural region, 42–3, 154, 217
Uvarov, Count Serge, 129
Uzbeg, Khan, 84

Varangians, 15, 56–7, 62–3, 67, 72; Normanist controversy, 52–4
Vasiliev, 63
Vasil'ko, Prince of Terebovl', 69
Vasily I, Grand Prince, 87–8, 89
Vasily II, Grand Prince, 89–90, 91, 95
Vasily III, Grand Prince, 96–7, 98, 99
veche (town assembly), 69–70, 72–4, 84–5, 91–2, 96
Velichkovsky, Paisy, 318–19
Venedi, 51
Vernadsky, G. V., 53
Vienna, Congress of, 139
Vil'na (Wilno), 171
Vishnyakov, I., 82
Vladimir, Prince of Staritsa, 102–3
Vladimir, principality, 75, 79, 81, 83, 85–7, 217
Vladimir I, Prince of Kiev, St 49, 60, 61–5, 66, 71, 73, 316

INDEX

Vladimir Monomakh, Prince of Kiev, 49, 69, 70–1, 72, 73–4
Vladislav, Prince, son of Sigismund III, 107–10, 114
Vladivostok, 207
Volga, 51, 52, 55, 78, 87, 90, 101, 112, 160, 165, 177, 206
Volhynia, 69, 72, 74, 75, 83
Vrubel', Mikhail, 210
Vseslav, Prince of Polotsk, 70
Vsevolod, Prince, son of Yaroslav, 66, 68–9, 71
Vsevolod III, Grand Prince, 75, 79
Vyatka, 92
Vyshinsky, A. Ya., 291

West, influence, 115, 121–4, 128–30, 132, 140, 152, 232; under Peter the Great, 170–2, 173
White Russia, 115, 204, 283, 295, 366–7
Wilno, see Vil'na
Witowt, Grand Prince of Lithuania, 88, 89
Witte, Count S. Yu., 208, 218, 226, 235; and economy, 216, 220–2, 231;

and government, 239, 242
Wrangel, Baron P. N., General, 281

Yagaylo, Grand Prince of Lithuania and King of Poland, 86–7, 88
Yaropolk, Prince of Kiev, 60, 61–2
Yaroslav the Wise, Prince of Kiev, 49, 62, 64, 65–9, 71, 73
Yelena Glinsky, 98
Yermak, 103
Yermolov, A. P., 136
Yezhov, N. I., 291
Yudenich, General N. N., 280
Yugoslavia, 297, 346, 371, 374, 376
Yury, Prince of Moscow, 83–4
Yury Dolgoruky, Prince of Suzdal', 74–5
Yur'yev (Tartu, Dorpat), 93, 171

Zhdanov, A. A., 298
Zinoviev, G., 275, 284–5, 289, 290–291
Żółkiewski, S., Polish hetman, 107–8
Zosima, Metropolitan, 91
Zubatov, S. V., 237
Zyrians (Komi), 317